W9-AZJ-166

Live Oak

Jacksonville

THE
NORTHEAST

Gainesville

St. Augustine

**The Northeast**
Pages 206–227

Daytona
Beach

Cedar Key

Ocala

Crystal River

Gulf of Mexico

Orlando

Cape
Canaveral

Walt Disney World

ORLANDO AND
THE SPACE
COAST

**Orlando and the
Space Coast**
Pages 142–205

Tampa

St. Petersburg

THE GULF
COAST

Fort
Pierce

Arcadia

THE GOLD AND
TREASURE
COASTS

**The Gold and
Treasure Coasts**
Pages 114–141

Palm
Beach

Fort
Myers

Belle
Glade

Naples

THE
EVERGLADES
AND THE KEYS

Fort
Lauderdale

Everglades
City

MIAMI

**The Everglades
and The Keys**
Pages 284–307

Flamingo

Key Largo

Islamorada

Marathon

Key West

# EYEWITNESS TRAVEL

# Florida

DK EYEWITNESS TRAVEL

# Florida

**Project Editor** Emily Hatchwell
**Art Editors** Janice English, Robert Purnell
**Editors** Freddy Hamilton, Jane Oliver,
Naomi Peck, Andrew Szudek
**Designers** Jill Andrews, Frank Cawley,
Dawn Davies-Cook, Eli Estaugh,
Simon Oon, Edmund White

**Contributors**
Ruth and Eric Bailey, Richard Cawthorne,
David Dick, Guy Mansell, Fred Mawer,
Emma Stanford, Phyllis Steinberg,
Ian Williams

**Photographers**
Max Alexander, Dave King,
Stephen Whitehorne, Linda Whitwam

**Illustrators**
Richard Bonson, Richard Draper, Chris Orr &
Assocs, Pat Thorne, John Woodcock

Printed and bound in China

First American Edition, 1997
18 19 20 21 10 9 8 7 6 5 4 3 2 1

Published in the United States by
DK Publishing, 345 Hudson Street,
New York, NY 10014
**Reprinted with revisions 1999, 2000,
2001, 2002, 2004, 2005, 2006, 2008,
2010, 2012, 2014, 2016, 2018**

Copyright 1997, 2018
© Dorling Kindersley Limited, London
A Penguin Random House Company

A catalog record for this book is available
from the Library of Congress.

ISSN 1542-1554
ISBN 978-1-4654-6871-0

This book makes reference to various
trademarks, marks, and registered marks
owned by the Disney Company and
Disney Enterprises, Inc.

Throughout this book, floors are referred
to in accordance with American usage,
ie the "first floor" is at ground level.

MIX
Paper from
responsible sources
FSC™ C018179
www.fsc.org

The historic Ponce de León Inlet Lighthouse offers spectacular views of Daytona Beach

# Introducing Florida

Flamingos at the Everglades National Park,
a mecca for birdwatchers

# Miami Area by Area

◀ **Title page** A lifeguard tower on a serene Florida beach  **Front cover main image** The palm-lined Fort Lauderdale beach in Florida
**Back cover image** Disney's iconic Cinderella Castle, Orlando

# Contents

A Tiffany window in St Augustine *(see p217)*

The breathtaking skyline of Fort Lauderdale, Florida

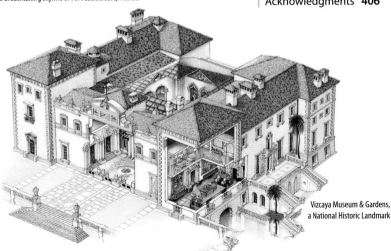

Vizcaya Museum & Gardens, a National Historic Landmark

# HOW TO USE THIS GUIDE

This guide helps visitors to get the most from a visit to Florida. It provides expert recommendations as well as detailed practical information. *Introducing Florida* maps the whole state and sets Florida in its historical and cultural context. *Miami Area by Area* and the six regional chapters describe all the important sights, using maps, pictures, and illustrations. Features cover topics from architecture to food and sport. Hotel and restaurant recommendations can be found in *Travelers' Needs*, while the *Survival Guide* includes tips on everything from transportation to safety.

## Miami Area by Area

Miami is divided into three sightseeing areas. Each has its own chapter, which opens with a list of the sights described. A fourth chapter, *Farther Afield*, covers outlying sights. All sights are numbered and plotted on an *Area Map*. Descriptions of each sight follow the map's numerical order, making sights easy to locate within the chapter.

**Sights at a Glance** lists the chapter's sights by category: Museums and Galleries, Streets and Neighborhoods, Historic Buildings, for example.

**All pages** relating to Miami have red thumb tabs.

**1 Area Map**
For easy reference, the sights are numbered and located on a map. Sights are also shown on the Miami Street Finder on pages 104–109.

**A locator map** shows where you are in relation to other areas of the city center.

**2 Street-by-Street Map**
This gives a bird's-eye view of the heart of each sightseeing area.

**A suggested route** for a walk is shown in red.

**Stars** indicate the sights that no visitor should miss.

**3 Detailed Information**
All the sights in Miami are described individually, with addresses, opening hours, and other practical information. The key to the symbols used in the information block is found on the back flap.

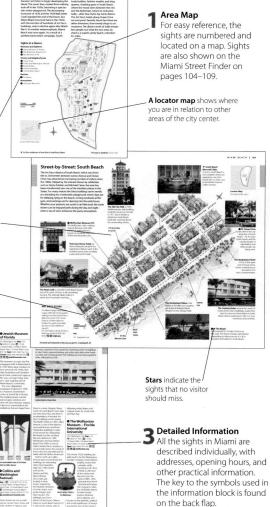

## Florida Area by Area

Apart from Miami, Florida has been divided into six regions, each of which has a separate chapter. The most interesting cities, towns, and places to visit in each area are numbered on a *Regional Map*.

**1 Introduction**
The landscape, history, and character of each region is described here, showing how the area has developed over the centuries and what it offers to the visitor today.

**Each region** of Florida can be quickly identified by its color coding, shown on the inside front cover.

**2 Regional Map**
This shows the main road network and gives an illustrated overview of the whole region. All entries are numbered, and there are also useful tips on getting around by car and public transportation.

**3 Detailed Information**
All the important towns and other places to visit are described individually. They are listed in order, following the numbering given on the Regional Map. Within each town or city there is detailed information on important buildings and other sights.

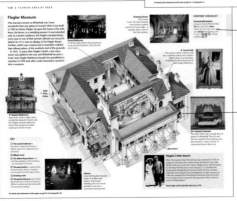

**The Visitors' Checklist**
provides all the practical information needed to plan a visit to all the top sights.

**4 Florida's Top Sights**
These are given two or more full pages. Historic buildings are dissected to reveal their interiors; art galleries have color-coded floor plans to help you to locate the best exhibits; theme parks are shown as a bird's-eye view, with the top attractions picked out.

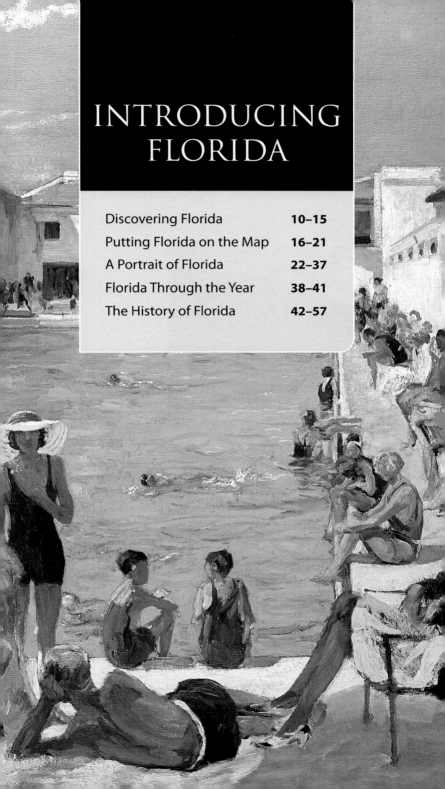

# INTRODUCING FLORIDA

# DISCOVERING FLORIDA

Florida spans two time zones and it takes more than 12 hours to drive from Key West to Pensacola. This state is packed with things to see and do, and these itineraries sample some of the best that Florida has to offer. They focus on areas within an easy drive of the two major gateway cities for air travel, Miami and Orlando, keeping long drives between stops to a minimum.

A two-day tour of Miami introduces you to this vibrant city, while a week-long tour encompassing Miami, the Florida Keys, and the Everglades immerses you in tropical Florida. A five-day tour in Orlando and the Space Coast is an easy add-on to a planned trip to the theme parks, or a new route to explore in a popular destination. A two-week tour sweeps through Central and North Florida, introducing you to natural and cultural attractions. Use these tours to inspire your next Florida adventure.

**The Daytona International Speedway**
This is an adrenalin-fueled day out, featuring exciting racing events from Superbike and Motocross to the fast and furious NASCAR races.

## Two Weeks in Central and North Florida

- Savor the views from **Bok Tower Gardens** atop the highest accessible point in the Florida peninsula, then head to **LEGOLAND® Florida**.
- Discover the impressive legacy of circus magnate John Ringling in **Sarasota**.
- Watch mermaids perform underwater acrobatics at **Weeki Wachee**.
- Splash in crystalline springs in the **Ocala National Forest**.
- Experience the world of racing at the **Daytona International Speedway**.
- See the remains of a 1790s Loyalist plantation on **Fort George Island**.

## One Week in South Florida

- Wander shaded paths in **Miami's** tropical gardens.
- Drive America's most scenic highway, the Overseas Highway, to **Key West**.
- Snorkel or swim the coral reefs of the **Florida Keys**.
- Be amazed by the vast landscapes of the **Everglades** and **Big Cypress Swamp**.
- See Florida history through the eyes of the **Seminole** and **Miccosukee**.
- Walk among ancient cypress trees in **Corkscrew Swamp Sanctuary**.

0 kilometers     80

0 miles        40

### Key

— Two Weeks in Central and North Florida

— One Week in South Florida

— Five Days in Orlando and the Space Coast

◄ *Winter in Florida*, an oil on canvas by Sir John Lavery (1856-1941)

## Five Days in Orlando and the Space Coast

- Visit **Cocoa Beach**, the heart of Florida's surf culture.

- Come nose-to-nose with a Space Shuttle at **Kennedy Space Center**.

- See the world's finest collection of Tiffany glass in **Winter Park**.

- Discover Florida's largest rose garden in Orlando's **Leu Gardens**.

- Feed hungry alligators and see native snakes at **Gatorland**.

- Soar high over **International Drive** on **The Orlando Eye**.

**Key Largo**
Take a boat trip and snorkel amidst the abundant underwater sealife and kaleidoscopic colors of Key Largo's coral reef.

## Two Days in Miami

*Florida's tightest ties to Latin America flow through this sprawling metropolis, which has a central core of vibrant culture.*

- **Arriving** Miami International Airport is 12 miles (19 km) west of Miami Beach.
- **Transport** From the airport take a taxi or Metrobus 150 Airport Flyer express to Miami Beach.
- **Reserving Ahead** It's always a smart idea to reserve hotel rooms ahead, especially in the Miami metro area.

**Day 1**
**Morning** Watch the sunrise across the ocean, when **Miami Beach** is at its quietest, before heading downtown to **Bayside Marketplace** (p78), the launch point for many **Biscayne Bay** boat trips (p78). A 90-minute cruise passes the mansions of the rich and famous, and the Miami skyline. The ten-minute loop around downtown on the Metromover (p77) offers a good overview of architecture in the city center, or you can walk the streets and admire the buildings.

**Afternoon** Stop at the **Miami-Dade Cultural County Plaza** (p78) for the history of how Miami has grown, then relax on **South Beach** (p70) before trying out

Touch panels of the Atlantis Space Shuttle at the Kennedy Space Center

one of its famed clubs, such as the Marlin Hotel (p69).

**Day 2**
**Morning** Recharge on the beach, then wander down **Ocean Drive** (pp64–7), between 6th and 13th Streets, to view the most concentrated collection of tropical-motif Art Deco buildings in the world – the Miami Design Preservation League offers a walking tour (p68). Stroll around the shops in **Lincoln Road Mall** (p72) before settling in a sidewalk café.

**Afternoon** With more than 80,000 historic fine art objects on display, the **Wolfsonian Museum** (p71) will keep you busy for several hours. Miami has one of the largest populations of Holocaust survivors in the world, and the city's Jewish heritage is well-documented at the **Florida Jewish Museum** (p71) and **Holocaust Memorial** (p72).

## Five Days in Orlando and the Space Coast

*The Disney theme parks and Universal Studios bring people from afar to Orlando, but this exciting region has plenty more attractions to offer and activities to be enjoyed.*

- **Arriving** Arrive and depart from Orlando International Airport or Orlando Sanford International Airport.
- **Transport** A car is essential in which to explore Orlando and the Space Coast.

**Day 1: Cocoa and Cocoa Beach**
From Orlando, head to the pretty, historic community of **Cocoa Village** (p199). Rambling around the village will show visitors many eclectic shops and historic sites, such as the **Porcher House** (p199). Lunch in one of the little cafés before crossing the bridge to **Cocoa Beach** (p199), the heart of Florida's surf culture. **Ron Jon Surf Shop** (p199) is a destination in itself, offering rentals and surfing classes. To end the day, relax on the beach: **Lori Wilson Park** is the best natural stretch.

**Day 2: KSC and Merritt Island**
The heart of America's connection to space is **Kennedy Space Center Visitor Complex** (pp200–205). Visit Heroes & Legends and the U.S. Astronaut Hall of Fame to experience space age and explore the history through 4D multisensory theater. The IMAX Theater (p202) and the Space Shuttle Atlantis (p201) are not to be missed; the Shuttle Launch Experience (p201) simulates the power of a Shuttle launch. After lunch with an astronaut (p200), take the KSC bus tour (p201). To finish, follow the Black Point Wildlife Drive through **Merritt Island National Wildlife Refuge** (p198) for close range animal sightings.

> **To extend your trip...**
> Spend a day in **New Smyrna Beach** enjoying the historic downtown and quiet shoreline parks.

**Day 3: Orlando and Winter Park**
Arrive early in **Winter Park** (p191) to see the finest Tiffany glass collection in the world at **Charles Hosmer Morse Museum of American Art** (p191). Lunch at a sidewalk café along trendy **Park Avenue** (p191), then seek out the Scenic Boat Tour (p191). End the day at **Cornell Fine Arts Museum** (p191) at Rollins College.

**Day 4: Orlando and International Drive**
Enjoy a morning walk through Florida's largest rose garden at **Harry P. Leu Gardens** (p190). Then explore **Orlando Science Center** (p191) before heading downtown to **Lake Eola** (p190) for a lunchtime stroll. Stop off at **Orange County Regional History Center** (p190) to see life-size dioramas of the area's history, and then finish the day on International Drive, where you can soar above the town on **The Orlando Eye** (p180). For an evening of family fun, head to **WonderWorks** (p192).

> **To extend your trip...**
> spend some time exploring **SeaLife Orlando** and **Madame Tussauds** (p181).

Coral Gables City Hall lit up in Miracle Mile

### Day 5: Kissimmee

Alligators and crocs are the star attractions at **Gatorland** (p192), but there are also ziplines over the alligator ponds and a rookery of colorful wading birds. Next, head to **Lake Toho** (p194) to enjoy Kissimmee Lakefront Park shoreline. If there is time, a stop at **Old Town** (p193) is fun for the family. Top off your evening with a rousing spectacle of a dinner show at **Medieval Times** (p193).

## One Week in South Florida

- **Arriving** Arrive and depart from Miami International Airport.

- **Transport** A car is essential to explore this part of Florida.

### Day 1: Tropical Miami-Dade

The tropical vibe of South Florida is easy to slip into as you head to **Coconut Grove** (p88), a leafy neighborhood fronting Biscayne Bay. A walk through **The Barnacle** (p88) will put you in touch with pioneer life inside a tropical forest. Continue south into **Coral Gables** (pp83–5) to spend the rest of the day amid the beautiful **Fairchild Tropical Gardens** (p96). Relax in Coconut Grove in the evening.

### Day 2: Everglades Main Park Road

Enter **Everglades National Park** (pp290–95), laden with water, sun screen, insect repellent, and a picnic lunch, via Main Park Road for a 39 mile (63 km) scenic drive. Stop at the **Visitor Center** (p291) for an introduction to the Everglades and its unique habitats. At **Royal Palm Hammock** (p294), take a walk

along the short and wildlife-rich **Anhinga Trail** (p291). On the Pinelands Trail (p294), look out for colorful liguus tree snails. Stop off at **Pa-hay-okee Overlook** (p295) for a panoramic view of the vast "river of grass," and walk the tunneling boardwalk through the mangrove forest at **West Lake** (p295). At **Flamingo** (p295), manatees and American crocs may be spotted near the marina. On your return trip, stroll down the **Mahogany Hammock Boardwalk** (p291) through one of the Everglades' tree islands.

### Day 3: Key Largo, Big Pine Key, and Key West

Drive down the Overseas Highway (US 1) into the Florida Keys. At **Key Largo** (p296), head for **John Pennekamp Coral Reef State Park** (pp296–7) to arrange a boat tour (3 hours) to the coral reef. After lunch, continue along US 1 towards Key West, taking a peek into the National Key Deer Refuge at **Blue Hole** (p301), an excellent observation spot for deer. Then drive on to **Key West** (pp302–7) for a walk along Duval Street (p302) and sunset at Mallory Square (p304).

> **To extend your trip...**
> Spend two days in Key West (pp302–7) to explore the plethora of attractions the island has to offer.

### Day 4: Key West, Marathon, and Key Largo

Tour **Fort Zachary Taylor Historic State Park** (p302) in the morning, then hop on the Conch Train (p304) for a narrated overview of the city. Stop at **The Oldest House Museum** (p306), which

illustrates the Keys' long maritime history. Driving back north along the Overseas Highway, take a break at **Crane Point Hammock** (p300) in Marathon, site of the oldest home in the Keys, to admire the views of Florida Bay. Spend the evening along **Key Largo**'s (p296) beach.

### Day 5: Everglades and Big Cypress

From Key Largo, continue north to the **Tamiami Trail** (p285) – the scenic highway across the Everglades. At **Shark Valley** (p291), hop on a trolley, or cycle the 15 mile (24 km) paved loop, stopping at the tall observation tower. Try native favorites such as fry bread at the adjacent **Miccosukee Indian Village** (p289). Back in the car, head to **Big Cypress National Preserve** (pp288–9), and stop at Oasis Visitor Center (p289) for an orientation to this unusual mosaic of ecosystems.

### Day 6: Everglades, Big Cypress, and Naples

Take an early morning boat tour from the **Gulf Coast Visitor Center** (p291) to see the west side of Everglades National Park in the **Ten Thousand Islands** (p290). Head north and pass through **Fakahatchee Strand Preserve State Park** (p289), a high bio-diversity area, en route to **Corkscrew Swamp Sanctuary** (p289) – a virgin forest of ancient cypress trees. Spend the evening in **Naples** (p288).

> **To extend your trip...**
> Continue north on the Tamiami Trail, for two days in **Fort Myers** (pp280–81) and **Sanibel Island** (pp282–3).

### Day 7: Naples, Big Cypress, and Coral Gables

Drive east across the Big Cypress Swamp on the Alligator Alley expressway (I-75). Exit at the **Big Cypress Seminole Preservation** (p289), home to the **Ah-Tah-Thi-Ki Museum** (p289). At **Billie Swamp Safari** (p289), take a swamp buggy or airboat ride. Finally finish your journey in **Coral Gables** (p83–5).

## Two Weeks in Central and North Florida

- **Arriving** Arrive and depart from Orlando International Airport.
- **Transport** A car is essential in which to explore Florida.

### Day 1: Orlando to Bradenton
From Orlando, follow Scenic Highway 17 south to Lake Wales. Spend several hours savoring the views and beauty of **Bok Tower Gardens** (p195). Continue southwest across the state, visiting the antebellum **Gamble Plantation** (pp270–71) en route to **Anna Maria Island** (p271).

**To extend your trip...**
Spend a day at **Legoland** (pp196–7), which includes the botanical beauty of historic **Cypress Gardens**.

### Day 2: Bradenton and Sarasota
Rise early for a walk at **De Soto National Memorial** (p271) before heading into Sarasota to spend most of your day on the expansive grounds of the **Ringling Museum** (pp274–7). Take in a spot of window shopping on Main Street in **downtown Sarasota** (p272) before crossing the bridge to **St. Armands Circle** (p273) for dinner.

### Day 3: Tampa and Ybor City
The **Florida Aquarium** (p266) is one of America's largest, featuring a tropical atrium on top of the building and marine galleries on multiple floors below. It connects to historic **Ybor City** (pp264–5) via the TECO Line Streetcar System (p262). Learn about the area's Cuban roots at the **Ybor City State Museum** (p265), and plan your dinner at one of Ybor City's restaurants.

**To extend your trip...**
Spend two days in Tampa to visit **Busch Gardens** (pp268–9) and the **Lowry Park Zoo** (p266).

### Day 4: St. Petersburg and Clearwater Beach
A pleasant place to explore on foot, **St. Petersburg** (p258) is home to the **Salvador Dalí Museum** (pp260–61) and the **Museum of Fine Arts** (p259) – notable cultural attractions in arts-focused downtown. For a taste of the tropics, wander through **Sunken Gardens** (p259) before working your way to the nearby coast for some beach time at **Sand Key Park** (p257). Spend the night at **Clearwater Beach** (p256), where there are many small motels on the bay side.

### Day 5: Dunedin and Tarpon Springs
Founded by a Scotsman, **Dunedin** (p255) has a village feel and is a pleasant destin-ation for buying or admiring antiques and art. It is bisected by the **Pinellas Trail** (p255). You can rent a bicycle to follow the trail north, or continue your drive to **Honeymoon Island State Park** (p255), one of the best places in Florida to see nesting ospreys. The Pinellas Trail also connects to **Tarpon Springs** (p255), your final destination for the day.

### Day 6: The Nature Coast
Continue up the Gulf Coast on US 19 to **Weeki Wachee Springs** (pp254–5), the home of "real live mermaids". At **Homosassa Springs Wildlife State Park** (p254), meet Florida's native wildlife, especially the manatee. Spend the evening in **Crystal River** (p254) enjoying one of the

Flamingos at Homosassa Springs Wildlife State Park

best sunsets in the region at the end of the Fort Island Trail – a driving route through the salt marsh, that ends on an island on the Gulf of Mexico.

**To extend your trip...**
Go snorkeling with the manatees (in winter) at **Crystal River National Wildlife Refuge** (p255).

### Day 7: Ocala
Best known for its horse farms – of which you will see many if approaching via SR 40 – **Ocala** (p226) is also a hub for outdoor recreation. Visit **Silver Springs** (p225) and cruise down the crystalline river, surrounded by jungle-like floodplain forests, by boat, or paddle with a kayak if you're feeling energetic. The Black Bear Scenic Byway leads into the **Ocala National Forest** (p225), where Juniper Springs boasts a compelling pair of tributaries linked by glassy waterways.

The picture-perfect St. Petersburg skyline and marina

### Day 8: Gainesville
Centered around the University of Florida, Gainesville is surrounded by natural and cultural attractions. At Cross Creek, **Marjorie Kinnan Rawlings Historic State Park** *(p226)* provides a peek into 1940s Florida life. From here, continue to **Micanopy** *(p226)* to explore this old trading post, established in 1821. Spend some time admiring the antiques and art that dominate the quaint downtown, then watch the wildlife at **Paynes Prairie Preserve State Park** *(p227)* for the rest of the day.

### Day 9: Gainesville and the Suwannee River
Start your morning with a visit to the **Florida Museum of Natural History** *(p227)* for a deeper understanding of Florida's natural habitats. Take a gentle drive north via US 41 through small historic towns to White Springs, home of **Stephen Foster Folk Culture Center State Park** *(p248)*, where Florida folkways are preserved in a beautiful setting along the Suwannee River.

> **To extend your trip…**
> Spend two days in the Florida Panhandle to visit the state capital of **Tallahassee** *(p246)*, where the plantation home of Goodwood *(p247)*, and the **Tallahassee Museum** *(p247)*, interpret Florida's early history.

### Day 10: Jacksonville
Along the St. Johns River waterfront, the **Cummer Museum of Art and Gardens** *(p213)* is a perfect blend of cultural and natural spaces. Follow Heckscher Drive to Fort George Island, home to the **Kingsley Plantation** *(p211)*, the oldest plantation home in Florida. Use the Mayport Ferry to cross the St. Johns River to **Mayport** *(p213)* for a splash in the surf at the beautiful **Kathryn Abbey Hanna Park** *(p213)* before dinner.

The expansive Daytona Beach

### Day 11: St. Augustine
Take A1A south along the coast for a scenic approach to **St. Augustine** *(pp214–19)*, and explore the **Fort Mose Historic State Park** *(p217)* – the site of the first free African settlement in North America. Continue into the hubbub of **St. Georges Street** *(p216)* to start exploring on foot. Early life in the city is well illustrated at the **Colonial Quarter** *(p216)*, and the **Lightner Museum** *(p217)* has many fascinating collections. Browse shops, galleries, and historic sites into the evening before taking on a pub crawl through the Old City.

### Day 12: St. Augustine
Walk through the **Castillo de San Marcos** *(pp218–19)* before driving to cross the Bridge of Lions to Anastasia Island. The **St. Augustine Alligator Farm Zoological Park** *(p217)* is Florida's oldest zoo. Continue across the street to the **St. Augustine Lighthouse** *(p217)*, the oldest brick structure in the city, and climb the 219 stairs to the top for the must-see view.

### Day 13: Scenic A1A
Following Florida A1A south from St. Augustine, stop for a tour of **Fort Matanzas National Monument** *(p220)* – the site of a coquina fortress. At **Washington Oaks Gardens State Park** *(p220)*, do not miss the unique coquina beach on the ocean side of the park. Continuing along the route, the quaint downtown of **Flagler Beach** *(p220)*, perched on bluffs above the sea, is a delightful stop en route to **Bulow Plantation Ruins Historic State Park** *(p220)*. Return to A1A south on the very scenic "The Loop." End your day at **Ormond Beach** *(p220–21)*.

### Day 14: Daytona Beach
A visit to the **Daytona International Speedway** *(p222)*, the home of racing, is a must, as is a visit to the **Museum of Arts and Sciences** *(p221)* for its extensive collection of Cuban art. Catch your last glimpse of the Florida coastline from the top of the **Ponce de León Inlet Lighthouse** *(p222)*.

Formal gardens adorn the natural beauty of Washington Oaks Gardens State Park

# Putting Florida on the Map

Florida, with a population of about 20 million, is the southernmost state of the continental US, jutting down toward the Caribbean between the Atlantic Ocean and the Gulf of Mexico. The Florida peninsula measures about 430 miles (690 km) north to south, and the state as a whole covers an area of 58,560 sq miles (151,714 sq km) – roughly the same size as England. The state capital is Tallahassee, a comparatively small city in the Panhandle – the narrow strip of land extending west along the shore of the Gulf of Mexico. Florida's principal international gateways, however, are Miami, Tampa, and Orlando.

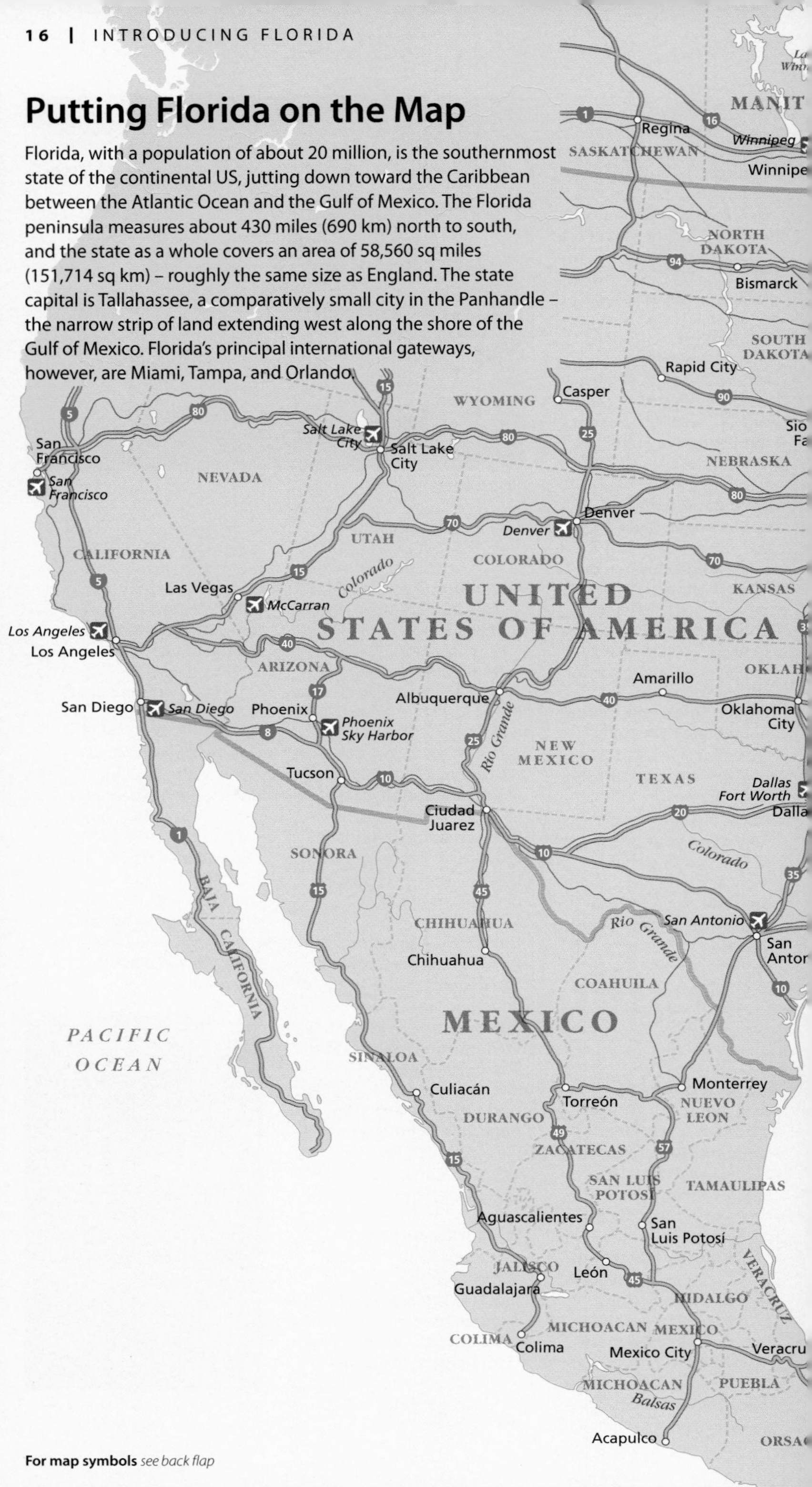

MANIT

Regina

*Winnipeg*

SASKATCHEWAN

Winnipe

NORTH
DAKOTA

Bismarck

SOUTH
DAKOTA

Rapid City

Casper

WYOMING

Sio
Fa

*Salt Lake City*

Salt Lake
City

NEBRASKA

San
Francisco

*San Francisco*

NEVADA

UTAH

*Colorado*

Denver

*Denver*

COLORADO

KANSAS

CALIFORNIA

Las Vegas

*McCarran*

UNITED
STATES OF AMERICA

*Los Angeles*

Los Angeles

ARIZONA

Albuquerque

Amarillo

OKLAH

San Diego

*San Diego*

Phoenix

*Phoenix
Sky Harbor*

NEW
MEXICO

*Rio Grande*

Oklahoma
City

Tucson

TEXAS

*Dallas
Fort Worth*

Dalla

Ciudad
Juarez

*Colorado*

SONORA

BAJA
CALIFORNIA

CHIHUAHUA

*Rio Grande*

San Antonio

San
Antor

Chihuahua

COAHUILA

PACIFIC
OCEAN

MEXICO

SINALOA

Culiacán

Torreón

Monterrey

DURANGO

NUEVO
LEON

ZACATECAS

SAN LUIS
POTOSI

TAMAULIPAS

Aguascalientes

San
Luis Potosí

JALISCO

León

VERACRU

Guadalajara

HIDALGO

COLIMA

Colima

MICHOACAN

MEXICO

Mexico City

Veracru

MICHOACAN

*Balsas*

PUEBLA

ORSAR

Acapulco

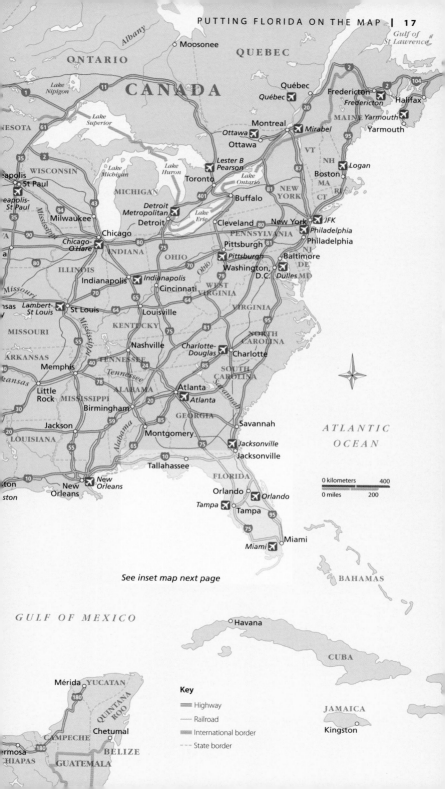

See inset map next page

**Key**

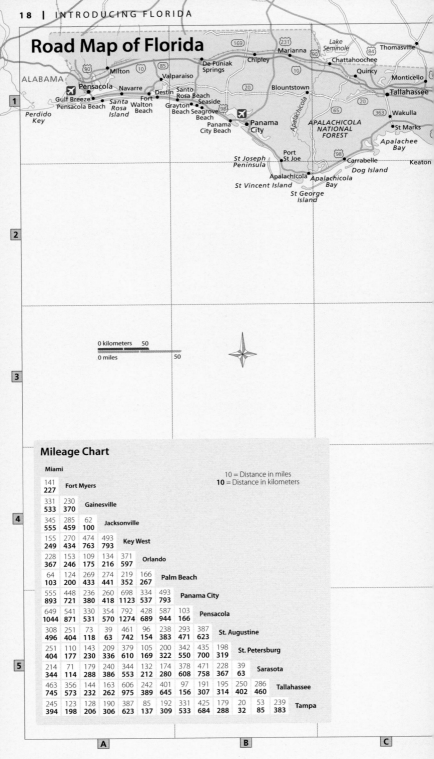

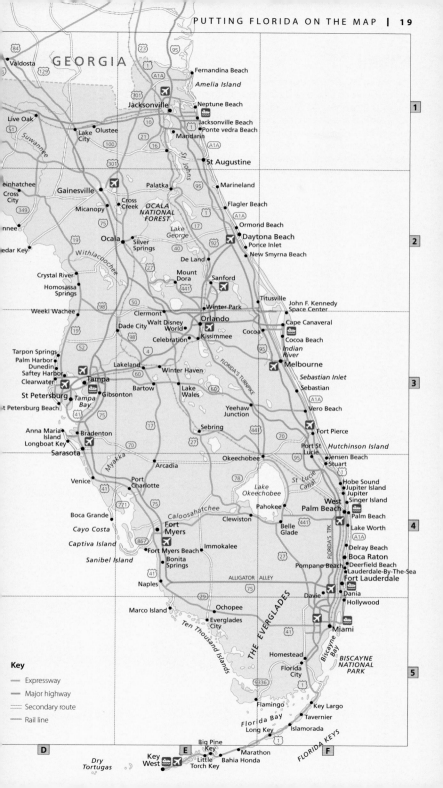

# Miami

The metropolis, often referred to simply as Miami or Greater Miami, is more accurately called Miami-Dade County. It covers 2,000 sq miles (5,180 sq km) and incorporates many districts and several cities. In this book, Miami has been divided up into three sightseeing areas: Miami Beach, including the resort of South Beach; Downtown and Little Havana, more traditionally urban areas; and the leafy suburbs of Coral Gables and Coconut Grove.

Coral Gables City Hall, a landmark in Miami's most desirable residential district

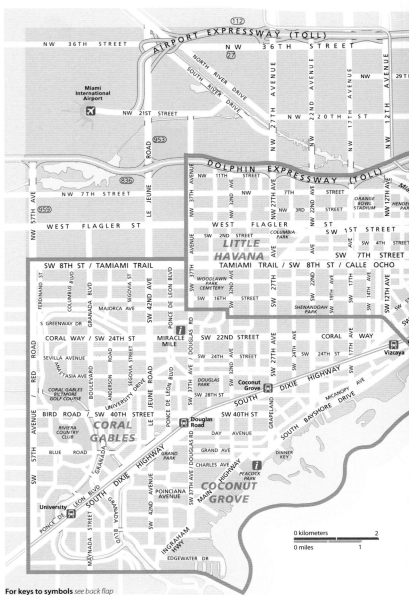

Miami Beach: a popular destination with tourists, near west Florida

Downtown: the visual and commercial focus of the metropolis, with high-rises built along the Miami River

**Key**

Expressway

Metrorail line

# A PORTRAIT OF FLORIDA

For the majority of Florida's 112 million-plus annual visitors, the typical travel poster images of the region – sun, sea, sand, and Mickey Mouse – are reason enough to jump on the next plane. The Sunshine State deserves its reputation as the perfect family vacation spot, but Florida is much richer in its culture, landscape, and character than its stereotypical image suggests.

It is easy to turn a blind eye to what lies beyond the Florida coast, where the beaches are varied and abundant enough to satisfy every visitor – whether you want simply to relax beneath azure skies or to make the most of the state's fine sports facilities. However, great rewards await those who put aside their suntan lotion and beach towels to explore.

The lush forests, the rolling hills of the north, and the colorful displays of bougainvillea and azaleas in spring shatter the myth that Florida's landscape is totally dull and flat. Wherever you are, it is only a short trip from civilization to wild areas, such as the Everglades, which harbor an extraordinary diversity of plant and animal life, and where the abundance of alligators and snakes is a reminder that the wildlife of Florida is a real threat and can be dangerous.

By world standards the state was a late developer (most of its historic districts date only from the early 1900s), but Florida boasts the nation's oldest town: St. Augustine, where a rare wealth of well-preserved buildings provide a glimpse of life in the 18th century.

Both climatically and culturally, Florida is a state divided – a bridge between temperate North America, and tropical Latin America and the Caribbean. In the north, roads are lined with stately live oak trees and people speak with a southern drawl, while, in the south, shade from the subtropical sun is cast by palm trees, and the inhabitants of Miami are as likely to speak Spanish as English.

The boardwalk in Everglades National Park offers stunning views

◀ The white, sandy beaches and warm, emerald waters of Panama City Beach viewed from above

A local resident enjoying some leisurely fishing off Naples pier, on the shores of the Gulf of Mexico

## People and Society

Florida, the state "where everyone is from somewhere else," has always been a cultural hodgepodge. The Seminoles, who arrived in the 17th century, have been in Florida longer than any other group. They live mostly on reservations, but you see them by the roadside in South Florida, selling their colorful, handmade crafts. The best candidates for the title of "true Floridian" are the Cracker farmers, whose ancestors settled in the state in the 1800s; their name comes perhaps from the cracking of their cattle whips, or the cracking of

corn to make grits. Unless you explore the interior, you probably will not meet a Cracker; along the affluent, heavily populated coast, you will rub shoulders mainly with people whose roots lie in more northerly states.

Immigrants have poured into Florida since World War II. It was the twentieth most populous state in the US in 1950, but is now ranked third. The largest

Miami Cubans playing dominoes

single group to move south has been the retirees, for whom Florida's climate and lifestyle of leisure (plus its tax concessions) hold great appeal after a life of hard work. Retirees take full advantage of Florida's recreational and cultural opportunities. You will see many seniors playing a round of golf, fishing, or browsing around one of Florida's shopping malls. While affluent communities such as Palm Beach fit the conservative and staid image that some people still have of Florida, the reality is very different. An increasing number of

A market trader selling clothes made by Seminoles

the new arrivals are young people, for whom Florida is a land of opportunity – a place to have fun and to enjoy the good life. It is this younger generation that has helped to turn Miami's South Beach, where beautiful bodies pose against a backdrop of Art Deco hotels, into one of the trendiest resorts in the US.

There has also been massive immigration from Latin America. Central Florida is home to a huge population of Puerto Ricans and immigrants from Mexico, whereas Miami has a large Cuban community. Here, salsa and merengue beats fill the air while exuberant festivals fill the calendar. The ethnic diversity is also celebrated in the local food: as well as genuine re-creations of Caribbean and other ethnic dishes, you can enjoy the exciting and innovative dishes that have emerged with the craze for cross-cultural cuisine.

Children having fun at a water park in Florida

Oranges, Florida's juiciest crop

### Economics and Tourism

Economically, Florida is in relatively good shape compared with other US states.

For most of its history, the state's main source of revenue has been agriculture: citrus fruits, vegetables, sugar, and cattle. Citrus grows mainly in southern central Florida, where fruit trees can stretch as far as the eye can see. High-tech industry is also significant, while the proximity of Miami to Latin America and the Caribbean has made it the natural route for US trade with the region. Florida's warm climate has also generated high-profile moneyspinners: spring baseball training attracts teams and many fans south, while the fashion trade brings models by the hundreds and plenty of glamor to Miami.

It is tourism that fills the state's coffers. The Walt Disney World® Resort may appear to dominate the industry, but Florida makes the most of all its assets: its superb beaches, its location near the Bahamas and the Caribbean (its cruise industry is flourishing), and its natural habitats. After decades of unbridled development, Florida has learned the importance of safeguarding its natural heritage. Vast areas of land have already disappeared beneath factories, condos, and sugarcane fields, but those involved in industry and agriculture are acting more responsibly, and water use is strictly monitored. Florida's natural treasures, from its swamps to its last remaining panthers, are now protected for posterity.

Flamingos – a popular icon seen in some parks

# The Landscape of Florida

Florida's landscape is relentlessly low-lying, the highest point in the state being just 345 ft (105 m) above sea level. The rare, rolling hills of the Panhandle provide some of the loveliest countryside in the state, whose flat peninsula is otherwise dominated by grassland and forests, punctuated by swamps and thousands of lakes. Great swathes of the natural landscape have had to surrender to the onslaught of urban development and agriculture – second only to tourism as the state's main economic resource. However, it's still possible to find areas that are surprisingly wild and unpopulated.

**Wetlands** consist mainly of tree-covered swamps, such as this cypress swamp, and more open, grassy marshes.

**Sandy beaches** account for more than 1,000 miles (1,600 km) of Florida's coastline. In contrast with the coral sand on the Atlantic side, the fine quartz sand in the Panhandle is so white that legend has it that unscrupulous traders sold it as sugar during World War II.

## Florida's Sinkholes

Many of Florida's 30,000 lakes and ponds started out as sinkholes, or "sinks." This curious phenomenon, which occurs mainly in northern and central Florida, is a result of the natural erosion of the limestone that forms the bedrock of much of the state. Most sinkholes form gradually, as the soil sinks slowly into a depression; others appear more dramatically, often after heavy rain, when an underground cavern collapses beneath the weight of the ground above. The largest recorded sinkhole occurred in Winter Park in 1981. It swallowed six cars and a house, and formed a crater more than 300 ft (90 m) in diameter. There is no sure way to predict sinkhole development, and many homeowners take out sinkhole insurance.

City workers surveying a sinkhole in the middle of a road

**Barrier islands**, formed by the piling up of drifting sand, encircle much of Florida's coast.

Pensacola

Tallahassee

Panama City

APALACHICOLA NATIONAL FOREST

0 kilometers 50
0 miles 50

Gainesville

Oca

Withlacooche

Hillsboro

St Petersburg

Tam

Sara

### Key

◼ Main urban areas

◼ Main wetland areas

◼ Main forest areas

-- Intracoastal waterway

🐄 Cattle

🐟 Fish and seafood

🍊 Citrus fruit

🎋 Sugarcane

🖊 Tobacco

🖊 Peanuts

**The Intracoastal waterway** is a natural but dredged channel, whose main section along the east coast is a continuation of a route that begins farther north in Maryland; some of the Florida sections were dredged back in the 1880s. It is a popular boating route *(see p364)*.

**Cattle** were shipped from Florida to market in Cuba under the Spanish. Today, Florida is second only to Kentucky in the raising of beef cattle in the southeastern states – its industry based largely on the Brahman, a hardy breed of cattle originally from India. The state's principal cattle ranching country lies along the Kissimmee River, and the town of Kissimmee is known as the "cow capital of Florida" *(see p193)*.

**Forest**, mostly pine, covers 50 per cent of the state's land area, but more than half of this is grown for commercial use.

acksonville

**Florida's citrus industry** produces more than 70 per cent of the citrus fruits consumed in the US. Oranges are grown mainly for their juice, for which the state is famous.

• Daytona
  Beach

• Orlando

**Sugarcane** thrives on the rich soil south of Lake Okeechobee *(see p132)*. Once reliant on migrant laborers from the Caribbean, who cut the cane by machete, the industry is now largely mechanized.

•Fort Pierce

*Lake Okeechobee*

sahatchee

t Myers

• Naples

• Palm Beach

• Fort Lauderdale

•MIAMI

*Miami Canal*

*Tamiami Canal*

*EVERGLADES*

**The Florida Keys** are a chain of fossilized coral islands, many of which are tiny and uninhabited.

**Urban growth** is the inevitable result of the constant influx of migrants from other US states and abroad, as well as of the general movement from rural to urban areas. The southeastern coast of Florida is almost completely built up – as seen at Delray Beach, which straddles the Intracoastal Waterway on the Gold Coast.

*FLORIDA KEYS*

─ Key West

# Wildlife and Natural Habitats

Florida's great variety of habitats and wildlife is due in part to the convergence of temperate north Florida with the subtropical south. Other factors include the state's humidity, sandy soils, low elevation, and proximity to water. Some plants and animals can live in several habitats, while others can survive only in one. The birdlife in Florida is particularly rich in winter, when migratory birds arrive from the colder northern states.

A tropical hardwood hammock in southern Florida

---

## Coastal Areas

Florida's coasts are rich in wildlife despite the often exposed conditions. Apart from wading birds, many animals remain hidden during the day. Some lie buried in the sand, while others leave the water only in darkness. Salt marshes and lagoons, protected from the ocean by dunes, are a particularly rich habitat.

**Saltwater lagoons** are fertile territory for fish and shellfish.

**Ocean**

**Limestone bedrock**

**Horseshoe crabs** emerge from the ocean in great hordes, usually in spring. They congregate on the beaches to breed.

**Shrubs** on the dunes are "pruned" by the ocean's salty spray and bent by the wind.

**Clay, sand, and shells**

**Bald eagles**, an endangered species found throughout the entire state, have a wingspan of 7 ft (2 m).

**Dunes** shift all the time, shaped by the wind and waves, but are stabilized by the roots of sea oats and other plants.

**Sea grapes**, which grow on dunes mainly in southeast Florida, are named after the oval fruit that hangs in grapelike clusters.

---

## Pine Flatwoods

These woods, where pines tower over an understory of plants and shrubs, cover about half of Florida, and are often interspersed with swamps and other habitats. They thrive when swept by fire periodically, and the plants and animals that live here have adapted to survive the difficult conditions.

**Saw palmetto**, as well as shrubs such as wax myrtle, do well in the open woodlands.

**Slash pine** is the most common tree in the flatwoods.

**Clay and sand**

**Sand**

**White-tailed deer** are solitary creatures. Those in Florida are smaller than the white-tailed deer found in more northerly states of the US.

**Pygmy rattlesnakes** are well camouflaged to blend easily into a background of grass and scrub.

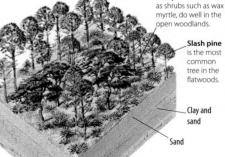

**The red-bellied woodpecker** nests in dead trees and may use the same nest in successive years.

## Freshwater Swamps

Many swamps have been drained to make way for agriculture or development, but they are still found all over Florida. They are often dominated by cypress trees, which are well suited to the watery conditions, requiring little soil to grow. The dwarf cypress is the most common species, the larger giant or bald cypress tree being rare these days.

**White ibis** find ample food in freshwater marshes and swamps. They nest in large colonies in high trees, or among reeds.

Peat

**Bobcats** have a distinctive short tail, facial ruff, and spotted coat.

**Cypress trees** often form a "dome." The trees at the water's edge are shorter than those at the center.

Sawgrass

**Cypress knees** are special roots that supply oxygen to the tree, which would otherwise die in the wet soil.

Water and organic matter

**Anole lizards** are usually green but can change to dark brown, depending on body heat or levels of stress.

**Water lilies** are the most spectacular freshwater flowering plants. The large leaf is a common resting site for frogs.

## Hardwood Forests

These are among the most verdant habitats in the state. Hardwood-dominated forests are called "hammocks." Unlike the tropical hardwood hammocks of southern Florida, those in the north are dominated by the splendid Spanish moss-laden live oak tree, interspersed with other species such as hickory and magnolia.

**Spanish moss**, like other epiphytes or air plants, grows on (but does no harm to) its host tree.

**Wild turkeys** are easily recognized by their colored plumage and "beard."

Cabbage or sabal palm

Live oak

**Magnolia**, one of the oldest known flowering plants, is characterized by its showy ornamental flowers and aromatic bark.

Sand and clay

**Hammocks** occur mainly in patches or in narrow bands along rivers.

**Opossums** are proficient climbers, with hands, feet, and tail well adapted to grasping thin branches.

**Armadillos** are mainly nocturnal. When threatened they roll into a ball, the hard armor protecting the soft body from predators such as bobcats.

# Hurricanes in Florida

A hurricane is a tropical cyclone with wind speeds of at least 74 mph (119 km/h). One in ten of the hurricanes to occur in the North Atlantic hits Florida – resulting in an average of one big storm every two years. The hurricane season runs from June 1 to November 30, but the greatest threat is from August to October. The Saffir-Simpson Hurricane Scale, which measures the winds and ocean flooding expected, categorizes hurricanes from one to five; category five is the worst, with winds of more than 155 mph (249 km/h).

Monument to the 1935 hurricane *(see p298)*

Hurricane names derive from a recognized alphabetical list of names, which rotates every six years. Originally, only women's names were used, but since 1979 men's and women's names have been alternated.

**The areas** of Florida most likely to be hit by a hurricane are the south-east coast, including the Florida Keys, the west coast of the Everglades, and the western Panhandle.

### The Life of a Hurricane

The development of a hurricane is influenced by several factors – primarily heat and wind. First the sun must warm the ocean's surface enough for water to evaporate. This rises and condenses into thunderclouds, which are sent spinning by the earth's rotation. The hurricane moves forward and can be tracked using satellite images similar to this one. Upon hitting land, the storm loses power because it is cut off from its source of energy – the warm ocean.

A boat lifted out of the water onto Miami's Rickenbacker Causeway by the force of the hurricane

An apartment building after its façade was ripped off by Andrew's ferocious winds

A tent camp, set up to house some of the 250,000 left temporarily homeless by Hurricane Andrew

### Hurricane Andrew

On August 24, 1992 Hurricane Andrew devastated South Florida. It measured only "4" on the Saffir-Simpson Scale (less than the 1935 hurricane that hit the Florida Keys), but until Katrina in 2005 it was the country's costliest ever natural disaster, causing $35 billion worth of damage. Astonishingly, only 15 people died in Florida (23 in the whole country) from the direct effects of Hurricane Andrew.

**The Eye**
Encircled by the fastest winds, the "eye" at the heart of the storm is a calm area. Once the eye has passed by, the winds return to their full force.

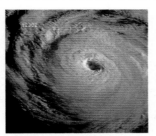

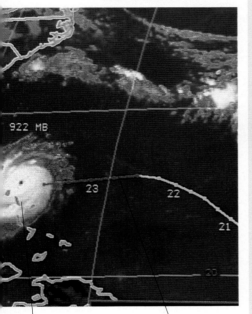

922 MB

**A typical hurricane** is 300 miles (480 km) wide and can rise 50,000–60,000 ft (15,250–18,300 m) above the ocean. It moves forward at a speed of 10–45 mph (15–70 km/h).

**Many hurricanes** form off the coast of Africa and then move west across the Atlantic.

## The Storm Surge

Most damage and deaths during a hurricane are not a result of wind and rain, but of flooding from the storm surge. This wall of water is whipped up by fierce winds near the eye of the storm and then crashes onto the shore; it can span more than 50 miles (80 km) and reach a height of 20 ft (6 m), or more.

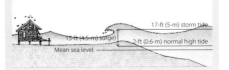

17-ft (5-m) storm tide
15-ft (4.5-m) surge
2-ft (0.6-m) normal high tide
Mean sea level

## Monitoring a Hurricane

Using satellites, computer models, and radar, the National Hurricane Center in Miami can detect a hurricane long before it reaches Florida. The most detailed information, however, is provided by pilots known as Hurricane Hunters, who fly in and out of the hurricane gathering data.

The damage from a hurricane is greatly reduced by being prepared: television and radio bulletins keep the public informed, and everyone is encouraged to follow the route of the storm on special hurricane tracking maps.

Trees bent by hurricane force winds

**1 Hurricane Alerts** The issuing of a Hurricane Watch is the first indication that a hurricane could hit Florida. This means that a storm may arrive within 36–48 hours. A Hurricane Warning heralds the storm's likely arrival within 24 hours. Airports are likely to close during these alerts.

Traditional hurricane alert flag

**2 Evacuation** Emergency management officials may issue evacuation orders via the local news media before a hurricane hits. People living in high-rise buildings, mobile homes, and low-lying areas are particularly vulnerable. Signs bearing the hurricane symbol direct people along safe routes. The Red Cross shelters those people who have nowhere else to go.

Evacuation sign

**3 The All Clear** After a hurricane dissipates or moves on, the all clear is given for people to return home. However, safety is still a concern after the storm because of fallen power lines, flooding, and cleanup-related accidents.

# Shipwrecks and Salvage

The waters off Florida are littered with thousands of shipwrecks that have accumulated over hundreds of years. Many sank during storms at sea, while others foundered on sandbars or the reefs off the Keys. The salvaged wrecks illustrated on the map are those that have had a large amount of their cargo recovered. Spain's treasure ships are the greatest prize among salvagers, just as they were once the favored target of pirates. In museums all across Florida, treasure and everyday objects offer an insight into the lives and riches of the Spanish.

**Lighthouses**
Since the 1800s, lighthouses like the one at Jupiter have helped ships to stay on course.

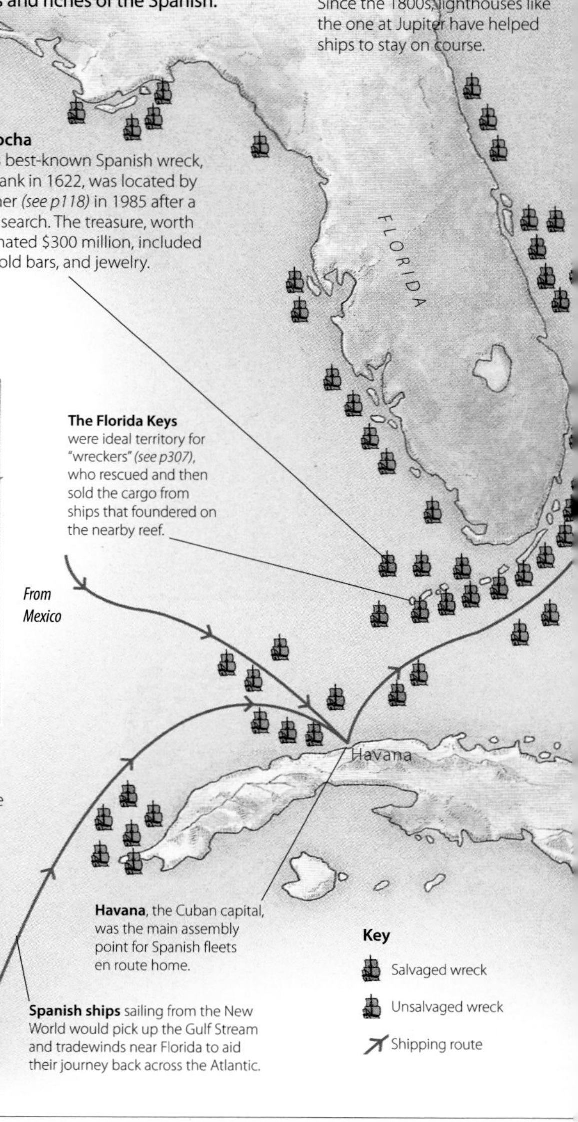

**The Atocha**
Florida's best-known Spanish wreck, which sank in 1622, was located by Mel Fisher *(see p118)* in 1985 after a 16-year search. The treasure, worth an estimated $300 million, included coins, gold bars, and jewelry.

FLORIDA

**The Florida Keys**
were ideal territory for "wreckers" *(see p307)*, who rescued and then sold the cargo from ships that foundered on the nearby reef.

*From Mexico*

**Salvaging Treasure**
Salvaging has always required ingenuity. This manuscript from 1623 shows a Spanish technique invented to rescue sunken treasure in the Keys.

MEXICO

*From South America*

Havana

**Havana**, the Cuban capital, was the main assembly point for Spanish fleets en route home.

**Spanish ships** sailing from the New World would pick up the Gulf Stream and tradewinds near Florida to aid their journey back across the Atlantic.

**Key**

 Salvaged wreck

 Unsalvaged wreck

 Shipping route

## Treasure Seekers

It took Mel Fisher more than 100 court hearings to establish his right to keep the treasures of the *Atocha*. Federal law states that wrecks located up to 3 miles (5 km)

offshore belong to the state in whose waters they are found, but the law is unclear when it comes to ships lying outside that limit. Amateurs who find coins with metal detectors on land can keep what they find, but in Florida a license is required to remove anything from an offshore wreck within its jurisdiction.

**A treasure hunter on the beach**

### Where to See Spanish Treasure in Florida

**McLarty Treasure Museum**
*see p118*
**Mel Fisher Maritime Museum**
*see p306*
**Mel Fisher's Treasure Museum**
*see p118*
**Museum of Man in the Sea**
*see p242*
**St. Lucie County Historical Museum**
*see p119*

**A Spanish treasure fleet** that sank here in 1715 *(see p118)* is still being salvaged. Amateurs scour nearby beaches for coins that are sometimes washed up after a storm.

*To Spain*

**Spanish Ships**
Caravels and galleons transported treasure back to Spain. These ships could carry a crew of about 200. The chests of gold and silver were usually kept under guard in a room on the lower deck.

**Blackbeard**
Notorious for his cruelty – and also for his habit of setting fire to hemp cords attached to his hat in order to intimidate his victims – Blackbeard preyed on Spanish ships in the early 18th century. He was killed by the British Navy in 1718.

*BAHAMAS*

*CUBA*

**Hispaniola** and nearby Tortuga were favorite haunts of French and English pirates, who would launch attacks on Spanish ships from here.

*TORTUGA*

0 kilometers 200
0 miles 200

*CARIBBEAN SEA*

*HISPANIOLA*

# Florida's Architecture

Buildings in Florida are perhaps most interesting as a reflection of the way in which the state was settled. Early pioneers built simple homes, but aspirations grew from the railroad era onward. Entrepreneurs, eager to lure people south, imitated styles with which northerners would be familiar. This trend, plus the speed of settlement, meant that Florida never developed an indigenous style. However, the Sunshine State has some quirky and memorable architecture, often inspired by the need to adapt to the warm climate.

High-rise architecture in downtown Jacksonville

## Florida's Vernacular Style

The early pioneers of the 1800s built houses whose design was dictated mainly by the climate and the location: the most identifiable common elements are the devices to maximize natural ventilation. Local materials, usually wood, were used. Original "Cracker" homes, so named after the people who built and lived in them (*see p24*), do not survive in great numbers, but the vernacular style has influenced Florida's architecture ever since.

A chickee, the traditional simple home of Florida's native people

**The brick chimney** replaced the original one, which was made of mud and sticks.

**A dog trot,** or open walk-through, was often added if, as here, the original house was extended.

**The roof,** here made of cypress shingle, was usually steeply pitched.

**The McMullen Log House,** a pine log cabin completed in 1852, is a typical Cracker dwelling. It is now preserved in Pinellas County Heritage Village (*see p256*).

**Overhanging eaves** shade both the porch and the windows.

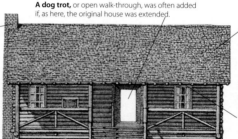

## The Gilded Age

From the 1880s, the railroads and tourism brought new wealth and ideas from outside the state. The love affair with Mediterranean Revivalism began and can be seen in Flagler's brick hotels in St. Augustine. Wood was still the favored material, though, and was used more decoratively – most famously in Key West. Other concentrations of Victorian houses are found in Fernandina Beach (*see p210*) and Mount Dora (*see p224*).

**A tower** fulfilled a decorative more than a practical purpose.

**Gabled roofs** were popular and were high enough to fit in an attic.

**Ventilation** was still a primary concern, hence the generous number of windows.

**Verandahs** that wrapped around the house were quite common.

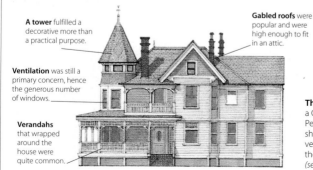

Moorish tower, former Tampa Bay Hotel

**The McCreary House,** a Queen Anne home in Pensacola dated c.1900, shows the refinement of vernacular styles during the Victorian period (*see p235*).

## The Fantasy of the Boom Years

The most notable buildings of the period 1920–50 set out to inspire romantic images of faraway places. Each new development had a theme, spawning islands of architectural styles from Moorish to Art Deco – the latter in Miami's South Beach district *(see pp64–71)*. Mediterranean Revivalism dominated, however. Its chief exponents were Addison Mizner in Palm Beach *(see pp122–9)*, and George Merrick in Coral Gables *(see pp84–7)*.

The Art Deco Celino Hotel on Miami's Ocean Drive

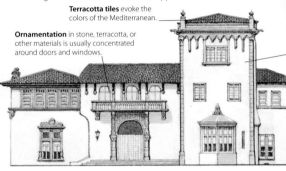

**Terracotta tiles** evoke the colors of the Mediterranean.

**Ornamentation** in stone, terracotta, or other materials is usually concentrated around doors and windows.

**Balconies**, turrets, and irregular roof levels are all recurrent features.

**Palm Beach mansions** are primarily Spanish Revival in style. This one on South Ocean Boulevard was built by Julius Jacobs, one of Mizner's chief designers, in 1929.

## Postwar Architecture

Many of Florida's most striking modern buildings are either shopping malls or public buildings, such as theaters or sports stadiums, which are often as impressive for their scale as for their design. More of a curiosity are the new towns of Seaside and Disney's Celebration *(see p156)*, which have arisen out of nostalgia for small-town America, and as a reaction to the impersonal nature of the modern city.

Van Wezel Performing Arts Hall in Sarasota *(see p272)*

**Large sash windows** allow abundant sunlight and sea breezes to enter the house.

**Seaside**, a piece of award-winning town planning in Florida's Panhandle, has houses with picket fences and other quaint pseudo-Victorian features *(see p240)*.

**A verandah** on the second floor offers a shady place to sit or to enjoy the ocean views.

**Wood**, characteristic of vernacular architecture in Florida, is the favored material in Seaside.

Neon signs along International Drive, Orlando

### The Highway

In the 20th century, the flood of visitors and settlers speeding south along Florida's highways has spawned buildings unique to the road. Alongside the drive-in banks and restaurants sit buildings shaped like ice-cream cones or alligators – designed to catch the eye of the motorist driving past at speed. Such outlandish style, aided by colorful neon signs, breaks up the monotonous strips of motels and fast food outlets.

# Spectator Sports in Florida

Florida offers a wide choice of sports entertainment. Thrilling and exciting events ranging from football, baseball, and basketball to horse, greyhound, and motor racing can be watched and enjoyed throughout the state. Soccer is gaining popularity, and stadiums are springing up from Orlando to Miami. Florida's sunny climate makes participation sports such as tennis, golf, and watersports popular throughout the year *(see pp362–7)*, and provides the perfect setting for national and international level tournaments.

College football game at EverBank Field stadium in Jacksonville

## Football

Florida presently boasts three teams in the National Football League (NFL): the Miami Dolphins, the Tampa Bay Buccaneers, and the Jacksonville Jaguars. The Miami Dolphins, have appeared in five Super Bowls, winning twice. The season runs from September to December *(see p100)*.

Among the college teams, the Seminoles of Tallahassee, the Miami Hurricanes, and the Gators from Gainesville often finish high in national football ratings; their rivalry is fierce. Florida holds more college bowl games than any other state.

## Soccer

Florida's growing soccer scene sees Orlando City, a member of the 22-team Major League Soccer league, play from March to October. The women's professional team, Orlando Pride, shares the Orlando City Stadium. Miami FC, a member of the North American Soccer League, plays at the Riccardo Silva Stadium at Florida International University. Miami Fusion and Miami United are National Premier Soccer League (NPSL) members.

## Baseball

Set up in 1993, the Florida Marlins was the state's first major league baseball team. Now called the Miami Marlins, the team has won two World Series and plays home games at Marlins Park in downtown Miami. The second Florida team to join the major leagues was the Tampa Bay Rays, based at St. Petersburg Tropicana Field stadium. The baseball season runs from April to October.

Fifteen major league baseball teams hold spring training in Florida. In March the teams play friendly games in the so-called **Grapefruit League**. These games, which take place throughout the week, attract large crowds, with fans often coming from outside the state. For dates and tickets contact the individual stadiums in advance. A more comprehensive list is also available from the Florida Sports Foundation *(see p364)*.

## Horse Racing

Florida boasts the country's second largest thoroughbred industry, centered on

### Grapefruit League: Who Plays Where

**Atlanta Braves**
Walt Disney World.
**Tel** (407) 939-4263.

**Baltimore Orioles**
Sarasota. **Tel** (941) 893-6300, (800) 745-3000.

**Boston Red Sox**
Fort Myers. **Tel** (617) 482-4769.

**Houston Astros**
West Palm Beach.
**Tel** (844) 676-2017.

**Minnesota Twins**
Fort Myers.
**Tel** (800) 338-9467.

**New York Yankees**
Tampa.
**Tel** (813) 875-7753.

**Philadelphia Phillies**
Clearwater.
**Tel** (727) 467-4457.

**St. Louis Cardinals**
Jupiter.
**Tel** (561) 775-1818.

**Tampa Bay Rays**
Port Charlotte. **Tel** (727) 825-3250.
A complete list is available from the Florida Sports Foundation *(see p373)*.
**w** flasports.com

New York Yankees baseball team, at Tampa for spring training

Ocala *(see p226)*. Gulfstream Park in Hallandale hosts racing from January to April. This is the home of the prestigious one million dollar Florida Derby which is run in March, or in the first part of April. The famous Breeders' Cup is also often held at Gulfstream. However, the heyday of horse racing has passed in Florida, and much of the gambling now takes place in casinos. Races are still held in October and November at the site of the former Calder Race Course, now Calder Casino. Thoroughbred racing also takes place at Tampa Bay Downs in Tampa from December to May. There is one harness racing track in Florida, Pompano Park in Pompano Beach, where top-ranked standardbred trotters and pacers strut their stuff from October to June.

Jai alai, claimed by its fans to be the oldest and fastest game in the world

Horse racing at Gulfstream Park, Florida's premier venue

## Ice Hockey

Although ice hockey is usually thought of as a cold weather sport, Florida has two teams in the National Hockey League. The Florida Panthers play at the BB&T Center in Sunrise, and the Tampa Bay Lightning, the 2004 Stanley Cup champions, play at the Amalie Arena. Thousands of Floridians have taken to watching the sport. The season runs from October to April.

## Jai Alai

Florida's game of jai alai is a type of pelota that originated in Europe and came to the US in the 1900s *(see p141)*. Games take place on a three-walled court, where players use a curved wicker basket to catch and hurl the ball, generating speeds in excess of 150 mph (240 km/h). The back wall is made of granite to absorb the resultant force.

One of the major attractions of this historic and fascinating game has always been the chance to gamble. During the past few years, the emphasis on gambling has resulted in many of the indoor arenas, or frontons, being transformed into casinos or places for poker tournaments. However, there are still a few frontons operating in Miami and Central Florida.

## Motor Racing

Auto and motorcycle racing are big in Florida. The season starts in February at the Daytona International Speedway *(see p222)*, one of the world's fastest tracks, with two very popular races. The IMSA Rolex 24 Hours at Daytona, like its older brother at Le Mans, runs all day and all night, and the Daytona 500 is a season highlight for

The Daytona 500, first held in 1959

the National Association of Stock Car Auto Racing (NASCAR). Other big races take place in Homestead, Pensacola, and Sebring. Hot rods come to Gainesville in March for the Gatornationals, the top drag-racing event on the Atlantic seaboard. Motorcycles also race in the annual Daytona 200.

## Basketball

Both professional and college basketball have a huge fan following in Florida. The Miami Heat, based at the American Airlines Arena, and the Orlando Magic, whose home court is the Amway Center, provide the best in exciting NBA action. The season runs from October to April.

**Action at Orlando Magic**

## Golf and Tennis

Golf tournaments abound in Florida, birthplace of golf ace Jack Nicklaus. Top of the bill are the Bay Hill Invitational in Orlando, and the PGA Players Championship in Ponte Vedra Beach near Jacksonville; both are held at the end of March.

Tennis is also popular. For example, Key Biscayne's Crandon Park Tennis Center is famous for its annual Miami Open in March, which attracts huge crowds.

# FLORIDA THROUGH THE YEAR

With its warm climate, Florida is a year-round destination, but the difference in the weather between north and south means it has two distinct tourist seasons. In south Florida (including Orlando), the busiest time is from October to April, when tourists come to enjoy the mild winters. Most will have left well before summer arrives, when it can be uncomfortably hot. Orlando's theme parks still attract families with children on school vacations, but in summer the Panhandle sees some of the biggest crowds. Be warned that prices in the tourist seasons can be double those charged during the rest of the year. Visitors are bound to encounter a festival of some kind round the year, but apart from national holidays *(see p41)*, only a few of these are Florida-wide. For a full list of festivals contact the local tourist office.

## Spring

In late February, college students invade Florida for Spring Break, pouring in by the thousands. For the next six weeks coastal resorts are bursting, particularly Daytona Beach, Panama City Beach, Fort Lauderdale, and Miami.

Baseball training *(see p36)* is also a big attraction in the spring. In the north, feast your eyes on the blooming azaleas and dogwood trees.

Daytona Beach swarming with pleasure seekers on Spring Break

### March
**Sanibel Shell Show** *(first week).* Shell collectors and artists come to Sanibel Island *(see pp282–3).*
**Florida Strawberry Festival** *(first week),* Plant City near Tampa. Strawberry shortcake and country music.
**Carnaval Miami** *(early Mar).* Ten days of Latino Miami festivities with beauty pageants, sports, food, and concerts. The Calle Ocho street festival finale is the largest in the world.

Little Havana's Calle Ocho, hub of the party at Carnival Miami *(see p40)*

### The Miami International Film Festival *(early Mar).* The Miami Film Society hosts a broad array of films for ten days *(see p359).*
**Motorcycle Races "Bike Week"** *(early Mar),* Daytona Beach *(see pp222–3).* Bikers converge from near and far, on vintage and modern bikes.
**Winter Park Sidewalk Art Festival** *(mid- Mar).* One of the country's best art festivals.
**Sunnyland Boat Festival** *(mid– Mar),* Lake Dora at Tavares. Antique boats race on the lake while visitors attend exhibitions.
**Springtime Tallahassee** *(late Mar, early Apr).* One of the South's largest festivals, with parades, balloon races, great food, and plenty of live music.

### April
**Easter** *(Mar/Apr).* Celebrate sunrise services at the Castillo de San Marcos *(see pp218–9),* and take carriage rides around St. Augustine.
**Conch Republic Celebration** *(mid-Apr–early May),* Key West. Party all week with parades, bed races, and dancing – all in honor of the town's founding fathers.

### May
**SunFest** *(first week),* West Palm Beach. Cultural and sports events.
**Pensacola Crawfish Festival** *(first week).* Enjoy boiled crawfish and fried 'gator to the music of Cajun bands.
**Isle of Eight Flags Shrimp Festival** *(first weekend),* Fernandina Beach. Shrimp and other seafood.
**Florida Folk Festival** *(late May).* A renowned three-day fiddle and food festival.
**Jacksonville Jazz Festival** *(mid- to late May).* Art and craft exhibitions mixed with three days of international jazz.
**Orlando International Fringe Festival** *(late May).* Ten days of comedy, drama, dance, mime, and musicals.
**Tampa Bay Margarita Festival** *(late May).* Features performances by renowned national artists and plenty of margaritas, as well as tasty bites to soak them up.

Emblem of the Conch Republic

## Average Daily Hours of Sunshine

Hours

[bar chart showing average daily hours of sunshine by month: Jan 8, Feb 8, Mar 9, Apr 9, May 9, Jun 9, Jul 9, Aug 8, Sep 7, Oct 6, Nov 7, Dec 7]

### Sunshine Chart
The chart shows the figures for the entire state. The west coast near St. Petersburg, which boasts an average of 361 days of sunshine per year, enjoys more sun than elsewhere, but blue skies are a fairly consistent feature everywhere. Even in southern Florida's wetter summer months, the clouds generally disperse quickly.

Young boy in patriotic colors at a Fourth of July celebration

## Summer

Temperatures and humidity rise as summer progresses, with only Atlantic breezes and almost daily afternoon storms to bring some relief. Florida's hurricane season *(see pp30–31)* is also underway. Travelers on a tight budget can make the most of the off-season hotel prices.

The big summer holiday is Independence Day on July 4, celebrated with street pageants, fireworks, barbecues, picnics, and mass cooling off in the water.

### June
**Fiesta of Five Flags** *(early Jun)*, Pensacola. Two weeks of parades, marathons, fishing rodeos, plus the reenactment of Tristán de Luna's beach landing in 1559.
**Monticello Watermelon Festival** *(mid-Jun)*, Monticello *(see p247)*. The harvest is celebrated in back-country style with barbecues and hoedowns.

**Silver Spurs Rodeo**
*(Jun, Feb)*, Osceola Heritage Park, Kissimmee *(see p193)*. This is the state's oldest and wildest rodeo, now housed in an indoor air-conditioned arena.

### July
**America's Birthday Bash**
*(Jul 4)*, Miami. Fireworks at midnight are preceded by picnics and fun for all the family, in south Florida's largest Independence Day celebration.
**Goombay Festival** *(mid–Jul)*, Coconut Grove, Miami *(see p88)*. Enjoy the parade at this Bahamian party offering great food along with Caribbean music.
**Hemingway Days Festival** *(mid-Jul)*, Key West. The city offers a week of author signings, short story contests, theatrical productions, and a very entertaining Hemingway lookalike contest.

### August
**Key West Lobsterfest**
*(early Aug)*, Key West. Live music, cold drinks, and fresh lobster at this end-of-summer party, complete with a sunset Duval Street Crawl.
**Boca Festival Days**
*(all month)*, Boca Raton. This celebration features an arts-and-craft fair, barber-shop quartet performances, as well as a sand castle-building contest.
**Annual Wausau Possum Festival** *(first Saturday)*, Wausau. This town north of Panama City Beach honors the marsu-pial with activities such as corn-bread baking and greased-pole climbing, and offers the chance to sample possum-based dishes.

Bearded contenders at the Hemingway Days Festival lookalike contest

## Average Monthly Rainfall

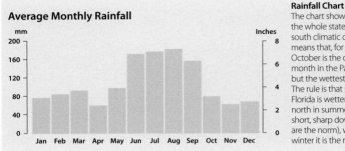

| | | | | | | | | | | | |
|---|---|---|---|---|---|---|---|---|---|---|---|

**Rainfall Chart**
The chart shows figures for the whole state. The north-south climatic divide means that, for example, October is the driest month in the Panhandle, but the wettest in the Keys. The rule is that southern Florida is wetter than the north in summer (when short, sharp downpours are the norm), while in winter it is the reverse.

## Fall (Autumn)

The temperatures begin to cool, and although storms are still a threat, the weather is pleasant. The fall months are a good time to visit because they are usually quiet: beaches, attractions, and highways are all much less crowded.

Thanksgiving, on the fourth Thursday in November, is the highlight of fall for many, when families come together to eat turkey and pumpkin pie. It is followed by the biggest shopping day of the year, called Black Friday, which commercially launches the countdown to Christmas.

### September

**St. Augustine's Founding Anniversary** *(Saturday nearest 8th)*. This period-dress reenactment of the Spanish landing in 1565 is held near the spot where the first settlers stepped off their ships.
**Junior Orange Bowl** *(Sep–Mar)*, Miami. This youth festival

*Sleek craft on display at the Fort Lauderdale Boat Show*

presents more than 15 sports and cultural events.

### October

**Carnival Miami** *(second Sunday)*. A nine-day street party in Miami's Latin district *(see pp80–81)*.
**Destin Fishing Rodeo** *(all month)*. Hordes of competitive anglers show up for a frenzy of fishing that includes a two-day seafood festival in the first week.

**Boggy Bayou Mullet Festival** *(mid-Oct)*, Valparaiso and Niceville. These twin cities near Fort Walton Beach celebrate the local fish with fine food, arts, and entertainment.
**Fort Lauderdale Boat Show** *(late Oct)*. The largest in-water boat show in the world attracts yachting enthusiasts to four separate city locations.
**Fantasy Fest** *(last week)*, Key West. This wild, week-long Halloween celebration features gay festivities, masked balls, a costume contest, and lively street processions.
**Johns Pass Seafood Festival** *(last weekend)*, Madeira Beach. This popular festival attracts seafood lovers to Johns Pass Village *(see p256)*.
**Guavaween** *(last Saturday)*, Tampa. This zany Halloween parade pokes fun at the life and history of the city, especially at an early attempt to grow guavas in the area.

### November

**Florida Seafood Festival** *(first weekend)*. Billed as Florida's oldest maritime event, Apalachicola offers a blessing of the fishing fleet, net-making lessons, oyster-shucking contests, and best of all, seafood eating.
**Great Gulf Coast Arts Festival** *(early Nov)* Pensacola. Enjoy visual and performance arts, along with good music and local food.
**Miami Book Fair International** *(mid-Nov)*. Publishers, authors, and bookworms congregate for this cultural highlight.
**St. Augustine Art & Craft Festival** *(last weekend)*. Juried fine art and craft fair is a fundraiser for the local Art Association.

*A vendor preparing shrimps at the Florida Seafood Festival*

## Average Monthly Temperature

**Temperature Chart**
This chart shows the average temperature in Florida in centigrade and Fahrenheit. In the north, even in winter, the evenings are only mildly chilly, and snow is very rare, although it is too cold for swimming. In southern Florida, the hot summer temperatures are exacerbated by the high humidity.

## Winter

Winter months are full of excitement in anticipation of Christmas and New Year's. The flood of "snowbirds" from the north intensifies. The celebrities arrive too, some to relax, others to perform during the state's busiest entertainment season. The crowds multiply at Walt Disney World®, and the Magic Kingdom® is at its most colorful.

### December

**Winterfest Boat Parade** *(early Dec)*, Fort Lauderdale. Boats decked with lights cruise the Intracoastal Waterway in a magical night-time display.
**St. Augustine Grand Illumination** *(early Dec)*. Torchlight parade through the old town, and a boat parade in front of the Castillo de San Marcos.

Santa on the Intracoastal Waterway for a sunny Florida Christmas

### January

**Orange Bowl** *(New Year's Day)*, Miami. The big post-season college football game.
**Las Olas Art Fair** *(early Jan)*, Fort Lauderdale. Las Olas Boulevard's street fair offers art displays, tasty food, and music.
**Greek Epiphany Day** *(Jan 6)*, Tarpon Springs. Ceremonies, feasts, and music at the St. Nicholas Greek Orthodox Cathedral *(see p255)*.

Pirates arriving for mock invasion at Tampa's annual Gasparilla Festival

**Art Deco Weekend** *(mid-Jan)*, Miami Beach. A street party in the Art Deco area *(see pp64–72)*.
**Winter Equestrian Festival** *(Jan–Mar)*, Wellington. Seven major equestrian events.
**Downtown Venice Craft Festival** *(late Jan)*. Quiet, romantic Venice spruces up its downtown streets for this very popular crafts bazaar.
**Gasparilla Festival** *(late Jan)*, Tampa. A boisterous party, with boat parades and locals in appropriate dress, in memory of the pirates who ravaged the coast *(see p267)*.

### February

**Florida State Fair** *(early-Feb)*, Tampa. A range of Carnival rides and big-name performers can be enjoyed at this fair.
**Speed Weeks** *(first three weeks)*, Daytona Beach. These motor races build up to the famous Daytona 500 on the final Sunday *(see pp222–3)*.
**Coconut Grove Arts Festival** *(mid-Feb)*, Miami. This avant-garde art show is one of the country's largest *(see p88)*.
**Swamp Cabbage Festival** *(last weekend)*, La Belle, east of Fort Myers. Rodeos, dancing, as well as delicacies made from the heart of the Palmetto, the palm tree, which is the state symbol of Florida.

### Public Holidays

**New Year's Day**
(Jan 1)
**Martin Luther King Day**
(3rd Mon, Jan)
**Presidents' Day**
(3rd Mon, Feb)
**Memorial Day**
(last Mon, May)
**Independence Day**
(Jul 4)
**Labor Day**
(1st Mon, Sep)
**Columbus Day**
(2nd Mon, Oct)
**Election Day**
(1st Tue, Nov)
**Veterans Day** (Nov 11)
**Thanksgiving** (4th Thu, Nov)
**Christmas Day** (Dec 25)

# THE HISTORY OF FLORIDA

At first glance, Florida appears to be a state with little history, but behind the state's modern veneer lies a long and rich past, molded by many different nationalities and cultures.

Until the 16th century, Florida supported a large indigenous population. Many of its tribes had complex political and religious systems that demonstrated a high degree of social organization. However, after Ponce de León first sighted "La Florida" in 1513, Spanish colonization quickly decimated the Native American population through warfare and disease.

French explorers troubled the Spanish initially, but a real threat to their control came only much later. In 1742 English colonists from Georgia defeated the Spanish, and thus acquired Florida through the Treaty of Paris in 1763. Florida was returned to Spain in 1783, but numerous boundary disputes and the War of 1812 soon followed; Andrew Jackson captured Pensacola from the British in 1819, and the official US occupation took place in 1821.

American attempts to remove the Seminoles from Florida led to conflicts that lasted more than 65 years. Soon after the Seminole Wars came the Civil War, by the end of which, in 1865, the state was in ruins. However Florida soon recovered. Entrepreneurs such as Henry Flagler built a network of railroads and luxurious hotels that attracted wealthy tourists from the north. Tourism flourished during the early 20th century, and by 1950 it had become Florida's top industry.

As the state opened up, agriculture expanded and migrants flooded in. The recession of the 1920s and 1930s was only a short hiatus in the state's growth, and between 1940 and 1990 the population increased sixfold.

Today, Florida is home to a sizeable Hispanic community, with a strong Cuban presence, as well as many other ethnic groups. Economic inequalities have led to social problems, and the state's relentless urbanization has put a severe strain on the environment, but Florida is still booming.

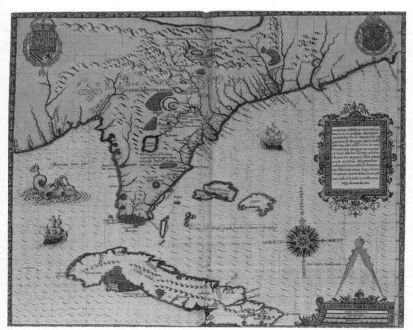

Theodore de Brys' 16th-century map of Florida, one of the earliest in existence

◀ An early postcard from Florida, a popular vacation destination in the 1920s

# Prehistoric Florida

Florida was once part of the volcanic chain that formed the Caribbean islands. This eroded over millions of years and was submerged. When the land finally re-emerged, Florida was connected to North America. Humans first arrived in Florida after the last Ice Age and formed distinct tribes. Some started as nomadic hunter-gatherer societies, developing into ones with permanent settlements along Florida's bountiful rivers and rich seaboard. A high degree of religious and political organization was common to many groups by around AD 1000, and was manifested especially in the building of burial and temple mounds.

**Early Tribal Contacts**
— Areas in contact

**Human Effigy Vessel**
This painted ceramic burial urn dates from AD 400–600. Such vessels were often very ornate and usually depicted birds and animals. "Kill holes" were often made in the pots to allow the soul of the pottery to accompany that of the dead.

**Pots** were often incised. This added to the surface area of the vessel and increased its resistance to heat, as well as making it more aesthetically pleasing.

**Copper headdress plate** were made of hammered copper that came from as far away as the Great Lakes

## Florida's Prehistoric Tribes

*Agriculture and burial mounds, traits shared with groups elsewhere in the southeast US, were associated with the Timucua and other tribes in north Florida. Southern tribes, such as the Calusa and Tequesta, left a legacy of woodcarvings and midden mounds, which indicate a diet based on fish and shellfish.*

### Marco Island's Secret

In 1896, a unique discovery was made on Marco Island *(see p288)*. Many ancient Calusa Native American artifacts of perishable organic material were found perfectly preserved in swampland. However, once out of the protective mangrove sludge, the objects quickly crumbled away. Today, sadly, just one or two of these extraordinary pieces, which include ceremonial items such as carvings and masks, survive.

**Calusa woodcarving**

**Fired Bowl**
Made c. AD 800, this ceramic bowl probably had a ceremonial use. Markings help archaeologists to identify the makers of the pot.

**c. 10,000** Palaeo-Indian stone tools are first made by Florida's earliest inhabitants

*Atlatls or throwing sticks, part of the tool-kit after 6000 BC*

| 10,000 BC | 9000 BC | 8000 BC | 7000 BC | 6000 BC | 5000 B |

*The skeleton of a mastodon, an Ice Age animal that once lived in Florida*

**c. 7500** The temperature rises and people start to hunt smaller animals such as deer, and include more plant foods in their diet

**c. 5000** The first semipermanent settlements are built along the St. Johns River, creating large midden mounds

**Timucua Native American Woman**
The first drawings of Native Americans of Florida show that they were heavily tattooed. Wooden ear plugs and shell jewelry were widely used, and clothing – animal skins and Spanish moss – was minimal.

**Clay Pipe**
Ancient Floridians ritually used a very powerful tobacco. Whether drunk as an infusion, chewed, or smoked in clay or stone pipes, the tobacco produced vivid hallucinations.

## Where to See Prehistoric Florida

Historical museums all over the state contain items relating to Florida's prehistory. Most notable is the Florida Museum of Natural History in Gainesville *(see p227)*. Temple mound sites at Crystal River and Fort Walton Beach both have museums attached – Crystal River *(p254)* is in a particularly attractive setting.

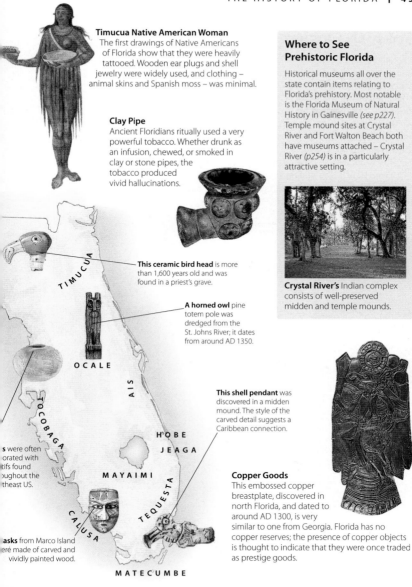

**Crystal River's** Indian complex consists of well-preserved midden and temple mounds.

**This ceramic bird head** is more than 1,600 years old and was found in a priest's grave.

**A horned owl** pine totem pole was dredged from the St. Johns River; it dates from around AD 1350.

TIMUCUA

OCALE

AIS

TOCOBAGA

HOBE

JEAGA

MAYAIMI

CALUSA

TEQUESTA

MATECUMBE

**This shell pendant** was discovered in a midden mound. The style of the carved detail suggests a Caribbean connection.

**Copper Goods**
This embossed copper breastplate, discovered in north Florida, and dated to around AD 1300, is very similar to one from Georgia. Florida has no copper reserves; the presence of copper objects is thought to indicate that they were once traded as prestige goods.

...s were often ...orated with ...tifs found ...oughout the ...heast US.

...asks from Marco Island ...ere made of carved and ...vividly painted wood.

c. 1000 Northern Florida sees a shift from a basic hunter-gatherer economy to one of cultivation. The settled communities develop more complex societies, and the first burial mounds are built

c.1000 Political systems and religious practices develop, and temple mounds are built. Increased contact with tribal groups outside Florida

| 4000 BC | 3000 BC | 2000 BC | 1000 BC | AD 1 | AD 1000 |

c. 3000 From this time, Florida enjoys a climate that is similar to that of today

c. 2000 The first crude pottery appears in Florida

*A temple structure, built on top of a burial mound*

c. 800 First evidence of corn crops being grown in north Florida

# Spanish Florida

After Juan Ponce de León first sighted Florida in 1513, several Spanish conquistadors attempted unsuccessfully to find gold and to colonize the region. The French were the first to establish a fort in 1564, but it was soon destroyed by the Spanish: the Gulf Stream carried Spanish treasure ships from other New World colonies past Florida's coast, and it was vital that "La Florida" did not fall into enemy hands. The Spanish introduced Christianity, horses, and cattle. European diseases, in addition to the brutality of the conquistadors, decimated local Native American populations. Britain, eager to expand her American colonies, led several raids into Florida in the 1700s, in an attempt to supplant Spanish rule.

**Spanish Fleet Sea Routes**
— Sea routes

**Ribault's Column,** erected in 1562 *(see p211)*, marked the French claim to north Florida.

**Juan Ponce de León**
While searching for gold, Ponce de León found land that he named *Pascua Florida,* after the Feast of Flowers (Easter).

**Corn,** native to Florida, was a staple crop for indigenous peoples.

## Fort Mose

Runaway slaves escaping the harsh conditions in the British Carolinas fled to Florida, where, as in other Spanish colonies, slaves enjoyed certain rights. The Spanish saw the advantage of helping Britain's enemies, and in 1738 created Fort Mose, near the garrison town of St. Augustine *(see p216–17)*, for the run-aways. This fort, with its own militia and businesses, is regarded as North America's first independent black community.

Black militiaman in the Spanish colonies

## Florida's First Settlement

*The Huguenot René Goulaine de Laudonnière founded "La Caroline," Florida's first successful European settlement, in 1564. Another Frenchman, Le Moyne, painted the Timucua greeting the colonizers.*

**1513** Ponce de León discovers Florida. He tries to establish a Spanish colony eight years later, but is unsuccessful

*Hernando de Soto's signature*

**1622** The Spanish ships *Atocha* and *Santa Margarita* sink during a hurricane

**c.1609** *A History of the Conquest of Florida* is published by Garcilasso Inca del Vega

| 1520 | 1540 | 1560 | 1580 | 1600 | 1620 |
|------|------|------|------|------|------|

**1528** Pánfilo de Narváez lands in Tampa Bay in search of El Dorado, the land of gold

**1539** Hernando de Soto arrives at Tampa Bay with 600 men, but he dies by the Mississippi River three years later

**1566** The Jesuits arrive in Florida

**1565** Pedro Menéndez de Avilés founds San Agustín (St. Augustine) after defeating the French

*Cross-section of the Atocha*

### Hernando de Soto
De Soto was the most ruthless of the conquistadors. His search for gold led to the massacre of many native people – only a third of his own party survived.

### Silver and Gold Hair Ornament
Native artifacts made of precious metals fueled the Spanish myth of El Dorado. In fact, the metals came from Spanish wrecks.

### Where to See Spanish Florida

In St. Petersburg, the De Soto National Memorial marks the spot where de Soto landed *(see p271)*. A reconstruction of Fort Caroline *(p211)* lies just outside Jacksonville. However, the best place to see the Spanish legacy is in St. Augustine *(pp214–15)* and its imposing Castillo de San Marcos *(pp218–19)*.

**Nuestra Senora de la Leche** is a shrine in St. Augustine founded by de Avilés in 1565.

**René Goulaine de Laudonnière** surveys the offerings of the Native Americans.

### Sir Francis Drake
Spain's power in the New World colonies worried the British. Drake, an English buccaneer, burned down St. Augustine in 1586.

**Athore,** the chief of the Timucua, shows the French colonizers his tribe worshiping at Ribault's Column.

### Codice Osuna
This 16th-century manuscript depicts members of Tristan de Luna's expedition to Florida. In 1559, a hurricane destroyed his camp at Pensacola Bay, destroying his attempts at colonization.

---

**1670** The Treaty of Madrid defines the Spanish claim to the New World

*The pirate Blackbeard's flag*

**1718** Blackbeard, who terrorized the east coast of Florida, is killed off North Carolina

**1740** The British, based in Georgia, besiege the Castillo de San Marcos

**1763** Under the Treaty of Paris, Britain gets Florida and returns recently captured Cuba to Spain

| 640 | 1660 | 1680 | 1700 | 1720 | 1740 | 1760 |

**1687** The first eight slaves fleeing the British plantations in the Carolinas arrive in Florida

**1693** The Spanish establish Pensacola, which is permanently settled five years later

**1702** The British raze St. Augustine

*Castillo de San Marcos, St. Augustine*

**1756** Castillo de San Marcos is completed

# The Fight for Florida

A plentiful supply of hides and furs, and the opportunity to expand the plantation system, attracted the British to Florida. After taking control in 1763, they divided the colony in two. Florida was subsidized by Britain and so stayed loyal during the American Revolution. However, Spain regained West Florida in 1781, and East Florida was handed back two years later. American slaves fled to Florida creating antagonism between Spain and the US. This was exacerbated by Native American raids to the north and their alliance with the runaway slaves. General Andrew Jackson invaded Spanish Florida, captured Pensacola, and even occupied West Florida, thus provoking the First Seminole War.

**British Florida 1763–83**
    East Florida
    West Florida

**The Spanish Caste System**
Few Spanish women came to the colonies, so Spanish men often took wives from native tribes, as well as African-American wives. A hierarchical caste system emerged – with those of pure Spanish blood at the top.

**Fort George** was the main British fortification at Pensacola.

**A drummer** kept the marching beat, and led soldiers into battle.

**Brazier**
Used for warmth during northern Florida winters, a brazier could also smoke out mosquitoes in summer.

**The Capture of Pensacola**
*In 1781, after a month-long siege, the Spaniard Bernardo de Gálvez defeated the British and captured Pensacola for Spain. His victory undoubtedly helped th bid for independence made by the American colonies.*

**1776** American Revolution leaves Britain's reserves heavily depleted, and British loyalists begin to abandon Florida

**1783** Under the Second Treaty of Paris, Britain recognizes American independence, gains the Bahamas and Gibraltar, and returns Florida to the Spanish, who start to colonize it in earnest

**1785–1821** Several Spanish-American border disputes occur

| 1765 | 1770 | 1775 | 1780 | 1785 |

*British soldier in the American Revolution*

**1781** Under de Gálvez, the Spanish land at Pensacola and capture West Florida

**1782** US Congress chooses the bald eagle as the emblem of the new republic

*National emblem*

### General Jackson

An ambitious soldier, Andrew Jackson led many raids into Florida and eventually conquered it. His successes made him the ideal candidate to become Florida's first American governor in 1821 and, later, the seventh US president.

### William Bartram's Illustrations

In 1765, William Bartram was appointed the royal botanist in America. He documented Florida's wildlife and her indigenous peoples.

### Bernardo de Gálvez,

the 27-year-old Spanish governor of Louisiana, was wounded in action in the battle for Pensacola.

### Political Cartoon

This cartoon shows the horse America throwing his master. British loyalists in East Florida were dismayed by the loss of the Colonies after 1783, and soon chose to leave Florida.

### Where to See the Fight for Florida

The Kingsley Plantation (see p211) near Jacksonville is the state's oldest surviving plantation house. Pensacola's historic Seville District (p234) was laid out by the British during their occupation, and St. Augustine (pp214–17) contains several buildings dating from this era; they include the British Government House, and the Ximenez-Fatio house, from the second period of Spanish rule.

**Kingsley Plantation** occupies a lovely setting at the mouth of the St. Johns River.

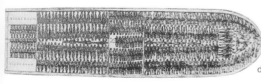

### The Slave Trade

Slavery fueled the plantation system. The journey from Africa to America could take months, and slaves were so tightly packed on board ship that many died en route.

---

**1800** Spain cedes West Florida's Louisiana territories to the French

**1803** The US buys Louisiana and pushes east, creating Florida's present western boundary. The US claims West Florida

**1808** A law banning the slave trade is enacted by the US Congress, but it is widely ignored

*Slave manacles*

**1817** First Seminole War begins

| 1795 | 1800 | 1805 | 1810 | 1815 |

**1795** Spain cedes territory north of the 31st parallel to the US

*The Patriots of East Florida's flag*

**1812** American patriots capture Amelia Island, demanding that the US annex East Florida from the Spanish. Their attempt fails but instills the feeling that Florida should belong to America

**1819** To settle Spain's $5 million debt to the US, all Spanish territories east of the Mississippi (including Florida) are ceded to the US.

# Antebellum Florida

After Florida became part of the US in 1821, American settlement proceeded quickly, and the plantation system was firmly established in north Florida. The settlers wanted good land, so the Federal government tried to remove all Native Americans to west of the Mississippi; resulting conflicts developed into the Second and Third Seminole Wars. After Abraham Lincoln, an opponent of slavery, was elected president in 1860, Florida became the third state to secede from the Union. During the ensuing Civil War it saw little action; Florida's chief role was to supply food (especially beef and salt) to the Confederates.

**Native Lands 1823–32**
Native reservation land

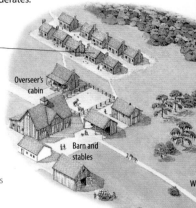

**Slave cabins** were often log huts, built away from the main residence.

**Overseer's cabin**

**Barn and stables**

**Osceola**
The influential leader Osceola refused to move from Florida with his tribe. In 1835 he started the Second Seminole War, during which many plantations were destroyed.

## Uncle Tom's Cabin

In 1852, Harriet Beecher Stowe, a religious northerner who spent her later years in Florida, published a novel that helped to change the face of America. *Uncle Tom's Cabin* is a tale about a slave who, having rescued a white child, is sold to a sadistic master and is eventually flogged to death. It was hugely successful and furthered the cause of the antislavery lobby. During the Civil War, President Lincoln joked that Mrs. Stowe was the "little woman who started this big war."

135,000 SETS, 270,000 VOLUMES SOLD.
**UNCLE TOM'S CABIN**
FOR SALE HERE.
**The Greatest Book of the Age.**

Poster for *Uncle Tom's Cabin*

**Cotton**
The principal cash crop on plantations was cotton. It required intensive labor and the work was grueling – especially picking the cotton off the spiny bushes.

---

**1821** Jackson becomes governor of the territory of Florida

**1823** Treaty of Moultrie Creek requires the Seminoles to move from north to central Florida

**1832** Under the Treaty of Payne's Creek, 15 Seminole chiefs cede their land in Florida to the US, and agree to move west

**1835** Second Seminole War begins

*Early horse-drawn train*

| 1820 | 1825 | 1830 | 1835 | 1840 |

*Osceola refusing to sign 1832 treaty*

**c.1824** The native village of Talasi is chosen as the site of the new state capital and is renamed Tallahassee

**1832** JJ Audubon, the naturalist, visits Key West

**1829** General Jackson becomes President of the US

**1842** Second Seminole War ends

**1836** The first railroads in Florida begin operating

**Paddlesteamer**
During the Seminole and Civil Wars, steamboats were used to transport troops and supplies to the interior.

**Chief Billy Bowlegs**
In 1855, a group of surveyors pillaged Seminole land. Chief Billy Bowlegs retaliated, starting the Third Seminole War. He surrendered in 1858; however, other Seminoles retreated into the Everglades.

**Goodwood House** was built in a grand style that befitted its wealth and importance within the local community.

Laundry

Privy

Guest House

Spring House

**The kitchen** was in a separate building because of the risk of fire.

## Plantation Life

*Antebellum plantations such as Goodwood (see p247), reconstructed here, were almost self-sufficient. They had their own laws, and some housed more than 200 slaves who tended cotton, corn, and other crops.*

## Where to See Antebellum Florida

Gamble Plantation (*see p270*) sheds light on the lifestyle of a wealthy plantation owner, while at Bulow Plantation (*p220*), and Indian Key (*p298*), you can see the ruins of communities destroyed by the Seminoles. The Museum of Science and History (*p212*) in Jacksonville contains Civil War artifacts, including some from the US army steamboat *Maple Leaf*. Key West's East Martello Tower (*p304*) and Fort Zachary (*p306*), and Fort Clinch (*p210*), in the north-east, are fine examples of 19th-century forts.

**The East Martello Tower** was built by Union forces to defend Key West's Atlantic coast.

**Battle of Olustee**
In February 1864, Union forces, including two Negro regiments, were defeated by Confederate troops in the northeast. Some 10,000 men fought in the six-hour battle; 2,000 were injured and 300 died.

---

**1845** On July 4 Florida becomes the 27th state to join the United States of America. The Capitol building in Tallahassee is completed

**1848** John Gorrie invents an ice-making machine

**1855** Third Seminole War begins; three years later 163 Seminoles surrender (including Billy Bowlegs) and are forcibly removed from Florida

**1861** Civil War begins

**1865** The northern army is defeated at the Battle of Natural Bridge. The Civil War ends in the same year

| 1845 | 1850 | 1855 | 1860 | 1865 |
|------|------|------|------|------|

*Florida's first state seal*

**1852** Harriet Beecher Stowe publishes the antislavery epic, *Uncle Tom's Cabin*

**1860s** Scottish merchants found Dunedin on Florida's west coast

*Civil War bond*

# Florida's Golden Age

After the Civil War, Florida's economy was devastated, but its fine climate and small population made it a land ripe for investment. The railroad barons Henry Flagler and Henry Plant forged their lines down the east and west coasts of Florida during the late 1880s and 1890s, and tourists followed in increasing numbers, stimulating the economy. A diverse agricultural base also sheltered Florida from the depression of the 1890s that ravaged other cotton-producing states. Fortunes were made and fine mansions were built. African-Americans were less fortunate; most lost the right to vote, Ku Klux Klan violence grew, and segregation was the norm.

**Growth of the Railroads**
— Railroads by 1860
— Railroads by 1890
— Overseas Railroad by 1912

**Steamboat Tourism**
Before the advent of the railroads, tourists explored Florida's interior by paddlesteamer. Steamboats plied scenic rivers such as the Oklawaha and the St. Johns.

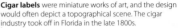

**Cigar labels** were miniature works of art, and the design would often depict a topographical scene. The cigar industry took off in Florida in the late 1800s.

**Jacob Summerlin**
After the Civil War, Jacob Summerlin, the "King of the Crackers" *(see p24)*, made his fortune by selling beef to Spanish Cuba. His wild cattle were descended, ironically, from animals that had been introduced to Florida by the conquistadors.

**Grand Hotels**
*Both Plant and Flagler built opulent palaces for rich tourists who used the railroads to escape the northern winters; these "snowbirds" would spend the winter season in style, in towns such as Tampa and St. Augustine.*

---

**1869** The first African-American Cabinet member is appointed as Secretary of State in Florida

*A Ringling Brothers' circus act*

**1885** Vincente Ybor transfers his cigar industry to Tampa

**1870s** More than 100 African-Americans are killed by the Ku Klux Klan in Jackson County

**1892** In the election, only 1 per cent of African-Americans remain eligible to vote

| 1870 | 1875 | 1880 | 1885 | 18 |
|---|---|---|---|---|

**1870** Steamboats start to take tourists, as well as goods, into the interior of Florida

**1884** Ringling brothers set up their traveling circus

**1891** The Cuban, José Martí, makes a speech in Tampa to drum up support for his independence movement

**1886** Flagler starts construction of the Florida East Coast Railroad

**1868** Vote granted to all male American citizens aged 21 and over, including African-Americans

**Rail Travel**
Many rich tourists had private railroad cars. Today Henry Flagler's can be seen at his former Palm Beach home (*see p128*).

**Where to See The Golden Age**

St. Augustine (*see pp214–19*) boasts several of Flagler's buildings, including what is today the Lightner Museum. The Tampa Bay Hotel is now the Henry B. Plant Museum (*p262*), and Fernandina has some fine examples of steam-boat architecture (*p210*). On Pigeon Key (*p300*) visitors will find Flagler's Overseas Railroad construction camp.

**Spanish-American War**
When America joined Cuba's fight against Spain in 1898, Florida boomed. Thousands of troops converged on Tampa, Miami, and Key West, and money from the nation's coffers poured in to support the war effort.

**Flagler College** in St. Augustine was once Henry Flagler's magnificent Ponce de Leon Hotel.

**The Tampa Bay Hotel,** built by Henry Plant in 1891, operated as a hotel until 1932. It had 511 rooms, and during the Spanish-American War served as the officers' quarters.

**Gilded Rocking Chair**
Representative of the decorative excesses of the 19th century, this rocking chair from the Lightner Museum (*see p217*) is elaborately embellished with scrolls and swans.

**The Birth of a Nation**
On its release in 1915, this epic film provoked a resurgence of violence by the Ku Klux Klan in Florida.

The Hillsborough River and nearby Tampa Bay helped to turn Tampa into one of the three largest Gulf ports by 1900.

**1895** Blossoming citrus groves are hit by the "Great Freeze." Julia Tuttle sends some orange blossoms to Flagler in Palm Beach to persuade him to continue his railroad to Miami

**1905** The University of Florida is established at Gainesville

*Driving on the sand at Daytona Beach*

**1918** Prohibition starts in Florida

| 1895 | 1900 | 1905 | 1910 | 1915 |

**1898** Teddy Roosevelt and his Rough Riders arrive in Tampa en route to fight in the Spanish-American War in Cuba

**1903** Alexander Winton sets a 68-mph (109-km/h) land speed record on the hard sand at Daytona Beach

**1912** Flagler steams into Key West

**1915** Dredging doubles the size of Miami Beach

**1916** Florida's cotton crop is wiped out by the boll weevil

*orange blossom*

# Boom, Bust, and Recovery

Like the rest of the US, Florida experienced times of both rapid growth and depression during the first half of the 20th century. Excited by the rampant development during the 1920s land boom, northerners poured in, many as "Tin Can Tourists" in their Model T Fords. Then, in 1926, three years before the Wall Street Crash, a real estate slump ruined many in the state. However economic recovery came earlier than in the rest of the US, with the growth of tourism and the introduction of federal schemes – many unemployed fled to Florida from the north looking for work. During and after World War II, the state continued to prosper, and in the 1950s it was boosted by the launch of the NASA space program.

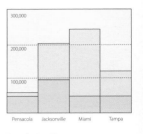

**Population Figures**
☐ 1920   ☐ 1950

### Land Boom
At the height of the boom, prime land could fetch $26,000 per acre. A great many northerners were bankrupted after unwittingly investing in swampland far from the waterfront.

### The American Dream in Florida
*Florida's warm winter climate and economic upswing attracted floods of northerners. Many who first came as visitors returned to settle, and foreign immigrants also favored the state. It was a land of opportunity with rapid urban growth and industries that provided good jobs – even the young could expect a good standard of living.*

### Hurricane of 1926
On September 18 a hurricane hit South Florida, destroying 5,000 homes. Locals said the winds "blowed a crooked road straight."

**1928** The Tamiami Trail between Tampa and Miami is officially opened

**1929** The first commercial flight between Miami to Havana is made by Pan American World Airways

**1931** Ernest Hemingway buys a house in Key West

**1935** Hurricane destroys Flagler's Overseas Railroad

1920   1925   1930   1935   194

**1926** Florida land prices crash, two banks collapse, and a hurricane hits the southeast and the Everglades, devastating Miami

**1931** Hialeah Park race track opens after pari-mutuel betting *(see p141)* is legalized

*Horse race at Hialeah Park*

**1939** Gangster Al Capone retires to an estate on Palm Island in Miami

**Tin Can Tourists**
Each winter, this new breed of tourist loaded up their cars and headed south. They stayed en masse in trailer parks, sharing their canned food and enjoying the Florida sun.

## Where to See Boomtime Florida

The Wolfsonian Foundation *(see p71)* and Miami Beach's Art Deco buildings *(pp64–71)* should not be missed. Mizner's whimsical Palm Beach legacy *(pp122–7)* is also worth visiting. Frank Lloyd Wright's college in Lakeland *(p270)* is very impressive; Henry Ford's winter home in Fort Myers *(p280)* is more modest.

**Miami Beach** contains a striking assortment of restored Art Deco buildings.

**Zora Neale Hurston**
Zora wrote about the lives of rural African-Americans. Her best known novel, *Their Eyes Were Watching God*, was written in 1937.

**Roosevelt's New Deal**
The president's New Deal, which allowed farmers to borrow money, helped Florida to recover from the Great Depression. Writers and photographers documented the policy's effects.

**World War II**
Florida was a training ground for many thousands of troops from 1941 to 1945. War reduced tourism, but the camps helped the economy.

**Citrus Industry**
Florida became the largest citrus producer in the country, helping it to survive the Depression of the 1930s.

---

**1947** President Truman opens Everglades National Park

*Racing car in the Daytona 200*

**1954** The first span of the Sunshine Skyway bridge over Tampa Bay opens

**1959** Lee Perry wins the first Daytona 200 race at the Daytona Speedway

| **1945** | **1950** | **1955** | **1960** |
|---|---|---|---|

**1945** On December 5, the disappearance of Flight 19 starts the myth of the Bermuda Triangle

**1942** In February, German U-boats torpedo a tanker just off the coast of Florida, in full view of bathers

**1958** The first Earth satellite, *Explorer I*, is launched from Florida after NASA chooses Cape Canaveral as the site of its satellite and rocket programs

*NASA logo*

# The Sixties and Beyond

Since 1960, Florida has flourished. Tourism has expanded at an unprecedented rate, and countless hotels have been built to cater to all budgets. Theme parks such as Walt Disney World®, Universal Studios®, and the Kennedy Space Center, home to NASA's space program, have brought both worldwide fame and crowds of visitors to the Sunshine State. The population has also grown rapidly, through migration from within the US and from abroad – modern Florida is home to many ethnic groups. The rapidly growing Hispanic community includes the largest Cuban population outside of Cuba. Florida is also home to a large Asian community. The negative effects of development have led to increased steps to protect natural resources: conservation has become a major issue.

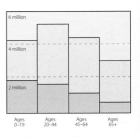

| | | | |
| 6 million | | | |
| 4 million | | | |
| 2 million | | | |
| Ages 0–19 | Ages 20–44 | Ages 45–64 | Ages 65+ |

**State Population Figures**
☐ 1960    ☐ 2010

**The Cuban Exodus**
More than 300,000 Cubans fled to Florida during the Castro regime, which began in 1959. Early arrivals came on "freedom flights," but later refugees had to make the trip by season flimsy rafts. Relations between the countries have changed since Fidel Castro's death in 2016.

**Martin Luther King**
The Civil Rights movement reached Florida in the 1960s. Martin Luther King Jr, (the movement's most prominent leader), was arrested while on a march in St. Augustine in 1964.

**SpaceX Dragon**
*In 2012, Space X became the world's first commercial space company to deliver cargo to the International Space Station. Under an agreement with NASA, SpaceX is developing the vessel to fly crew for manned flights.*

**1964** Martin Luther King Jr. is arrested and imprisoned in St. Augustine

**1962** Cuban missile crisis

**1961** Alan Shephard becomes the first US man in space

*Alan Shephard, NASA astronaut*

**1969** Apollo II is launched from Cape Canaveral. Buzz Aldrin and Neil Armstrong are the first men to walk on the moon

**1973** Dade County is officially bilingual, and English-Spanish road signs are erected

**1970**

**1971** The Magic Kingdom®, Walt Disney's first venture in Florida, opens in Orlando at a cost of $700 million

**1977** Snow falls on Miami in January

**1981** Maiden voyage of the Space Shuttle

**1980** 125,000 Cubans arrive in Florida in the Mariel boatlift, which is launched by Fidel Castro and lasts for five months

**1980**

**1982** Key West declares itself the "Conch Republic" for just one week

**1986** The space shuttle *Challenge* explodes, killing seven crew mem

**1990** General Noriega, the former ruler of Panama, faces drugs charges in Miami

### Conservation
One way Floridians can support the conservation movement is by buying a special license plate. Money raised goes to the cause depicted.

**Miami Art**
Graffiti is now considered high art in the Wynwood area. The downtown Perez Art Museum boasts a vast collection of art from the Americas.

## Where to See Modern Florida

Florida has plenty of fine modern architecture, from the skyscrapers in downtown Miami *(see pp74–81)* and Jacksonville *(see p212)* to the Florida Aquarium in Tampa *(see p266)*. To see a more nostalgic approach to modern architecture, visit Seaside in the Panhandle *(see p240)*.

**Naturalization**
Becoming a US citizen is the dream of many immigrants. Thousands pledge an oath of allegiance together at mass ceremonies.

**Downtown Miami's** modern skyscrapers create a distinctive and impressive city skyline.

**SpaceX Falcon 9** rocket launches the Dragon capsule into orbit from Cape Canaveral.

**Florida's Elderly**
Just less than 20 per cent of Florida's population is over 65 years old. Many retirees are attracted to the state by its low taxes and easy, outdoors lifestyle.

**Caribbean Cruises**
Tourism is big business in Florida, and cruises in state-of-the-art ships are an increasingly popular vacation choice.

---

**1992** Hurricane Andrew wreaks havoc on South Florida

**1993** The Task Force on Tourist Safety is created

**1994** Another influx of Cubans arrives in Florida

**2000** George Bush wins controversial presidential elections

**2002** Jimmy Carter becomes the first US President to visit Cuba since the embargo began

**2003** Space shuttle *Columbia* explodes on re-entry into Earth's atmosphere, killing all its crew

**2004** One of the deadliest hurricane seasons in history inflicts more than $40 billion in damage

*George W. Bush*

**2011** After operating for 30 years, NASA's Space Shuttle program ends with its final mission, *Atlantis*

**2012** The first commercial space company, SpaceX, delivers cargo to the International Space Station, carried on the Dragon spacecraft

**2014** President Barack Obama opens relations with Cuba. Regular flights from Florida to the island begin

**2016** 49 young people were gunned down at Pulse nightclub in Orlando

**2000** **2010** **2020**

# MIAMI
# AREA BY AREA

# Miami at a Glance

Miami has been called the Magic City because what was merely a trading outpost a century ago now sprawls for 2,000 sq miles (5,200 sq km) and boasts a population of more than five million. Visitors are most likely to remember Miami for its fun-filled South Beach, for its beautiful beaches, and for the Latin and Caribbean culture that permeates daily life. Greater Miami attracts more than 15.8 million visitors each year.

**Little Havana,** the original heart of the city's Cuban community, is Miami's most welcoming neighborhood. Life in the streets is fun, with domino games and busy cafés (*see pp80–81*).

**The Biltmore Hotel** epitomizes Coral Gables, the exclusive minicity developed during the 1920s real estate boom. Tales of celebrity guests and Mafia murders add to the mystique of the luxurious hotel (*see pp84–7*).

**CORAL GABLES AND COCONUT GROVE** (*See pp82–91*)

WEST FLAGLER ST

SW 8TH STREET

SW 22ND STREET

GRANADA BLVD

SW 42ND AVE

S DIXIE HWY

HARDEE RD

**The "International Villages"** are clusters of ethnic architecture, from French to Chinese, hidden away along the shady streets of Coral Gables. A tour of them will provide a taste of Miami's loveliest suburb (*see pp84–5*).

**Coconut Grove Village** is a small, friendly area which focuses on entertainment. Enjoy a relaxing amble or shop in the daytime, before heading for the restaurants and bars, which come to life in the evening (*see p88*).

◄ Aerial view of Downtown Miami

**Downtown Miami** is the commercial hub of the city. Its appeal lies in its eye-catching high-rise architecture, such as the Southeast Financial Center, pictured here, and in the Hispanic bustle on the streets (*see pp76–9*).

W 41ST ST

MIAMI BEACH
(*See pp62–73*)

ALTON RD

**South Beach** is ideal for people-watching or taking part in the fun and games of the resort. During the daytime you can take it easy on the fabulous sandy beach (*see pp68–70*).

8TH STREET

VNTOWN AND
TLE HAVANA
(*See pp74–81*)

0 kilometers    2
0 miles    1

**The Art Deco District** of South Beach boasts many dazzling 1930s buildings, with decorative features unique to Florida (*see pp64–71*).

**Vizcaya** is Miami's top premier sight. The early 20th-century Italianate mansion has rooms decorated in all imaginable styles, while the gardens are dotted with statues, and picturesque buildings, such as this romantic teahouse (*see pp90–91*).

# MIAMI BEACH

Often referred to as the American Riviera, Miami Beach was a sandbar accessible only by boat a century ago. It was the building of a bridge to the mainland in 1913 that enabled real estate investors such as millionaire Carl Fisher to begin developing the island. The resort they created from nothing took off in the 1920s, becoming a spectacular winter playground. The devastating hurricane of 1926 and the 1929 Wall Street Crash signaled the end of the boom, but Miami Beach bounced back in the 1930s with the erection of hundreds of Art Deco buildings, only to decline again after World War II. In another metamorphosis, Miami Beach rose once again. As a result of a spirited preservation campaign, South

Beach (the southern part of Miami Beach) has been given a new lease of life. It boasts the world's largest concentration of Art Deco buildings, whose funky colors are no less arresting than the local population of body builders, fashion models, and drag queens. Anything goes in South Beach, where the mood veers between the chic and the bohemian, hence its nickname SoBe – after New York's hip SoHo district. The Art Deco hotels along Ocean Drive are everyone's favorite haunt but there are other diversions, from trendy shops to art museums. The district north of SoBe tempts few people, but what the two areas do share is a superb sandy beach, unbroken for miles.

## Sights at a Glance

**Museums and Galleries**
- ❸ Jewish Museum of Florida
- ❺ The Wolfsonian Museum-FIU
- ❾ Bass Museum of Art

**Streets and Neighborhoods**
- ❶ Ocean Drive
- ❹ Collins and Washington Avenues
- ❻ Española Way
- ❼ Lincoln Road Mall
- ❿ Central Miami Beach

**Beaches**
- ❷ The Beach

**Monuments**
- ❽ Holocaust Memorial

0 meters 1,000
0 yards 1,000

See also Street Finder map 2

◀ Art Deco architecture at Ocean Drive in South Beach, Miami

For keys to symbols *see back flap*

# Ocean Drive: Deco Style

The cream of South Beach's Art Deco District, which consists of some 800 preserved buildings, is found on Ocean Drive. Its splendid array of buildings illustrates Miami's unique interpretation of the Art Deco style, which took the world by storm in the 1920s and 1930s. Florida's version, often called Tropical Deco, is fun and jaunty. Motifs such as flamingos and sunbursts are common, and South Beach's seaside location inspired features more befitting an ocean liner than a building. Using inexpensive materials, architects managed to create an impression of stylishness for what were, in fact, very modest hotels. The best of the buildings along Ocean Drive are illustrated here, and on pages 66–7.

**Ocean Drive: 6th to 9th Streets**

**White, blue, and green** were popular colors in the 1930s and 1940s; they echo Miami's tropical vegetation and the ocean.

**Windows** are often continuous around corners.

**View along Ocean Drive**

① **The Celino** (1937) Henry Hohauser, the most famous architect to work in Miami, designed this hotel. It has fine etched windows.

**Angular edges** exemplify the influence of Cubism.

**Bands of windows** provide plenty of light and, when open, encourage the circulation of cooling sea breezes.

**A flamingo** is etched into glass doors in the Beacon's lobby.

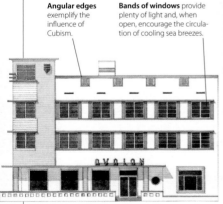

④ **Avalon** (1941) The Avalon is a fine example of Streamline Moderne. The lack of ornamentation and the asymmetrical design are typical, as is the emphasis on horizontal as opposed to vertical lines.

⑤ **Beacon** (1936) The traditional abstract decoration above the ground floor windows of the Beacon has been brightened by a contemporary color scheme, an example of Leonard Horowitz's Deco Dazzle *(see p71)*.

## Art Deco: from Paris to Miami

The Art Deco style emerged following the 1925 Exposition Internationale des Arts Décoratifs et Industriels Modernes in Paris. Traditional Art Deco combined all kinds of influences, from Art Nouveau's flowery forms and Egyptian imagery, to the geometric

patterns of Cubism. In 1930s America, Art Deco buildings reflected the belief that technology was the way forward, absorbing features that embodied the Machine Age and the fantasies of science fiction. Art Deco evolved into a style called Stream-line Moderne, which dominates along Ocean Drive. Few buildings in South Beach stick to just one style. Indeed it is the creative mix of classic Art Deco details with streamlining and tropical motifs that has made the architecture along Ocean Drive unique.

**Deco-style postcard of the Avalon Hotel**

**The Berkeley Shore**, behind Ocean Drive on Collins Avenue, has classic Streamline Moderne features such as this stepped parapet.

**Circles**, as decoration or as windows, were inspired by the portholes used in ship design.

**The lobby** of the Majestic has splendid brass elevator doors.

**Bas-relief friezes** are a recurrent decorative element on Ocean Drive façades.

② **Imperial** (1939) The design of the Imperial echoes that of the earlier Park Central next door.

③ **Majestic** (1940) This hotel was the work of Albert Anis, the architect also responsible for the nearby Avalon and Waldorf hotels.

**Racing stripes** are typical of Streamline Moderne.

**"Eyebrows"** – flat overhangs above the windows – are ideal for providing shade against the unrelenting Miami sun.

**This ornamental lighthouse** is one of the most evocative examples of Ocean Drive's "architecture for the seashore."

**Neon lighting** was frequently used to highlight hotel signs and architectural features, so that they could be enjoyed after dark.

**Porthole windows**

⑥ **Colony** (1935) One of Henry Hohauser's finest hotels, the Colony has Ocean Drive's most famous neon sign and an interesting mural in the lobby.

⑦ **Waldorf Towers** (1937) The maritime influence on the design of the Waldorf and some other hotels led to the coining of the phrase "Nautical Moderne."

# Ocean Drive: Deco Style

Three principal Art Deco styles exist in South Beach: traditional Art Deco, the more futuristic Streamline Moderne, and Mediterranean Revival, which is derived from French, Italian, and Spanish architecture. The unusual injection of Mediterranean Revival influences along Ocean Drive is noticeable mainly between 9th and 13th streets. It is here that visitors will find some of South Beach's best known Art Deco buildings.

**Ocean Drive: 10th to 13th Streets**

**The central tower** imitates both a ship's funnel and the totems of Native American culture.

**Colored strips,** or "racing stripes," invoke a feeling of speed and motion.

**The railings** edging the roof imitate those on a ship's deck.

**⑧ Breakwater** (1939)
The Breakwater, by Anton Skislewicz, is a classic Streamline Moderne hotel with its racing stripes and a striking central tower. A multimillion-dollar renovation has seen the hotel restored to its original splendor.

**The window arches** and columned porch are evocative of Mediterranean architecture.

**⑨ Edison** (1935) Hohauser
*(see p64)* experimented here with Mediterranean Revivalism, although he was preceded by the architect of the nearby Adrian.

**The sign** for the Leslie Hotel is simple, like the building – in contrast with the more exuberant Carlyle next door.

Corner windows

**Flat roofs** are the norm along Ocean Drive, but these are often interrupted by a tower or other vertical projection.

**⑫ Leslie** (1937)
This classic Art Deco hotel's vertical lines are picked out in pale yellow, as the bright colors of the past decade are being replaced by white and pastels.

**⑬ Carlyle** (1941)
With its three stories and three vertical columns, the Carlyle makes use of the classic Deco divisions, sometimes known as the "holy three." Most hotels along Ocean Drive have three floors.

**A salamander** in stucco above the front entrance to the Abbey Hotel, on 21st Street, adds a colorful and playful touch to the building's façade.

**Vertical fluting** occurs frequently along Ocean Drive.

**"Eyebrow" overhangs** shade the windows.

## Preserving South Beach

The campaign to save the Art Deco architecture of South Beach began in 1976, when Barbara Capitman (1920–90) set up the Miami Design Preservation League – at a time when much of the area was destined to disappear under a sea of high-rises. Three years later, 1 sq m (2.5 sq km) of South Beach became the first 20th-century district in the country's National Register of Historic Places. Battles still raged against developers throughout the 1980s and 1990s, when candlelit vigils helped to save some buildings.

Barbara Capitman in 1981

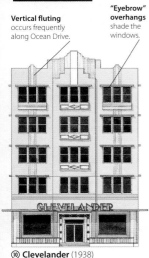

**⑩ Clevelander** (1938)
This hotel's architect, Albert Anis, used classic Deco materials, such as glass blocks in the hotel's bar – now a top South Beach nightspot.

Terracotta tiles

**Reinforced concrete** was the most common building material used along Ocean Drive, with walls generally covered in stucco.

**A verandah** is a prerequisite for most Ocean Drive hotels.

**⑪ Adrian** (1934)
With its subdued colors and chiefly Mediterranean inspiration, the Adrian stands out among neighboring buildings.

**The corners** of the building are beautifully rounded.

**The terrazzo floor** in the bar is a mix of stone chips and mortar – a cheap version of marble that produced style at minimal cost.

**The frieze** recalls the abstract designs of the Aztecs.

**⑭ Cardozo** (1939)
A late Hohauser work and Barbara Capitman's favorite hotel, this is a Streamline masterpiece, in which the detail of traditional Art Deco is replaced with curved sides and other expressions of the modern age.

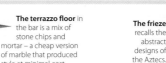

**⑮ Cavalier** (1936)
With its sharp edges, this traditional Art Deco hotel provides quite a contrast to the later Cardozo next door.

# Street-by-Street: South Beach

The Art Deco district of South Beach, which runs from 6th to 23rd streets between Lenox Avenue and Ocean Drive, has attracted an increasing number of visitors since the 1980s. Helped by the interest shown by celebrities such as Gloria Estefan and Michael Caine, the area has been transformed into one of the trendiest places in the States. For many visitors the Deco buildings serve merely as a backdrop for a hedonistic playground, where days are for sleeping, lying on the beach, or long workouts at the gym, and evenings are for dancing into the early hours. Whether your passions are social or architectural, the route shown can be enjoyed both during the day and night – when a sea of neon enhances the party atmosphere.

**The Old City Hall,** a 1920s Mediterranean-style building, ended its service as city hall in 1977, but it remains a distinctive South Beach landmark, towering above the surrounding streets.

**11th Street Diner**
*(see p329)*

**❺ Wolfsonian Museum-FIU**
The Wolfsonian, with a striking Spanish Baroque-style relief around its main entrance, houses an excellent collection of fine and decorative arts.

**The Essex House Hotel,** by Henry Hohauser *(see p64)*, has typical Deco features such as the rounded corner entry. Its lobby is also well worth a look.

**The News Café** is a favorite South Beach haunt *(see p329)*, open 24 hours a day and always buzzing. The sidewalk tables make it a prime spot for people-watching.

WASHINGTON AVENUE

9TH STREET

COLLINS AVENUE

11TH STREET

10TH STREET

## ART DECO TOURS

The Miami Design Preservation League offers 90-minute guided walking tours from the Art Deco Welcome Center (1001 Ocean Drive) at 10:30am daily and 6:30pm Thu; audio tours daily; also the Art Deco Weekend *(see p41)*.
For information call the Art Deco Welcome Center at (305) 763-8026. 🚶 Ⓦ **mdpl.org**

| 0 meters | 75 |
| 0 yards | 75 |

**Key**

— Suggested route

**Art Deco Welcome Center**

**Beach Patrol Station**

*For hotels and restaurants in this area see pp314–15 and pp329–30*

**★ South Beach Bars and Clubs**
A visit to South Beach is not complete unless you experience one of its trendy bars or clubs, such as the Marlin Hotel on Collins Avenue.

**Locator Map**
See Street Finder map 2

**❶ ★ Ocean Drive**
Ocean Drive is the star attraction of South Beach – for its many stylish hotels, and the colorful parade of rollerbladers and other people out being seen.

**The Netherland Hotel**
*(1935)*, at the quiet end of Ocean Drive, boasts colorful stucco decoration. It is now a condominium.

**The Amsterdam Palace**, now known as The Villa Casa Casuarina, was home of designer Gianni Versace. It is now a luxury hotel.

Lummus Park

**The Cardozo Hotel**, among the cream of Ocean Drive's Deco buildings, marked the start of a new era of restoration in South Beach when it reopened in 1982. It is now owned by Gloria Estefan.

**❷ ★ The Beach**
Sand extends for 10 miles (16 km) up the coast. The beach changes atmosphere depending on where you are. It is at its broadest and liveliest in South Beach.

# South Beach

Ocean Drive has the most well-known Deco buildings in South Beach. There are also wonderful discoveries to be made on Collins and Washington Avenues, as well as farther west in quieter residential streets, such as Lenox Avenue, where visitors will find doors etched with flamingos and other Deco features.

South Beach, or SoBe, is best explored on foot since parking is difficult. Alternatively, join the locals on rollerblades or bicycles – both of which can be rented locally.

The Amsterdam Palace, one of Ocean Drive's few non-Deco buildings

## ❶ Ocean Drive

**Map** 2 F3, F4. 150 Miami Beach Airport Flyer, M (113), S (119), C (103), 120 Beach MAX. ℹ 1001 Ocean Drive, (305) 672-2014; Art Deco Welcome Center, (305) 763-8026. 🌐 mdpl.org

Spending time at one of the bars or cafés on the waterfront is arguably the best way to experience Ocean Drive. It is effectively a catwalk for a constant procession of well-toned flesh and avant-garde outfits; even the street cleaners look cool in

their white uniforms, while police officers in skintight shorts cruise past on mountain bikes. But a more active exploration need not involve more than a stroll.

At No. 1114 is the 1930 Mediterranean Revival Amsterdam Palace, also known as Casa Casuarina, which the late designer Gianni Versace purchased in 1993 for $3.7 million. This is now a luxury boutique hotel. Nearby, behind the Art Deco Welcome Center, the Beach Patrol Station is a classic Nautical Moderne building *(see p65)*, with ship's railings along the top and porthole windows; it still functions as the base for local lifeguards.

There is little to lure visitors south of 6th Street, but from the tip of South Pointe Park you can watch cruise liners entering Government Cut *(see p79)*.

## ❷ The Beach

**Map** 2. M (113), S (119), C (103), 120 Beach MAX, 150 Miami Beach Airport Flyer, A (101).

Much of the sand flanking Miami Beach was imported a few decades ago, and it continues to be replenished to counter coastal erosion. The vast stretches of sand are still impressive and people flock to them.

Up to 5th Street the beach is popular with surfers. The immense beach beyond is an extension of SoBe's persona, with colorful lifeguard huts and hordes of posing bathers. Alongside runs Lummus Park, where there are still Jewish folk chatting in Yiddish – evidence of the district's pre-gentrification era. The beach around 12th Street is particularly popular with the gay community.

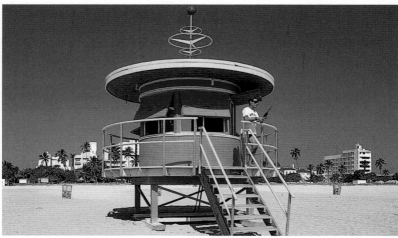

Lifeguard huts in South Beach, with the colors and style to match Ocean Drive

### ❸ Jewish Museum of Florida

301 Washington Ave. **Map** 2 E4.
**Tel** (305) 672-5044. 🚍 C (103),
120 Beach MAX, 150 Miami Beach
Airport Flyer, 123 South Beach Local,
M (113). **Open** 10am–5pm Tue–Sun.
**Closed** Jewish and national hols. 🦽
📷 💺 🆆 **jewishmuseum.com**

This museum occupies the first synagogue built in Miami Beach, in 1936. When large numbers of Jews arrived in the 1930s, they often faced fierce anti-Semitism – local hotels carried such signs as "No Jews or Dogs." Today, Jews are a vital, if ageing, part of Miami Beach's community.

The once dilapidated synagogue reopened in 1995 as a museum and research center of Jewish life in Florida. The building boasts colorful stained-glass windows and other Art Deco features, making it almost as memorable as the exhibitions that are staged here.

The unmistakable tower of the Delano Hotel on Collins Avenue

### ❹ Collins and Washington Avenues

**Map** 2. 🚍 C (103), M (113), S (119),
120 Beach MAX, 150 Miami Beach
Airport Flyer, 123 South Beach Local.
ℹ️ 1920 Meridian Avenue (Miami
Beach Visitor Center), (305) 672-1270.
🆆 **miamibeachchamber.com**

These streets are not as well-kept as Ocean Drive: stores sell kinky clothes or tattoos, and

### Changing Colors in South Beach

Art Deco buildings were originally very plain, typically in white with only the trim in bright colors. The paint never extended to the backs of the buildings since money was too tight in the 1930s to allow anything more than a jazzy façade. In the 1980s, designer Leonard Horowitz created the "Deco dazzle" by smothering some 150 buildings in color. Purists expressed dismay, and as the colors fade in the Florida sun, their wish is being granted. The buildings are now being repainted white, with pastel accents.

Cardozo Hotel on Ocean Drive

there is a more Hispanic flavor. Some of South Beach's top clubs are here (see p102), and there is an abundance of modest Art Deco buildings worth seeing. The Marlin Hotel, at 1200 Collins Avenue, is one of the district's most well-known and finest Streamline buildings. It used to be owned by Christopher Blackwell, founder of Island Records. Behind, at 1300 Washington Avenue, Miami Beach Post Office is one of SoBe's starker Deco creations; a mural inside shows the arrival of Ponce de León (see p46) and his battle with the Native Americans.

Farther north up Collins Avenue past Lincoln Road, the buildings are interesting rather than beautiful. High-rise 1940s hotels such as the Delano and Ritz Plaza still bear Deco traits, particularly in their towers inspired by the futuristic fantasies of comic strips, such as *Buck Rogers* and *Flash Gordon*. The strikingly non-Deco interior of the luxury Delano Hotel on South Beach (see p315) is well worth seeing, with its

Electric kettle (1909) in the Wolfsonian

billowing white drapes and original works by Gaudí, Dalí, and Man Ray.

### ❺ The Wolfsonian Museum – Florida International University

1001 Washington Ave. **Map** 2 E3.
**Tel** (305) 531-1001. 🚍 C (103),
120 Beach MAX, 150 Miami Beach
Airport Flyer, 123 South Beach Local.
**Open** noon–6pm Thu–Tue. 🦽 🚫
📷 💺 🆆 **wolfsonian.org**

This sturdy 1920s building (see p68) used to be the Washington Storage Company, where Miami's wealthy stored their valuables while traveling north. Now it holds a collection of decorative and fine arts from the period 1885–1945, primarily from North America and Europe. The museum's collection of 80,000 objects includes books, posters, furniture, and sculpture, and focuses on the aesthetic, political, and social significance of design around the turn of the century.

Española Way, a leafy Mediterranean-style shopping street

## ❻ Española Way

**Map** 2 E2. 🚌 C (103), 123 South Beach Local.

Between Washington and Drexel Avenues, Española Way is a tiny, tree-lined enclave of Mediterranean Revival buildings, where ornate arches, capitals, and balconies adorn salmon-colored, stuccoed frontages. Built from 1922–5, it is said to have been the inspiration for Addison Mizner's Worth Avenue in Palm Beach *(see pp122–3)*.

Española Way was originally an artists' colony but instead became an infamous red-light district. During the last couple of decades, however, its intended use has been resurrected in its dozen or more boutiques and offbeat art galleries *(see p99)*.

## ❼ Lincoln Road Mall

**Map** 2 E2. 🚌 A (101), 120 Beach MAX, 150 Miami Beach Airport Flyer, 123 South Beach Local, S (119), M (113), L (112), C (103). **Tel** (305) 538-7887. **Open** 11am–10pm Mon–Wed, 11am–11pm Thu–Sun. **Closed** Jan 1, Thanksgiving, Dec 25. ♿

One of the cultural corners of South Beach has had a roller-coaster history. Developer Carl Fisher *(see p63)* envisaged it as the "Fifth Avenue of the South" when it was planned in the 1920s, and its stores did indeed become the height of fashion. Four decades later, Morris Lapidus (designer of the Fontainebleau Hotel) turned the street into one of the country's first pedestrian malls, but this did not prevent

Lincoln Road's decline in the 1970s – the concrete pavilions that Lapidus introduced may not have helped.

The street's revival was initiated by the establishment of the ArtCenter South Florida here in 1984. Between Lenox and Meridian Avenues there are three exhibition areas and some dozen studios, as well as other independent galleries *(see p99)*. Education programs are also on offer. The art may be too experimental for most living rooms.

The galleries are usually open in the evenings. This is when the mall comes alive, because theater-goers frequent the restored Art Deco Lincoln and Colony theaters *(see p103)*. Those searching for a less intense alternative to Ocean Drive hang out at voguish

restaurants and cafés, such as the Paul Bakery at No. 846 – Lincoln Road's answer to the News Café *(see p68)*. At night, the Streamline Moderne Sterling Building at No. 927 looks terrific – its glass blocks emanating a blue glow.

## ❽ Holocaust Memorial

1933–45 Meridian Ave. **Map** 2 E1. **Tel** (305) 538-1663. 🚌 A (101), L (112), M (113), S (119), 123 South Beach Local. **Open** 9am–9pm daily. ♿

Miami Beach has one of the largest populations of Holocaust survivors in the world, hence the great appropriateness of Kenneth Treister's gut-wrenching memorial, finished in 1990. The centerpiece is an enormous bronze arm and hand stretching skyward, representing the final grasp of a dying person. It is stamped with a number from Auschwitz and covered with nearly 100 life-size bronze statues of men, women, and children in the throes of unbearable grief. Around this central plaza is a tunnel lined with the names of Europe's concentration camps, a graphic pictorial history of the Holocaust, and a granite wall inscribed with the names of thousands of victims.

The Holocaust Memorial

Food enthusiasts at the popular Paul Bakery, Lincoln Road Mall

*For hotels and restaurants in this area see pp314–15 and pp329–30*

*Coronation of the Virgin* (c.1492) by Domenico Ghirlandaio

## ❾ Bass Museum of Art

2100 Collins Ave. **Map** 2 F1. **Tel** (305) 673-7530. 🚍 C (103), S (119), L (112), M (113), 120 Beach MAX, 150 Miami Beach Airport Flyer, 123 South Beach Local. **Open** noon–5pm Wed–Sun. **Closed** Mon, Tue & public hols. 🖼 ♿ 🆆 **thebass.org**

This Mayan-influenced Deco building was erected in 1930 as the city's library and art center. As a museum, it came of age in 1964 when philanthropists John and Johanna Bass donated their art collection – European paintings, sculpture, and textiles from the 15th to 17th centuries.

Gallery space is divided between permanent and temporary exhibitions, the former displaying more than 2,800 pieces of sculpture, graphic art, and photography. Highlights include Renaissance works, paintings from the northern European schools, and 16th-century Flemish tapestries. There are also exhibits on contemporary architecture. The museum underwent renovation and the programmable space has been expanded.

### Shooting Fashion in Miami Beach

Thanks to its combination of Art Deco buildings, palm trees, beach, and warm climate, South Beach is one of the world's most popular places for fashion shoots. Around 1,500 models live here, but this does not include the thousands of young hopefuls who flock here uninvited during the season, and stroll around looking cool in the bars and on the beach. The season runs from October through to March, when the weather in Europe and northern America is too cold for outdoor shoots.

Stroll around SoBe in the early morning and visitors cannot fail to spot the teams of directors, photographers, make-up artists, and their assistants as well as, of course, the models themselves. Ocean Drive is the top spot for shoots, but it is possible to surprise a team at work even in the quieter backstreets.

Photographer and crew shooting a model in Miami Beach

## ❿ Central Miami Beach

**Map** 2 F1. 🚍 C (103), M (113), S (119), J (110), L (112), 120 Beach MAX, 150 Miami Beach Airport Flyer.

Miami Beach north of 23rd Street, sometimes called Central Miami Beach, is a largely unprepossessing sight, with endless 1950s and 1960s high-rise apartments separating the Atlantic from busy Collins Avenue. A boardwalk running all the way from 23rd to 46th Street overlooks a narrow beach, frequented primarily by families. The most eye-catching sight in the area is the **Fontainebleau Hotel**

(which is pronounced as "Fountain-blue", locally).

Completed in 1954, the curvaceous Fontainebleau is apparently the nearest the architect Morris Lapidus (b.1903) could get to his client's wishes for a modern French château style. The hotel's dated grandeur still impresses, particularly the pool with waterfall, and the lobby with Lapidus's signature bow ties on the tiles. The hotel was an ideal setting for the James Bond film *Goldfinger* in the 1960s.

Star guests have included Frank Sinatra, Elvis Presley, Bob Hope, Sammy Davis Jr., and Lucille Ball. Today the lobby is still one of the best places to spot celebrities in Central Miami Beach.

From the Bayside Market-place *(see p78)* visitors can take a tour on any of several cruise boats available. The tours provide a more leisurely view of many of the millionaires' mansions in Biscayne Bay *(see p78)*. Several water taxi companies offer trips between Miami and Miami Beach.

Poolside view of the Fontainebleau Hotel, Central Miami Beach

# DOWNTOWN AND LITTLE HAVANA

When the development of Miami took off with the arrival of the Florida East Coast Railroad in 1896, the early city existed on one square mile (2.5 sq km) on the banks of the Miami River, site of the present downtown area. Wealthy industrialists from the northern US set up banks and other institutions and built winter estates along Brickell Avenue. This is now the hub of Miami's financial district that was spawned by a banking boom in the 1980s. Downtown's futuristic skyscrapers, bathed nightly in neon, demonstrate the city's status as a major financial and trade center.

Even after World War II, Miami was still little more than a resort. It was largely the arrival of Cuban exiles from 1959 onward (see p56) that

turned Miami into a metropolis. The effect of this Cuban influx is visible most clearly on the streets both Downtown and in Little Havana. The chatter, faces, and food make both districts feel more like an Hispanic city with an American flavor than the other way around.

Downtown and Little Havana are enjoyable as much for their atmosphere as for their sights. Downtown has the Miami-Dade Cultural Plaza, which houses the History Miami Museum, one of Florida's best historical museums, and the Pérez Art Museum Miami on Biscayne Bay. However, tourists are catered to primarily at the shopping and entertainment mall of Bayside Marketplace – a starting point for relaxing boat trips around Biscayne Bay.

## Sights at a Glance

### Museums and Galleries
1 Miami-Dade Cultural Plaza
3 Pérez Art Museum Miami
5 Philip and Patricia Frost Museum of Science

### Historic Buildings
2 US Federal Courthouse Complex

### Modern Architecture
7 Brickell Avenue

### Neighborhoods
8 Little Havana

### Shops and Restaurants
4 Bayside Marketplace

### Boat Trips
6 Port of Miami Boat Trips

See also Street Finder maps 2, 3

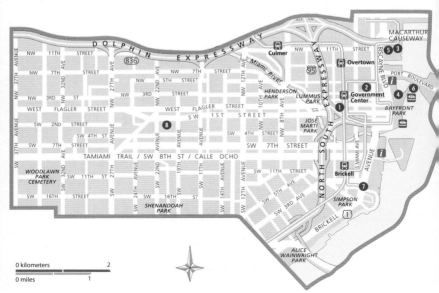

◄ Downtown Miami's Bayside Marketplace at night

For keys to symbols see back flap

# Street-by-Street: Downtown

Downtown's skyline is sublime. It undoubtedly looks best from a distance, particularly at night, but the architecture can also be enjoyed close-up. The raised track of the Metromover provides a good overall view; or visitors can explore at ground level, in order to investigate the attractive interiors of some of Downtown's public buildings.

The commercial district that lurks beneath the flash high-rises is surprisingly downscale, full of cut-price jewelry and electronics stores, but the Latin street life is vibrant: cafés specialize in Cuban coffee, and street vendors sell freshly peeled oranges, Caribbean-style. Flagler Street, Downtown's main thoroughfare, is the best place to feel the Hispanic buzz. While the area has a vibrant scene and is home to an increasing number of shops, restaurants, and condos, visitors still need to be aware of their surroundings.

**The Downtown Skyline** is a monument to the banking boom of the 1980s. There is an excellent view of it from the MacArthur Causeway.

**❷ US Federal Courthouse Complex**
This detail from the mural inside the courtroom depicts Miami's transformation from a wilderness to a modern city.

**Dade County Courthouse** has an impressive lobby, with ceiling mosaics that feature this copy of the earliest version of Florida's state seal, complete with mountains.

| 0 meters | 150 |
|---|---|
| 0 yards | 150 |

**Key**

— Suggested route

**❶ ★ Miami-Dade Cultural Plaza**
This large complex, with a Mediterranean-style central courtyard and fountains, is home to the HistoryMiami Museum, one of the best history museums in Florida.

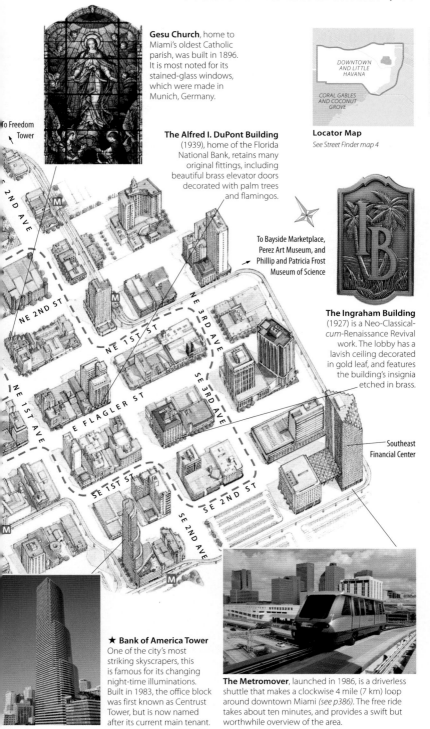

**Gesu Church**, home to Miami's oldest Catholic parish, was built in 1896. It is most noted for its stained-glass windows, which were made in Munich, Germany.

To Freedom Tower

**The Alfred I. DuPont Building** (1939), home of the Florida National Bank, retains many original fittings, including beautiful brass elevator doors decorated with palm trees and flamingos.

**Locator Map**
See Street Finder map 4

DOWNTOWN AND LITTLE HAVANA

CORAL GABLES AND COCONUT GROVE

To Bayside Marketplace, Perez Art Museum, and Phillip and Patricia Frost Museum of Science

**The Ingraham Building** (1927) is a Neo-Classical-*cum*-Renaissance Revival work. The lobby has a lavish ceiling decorated in gold leaf, and features the building's insignia etched in brass.

NE 2ND AVE

NE 2ND ST

NE 1ST ST

NE 3RD AVE

NE 1ST AVE

E FLAGLER ST

SE 3RD AVE

Southeast Financial Center

SE 1ST ST

SE 2ND ST

SE 2ND AVE

★ **Bank of America Tower**
One of the city's most striking skyscrapers, this is famous for its changing night-time illuminations. Built in 1983, the office block was first known as Centrust Tower, but is now named after its current main tenant.

**The Metromover**, launched in 1986, is a driverless shuttle that makes a clockwise 4 mile (7 km) loop around downtown Miami (see p386). The free ride takes about ten minutes, and provides a swift but worthwhile overview of the area.

# Downtown

Downtown's grand early 20th-century buildings, scattered among modern high-rises, are very evocative of the confidence of those boom years. The Mediterranean Revival and Neo-Classical styles were both popular. A fine example of the latter is Freedom Tower (1925) on Biscayne Boulevard, modeled very loosely on the Giralda in Seville. At first home to the now-defunct *Miami News,* its role and name changed in the 1960s when it became the reception center for Cubans fleeing from Castro *(see p56).* Downtown has a few Deco buildings, such as Macy's (formerly Burdines) on Flagler Street *(see p98).*

## ❶ Miami-Dade Cultural Plaza

101 West Flagler St. **Map** 4 E1.
🚇 Metrorail (Government Center).
🚌 2, 3, 66, 77, all buses to Government Center. **Tel** (305) 375-1492. **Open** 10am–5pm Mon–Wed, Fri, Sat, noon–5pm Sun. 🅿 🅰 🆆 historymiami.org

Designed by the celebrated American architect Philip Johnson in 1982, the Miami-Dade Cultural Plaza houses a splendid history museum, and library.

HistoryMiami concentrates on pre-1945 Miami. There are informative displays on the Spanish colonization and Seminole culture among other topics, but it is the old photographs that really bring Miami's history to life: from the hardships endured by the early pioneers, to the fun and games of the Roaring Twenties.

## ❷ US Federal Court-house Complex

301 N Miami Ave. **Map** 4 E1.
**Tel** (305) 523-5100. 🅼 Wilkie D. Ferguson. 🚇 Metrorail (Historic Overtown/Lyric Theater). 🚌 6, all downtown routes. **Open** 8am–5pm Mon–Fri. **Closed** public hols. 🅰

This complex houses the modern, glass-encased Wilkie D. Ferguson building and the interesting Neo-Classical C. Clyde Atkins building. It has a pleasant, thoroughly Mediterranean courtyard, but the main attraction (for the casual visitor at least) is the mural entitled *Law Guides Florida's Progress (see p76)* on the second floor, which was designed by Denman Fink, famous for his

work in Coral Gables *(see p86).* Public access to the courthouse is often restricted, especially during important cases.

## ❸ Pérez Art Museum Miami

1075 Biscayne Blvd. **Map** 4 F1.
**Tel** (305) 375-3000. 🅼 College/Bayside. **Open** 10am–5pm Tue–Sun. **Closed** Thanksgiving, Dec 25. 🅰
🆆 pamm.org

A modern and contemporary art museum displaying 20th- and 21st-century international art, the Pérez Art Museum Miami (PAMM) opened in December 2013 after the Miami Art Museum outgrew the Miami-Dade Cultural Plaza. Located in an impressive building designed by Swiss architects Herzog and de Meuron, and overlooking Biscayne Bay, the museum is named after its benefactor, real-estate developer Jorge Pérez.

## ❹ Bayside Marketplace

401 Biscayne Blvd. **Map** 4 F1.
**Tel** (305) 577-3344. 🅼 College/Bayside. 🚌 3, 11, C (103), S (119), 95, 93 Biscayne MAX, 120 Beach MAX. **Open** 10am–10pm Mon–Thu, 10am–11pm Fri & Sat, 11am–9pm Sun. **Closed** Thanksgiving, Dec 25. 🅰

By far the most popular spot among tourists Downtown (as well as the best place to park in the area), Bayside Marketplace is an undeniably fun complex. It curves around Miamarina, where a plethora of boats, some private, some offering trips around Biscayne Bay, lie docked.

With its numerous bars and restaurants, Bayside is a good place to eat as well as to shop. The food court on the first floor does not serve *haute cuisine* but is fine for a fast-food meal. Bands often play in the waterfront esplanade.

## ❺ Phillip and Patricia Frost Museum of Science

1101 Biscayne Blvd. **Map** 4 F1.
**Tel** (305) 434-9600. 🅼 College/Bayside. **Open** 9am–6pm daily.
🆆 frostscience.org

The new jewel in Miami's crown is the striking Phillip and Patricia Frost Museum of Science, located in the bayfront area called Museum Park. The museum features the Frost Planetarium, Aquarium, and the North and West Wings.

The stunningly modern exterior of Pérez Art Museum Miami

*For hotels and restaurants in this area see p315 and pp330–31*

The interactive MeLab at the Phillip and Patricia Frost Museum of Science

It's mission is to help visitors explore and understand the power of science.

## ❻ Port of Miami Boat Trips

Bayside Marketplace. **Map** 4 F1. Ⓜ College/Bayside. 🚌 3, 16, A (101), C (103), S (119), 11, 120 Beach MAX, 93 Biscayne MAX. Island Queen Cruises: (305) 379-5119. Duck Tours: (305) 673-2217.

The world's busiest cruise port, and a sprinkling of exclusive private island communities, occupy Biscayne Bay between Downtown and Miami Beach. Since racing along MacArthur Causeway in a car provides only a brief glimpse of this area, cruises from Bayside Marketplace offer a better, more leisurely view. "Estates of the Rich and Famous" tours run by Island Queen Cruises and other companies leave regularly and last for about 90 minutes.

Tours begin by sailing past the port, situated on Dodge and Lummus islands. The port contributes more than $18 billion a year to the local economy, handling over four million cruise passengers annually. The mammoth ships make an impressive sight when they are in dock, or heading to or from port (usually on weekends).

Near the eastern end of MacArthur Causeway passengers pass the US Coastguard's fleet of high-speed craft. Opposite lies unbridged

ISLAND QUEEN

Port of Miami tour boat sign

Fisher Island, separated from South Beach by Government Cut, a deep water channel dredged in 1905. A beach for African-Americans in the 1920s, Fisher Island has ironically become a highly exclusive residential enclave, with homes rarely costing less than $500,000. The tour continues north around Star, Palm, and Hibiscus islands, which were all man-made in the second decade of the 20th century, when real estate lots were sometimes sold "by the gallon." Mansions in every possible architectural style lurk beneath the tropical foliage, among them the former homes of Frank Sinatra and Al Capone, as well as the abodes of celebrities such as Gloria Estefan and Julio Iglesias.

Other boat trips from Bayside Marketplace include night-time cruises, deep-sea fishing excursions, and even a tall ship cruise. A particularly good tour is run by Duck Tours which has an amphibious vehicle that departs several times a day from South

Beach, and splashes down in Biscayne Bay for a closer look at the many mansions.

## ❼ Brickell Avenue

**Map** 4 E2–E4. Ⓜ various stations. Ⓡ Metrorail (Brickell & Government Center). 🚌 6, 8, 48, B (102), 207, 208, 95, 500 Midnight Owl . 🛈 Greater Miami Beaches Convention and Visitors Bureau, 701 Brickell Ave, Suite 2700, (305) 539-3000.
🆆 **miamiandbeaches.com**

In the early 20th century, the building of palatial mansions along Brickell Avenue earned it the name Millionaires' Row. Today, its northern section is Miami's palm-lined version of New York's Wall Street – its international banks enclosed in modern, glass blocks. South of the bend at Southwest 15th Road is a series of startling apartment houses glimpsed in the opening credits of TV series *Miami Vice*. Created in the early 1980s by an iconoclastic firm of Postmodernist architects called Arquitectonica, the buildings, now condos, still impress.

The most memorable is the Atlantis (at No. 2025), for its "skycourt" – a hole high up in its façade containing a palm tree and Jacuzzi. The punched-out hole reappears as an identically sized cube in the grounds below. Arquitectonica also designed the Palace, at No. 1541, and the Imperial, at No. 1627. Described as "architecture for 55 mph" (that is, best seen when passing in a car), these exclusive residences and high-rise office buildings were designed to be admired from a distance.

One of the lavish mansions seen during a Port of Miami boat tour

# ❽ Little Havana

**Map** 3 C2. 🚌 207 and 208 Little Havana Connections. **El Titan de Bronze Cigar Mfg.:** 1071 W. 8th St. **Tel** (305) 860-1412. **Open** 9am–5pm Mon–Fri, 8am–4pm Sat. **Closed** Sun, public hols. **El Aguila Vidente (The Seeing Eagle):** 1122 SW 8th St. **Map** 3 C2. **Tel** (305) 854-4086. **Open** 10:30am–5:30pm Mon–Sat. **Closed** Sun, public hols.

Cubans live all over Greater Miami, but it is the 3.5 sq miles (9 sq km) making up Little Havana that, as its name suggests, have been their surrogate homeland since they first started fleeing Cuba in the 1960s (see p56). Other Hispanic groups have now settled here, too.

Time in Little Havana is best spent out in the streets, where the bustling workday atmosphere is vibrant. A salsa beat emanates from every other shop; *bodegas* (canteens) sell Cuban specialties such as *moros y cristianos*, while elderly men knock back thimblefuls of *café cubano*.

Little Havana's principal commercial thoroughfare and sentimental heart is Southwest 8th Street, better known as **Calle Ocho.** Its liveliest stretch, between 11th and 17th Avenues, is best enjoyed on foot, but other points of interest are more easily explored by car.

Recalling the spirit of Havana cigar factories, **El Titan de Bronze**, on Calle Ocho, is family owned, and all the cigars are made by "Level 9" masters. Visitors are welcome to watch the handful of cigar rollers at work. The leaves are grown in Nicaragua – reputedly from Cuban tobacco seeds, the world's best. Local smokers, mainly non-Cuban, come to buy boxes of the wide range of cigars on sale (see p99).

Also found on 8th Street are several *botánicas*, and spiritual stores dedicated to the practice of the Afro-Cuban religion Santería. The merchandise includes herbs, potions, and ceramic figures of saints. Southwest 13th Avenue, south from Calle Ocho, is known as **Cuban Memorial Boulevard** and is the district's nationalistic focal point. The eternal flame of the Brigade 2506 Memorial remembers the Cubans who died in the Bay of Pigs invasion of Cuba in 1961. Every year people gather here on April 17 to remember the disastrous attempt to overthrow Fidel Castro's regime. Beyond, other memorials pay tribute to Cuban heroes Antonio Maceo and José Martí, who fought against Cuba's Spanish colonialists in the 1800s (see pp52–3). At intervals along Calle Ocho between 12th and 17th Avenues, more recent Latin celebrities such as Julio Iglesias and Gloria Estefan are honored with stars on the pavement in

Waitress at the Versailles

The eternal flame commemorating the Bay of Pigs invasion

Little Havana's version of Hollywood's Walk of Fame.

At the corner of 15th Avenue, older male Cubans match their wits over dominoes in tiny **Máximo Gómez Park** – also known as Domino Park. According to a list of rules, players can be banned from the park for foul language, spitting, or shouting.

North of Calle Ocho at West Flagler Street and Southwest 17th Avenue, **Plaza de la Cubanidad** has a map of Cuba sculpted in bronze. José Martí's enigmatic words alongside translate as "the palm trees are sweethearts that wait." Behind, a flourish of flags and banners advertises the headquarters of Alpha 66, Miami's most hardline grouping of anti-Castro Cubans, whose supporters once trained in the Everglades.

Much farther west, at 3260 Calle Ocho, lies **Woodlawn Cemetery**. Visitors can ask for directions to the memorials to the unknown Cuban freedom fighter in plot 31, with Cuban and US flags flying alongside, or to the tomb of Gerardo Machado, an infamous Cuban dictator of the 1930s.

Finish off a tour of Little Havana with a snack or full meal at the nearby **Versailles** restaurant (see p331). This is a cultural and culinary bastion of Miami's Cuban community that has served nostalgic exiles, as well as tourists, since 1971.

Cubans enjoying a game of dominoes in Máximo Gómez Park

# Miami's Cuban Community

The Cuban community in Miami is unusually cohesive, thanks to a shared passion for its homeland and a common hatred for the Castro regime. The exiles, as they often call themselves, come from all walks of life. Early immigrants were largely wealthy white (and conservative) professionals, who now sit on the boards of some of Miami's biggest companies, and live in the city's stylish and upscale suburbs. The "Marielitos", who came in 1980 (see p56), were mostly working class, like many of those who have arrived since. Some second-generation Cubans, such as pop star Gloria Estefan, now have very successful careers. Nowadays these professionals are often dubbed "yucas," or Young, Up-and-coming Cuban-Americans. The Cuban presence is felt in every layer of Miami society – seen in everything from the food to the Spanish spoken on the street, and visible everywhere from Little Havana to elite Coral Gables.

**Images of Old Cuba**
Murals, such as this one of the Cuban resort of Varadero, symbolize the nostalgia and love for the homeland felt by Cubans of all generations. Many hope to return to the island one day.

**Political Action**
Cubans in Miami eagerly follow events in Cuba. They often take to the streets to wave the Cuban flag, and protest against the Castro regime or the US government's Cuban policy.

Salsa music, recorded by Cubans in Miami and popular in the city

## Cuban Culture in Miami

*The Cubans have brought their music, their religion, their whole way of life to Miami. They are nominally Catholic, but many Cubans adhere to Santería, a blend of Catholic beliefs and the animist cults taken to Cuba by African slaves during the Colonial period.*

A Cuban-style hole in the wall café, where coffee, snacks, and conversation are enjoyed

A religious shop or *botánica* in Little Havana selling the paraphernalia of Santería

# CORAL GABLES AND COCONUT GROVE

Coral Gables, one of the country's richest neighborhoods, is (and feels like) a separate city within Greater Miami. Aptly named the City Beautiful, its elegant homes line winding avenues shaded by banyans and live oaks. They back up to hidden canals and many have their own jetties. Regulations ensure that new buildings use the same architectural vocabulary advocated by George Merrick when he planned Coral Gables in the 1920s *(see p86)*. As well as exploring Merrick's legacy, visitors can peer into some of Miami's most stylish shops. Coconut Grove is Miami's oldest

community. Wreckers *(see p307)* lived here from the mid-1800s, but the area attracted few people until the late 1880s, when Ralph Monroe *(see p88)* persuaded some friends to open a hotel. It was staffed by Bahamians and frequented by Monroe's intellectual friends. Ever since, the area has attracted an eclectic group of artists and entrepreneurs. A mix of shops, cafés and sailboats adds to the bohemian feel. Affordable restaurants and shops draw weekend and evening crowds, making Coconut Grove one of the liveliest districts in Miami.

## Sights at a Glance

**Museums and Galleries**
6 Lowe Art Museum
11 Coral Gables Museum

**Streets and Neighborhoods**
1 Miracle Mile
7 Coconut Grove Village

**Historic Buildings**
2 Coral Gables City Hall
3 Coral Gables Merrick House
4 Venetian Pool

5 Biltmore Hotel
8 The Barnacle
12 *Vizcaya Museum and Gardens pp90–91*

**Churches**
10 Ermita de la Caridad

**Marinas**
9 Dinner Key

*See also Driving tour map pp84–5*

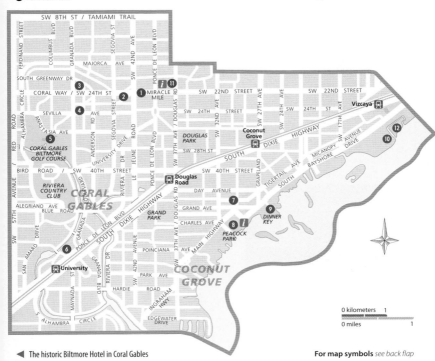

◄ The historic Biltmore Hotel in Coral Gables

For map symbols *see back flap*

# Coral Gables Driving Tour

This driving tour wends its way along Coral Gables' lush and peaceful lanes, connecting the major landmarks of George Merrick's 1920s dream city *(see pp86–7)*. As well as much-admired public buildings such as the Biltmore Hotel, it takes in two of the original four grand entrances and six of Merrick's Disneyesque international "villages."

It is quite possible to visit all the sights on the tour in one busy day. Allow time to get lost; Coral Gables is very confusing for a planned city. Signs for streets, named after Spanish places that Merrick allegedly pulled out of a dictionary, are often hard to spot, lurking on white stone blocks in the grass.

③ **Alhambra Water Tower**
This folly, built in 1925, was the work of Denman Fink *(see p86)*.

⑥ **Venetian Pool** is a beautiful public swimming pool embellished with Venetian-style buildings.

⑦ **Coral Gables Congregational Church**
Coral Gables' first church, built by Merrick in Spanish Baroque style, has an elaborate bell tower and portal.

⑩ **The Lowe Art Museum** boasts an excellent collection, including some fine European and Native American art.

⑧ **Biltmore Hotel**
One of the most stunning hotels in the country, the Biltmore has been beautifully restored to its 1920s grandeur.

⑪ **French City Village**
This is one of seven international villages that were built to add variety to the mostly Mediterranean-style city.

| 0 meters | 500 |
| 0 yards | 500 |

**① The Granada Entrance** is a copy of the gate to Granada in Spain.

**② The Country Club Prado Entrance**, complete with ornamental pillars, is the most elegant of the grand entrances.

**Locator Map**
*See Street Finder map 5*

**④ Coral Way**
Live oaks and Spanish-style houses line one of Coral Gables' loveliest and oldest streets.

**⑤ Coral Gables Merrick House** was once the home of George Merrick and is now a museum.

**⑯ Coral Gables City Hall** has a decorative interior, featuring murals painted in the 1920s and 1950s.

**⑰ Miracle Mile**
Conservative bridal, fashion, and jewelry stores set the tone along the district's most important shopping street.

**Key**

⚎ Expressway
▬ Tour route
— Metrorail line
⚌ Other Road
⚏ Trolley Route

## Tips for Drivers

**Tour length:** 14 miles (23 km).
**Starting point:** Anywhere, but the route is best made in a counterclockwise direction.
**Stopping-off points:** There are some highly rated restaurants off Miracle Mile, and you can enjoy an English-style tea at the Biltmore if you reserve 24 hours in advance. Or, you can take a dip at the Venetian Pool.
**When to go:** Wednesdays and Sundays are the best days to visit because of the hours of the Coral Gables Merrick House, Lowe Art Museum, and the Biltmore tours *(see pp86–7)*. Avoid the rush hours (7–9:30am, 4:30–6:30pm).

A private boat moored on one of Coral Gables' canals

## Finding the Sights

① Granada Entrance
② Country Club Prado Entrance
③ Alhambra Water Tower
④ Coral Way
⑤ Coral Gables Merrick House
⑥ Venetian Pool
⑦ Coral Gables Congregational Church
⑧ Biltmore Hotel
⑨ Colonial Village
⑩ Lowe Art Museum
⑪ French City Village
⑫ Dutch South African Village
⑬ French Country Village
⑭ Chinese Village
⑮ French Normandy Village
⑯ Coral Gables City Hall
⑰ Miracle Mile

Galleried rotunda inside the Colonnade Building on Miracle Mile

# ❶ Miracle Mile

Coral Way between Douglas and Le Jeune roads. **Map** 5 C1. 🚇 Metrorail (Douglas Rd, Vizcaya) 🚌 37, 42 (both from Douglas Rd), 24 (from Vizcaya).

In 1940, a developer hyped Coral Gables' main shopping street by naming it Miracle Mile (the walk along one side and down the other equating a mile). Colorful canopies adorn shops as prim and proper as their clientele (see p98). High prices and competition from out-of-town malls ensure that the street is rarely busy.

The Colonnade Building, at No. 169, was built in 1926 by George Merrick as the sales headquarters for his real estate business. Its superb rotunda is now a lobby for the deceptively modern and very impressive Colonnade Hotel. Caffe Abbracci (see p332) offers Italian food and celebrity-viewing opportunities. Nearby, at Salzedo Street and Aragon Avenue, the Old Police and Fire Station Building, built in 1939, features a fine pair of sculpted firemen.

# ❷ Coral Gables City Hall

405 Biltmore Way. **Map** 5 C1. **Tel** (305) 446-6800. 🚇 Metrorail (Douglas Rd). 🚌 24, 42, 56. **Open** 8am–5pm Mon–Fri. **Closed** public hols. ♿
Ⓦ **coralgables.com**

Built in 1928, Coral Gables City Hall epitomizes the Spanish Renaissance style favored by Merrick and his colleagues. Its semicircular façade even has a Spanish-style coat of arms, which was designed for the new city of Coral Gables by Denman Fink, George Merrick's uncle. Fink was also responsible for the mural of the four seasons that decorates the dome of the bell tower: winter is represented as an old man, the other seasons as young women. Above the stairs, a mural that illustrates Coral Gables' early days, *Landmarks of the Twenties*, was the work of John St. John in the 1950s; he artificially aged it by chain-smoking and exhaling onto the paint as it dried.

**Coat of arms on Coral Gables City Hall**

# ❸ Coral Gables Merrick House

907 Coral Way. **Map** 5 B1. **Tel** (305) 460-5361. 🚌 24, 42. **Open** 1–4pm Wed & Sun. 🚫 ♿ 🚫 ♿ 🚫

Make the effort to visit the Merrick family home to appreciate the comparatively modest background of Coral Gables' creator. However, its opening hours are limited.

When Reverend Solomon Merrick brought his family to Florida from New England in 1899, they settled in a wooden cabin south of the growing city of Miami. They later added a much larger extension and named the house Coral Gables, thinking the local oolitic limestone used to build it was coral because of the fossilized marine life it contained.

Now a museum, the emphasis is on the family, particularly Solomon's famous son, George. Some of the furniture was owned by the Merricks, and there are family portraits and paintings by George's mother and his uncle. The grounds have been reduced in size, but the small garden is awash with tropical trees and plants.

## George Merrick's Dream City

The dream of George Merrick was to build a new city. With the help of Denman Fink as artistic advisor, Frank Button as landscaper, and Phineas Paist as architectural director, he conjured up a wholly planned aesthetic wonderland. Its architecture was to be part-Spanish, part-Italian – in Merrick's words "a combination of what seemed best in each, with an added touch of gaiety to suit the Florida mood." The dream spawned the biggest real estate venture of the 1920s, costing around $100 million. Some $3 million a year was spent on advertising alone, with posters promoting idyllic canal scenes while they were still on the drawing board. The 1926 hurricane (see p54) and the Wall Street crash left Merrick's city incomplete, but what remains, together with subsequent imitations, is a great testament to his imagination.

Portrait of George Merrick, on display in his family home

Venetian Pool, ingeniously created in the 1920s out of an old coral rock quarry

## ❹ Venetian Pool

2701 De Soto Blvd. **Map** 5 B2. **Tel** (305) 460-5306. 🚇 Metrorail (Douglas Rd, Vizcaya). 🚌 42 (from Douglas Rd), 24 (from Vizcaya). **Open** Apr–May & Sep–Oct: 11am–5:30pm Tue–Thu; mid-Jun–mid-Aug: 11am–7:30pm Mon–Fri; Nov–Mar: 10am–4:30pm Tue–Thu; all year: 10am–4:30pm Sat & Sun. **Closed** Jan 1, national holidays. 🅿 ♿ 🆆 **coral gablesvenetianpool.com**

This may be the most beautiful swimming pool in the world. It was fashioned from a coral rock quarry in 1923 by Denman Fink and Phineas Paist. Pink stucco towers and loggias, candy-cane Venetian poles, a cobblestone bridge, caves, and waterfalls surround the clear, spring-fed waters. The pool was originally one of the most fashionable social spots in Coral Gables: see the photographs in the lobby of beauty pageants staged here during the 1920s.

## ❺ Biltmore Hotel

1200 Anastasia Ave. **Map** 5 A2. **Tel** (305) 445-1926. 🚇 Metrorail (Douglas Rd). 🚌 42. ♿ 🚗 Sun only. 🆆 **biltmorehotel.com**

Coral Gables' outstanding single building was completed in 1926. In its heyday, when it hosted celebrities such as Al Capone (who had a speakeasy here), Judy Garland, and the Duke and Duchess of Windsor, guests hunted foxes in the vast grounds

(now a golf course) and were punted along canals in gondolas. The Biltmore served as a military hospital during World War II, when its marble floors were covered in linoleum, and it remained a veterans' hospital until 1968. Following a \$55-million restoration in 1986 the hotel went bankrupt in 1990, but then opened its doors again two years later.

A 315-ft (96-m) near replica of Seville Cathedral's Giralda tower, which was also the model for Miami's Freedom Tower *(see p78)*, rises from the hotel's imposing façade. Inside, Herculean pillars line the grand lobby, while from the terrace behind you can survey one of the largest hotel swimming pools in the US. The Biltmore's famous swimming instructor, Johnny Weismuller, known for his role as Tarzan, set a world record here in the 1930s.

Weekly tours of the hotel depart from the desk.

Han dynasty horse, Lowe Art Museum

## ❻ Lowe Art Museum

1301 Stanford Drive. **Map** 5 A5. **Tel** (305) 284-3535. 🚇 Metrorail (University). 🚌 48, 56. **Open** 10am–4pm Tue–Sat, noon–4pm Sun. **Closed** Mon, public holidays. 🅿 ♿ 🆆 **lowemuseum.org**

This museum is located in the middle of the campus of the University of Miami, founded in 1925 thanks to a \$5-million donation from George Merrick. Among the 8,000 permanent exhibits are impressive Renaissance and Baroque works, and an excellent collection of Native American art. There is also an Egyptian collection, some fine works in the 17th-century and contemporary European and American collections, Afro-Cuban lore, and historical memorabilia. Ancient art from Latin America and Asia, and 20th-century photography are also well represented.

South view of the Biltmore Hotel, Coral Gables' most famous landmark

## ❼ Coconut Grove Village

**Map** 6 E4, F4. 🚇 Metrorail (Coconut Grove, Douglas Rd). 🚌 48, 249 Coconut Grove Circulator.

A fabled hippy hangout in the 1960s, these days the focal point of Coconut Grove cultivates a more salubrious air. Well-groomed young couples wining and dining beneath old-fashioned streetlamps now typify what is often known simply as "the village." Only the odd snake charmer and neck masseur, plus a few New Age shops, offer glimpses of alternative lifestyles. Come at night or on the weekend to see the Grove at its best.

The village's nerve center is at the intersection of Grand Avenue, McFarlane Avenue, and Main Highway, where visitors will find the lively **CocoWalk**. This outdoor mall *(see p98)* is one of the most popular destinations here. Its courtyard is full of cafés and souvenir stands, while on upper floors a band often plays. There are also family restaurants *(see pp329–49)*, a movie theater, and a nightclub. It is undergoing renovations. However, many shops and cafés are still open.

A short distance east along Grand Avenue, a stylish shopping area called **Mayfair in the Grove** *(see p98)* is worth visiting as much for its striking

CocoWalk open-air mall in Coconut Grove Village

ensemble of Spanish tiles, waterfalls, and foliage, as for its shops. But in order to better appreciate Coconut Grove's relaxed café lifestyle, head along the sidestreets of Commodore Plaza and Fuller Street.

For a different atmosphere, browse among the food stands of the colorful **Farmers' Market**, held on Saturdays at McDonald Street and Grand Avenue. Farther along Grand Avenue are the simple homes of the local Bahamian community. This neighborhood comes alive during Coconut Grove's exuberant Goombay Festival during July (see p39).

A five-minute stroll south along Main Highway will pass through a shady, affluent neighborhood where palms, bougainvillea, and hibiscus conceal elegant clapboard

villas. At 3400 Devon Road stands the picturesque **Plymouth Congregational Church**, which appears to have been built much longer ago than 1916. It is usually locked, but the ivy-covered façade and setting are the main attraction.

Munroe, designer of the Barnacle, painted by Lewis Benton in 1931

## ❽ The Barnacle

3485 Main Highway, Coconut Grove. **Map** 6 E4. **Tel** (305) 442-6866. 🚌 37 (with a short walk), 48, 249 Coconut Grove Circulator. **Open** 9am–5pm Fri-Mon. **Closed** Tue, Jan 1, Thanksgiving, Dec 25. 🅿 📷 🅦 **floridastateparks. org/thebarnacle**

Hidden from Main Highway by tropical hardwood trees, the Barnacle is Dade County's oldest home. It was designed and occupied by Ralph Munroe, a Renaissance man who made his living from boat building and wrecking *(see p307)*. A botanist and photographer, he was also an avid environmentalist with a strong belief in the importance of self-sufficiency.

### Miami: Fact Meets Fiction

Hiaasen's bestsellers

In the 1980s, the public perception of Miami was as the drug and crime capital of the entire country. Ironically, the popular TV series *Miami Vice (see p57)* played on this reputation, glamorizing both the city and the violence. The best novels about Miami in the 1990s also emanated from its seedier side. Its two most renowned crime writers are Edna Buchanan, winner of a Pulitzer prize for news reporting on the *Miami Herald*, and Carl Hiaasen, a columnist for the same newspaper. However fanciful his plots might seem (building inspectors practicing voodoo, or talk-show hosts having plastic surgery on the air), Carl Hiaasen claims the ideas come straight from the *Herald's* news pages. *Striptease* was the first of his novels to be made into a movie.

When first constructed in 1891 the house was a bungalow, built of wood salvaged from wrecks and laid out to allow air to circulate (essential in those pre-air-conditioning times). Then, in 1908, Munroe raised the building and added a new ground floor to accommodate his family.

Inside the two-story house visitors can explore rooms stuffed with old family heirlooms and wonderful, dated practical appliances, such as an early refrigerator. The hour-long tours of the property also take in Munroe's clapboard boat-house, full of his tools and work-benches. Alongside, you can see the rail track that Munroe used to winch boats out of the bay.

## 9 Dinner Key

3400 Pan American Drive. **Map** 6 F4. Metrorail (Coconut Grove). 22, 249 Coconut Grove Circulator (both from Coconut Grove), 48.

In the 1930s, Pan American Airways transformed Dinner Key into the busiest seaplane base in the US. It was also the point of departure for Amelia Earhart's doomed round-the-world flight in 1937. Visitors can still see the airline's sleek Streamline Moderne-style *(see p65)* terminal, which houses Miami City Hall – the hangars where seaplanes were

Deco detail on Miami City Hall façade, Dinner Key

An elegant fountain at the entrance to Country Club Prado in Coral Gables

once harbored are now boatyards. To see how some people enjoy their leisure time, walk among the yachts moored in Miami's most prestigious marina.

## 10 Ermita de la Caridad

3609 S Miami Ave. **Map** 3 C5. **Tel** (305) 854-2404. Metrorail (Vizcaya). 12, 48. **Open** noon–8pm, Spanish mass daily, 3pm Sun vigil.

This distinctive conical church, erected in 1966, is a very holy place for Miami's Cuban exiles – a shrine to their patron saint, the Virgin of Charity. A mural above the altar (which faces Cuba rather than being oriented eastward), illustrates the history of the Catholic church in Cuba, showing the Virgin and her shrine on the island. The church is hard to find: take the first turn north of the Mercy Hospital.

## 11 Coral Gables Museum

285 Aragon Ave **Map** 5 C1 **Tel** (305) 603-8067 Metrorail (Douglas Rd.) 24, 42, 56. **Open** noon-6pm Tue-Fri; 11am-5pm Sat; noon-5pm Sun.

Housed in the historic police and fire station building, this local museum offers a wide variety of exhibitions about Coral Gables and the surrounding area. A show of photographer Clyde Butcher's large format images focus on the natural beauty of the Tamiami Trail, along with a separate exhibition of the history and culture of the trail that does not shy away from describing its devastating impact on the Everglades.

Coral Gables' founder and developer, George Merrick, is the focus of another exhibition, showing how he was inspired to build a place where "your castles in Spain are made real." The museum is also the City of Coral Gables official visitors center and a great starting point for a wide variety of tours.

The Ermita de la Caridad, right on the edge of Biscayne Bay, which attracts many Cuban worshipers

# ⑫ Vizcaya Museum and Gardens

Florida's grandest residence was completed in 1916 as the winter retreat for millionaire industrialist James Deering. His vision was to replicate a 16th-century Italian estate, but one that had been altered by succeeding generations. Hence, Vizcaya and its opulent rooms are a blend of styles from Renaissance to Neo-Classical, furnished with the fruits of Deering's shopping sprees around Europe. The formal gardens combine the features of Italian and French gardens with Florida's tropical foliage.

Deering would constantly enquire of his ambitious architect: "Must we be so grand?" fearing that Vizcaya would be too costly to support. After his death in 1925, it proved to be so until 1952, when it was bought by Miami-Dade County. The house and gardens were opened to the public soon after.

★ **Deering Bathroom**
Deering's elaborate bathroom has marble walls, silver plaques, and a canopied ceiling reminiscent of a Napoleonic campaign tent.

**Pulcinella**
The 18th-century English statue of Pulcinella, in the intimate Theater Garden, is one of many European sculptures in the grounds of the villa.

## KEY

① **The East Loggia**, used for informal entertaining, contains a model caravel, a favorite Deering motif.

② **The Dining Room** resembles a Renaissance banquet hall, complete with tapestries and a 16th-century refectory table.

③ **Seahorse weathervane**

④ **The courtyard**, now protected by glass, was once open to the sky.

⑤ **The roof** is covered with barrel tiles taken from buildings in Cuba.

⑥ **The Living Room**, is a grand Renaissance hall with the curious addition of an organ, made especially for Vizcaya.

⑦ **The Swimming Pool** extends under the house and was accessible via an interior staircase.

★ **Music Room**
This Rococo room is arguably the loveliest in the house. It is lit by a striking chandelier of multicolored glass flowers.

★ **Gardens**
Formal gardens like those at Vizcaya are a rarity in Florida. The Mound provides a lovely view down the symmetrical Center Island to the South Terrace of the villa.

Entrance
5
4
6
7

**Cathay Bedroom**
Overwhelmed by the luxurious canopied bed, the Cathay Bedroom is decorated with chinoiserie, which was immensely popular in Europe in the 18th century.

**ering Sitting Room**
ceiling decoration of this -Classical room features a horse, one of Vizcaya's rrent motifs.

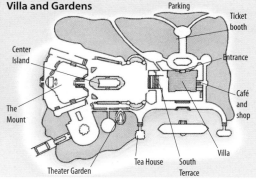

**Villa and Gardens**

Parking
Ticket booth
Center Island
Entrance
The Mount
Café and shop
Theater Garden
Tea House
South Terrace
Villa

# FARTHER AFIELD

The areas north of Miami Beach and Downtown, and south of Coral Gables are seldom very scenic, but they are well worth exploring for the great beaches and fun family attractions, as well as for some fascinating art-inspired sights.

Much of northern Miami has a reputation for crime and poverty, in particular Liberty City and Overtown. It is best to avoid these areas, and follow the safety tips on page 372. Be careful, too, when driving through Hialeah or Little Haiti – both atmospheric neighborhoods but ones that may appeal

only to the most adventurous sightseer. Wynwood Arts District, a former manufacturing and warehouse area just north of Downtown, is fast becoming known for its open air street-art, galleries, antiques shops, and eclectic bars.

Southern Miami's dull, non-descript suburbs give way to mile after mile of citrus orchards and nurseries. Many of this area's attractions, which consist primarily of zoos, parks, and gardens, offer visitors a glimpse of tropical flora and fauna, as well as a chance to enjoy the area's abundant marine life.

## Sights at a Glance

**Historic Buildings**
2 Ancient Spanish Monastery
14 Coral Castle

**Museums and Galleries**
10 Wings Over Miami
11 Gold Coast Railroad Museum

**Parks, Gardens, and Zoos**
5 Miami Seaquarium
7 Fairchild Tropical Botanic Garden
8 Charles Deering Estate
9 Jungle Island
12 Zoo Miami
13 Monkey Jungle

**Beaches**
1 North Beaches
6 Key Biscayne

**Neighborhoods**
3 Wynwood Arts District
4 Little Haiti

## Key

| | |
|---|---|
| ▨ | Main sightseeing areas |
| ▨ | Urban area |
| ▭ | Expressway |
| ▭ | Major highway |
| ⋯ | Secondary route |
| — | Rail line |

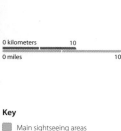

◀ Palm trees and blue skies at Crandon Park Beach, Key Biscayne

**For map symbols** see back flap

## ❶ North Beaches

Collins Avenue. 🚌 G (107), H (108), E (105), S (119), 120 Beach MAX.

The barrier islands north of Miami Beach are occupied mainly by exclusively smart residential areas and a few oceanfront resorts, strung out along Collins Avenue. The North Beach areas are quieter than the more vibrant South Beach, but the hotels are right on the sands, and are less expensive.

A peaceful strip of sand between 79th and 87th Streets separates Miami Beach from **Surfside**, a simple community

Beach at Haulover Park, under the protective eye of a lifeguard

very popular with French Canadians. At 96th Street Surfside merges with **Bal Harbour**, a stylish enclave known for some flashy hotels and one of the swankiest malls

around *(see p98)*. Northward is the pleasant **Haulover Park**, with a marina on the creek side and dune-backed sands facing the ocean.

## ❷ The Ancient Spanish Monastery

16711 W Dixie Hwy, N Miami Beach. **Tel** (305) 945-1462. 🚌 3 (from downtown Miami), 93, E (105), H (108). **Open** 10am–4pm Mon–Sat, 11am–4pm Sun. **Closed** some weekends (call to check), public hols. 🅿️ ♿ 🅦 spanishmonastery.com

These monastery cloisters have an unusual history. Built between 1133–41 in Spain, in 1925 they were bought by newspaper tycoon William Randolph Hearst, who had their 35,000 stones packed into crates. An outbreak of foot-and-

mouth disease led to the crates being opened (for the packing straw to be checked), and the stones were repacked incorrectly. Once in New York, they remained there until 1952, when it was decided

to piece together "the world's largest and most expensive jigsaw puzzle." The cloisters resemble the original version, but there is still a pile of unidentified stones in one corner of the gardens.

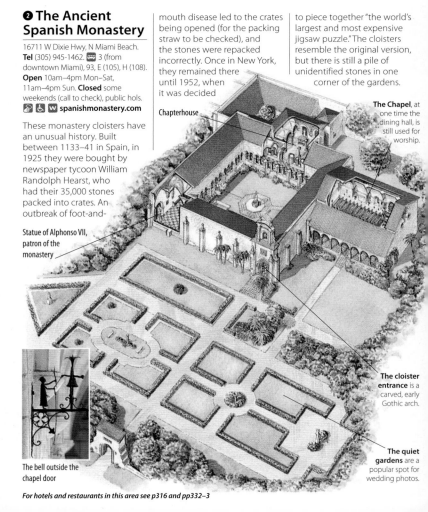

**Statue of Alphonso VII**, patron of the monastery

**Chapterhouse**

**The Chapel**, at one time the dining hall, is still used for worship.

**The cloister entrance** is a carved, early Gothic arch.

**The quiet gardens** are a popular spot for wedding photos.

The bell outside the chapel door

## ❸ Wynwood Arts District

NE 20th to 29th Streets, E of I-95,
2.7 miles (4.3 km) N of Downtown.
🚌 2. **W** wynwoodmiami.com

A vibrant arts district in the former manufacturing area of Greater Miami, Wynwood is known for its outdoor arts scene, where blocks of gray industrial buildings have seen a rebirth through colorful murals and graffiti. The gathering of artists promoted the opening of galleries and performing arts spaces. Restaurants and cafés followed, bringing more creative businesses. Now it is one of the top spots for hip culture. Wynwood features food tours, art walks, retail shops with interesting fashion, design companies, office space for entrepreneurs, and much more. At its heart and soul is the project that started it all – The Wynwood Walls. The late Tony Goldman's creative spotlight turned to the street art in the area and transformed the community.

## ❹ Little Haiti

46th to 79th Streets, E of I-95. 🚌 2 &
202 Little Haiti Connection.

Since the 1980s, many Haitian refugees have settled in this part of Miami. It is a visibly impoverished but colorful community, and fairly safe if you stick to the main streets, 54th Street and NE 2nd Avenue.

The **Caribbean Market-place**, at NE 2nd Avenue and 60th Street, has a few craft stalls, but more interesting are the surrounding shops painted

Waterfront homes and boats at a canal in Key Biscayne

in dazzling colors. High-decibel Haitian music blares out of some; others are *botánicas (see p81),* stocking herbal potions and saints' ephemera; and many more sell "Caribbean-style" chicken and plantains.

## ❺ Miami Seaquarium

4400 Rickenbacker Cswy,
Virginia Key. **Tel** (305) 361–5705.
🚇 Metrorail (Brickell). 🚌 B from Brickell station. **Open** 10am–6pm daily. 🅿 ♿ **W** miamiseaquarium. com

This tropical complex combines entertainment with conservation and education, and houses sea lions, dolphins, and killer whales. "Penguin Isle" houses a colony of African Penguins and has displays exploring the challenges faced by these birds in the wild. The Seaquarium is also home to five species of sea turtles, all of

which are found in Florida's waters. Other attractions include sharks, viewing areas for manatees, a mangrove swamp full of pelicans, and a tropical fish aquarium with coral, fish, and other marine life.

## ❻ Key Biscayne

7 miles (11 km) SE of Downtown.
🚌 B (102). Bill Baggs Cape Florida State Park: **Tel** (305) 361–5811.
**Open** daily. **W** floridastateparks.org

The view of Downtown from Rickenbacker Causeway, connecting the mainland to Virginia Key and Key Biscayne, is one of Miami's best. Views aside, Key Biscayne has some of the city's best beaches. Most impressive is the beach in **Crandon Park** in the upper half of the key, which is 3 miles (5 km) long with palm trees and an offshore sandbar. There is also a fenced beachfront picnic area which can accommodate up to 2,000 people. At the key's southern end, the **Bill Baggs Cape Florida State Park** has a shorter beach joined to more picnic areas by boardwalks across dunes. The lighthouse near the tip, built in 1825, is the oldest building in South Florida.

A mix of mini-malls and oceanfront apartments line Crandon Boulevard between the two parks, as well as a golf course and tennis center, which is open to the public.

A beautifully painted shop at the Caribbean Market in Little Haiti

### ❼ Fairchild Tropical Botanic Garden

10901 Old Cutler Rd. **Tel** (305) 667-1651. 🚌 57, 136 (both require a walk). **Open** sunrise–sunset (office: 8am–5pm). **Closed** Dec 25. 🚫 📷 ♿ 🆆 **fairchildgarden.org**
Mattheson Hammock Park: **Tel** (305) 665-5475. **Open** 7:30am–4:30pm daily. 🆆 **fairchildgarden.org**

This huge and incredibly beautiful tropical garden, established in 1938, doubles as a major botanical research institution. Around a series of man-made lakes stands one of the largest collections of palm trees in the world (550 of the 2,500 known species), as well as an impressive array of cycads – relatives of palms and ferns that bear unusual giant red cones. There are countless other wonderful trees and plants, including a comical-looking sausage tree.

During 40-minute trolley tours, guides describe how plants are used in the manu-facture of medicines and perfumes (the flowers of the ylang-ylang tree, for example, are used in Chanel No. 5). Allow another two hours to explore independently.

Next to the Fairchild Tropical Botanic Garden is the waterfront Mattheson Hammock Park. There are walking and cycling trails through mangrove swamps, but most visitors head for the Atoll Pool, an artificial salt-water swimming pool, encircled by sand and palm trees alongside Biscayne Bay. There is also a marina with a sailing school, and a first-rate beachfront restaurant.

### ❽ Charles Deering Estate

16701 SW 72nd Ave. **Tel** (305) 235-1668. **Open** 10am–5pm daily. 🚫 📷 ♿ **Closed** Thanksgiving, Dec 25. 🆆 **deeringestate.com**

While his brother James enjoyed the splendor of Vizcaya (*see pp90–91*), Charles Deering had his own stylish winter retreat on Biscayne Bay, which he used regularly between 1916 and 1927. His 444 acre (180 ha) estate, including a Mediterranean Revival mansion, was acquired by the state in 1985, and offers public access to Biscayne Bay.

The estate's buildings include the main house and a 19th-century inn called Richmond Cottage, which, when it was built, was the southernmost hotel on the US mainland .

The grounds are the main attraction, with mangrove and rockland pine forests, a salt marsh, and what is apparently the largest virgin coastal tropical hardwood hammock on the US mainland. There is an extensive fossil site on the grounds, and youth camps, conservation programs, and canoe tours on the weekend.

The Charles Deering Estate offers ecotours and access to Biscayne Bay

### ❾ Jungle Island

1111 Parrot Jungle Trail, Watson Island. **Tel** (305) 400-7000. 🚌 C (103), M (113), S (119), 120 Beach MAX. **Open** 10am–6pm daily. 🚫 ♿ 🆆 **jungleisland.com**

This beautifully maintained tropical garden, populated by hundreds of birds and exotic animals, has been a Miami landmark for 80 years. Some birds are caged, some, such as the flamingos, roam wild, while others perform in the Winged Wonders or Wild Encounters shows.

Visitors can interact with lemurs and sloths, and see how the staff care for the animals. There is also a children's playground, and a wide range of tropical trees.

The tranquil, palm-fringed lakes of the Fairchild Tropical Botanic Garden

*For hotels and restaurants in this area see p316 and pp332–3*

A Bengal tiger in front of a mock Khmer temple at Zoo Miami

Still run by the family that founded it back in 1933, Monkey Jungle's best selling point is that human visitors are caged while the animals roam free. Visitors walk through a caged area with Java macaques clambering above you, or can observe South American monkeys at close quarters in a simulated rainforest. Other primates, including gorillas and gibbons, are kept conventionally in cages.

Demonstrations showing the various capabilities of macaques, chimpanzees, and other species take place regularly throughout the day.

## ⓾ Wings Over Miami

14710 SW 128th St, adjacent to Tamiami Airport. **Tel** (305) 233-5197. 🚌 136, 137 (both require a walk). **Open** 10am–5pm Wed–Sun. **Closed** public holidays. 🅿️ ♿ 🆆 wingsovermiami.com

This museum is dedicated to the preservation of old aircraft. Its hangars contain a superb collection of finely preserved examples of operating aircraft, including a 1943 AT6D Texan "Old Timer," a Douglas B-23 Dragon, and a British Provost jet, as well as other exhibits such as a machine-gun turret.

All these planes take to the sky during the Memorial Day weekend celebration. In January or February they are sometimes joined by B-17 and B-24 bombers in the Wings of Freedom event.

## ⓫ Gold Coast Railroad Museum

12450 SW 152nd St, Miami. **Tel** (305) 253-0063. 🚇 Metrorail (Dadeland North) then Zoo Bus. 🚌 **Open** 10am–4pm Mon–Fri, 11am–4pm Sat–Sun. 🅿️ ♿ 🆆 gcrm.org

Located next to the Zoo Miami, this unusual museum is a must-see for railroad enthusiasts. Highlights include the presidential railroad car "Ferdinand Magellan," two California Zephyr cars, and three old Florida East Coast Railway steam locomotives. There is even a two-foot gauge railroad for children to ride on weekends.

## ⓬ Zoo Miami

12400 SW 152nd St, Miami. **Tel** (305) 251-0400. 🚇 Metrorail (Dadeland North) then Zoo Bus. **Open** 10am–5pm Mon–Fri, 9:30am–5:30pm Sat–Sun. 🅿️ ♿ 🆆 zoomiami.com

This giant zoo is one of the country's best. Animals are kept in spacious landscaped habitats, separated from humans by moats. Highlights include lowland gorillas, Malayan sun bears, and white Bengal tigers. The Petting Zoo is a hit with children, and the Wildlife Show demonstrates the agility of big cats.

Take the 20-minute ride on the monorail for an overview, and then decide what to visit. Alternatively, take the monorail to Station 4 and then walk back.

## ⓭ Monkey Jungle

14805 SW 216th St, Miami. **Tel** (305) 235-1611. 🚇 Metrorail (Dadeland South) then bus 31, 38 (or Busway flyer during peak hours) to Cutler Ridge Mall, then taxi. **Open** 9:30am–5pm daily. ♿ 🆆 monkeyjungle.com

A macaque, one of the most active primates at Monkey Jungle

Crescent moon sculpted from rock at Coral Castle

## ⓮ Coral Castle

28655 S Dixie Hwy, Homestead. **Tel** (305) 248-6345. 🚇 Metrorail (Dadeland South) then bus Busway Max. 🚌 38, 70. **Open** 7am–8pm daily. **Closed** Dec 25. 🅿️ ♿ 🆆 coralcastle.com

From 1920 to 1940, a Latvian named Edward Leedskalnin single-handedly built this series of giant castle-like sculptures out of coral rock, using tools assembled from automobile parts. He sculpted most of the stones 10 miles (16 km) away in Florida City, moving them again on his own to their present site. Some, such as a working telescope, represent their creator's great passion for astrology. Others, such as the heart-shaped table, remember a Latvian girl who refused to marry him.

# SHOPPING IN MIAMI

Miami's shops range from the ultra chic to the quirky and colorful, reflecting the nature of the city. Being made up of neighborhoods, Miami offers a choice of districts in which to shop. Serious shoppers will probably gravitate toward the malls, which attract visitors from all over Latin America and the Caribbean. Some of these double as entertainment centers *(see p354)*, often staying open until 11pm, but most of the stores tend to keep normal hours.

If your shopping tastes are more offbeat, head for Coconut Grove or South Beach, where shops are aimed at a totally different market. Here, wild leather gear, motorized skateboards, cardboard art, and the like are available, and visitors can pick up fun souvenirs, too. Most stores in Coconut Grove stay open late, especially on weekends. Stores in South Beach keep irregular hours, with most opening up late in the day, and some not opening until 11am or noon.

### Where to Shop

South Beach is a fun place to shop, but the most relaxed shopping area is Coconut Grove. It has numerous boutiques concentrated in a small area and boasts two malls *(see p88)*: **CocoWalk**, whose jewelry, gift, and clothing stores play second fiddle to cafés and restaurants, and **Mayfair in the Grove** – where pricey boutiques are suitable mainly for window-shopping.

**Bayside Marketplace** *(see p78)* has a wide range of stores, with all kinds of gift emporia and fashion stores. Otherwise, Downtown offers cut-price electronics and jewelry, although **Macy's** department store, founded in 1898, is of more general interest.

Entirely different in tone is Coral Gables, with its demure stores along Miracle Mile *(see p86)* and its smart art galleries. The **Village of Merrick Park** offers an added dimension to Coral Gables with its luxury retail stores complete with concierge services.

Dedicated shoppers head for Miami's famous malls. **Bal Harbour Shops** is an alluring upscale mall in a tropical garden setting where the increasing number of retail shops provide luxury goods to the rich and famous. **Aventura Mall**, also in North Miami, boasts more than 200 shops including four department stores, one of which is **Macy's**.

Typical window-dressing in a South Beach boutique

### Fashion and Jewelry

Miami has everything, from top designer to discount clothes. In Bal Harbour Shops, jewelers and fashion stores with names such as Tiffany & Co., Gucci, and Cartier stand alongside shops such as J. W. Cooper, specializing in Western gear. By contrast, **Stein Mart**, in nearby Aventura, deals in cut-rate designer clothes. More good deals can be found in the 100 or so discount stores of Downtown's Fashion District – on 5th Avenue, between 24th and 29th Streets. The **Seybold Building**, also Downtown, is famous for its cut-rate gold, diamonds, and watches.

In South Beach, stores on Lincoln Road and Washington Avenue deal primarily in leather and party outfits, but there are more chic stores, too. The boutiques along Miracle Mile in Coral Gables are more consistently up-scale: **Bolado Clothiers**, for made-to-measure clothes, is typical.

### Gifts and Souvenirs

Bayside marketplace is reliable gift-buying territory, with shops such as the **Caribbean Life** store and the **Disney Store**, and plenty ofof pushcarts laden with espadrilles, ties, and other items. In Coconut Grove, alongside numerous shops selling T-shirts

CocoWalk Mall in Coconut Grove

Cigarmaker in action

and sunglasses, are shops specializing in anything from oriental crafts to condoms. In North Miami visit **Edwin Watts Golf Shop**. This is the place to go for everything golf, including discounts on greens fees.

Macy's is not a classic hunting-ground for souvenirs, but visitors can sometimes pick up unusual items, such as genuine artifacts from the wreck of the *Atocha* salvaged by Mel Fisher *(see p32)*.

**Intermix** is an upscale, pricey boutique and epitomizes all that is exciting about Miami Beach.

South Beach is probably the best place for fun mementos and gifts. The **Art Deco Welcome Center** on Ocean Drive has a small but good choice, including T-shirts,

posters, and models of Ocean Drive buildings, in addition to a few genuine Art Deco antiques. The shop also maintains an impressive selection of pertinent books. A mix of tourists and locals come to buy handmade cigars at the well-known **El Titan de Bronze** in Little Havana *(see p80)*. A favorite brand among locals is La Palina, which celebrates the role of women in the cigar industry. **Sosa Family Cigars** also has an excellent selection.

A good shop for edible souvenirs, such as Florida jellies and sauces, is **Epicure** in South Beach, although tourists are not targeted at this gourmet supermarket.

Craft stalls are set up in Española Way *(see p72)* on weekends, and locally made crafts can be found in the small shops of the Wynwood area, north of Downtown.. Fine art is a much easier proposition. Española Way itself has a few avant-garde galleries, but a greater concentration of better quality

fine art is found along Lincoln Road. Most of the galleries, including the Art Center South Florida *(see p72)*, feature contemporary paintings, sculpture, ceramics, and furniture in provocative or Pop Art style. The art in Coral Gables' galleries is more traditional.

## Books and Music

**Books & Books** in Coral Gables, Miami Beach, and at the Adrienne Arsht Center, are the town's favorite bookstores. The original, with shelves from floor to ceiling, was founded by Mitchell Kaplan in 1982. The store has developed a large following for its vast collection of books on art, architecture, travel, and photography. Both stores have know-ledgeable staff and well-curated stock. Visitors will find branches of chain bookstores, such as Barnes & Noble, in many shopping malls.

A ceramic Art Deco hotel

With a coffee shop, café, and an event space, **Sweat Records** in the the Little Haiti/ Wynwood area is the home of indie music in Miami.

## DIRECTORY

### Shopping Malls and Department Stores

**Aventura Mall**
Biscayne Blvd at 195th St.
**Tel** (305) 935-1110.

**Bal Harbour Shops**
9700 Collins Ave.
**Tel** (305) 866-0311.

**Bayside Marketplace**
401 Biscayne Blvd. **Map** 4 F1. **Tel** (305) 577-3344.

**CocoWalk**
3015 Grand Ave.
**Map** 6 E4.
**Tel** (305) 444-0777.

**Macy's**
22 E Flagler St.
**Map** 4 E1.
**Tel** (305) 577-1500.

**Mayfair in the Grove**
2911 Grand Ave.
**Map** 6 F4.
**Tel** (305) 448-1700.

**Village of Merrick Park**
358 San Lorenzo Ave.
**Map** 3 C3.
**Tel** (305) 529-0200.

### Fashion and Jewelry

**Bolado Clothiers**
314 Miracle Mile.
**Map** 5 C1.
**Tel** (305) 448-5905.

**Seybold Building**
36 NE 1st St. **Map** 4 E1.
**Tel** (305) 374-7922.

**Stein Mart**
19915 Biscayne Blvd. **Map** 4 E1. **Tel** (305) 932-4171.

### Gifts and Souvenirs

**Art Deco Welcome Center**
1001 Ocean Drive.
**Map** 2 F3. **Tel** (305) 672-2014.

**Caribbean Life**
Bayside Marketplace. **Map** 4 F1. **Tel** (305) 416-9695.

**Disney Store**
Bayside Marketplace.
**Map** 4 F1. **Tel** (305) 371-7621.

**Edwin Watts Golf Shop**
15100 N. Biscayne Blvd.
**Tel** (305) 944-2925.

**El Titan de Bronze**
1071 SW 8th St. **Map** 3 B2.
**Tel** (305) 860-1412.

**Epicure**
1656 Alton Rd.
**Map** 2 D2.
**Tel** (305) 672-1861.

**Intermix**
634 Collins Avenue.
**Map** 2 E4.
**Tel** (305) 531-5950.

**Sosa Family Cigars**
3475 SW 8th St.
**Map** 3 B2.
**Tel** (305) 446-2606

### Books and Music

**Books & Books**
265 Aragon Ave. **Map** 5 C1. **Tel** (305) 442-4408.

**Sweat Records**
5505 NE 2nd Ave.
**Map** E1.
**Tel** (786) 693-9309

# ENTERTAINMENT IN MIAMI

A fleet of stretch limos parked outside the hottest nightspots attests to the fact that South Beach is one of the trendiest places on the planet. For many people, the chance to party in style is one of the city's chief attractions. Most visitors make for the nightclubs, which are surprisingly laid-back, and these are also ideal spots for live music. For anyone not into celebrity-spotting or dancing, Miami offers a wide range of cultural and sports events. The city's performing arts scene is buoyant.

The Arsht Center is the biggest venue, with its resident symphony and ballet companies. The New World Center merges music education with state-of-the-art technical capabilities. The winter season is the busiest, when Miami attracts many internationally renowned artists. If you are lucky, your visit may coincide with one of the city's colorful and large-scale festivals. The easiest way to purchase tickets for most events is to call Ticketmaster *(see p361)*. Otherwise, contact the venue directly.

## Information

Two essential sources of information are the weekend section of Friday's edition of the *Miami Herald*, and the free and more comprehensive *New Times*, which is published every Wednesday.

For hot tips about the latest and most happening spots in the city, check out the **Night Guide Miami** website. The vibrant gay nightlife of South Beach is covered in detail in several free and widely available magazines.

## Performing Arts

Major touring companies usually perform at **Adrienne Arsht Center for the Performing Arts**, consisting of the Ziff Ballet Opera House and the Knight Concert Hall; the **Miami/Dade County Auditorium**; the **Jackie Gleason Theater** in South Beach; and Downtown's **Olympia Theater**, a fabulous 1920s theater with an ornate Moorish interior, which was one of the last theaters in the

country to stage Vaudeville acts. The Broadway Series (November to April) in the Ziff Ballet Opera House leads Miami's drama scene. More intimate spots include the **Miami Theater Center** in Miami Shores, and **Gable Stage** and the **Actors' Playhouse** in Coral Gables for new shows and old favorites.

**Miami City Ballet** performs classical and contemporary work at its home at the Arsht Center, and you can sometimes see dancers rehearse at the company's base on Liberty Avenue. The **Performing Arts Network** in North Miami is home to a startling array of dancers and artists.

Miami's most acclaimed classical orchestra is Michael Tilson Thomas's New World Symphony *(see p359)*, which comprises some of the most stellar musicians in the country. The orchestra performs at the **New World Center**, from October to May. The Concert Association of Florida organizes most of Miami's top concerts.

A crowd of spectators at the Gulfstream Park Racetrack

## Spectator Sports

Miami boasts a wide variety of spectator sports. The Miami Dolphins football team compete at the **Hard Rock Stadium**, while the Major League baseball team, Miami Marlins play at **Marlins Park**, under a retractable roof. The Hurricanes from the University of Miami are one of Florida's top college football squads, and attract large crowds. The popular Miami Heat basketball team play at the **American Airlines Arena**.

For some Hispanic flair, catch a game of jai alai *(see p37)*. A primary venue for this uniquely Floridian version of pelota is the **Miami Jai Alai Fronton**. Betting is *de rigueur* here, just as it is at **Gulfstream Park Racetrack**, **Calder Casino**, and **Flagler Dog Track**.

## Latin Sounds

**Mango's Tropical Café** on Ocean Drive in South Beach specializes in loud, brassy Latin music, and it is routine for

Adrienne Arsht Center for the Performing Arts

Interior of the 2,400-seat Ziff Ballet Opera House

female as well as male staff to dance upon the bar tops. Very touristy, but also a lot of fun. Also in the South Beach area, **Tapas y Tintos** is a great place for a few drinks and a light bite to eat on a Saturday, while watching live Flamenco.

**Hoy Como Ayer** offers energetic and smoky cabaret right on Calle Ocho, in the heart of Little Havana. Brimming with an array of Cuban memorabilia, this popular nightclub promises late-night dancing to Cuban musicians playing mambo, rumba, cha-cha-cha, and sou cubano. Live bands play some nights, while DJs spin Afro Cuban, funk, Latin, and jazz on others.

If in doubt about your dancing skills, take a free lesson from some of Miami's best. Instructors are on hand on Wednesdays at Salsa Mia in **Mango's Tropical Café**, and on Fridays and Saturdays at **Bongo's Cuban Café**, at the American Airlines Arena.

## Live Music

Most of the bars on Ocean Drive offer live music, which is typically Latin, jazz, reggae, or salsa. A few blocks away, **Jazid** hosts live jazz, blues, and funk, with Latin bands on the lower level, and a DJ spinning fusion and trance upstairs.

In the Art Deco district of South Beach, The Fillmore Miami Beach at the Jackie Gleason Theater, which seats up to 2,500 concert goers, hosts a variety of live music events.

Coral Gables is where you will find **The Globe Café & Bar**, an intimate, European style bistro, that features live jazz every Saturday night.

## Bars

For that extra touch of sophistication, head to **Repour Bar & Lounge** at the Albion Hotel for one of its renowned hand-crafted cocktails. To watch another craft-cocktail

alchemist at work, a visit to **The Drawing Room** at the Shelborne South Beach is a must. Nearby, enjoy a drink and a range of musical styles at swanky **Marlin Bar**. A celebrity favorite, **Skybar** features three distinct areas on the rooftop, and is one of SoBe's most happening and glamorous hangout zones.

The glitzy **Rose Bar** at the Delano pours out top-dollar martinis, while **Raleigh Hotel's** pool bar has been pouring midday mojitos since Esther Williams made her movies there. At the other end of the spectrum, the pool bars and rooftop terrace at **The Clevelander** offer great views and a party atmosphere day and night.

Outside SoBe, immerse yourself in the artsy funk of **The Wynwood Yard** for live music, cocktails, craft beers, and tasty and creative food options from various food trucks.

People enjoying a music performance at The Wynwood Yard

One of the four bars at The Clevelander on Ocean Drive

## Nightclubs

Miami has long been reputed as a hardcore party town, and with good reason. Most of the city's hottest venues have long lines of would-be party-goers waiting at the entrances. To get in, tip the scales in your favor by dressing to impress. Groups of men hoping to make it past the bouncer stand a better chance of gaining entry if they invite some female friends to accompany them. Most clubs prefer to keep the customer ratio heavily skewed toward the feminine. You have been warned!

Greater Miami boasts three areas that really live up after dark: South Beach; Downtown, which includes the trendy Wynwood Arts District; and the more understated Coconut Grove, which offers the best wining and dining options.

In SoBe, the bars along Ocean Drive and nearby streets are busy all day, but the nightclubs only really get going after midnight. It is not uncommon to see people winding their way out as the sun rises the next day. You can start your party during the day at **Nikki Beach**, an oceanfront complex with laidback cabanas, an award-winning restaurant serving delectable Sunday brunch, a lifestyle boutique, and a nightclub. For a more sophisticated experience, **Pearl Champagne Lounge** next door offers sleek surroundings and live burlesque.

**LIV** is a mega nightclub inside the iconic Fontainebleu Hotel, which in the 60s hosted Frank Sinatra and Elvis, that draws renowned DJs and a large crowd. The cavernous **Mansion Night-club** is a SoBe institution – home to late-night, high-energy dancing, eye-catching entertainment, a pricey cover charge, and expensive drinks. The club attracts long lines of tourists and locals. and it is almost impossible to get in on the weekends.

Moving farther south, the opulent nightclub **STORY** is a venue for dancing, with stunning lighting effects,

Sushi Samba, a top destination for sushi lovers

exorbitant entrance fee, lots of security and, sometimes, celebrity DJs.

If you seek Latin rhythms, **Mango's Tropical Café** has live bands and DJs playing high-energy salsa, merengue, and popular songs in several dance rooms. Live entertainment also includes male and female dancers performing Latin dance routines on the bar.

Farther up, near the Delano, you will find **Mynt Lounge**, which is known for its exclusivity; gaining entry can be rather difficult.

Sophisticated cocktails and DJs are the attraction at the Shore Club's **Skybar** nightclub areas: The Red Room, with its rich scarlet and gold decor; the Moroccan-themed garden area; and the Sand Bar on the beach.

Rivaling SoBe, Downtown Miami has a buzzing clubbing scene, but the venues change rather quickly. The **Fifty Ultra Lounge** atop the Viceroy Hotel on Brickell Ave, offers stunning views of the city and the port.

Slightly north of Downtown, in the very hip and evolving neighborhood of Wynwood, the clubbing scene is booming but with an entirely different vibe and relatively cheaper drinks. **SHOTS Miami** offers theme DJs, playing hip-hop and a variety of dance music. **Lagniappe's** is a wine bar with live music and a romantic vibe. The outdoor patio offers spots to sit under twinkling lights while drinking wine and enjoying charcuterie and cheese. **Gramps**, another popular spot for live music and craft cocktails, has an eccentrically furnished outdoor patio.

Over in the more refined area of Coral Gables, **Son Cubano** is decorated to reflect a bar and restaurant in the 1950s. Food and drinks are a fusion of Cuban and Asian cuisines, and local Cuban jazz musicians perform on the weekends. At Lincoln Road's **Sushi Samba**, Wasabi Tuesdays are a must for lovers of sushi, sake, and karaoke.

Many clubs have a gay night, while others categorically advertise themselves as exclusively gay. However, most venues seem to draw a mixed crowd. **Twist**, with a Key West-style terrace, is a very popular gay bar and also sports a dance floor. **Club Space** attracts a massive gay crowd into its cavernous building, though you will find that Friday night brings in a wide cross-section of club goers.

## Festivals

If you are lucky, your visit may coincide with one of the city's colorful and large-scale festivals (see pp38–41).

Two of the largest and best known festivals are very different but equally popular: the Winter Music Conference in March, when thousands of DJs and club kids flood South Beach, and the South Beach Wine & Food Festival, also in March, which offers opportunities to meet celebrity chefs.

Both festivals bring in plenty of visitors to the packed SoBe area, so the downside is that the already-crowded clubs are that much harder to get into. However, celebrity-spotters can have a field day at these festivals.

# DIRECTORY

## Information

**Night Guide Miami**
[w] miami.nightguide.com

## Performing Arts

**Actors' Playhouse**
280 Miracle Mile.
**Map** 5 C1.
**Tel** (305) 444-9293.

**Adrienne Arsht Center for the Performing Arts**
1300 Biscayne Blvd.
**Map** 4 F1.
**Tel** (305) 949-6722.

**Colony Theatre**
1040 Lincoln Rd.
**Map** 2 D2.
**Tel** (305) 674-1026.

**Gable Stage**
1200 Anastasia Ave,
Coral Gables.
**Map** 5 A2.
**Tel** (305) 445-1119.

**Jackie Gleason Theater**
1700 Washington Ave.
**Map** 2 E2.
**Tel** (305) 673-7300.

**Miami City Ballet**
2200 Liberty Ave.
**Map** 2 E2.
**Tel** (305) 929-7010.

**Miami/Dade County Auditorium**
2901 W Flagler St.
**Tel** (305) 547-5414.

**Miami Theater Center**
9806 NE 2nd Ave, Miami
Shores. **Map** 4 E1.
**Tel** (305) 751-9550.

**New World Center**
541 Lincoln Rd.
**Map** 2 E2.
**Tel** (305) 673-3330.

**Olympia Theater**
174 E Flagler St.
**Map** 4 E1.
**Tel** (305) 374-2444.

**Performing Arts Network**
13124 West Dixie Hwy,
North Miami
**Tel** (305) 899-7730.

## Spectator Sports

**American Airlines Arena**
601 Biscayne Blvd.
**Tel** (786) 777-1000.

**Calder Casino**
21001 NW 27th Ave.
**Tel** (305) 625-1311.

**Casino Miami Jai-Alai**
3500 NW 37th Ave.
**Tel** (305) 633-6400.

**Gulfstream Park Racetrack**
901 S Federal Hwy.
**Tel** (954) 454-7000.

**Hard Rock Stadium**
347 Don Shula Dr.
**Tel** (305) 943-8000.

**Magic City Casino**
450 NW 37th Ave.
**Tel** (305) 649-3000.

**Marlins Park**
501 Marlins Way
**Tel** (305) 480-1300.

## Latin Sounds

**Bongo's Cuban Café**
601 Biscayne Blvd.
**Tel** (786) 777-2100.

**Hoy Como Ayer**
2212 SW 8th St.
**Tel** (305) 541-2631

**Mango's Tropical Café**
900 Ocean Drive.
**Map** 2 E5.
**Tel** (305) 673-4422.

**Salsa Mia**
900 Ocean Drive.
**Map** 2 E5.
**Tel** (305) 458-4558.

**Son Cubano**
2530 Ponce De Leon Blvd,
Coral Gables. **Map** 5 A2.
**Tel** (305) 902-6220

**Tapas y Tintos**
448 Española Way.
**Map** 2 E2.
**Tel** (305) 538-8272.

## Live Music

**The Globe Café & Bar**
377 Alhambra Circle,
Coral Gables.
**Map** 5 C1.
**Tel** (305) 445-3555.

**Gramps**
176 NW 24th St.
**Map** 5 C1.
**Tel** (302) 699-2669.

**Jazid**
1342 Washington Ave.
**Map** 2 E2.
**Tel** (305) 673-9372.

## Bars

**The Bar at 1220**
The Tides Hotel, 1220
Ocean Drive.
**Map** 2 F3.
**Tel** (305) 604-5070.

**The Clevelander**
1020 Ocean Drive.
**Map** 2 F3.
**Tel** (786) 276-1414.

**The Drawing Room**
1801 Collins Ave.
**Map** 2 F3.
**Tel** (305) 531-1271.

**Marlin Bar**
1200 Collins Ave.
**Map** 2 E3.
**Tel** (305) 604-3595.

**Raleigh Hotel**
1775 Collins Ave.
**Map** 2 F1.
**Tel** (305) 534-6300.

**Rose Bar**
The Delano Hotel,
1685 Collins Ave.
**Map** 2 F1.
**Tel** (305) 672-2000.

**Skybar**
The Shore Club Hotel,
1901 Collins Ave.
**Map** 2 F1.
**Tel** (305) 695-3100.

**The Wynwood Yard**
56 NW 29th St.
**Tel** (305) 351-0366.

## Nightclubs

**Club Space**
142 NE 11th St.
**Tel** (305) 375-0001.

**Fifty Ultra Lounge**
485 Brickell Avenue.
**Map** 4 F2.
**Tel** (305) 503-4400.

**LIV at Fontainebleau Miami Beach**
4441 Collins Ave.
**Map** 2 F1
**Tel** (305) 674-4680

**Mansion Nightclub**
1235 Washington Ave.
**Map** 2 E3.
**Tel** (305) 695-8411.

**Mynt Lounge**
1921 Collins Ave.
**Map** 2 F1.
**Tel** (786) 276-6132.

**Nikki Beach**
1 Ocean Drive.
**Map** 2 E5.
**Tel** (305) 538-1111.

**Pearl Champagne Lounge**
1 Ocean Drive.
**Map** 2 E5.
**Tel** (305) 510-6524.

**Skybar**
The Shore Club Hotel,
1901 Collins Ave.
**Map** 2 F1.
**Tel** (305) 695-3100.

**SHOTS Miami**
311 NW 23rd St.
**Map** 2 E3.
**Tel** (305) 571-0439.

**STORY**
136 Collins Ave.
**Map** 2 E5
**Tel** (305) 538-2424

**Sushi Samba**
600 Lincoln Rd.
**Map** 2 E2.
**Tel** (305) 673-5337.

**Twist**
1057 Washington Ave.
**Map** 2 E3.
**Tel** (305) 538-9478.

# MIAMI STREET FINDER

The map references given with all sights, shops, and entertainment venues described in the Miami chapter refer to the six pages of maps in this section. The key map below shows the area of the city that is covered, with the three major sightseeing districts color-coded pink. All the principal sights mentioned

in the text are marked, as well as useful information, such as transit stops, tourist offices, and post offices; a full list is given in the key. Map references are also given for Miami's hotels *(see pp314–25)*, restaurants *(see pp329–49)*, and bars and cafés *(see pp348–9)* included in the Travelers' Needs section.

*Belle*

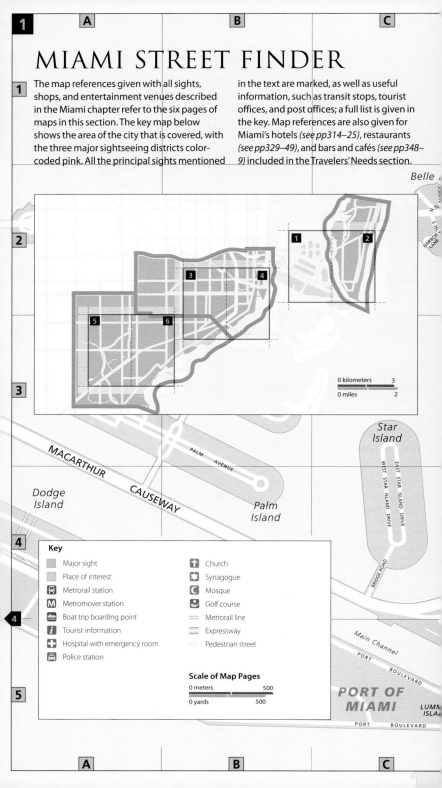

0 kilometers 3

0 miles 2

*Star Island*

MACARTHUR    CAUSEWAY    PALM AVENUE

*Dodge Island*

*Palm Island*

WEST STAR ISLAND DRIVE   EAST STAR ISLAND DRIVE

BRIDGE ROAD

### Key

| | |
|---|---|
| ▢ Major sight | ✝ Church |
| ▢ Place of interest | ✡ Synagogue |
| 🚇 Metrorail station | ☪ Mosque |
| Ⓜ Metromover station | ⛳ Golf course |
| 🚢 Boat trip boarding point | ═ Metrorail line |
| ℹ Tourist information | ═ Expressway |
| ✚ Hospital with emergency room | Pedestrian street |
| 🏛 Police station | |

*Main Channel*

PORT   BOULEVARD

**PORT OF MIAMI**

LUMN ISLA

PORT   BOULEVARD

### Scale of Map Pages

0 meters 500

0 yards 500

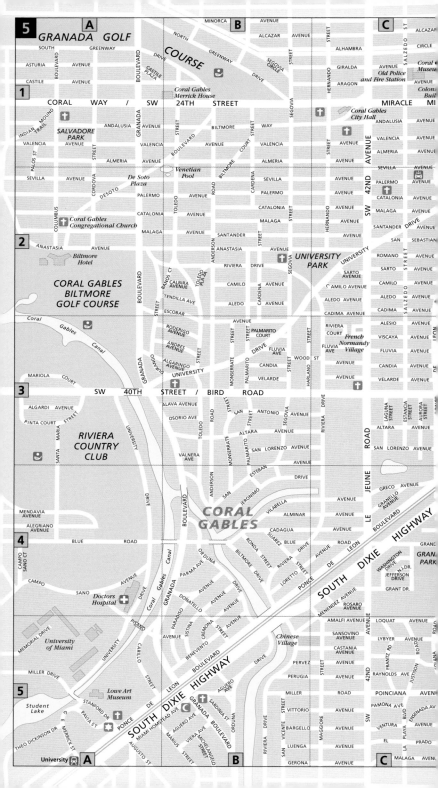

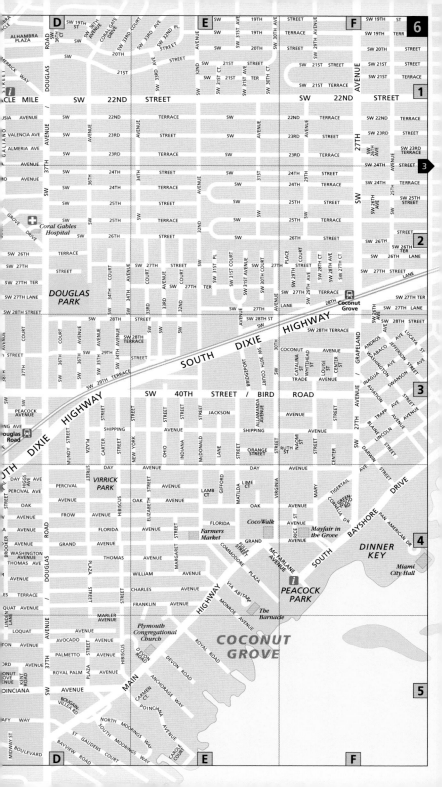

# FLORIDA AREA BY AREA

# Florida at a Glance

Walt Disney World aside, Florida is best known for its beaches; there are so many of these that everyone should be able to find one to suit his or her taste. Most tourist attractions, from state-of-the-art museums to historic towns, are also found along the coast. The joy of Florida, however, is that inland destinations are within easy reach. It is well worth venturing away from the coast to explore some of the state's richest natural landscapes and appreciate the full flavor of Florida.

**Canoeing** is very popular in the Panhandle, where rivers such as the Suwannee are frequently flanked by lush vegetation *(see p248).*

Milton

De Funiak Springs

Pensacola

**THE PANHANDLE**
*(See pp228–249)*

Tallahassee

Panama City

Carrabelle

Steinhatchee

Gaines

Suwannee

Homosassa Springs

Weeki Wachee

**Beaches** in the Panhandle boast the finest sand in Florida, washed by the warm waters of the Gulf of Mexico. Resorts like Panama City Beach throng with people in the summer *(see pp240–41).*

T...

St Petersburg

**Busch Gardens**, which combines a wildlife park with roller coasters and other rides, is the top large-scale family attraction outside Orlando *(see pp268–9).*

Sarasot

**The Ringling Museum of Art** boasts one of the state's top art collections and has an elegant courtyard filled with copies of Classical statuary, including this *Lygia and the Bull (see pp274–7).*

0 kilometers 75
0 miles 75

◄ Dawn at Long Pine Key Lake in Everglades National Park

**Castillo de San Marcos** is a 17th-century Spanish fort in Florida's oldest town, St. Augustine. Its well-preserved state is due to both its design, and its 18 ft (6 m) thick walls (see pp218–19).

**Orlando's theme parks** are Florida's principal attraction away from the coast. Here, you can escape into a man-made fantasy world, where an extraordinary array of shows and rides provide the entertainment. Most famous is Walt Disney World® (see pp146–79), but Universal Orlando® (see pp182–9), pictured here, and SeaWorld® (see p180) draw their own vast crowds.

Daytona Beach (see pp221–3)

nville

: Augustine

NORTHEAST
(see pp206–227)

la

Daytona Beach

Kennedy Space Center (see pp200–205)

Orlando

ORLANDO AND THE SPACE COAST
(See pp142–205)

Melbourne

Yeehaw Junction

Vero Beach

Fort Pierce

GULF
AST
250–283)

THE GOLD AND TREASURE COASTS
(See pp114–141)

Lake Okeechobee

Jupiter

rt
arlotte

Fort Myers

Palm Beach

Boca Raton

Fort Lauderdale

les

THE EVERGLADES AND THE KEYS
(See pp284–307)

Miami

Florida City

John Pennekamp Coral Reef State Park
(see pp296–7)

Islamorada

Marathon

ey
est

**The Gold Coast** is full of luxurious homes. In Palm Beach you can visit the 1920s home of Henry Flagler, and marvel at the mansions and yachts along the Intracoastal Waterway (see pp122–9).

**Everglades National Park**, a vast expanse of prairie, swamp, and mangrove that teems with wildlife, is as wild as Florida gets. It is just a short drive from Miami (See pp290–91).

# THE GOLD AND TREASURE COASTS

Named after booty found in Spanish galleons wrecked along their shores, the Gold and Treasure coasts today are two of the state's wealthiest regions. The promise of winter sunshine once lured only the well-to-do, but now it entices millions of vacationers.

Vacations center on the pencil-thin barrier islands that extend right along the coast, squeezed between prime beaches and the Intracoastal Waterway *(see p27)*. The Treasure Coast, stretching from Sebastian Inlet down to Jupiter Inlet, is relatively undeveloped, with great sweeps of wild, sandy beaches and affluent but unshowy communities.

Wedged between the Atlantic and the Everglades, the 60-mile (97-km) Gold Coast extends from just north of West Palm Beach down to Miami. Before being opened up by Flagler's East Coast Railroad in the late 19th century, this part of Florida was a wilderness populated by Seminoles and the occasional settler. Today, except for golf courses and scattered parks, it is

unremittingly built up. The Gold Coast divides into two counties. In Palm Beach County, rich northerners, most of whom have made their fortunes elsewhere, display their privileged lifestyle in million-dollar homes and on croquet lawns and polo fields. The winter resorts of Palm Beach and Boca Raton offer memorable glimpses of how affluent Americans spend their time and money. Broward County, synonymous with Greater Fort Lauderdale, is one huge metropolis. Its relentless urbanization is relieved by waterways and beaches, including in Fort Lauderdale itself, one of several local resorts in which visitors let their hair down more than their formal Palm Beach County counterparts.

Seagulls circling at the picturesque Palm Beach

◀ Aerial view of Fort Pierce

# Exploring the Gold and Treasure Coasts

Most visitors come here for a stay-put beach vacation. North of Palm Beach lies an unspoiled, uncrowded coastal stretch, while to the south visitors will find condos, sunbeds, and plenty of company. Coastal parks rich in bird life provide reminders of how the land looked in its virgin state. Cultural sight-seeing comes fairly low on the agenda, but West Palm Beach's superb Norton Museum of Art and the exclusive town of Palm Beach should not be missed. The more active can play golf, shop, and fish – the main reason to head inland is for the excellent fishing on Lake Okeechobee. All along the coast, hotel rooms are hard to come by and twice the price from December to April; in summer visitors take advantage of lower rates.

Boca Raton's Old Town Hall, the work of Addison Mizner *(see p124)*

## Sights at a Glance

1. Sebastian Inlet
2. Mel Fisher's Treasure Museum
3. Vero Beach
4. Fort Pierce
5. Hutchinson Island
6. Stuart
7. Jupiter Island
8. Jupiter
9. Juno Beach
10. *Palm Beach pp122–9*
11. West Palm Beach
12. Lion Country Safari
13. Lake Okeechobee
14. Lake Worth
15. Delray Beach
16. Loxahatchee National Wildlife Refuge
17. Morikami Museum and Japanese Gardens
18. Butterfly World
19. Boca Raton
20. *Fort Lauderdale pp136–9*
21. Dania
22. Hollywood
23. Davie
24. Flamingo Gardens

### Key

0 kilometers 20
0 miles 20

═══ Highway
═══ Major road
─── Secondary road
····· Minor road
─── Scenic route
─── Main railroad

*For hotels and restaurants in this region see pp316–17 and pp336–9*

Designer shops and cars in exclusive Palm Beach

## Getting Around

A car is absolutely essential, because public transportation is either limited or nonexistent. Amtrak basically offers ways to get to (rather than around) the area, but Tri-Rail *(see p384)* has services stopping at towns and airports between Miami and West Palm Beach. Three main highways run the length of the coast. Use the fast-moving, multilaned I-95 to travel any distance. Avoid US 1 where possible: it trawls slowly through the unscenic center of every significant urban area. Route A1A can be slower still but is usually far less congested, and often delivers picturesque views. Avoid traveling on major roads anywhere along the Gold Coast and around the Treasure Coast's main centers during rush hours (weekdays 7:30–9:30am and 4:30–7pm).

The skyline of Fort Lauderdale dotted with high-rise buildings

**For keys to symbols** *see back flap*

# ❶ Sebastian Inlet

**Road map** F3. Indian River Co.
🚌 Sebastian. 🛈 700 Main St, (772)
589-5969. 🔲 sebastianchamber.com

At Sebastian Inlet, the Atlantic Ocean mingles with the brackish waters of the Indian River section of the Intracoastal Waterway *(see p27)*. The **Sebastian Inlet State Park** spans this channel and, with its 3 miles (5 km) of pristine beaches, is one of the most popular state parks in Florida.

A tranquil cove on the northern side of the inlet is an ideal place to swim – avoiding the waves that make the southern shores (on Orchid Island) one of the best surfing spots on

Spanish plate, McLarty Museum

Florida's east coast. Competitions take place on many weekends, and there are boards for rent. The park is also famous for its fishing, and the inlet's mouth is invariably crowded with fishing boats. The two jetties jutting out into the Atlantic Ocean on either side are also crammed with anglers, while more lines dangle in the clear waters of the Indian River.

At the southern end of the park, the **McLarty Treasure Museum** takes a detailed look at the history surrounding the loss of a Spanish Plate Fleet in 1715. On July 31 a hurricane wrecked 11 galleons on the shallow reefs off the coast between Sebastian Inlet and Fort Pierce. The ships were en route from Havana back to Spain, riding the waters of the warm Gulf Stream,

and laden with booty from Spain's New World colonies. About a third of the 2,100 sailors lost their lives, while the survivors set up a camp where the McLarty Treasure Museum now stands.

Immediately following this tragedy, some 80 per cent of the cargo was salvaged by the survivors, helped by local Ais Indians. The fleet then lay undisturbed until 1928, when one of the wrecks was rediscovered. Salvaging resumed in the early 1960s; since then, millions of dollars worth of treasures have been recovered. Finds on display include gold and silver coins but feature mostly domestic items.

🏛 **Sebastian Inlet State Park**
9700 S A1A, Melbourne Beach.
**Tel** (321) 984-4852. **Open** daily. 🅿️
🚻 ♿ 🔲 floridastateparks.com

🏛 **McLarty Treasure Museum**
13180 N Highway A1A. **Tel** (772) 589-2147. **Open** 10am–4pm daily 🅿️ ♿

# ❷ Mel Fisher's Treasure Museum

**Road map** F3. Indian River Co.
**Tel** (772) 589-9875. 🚌 Sebastian.
**Open** 10am–5pm Mon–Sat (from noon Sun). **Closed** Jan 1, Easter, Sep, Thanksgiving, Dec 25. 🅿️ ♿
🔲 melfisher.com

One of the great rags-to-riches stories is presented at this amazing museum. Billed as "The World's Greatest Treasure Hunter," Mel Fisher died in

The late Mel Fisher: treasure hunter and founder of the Mel Fisher's Treasure Museum

1998, but his treasure-hunting team of divers lives on.

The museum boasts treasures from different wrecks, including the 1715 fleet (which his team has been salvaging for decades), and the Atocha *(see pp32–3)*. There are jewels, a gold bar, and more everyday items. In the Bounty Room, visitors can buy original Spanish reales, or copies of historic jewelry. See also The Mel Fisher Maritime Museum on p306.

# ❸ Vero Beach

**Road map** F3. Indian River Co.
🚉 15,500. 🚌 🛈 1216 21st St, (772) 567-3491. 🔲 indianriver chamber.com

The main town of Indian River County, Vero Beach, and in particular its resort community on Orchid Island, is a wealthy place. Mature live oaks line the residential streets, and buildings are restricted to four stories. Pretty clapboard houses along Ocean Drive contain galleries, boutiques, and antique shops.

The **Vero Beach Museum of Art** in Riverside Park on Orchid Island shows high-profile exhibitions, but the town is most famous for its beaches and two hotels. The Driftwood Resort, in the heart of oceanfront Vero Beach, began life in 1935 as a beach house. It was created out of reclaimed wood and driftwood by a local eccentric and filled with an amazing array of bric-a-brac, still present today. Seven miles (11 km) north at Wabasso Beach, one of the best of the superb shell-strewn sands

Catching the waves at the Gold Coast's Sebastian Inlet

on Orchid Island, is the Vero Beach Resort – Disney's first Florida hotel outside Orlando. It is a model of measured elegance.

The **Indian River Citrus Museum**, on the mainland, is dedicated to the area's chief crop. All kinds of items relevant to the citrus industry are displayed, including some old photographs, harvesting equipment, and brand labels.

🏛 **Vero Beach Museum of Art**
3001 Riverside Park Drive. **Tel** (772) 231-0707. **Closed** Jan 1, Thanksgiving, Dec 25. ♿ 🆆 verobeachmuseum.com

🏛 **Indian River Citrus Museum**
2140 14th Ave. **Tel** (772) 770-2263. **Open** 10am–4pm Tue–Fri. **Closed** public hols. ♿ 🆆 veroheritage.com

## ❹ Fort Pierce

**Road map** F3. St. Lucie Co. 👥 41,500. ✈ 🚌 ℹ 2300 Virginia Ave, (772) 462-1535. 🆆 visitstluciefla.com

Named after a military post built during the Second Seminole War (see pp50–51), Fort Pierce is not considered a tourist mecca. The town's biggest draw is its barrier islands, reached by crossing two causeways that sweep across the Intracoastal Waterway.

Take the North Beach Causeway to reach North Hutchinson Island. Its southern tip is occupied by the **Fort Pierce Inlet State Park**, which includes the town's best beach, backed by dunes and popular with surfers. Just to the north, on the site of a World War II training school, is the **National Navy UDT-SEAL Museum**. From 1943 to 1946,

Vero Beach's Driftwood Resort, built using reclaimed wood

more than 3,000 US Navy frogmen of the Underwater Demolition Teams (UDTs) trained here, learning how to disarm sea mines and beach defenses. By the 1960s, they had become an elite advance fighting force known as SEALs (Sea, Air, Land commandos). The museum explains the frogmen's roles in World War II, Korea, Vietnam, and in the present.

Half a mile (1 km) away is Jack Island – actually a peninsula on the Indian River. This mangrove-covered preserve teems with bird life and is crossed by a short trail leading to an observation tower. Situated on the southern causeway linking Fort Pierce to Hutchinson Island is the **St. Lucie County Historical Museum**. This has an enjoyable array of displays, which include finds from the 1715 wrecks in the Galleon Room, and reconstructions of a Seminole camp and an early 20th-century general store. Visitors can also look

around the adjacent "Cracker" home (see p34).

Back on the mainland, literature buffs and fans of writer Zora Neale Hurston can follow a heritage trail dedicated to her final years.

🏞 **Fort Pierce Inlet State Park**
905 Shorewinds Drive, N Hutchinson Island. **Tel** (772) 468-3985. 🅿 ♿ limited.

🏛 **National Navy UDT-SEAL Museum**
3300 N Highway A1A. **Tel** (772) 595-5845. **Open** Jan–Apr: daily; May–Dec: Tue–Sun. **Closed** public hols. 🅿 ♿ 🆆 navysealmuseum.com

🏛 **St. Lucie County Historical Museum**
414 Seaway Drive. **Tel** (772) 462-1795. **Open** 10am–4pm Tue–Sat (from noon Sun). **Closed** public hols. 🅿 ♿ limited. 🆆 stlucieco.gov

🚏 **Zora Neale Hurston Dust Tracks Heritage Trail**
Garden of Heavenly Rest Cemetery, Avenue S and 17th St. 🆆 stlucieco.gov/zora

A 1937 brand label from central Florida using the Indian River name

## Indian River's Citrus Industry

Citrus fruits were brought to Florida by the Spanish in the 16th century: each ship was purportedly required to leave Spain with 100 citrus seeds to be planted in the new colonies. Conditions in Florida proved ideal, and the fruit trees flourished, particularly along the Indian River between Daytona and West Palm Beach. In 1931, local farmers created the Indian River Citrus League to stop growers outside the area from describing their fruit as "Indian River." One third of Florida's citrus crop, and 75 per cent of its grapefruit yield, is produced here. The majority of the oranges are used to make juice. Unfortunately, the industry has been afflicted by a bacterial infection, which has decimated the crops. State scientists are battling to find a cure for it so that this economically-important product can recover.

Gilbert's Bar House of Refuge Museum, on the Atlantic shore of Hutchinson Island

## ❺ Hutchinson Island

**Road map** F3. St. Lucie Co/Martin Co. 🚗 5,000. ℹ️ 1900 Ricou Jensen Beach, (772) 334-3444. 🅦 **jensenbeach.biz**

Extending for more than 20 miles (32 km), this barrier island is most memorable for its breathtaking beaches. In the south, sun-worshipers head for Sea Turtle Beach and the adjacent Jensen Beach Park, close to the junction of routes 707 and A1A. Stuart Beach, at the head of the causeway across the Indian River from Stuart, is well frequented, too.

Near Stuart Beach is the **Elliott Museum**, created in 1961 in honor of inventor Sterling Elliott, some of whose quirky contraptions are on show. Focusing on art, history, technology, and innovation, the museum was completely rebuilt in 2013.

Continuing south for about a mile (1.5 km), you will reach **Gilbert's Bar House of Refuge Museum**. Erected in 1875, it is one of ten such shelters along the east coast, established by the Lifesaving Service

(predecessors of the US Coast Guard) for shipwreck victims. The stark rooms in the charming clapboard house show how hard life was for the early caretakers, who often stayed only a year. A replica of an 1840s "surf boat" used on rescue missions sits outside.

Beyond the refuge is **Bathtub Beach,** the best on the island. The natural pool formed by a sandstone reef offshore provides a safe, popular swimming spot.

### 🏛 Elliott Museum

825 NE Ocean Blvd. **Tel** (772) 225-1961. **Open** 10am–5pm daily. **Closed** Jan 1, Easter, Jul 4, Thanksgiving, Dec 25. ♿ 🅿

### 🏛 Gilbert's Bar House of Refuge Museum

301 SE MacArthur Blvd. **Tel** (772) 225-1875. **Open** 10am–4pm Mon–Sat (from 1pm Sun). **Closed** Jan 1, Easter, Thanksgiving, Dec 25. ♿ 🅿

## ❻ Stuart

**Road map** F3. Martin Co. 🚗 17,000. ℹ️ 1650 S Kanner Highway, (772) 287-1088. 🅦 **goodnature.org**

The magnificent causeway across the island-speckled Indian River from Hutchinson Island offers a fine approach to Martin County's main town. Ringed by affluent waterfront enclaves and residential golf developments, Stuart has a fetching, rejuvenated

downtown area, which is by-passed by the busy coastal highways. South of Roosevelt Bridge, along Flagler Avenue and Osceola Street, is a short riverside boardwalk, a smattering of 1920s brick and stucco buildings, and a number of art galleries. In the evenings, live music emanates from buzzing restaurants and bars.

The Florida scrub jay, a resident of Jupiter Island's sand pine scrub

## ❼ Jupiter Island

**Road map** F4. Martin Co. 🚗 200. ℹ️ 800 N US 1, (561) 746-7111. 🅦 **townofjupiterisland.com**

Much of this long, thin island is a well-to-do residential neighborhood, but there are also several excellent public beaches.

Toward Jupiter Island's northern end, **Hobe Sound National Wildlife Refuge** beckons with more than 3 miles (5 km) of beach, mangroves, and magnificent unspoiled dunes. The other half of the refuge, a strip of pine scrub flanking the Intracoastal Waterway, is a haven for birds, including the Florida scrub jay. There is a nature center by the junction of US 1 and A1A.

**Blowing Rocks Preserve,** a short distance south, has a fine beach. During storms, holes in the shoreline's limestone escarpment shoot water skyward – hence the name.

### 🗺 Hobe Sound National Wildlife Refuge

13640 SE Federal Hwy. **Tel** (772) 546-6141. 🏖 to the beach. Beach: **Open** daily. Nature Center: **Tel** (772) 546-2067. **Open** Mon–Fri. **Closed** public hols.

The brightly painted Riverwalk Café, St. Lucie Street, downtown Stuart

## Environs

Named after a man who was shipwrecked nearby in 1696, **Jonathan Dickinson State Park** comprises habitats as diverse as mangrove swamps, pine flatwoods, and a cypress-canopied stretch of the Loxahatchee River. As well as walking and horseback riding trails, there are canoes for rent and boat trips along the river. Manatees, alligators, ospreys, and herons are often sighted along the way.

Jupiter Inlet Lighthouse as seen from Jupiter Beach Park

🏞 **Jonathan Dickinson State Park**
16450 SE Federal Hwy. **Tel** (772) 546-2771. **Open** daily. 🅿 ♿ limited.

## ❽ Jupiter

**Road map** F4. Palm Beach Co.
🏙 63,800. ℹ 800 N US 1, (561) 746-7111. 🌐 jupiter.fl.us

This small town is best known for its fine beaches and spring-training camps of the Miami Marlins and the St. Louis Cardinals. The **John D. MacArthur Beach** on Singer Island is one of the state's best (*see p131*). The Loxahatchee River Historical Society runs the **Jupiter Inlet Lighthouse and Museum** and has exhibits on the area's original inhabitants (the Hobe Indians), and 18th-century English settlers.

🏞 **John D. MacArthur State Park**
Singer Island (cross the Intracoastal Waterway on Blue Heron Blvd, turn north on Ocean Blvd). **Open** daily.

## Environs

Close by, on the south side of Jupiter Inlet, is a beautiful county park, **Jupiter Beach Park**. It is easily accessible and has a superb beach of chocolate-colored sand, complete with lifeguards – it is also a Mecca for anglers and pelicans. There are picnic pavilions, tables, a children's play area, rest rooms, and a fishing jetty. Visitors can enjoy a good view across to scenic **Jupiter Inlet Lighthouse**, dating from 1860, and the oldest structure in the county, which can be climbed for a wider perspective. The old oil house at its base is now a small museum. In addition to the Lighthouse, there is an added bonus for Sunday visitors: the 1896 Dubois House Museum, operated by the Loxahatchee River Historical Society, and furnished in turn-of-the-century pioneer style, offers free tours. Nearby is the huge **Carlin Park,**

operated by the Parks and Recreation Department of Palm Beach County. It offers playing fields, picnic areas, tennis courts, rest rooms, and a guarded beach.

🏛 **Jupiter Inlet Lighthouse and Museum**
500 Captain Armour's Way. **Tel** (561) 747-8380. **Open** 10am–5pm Tue–Sun. **Closed** public hols. 🅿 🌐 jupiterlighthouse.org

🏖 **Carlin Park**
400 South State Road A1A. **Tel** (561) 966-6600. **Open** daily. Lifeguards on duty from 9am to 5:20pm.

## ❾ Juno Beach

**Road map** F4. Palm Beach Co.
🏙 3,100. **Open** 1555 Palm Beach Lakes Blvd, Suite 800, (561) 471-3995.

The pristine sands by Juno Beach, a small community that stretches north to Jupiter Inlet, are one of the world's most productive nesting sites for loggerhead turtles. In Loggerhead Park, nestled between US 1 and Route A1A, the fascinating **Loggerhead Marinelife Center** is an eco-science center and nature trail. Injured turtles, perhaps cut by boat propellers, or snagged on fishing lines, recuperate in tanks. A path leads to the beach where turtles nest during the summer. Advance reservations are a must.

🏞 **Loggerhead Marinelife Center**
14200 US 1. **Tel** (561) 627-8280. **Open** 10am–5pm Mon–Sat, 11am–5pm Sun. **Closed** Dec 25. ♿ 🌐 marinelife.org

### Florida's Sea Turtles

Florida's central east coast is the top sea turtle nesting area in the US. From May to September female turtles lumber up the beaches at night to lay about 100 eggs in the sand. Two months later the hatchlings emerge and dash for the ocean, again under the cover of darkness. Sea turtles, including Florida's most common species, the loggerhead, are threatened partly because hatchlings are disoriented by lights from buildings.

The approved way to see a turtle laying eggs is to join an organized turtle watch. These nocturnal expeditions are popular all along the coast: call local chambers of commerce, such as the one in Juno Beach, for details.

A loggerhead hatchling's first encounter with the sea

# ⑩ Palm Beach

Literally and metaphorically insular, Palm Beach has long provided revealing facts about serious American wealth. Henry Flagler, pioneer developer of South Florida *(see p129)*, created this winter playground for the rich at the end of the 19th century. In the 1920s, the architect Addison Mizner *(see p124)* gave the resort a further boost and transformed the look of Palm Beach by building lavish Spanish-style mansions for its seasonal residents. In the 1960s, the town virtually closed down in summer – even traffic lights were dismantled. Nowadays, Palm Beach stays open all year, but it is still essentially a winter resort. In what is claimed to be the richest town in the US, visitors can observe members of the fashionable society as they idle away the hours in some of the state's most stylish shops and restaurants, or make their way to private clubs and glamorous charity balls.

Via Roma's grand entrance belies the charming alleyway beyond

Stylish Worth Avenue, shopping mecca for the very rich

### Worth Avenue

For an insight into the Palm Beach lifestyle, Worth Avenue is compulsory viewing. While their employers toy over an Armani dress or an antique Russian icon, chauffeurs keep the air conditioning turning over in the Rolls Royces outside. Stretching four fabulous blocks from Lake Worth to the Atlantic Ocean, it is the town's best known thoroughfare.

Worth Avenue, as well as the architecture of Addison Mizner, first became fashionable with the construction of the exclusive Everglades Club, at the western end, in 1918. This was the result of the collaboration between Mizner and Paris Singer, the heir to the sewing machine fortune, who had first invited the architect down to Florida. Originally intended as a hospital for officers shellshocked during World War I, it never housed a single patient, and instead became the town's social hub. Today, the building's loggias and Spanish-style courtyards are still a very upscale, members-only enclave.

Across the street, and in stark contrast to the club's rather plain exterior, are Via Mizner and Via Parigi, lined with colorful shops and restaurants. These interlinking pedestrian alleys were created by Mizner in the 1920s, and are Worth Avenue's aesthetic highlights. Inspired by the backstreets of Spanish villages, the lanes are a riot of arches, tiled and twisting flights of steps, bougainvillea, fountains, and pretty courtyards. Overlooking the alleys' entrances are the office tower and villa that Mizner designed for himself. The tower's first floor originally housed display space for his ceramics business, and was the avenue's first commercial unit. Connecting the two buildings is a walkway that forms the entrance to Via Mizner's shopping area. The other vias off Worth Avenue are more modern but, built in the same style and decorated with flowers and attractive window displays, they are nonetheless charming. Don't miss Via Roma or the courtyards joining Via de Lela and Via Flora.

Water fountain, Via Mizner

Worth Avenue in 1939, captured by society photographer Bert Morgan

*For hotels and restaurants in this area see pp316–17 and pp333–6*

# Shopping on Worth Avenue

The epitome of Palm Beach, Worth Avenue and the alleyways that connect with it, contain some 250 exquisitely designed clothing boutiques, art galleries, and antique shops. The shop fronts, ranging in style from Mizner's signature Spanish look to Art Deco, form an eclectic and pleasing mix. The artful window displays of Florida's most famous shopping street look their best when brightly lit up at night. Some windows flaunt wonderfully ironic symbols of wealth, such as fake caviar on toast or a life-size model of a butler. In 1979, a Rolls Royce fitted with a bulldozer blade symbolically broke the ground for 150 Worth, an open-air mall at the Avenue's eastern end. It is this sort of showy display that typifies Worth Avenue, and distinguishes it from other prestigious shopping areas.

## Worth Avenue's Exclusive Shops

*Worth Avenue boasts a spectacular mix of glitzy shops. Jewelry stores abound, including those specializing in high quality imitations. Visitors will also find elegant ready-to-wear houses, fancy gift shops, designer boutiques, and luxury department stores.*

**Cartier** has the ultimate in gifts and souvenirs. Choose from gold jewelry, pens, and, of course, their signature watches.

**Tiffany & Co**. is one of the most famous names on Worth Avenue. Best known for its jewelry (including exclusive designs by Paloma Picasso) and silverware, it also sells perfume and leather goods.

**Saks Fifth Avenue**, located in the elegant Esplanade mall, has two floors of luxury apparel from lingerie to designer menswear.

**Betteridge, Greenleaf, and Crosby**, specialist jewelers, in Palm Beach since 1896.

**Giorgio's boutique** offers luxury, handmade clothing, plus bags, shoes, and accessories made of alligator and ostrich leather. It also offers executive furniture fashioned from alligator leather and wood.

**Richter's of Palm Beach** are specialists in rare estate jewelry, and purveyors of unique gems.

# Exploring Palm Beach

The spirit and imagination of Addison Mizner infuses the whole of Palm Beach. As well as those buildings he designed himself, he influenced the look of countless others. Mizner's architecture, described by a biographer as a "Bastard-Spanish-Moorish-Romanesque-Gothic-Renaissance-Bull-Market-Damn-the-Expense Style," gave his contemporaries plenty of ideas to work from. Palm Beach is full of the splendid creations of men such as Marion Wyeth, Maurice Fatio, and Howard Major, all active in the 1920s, as well as more recent imitations. Gazing at the luxurious mansions of the rich and famous in the exclusive "suburbs" is an essential activity in Palm Beach.

A panel, representing drama, from the mural in the Four Arts Library

### Exploring Palm Beach

After the opulence of Worth Avenue, the atmosphere along the mainly residential streets to the north is more restrained. Leafy Cocoanut Row features some luxurious private homes, but along South County Road, which runs parallel, Mizner's influence is more in evidence – in the street's eclectic architecture, such as the immaculately restored Town Hall, built in 1926. Nearby is the attractive Mizner Memorial Park, where the centerpiece is a fountain and narrow pool flanked by palm trees, and Phipps Plaza – a quiet, shady close containing some delightful buildings with tiled windowsills and flower-decked gates. Mizner himself designed the fine coral

Mizner Memorial Fountain

house at No. 264. Also memorable is Howard Major's tropical cottage (1939), which features delicate Chinese influences.

If there is time to spare, it is worth strolling along some of the streets to the west of South County Road, where there is a mix of Mizneresque houses and early 20th-century bungalows set in shady gardens. In contrast, the most imposing street in this area is Royal Palm Way. Its rank of palm trees makes a fine approach to Royal Palm Bridge, which is an excellent platform for admiring the luxury yachts on Lake Worth. This is particularly worthwhile in December, when they are decked out in colored lights for the annual boat parade.

### 🏛 Society of the Four Arts

2 Four Arts Plaza. **Tel** (561) 655-7226.
Gallery: **Open** Dec–Apr: 10am–5pm
Mon–Sat, 2–5pm Sun. **Closed** Sun (May–Oct), public hols. Gardens:
**Open** 10am–5pm Mon–Sun. Library:
**Open** 10am–4:45pm Mon–Fri, 10am–12:45pm Sat. **Closed** Sat (May–Oct), Sun, public hols. ♿

Founded in 1936, the Society of the Four Arts incorporates two libraries, exhibition space, and an auditorium for lectures, concerts, and films.

The gallery and auditorium were originally part of a private club designed by Mizner, but Maurice Fatio's Italianate Four Arts Library building is far more striking. The murals in its loggia represent art, music, drama, and literature. The grounds include modern sculptures.

Via Mizner *(see p122)*, a classic example of Mizner's work

## Mizner's Spanish Fantasy

Addison Mizner (1872–1933) came to Palm Beach from New York in 1918 to convalesce after an accident. An architect by profession, he soon began to design houses, and in the process changed the face of Palm Beach and, essentially, Florida *(see pp34–5)*. By adapting the design of old Spanish buildings to suit his environment, Mizner created a new style of architecture. He incorporated features such as loggias and external staircases to accommodate the region's high temperatures, and his workmen covered walls in condensed milk and rubbed them with steel wool to fake centuries-old dirt.

Addison Mizner in the mid-1920s

Addison Mizner became a multimillionaire, successful because of both his architectural vision and his ability to ingratiate himself into his prospective clients' milieu. He later turned his attention to Boca Raton *(see pp134–5)*, but the collapse of the Florida land boom at the end of the 1920s hit him heavily, and by the end of his life Mizner had to rely on friends to pay his bills.

### 🏛 Hibel Museum of Art
5353 Parkside Drive, Jupiter. **Tel** (561) 622-5560. **Open** 11am–4pm Tue–Fri (call first). **Closed** public hols. ♿
**W** hibelmuseum.org

Typical works of Edna Hibel, born in Boston in 1917 and a resident of neighboring Singer Island *(see p131)* until her death in 2014, are idealized portraits of mothers and children from around the world. She painted on all types of surfaces, ranging from wood and silk to crystal and porcelain.

The museum, founded in 1977, holds more than 1,500 of the artist's creations.

*Brittany and Child* (1994) by Edna Hibel (oil, gesso, and gold on silk)

### 🛏 The Breakers
1 South County Rd. **Tel** (561) 655-6611. 📷 Wed pm. ♿
**W** the breakers.com

Rising above Florida's oldest golf course, this mammoth Italian Renaissance structure is the third hotel on the site: the first Breakers, built in 1896, burned down in 1903. Its replacement suffered the same fate in 1925, destroyed by a fire supposedly started by a guest's curling iron. Miraculously, the present Breakers was built in less than a year. The hotel has always been a focal point for the town's social life, hosting numerous galas in its magnificent ballrooms.

Palm Beach's grandest hotel is refreshingly welcoming to nonresidents: feel free to watch a game of croquet, have a milkshake in its old-fashioned soda shop, or explore the lobby (with its hand-painted ceiling) and the palatial public rooms.

For a more in-depth look, take the weekly guided tour with the

The façade of the Breakers Hotel, designed by New York firm Schultze and Weaver

"resident historian." South of the hotel are three 19th-century wooden mansions, all that remain of **Breakers Row.** These were originally rented out to Palm Beach's wealthiest visitors for the winter season.

### 🏘 Palm Beach Suburbs
Palm Beach's high society usually hides away behind appropriately high hedges in multimillion-dollar mansions. Some of these were built by Addison Mizner and his imitators in the 1920s, but since then hundreds of others have proliferated, in all kinds of architectural styles, from Neo-Classical to Art Deco.

The most easily visible accommodation can be seen sitting on a ridge along South Ocean Boulevard, nicknamed "Mansion Row." At the top end, the Georgian residence at No. 126 belongs to Estée Lauder. No. 720, built by Mizner for himself in 1919, was for a time owned by John Lennon. Eight blocks beyond, Mar-a-Lago (No. 1100) is Palm Beach's

grandest residence, with 58 bedrooms, 33 bathrooms, and three bomb shelters. Built by Joseph Urban and Marion Wyeth in 1927, it was bought in 1985 by Donald Trump, who converted it into an expensive private club.

The homes in the northern suburbs are more secluded. North County Road passes Palm Beach's largest domestic property at No. 513. Beyond, No. 1095 North Ocean Boulevard was used as a winter retreat by the Kennedy family until 1995.

Glimpsing how the other half lives is discouraged by setting a minimum speed limit of 25 mph (40 km/h). This makes cycling an attractive option. Bikes are easy to rent *(see p127)*, and there are various bicycle routes. The most scenic of these is the 3-mile (5-km) Lake Trail, which doubles as an exercise track for the locals. It runs from Worth Avenue almost to the island's northern tip, hugging Lake Worth and skirting the backs of mansions. Its prettiest section is north of Dunbar Road.

Mar-a-Lago, the most extravagant home in the Palm Beach suburbs

# A Tour of Palm Beach

Circled by the main thoroughfares of South County Road and Cocoanut Row, this tour links all the major sights of central Palm Beach, including Henry Flagler's impressive home, Whitehall. The section of the tour along Lake Drive South forms part of the scenic Palm Beach bicycle trail, which flanks Lake Worth and extends into the suburbs. Although the tour is intended to be made by car, parts (or all) could equally be made by bicycle, on foot, or even on skates. These alternatives avoid the problem of Palm Beach's zealous traffic cops who patrol the streets in motorized golf carts.

**① Flagler Museum**
Formerly Flagler's private winter residence, "Whitehall" opened to the public in 1959. Beautifully restored, most of its furniture is original.

**② Sea Gull Cottage**
Built in 1886, this is Palm Beach's oldest building. It was Flagler's first winter home.

**③ Royal Poinciana Chapel** was built by Flagler for his guests in 1896.

*LAKE WORTH*

Royal Park Bridge

**⑤ Casa de Leoni**
No. 450 Worth Avenue is one of Mizner's most enchanting buildings. It set a trend for the Venetian Gothic style.

| 0 meters | 250 |
|---|---|
| 0 yards | 250 |

**Key**

▬▬ Route of tour

EVERGLADES CLUB GOLF LINKS

**⑦ Public Beach**
Despite the town's name, its public beach is perhaps surprisingly unspectacular, but it is free and open to all.

**⑧ Town Hall** was designed in 1926 and is a well-known Palm Beach landmark.

**⑬ Green's Pharmacy**, open since 1937, is a drugstore with a diner attached. People come for the great breakfasts, the traditional ice-cream sodas, and terrific burgers – all served in a lively atmosphere.

## VISITORS' CHECKLIST

**Practical Information**
Road map F4. Palm Beach Co.
🏠 8,500 ℹ️ 45 Cocoanut Row,
(561) 655-3282. 🎭 Artigras (Feb).

**Transport**
✈️ 3 miles (5 km) W. 🚉 Amtrak and Tri-Rail, 201 S Tamarind Ave, West Palm Beach, (800) 872-7245.
🚌 201 S Tamarind Ave, West Palm Beach, (800) 231-2222.
🚌 41, 42 from West Palm Beach.

**⑫ The Breakers**, originally called the Palm Beach Inn, was the fourth of Henry Flagler's impressive east coast hotels.

**⑮ The Hotel Royal Poinciana**
This lavish 2,000-room, wooden hotel was a winter retreat for the very rich. It burned down in 1935; today only the green house cupola survives.

**⑪ Bethesda-by-the-Sea Church** is Gothic Revival in style, and has a cloistered courtyard and pleasant, quiet gardens to the rear.

ATLANTIC OCEAN

**⑭ St. Edward's Church**
Completed in 1927, St. Edward's was built in a Spanish Revival style and features a decorative, cast stone Baroque bell tower and entrance.

**⑩ Phipps Plaza** contains some attractive buildings in fanciful designs, including Mediterranean and Southwest Spanish styles.

### Tips for Drivers
**Tour length:** 4 miles (7 km).
**Starting point:** Anywhere. The tour is best followed in a clockwise direction since Worth Avenue is one way, running from east to west. The Palm Beach Bicycle Trail Shop, 223 Sunrise Ave, tel (561) 659-4583 (open daily), is a good starting point if you want to rent a bicycle, tandem, or skates.
**Parking:** Meters accept payments both in cash and by card. There are also plenty of spaces to park free for an hour, but remember not to overstay.

**⑨ The Memorial Park fountain in downtown Palm Beach**

### Finding the Sights
① Flagler Museum (see pp128–9)
② Sea Gull Cottage
③ Royal Poinciana Chapel
④ Society of Four Arts (see p124)
⑤ Casa de Leoni
⑥ Worth Avenue (see pp122–3)
⑦ Public Beach
⑧ Town Hall (see p124)
⑨ Memorial Park (see p124)
⑩ Phipps Plaza (see p1204)
⑪ Bethesda-by-the-Sea Church
⑫ The Breakers (see p125)
⑬ Green's Pharmacy
⑭ St. Edward's Church
⑮ The Hotel Royal Poinciana
⑯ Hibel Museum of Art (see p125)

# Flagler Museum

This mansion, known as Whitehall, was described as "more wonderful than any palace in Europe" after it was built in 1902 by Henry Flagler. He gave the home to his wife, Mary Lily Kenan, as a wedding present. It was intended only as a winter residence; the Flaglers traveled down every year in one of their private railroad cars *(see p53)*. Railcar No. 91 is now on display in the Flagler Kenan Pavilion, which was constructed to resemble a Gilded Age railway palace, at the southern end of the grounds.

In 1925, 12 years after Flagler's death, a ten-story tower was added to the rear, and Whitehall became a hotel. Jean Flagler Matthews bought her grandfather's mansion in 1959 and, after costly restoration, turned it into a museum.

**Grand Ballroom**
Of all the balls held in this sumptuous room, the *Bal Poudré* in 1903 was the most lavish.

Flagler
← Kenan
Pavilion

**★ Master Bathroom**
Apart from a tub, a toilet, and a wonderful separate shower unit, the Flaglers' private bathroom boasts this gorgeous double washstand made of onyx.

## KEY

① **The master bedroom** is furnished in yellow silk damask, a faithful copy of the original Rococo-style fabric.

② **Billiard room**

③ **The Yellow Roses Room** had matching wallpaper and furnishings – an innovation for its time.

④ **The east portico** is supported by massive fluted columns. Outsized urns are placed on the steps in front.

⑤ **Drawing room**

⑥ **The grand staircase** leads off the grand hall and is itself constructed of different marbles and decorated with intricate bronze railings.

**Library**
Lined with leather-bound books and filled with objects and ornate detailing, this red, wood-paneled room has a somewhat intimate feel.

*For hotels and restaurants in this area see pp316–17 and pp333–6*

**Drawing Room**
This ornate
Louis XVI-style drawing
room boasts a piano
and French Gray walls –
a popular decor color in
the 19th century.

## VISITORS' CHECKLIST

**Practical Information**
Cocoanut Row & Whitehall Way.
**Tel** (561) 655-2833. **Open** 10am–
5pm Tue–Sat, noon–5pm Sun.
**Closed** Thanksgiving, Dec 25,
Jan 1. 🦽 📷 normally available.
♿ 🚻 📷

**★ Grand Hall**
This grand marble entrance hall
has a painted ceiling and contains
gilded chairs and paintings,
including this formal portrait of
Jean Flagler Matthews.

**★ Colonial Chamber**
The early 1900s saw a steady flow
of guests to Whitehall. The rich and
famous stayed in this inviting room,
decorated in a color scheme of
cream and *Rose de Barry* red.

Main entrance

## Flagler's Palm Beach

After the Spanish ship *Providencia* was wrecked in 1878, its
cargo of coconuts was strewn along the beach near Lake
Worth and soon took root. Henry Flagler, busy with his
plans to develop Florida's east coast *(see pp52–3)*, spotted
the lovely palm-fringed beach around 1890. He was smitten
with the area's beauty and immediately bought up land. In
1894, he opened the Hotel Royal Poinciana *(see p127)* and
in so doing set the course for the growth of the exclusive
resort of Palm Beach.

Henry Flagler and his third wife, Mary Lily, in 1910

High-rises towering over the still waters of Lake Worth in West Palm Beach

# ⓫ West Palm Beach

**Road map** F4. Palm Beach Co.
⛟ 108,000. ✈ 🚂 Amtrak & Tri-Rail.
🚌 ℹ 1555 Palm Beach Lakes Blvd,
(561) 233-3000. 🖥 palmbeachfl.com

At the end of the 19th century, Henry Flagler *(see pp128–9)* decided to move the service businesses and unsightly homes of Palm Beach's workers to the mainland, out of sight of the tourists. He thus created West Palm Beach, which has been the commercial center of Palm Beach County ever since.

The city has succeeded in forging a stronger identity for itself, but it still plays second fiddle to its infinitely more glamorous (and smaller) neighbor.

The Downtown Waterfront Commons on Clematis Street is alive with visitors enjoying the picturesque Lake Worth, and is home to an extensive calendar of events. Northwood Village is also worth a visit, boasting ethnic restaurants, antique and vintage shops, and boutiques. This eclectic neighborhood, just north of Downtown West Palm Beach, is rich with cultural history.

West Palm Beach may not be the place to spend an entire vacation, but it enjoys a fine setting by Lake Worth, and its few attractions are well worth a visit – in particular the excellent Norton Museum of Art, rated the top museum in the southeastern US by *The New York Times*.

## 🏛 South Florida Science Center and Aquarium

4801 Dreher Trail N. **Tel** (561) 832-1988. **Open** 9am–5pm Mon–Fri, 10am–6pm Sat–Sun. **Closed** Thanksgiving, Dec 25. 🏵 ♿ 🖥 sfsciencecenter.org

This science museum is aimed at children. There are plenty of hands-on exhibits to teach visitors about subjects such as light, sound, color, and the weather. You can attempt to create your own clouds, and even touch a mini-tornado. The best time to visit is on the last Friday night of the month, when visitors can look through a giant telescope in its observatory, and watch laser light shows in the Dekelboum planetarium.

## 🏛 Norton Museum of Art

1451 South Olive Ave. **Tel** (561) 832-5196. **Open** 10am–5pm Tue–Sat (9pm Thu), 11am–5pm Sun. **Closed** Mon, public hols. 🏵 ♿ 🖥 norton.org

This art museum, the largest in Florida, has possibly the finest art collection in the state; it also attracts traveling exhibitions. The museum was established in 1941 with about 100 canvases belonging to Ralph Norton, a Chicago steel magnate who had retired to West Palm Beach. He and his wife had wide-ranging tastes, which is reflected in the art on display.

The collection falls into three main fields. First among these are the French Impressionist and Post-Impressionist art, which

## Polo and Equestrian Season

The Palm Beaches' west-central community of Wellington is one of the top three places for polo and equestrian activities in the world. The International Polo Club Palm Beach features the world's top Polo players, and is the epicenter of social activity among Palm Beaches' elite from January to April.

It also has a Polo School for both children and adults.

The Palm Beach International Equestrian Center hosts equestrian competitions, attracting thousands of visitors, followed by an energetic nightlife scene. For information about dates call the clubs at Wellington, (561) 204-5687; Boca Raton, (561) 994-1876; or Lake Worth, (561) 965-2057.

Close quarters polo action, popular entertainment in Palm Beach County

includes paintings by Cézanne, Braque, Picasso, Matisse, and Gauguin, whose moving work *Agony in the Garden* is the most famous painting in the museum. *Night Mist* (1945) by Jackson Pollock is another proud possession, forming part of the Norton's impressive store of 20th-century American art. This gallery also features some fine works by Winslow Homer, Georgia O'Keeffe, Edward Hopper, and Andy Warhol.

*Agony in the Garden by Paul Gauguin (1889)*

The third principal collection comprises an outstanding array of artifacts from China, including tomb jades dating from about 1500 BC, and ceramic figures of animals and courtiers from the T'ang Dynasty (4th–11th centuries AD). There is also much fine Buddhist carving, in addition to more modern sculptures by Brancusi, Degas, and Rodin.

A rare Florida panther at the Palm Beach Zoo

### 🗺 Palm Beach Zoo at Dreher Park

1301 Summit Blvd. **Tel** (561) 547-9453. **Open** daily. **Closed** Thanksgiving, Dec 25. 🐾 ♿ 🖥 palmbeachzoo.org

This little zoo is as appealing to youngsters as the nearby South Florida Science Center and Aquarium. Of the 100 or more species represented, most interesting are the endangered Florida panther and the giant tortoises, which can live for up to 200 years. At the re-created South American plain visitors can see llamas, rheas, and tapirs from an observation deck, follow a boardwalk trail through exotic foliage, or cruise around a lake alive with a huge population of pelicans.

### Environs

A more pleasant alternative to staying in West Palm Beach (and a considerably cheaper option than Palm Beach), is to find accommodation north across the inlet at **Singer Island or Palm Beach Shores**. These are relaxing, slow-paced communities, and the wide beach is splendid, but spoiled by a skyline of apartment buildings.

Boating and fishing are popular activities here. Palm Beach Shores has sport-fishing boats for charter, as well as boats that offer cruises around Lake Worth. The Manatee Queen is a catamaran *(see p360)* offering tours of the mansions along the Intracoastal Waterway.

At the north end of Singer Island is **John D. MacArthur Beach State Park**. Here, a dramatic boardwalk bridge meanders across a mangrove-lined inlet of Lake Worth to a hardwood hammock and a lovely beach. Brochures from the Nature Center illustrate plants and wading birds, and in the summer visitors can see nesting loggerhead turtles while on a guided walk *(see p121)*.

**The Gardens Mall**, 2 miles (3 km) inland in Palm Beach Gardens has fragrant walkways and glass elevators that link approximately 200 shops.

### 🗺 John D. MacArthur Beach State Park

A1A, 2 miles (3 km) N of Riviera Bridge. **Tel** (561) 624-6950. **Open** daily; Nature Center: 🐾 ♿ 🏠 🖥 macarthurbeach.org

### 🏠 The Gardens Mall

3101 PGA Blvd. **Tel** (561) 622-2115. **Open** daily. **Closed** Easter Sun, Thanksgiving, Dec 25. ♿ 🖥 thegardensmall.com

## ⓬ Lion Country Safari

**Road map** F4. Palm Beach Co. 2003 Lion Country Safari Rd, Loxahatchee. **Tel** (561) 793-1084. 🚉 West Palm Beach. 🚌 West Palm Beach. **Open** daily. ♿ 🖥 lioncountrysafari.com

Twenty miles (32 km) inland from West Palm Beach, off US 441, this park is the area's big family attraction.

There are two parts: firstly, you can drive through a 500 acre (200 ha) enclosure and observe lions, giraffes, rhinos, and other wildlife at close quarters. If you have a convertible car you can rent a vehicle with a hard roof. Secondly, there is a zoo and amusement park. Along with aviaries, petting areas, and islands inhabited by monkeys, there are fairground rides, boat tours, and a park populated by plastic dinosaurs. A camping area is also available. All parts of this park become very busy on weekends.

Antelope resting in the shade at Lion Country Safari

A fisherman enjoying early evening angling on Lake Okeechobee

### ⑬ Lake Okeechobee

**Road map** E4, F4. 🚌 Palm Trans bus to Pahokee, (561) 841-4200.
ℹ️ 115 E Main St, Pahokee, (561) 924-5579. 🌐 **pahokee.com** Roland Martin: 920 E Del Monte Ave, Clewiston.
**Tel** (800) 473-6766. 🌐 **rolandmartin marina.com**

Meaning "big water" in the Seminole language, Okeechobee is the second largest freshwater lake in the US, covering 750 sq miles (1,942 sq km). The "Big O," as the lake is often called, is famous for its abundance of fish, particularly largemouth bass. Roland Martin or any of the many marinas will rent visitors a boat, tackle, bait, picnic food, or a guide and chartered boat. Nearby **Clewiston** offers the best facilities, with three marinas and a choice of decent motels.

For those who are not anglers, time in Florida is better spent elsewhere. The bird life is rich along the shore, but the lake is too big to be scenic, and a high encircling dike, which protects the countryside from floods, prevents views from the road. **Pahokee** is one of the few places to offer easy lakeside access, and it boasts possibly the best sunsets in Florida, after the Gulf Coast.

The grim and hardworking communities at the lake's southern end are dependent on sugar for their prosperity. Half the sugarcane in the country is grown in the plains around Belle Glade and Clewiston ("America's Sweetest Town"),

A Lake Okeechobee sugar town proclaims its wealth

where the rich soil is even darker than chocolate.

A one-time federal plan to buy the sugarcane land south of Lake Okeechobee and return it to marshland, in order to cleanse the water draining into the Everglades, has hit some stumbling blocks. Meanwhile, Big Sugar continues to produce its sweet product near the Big Water.

### ⑭ Lake Worth

**Road map** F4. Palm Beach Co.
🏛️ 37,800. 🚌 ℹ️ 501 Lake Ave, (561) 790-6200. 🌐 **cpb chamber.com**

Lake Worth is a civilized, unpretentious community. On its barrier island side there is a jolly, public beach scene; on the mainland, a dozen or more antique shops set the tone along Lake and Lucerne Avenues, the heart of Lake Worth's low-key downtown area. Visitors will find an Art Deco movie theater converted into an exciting space for art exhibitions, live music clubs, coffee houses, art galleries, antique malls, retail stores, and

restaurants. The community has worked hard to retain its old Florida flavor, with rules in place that protect the town from insensitive development. Facilities include fresh and saltwater for boating, a golf course, fishing pier, a waterfront amphitheater, parks, and athletic facilities.

### ⑮ Delray Beach

**Road map** F4. Palm Beach Co.
🏛️ 66,200. 🚆 Amtrak and Tri-Rail. 🚌 ℹ️ 64 SE 5th Ave, (561) 278-0424. Cruises: **Tel** (561) 243-0686. 🌐 **delraybeach.com**

The most welcoming place between Palm Beach and Boca Raton, Delray Beach has an upscale but friendly air. The town is proud of the national awards for "civic-mindness" and being the "Most Fun Small Town in America" that it has consistently received in recent decades.

The long stretch of sedate beach, with direct access and good facilities, is magnificent, and between November and April Delray Yacht Cruises runs daily paddleboat trips along the Intracoastal Waterway. Drift fishing boats also offer rides.

Delray's heart lies inland, along Atlantic Avenue – an inviting street softly lit at night by old-fashioned lamps and lined with palm trees, chic cafés, antique shops, and art galleries. Alongside lies Old School Square, with a cluster of attractive 1920s buildings. Nearby, snug **Cason Cottage** has been meticulously restored to the way it might have looked originally, around 1915.

**🏚️ Cason Cottage**
5 NE 1st St. **Tel** (561) 274-9578. **Closed** public hols. 📷 by appt. ♿

A peaceful springtime scene by the ocean at Delray Beach

## ⓰ Loxahatchee National Wildlife Refuge

**Road map** F4. Palm Beach Co. 10216 Lee Rd. **Tel** (561) 732-3684. 🚇 Boynton Beach. 🚌 Delray Beach. Refuge: **Open** daily. **Closed** Thanksgiving, Dec 25. ♿ 🅿 ♿ Visitor Center: **Open** daily. **Closed** Thanksgiving, Dec 25. 🆆 fws.gov/loxahatchee

This 221-sq mile (572-sq km) refuge, which contains the most northerly remaining part of the Everglades, has superb and abundant wildlife. The best time to visit is early or late in the day, and ideally in winter, when many migrating birds make temporary homes here.

The visitor center, off Route 441 on the refuge's eastern side, 10 miles (16 km) west of Delray Beach, has a good information center explaining the Everglades' ecology; it is also the starting point for two memorable trails. The half-mile (1 km) Cypress Swamp Boardwalk enters a magical natural world, with guava and wax myrtle trees and many epiphytes *(see p294)* growing beneath the canopy. The longer Marsh Trail passes by marshland, whose water levels are manipulated to produce the best possible environment for waders and waterfowl. On a winter afternoon it is a bird-watcher's paradise, with a cacophony of sound from herons, grebe, ibis,

A blue heron standing alert in the wildlife refuge at Loxahatchee

A schoolboy's bedroom, Japanese style, at the Morikami Museum

and other birds. Visitors may also spot turtles and alligators.

Those with their own canoes can embark on the 6 mile (9 km) canoe trail. There is also an extensive program of guided nature walks.

## ⓱ Morikami Museum and Japanese Gardens

**Road map** F4. Palm Beach Co. 4000 Morikami Park Rd. **Tel** (561) 495-0233. 🚇 Delray Beach. 🚌 Delray Beach. **Open** 10am–5pm Tue–Sun. **Closed** public hols. ♿ ♿ 🆆 morikami.org

The country's only museum devoted exclusively to Japanese culture is located on land donated by a farmer named George Morikami; he was one of a group of Japanese pioneers who established the Yamato Colony (named after ancient Japan) on the northern edge of Boca Raton in 1905. With the help of money from a development company owned by Henry Flagler *(see pp128–9)*, they hoped to grow rice, tea, and silk. The project never took off, however, and the colony gradually petered out in the 1920s.

A blue morpho at Butterfly World

Displays in the Yamato-kan villa, on a small island in a lake, show the settlers' story and also delve into past and present Japanese culture. There are interesting reconstructions of

a bathroom, a schoolboy's bedroom, and eel-and-sake restaurants. Six historic garden sites surround the villa, and paths lead into serene pinewoods.

A building across the lake holds exhibitions on all matters Japanese, a café serving Japanese food, and a traditional teahouse where tea ceremonies are performed once a month. Also, origami workshops are offered.

## ⓲ Butterfly World

**Road map** F4. Broward Co. 3600 W Sample Rd, Coconut Creek. **Tel** (954) 977-4400. 🚇 Deerfield Beach (Amtrak & Tri-Rail). 🚌 Pompano Beach. **Open** daily. **Closed** Easter, Thanksgiving, Dec 25. ♿ ♿ 🆆 butterflyworld.com

Within giant walk-through aviaries brimming with tropical flowers, thousands of dazzling butterflies from all over the world flit about, often landing on visitors' shoulders. Since the aviaries are effectively solar powered, the butterflies are most active on warm, sunny days, so plan a visit accordingly. There are also cabinets of emerging pupae and a fascinating collection of mounted insects – including morpho butterflies, with their incredible metallic blue wings, and beetles and grasshoppers the size of an adult hand. Outside, enjoy a wander around the extensive gardens.

# ⑲ Boca Raton

In 1925, an advertisement for Boca Raton announced: "I am the greatest resort in the world." Although the city imagined by the architect Addison Mizner *(see p124)* did not materialize in his lifetime, Boca Raton has today become one of Florida's most affluent cities. Corporate headquarters and high-tech companies are located here, and executives in a national survey have judged it Florida's most enticing place to live. What must attract them are the country clubs, plush shopping malls, and gorgeous beachfront parks, not to mention desirable homes inspired, if not built, by Mizner.

Young musician performing at the Lynn University Conservatory of Music

Peach-pink Mizner Park, one of Boca's shopping malls

## Exploring Boca Raton

After initiating the development of Palm Beach, Addison Mizner turned his attention to a sleepy pineapple-growing settlement to the south. However, instead of his envisaged masterpiece of city planning, only a handful of buildings were completed by the time Florida's property bubble burst in 1926 *(see p54)*. Boca, as it is often called today, remained little more than a hamlet until the late 1940s.

The nucleus of Mizner's vision was the ultra-luxurious Cloister Inn, finished in 1926 with his trademark Spanish details. It stands off the eastern end of Camino Real, which was intended as the city's main thoroughfare, complete with a central canal for gondolas. The hotel is now part of the greatly expanded and exclusive **Boca Raton Resort and Club** *(see p316)*. Nonresidents can visit only on a weekly tour arranged by the Boca Raton Historical

Society, which is based at the **Town Hall** on Palmetto Park Road. A few rooms here have simple displays regarding local history.

Just opposite, built in a style that epitomizes Mizner's work, is the open-air **Mizner Park**. This is perhaps the most impressive of Boca's dazzling malls that provide the best illustrations of the city's rarefied lifestyle. Even more Mizneresque is the nearby **Royal Palm Place**, with chic boutiques tucked away in hidden courtyards.

The verdant and historic **Old Floresta** district, about a mile (1.5 km) west of the town hall, contains 29 Mediterranean-style homes built by Mizner for his company directors. It is a pleasant area to explore.

### 🏛 Boca Raton Museum of Art

501 Plaza Real, Mizner Park.
**Tel** (561) 392-2500. **Open** Tue–Sun.
**Closed** public hols. 🅿 ♿
W bocamuseum.org

Located in a spectacular setting within beautiful Mizner Park in downtown Boca Raton, this museum contains 44,000 sq ft (4,088 sq m) of space for world class exhibitions, and an impressive display of contemporary art.

### 🏛 Lynn University Conservatory of Music

3601 N Military Trail. **Tel** (561) 237-9000. W lynn.edu/music

The Conservatory of Music at Lynn University admits a highly select group of gifted music students from all over the world to train for a career in solo, chamber, and orchestral music performance – many achieving worldwide acclaim. As a center for the celebration of music, the Conservatory attracts thousands of music lovers who attend around 100 student, faculty and guest artist performances, as well as master classes and lectures each year.

### 🏛 Sports Immortals Museum

6830 N Federal Hwy. **Tel** (561) 997-2575.
**Open** 10am–6pm Mon–Fri, 11am–5pm Sat–Sun. **Closed** Sun, Jan 1, Dec 25. ♿
♿ W sportsimmortals.com

Among the 10,000 sports mementos at this museum are Babe Ruth's baseball bat and Muhammad Ali's boxing robes. The most prized item is a rare cigarette card worth an astonishing $1,000,000: the card was

Boca's attractive town hall, designed by Addison Mizner and built in 1927

Deerfield Beach, a quiet coastal resort within easy reach of Boca Raton

withdrawn when the baseball player depicted objected to any association with tobacco.

### The Beaches
North of Boca Raton's inlet stretches a seductively long, undeveloped, dune-backed beach, reached via beachside parks. The most northerly of these, **Spanish River Park**, is also the most attractive, with pleasant picnic areas shaded by pines and palm trees. Its loveliest spot is a lagoon on the Intracoastal Waterway next to an observation tower. At **Red Reef Park** visitors can stroll along the boardwalk on top of the dunes and snorkel around an artificial reef *(see p362)* just offshore. The sands are usually uncrowded, perhaps because of the exorbitant parking fees.

### Gumbo Limbo Nature Center
1801 North Ocean Blvd.
**Tel** (561) 338-1473.
**Open** daily. **Closed** public hols.
**gumbolimbo.org**
This first-rate, highly informative center lies next to the Intra-coastal, within Red Reef Park. The boardwalk winds through mangroves and a tropical hardwood hammock to a tower, which offers sensational panoramic views.

### Environs
High-rise development continues unabated south along Route A1A. **Deerfield Beach** is the area's most inviting community, thanks to its fishing pier and its fine beach, backed by a palm-lined prome-nade. Five miles (8 km) south, **Pompano** is forever tied to its status as "swordfish capital of the world," corroborated by photos of giant catches displayed on its pier.

## Boca Raton City Center

① Old Floresta
② Boca Raton Museum of Art
③ Town Hall
④ Lynn University Conservatory of Music
⑤ Mizner Park
⑥ Boca Raton Resort and Club
⑦ Red Reef Park
⑧ Gumbo Limbo Nature Center
⑨ Spanish River Park

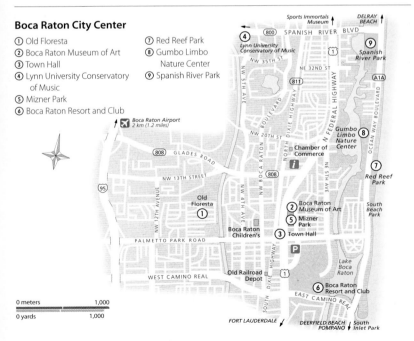

# ⑳ Fort Lauderdale

During the second Seminole War *(see p50)*, Fort Lauderdale consisted of little more than three forts. By 1900, it had become a busy trading post on the New River, which meanders through what has become a sprawling city.

Today, Greater Fort Lauderdale wears many hats: it is an important business and cultural center, a popular beach resort, and a giant cruise port. However, it is still the city's waterways *(see p139)* that define its unique character.

Appel's *Big Bird with Child*, Museum of Art

## Exploring Downtown Fort Lauderdale

Downtown Fort Lauderdale, with its modern, sleek, glass-sided office buildings, presents the city's business face. The **Riverwalk** follows a 1.5 mile (2.4 km) stretch of the New River's north bank and links most of the city's historical landmarks and cultural institutions. This promenade starts near Stranahan House, built on the site of the city's first trading post, goes through a strip of parkland, and ends up by the Broward Center for the Performing Arts *(see p358)*.

Old Fort Lauderdale extends along Southwest 2nd Avenue. It is comprised of an attractive group of early 1900s' buildings administered by the Fort Lauderdale Historical Society, which is based at the Fort Lauderdale Historical Museum. The King-Cromartie House, built in 1907 on the south bank of the river, was transported by barge to its present site in 1971. Its modest furnishings reflect the basic living conditions of Florida's early settlers. Behind the home is a replica of the city's first schoolhouse, which

opened in 1899. The cafés and restaurants in old brick buildings along adjacent Southwest 2nd Street are buzzing at lunchtime and in the early evening.

A hop-on hop-off trolley tour provides an easy way to get to explore the heart of the city. The tour links Fort Lauderdale's downtown area and the beach, taking in all the principal sights.

### 🏛 Fort Lauderdale History Center
219 SW 2nd Ave.
**Tel** (954) 463-4431.
**Open** Tue–Sun.
**Closed** Jan 1, Jul 4, Dec 25. 📷 ♿

The New River Inn in Old Fort Lauderdale was built using concrete, in 1905. Now a museum, it contains various fascinating exhibits that chart the area's history and the growth of the city up to the 1940s. A small theater shows amusing silent movies that were made during the 1920s, heyday of south Florida's movie industry.

## Sights at a Glance

① Museum of Discovery and Science
② Broward Center for the Performing Arts
③ Fort Lauderdale History Center
④ Museum of Art
⑤ Stranahan House
⑥ International Swimming Hall of Fame
⑦ Bonnet House
⑧ Hugh Taylor Birch State Park

The shady Riverwalk, winding along the north bank of the New River

*For hotels and restaurants in this area see pp316–17 and pp333–6*

## 🏛 Museum of Art

1 E Las Olas Blvd. **Tel** (954) 525-5500. **Open** 11am–6pm Tue–Sun. **Closed** Mon, public hols. ♿ 🅦 **moafl.org**

This fine art museum, housed in an impressive postmodern building, is best known for its large assemblage of works of CoBrA art. The name CoBrA derives from the initial letters of Copenhagen, Brussels, and Amsterdam, the capitals of the home countries of a group of Expressionist painters who worked from 1948–51. The museum displays works by Karel Appel, Pierre Alechinsky, and Asger Jorn, the movement's leading exponents. The William Glackens Wing features this American Impressionist's work.

## 🏛 Museum of Discovery and Science

401 SW 2nd St. **Tel** (954) 467-6637. **Open** daily year-round. ♿ 🅦 **mods.org**

This is one of the largest and best museums of its kind in Florida. Here, all types of creatures, including alligators, turtles, snakes, and bats, appear in re-created Florida "ecoscapes." You can even take a simulated ride to Mars. In the AutoNation® IMAX® theater, movies are projected on to a huge 60 ft (18 m) high screen. This is also one of the few places in the world to show 3-D IMAX movies where the audience uses special glasses and personal headsets for 360-degree sound. The EcoDiscovery Center, the latest addition to the museum, offers a vast array of interactive exhibits, including an outdoor otter habitat.

## 🏠 Stranahan House

335 SE 6th Ave. **Tel** (954) 524-4736. **Open** Wed–Sun. **Closed** public hols; Jul–Aug: hours vary. ♿ 🎫 🅦 limited. 🅦 **stranahanhouse.org**

The city's oldest surviving house, a pine and oak building, built by the pioneer Frank Stranahan in 1901, became the center of Fort Lauderdale's community, serving as a trading post, meeting hall, post office, and bank. The photos of Stranahan trading with the local Seminoles (see p289) are more evocative of the early days than the furnishings inside. Goods such as alligator hides, otter pelts, and egret plumes – used in the fashions of the day – were brought by the Seminoles from the nearby Everglades in their dugout canoes.

## Las Olas Boulevard

Despite a constant stream of traffic, the section of Las Olas Boulevard between 6th and 11th Avenues is Fort Lauderdale's most picturesque and busiest street – although a crossing system has made it more pedestrian friendly. A winning mix of formal, casual, and chic boutiques and eateries line this thoroughfare, where it is possible to buy anything from a fur coat to Haitian art.

For those who are not serious shoppers, visit in the evenings when the sidewalks overflow with drinkers and diners, and the palm trees are outlined with twinkling lights.

Heading toward the beach, the boulevard passes a canal-lined area from which there is a closer look at a more lavish Fort Lauderdale lifestyle (see p139).

### VISITORS' CHECKLIST

**Practical Information**
**Road map** F4. Broward Co.
🗺 178,700. 🛈 100 East Broward Blvd, (954) 765-4466. Trolley charters: **Tel** (954) 429-3100. 🎭 Winter Fest Boat Parade (Dec).

**Transport**
✈ 5 miles (8 km) S. 🚆 200 SW 21st Terrace, (800) 872-7245. 🚌 515 NE 3rd St, (800) 231-2222. 🚌 1850 Eller Dr., (954) 523-3404.

Map labels: BOCA RATON; N FED HWY; Middle River; Hugh Taylor Birch State Park; Intracoastal Waterway; E SUNRISE BOULEVARD; NORTH OCEAN BLVD; Bonnet House; A1A; BAYSHORE DR.; N BIRCH RD.; SOUTH OCEAN BOULEVARD; LAS OLAS BOULEVARD; Beach Place; The Isles; International Swimming Hall of Fame; New River; Bahia Mar Yachting Centre; SEABREEZE BOULEVARD; Pier 66 Marina; CAUSEWAY; 8; 7; 6

0 kilometers 1
0 miles 1

Stranahan House on the New River, Broward County's oldest residence

# Exploring Fort Lauderdale: Beyond Downtown

Even if you miss the signs proclaiming "Welcome to Fort Lauderdale – Yachting Capital of the World," it won't take you long to recognize the real focus of the city. For tourists and residents alike, the appeal of Fort Lauderdale lies, above all, in its attractive beaches and in the waterways that branch from the city's historical lifeblood – the New River and the Intracoastal Waterway.

Cyclists and pedestrians enjoying the shady beachfront promenade

## The Beach

Until the mid-1980s, when the local authorities began to discourage them, students by the thousand would descend on Fort Lauderdale for Spring Break. Today, the excellent beach is still the liveliest along the Gold Coast – especially at the end of Las Olas Boulevard, where in-line skaters cruise, and strollers enjoy the beachfront promenade.

Beachside Fort Lauderdale offers plenty for family visits; Hugh Taylor Birch State Park offers canoeing in a lagoon, and South Beach Park has the most pleasant strip of sand.

The outdoor pools at Fort Lauderdale's International Swimming Hall of Fame

## 🏛 International Swimming Hall of Fame

1 Hall of Fame Drive. **Tel** (954) 462-6536. **Open** daily. 🈺 🦽

If you ever wanted to know about the history of Oman's aquatic sports, or the evolution of diving positions, this is the place to come. This detailed museum displays an odd mix of exhibits, from ancient wooly bathing suits to amusing mannequins of stars, such as Johnny "Tarzan" Weismuller, holder of 57 world swimming records.

## 🏛 Bonnet House Museum and Gardens

900 N Birch Rd. **Tel** (954) 563-5393. 🈺 compulsory, 9am–4pm Tue–Sun. **Closed** Mon, public hols. 🈺

**w** bonnethouse.org

This unusually furnished house, close to the waterfront, is by far the most enjoyable piece of old Fort Lauderdale. It stands amid idyllic tropical grounds, where the bonnet water lily, from which the house took its name, once grew. Artist Frederic Bartlett built this cozy, plantation-style winter home himself in 1920, and examples of his work, especially murals, are everywhere. Swans and monkeys inhabit the grounds, which are also home to one of the largest orchid collections in southeast US.

## 🏛 Sawgrass Mills Mall

12801 W Sunrise Blvd. **Tel** (954) 846-2300. **Open** 10am–9:30pm Mon–Sat, 11am–8pm Sun. **Closed** Dec 25. 🦽

**w** sawgrassmillsmall.com

The largest outlet mall in Florida and one of the state's largest tourist attractions after Orlando's Disneyworld. There are some 300 stores, plus cinemas, restaurants, and a life-size Barbie house – the Barbie Dream House Experience.

## 🦋 Hugh Taylor Birch State Park

3109 E Sunrise Blvd. **Tel** (954) 564-4521. **Open** daily. 🈺 🦽

These 180 acres (73 ha), part of 3 miles (5 km) of barrier island that Chicago lawyer Hugh Taylor Birch bought in 1894, amount to one of the Gold Coast's few undeveloped oases of greenery. Visitors come to rent canoes on the lagoon, wander along a trail through a tropical hammock, and, above all, to exercise along a scenic circular road.

Jewelry stalls and neon lights at the Swap Shop of Fort Lauderdale

## Environs

Bargain-hunters will love the **Swap Shop of Fort Lauderdale**, covering an incredible 75 acres (30 ha). This place is an American version of a bazaar or souk, with whole rows devoted to jewelry, sunglasses, and other trinkets. Many of the 12 million annual visitors are lured by the fresh produce, and nursery which sells indoor and outdoor plants. The parking lot becomes a huge drive-in movie theater in the evenings.

## 🏛 Swap Shop of Fort Lauderdale

3291 W Sunrise Blvd. **Tel** (954) 791-7927. **Open** daily. 🦽

The Jungle Queen, Fort Lauderdale's most famous cruise boat

## The Waterways

Around the mouth of the New River lie dozens of parallel, arrow-straight canals. The area is known as **The Isles**, named after the rows of slender peninsulas created from mud when the canals were dug in the 1920s. This is the most desirable place to live in the city: looming behind lush foliage and luxurious yachts are ostentatious mansions worth millions of dollars. Their residents, such as Wayne Huizenga, former owner of the Block-buster Video empire and present co-owner of the Miami Dolphins football team, are chiefly rich businesspeople.

The islands flank the Intracoastal Waterway, which also crosses **Port Everglades**. This is the world's second-largest cruise port after Miami,

A water taxi on the New River

as well as a destination for container ships, oil tankers, destroyers, and submarines.

The best way to view the Intracoastal waterway is from a boat ride, because the mansions, yachts, and port can really only be properly viewed from the water. Visitors can choose from all the different types of boat trips that are on offer. The **Jungle Queen** is a wonderful old-fashioned river-boat that has been taking visitors up the New River for more than eight decades; there are daytime trips that take three hours, including a visit to a tropical island, and evening cruises, which include a vaudeville show and barbecue dinner.

Alternatively, 90-minute **Carrie B** riverboat tours depart from the Riverwalk, pass various mansions, browse around the port, and then visit the warm waters of a power plant discharge where large numbers of manatees (*see p254*) gather.

**Water Taxis**, operating like shared land taxis, travel up New River to Downtown and anywhere from the port north to Oakland Park Boulevard. The taxis are on an hourly schedule for one flat-rate all-day pass. Boats can be rented from the Bahia Mar Yachting Center and Pier 66 Marina.

Finally, a family adventure for anyone wishing to sail, talk, dress, and shoot cannons like a pirate: Bluefoot Pirate Adventures takes visitors on a treasure hunt that finishes with a battle on the high Intracoastal Waterway.

## Useful Addresses

**Carrie B**
440 N New River Dr E.
**Tel** (954) 768-9920.

**Bluefoot Pirate Adventures**
801 Seabreeze Blvd.
**Tel** (954) 530-8302.
W **bluefootpirates.com**

**Jungle Queen**
Bahia Mar Yachting Center,
A1A, Fort Lauderdale Beach.
**Tel** (954) 462-5596.
W **junglequeen.com**

**Water Taxi**
413 SW 3rd Ave.
**Tel** (954) 467-6677.
W **watertaxi.com**

Panoramic view over Fort Lauderdale's scenic waterways, with its luxurious yachts and mansion-lined canals

Pristine views of the Dania fishing pier at Hollywood beach

### ㉑ Dania

**Road map** F4. Broward Co.
🅰 30,000. 🚆 Hollywood.
🚌 Hollywood. 🛈 Dania, (954) 926-
2323. 🌐 greaterdania.org

Dania blends seamlessly into the coastal conurbation. Some locals visit the town only to watch a game of jai alai, but the other main attraction is the **John U. Lloyd Beach State Park**, a chunk of virgin barrier island that contrasts acutely with nearby Port Everglades *(see p139)*. From the park's northern tip, you can watch ships come and go; to the south stretches one of the Gold Coast's loveliest beaches: more than 2 miles (3 km) in length and backed by pine trees. Canoes can be rented to explore the scenic, mangrove-lined creek that runs through the heart of the park.

The **Dania Beach Pier**, like others along the coastline of Florida, will appeal to those who enjoy strolling by the ocean or sea fishing. The magnificent views of the coastline from the pier are well worth the small entrance fee.

Along the northern part of US 1 are some 150 antique shops. Despite their poor location, alongside the traffic-ridden road, they make entertaining browsing.

🔷 **John U. Lloyd Beach State Park**
6503 N Ocean Drive. **Tel** (954)
923-2833. **Open** daily. 🏖 ♿

🔁 **Dania Beach Pier**
300 N Beach Rd, Dania
Beach. **Tel** (954) 924-3613.
**Open** 6am–midnight daily.
🏖 ♿ 🌐 ci.dania-beach.fl.us

### ㉒ Hollywood

**Road map** F4. Broward Co.
🅰 150,000. 🚆 Amtrak and Tri-Rail.
🚌 🛈 330 N Federal Hwy, (954) 923-
4000. 🌐 hollywoodchamber.org

Founded by a Californian in the 1920s, this large and unpretentious resort is the destination for of the 300,000 French Canadians who migrate to Greater Fort Lauderdale every winter.

The development in Hollywood has since been concentrated in the historic downtown arts district around Young Circle. The area has many restaurants and the **Art and Culture Center of Hollywood**, which holds art exhibitions, theater, music, and dance performances. The community's sandy beach is excellent for families. Visit the Hollywood Beach Broadwalk, a 2.5-mile (4-km) cycling and walking path along the beach, dotted with live music venues and restaurants.

The **Anne Kolb Nature Center** includes a five-level observation fishing pier, two nature trails, outdoor amphitheater, and exhibit hall. The **Topeekeegee Yugnee Park** offers picnic and playground areas, a water park, paved pathways for walking and biking, basketball and tennis courts, and a fishing pier.

🏛 **Art and Culture Center of Hollywood**
1650 Harrison Street. **Tel** (954) 921- 3274.
**Open** 10am–5pm Mon–Sat, noon–4pm
Sun. 🌐 artandculturecenter.org

🏛 **Anne Kolb Nature Center**
751 Sheridan. **Tel** (954) 357-5161.
🌐 broward.org/Parks/WestLakePark/
Pages/AnneKolbNatureCenter.aspx

🌳 **Topeekeegee Yugnee Park**
3300 N Park Rd. **Tel** (954) 357-8811.
**Open** 9am–5pm daily.
**Closed** Thanksgiving, Dec 25.
🌐 broward.org/Parks/topeekeegee
yugneepark

**Environs**
At the crossroads of State Road 7/441 and Route 848/Stirling Road, on the western edge of

Sun worshipers enjoying the pristine sands of Hollywood Beach

Inside the huge Seminole Hard Rock Hotel and Casino

Hollywood, is the Seminole Tribe of Florida Hollywood Reservation, home of the tribal headquarters. Since casino gambling is legal on the reservations, the reservations have seen much financial benefit. Covering 480 acres (194 ha), it is Florida's smallest Indian reservation.

**Seminole Classic Casino in Hollywood** is open 24 hours a day, offering poker, bingo, and other gaming. Reservations are exempt from state gambling laws, and in the cavernous bingo hall as many as 1,400 players compete for five-figure cash prizes. The main attraction is the **Seminole Hard Rock Hotel and Casino**. This resort and hotel features a huge casino, tropical pool area, Hard Rock Live, and Seminole Paradise.

**Seminole Classic Casino in Hollywood**
4150 N State Rd 7. **Tel** (954) 961-3220. **Open** 24 hours. **Closed** Dec 25.
**W** seminoleclassiccasino.com

**Seminole Hard Rock Hotel and Casino**
1 Seminole Way. **Tel** (866) 502-7529, (924) 327-7625. **Open** 24 hours.
**W** seminolehardrockhollywood.com

## ㉓ Davie

**Road map** F4. Broward Co. 70,000. Fort Lauderdale. 4185 Davie Rd, (954) 581-0790. **W** davie-coopercity.org

Centered on Orange Drive and Davie Road, and surrounded by paddocks and stables, the town of Davie reflects Florida's long cowboy history, much older than California's. Cacti grow outside the town hall's wooden

huts, and the local McDonald's even has a corral at the back. Drop in on Grif's Western Wear, a cowboy supermarket at 6211 South West 45th Street, to stock up on saddles, cowboy hats, and boots. The only way to sample the town's real flavor, however, is to watch bronco busting, bull riding, and steer wrestling in a rodeo at the **Bergeron Rodeo**

Stetsons for sale at Grif's Western Wear shop in Davie

**Grounds**, home to the Davie Rodeo Association. In addition to the many rodeo events, the arena hosts a diverse program of concerts and circuses, plus monster truck and airboat shows.

**Bergeron Rodeo Grounds**
4271 Davie Road. **Tel** (954) 797-1153. **W** davie-fl.gov

## ㉔ Flamingo Gardens

**Road map** F4. Broward Co. 3750 South Flamingo Rd, Davie. **Tel** (954) 473-2955. Fort Lauderdale. Fort Lauderdale. **Open** daily. **Closed** Mon (Jun–Oct), Thanksgiving, Dec 25. **W** flamingogardens.org

These beautiful gardens started out in 1927 as a weekend retreat for the Wrays, a citrus-farming family. You can tour the family's 1930s home, furnished in period style, but the gardens are the main attraction. Trolley tours pass groves of lemon and kumquat trees, live oaks, banyans, and other exotic vegetation.

The gardens are home to many Florida birds, including the bald eagle *(see p28)* and flamingos. Several species of ducks, gulls, doves, and waders – including the roseate spoonbill *(see p293)* – inhabit a walk-through aviary split into habitats such as cypress forest and mangrove swamp. Wildlife Encounter shows are held here in the afternoons.

### Jai Alai – a Merry Sport

This curious game originated some 300 years ago in the Basque Country (jai alai means "merry festival" in Basque), and was brought to the US in the early 1900s via Cuba. Florida has several arenas, or "frontons."

Watching a game of jai alai makes for a cheap night out (if you don't bet). The program explains both the scoring and the intricacies of pari-mutuel betting, where those who bet on the winners share in the total amount wagered. People yell and cheer loudly during the points, since many will have put money on the outcome. Although the increase in the number of gaming casinos has dwindled jai alai frontons in the state, the game can still be seen in South Florida frontons. The rules of the game are explained on page 37.

Jai alai player poised for a hit

# ORLANDO AND THE SPACE COAST

With everything from roller coasters to wizarding worlds and a well-known mouse with very big ears, Orlando is a family-oriented fantasyland and the undisputed theme park capital of the world, attracting more than 68 million visitors every year.

Orlando started out as an army post, Fort Gatlin, which was established during the Seminole Wars *(see pp50–51)*. History has it that the fort was later renamed after a soldier called Orlando Reeves, who was hit by a Seminole arrow in 1835. A town developed, but even through the first half of the 20th century Orlando and neighboring towns such as Kissimmee were only small, sleepy places dependent on cattle and the citrus crop.

Everything changed in the 1960s. First of all came the job opportunities associated with the space program at Cape Canaveral. Then Walt Disney World® started to take shape: its first theme park, the Magic Kingdom®, opened in 1971. Since then, Disney claims that more than 600 million visitors have made the pilgrimage, with more than 60 million of those visitors

arriving in 2016 alone. Its success has generated a booming entertainment industry in Greater Orlando, as an increasing number of attractions appear on the scene, all eager to cash in on the captive market. The region has a subtle beauty, with hundreds of lakes bordered by moss-draped oaks or stands of cypress trees, spring-fed rivers, ancient forests, and verdant farmlands. Along the Space Coast, the communities on the mainland shore hold little appeal. However, the barrier islands across the broad Indian River boast 72 miles (116 km) of stunning sandy beaches, and there are two nature preserves rich in bird life. Amid all this, set in a preserved marshy vastness beneath giant skies, in surprising harmony with nature, is the Kennedy Space Center, from which rockets have been launched to the moon, and in the near future, to Mars.

The expansive and unspoiled watery landscape of Merritt Island on the Space Coast

◄ Guests enjoying the Astro Orbiter ride at Tomorrowland in Walt Disney World®

# Exploring Orlando and the Space Coast

The reason so many vacationers come to Orlando is to experience the big theme parks, especially Walt Disney World®, SeaWorld®, and Universal Studios®. In and around the theme parks, International Drive, and in Kissimmee, there are more than 119,000 hotel rooms – a greater number than in the whole of New York. Those with time to spare should visit the serene Bok Tower Gardens or, just up the road, the fun LEGOLAND®. At night, experience the razzmatazz at the fantastic entertainment complex of Universal's CityWalk®. The quaint boutiques and sidewalk cafés of Orlando's upscale neighbor, Winter Park, appeal to those seeking more sophisticated fare. Just 50 miles (80 km) away, the Space Coast is an easy day trip from Orlando. Here, beaches range from empty, wild sands, to the buzzing surfing mecca of brash Cocoa Beach.

## Key

═══ Highway
═══ Major road
═══ Secondary road
═══ Minor road
─── Scenic route
▬▪▬ Main railroad

The Singing Tower as seen from the Reflection Pool at Bok Tower Gardens

Rockets from the early days of space exploration, at the Kennedy Space Center

## Getting Around

If you are exploring beyond the theme parks, rent a car. With an extensive network of divided highways, driving is relaxing and fast: from Walt Disney World®, downtown Orlando is half an hour's drive north, and LEGOLAND® an hour south. If you are spending your whole vacation on Disney property, see pages 147 and 178 for transit options. Many hotels offer free shuttle bus services to the theme parks, and Lynx buses (see p387) serve most tourist destinations in Greater Orlando. The Space Coast is an hour east from Orlando on Route 528 (Beachline Expressway). I-95 is the main north-south route along the coast. Route A1A connects the beaches on the barrier islands.

## Sights at a Glance

*For hotels and restaurants in this area see pp317–18 and pp336–9*

# ➊ Walt Disney World® Resort

Let your imagination take flight at this world-class entertainment center, where there is something for everyone, regardless of age. Plan to spend at least a day in each of Disney's "big four" – Magic Kingdom®, Epcot®, Disney's Hollywood Studios®, and Disney's Animal Kingdom®. Don't miss a chance to cool off at the two water parks – Blizzard Beach and Typhoon Lagoon. Alternatively, choose to let off steam at Disney's Wide World of Sports complex; golf courses; hiking and riding trails; and pools and lakes for swimming, boating, waterskiing and much more. With more than 30 resorts on the premises, visitors can go back to their hotel to rest before returning to one of the parks for the fireworks finale, or to check out a show at Disney Springs®, formerly Downtown Disney®.

**Magic Kingdom®**
Seven Lands of fantasy and adventure encircle the stunningly beautiful Cinderella's Castle.

## Sights at a Glance

**Disney's Animal Kingdom®**
Experience the thrill of the wild through encounters with animals, as well as the pure fun of African safaris, river rafting, and treks, along with a virtual ride through an alien planet.

| 0 meters | 500 |
| 0 yards | 500 |

## Key

- - - - Monorail

▬▬▬ Interstate highway

**Blizzard Beach**
Thrilling rides and exhilarating water slides are on offer at this cleverly designed 66 acre (27 ha) water theme park.

### Epcot®

Travel across continents, blast into space on a rocket to Mars, embark on an underwater adventure, and take a peek into the future with remarkable discoveries and inventions.

### Disney's Hollywood Studios®

There's no business like show business at Disney's Hollywood Studios®, where guests of all ages are immersed in the glitz, glamor, and magic of Hollywood.

### Getting Around

An extensive, efficient transportation system handles more than 200,000 guests each day. The transportation hub of Walt Disney World® is the Ticket and Transportation Center (TTC). Monorails, ferryboats, and motorcoach shuttle services operate daily. Additionally, hotels outside the resort area offer free shuttle services to the parks. For further details, *see page 178*.

### Disney Springs®

Themed celebrity restaurants, nightclubs, shows, and the largest outlet for Disney merchandise – all this and much more is on offer at this exciting entertainment and shopping complex.

**Key**

Main sites

**For keys to symbols** *see back flap*

# The Magic Kingdom®

Reappearing in similar form in California, Japan, and France, the Magic Kingdom® is the essential Disney theme park. Cartoon characters and nostalgic visions of how the world (and particularly America) once was, and how it might be again, fill its unrelenting cheerful 107 acres. The park is made up of seven "lands" evoking a particular theme or era, such as the Wild West, Colonial America, and the future. Binding the park together are stunning parades, musical street performers, and Disney characters ready to greet their guests.

Fantasyland®'s landmark castle

## Tackling the Park

Disney hotel guests can take advantage of Extra Magic Hours, which offer time in the park before and after regular opening hours.

If you are a Disney resort guest, plan to reach the entrance turnstiles one and a half hours before the official opening time. This will allow you to enjoy Fantasyland® and Tomorrowland® for an hour before the rest of the park opens. On arrival, you can pick up a map that shows the lands and rides, and lists the show and parade times. A notice board at the top of Main Street® also shows this, and gives a list of waiting times at various attractions. To make use of waiting times for rides, you can book FastPass+ reservations for specific times, up to 30 days in advance. The reservations can also be changed on the day using the kiosks dotted around the parks. Disney's MagicBands, worn on the wrist, or Magic Cards, also allow for quick access to FastPass+ entrances to rides. Getting around the Park is relatively easy because the lands radiate from the central hub, in front of Cinderella's Castle.

The major attractions lie at opposite sides of the park, so you will have to walk a fair way to avoid long waits in line. There are also more novel forms of transport. Main Street® has vehicles which, true to the Disney story-telling ideal, tell the story of transport from the horse-drawn trolley to the motor car. A steam train circles the park, calling at Main Street®, Fantasyland®, and Frontierland®.

## Eating and Drinking

Food is mostly fast. For a reasonable meal, try Be Our Guest inside the Beast's enchanted castle, which offers a quick-service lunch or sit-down dinner, or The Liberty Tree Tavern or the Crystal Palace for quieter dining. Cinderella's Royal Table in the castle can provide – for a hefty price – a setting regal enough for any princess.

## Main Street, USA®

This is a Disney fantasy of a small-town, Victorian America that never was. As you enter Main Street®, you pass beneath Main Street Station from where you can ride the train around the park. Trains run every 10 minutes. Beneath the station are lockers where, for a small fee, you can store valuables and bags. As you enter the town square, City Hall lies to your left and is the place to visit first for any information, such as which shows are running, and what special events might be happening. Main Street® itself is a magnificent mixture of color, shapes, and music, all in astonishing detail. In Town Square Theater, to the right as you enter the square, you can meet Mickey Mouse, starring as a magician, before heading for the shop-lined Main Street®.

At night, this area assumes a magical ambience when thousands of lights bring a warm glow to the spotlessly clean paving. It is also an excellent place to see the Once Upon A Time projection, a light and music show, where scenes from Disney films are projected right onto the Cinderella Castle.

## Adventureland®

Lush foliage, evocative drumbeats, and Colonial buildings combine to conjure images of Africa and the Caribbean. Crossing a wooden bridge from the central hub, Adventureland® is an exciting and entertaining fusion of the exotic and the tropical.

**The Jungle Cruise** boat ride, which takes guests around a variety of animatronically animated settings of deepest Africa, India, and South America is very popular due, in most part, to the great

### Tips

- If you are an early entry guest, plan to wait at the rope barrier next to Peter Pan and "it's a small world" about 15–20 minutes before the official opening time.
- If you want to visit Splash Mountain® first, board the train at Main Street® before the park has opened. On opening time, the train will pull out and stop in Frontierland® about 7 minutes later. The station is next to Splash Mountain® and Big Thunder.
- In order to reduce the number of guests in attractions prior to closing, much of the internal queuing areas are roped off so the lines of waiting guests still appear long from the outside.
- The best place to see all the parades is Frontierland®, although during peak periods you will still have to find a spot about 45 minutes before the parade.
- Daytime parades run from Splash Mountain® area to Town Square and the night-time parades in the opposite direction.

## One Day Itinerary

If you really want to cover the Magic Kingdom® in one day, be warned, it is a daunting task, particularly in the summer. Begin early and follow these tips to ensure you get the most out of the day. Pick up the park map at the entrance, or download the **My Disney Experience** mobile app. It helps if you have arranged your FastPass+ in advance, but there are kiosks around the park where you can make new reservations or amend the ones you have.

1. After leaving the turnstiles, head immediately for the central hub. If the entire park is open, turn right and head for **Space Mountain®**. Those who like thrills should ride while others can head for **Buzz Lightyear's Space Ranger Spin®**.
2. After Space Mountain® head for **Fantasyland®** (keep the speedway on your right and turn left at the Mad Hatter's Teacups) and head for the **Seven Dwarfs Mine Ride** or the **Many Adventures of Winnie the Pooh**.
3. After Winnie, turn left and head toward **Peter Pan's Flight** and also ride **"it's a small world"®**.
4. Exit left, head to Liberty Square and visit **Haunted Mansion®** on the right.
5. Exit Haunted Mansion® to the right and continue to **Splash Mountain®**. Next, turn right and cross to **Big Thunder Mountain Railroad**.
6. Take the exit from Big Thunder and cross the bridge bearing right to **Pirates of the Caribbean®**.
7. Take a break on the **Jungle Cruise**. Continue relaxing at the **Enchanted Tiki Room**.
8. Good time for lunch. Eat light at a fast food restaurant.
9. Walk off lunch by clambering around at the **Swiss Family Treehouse** in Adventureland®.
10. Cross the central hub to **Tomorrowland®** and participate in **Stitch's Great Escape!**
11. Visit the **Monsters, Inc. Laugh® Floor Comedy Club** and choose between **Astro Orbiter** and the **Carousel of Progress**.
12. Head back to the Tea Cups, and turn right to ride **Dumbo the Flying Elephant®** or **The Barnstormer**.
13. Cross central hub to **Frontierland®**, and find a spot to stake out for the **afternoon parade**.
14. You will now have ridden and seen the top attractions in the Magic Kingdom®. This is a good time to rest before finding a good spot to see the Once Upon A Time projection, light and projection show at Cinderella's Castle.
15. Finally, stake out a bench in the park to see the **fireworks** in comfort.

entertainment value of the "boatman" whose often wacky and infectious humor cannot fail to amuse.

The **Enchanted Tiki Room** is an amusing and cleverly animated attraction, and is a pleasant way to spend 20 minutes or so if you want to escape the heat. Featuring animated flora and fauna from the tropics, its worth a visit to escape the crowds.

The **Pirates of the Caribbean®** is an extremely entertaining and remarkably detailed voyage where you cruise through crumbling, underground prisons, past fighting galleons of the 16th century, and past scenes of Disneyfied debauchery and mayhem, along with Captain Jack Sparrow and his crew. The ride is certainly a firm favorite with park visitors.

At the exit, there is a gift shop, which is very popular with fans of the movie franchise as a source for a range of pirate-themed accessories and memorabilia: swords, hats, plastic hooks, bandanas, jewels, and pirate treasure.

## Frontierland®

Set in Hollywood-inspired Wild West, this land abounds with raised walkways and trading posts. **The Frontierland Shootin' Arcade** is reminiscent of both the Wild West and of Country Fairs gone by, while the **Country Bear Jamboree** provides a completely audio animatronic animal show, popular with all youngsters and a welcome respite from the blazing Florida sun.

Opposite Big Thunder Mountain is the landing stage where a raft can be taken to Tom Sawyer's Island. Complete with a fort, swinging bridges, waterfalls and tunnels, it is a child's dream adventure playground.

A stunningly conceived and superbly executed journey through America's Wild West on an out of control mine train, **Big Thunder Mountain Railroad** remains one of the Park's enduring attractions. In roller coaster terms, it is a relatively gentle experience, although the rear cars provide a wilder ride than the front. It also attracts large lines of people from early in the day, so this is a ride to be enjoyed sooner, rather than later.

## Shows and Parades

Do not miss seeing at least one of each of these events. The shows – Mickey's PhilharMagic Orchestra, a 3-D animated movie, and The Enchanted Tiki Room – are superb in their own right but the parades are unique. Floats of towering proportions surrounded by a multitude of actors and dancers travel on a set route between Frontierland® and the Town Square on Main Street®. The Festival of Fantasy Parade winds its way through the park at noon and 3:30pm daily, featuring a garden of Princesses, Peter Pan and Wendy, Mickey and Minnie, and Maleficent as a clockwork dragon. The evening also features Once Upon A Time, which bathes the Cinderella Castle in multi-colored projections of scenes from Disney films.

An outstanding attraction which threatens to get you far wetter than it actually does is **Splash Mountain®**. This is the epitome of what Disney does best, with a seamless integration of music, special effects, and beautifully crafted creatures. This, combined with a multitude of small drops prior to the big one make this one of the finest flume rides in the world. Absolutely guaranteed to make you want to do it again, this ride develops long lines early on, and remains that way until closing.

## Liberty Square

The smallest of all the lands, Liberty Square is set in post-Colonial America and hosts the **Liberty Square Riverboat, Hall of Presidents**, and **The Haunted Mansion®**. Entertaining rather than scary, except perhaps for very small children, The Haunted Mansion® rarely has long lines and provides a cool respite, particularly in the middle of a hot summer day. The ride travels through a graveyard into the namesake mansion, where walls and floors are not what they seem, and gravestones sing jolly songs as you pass. Watch out, because when your ghostly transport leaves the mansion behind, a transparent hitchhiker will be sitting right next to you.

For a dose of reality, board the Liberty Square Riverboat, a mock paddle steamer, and take a slow journey around Tom Sawyer's Island, looking out for real tropical birds along the way. The steamer gently cruises through America's 19th-century past while you listen to a recorded narration delivered in the voice of Mark Twain.

Refuge from the crowds and heat can be found in the nearby Hall of Presidents, an audio animatronic presentation featuring all 45 US presidents, including President Donald Trump. Before the presidents are introduced, an interesting movie is shown that explores the history of America.

## Shopping

There are shops everywhere in the Magic Kingdom® and they sell just about every type of clothing, confectionery (except chewing gum!) and badged merchandise imaginable. All Lands have their own shops selling items based on the theme of the Land and of the nearest ride (much piratical memorabilia can be purchased near Pirates of the Caribbean®, for instance). However, some of the best shopping is in Disney Springs®, where you can browse through the largest Disney store in the world.

## Fantasyland®

Dominated by the soaring spires of Cinderella's Castle, this Land forms the core of the Magic Kingdom®. A major expansion that doubled the size of Fantasyland® added two new castles to the skyline: Beast's Castle and Prince Eric's Castle. The circus area evokes Disney's classic film, *Dumbo*, with a big top, and attractions such as **The Barnstormer**, where the Great Goofini performs daredevil acrobatics. But the big attraction of Fantasyland® is the **Seven Dwarves Mine Train®** roller coaster ride.

The delightfully designed attractions produce a feeling of amazement in even the most cynical, and this land is usually the first destination for kids. **Prince Charming Regal Carousel** (a genuine 1917 restoration) seems to entice both old and young onto its gallopers. **Peter Pan's Flight** is deservedly popular combining the feeling of flying with the delight of perfectly matched music and movement.

Opposite is **"it's a small world"®**, a water borne journey through a series of animated tableaux accompanied by a rather persistent melody which, if you're not careful, you'll find hard to get out of your head for the rest of the day. Lines are long here, so use a FastPass+ if possible. **The Many Adventures of Winnie the Pooh** incorporates the latest in ride vehicle technology, lighting, and multi-channel sound effects, producing an attraction which deserves its FastPass+ status. The playground across from the ride, "Pooh's Thoughtful Spot" is a good place to take a break. **Mickey's PhilharMagic®**

is an excellent 3-D animated movie starring an array of best-loved Disney characters.

In the summer heat, the long lines for some of the short, child-friendly rides can be a strain on all concerned. Try alternating between outdoor rides, such as Dumbo and the carousel, and indoor attractions such as "it's a small world", and Mickey's PhilharMagic®, which has an indoor line, giving visitors a chance to cool down.

## Tomorrowland®

**The Tomorrowland® Transit Authority** is a serene yet interesting 10-minute ride, which uses linear induction drives. This journey through Tomorrowland® provides some of the best views in the park and an opportunity to relax after a great deal of walking. Almost never busy, it travels through Space Mountain® and offers views inside several other attractions as well.

**Space Mountain®** is the fastest ride where you shoot through tight bends and sharp drops in stygian blackness against projections of asteroids and similar. The effects of traveling through space are excellent, but the ride, though wilder than Big Thunder Mountain, may seem tame for seasoned thrillseekers.

While the lining up experience is never really fun, Disney has perfected it, and provides distractions as guests wait in line for many of the rides, including Space Mountain®. Video-game stations dot the corridor approaching the Launch Pad, giving space visitors a way to test skills needed for survival.

*For hotels and restaurants in this area see pp317–18 and pp336–9*

Weary adults and kids will find unexpected fun at **Cosmic Ray's Starlight Café**. A giant alien, "Sonny Eclipse," holds court at a piano bar, and live dancers lead audience participation. It's also a great place to escape the heat or rain. There are three food areas with different menus at each.

Handling large crowds with ease, **Walt Disney's Carousel of Progress** is a sit-down attraction where the auditorium rotates around a central stage. The show examines domestic life through the ages and, although rather quaint, is a firm favorite, particularly late in the evening.

At **Monsters, Inc. Laugh Floor® Comedy Club** you'll discover the power of laughter in an interactive adventure, as you match your wits against the one-eyed hero Mike Wazowski and his two comedian wannabe friends.

One of Tomorrowland®'s greatest innovations is **Buzz Lightyear's Space Ranger Spin®**. A superb and highly addictive journey through *Toy Story* adventures sets you in a two seater car, fitted with laser cannons, electronic scoreboards, and a control which allows you to rotate the car rapidly for a better aim. A very fast loader, it's one of the best rides in the park.

Shooting at the targets with a red laser beam which evokes bangs, crashes, pings, and rapid increases in your scores. This has become one of the few rides that children tear their parents away from, such is its popularity.

## Tips

- Lines at attractions are shorter during parade times.
- Watch the fireworks from the top of Main Street® (near the hub), then enjoy the rides until the park closes.
- Ride the train around Magic Kingdom® for an overview of what is there.
- Grab a seat on the terrace at Cosmic Ray's for a perfect view of the fireworks and Cinderella Castle projection show.
- If you are staying on site, take the children back to the hotel for lunch and a swim during the heat of the day.
- If you have young children, rent a stroller when you enter the park.

## Rides and Shows Checklist

This chart is designed to help you to plan what to visit in the Magic Kingdom®. The rides and shows are listed in no particular order within each Land.

| | | WAITING TIME | HEIGHT / AGE RESTRICTION | BUSIEST TIME TO RIDE | FASTPASS | LOADING SPEED | MAY CAUSE MOTION SICKNESS | OVERALL RATING |
|---|---|---|---|---|---|---|---|---|
| **ADVENTURELAND®** | | | | | | | | |
| R | Jungle Cruise® | ● | | 11am–5pm | ➡ | ❷ | | ▼ |
| R | Pirates of the Carribbean® | ○ | | noon–4pm | | ❶ | | ◆ |
| S | Enchanted Tiki Room | ○ | | | | ❶ | | ▼ |
| R | Magic Carpets of Aladdin | ○ | | | | ❶ | | ▼ |
| **FRONTIERLAND®** | | | | | | | | |
| R | Big Thunder Mountain Railroad | ● | 1.02m | 10am–7pm | ➡ | ❶ | ✔ | ★ |
| R | Splash Mountain® | ● | 1.02m | 10am–7pm | ➡ | ❶ | | ★ |
| S | Country Bear Jamboree | ○ | | | | ❶ | | ▼ |
| S | Frontierland Shootin' Arcade | ◗ | | | | ❶ | | ◆ |
| **LIBERTY SQUARE** | | | | | | | | |
| R | Hall of Presidents | ○ | | | | ❶ | | ▼ |
| R | Haunted Mansion® | ◗ | | | | ❶ | | ◆ |
| R | Liberty Square Riverboat | ○ | | | | ❶ | | ▼ |
| **FANTASYLAND®** | | | | | | | | |
| R | Dumbo the Flying Elephant® | ◗ | | 9am–7pm | | ❸ | | ▼ |
| R | It's a Small World® | ○ | | | | ❶ | | ▼ |
| R | The Many Adventures of Winnie the Pooh | ● | | 10am–6pm | ➡ | ❸ | | ★ |
| R | Peter Pan's Flight | ● | | 9am–9pm | ➡ | ❸ | | ★ |
| R | The Barnstormer | ◗ | 89cm | 9am–7pm | | ❷ | | ▼ |
| R | Mad Tea Party | ○ | | | | ❶ | ✔ | ▼ |
| **TOMORROWLAND®** | | | | | | | | |
| R | Buzz Lightyear's Space Ranger Spin® | ◗ | | 10am–6pm | ➡ | ❶ | | ◆ |
| R | Space Mountain® | ● | 1.2m | 9am–7pm | ➡ | ❷ | | ★ |
| S | Cosmic Ray's Starlight Café | ○ | | | | | | ▼ |
| S | Monsters, Inc. Laugh Floor® Comedy Club | ◗ | | | | | | ▼ |
| R | Tomorrowland® Transit Authority | ○ | | | | ❶ | | ▼ |

**Key**: Ride – R  Show – S; Waiting Time Good – ○ Average – ◗ Bad – ●; Overall Rating Good – ▼ Excellent – ◆ Outstanding – ★  Loading Speed Fast – ❶ Leisurely – ❷ Slow – ❸

# Epcot®

Epcot®, an acronym for the Experimental Prototype Community of Tomorrow, was Walt Disney's dream of a technologically replete, living community. It was intended to represent a utopian vision of the future, but upon its opening in 1982, several changes had been made to the original dream, and Epcot® opened as an educational center and permanent world's fair.

The 250-acre park is divided into two distinct halves: Future World with an emphasis on entertainment and education, and World Showcase which represents the art, culture, and culinary expertise of different countries around the globe.

The France Pavilion in World Showcase

## Tips

- Early entry guests are allowed into the parks immediately to enjoy certain attractions, so it's a good idea to be at the turnstiles at least 15 minutes before they open.
- Test Track® and Mission: SPACE® are exceptionally popular but unreliable. This combination causes long lines from the outset. Try to ride these first and then, on leaving, take a FastPass+ ticket for another ride later.
- Boats cross the World Showcase Lagoon fairly regularly. A bonus is that they are air conditioned, so offer some respite from the heat in the middle of the day.
- Most people ride Spaceship Earth as soon as they arrive in Epcot®, and waiting times are therefore long. In the afternoon, however, you can walk on with virtually no wait.

## Tackling the Park

Epcot® is two and a half times the size of the Magic Kingdom® which means that at least two days are needed to see the Park in its entirety. World Showcase is not usually open until 11am so the early-morning crowds fill Future World. The "back gate" or International Gateway entrance opens at 9am, and visitors can enter World Showcase and eat breakfast at Les Halles Boulangerie and Patisserie in the French Pavilion. Arriving early is the key to a successful visit. If you are entitled to early entry privileges, arrive 1 hour and 40 minutes before the official opening time.

Although there are relatively few rides in Future World, two of these, Test Track® and Mission: SPACE® are besieged from the outset. To reach them, bear left through the huge Innoventions East building. It sometimes helps to think of Future World as a clock face; if the turnstiles are at 6 o'clock then Mission: SPACE® is at 9 o'clock and Test Track® is at 11 o'clock.

After leaving the Mission: SPACE®/Test Track® area, retrace your steps back through Innoventions East and cross through Innoventions West, emerging to see the Soarin'®and The Seas with Nemo & Friends®. If you are most interested in seeing the world architecture, and eating at one of the many restaurants in Epcot®, a more pleasant way to enter the park is through the International Gateway. Park at Disney's Boardwalk and walk, or take the boat and disembark at the entrance between France and England.

World Showcase holds far more interest for adults than children, but the transformation of Norway Pavilion's Maelstrom ride into Frozen Ever After brings the popular animated film *Frozen* and the kingdom of Arendelle to life, guaranteeing the presence of fans who just cannot get enough of princesses Anna and Elsa. There are minor rides (usually boat rides) in some pavilions and several show movies. The dining at some pavilions is excellent and should be reserved well in advance.

## IllumiNations: Reflections of Earth

The one Epcot® show that should not be missed is the nightly IllumiNations. Presented near closing time around World Showcase Lagoon, it is a rousing *son et lumière* show on an unbelievably extravagant scale with lasers, fire- and waterworks, and a symphonic soundtrack that highlights the 11 featured nations. Best viewing spots are a seat on the verandah at the Cantina de San Angel in Mexico, the outside restaurant balcony in Japan, and the International Gateway bridge near the United Kingdom.

Transport is not very efficient (you will always get there faster by walking), so good, comfortable shoes are essential. There is also not much shade so be sure to wear a hat.

## Future World

The first area to be encountered by guests arriving at the main turnstiles, Future World comprises a series of huge, modernistic buildings around the outside, the access to which is through Innoventions East and West. Some buildings house a single ride attraction, while others afford the opportunity to browse various exhibits – usually hands-on – and to enjoy smaller rides within the main pavilion. Most of the attractions here are sponsored by major manufacturers, which will be evident from the signs.

### Pin Trading

This answer to many a parent's prayer was introduced when Disney noticed that the lapel pins it had produced for special events were re-selling at several times the market value. In a flash of inspiration, they created Pin Stations – small booths in every park selling only the hundreds of different pins that Disney produces. They usually cost $6–15 each. Following this up with a stroke of genius, they also created Pin Traders – cast members who could be persuaded to swap pins with guests. The idea had a set of very simple trading rules, which cast members could break in favor of the guest. This has captured the imagination of children and teenagers who happily spend hours tracking down the pin they want and swapping another for it. The concept has been so successful with guests and cast members that Disney has no plans to end it. Depending on the type of hotel package you have reserved, you may be presented with a set of pins on arrival to start the ball rolling.

### Spaceship Earth

Housed in an enormous 7,500-ton geodesic sphere, this continuously loading ride takes visitors gently past well-crafted tableaux and anima-tronic scenes portraying mankind's progress in the field of technology. This incredible story of development, narrated by actress Dame Judi Dench, takes visitors through time beginning with prehistoric man's first words, and finishing with the cyber age of the 21st century. Almost as interesting as the ride itself is the fascinating dome which cunningly re-circulates rainwater into the World Showcase Lagoon.

## TOP 10 ATTRACTIONS

① **Test Track®**

② **Mission: Space®**

③ **Rock 'n' Roller Coaster®** **Starring Aerosmith**

④ **The Seas with Nemo & Friends®**

⑤ **Soarin'®**

⑥ **Frozen Ever After**

⑦ **Turtle Talk With Crush**

⑧ **Reflections of China**

⑨ **Impressions De France**

⑩ **Illuminations**

### Innoventions

Both buildings of the Innoventions attraction, East and West, form a hands-on exhibition of products of the near future which, through ties to consumer electronics manufacturers, is constantly updated. However, time is needed to make the most of Innoventions, and many of the games have now moved to Disney Springs®, with the result that the theme has become more adult.

The leafy expanse of the World Showcase Epcot®

# Epcot® Mission: SPACE®

The most impressive thrill ride at Epcot® Mission: SPACE® takes guests on a journey to the heavens that culminates with a crash landing on Mars. This extremely popular attraction is the ultimate in simulator thrill rides, combining high-speed spinning – to simulate g-forces – with a simulator and a 3-D visual interactive storyline. The result is a completely mesmerizing and convincing rocket launch and high-speed trip to Mars, which also involves a ride around the moon. Particularly impressive are the wholly realistic re-creations of a liftoff into space and a problem-fraught landing. The most technologically advanced of Disney's attractions, the ride is a creation of Disney imagination, but is based on scientific fact and theory provided by astronauts, scientists, and engineers.

## International Space Training Center

The story is set at the International Space Training Center (ISTC) in the year 2036. In this future time of space exploration, many countries have joined together to train a new generation of space explorers. Mission: SPACE® participants become astronaut candidates on their first training mission.

The ISTC building is a gleaming, metallic affair, complete with curved walls and a state-of-the-art, Space Age look. The curvy steel exterior surrounds the courtyard, called **Planetary Plaza**. From the moment visitors step into this courtyard, they are taken straight into a futuristic world. Huge replicas of Earth, Jupiter, and the moon fill Planetary Plaza, and its walls feature quotations from historical figures about space travel and exploration. The moon model displays brass plaques indicating the location of every US and Soviet manned and unmanned touchdown during the 1960s and 1970s. The interior of the ISTC is compartmentalized into various areas for different levels of training. There are four ride bays, with ten capsules in each bay – each capsule can hold four guests.

## Training

Before embarking on their flight, the explorers must follow a series of procedures in order to prepare for their "mission." These training and briefing sessions also go a long way in making the wait times for the show seem shorter, be they keep the crowds entertained prior to the actual ride portion of the show: the ambience is well-executed and slightly militaristic – a rare feature at Disney parks. At the **ISTC Astronaut Recruiting Center**, explorers learn about training and view a model of the X-2 Trainer, the futuristic spacecraft they will board for their journey into space.

The second station of the mission is the **Space Simulation Lab**, a slowly spinning 35-ft (10-m) high gravity wheel containing work quarters, exercise rooms, sleeping cubicles, and dining areas for space teams. One of the highlights of the lab is an authentic Apollo-era Lunar Rover display unit on loan from the Smithsonian National Air and Space Museum, which describes mankind's first exploration of the moon.

Participants then enter the **Training Operations Room**, which bustles with the activity of various training sessions in progress. Several large monitors show live video feeds of ongoing ISTC training sessions. In **Team Dispatch**, a dispatch officer meets participants. Here, participants are split into teams of four people and sent to the **Ready Room**. This is the point at which each team member accepts an assignment: commander, pilot, navigator, or engineer. Each member is supposed to carry out the tasks associated with his or her assigned role during the flight. It is here that the explorers meet Capcom –

Replicas of planets standing out dramatically against the metallic façade of the Mission: SPACE® building

*For hotels and restaurants in this area see pp317–18 and pp336–9*

the capsule communicator – who will act as the astronauts' guide through the flight. In the **Pre-flight Corridor**, explorers receive their final instructions for the mission. A uniformed flight crew member then escorts the team to a capsule – the X-2 Space Shuttle.

## Flight and Landing

The team members board the X-2 training capsule and are securely strapped in, with individual "windows" just inches away. The countdown begins and then there is a pulse-racing liftoff: the roar of engines, the clouds of exhaust, and the motion of the capsule all combine to generate sensations in the participants similar to those that astronauts feel during actual liftoff.

The cabin's windows are actually state-of-the-art video flat screens that use a combination of LCD glass and electronic video cards to present an ultra-sharp full-motion video based on actual data taken from Mars-orbiting

### Top Tips

- This is the first ride created with Disney's FastPass+ system in mind. A FastPass+ reservation is a must for this ride, as it is arguably the most popular in the park.
- Read all the warning signs at the entrance to Mission: SPACE® and take the ride only if you are sure you'll be able to handle it.
- You will be given a choice of experiences: Orange, with centrifugal spinning (known to induce nausea), or Green, the tamer, non-spinning version.
- The ride has a minimum guest height requirement of 3 ft 8 in (1.1 m).
- The entire Mission: SPACE® experience, from pre-show to the Advance Training Lab, can last from 45 minutes to more than an hour. The ride to Mars lasts approximately four minutes from capsule door closing to it reopening.

satellites. The spectacular views of planets Earth and Mars that participants glimpse through the capsule windows, reinforce their illusion of traveling through space.

The members of the space team must work in unison, performing the roles of pilot, commander, navigator, and engineer in order to successfully face challenges and accomplish their mission to Mars. Throughout the flight, crew members receive instructions from Capcom regarding their duties, which consists of pressing buttons; the capsule obeys the commands very convincingly. Unexpected twists and turns keep participants on the edge of their seats, and call for tricky maneuvers with joysticks. Apart from the exhilarating "slingshot" around the moon, other thrills include a brief experience of "weightlessness" and dodging asteroids on the way to Mars.

The four-minute ride comes to a crashing finale with the Mars landing, complemented by superb sound effects that are achieved by the use of a stereo woofer built right into the back of the space capsules. Pioneering astronauts such as Buzz Aldrin and Rhea Seddon have taken their turn on the ride, comparing it favorably to actual space travel.

The G-forces that come into play during Mission: SPACE® are, in fact, of lower intensity than in a typical roller coaster but they are of much greater duration.

## Advance Training Lab

After the ride, guests can visit the Advance Training Lab, a colorful interactive play area where they can test their skills in space-related games for people of all ages. Guests can explore this area even if they choose not to go on the ride itself. There is no minimum height requirement here.

In **Space Race**, two teams are involved in a race to be the first to complete a successful

### VISITORS' CHECKLIST

**Practical Information**
Future World, between Test Track & Wonders of Life. **Tel** (407) 934-7639. **Open** 9am–9pm daily.

mission from Mars back to Earth. The teams are composed of up to 60 guests, who are required to work together to overcome numerous challenges and setbacks in their mission. **Expedition: Mars** is another fun endeavor at the Advance Traning Lab. In this sophisticated video game, the player's mission is to locate four astronauts stranded on Mars. **Space Base** is targeted at junior astronauts. It is an excellent interactive play area where children can climb, slide, crawl, explore, and get rid of excess energy. Visitors can also send **Postcards from Space** at a kiosk in the Advanced Training Lab. Here, guests make a video of themselves in one of several space-related backdrops to create a fine memento of their Mission: SPACE® experience, and can email the result to friends and family.

Beyond the Advance Training Lab is the **Mission: SPACE® Cargo Bay**, a shopping area spreading across 1,500 sq ft (139 sq m). A 4 ft (1.2 m) high 3-D figure of Mickey Mouse dressed as an astronaut greets visitors, and the area is dominated by a 12 ft (3.6 m) mural depicting various Disney characters in space gear on the surface of Mars. Here, a large variety of souvenirs can be purchased, from inexpensive to costly, as a remembrance of a "space experience."

### Caution

This ride is not for everyone, and is certainly not for anyone prone to motion sickness, or sensitive to tight spaces, loud noises, or spinning. Younger children may find it too intense, and expectant mothers and people with high blood pressure or heart problems would be well advised to forgo it. Remember: there is no backing out after liftoff.

## Epcot® Continued

### The Seas with Nemo & Friends®

The technology behind this attraction is quite stunning in its own right, but most people come here to visit Sea Base Alpha, Epcot®'s most ambitious research project. A pre-show presentation prepares you for your journey to the bottom of the ocean, after which you take the "clamobiles" to ride through a stunning coral reef setting. Picking up where the motion picture left off, familiar characters like Dory, Bruce, Marlin, and Squirt inhabit a huge aquarium containing more than 65 species of marine life. **Turtle Talk with Crush** is a breakthrough experience into real-time animation with many interactive components.

Visitors can take several behind-the-scenes tours of the saltwater tank at The Seas. Dolphins in Depth gives visitors an opportunity to see the dolphin trainers and feeders at work. It culminates in an up-close encounter with one of several dolphins in the giant aquarium. Other tours include Epcot DiveQuest, which takes guests underwater to see some of the aquarium's 6,000 sea creatures, including sea turtles, angelfish, eagle rays, and sharks, and the Seas Aqua Tour, that allows guests to snorkel on the surface.

### Test Track®

One of the most popular rides in Epcot®, long lines form quickly at park opening time and increase rapidly. Test Track® uses the most sophisticated ride vehicle technology available placing guests in a simulator that moves on tracks at high speed. Essentially, you are the passengers in a six seater prototype sports car being tested prior to going into production. Although the ride puts you through brake tests, hill climbs, sharp turns, near crashes, and paint spraying bays, the climax is the outside lap of the ride where the vehicle exceeds 66 mph on a raised roadway around the outside of the Test Track® building. So advanced is the technology that the ride is kept running 24 hours a day, because the start up procedure is so lengthy. However, the system has frequent stops – usually because the advanced safety systems have cut in and halted the entire run. While this is obviously reassuring in some ways, the lines outside continue to grow until, by the evening, you can expect a wait of between 90 minutes and two hours for this 4 minute ride. The ride itself, however, is so good you will want to ride it again and again. FastPass+ reservations for the day are usually fully reserved by lunchtime.

### Top Tips

- Test Track is exceptionally popular but unreliable. To avoid the long lines, try to ride this first. On leaving, take a FastPass+ ticket for another ride later.
- If a breakdown occurs during your ride, after disembarking ask the cast member if you can ride again, immediately.
- Because Test Track runs continuously – even when the park is closed – you can jump back on it for a repeat ride in the last minutes before park closing.
- The Land is an agriculturist's dream pavilion. However, there's plenty for kids to see here, including giant tomatoes and squashes, Mickey-shaped pumpkins, massive lemons, and produce that is grown with no soil, and served in the adjacent restaurants. It also features the thrill ride Soarin', which takes you on a breathtaking trip around the world, and will appeal to all but the very young.
- A better bet for them is The Seas with Nemo & Friends, featuring characters from Finding Nemo, along with more than 6,000 sea creatures in the aquarium.

### The Imagination! Pavilion

The Imaginaton! Pavilion houses the Journey into Your Imagination with Figment ride, and the Imageworks Lab. The pavilion is air-conditioned, offering a cool respite from the heat.

**Phineas and Ferb: Agent P's World Showcase Adventure** is an interactive game, based on the animated Disney series, that sends visitors around World Showcase seeking clues in each of the world pavilions to help thwart Doofenshmirtz's evil plot. The **Journey into Imagination with Figment** ride is a very upbeat and light-hearted trip in search of ideas in the arts and sciences.

The **ImageworksLab** is an interactive playground of audio-visual sensory games and demonstrations.

### Celebration Florida

Materializing out of former swampland adjacent to Walt Disney World®, Celebration is a new town with old values. Inspired partly by the romantic streets of Charleston in South Carolina, Disney attempts to re-create the wholesome small-town atmosphere that many middle-aged Americans remember and miss. The residents experience a cookie-jar world of friendly neighbors and corner grocery stores.

People began moving here in 1996, the first of an expected total of 20,000 inhabitants. Now, more than 8,000 residents enjoy the pedestrian-friendly streets, the nostalgic architecture (designed by some respected architects), and the hospital that treats both "wellness" and illness. The residents are not daunted by Celebration's strict rules, which set out, for example, that visible curtains must be white or off-white, and that streetside shrubbery must be approved by Disney. In some ways, however, Celebration is like any other town: the public is free to visit and look around.

*For hotels and restaurants in this area see pp317–18 and pp336–9*

## The Land

Ecology and conservation form the main themes and permeate the three attractions housed around the fast food restaurant. These are consequently much busier during lunchtimes. Lion King characters lead **The Circle of Life**, a hymn to conservation expressed through movie and animation, while **Living with the Land** is a cruise through the past, present, and future of US farming, showing off Disney's famed hydroponic gardens, which supply onsite restaurants with fresh produce. However, the greatest attraction here has to be the thrill ride **Soarin'®**, where passengers are lifted off the ground in a simulated hang glider to experience the wonders of the world from above, including Australia's Sydney Harbour, the Great Wall of China, and the spectacular waterfalls of South America.

## One Day Itinerary

1 Arrive 1 hour 40 minutes before the official opening time on an early entry day, or an hour before on a normal day.

2 If you reserve your FastPass+ entries before your vacation, you are set. Otherwise, head directly to the nearest FastPass+ kiosk and reserve entry times for **Test Track®** and **Mission: SPACE®**. Head across **Future World** or **Imageworks**.

3 Leave and head back toward the entrance and ride **Spaceship Earth**.

4 From there, head to **The Land Pavilion** and collect FastPass+ tickets for **Soarin'®**.

5 Head to **Disney & Pixar Short Film Festival**.

6 Head towards **World Showcase**.

7 Head to the left around the lagoon and visit **Mexico**. Ride **Gran Fiesta Tour**.

8 Continue to the left around the lagoon and go to **Norway**. Ride **Frozen Ever After**.

9 Time to eat, then visit **China** (movie), **France** (movie), and **Canada** (movie).

10 Return to **Future World** and visit **The Land Pavilion**. Experience the attractions there.

11 Leave the Land Pavilion to the left and head for **The Seas with Nemo & Friends®**. Experience both attractions there.

12 Exit Living Seas to the right, pass through both **Innoventions East** and **West**.

It is now a good time to head back to your hotel and return by 7pm to reserve a good spot to see **IllumiNations**.

## Rides and Shows Checklist

This chart is designed to help you plan what to visit at Epcot®. The rides and shows are listed in no particular order within Future World and World Showcase.

| | | WAITING TIME | HEIGHT / AGE RESTRICTION | BUSIEST TIME TO RIDE | FASTPASS | MAY CAUSE MOTION SICKNESS | OVERALL RATING |
|---|---|---|---|---|---|---|---|
| **FUTURE WORLD** | | | | | | | |
| S | The Circle of Life | ○ | | noon–2pm | | | ▼ |
| R | Soarin'® | ● | 1.02m | All day | ➡ | ✔ | ★ |
| S | Living with the Land | ● | | noon–2pm | | | ◆ |
| R | Mission: Space® | ● | 1.3m | 9am–5pm | ➡ | ✔ | ◆ |
| R | Spaceship Earth | ◗ | | 9am–noon | | | ★ |
| R | Test Track® | ● | 1.1m | All day | ➡ | ✔ | ★ |
| S | The Seas with Nemo & Friends® / Turtle Talk with Crush | ○ | | 11am–3pm | | | ◆ |
| S | Phineas and Ferb: Agent P's World Showcase Adventure | ○ | | | | | ▼ |
| S | Journey into Imagination with Figment | ◗ | | | | | ▼ |
| | **WORLD SHOWCASE** | | | | | | |
| R | Gran Fiesta Tour | ○ | | noon–3pm | | | ▼ |
| S | Impressions De France | ○ | | | | | ▼ |
| R | Frozen Ever After | ● | | 11am–5pm | | | ◆ |
| S | The American Adventure | ○ | | | | | ◆ |
| S | O Canada | ○ | | | | | ◆ |
| S | Reflections of China | ○ | | | | | ★ |
| S | Japan Drummers | | | | | | ▼ |
| S | Germany Biergarten Oompah Band | | | | | | ▼ |

**Key:** Ride – R Show – S; Waiting Times Good – ○ Average – ◗ Bad – ●;
Overall Rating Good – ▼ Excellent – ◆ Outstanding – ★

## World Showcase

The temples, churches, town halls, and castles of these 11 pavilions or countries are sometimes replicas of genuine buildings, sometimes merely in vernacular style. But World Showcase is much more than just a series of architectural set pieces. Every pavilion is staffed by people from the country it represents, selling high-quality local products as well as surprisingly good ethnic cuisine.

At set times (which are given on the guidemap) native performers stage live shows in the forecourts of each country: the best are the excellent acrobats at China and drummers at Japan. Only a couple of pavilions include rides, while a number have stunning giant-screen introductions to their country's history, culture, and landscapes. A few even have art galleries, though these often go unnoticed.

There are ferries across World Showcase Lagoon, linking Canada to Morocco and Mexico to Germany, but it is also relatively quick and easy to get around World Showcase on foot.

 **Mexico**
A Mayan pyramid hides the most remarkable interior at World Showcase. Stalls selling sombreros, ponchos, and papier-mâché animals (*piñatas*), and musicians fill a plaza bathed in a purple twilight. The backdrop to this is a rumbling volcano. The **Gran Fiesta Tour** boat ride tells the story of the Three Caballeros, passing through Audio-Animatronics and cinematic scenes of Mexico past and present, while the two restaurants on the lagoon side of the pavilion offer the best viewing spot for IllumiNations later on.

 **Norway**
The architecture here includes replicas of a stave church (a medieval wooden church) and Akershus Castle (a 14th-century fortress above Oslo harbor), arranged attractively around a cobblestone square.

You can buy trolls and sweaters and other native crafts, but the essential element here is **Frozen Ever After**. Based on the animated film *Frozen*, and its popular princesses Anna and Elsa, parts of the Norway Pavilion have been transformed into the Kingdom of Arendelle. Guests can participate in the Winter in Summer Celebration.

 **China**
In this pavilion the *pièce de résistance* is the half-size replica of Beijing's well-known landmark, the Temple of Heaven. The peaceful scene here contrasts with the more rowdy atmosphere in some of the nearby pavilions.

For entertainment, there is **Reflections of China**, a Circle-Vision movie (shown on nine screens all around the audience simultaneously), which makes the most of the country's fabulous, little-seen ancient sites and scenery. Note that visitors must stand throughout the movie. The pavilion's extensive shopping emporium sells everything from Chinese lanterns and painted screens to tea bags.

 **Germany**
A mixture of gabled and spired buildings are gathered around a central square, St. Georgsplatz. They are based on real buildings from all over Germany, including a merchants' hall in Freiburg and a Rhine castle. Visitors with small children should try to time a visit so that it coincides with the hourly chime of the glockenspiel in the square.

An accordionist sometimes plays, and the shops are full of quirky or clever gifts such as beautifully crafted wooden dolls. However, you really need to dine here to experience the full flavor of Germany.

 **Italy**
The bulk of Italy's relatively small pavilion represents Venice: from gondolas moored alongside candycane poles in the lagoon, to the tremendous versions of the towering redbrick campanile and the 14th-century Doge's Palace of St. Mark's Square – even the fake marble looks authentic. The courtyard buildings behind are Veronese and Florentine in style, and the Neptune statue is a copy of a Bernini work.

The architecture is the big attraction, but visitors should also stop off to eat in one of the restaurants or browse around the shops where pasta, amaretti, and wine are available to buy.

 **The American Adventure**
The American pavilion is the centerpiece of World Showcase, but it lacks the charm found in most of the other countries. However, Americans usually find **The American Adventure** show, which takes place inside the vast Georgian-style building, very moving. For others it will provide an interesting insight into the American psyche. The show is an

---

## World Showcase: Behind the Scenes

If you wouldd like more than just a superficial view of Walt Disney World®, its behind-the-scenes tours may appeal. In Future World, a four-hour walking tour – the UnDISCOVERed Future World – shows you Walt Disney's original concepts for Epcot®, and takes you beneath the Test Track® to watch the cars pass directly overhead. It also goes backstage at IllumiNations to see the secrets of the fireworks show. The tour costs about $64 per person. If you have $249 and seven hours to spare, you might want to sign up for the Backstage Magic tour, which includes all three theme parks. One of the highlights is the visit to the famous tunnel network beneath the Magic Kingdom®. For information on all Disney tours call (407) 939-8687.

---

*For hotels and restaurants in this area see pp317–18 and pp336–9*

openly patriotic yet thought-provoking romp through the history of the United States up to the present day. It incorporates tableaus on screen and some excellent Audio-Animatronics® figures, particularly of the author Mark Twain and the great 18th-century statesman, Benjamin Franklin.

 **Japan**
This restrained, formal place has a traditional Japanese garden, a Samurai castle, and a pagoda where musicians play huge ceremonial drums several times a day. It is modeled on a 7th-century temple in Nara whose five levels represent earth, water, fire, wind, and sky.

The Mitsukoshi department store, a copy of the Imperial Palace's ceremonial hall in Kyoto, offers kimonos, bonsai trees, wind chimes, and the chance to pick a pearl from an oyster. Japan really comes to life in its restaurants.

 **Morocco**
Morocco's appeal lies in its enameled tiles, its keyhole-shaped doors, its ruddy fortress walls, and the twisting alleys of its *medina* (old city), which is reached via a reproduction of a gate into the city of Fez.

Morocco offers some of the best handmade crafts in World Showcase. The alleys of the old city leads visitors to a bustling market of little stores selling carpets, brassware, leather-ware, and shawls, with belly dancing and couscous in the Restaurant Marrakesh, and Mediterranean cuisine in Spice Road Table on the lagoon.

**France**
A Gallic flair infuses everything in the France pavilion from its architecture (including a one-tenth scale replica of the Eiffel Tower, Parisian Belle Epoque mansions, and a rustic village main street), to its upscale stores (perfume, wine, and berets). French food can be sampled in a couple of restaurants and a patis-serie selling croissants and cakes.

A movie titled **Impressions de France** is the main enter-tainment. The movie, shown on

## Eating and Drinking

 Dining well is fundamental to visiting Epcot® and particularly World Showcase. Some of the latter's pavilions have decent fast-food places, but the best restaurants (including those listed below unless otherwise stated) require reservations. Call (407) 939-3463 as soon as you know when you will be at Epcot®. Reserve early in the day. Most restaurants serve lunch and dinner; try unpopular hours such as 11am or 4pm if other times are unavailable. Lunch is usually about two-thirds of the price of dinner, and children's menus are available at even the most upscale restaurants.

Recommended in World Showcase are:
**Mexico:** La Hacienda de San Angel offers Mexican cuisine with a view of the lagoon and the fireworks. The San Angel Inn restaurant, inside the marketplace, offers views of the pyramid and the boat ride.
**Norway:** Restaurant Akershus offers a good-value *koldtbord* (buffet) of Norwegian dishes in a castle setting.
**Germany:** the Biergarten has a beer hall atmosphere, with a cheap and plentiful buffet and hearty oompah-pah music.
**Italy:** L'Originale Alfredo di Roma Ristorante is enormously popular and engagingly chaotic, with sophisticated dishes.
**Japan:** you can eat communally, either in the Teppan Yaki Dining Rooms around a grilling, stir-frying chef, or at the bar of Tempura Kiku for sushi and tempura (no reservations).
**France:** there are three top-notch restaurants here: the upscale Monsieur Paul (dinner only); Les Chefs de France, a family-friendly bistro with *haute cuisine* by acclaimed French chefs; and the Les Halles Boulangerie & Patisserie, which serves exquisite baked goods. It is the perfect spot for an early breakfast.
**Canada:** Le Cellier Steakhouse is excellent. Advance reservations are required.

Spring and Fall bring two wildly popular festivals to Epcot®: **Spring's International Flower & Garden Festival**: features the skills of the Disney horticulture team, plus tasty bites and drinks. **International Food & Wine Festival**: offers food and beverage tasting stations, along with seminars by celebrity chefs and authors.

five adjacent screens and set to the sounds of French classical music, offers a whirlwind tour through the country's most beautiful regions.

 **United Kingdom**
The Rose and Crown Pub is the focal point in this pavilion. It serves traditional English fare such as Cornish pasties, fish and chips, and even draft bitter – chilled to suit American tastes. Pleasant gardens surround the pub, as well as a medley of buildings of various historic architectural styles. These include a castle based on Hamp-ton Court, an imitation Regency terrace, and a thatched cottage.

There is not much to do here in this pavilion other than browse around the shops, which sell everything from quality tea and china to sweaters, tartan ties, teddy bears, and toy soldiers. The

terrace in the Rose and Crown, however, offers good views of IllumiNations.

 **Canada**
A log cabin, 30 ft (9 m) high totem poles, a replica of Ottawa's Victorian-style Château Laurier Hotel, a rocky chasm, and ornamental gardens make up the large but rather staid Canadian pavilion.

The country in all its diversity, and particularly its grand scenery, comes to life much better in the Circle-Vision movie **O Canada!** (though China's Circle-Vision movie is even better). The audience stands in the middle of the theater and turns around to follow the movie as it unfolds on no fewer than nine screens.

Shops at Canada sell a range of First Nation and Inuit crafts, as well as various edible special-ties, including wine.

Facade of the Tower of Terror at Hollywood Studios ▶

# Disney's Hollywood Studios®

Disney's Hollywood Studios® was launched in 1989 as a working movie and TV production facility. In 2004, however, the animation department was shut down and the production facility was almost completely abandoned. Regardless, the park remains a famed tourist destination, with top-notch shows and rides based on Disney and Metro-Goldwyn-Mayer movies and TV shows, offering a tribute to Hollywood. Popular rides like the Tower of Terror and The Star Tours®, and shows such as "Fantasmic!" and "Voyage of The Little Mermaid" have taken the park's popularity to new heights, and its educational yet highly entertaining interactive experiences are geared toward adults and teenagers.

The Star Tours® – The Adventure Continues at Disney's Hollywood Studios®

## Tackling the Park

This park is not laid out in the same way as the other theme parks, although Hollywood Boulevard acts as a sort of "Main Street USA" with the purpose of funneling guests toward the attractions. During the past few years, Disney has expanded the breadth and scope of the attractions here, building some of the finest in Orlando. The entertainment schedule changes frequently and streets can be closed off during the visit of a celebrity, or for a live filming session. Although most of this happens in winter, it is a good idea to find out times, locations, and events as soon as you enter the park from Guest Services, on the left of the main entrance.

As with the other theme parks, arriving early is the key to avoid waiting a long time in line. It is also worth bearing in mind that some attractions are particularly intense and can frighten young children.

At about 3:30pm, there is an afternoon parade. The open plan of the park means that guests may become hot while waiting for the parade, which is always based on one of the recent animated movies from Disney.

At night, **Fantasmic!** takes place. This superb event is held once a night during the slow season and twice during peak periods. Seating 10,000 people at a time, you will need to turn up at least two hours before, however, to get a good seat!

## Hollywood Boulevard

Delightful Art Deco styled buildings vie with a replica of Grauman's Chinese Theater to present an image of Hollywood that never was. It is here that your picture will be taken and where you might well see some of the cast members acting as reporters or police, chasing celebrities. More importantly, it is on the Boulevard that the cast members will try to direct you to the Indiana Jones™ Epic Stunt Spectacular – a live action show using many of the stunts from the Indiana Jones movies. However, the top attractions are based in the opposite direction.

Halfway up the boulevard, Sunset Boulevard breaks to the right, leading to the two most popular rides in the Park, The Twilight Zone Tower of Terror™ and the Rock 'n' Roller Coaster® Starring Aerosmith.

At the junction between Hollywood and Sunset Boulevard lies one of the ubiquitous pin stations where budding traders can ambush cast members and swap badges. At the top of Hollywood Boulevard lies the Central Plaza, dominated by the replica of Grauman's Chinese Theater, where you can experience **The Great Movie Ride®**. This is one of the few attractions where the lining up is almost as good as the ride itself. Here, huge ride vehicles carrying 60 guests apiece track silently past the largest movie sets ever built for a Disney ride. As always, the most realistic sets imaginable are combined with real live action sequences to make this an enjoyable, though sometimes scary for children, ride which ends on a very upbeat and optimistic note.

## Sunset Boulevard

Like Hollywood Boulevard, Sunset Boulevard is a rose-tinted evocation of the famous Hollywood street in the 1940s. Theaters and storefronts (some real, some fake) have been re-created with characteristic

### Top Tips

- The most popular rides here are the Twilight Zone Tower of Terror™ and the Rock 'n' Roller Coaster® so visit these early to avoid the lines.
- If you are too young, too short, or simply not a roller coaster fan, it is possible for your whole group to go through the beginning of the Rock 'n' Roller Coaster® ride, and break off just before boarding the limo. Child swapping is also possible. Ask a cast member for help.
- In the boiler room of the Twilight Zone Tower of Terror™, take any open gateway to the lifts – do not worry if others are not. You will get a better seat and a better view.

attention to detail, and the street is dominated at one end by the Hollywood Tower Hotel. This lightning-ravaged, decrepit Hotel is the spot for Orlando's scariest ride – **The Twilight Zone Tower of Terror**™ – in which you are strapped into the service elevator for a voyage inspired by the 1950s TV show *The Twilight Zone*. The pre-show area is a library into which you are ushered by a melancholic bell hop. From here you enter what appears to be the boiler room of the hotel and you walk through to the lifts – apparently freight elevators fitted with plank seats. The elevator doors sometimes open to allow glimpses of ghostly corridors, but it is hard to concentrate on anything other than the ghastly 13-story

plunge that everyone knows will come – but not exactly when. When you arrive on the 13th floor the elevator actually trundles horizontally across the hotel. Once you are in the drop shaft you get dropped no fewer than seven times.

This is a masterpiece of ride technology and imagination. The original single drop has been expanded to seven and, during the first drop, enormously powerful engines actually pull you down faster than free fall.

You can also enjoy the fleeting view of the whole park and indeed outside the park (a break with Disney tradition), before you begin the terrifying descent. This ride is not to everyone's taste, but die-hard enthusiasts and novices alike pack this ride from the outset.

A triumph of noise over everything else, the **Rock 'n' Roller Coaster® Starring Aerosmith** accelerates you to nearly 60mph in 2.8 seconds in the dark, and pulls 5G in the first corkscrew, of which there are several. The pre-show, a rather lame affair, links a recording session of the band Aerosmith to the ride. From

here you line up at two doors. If you prefer the front seats, you can reach these via the lower ramp. Replete with loops, corkscrews and steep drops, the Rock 'n' Roller Coaster® also employs a fully synchronized and very loud soundtrack as it hurls you toward the neon-lit equivalent of oblivion.

Sunset Boulevard houses the entrance to the **Theater of the Stars**, which shows a live stage show at indicated times and combines live action with animation and a great musical score. **The Music of Pixar Live!**, featuring the animated antics of popular Pixar characters such as Buzz Lightyear and Woody, alternates with *Beauty and the Beast Live on Stage*. Sunset Boulevard is also where you will find the entrance to the **Fantasmic!** show.

### Fantasmic!

This evening show tends to exhaust superlatives. It is, quite simply, the finest event of its kind in Florida. Combining music, lasers, fan fountain projection, animation, and a cast of more than a hundred actors and dancers, Fantasmic! manages to choreograph the entire event with split second accuracy to music, fireworks, and lighting. Set on an island in a lagoon, the story concerns the ongoing battle between good and evil. Illuminated boats, flying floats, and a lake which bursts into flames are but some features of this enchanting event which plays to audiences of 10,000 per showing.

To ensure a good seat you will have to be there at least two hours before it starts (alternatively, some restaurants offer a dinner package which includes reserved seating). Even in the quietest time of the off peak season, all 10,000 places are taken, up to 30 minutes before the show starts. However, this truly is one event you will never forgive yourself for missing.

The Rock 'n' Roller Coaster® Starring Aerosmith, Sunset Boulevard

## Animation Courtyard

The original idea behind Animation Courtyard was not just to give visitors an inside look into the history and process of animation, but also a glimpse at all forthcoming Disney animated movies as they were being made. With the expansion of the **Star Wars** franchise into the park, guests are seeing more of their favorite characters around the area. BB-8, the rolling robot of *Star Wars: The Force Awakens*, welcomes guests to the Star Wars Launch Bay, which contains artifacts and props from the films.

Muppet* Vision 3-D, an action-packed movie

The **Voyage of The Little Mermaid** show is enacted by cartoon, live, and Audio-Animatronic® characters. Lasers and water effects are used to create the feel of an underwater grotto. The show remains one of the most popular in the park, appealing to all ages, but young children sometimes find the lightning storm scary. **Disney Junior – Live on Stage!** is also aimed at youngsters and features singing and dancing Disney Junior characters.

## Mickey Avenue

Mickey Avenue is a great place to look out for Mickey Mouse who may be signing autographs.

Nearby is **Walt Disney Presents** (formerly called "One Man's Dream"), which tells the story of how the Disney brand came into being. This could be dismissed as propaganda, but it is difficult not to admire Walt's great vision and risk-taking. He would probably be shocked at the size of the company these days, having humbly said: "I only hope that we don't lose sight of one thing – that it was all started by a mouse."

Just off Mickey Avenue is **Pixar Place**, home to Toy Story Land, where Slinky Dog Dash takes riders on a roller coaster ride, and Alien Swirling Saucers put riders inside a toy playset from Pizza Planet. **Toy Story Mania!**®, is a 4-D interactive ride that transports youngsters into the film's toy box aboard a carnival ride tram. A variety of games are hosted by favourite Toy Story characters. Five shooting games, let them deploy weapons such as hardboiled eggs, baseballs, rings, and suction darts. The ride has proven so popular that it is on the FastPass+ list, and was extensively expanded in 2016.

The interactive 4D attraction at Toy Story Mania!

## Echo Lake

The interest here focuses on two shows and one thrill ride, Star Tours.

### Eating and Drinking

It is definitely worth going to the trouble of making a reservation at three of the full-service restaurants at Disney's Hollywood Studios®, though more for their atmosphere than for their food. You can reserve a table by calling (407) 939-3463/WDW-DINE, or by going directly to the Dining Reservation Booth, at the crossroads of Hollywood and Sunset boulevards, or to the restaurants themselves.

The civilized, costly Hollywood Brown Derby replicates the Original Brown Derby in Hollywood where the stars met in the 1930s, right down to the celebrities' caricatures on the walls and the house specialties of Cobb Salad and grapefruit cake. Children usually prefer the Sci-Fi Dine-In Theater Restaurant, a 1950s drive-in where customers sit in mini-Cadillacs under a starry sky to watch old science-fiction movies, while munching on popcorn and burgers. In the 1950's Prime Time Café you are served by maternal waitresses in 1950s kitchens with the TV tuned to period sitcoms; the food, such as meatloaf and pot roast, is homey.

The best place to eat without a reservation is the self-service Art Deco-themed cafeteria Hollywood & Vine, where you can choose from a varied buffet that includes pasta, salads, seafood, ribs, and steaks.

*For hotels and restaurants in this region see pp317–18 and pp336–9*

The area to the left of Echo Lake offers a taste of the Star Wars inspired land, Star Wars: Galaxy's Edge that will open in 2019. A short film, *Star Wars: Path of the Jedi* compiles the movies to retell the epic saga of the Jedi Order. Just beyond is Star Tours®.

The storyline of the sensational ride **Star Tours®** is based on the *Star Wars* movies. The spaceship, a flight simulator similar to those used to train astronauts, takes a wrong turn and has to evade meteors and cope in an inter-galactic battle. What spectators see on screen seems unbelievably real since the craft jolts in synchronicity with the action.

The large-scale show **Indiana Jones™ Epic Stunt Spectacular!** re-creates well-known scenes from the Indiana Jones movies to deliver plenty of big bangs and daredevil feats to thrill the audience. Death-defying stunt-men leap between buildings as they avoid sniper fire and sudden explosions. As an educational sideline, the stunt director and real stunt doubles

demonstrate how some of the action sequences are realized. Arrive early if you want to take part as an extra in the show.

The area formerly known as Streets of America has been permanently closed. The only remnant of the area is the Muppet Courtyard. In **Muppet\* Vision 3-D**, a highly enjoyable, slapstick 3-D movie (starring the Muppets), trombones, cars, and rocks launch themselves out of the screen at spectators; they are so realistic that children often grasp the air expecting to touch them.

## Shopping

Most of the best shops are on Hollywood Boulevard, which stays open half an hour after the rest of the theme park has closed. Mickey's of Hollywood is the big emporium for general Disney merchandise. Celebrity 5 & 10 has a range of affordable movie souvenirs, such as clapper boards and Oscars®, as well as books and posters. Much pricier is Sid Cahuenga's One-Of-A-Kind, where you can buy rare movie and TV memorabilia such as genuine autographed photos (of Boris Karloff and Greta Garbo, for example), or famous actors' clothes. Limited-edition "cels" in Animation Gallery in Animation Courtyard will make an even bigger dent in your wallet; the same shop sells good Disney posters and books, too.

Truck on fire at the Indiana Jones™ Epic Stunt Spectacular!

## Rides, Shows, and Tours Checklist

This chart is designed to help you to plan what to visit at Disney's Hollywood Studios®. The rides, shows, and tours are listed in no particular order within each area.

| | | WAITING TIME | HEIGHT/AGE RESTRICTION | BUSIEST TIME TO RIDE/ATTEND | FASTPASS | MAY CAUSE MOTION SICKNESS | RATING OVERALL |
|---|---|---|---|---|---|---|---|
| **SUNSET BOULEVARD** | | | | | | | |
| S | Fantasmic! | ● | | Any | | | ◆ |
| R | Rock 'n' Roller Coaster® Starring Aerosmith | ● | 1.2m | ➤11 | ➡ | ✔ | ◆ |
| R | Twilight Zone Tower of Terror™ | ● | 1.1m | ➤11 | ➡ | ✔ | ★ |
| **ANIMATION COURTYARD** | | | | | | | |
| S | Disney Junior – Live on Stage! | ◗ | | Any | | | ▼ |
| S | Voyage of the Little Mermaid | ● | | Any | ➡ | | ◆ |
| S | Star Wars Launch Bay | ◗ | | Any | | | ▼ |
| **PIXAR PLACE** | | | | | | | |
| T | Toy Story Mania!® | ◗ | | Any | ➡ | | ★ |
| T | Walt Disney Presents | ◗ | | Any | | | ▼ |
| **ECHO LAKE** | | | | | | | |
| S | Indiana Jones™ Epic Stunt Spectacular! | ● | | Any | | | ◆ |
| R | Star Tours® | ◗ | 1.1m | ➤11 | ➡ | ✔ | ★ |
| S | Muppet\* Vision 3-D | ● | | Any | | | ★ |

Key: Ride – R Show – S Tour – T; Waiting Times Good – ○ Average – ◗ Bad – ●; Overall Rating Good – ▼ Excellent – ◆ Outstanding – ★; Time to Ride Anytime – Any Before 11am – ➤11

# Disney's Animal Kingdom®

The largest of the theme parks, Disney's Animal Kingdom® is five times the size of the Magic Kingdom®. It is rather unique in that it is home to more than 1,700 animals of 250 species, and consequently every visit is likely to be different. The park is loosely based on the real, the mythical, the extinct, and the alien, and some areas are accessible only on a safari-type tour.

## Tackling the Park

The park is divided into seven lands: The Oasis, Discovery Island®, Dinoland USA®, Pandora – The World of Avatar, Africa, Asia, and Rafiki's Planet Watch®. Navigation within the park is also quite different from other parks. When visitors first pass through the turnstiles, they enter **The Oasis** – a foliage festooned area offering several routes to the park's central hub, Safari Village. The Oasis contains many little surprises, most of which are missed by visitors who race through to reach the attractions. Time spent waiting quietly at the various habitats will be well rewarded. For thrill seekers, the park offers few traditional thrills, however, the "rides" they do have are outstanding and become very crowded.

## Discovery Island

As visitors emerge into the open space of the village, the **Tree of Life®** looms – this is a massive, 14-story structure that is the signature landmark of the park. It holds sway over a pageant of brightly colored shop fronts and a multitude of pools and gardens, each

Re-creations of alien flora in Pandora – The World of Avatar

holding a variety of wildlife. The main shops, baby care, and first aid post all face the Tree of Life®.

Under its branches lie the bridges that cross to the other lands, and within the trunk itself is the **It's Tough to be a Bug®** show. This 3D theater presentation is really outstanding and not to be missed.

## Pandora – The World of Avatar

Disney's Imagineers bring to life the sights of Pandora (from James Cameron's movie *Avatar*). Opened in 2017, the mythical land features floating mountains, fantastical alien flora growing among real tropical plants, and the sights

and sounds of non-terrestrial wildlife. While the experience is beautiful during the day, it is magical after dark, when lit by the bioluminescence of Pandora's plants. One of the main attractions is **Avatar Flight of Passage**, a flight simulator-based ride designed to make visitors to feel as though they are flying on the winged banshees atop the floating mountains, down cliff faces to the sea, and through astonishingly detailed forests and caves. The Valley of Mo'ara features the **Na'vi River Journey**, a much gentler, but no less beautiful ride aboard a reed raft through the luminescent land.

## Africa

Entered through the village of Harambe, Africa is the largest of the lands. The architecture is closely modeled on a Kenyan village and conceals Disney cleanliness behind a façade of simple, run-down buildings and wobbly telegraph poles.

A very popular show, the **Festival of the Lion King** encourages cheering and singing like no other. The show is exceptionally well-choreographed and costumed, and is now housed in an air-conditioned auditorium – a welcome relief in summer.

The **Kilimanjaro Safaris®** is the park's busiest attraction, though it becomes quieter in the after-noon. Guests board open sided trucks driven into an astonishing replica of the East African land-scape. During this 20-minute drive over mud holes and creaking bridges guests have the oppor-tunity to see many African animals including hippos, rhinos, lions, and elephants, all roaming free and undisturbed. It is not unusual for a white rhino to roam close enough to sniff the truck! Affording an excellent opportunity to see gorillas close up, the

Animals roaming freely on the Kilimanjaro Safaris®

*For hotels and restaurants in this area see pp317–18 and pp336–9*

**Pangani Forest Exploration Trail®** leads visitors into a world of streams and waterfalls. It can get rather congested with guests exiting the Safaris. It is less busy in the late afternoon and guests can actually spend some time watching the animals. There are different vantage points to observe families of lowland gorillas foraging through trees and bushes. The pleasant Wildlife Express train ride takes you to **Rafiki's Planet Watch®**, featuring Conservation Station® and Habitat Habit, both educational programs, and Affection Section, a shaded petting yard.

## Asia

This land features gibbons, exotic birds, and tigers set in a re-creation of post-Colonial Indian ruins. **Kali River Rapids®** offers visitors a chance to get completely drenched. This short ride presents some of the most striking and detailed surroundings in the park, which may be missed as yet another wave saturates the parts still merely damp.

Tapirs, Komodo dragons, and giant fruit bats can be found on the **Maharaja Jungle Trek®**, the climax of which is undoubtedly the magnificent Bengal tigers roaming the palace ruins. Through glazed walled sections of the palace, visitors can get within arm's length of the tigers.

At the **Flights of Wonder** birds perform fascinating and complex maneuvers demonstrating the natural survival techniques used by the birds in the wild.

**Expedition Everest – Legend of the Forbidden Mountain™** takes passengers on a high-speed train adventure across the rugged terrain and icy slopes of the Himalayas.

## Dinoland USA®

This land gives visitors the chance to witness dinosaurs live and die. On the popular ride **DINOSAUR**, guests board a mobile motion simulator which bucks and weaves trying to ensnare and avoid carnivorous dinosaurs. This is a pretty wild ride, and mostly in the dark – best enjoyed by older children. For family entertainment try **Finding Nemo – The Musical** at the

Theater in the Wild, **Primeval Whirl®,** or TriceraTop Spin, a roller coaster with spinning cars. There is also **The Boneyard®**, where young children can dig for dinosaur bones.

### TOP 10 ATTRACTIONS

① **Avatar Flight of Passage®**

② **Na'Vi River Journey®**

③ **It's Tough to Be a Bug®**

④ **Kali River Rapids®**

⑤ **Dinosaur**

⑥ **Finding Nemo – the Musical**

⑦ **Flights of Wonder**

⑧ **Kilimanjaro Safaris®**

⑨ **Festival of the Lion King**

⑩ **Expedition Everest – Legend of the Forbidden Mountain™**

| Rides, Shows, and Tours Checklist — This chart is designed to help you plan what to visit at Animal Kingdom. The major rides, shows, and tours are listed in no particular order within each area. | WAITING TIME | HEIGHT/AGE RESTRICTION | BUSIEST TIME TO RIDE/ATTEND | FASTPASS | MAY CAUSE MOTION SICKNESS | OVERALL RATING |
|---|---|---|---|---|---|---|
| **PANDORA – THE WORLD OF AVATAR®** | | | | | | |
| R Avatar Flight of Passage® | ● | 44in | Any | ➡ | ✔ | ★ |
| R Na'vi River Journey® | ◗ | | Any | ➡ | | ★ |
| **DISCOVERY ISLAND®** | | | | | | |
| S It's Tough to Be a Bug® | ◯ | | Any | ➡ | | ◆ |
| **DINOLAND USA®** | | | | | | |
| R Dinosaur | ◗ | 3 ft 4 in | Any | ➡ | ✔ | ▼ |
| S Finding Nemo – the Musical | ◗ | | Any | | | ◆ |
| **AFRICA** | | | | | | |
| R Kilimanjaro Safaris® | ● | | Any | ➡ | ✔ | ★ |
| T Pangani Forest Exploration Trail® | ● | | Any | | | ◆ |
| S Festival of the Lion King | ◗ | | Any | | | ★ |
| **ASIA** | | | | | | |
| R Kali River Rapids® | ◗ | 3 ft 2 in | Any | ➡ | ✔ | ★ |
| S Flights of Wonder | ◗ | | Any | | | ★ |
| T Expedition Everest – Legend of the Forbidden Mountain™ | ● | 3 ft 8 in | ➤11 | ➡ | ✔ | ▼ |

**Key:** Ride – R Show – S Tour – T; Waiting Time Good – ◯ Average – ◗ Bad – ●; Time to Ride: Anytime – Any Before 11am –➤11; Overall Rating Good – ▼ Excellent – ◆ Outstanding – ★

# Water Parks

Walt Disney World® features two of the best water parks in the world, including the second-largest on record. A third water park, River Country – the first to be built in Walt Disney World® – is now closed. While playing second fiddle to the major theme parks of the resort, the water parks manage to attract huge numbers of visitors, particularly during the hot summer months.

Typhoon Lagoon bears only a pretense of a theme, a whimsical pirate/nautical motif that features everything from thrilling slides to winding rapids to gentle rivers. Apart from the chance to snorkel with real sharks and other fish, it is a regular water park, only Disney-fied. On the other hand, Disney's Blizzard Beach is a wonderful working "flooded ski resort" that throws visitors into a "failed" winter wonderland and substitutes flumes and slides for skis and toboggans. This truly clever idea keeps the area covered in "snow" but with pleasant warm water almost all year round.

Sliding down Mount Gushmore at Blizzard Beach

## Blizzard Beach

During a "freak" winter storm – or so legend has it – an entire section of the Disney property was buried under a pile of powdery snow. Disney Imagineers quickly set to work, building Florida's first ski resort, complete with ski lifts, toboggan runs, and a breathtaking ski slope. However, the snow started to melt quickly, and the Disney people thought all was lost until they spotted an alligator snow-boarding himself down the mountainside. In a flash, they reinvented the ski resort as a water/ski park, Blizzard Beach. They turned luge runs into slides and the mountain into the world's longest and highest flume, and created creeks for inner-tube enthusiasts to paddle around in.

The centerpiece of Blizzard Beach is the 120 ft (36 m) high **Summit Plummet**, which rockets particularly brave visitors at speeds of more than 60 mph (96 km/h). Incredibly popular with teenagers, it is slightly too intense for younger children – you must be at least 4 ft (1.2 m) tall to ride it. The Slusher Gusher and Toboggan Racer are similar, but less frightening, water slides. There's also the Snow Stormers flumes and Downhill Double Dipper racing slides, favorites with families. The Downhill Double Dipper pits two racers against each other in an inner-tube water-slide for big kids, teens, and adults. Race down the parallel flumes to the bottom of Mount Gushmore.

The thrills continue with the **Teamboat Springs** whitewater raft ride, a rollicking race through choppy waters that lasts far longer than expected but leaves you wanting more anyway. The Runoff Rapids is another speedy trip through harrowing water-ways, this time in an inner tube.

For those with a more relaxed agenda, there is the chair lift to carry passengers up the side of **Mount Gushmore**, where there is rock-climbing or hiking. Or you may choose to lazily float around the entire park by tubing down Cross Country Creek, or take a slide down the mild Cool Runners. The one-acre pool called Melt-Away Bay is no ordinary swimming hole, as it has waves big enough to ride, and a large, sandy beach with chairs for those who choose to relax and enjoy the sun.

Children's areas include the Blizzard Beach Ski Patrol Training Camp, aimed at older children, and Tike's Peak for the little ones, which has scaled down versions of the more intense attractions.

## Top Tips

- Blizzard Beach and Typhoon Lagoon have their own, free, parking lots; Winter Summerland shares the Blizzard Beach lot. You don't need to wait for Disney transportation if you've got a vehicle – you can drive to the water parks and park right there.

Swimmers head almost vertically down Summit Plummet

## Typhoon Lagoon

This water park offers less in the way of man-made thrills and more natural excitement, though it also features some traditional water park favorites. Where Blizzard Beach trades on its novelty, Typhoon Lagoon revels in natural beauty and sealife encounters, and boasts a surf pool that is the world's largest, at 650,000 cu ft (18,406 cu m). The park's motif is that of a shipwreck – the "Miss Tilly" which got caught in a storm so severe it landed on the peak of **Mount Mayday** – in a tropical paradise.

At the top of Mount Mayday, visitors will find three whitewater raft rides of varying intensity – the thrilling Gang Plank Falls, the incredibly high and wild Mayday Falls, or the relatively tame Keelhaul Falls.

Also on Mount Mayday are the body-slide rides known collectively as Humunga-Kowabunga. Great fun but highly intimidating, these rides involve falls of roughly 50 ft (15 m) at speeds of 30 mph (48 km/h). Visitors must be at least 4 ft (1.2 m) tall to ride these. The Storm Slides offer three flumes that go twisting and turning inside the mountain itself; these rides are less intense. Crush 'n' Gusher has torrents of gushing water taking the most daring of raft riders on a gravity-defying

The Wave Pool, with "Miss Tilly" in the backgound

adventure through twisting caverns. More relaxing is the powerful **Wave Pool** which offers 6 ft (1.8 m) high waves alternating with gentler periods. The other peaceful attraction in Typhoon Lagoon is the high-light of the park for adults – the meandering, relaxing, and stunningly beautiful **Castaway Creek**, where you can inner-tube your troubles away through waterfalls, grottoes and rain –

forests. Children can enjoy the aquatic playground, Ketchakiddee Creek, and the smaller wave pools. Of special note is the **Shark Reef**, which offers visitors the chance to either observe tropical fish and live, small sharks from the safety of a "overturned freighter", or to grab a snorkel and mask and go one-on-one with them. It's very safe and offers pleasant views of the colorful sealife.

Getting up close and personal with sealife at Shark Reef

## Winter Summerland

Although Fantasia Gardens, on Buena Vista Drive, was the first themed mini-golf park on Disney property, Winter Summerland is unique in that it continues the motifs of the neighboring water parks, Blizzard Beach and Typhoon Lagoon, but adds a Christmas twist, with two elaborately-designed 18-hole courses – the Winter and Summer courses. The two courses were supposedly built by St. Nick's elves, who were divided into two camps – those who missed the North Pole and those who preferred the Florida heat.

Both courses feature plenty of interactive elements, and are surprisingly challenging. Generally the most popular, the Winter Course is widely perceived as being slightly easier, with "snow" and holiday elements abounding. A few of the holes on each course are identical except for the substitution of snow for sand on the Summer holes. The Summer course features surfboards, water sprays, and other tropical obstacles, including a sand-buried snoozing Santa. The two courses converge for the final two holes in a log cabin-style lodge.

*For hotels and restaurants in this area see pp317–18 and pp336–9*

# Disney Cruise Line®

With a cruise line that offers four gorgeous, larger-than-average ships, private destinations, and an all-inclusive fare, Walt Disney World® has extended its reach to the high seas of the Caribbean, Mediterranean, Pacific, and Transatlantic cruises. In addition to the popular three- and four-night trips, there are extended itineraries available to passengers, which offer more island ports and longer duration cruises. Disney's Cruise Line® has a pair of powerful incentives no other cruise line can match: apart from its outstanding reputation for quality and comfort, it offers vacations that include stays at Walt Disney World® as part of the total package.

A Disney Cruise Line® ship docked at a pier

A Disney Cruise Line® ship at Castaway Cay

## The Ships and the Destination

The four Disney cruise ships, the **Disney Magic®**, the **Disney Wonder®**, the **Disney Dream®** and the **Disney Fantasy®** have staterooms that are around 25 per cent larger than those of most other cruise ships. The interiors reflect the stately elegance of European vessels of old, with an Art Deco theme for the Magic and Art Nouveau for the Wonder, and classic early 20th-century design for both

Dining in style at Palo restaurant aboard a Disney ship

the Dream® and the Fantasy®. All ships offer theater, restaurants, spas, and fitness centers among several other amenities.

**Castaway Cay**, Disney's own private island, is the end point of the Caribbean Disney cruise, and is very much a tropical extension of Walt Disney World®'s hotels and resorts. There are uncrowded beaches, snorkeling, bicycling, glass-bottom boat tours, watersports, and much more on offer. In addition, there is always plenty to do for children on board and off – so much so that you may see very little of them during your trip.

## The Short (Three–Four-night) Cruises

The itinerary on the shorter cruises is the same – after arriving at Port Canaveral by charter bus and checking in, passengers cast off and arrive in Nassau in the Bahamas the next day. The following day you arrive at Castaway Cay, and leave there in the evening to return to Canaveral at 9am the following morning. The four-night cruise adds a day at sea, with the occasional stop in Freeport before returning to Port Canaveral.

## The Long (Seven–Fourteen-night) Cruises

As well as Eastern Caribbean and Western Caribbean cruises, Disney offers European cruises. These take you to seven ports of call across Italy, France, Spain, Tunisia, Malta, and Corsica, or you can see the Northern European capitals on a 12-night cruise. There are also 14-night east and west-bound trans-atlantic journeys that begin or end in the Bahamas or the Mediterranean.

### Top Tips for Cruisers

- Bear in mind that the all-inclusive fare does not include things such as tips for servers, stateroom hostess, assistant server, and head server. Other additional charges are for soft drinks at the pool, and alcoholic beverages. There is a $10 per person charge for eating in the adults-only specialty restaurant. Shore excursions are also extra significant charges – port charges as well as government taxes are added to the fee.
- It is a good idea to plan ahead for shore excursions to avoid taking a chance and waiting in a line to sign up for them once on the ship. You can log on to the website (see p179) to sign up for shore excursions.

# Fort Wilderness Resort & Campground

A campground would seem to be at odds with the provide-every-luxury mentality of most Walt Disney World® accommodations but Fort Wilderness, which opened in 1971, still represents one of Walt Disney's aims – to foster an appreciation of nature and the outdoors. Located on Bay Lake in the Magic Kingdom® resort area, it has more than 750 shaded campsites and over 400 cabins to provide various levels of "roughing it." While wildlife is fairly sparse in this area, amenities and even entertainment are plentiful. The center of Fort Wilderness is Pioneer Hall, home to several restaurants and the hugely popular dinner show, Hoop-Dee-Doo Musical Revue *(see p177)*. There is convenient boat transportation to Magic Kingdom® and motorcoach transfers to all theme parks.

Riders enjoying a stroll at Fort Wilderness Resort & Campground

A caravan at Disney's Fort Wilderness Resort & Campground

## Accommodation and Community Areas

The campsites at Fort Wilderness are small but reasonably secluded, with electric and water "hookups" at all locations. All the cabins offer house-like comfort in confined quarters.

There are 15 air-conditioned "comfort stations" all around the campground, with facilities such as laundries, showers, telephones, and even ice machines, open 24 hours a day. Two "trading posts" offer groceries and rent out recreational equipment.

## Recreation

There is plenty to keep visitors happily occupied at Fort Wilderness Resort. The **Tri-Circle D Ranch** has two heated pools, guided horseback tours, and pony rides. Other recreational facilities include tennis, volleyball, and basketball courts, bike and boat rentals, fishing, an exercise trail, nightly wagon rides, horseshoes and shuffleboard, carriage rides, a petting zoo, and video arcades. You can also opt for skiing, parasailing, and wakeboarding. Equipment is usually available for rental. Reservations are required for fishing and for the guided tours on horse-back.

In addition, Fort Wilderness offers a **Campfire** program with singalongs and outdoor movies. Available to all Disney guests – and not just Fort Wilderness residents – the program features an hour of singalongs complete with toasted marshmallows and the American delicacy "s'mores" – melted marshmallow and chocolate on graham crackers. Hosted in part by the Disney chipmunks Chip 'n' Dale, the singalong leads into the screening of a Disney animated feature. An additional attraction is the night-time **Electrical Water Pageant** *(see p177)*, which goes by Fort Wilderness Resort at 9:45pm. There is a good all-you-can-eat breakfast buffet at the Trail's End Restaurant.

## Sports at Walt Disney World®

Besides Fort Wilderness, all Disney resorts have sports and fitness facilities, though available only for residents. In 1997, **Disney's Wide World of Sports®** complex was opened, primarily as a training camp and athletic haven for exhibition games, Olympic training, and other recreational activities. Now called the **ESPN Wide World of Sports,** the complex hosts sports events year round, ranging from amateur athletics to professional baseball spring training. The complex has 230 acres of excellent facilities for more than 60 sports where athletes of all ages compete. The sports-worshiping park includes a 9,500 seat champion baseball stadium, a dozen baseball and softball fields, 10 clay tennis courts, a sprawling stadium used for basketball, volleyball or gymnastics, and 17 playing fields that can be fitted out for football, soccer, lacrosse, and more.

# Disney Springs®

Shopping, fine dining, exciting shows, and concerts are on offer at Disney Springs®, formerly known as Downtown Disney®, giving visitors plenty to do at Walt Disney World® Resort after the theme parks have closed. Disney Springs® is a series of "islands" surrounded by bodies of water resembling Florida's magnificent freshwater springs. This lovely outdoor waterfront mall features shops, restaurants, and entertainment. The Marketplace, Town Center, and the Landing offer free musical entertainment among world-class restaurants. The West Side offers more eateries, plus the House of Blues. There is even a two-story, vintage bowling alley and dining complex called Splitsville Luxury Lanes, where families enjoy old-fashioned 10-pin bowling and nostalgic American food.

Disney Springs® offers free parking, free admission and buses run continually to the on-property resort hotels. It also has its own iconic attraction, a giant tethered balloon that takes guests 400 ft (122 m) into the air to view the amazing scenery of Walt Disney World® Resort and Orlando beyond.

Harley-Davidson store at Town Center, Disney Springs®

## Town Center

Most visitors will enter Disney Springs® via Town Center, as the main parking lots empty into this area. Internationally known brand-name shops fill this space. The **Orlando Harley-Davidson** store offers a huge selection of men's, women's, and children's apparel, gifts, and collectibles. There are two Harley-Davidson motorcycles for guests to sit on, and there is even a Harley-Davidson cookbook for sale. Dining experiences in Town Center include **Planet Hollywood Observatory**, the child-friendly **T-Rex Café**, and the Mexican eatery of chef Rick Bayless, **Frontera Cocina**.

## The Landing

Mostly a waterfront area, the Landing features several celebrity chef restaurants such as the serenely sophisticated **Morimoto Asia**, the energetic **Raglan Road Irish Pub**, or **Paddlefish**, aboard the iconic paddle steamer anchored on Lake Buena Vista. **The Boathouse** offers waterfront dining with views of small boats resembling 1950s cars buzzing around the lake. Free water taxis are also available. **The Edison**, a restaurant built to resemble a steam-punk era power plant containing a working steam engine, sits on the waterfront and offers American cuisine along with entertainment including jugglers, live music, aerialists, and cabaret acts.

Guests must be 21 or older to enter after 10 pm. **Maria & Enzo's Ristorante**, whose chef has earned a Michelin star, is right next door, but just across the street and down some stairs, you'll find a charming little speakeasy called **Enzo's Hideaway**, built into former employee tunnels beneath the streets.

## West Side

Each store, restaurant, or business on Disney Springs® West Side has a unique feel to it, making for a splendid evening of exploration. Among the do-not-miss shops are the popular **Candy Cauldron** where sweets are made on the spot, the **Dino Store**, where visitors can assemble a plush pet dino at the Build-A-Dino® Workshop. There is also a state-of-the-art **AMC 24 Theater** offering 24-hour dine-in movies.

Full-service restaurants here include the popular Cuban and Latin fare of **Bongos Cuban Café®** (which features a band and dancing), the Southern US cuisine of the **House of Blues®** restaurant, and the American food at **Splitzville Luxury Lanes**. Quick bites can be obtained from **Wetzel's Pretzels®**, featuring pretzels and Häagen-Dazs ice creams.

The West Side has special attractions that require separate admissionsm such as the House of Blues® concert hall (part of the national chain, which attracts major music acts). In addition to regular shows by

Disney Springs® West Side glittering in the evening

The lovely Marketplace at Disney Springs®

national artists, with a side stage for smaller acts, the House of Blues offers a Sunday Gospel Brunch that features live gospel performers showing off their uniquely American religious singing.

Visitors can take to the skies from Disney Springs® in an illuminated balloon operated by **Aerophile**. It is tethered so there is no chance of floating away. Passengers spend approximately 10 minutes enjoying breathtaking 360-degree views of Walt Disney World® Resort and, depending on the weather, there are views of up to 10 miles (16 km) away. The balloon is the world's largest

tethered gas balloon, and is attached to a gondola that can hold up to 29 guests and a pilot. Weather permitting, flights operate daily from 9am until midnight, and are wheelchair accessible. Flights cost $20 per adult and $15 per child (aged 3–9 years).

## Marketplace

An open-air mall with some excellent shops and a good variety of restaurants, the Marketplace makes for a relaxing walk if there is time. Among the highlights, especially for children, is the **LEGO® Imagination Center**, which features photo-op

A giant lego Woody in the Lego Imagination Center

displays of wonderful LEGO constructions, from a spaceship to a dragon, in the water next to the store. Also of interest to kids will be the **Once Upon a Toy** and **Disney's Days of Christmas** stores. Kids and adults alike will be awed by the sheer size of the **World of Disney** emporium, the largest Disney memorabilia store in the world and the "mother lode" for all Disney souvenirs. Restaurants include the colorful **Rainforest Café**™, with its fiery simulated volcanic eruption, best seen from across the lake, and **Ghirardelli's® Soda Fountain & Chocolate Shop** with its malt-shop atmosphere.

Quick bites can be found at **AristoCrepes** on the bridge, and the **McDonald's** and **Earl of Sandwich®** eateries.

### After Dark Events

Apart from the Disney Springs® attractions, other prime after-dark entertainment includes **dinner shows** and the **Electrical Water Pageant**. A floating parade that wanders around park resorts such as Polynesian and Contemporary, the Electrical Water Pageant is best viewed from the unobstructed beach in Fort Wilderness. This kids' favorite showcases 20 minutes of dazzling electrical animation – dolphins jumping out of the water, whales swimming by, even a fire-breathing dragon. Around since 1971, it often serves as an opening act or postscript for the Magic Kingdom® and Epcot® fireworks. Disney's two long-running dinner shows, Hoop-Dee-Doo Musical Revue and Disney's Spirit of Aloha, tempt visitors to stay longer at the theme parks. The first is a popular Western comedy show at Fort Wilderness' Pioneer Hall; the second features authentic Polynesian music, dance, and food. Another show, Mickey's Backyard BBQ, provides country 'n' western fun.

The superbly constructed LEGO® dragon at the Marketplace

# Essential Information

Spread over a large area of 47 sq miles (121 sq km) and brimming with attractions, Walt Disney World® Resort can provide entertainment for the whole family for at least a week. Guests on a shorter holiday need to plan carefully to make the most of their visit to this dream vacationland. The information here is geared toward aiding them in this task.

## When to Visit

The busiest times of the year are Christmas, the last week of February until Easter, and June to August. At these times some 90,000 people a day could visit Magic Kingdom® alone. All the rides will be operating and the parks are open for longer periods. During off-season, 10,000 guests a day might visit the Magic Kingdom®, only one water park may be operating, and certain attractions may be closed for maintenance. The weather is also a factor – in July and August, hot and humid afternoons are regularly punctuated by torrential thunderstorms. Between October and March, however, the temperatures and humidity are both more comfortable, and permit a more energetic touring schedule.

## Busiest Days

Each of the theme parks is packed on certain days. The busiest days are as follows: Magic Kingdom®: Monday, Thursday, and Saturday. Epcot®: Tuesday, Friday, and Saturday. Disney's Hollywood Studios®: Wednesday and Sunday. Note, however, that after a thunderstorm, the water parks are often almost empty – even at peak times of the year.

## Opening Hours

When the theme parks are busiest, opening hours are the longest, typically 9am to 10–11pm or midnight. In less busy periods, hours are usually 9am to 6–8pm. Call to check. The parks open at least 30 minutes early for pass holders and guests at any of the WDW hotels and resorts.

## Length of Visit

To enjoy Walt Disney World® to the full, you may want to give Magic Kingdom® and Epcot® two full days – or one and a half days, with half a day at a water park – each, leaving a day for Disney's Hollywood Studios® and Animal Kingdom®. Set aside three nights to see Fantasmic!, IllumiNations, and Wishes™ firework displays.

## The Ideal Schedule

To avoid the worst of the crowds and the heat:
• Arrive as early as possible and visit the most popular attractions first.
• Take a break in the early afternoon, when it's hottest and the parks are full.
• Return to the parks in the cool of the evening to see parades and fireworks.

## Tickets & Types of Passes

There are several customized package plans available. A base ticket gives each member of your travel party entry to one theme park every ticketed day. The longer you stay, the less you pay per day. You can then add on up to three options. The **Park Hopper®** lets you come and go through multiple parks and gives you extra visitor hours. See http://disneyworld.disney.go.com/tickets-passes for options and pricing. Disney has introduced a high-tech tool to speed up the ticketing and FastPass+ process. MagicBands, colorful wristbands with credit card and ID information coded into them, allow you park entry, let you unlock your hotel room door, and charge food and other purchases to your hotel room account.

Passes are available at Disney stores, the airport, the Tourist Information Center on I-Drive, and the official Disney website.

In addition, passes are sometimes included in package deals.

## Getting Around

An extensive, efficient transportation system handles an average of 200,000 guests each day. Even if you stay outside Walt Disney World® Resort, many nearby hotels offer free shuttle services to and from the theme parks, but you can check this when you make your reservation.

The transportation hub of Walt Disney World® is the **Ticket and Transportation Center (TTC)**. Connecting it to the Magic Kingdom® are two monorail services. A third monorail links the TTC to Epcot®. Ferries run from the TTC to the Magic Kingdom® across the Seven Seas Lagoon.

Ferries connect the Magic Kingdom® and Epcot® with the resorts in their respective areas, while buses link everything in Walt Disney World®, including direct links to the Magic Kingdom®. All ticket holders can use the entire transportation system for free.

Although Disney transportation is efficient, you may wish to rent a car if you want to enjoy the entire area without inconvenience. Disney, now offers a new transportation option called Minnie Van service. For more information visit https://disneyparks.disney.go.com/blog/2017/07/now-available-minnie-van-service-at-walt-disney-world-resort. The theme parks are spread out and, especially for visits to swimming attractions such as Blizzard Beach and Typhoon Lagoon, Disney transportation is not always the best option for children. Young children who are wet and tired from swimming will not welcome waiting for the Disney bus.

## Etiquette

This family park welcomes millions of visitors every year, and to facilitate a pleasant experience for all, they prescribe certain rules. Alcohol, plastic straws, selfie sticks, balloons and glass containers aren't allowed inside the park. Visitors should refrain from jumping the queue or littering. They ought to be mindful of staff requests, such as no flash photography, and should heed the no costume rule.

## Coping with Lines

Lines tend to be shortest at the beginning and end of the day, and during parade and meal times. Lines for the rides move slowly, but the wait for a show is rarely longer than the show itself. The **FastPass+** allows visitors to reserve time at 25 of the most popular attractions rather than wait in long lines. Disney parks fill rapidly after the first hour of opening. Until then, you can usually just walk onto rides for which you will have to line up later.

## Disabled Travelers

Wheelchairs can be borrowed at the park entrance and special bypass entrances allow disabled guests and carers to board rides without waiting in line. Staff, however, are not allowed to lift guests or assist with lifting for safety reasons.

## Very Young Children

As Walt Disney World® can be physically and emotionally tiring for children, try to adapt your schedule accordingly. If you've come with pre-school-age kids, focus on Magic Kingdom®.

The waiting and walking can exhaust young children quickly so visitors can rent a stroller, available at every park entrance. Each stroller is personalized when you rent it, but if it should go missing when you leave a ride, you can get a replacement with your rental receipt. Baby Care Centers for changing and feeding are located all around the parks.

In a system called "switching off," parents can enjoy a ride one at a time while the other parent stays with the child – without having to line up twice.

## Meeting Mickey

For many youngsters, the most exciting moment at Walt Disney World® Resort is meeting the Disney characters. You will spot them in all the theme parks, but you can have more relaxed encounters in a number of restaurants, usually at breakfast. Each theme park and many of the resorts also offer "character dining," though you must call well ahead of time to make a reservation.

## Safety

The resort's excellent safety record and first rate security force mean problems are rare and dealt with promptly. Cast members watch out for young unaccompanied children and escort them to lost children centers. Bags of all visitors are checked.

## Staying & Dining

Lodging in the Disney-run hotels and villa complexes is of a high standard. However, even the lowest-priced places are more expensive than many hotels outside Walt Disney World®. But keep in mind that, apart from Disney quality, your money also buys:
• Early entry into the theme parks (up to 60 minutes).
• Guaranteed admission to the theme parks even when the parks are otherwise full.
• The delivery of shopping purchases made anywhere in Walt Disney World® Resort.

For dining at any full-service restaurant in Walt Disney World®, especially in Epcot®, book a Priority Seating – the table reservation equivalent of the FastPass.

For more information, see pages 146–53 and 156–61.

## Parking

Visitors to Magic Kingdom® must park at the TTC and make their way by trolley or foot – Epcot®, Disney's Hollywood Studios®, and Animal Kingdom® have their own parking lots. Parking is free for Disney resort residents – others must pay, but only once a day no matter how many times they move their vehicle. The lots are large, so it's important to remember the character name and row of the section where you are parked.

# DIRECTORY

## General

**Accommodation Information/ Reservation**
Tel (407) 939-6244.

**Dining Reservations (including Dinner Shows)**
Tel (407) 939-3463. Operational 7am–11pm Sat–Sun.

**Disney Tours**
Tel (407) 939-8687.

**General Information**
Tel (407) 939-6244.
W disneyworld. disney.go. com/wdw

**Golf Reservations**
Tel (407) 939-4653.

## Theme Parks & Attractions

**Blizzard Beach**
Tel (407) 560-3400.

**Disney Cruise Line®**
Tel (800) 939-2784.
W disneytravelagents.com

**Disney's Animal Kingdom®**
Tel (407) 938-3000.

**Disney's Hollywood Studios®**
Tel (407) 824-4321.

**ESPN Wide World of Sports®**
Tel (407) 939-4263.

**Disney Springs®**
Tel (407) 828-3800.

**Epcot®**
Tel (407) 934-7639.

**Fort Wilderness Resort & Campground**
Tel (407) 824-2900.

**Magic Kingdom®**
Tel (407) 934-7639.

**Typhoon Lagoon**
Tel (407) 939-6244.

## ❷ SeaWorld® Orlando, Discovery Cove®, and Aquatica

**Road map** E3 7007. SeaWorld Dr.
**Open** 9am–5pm daily. **Tel** (407) 351-3600. **W** seaworld.com

The SeaWorld® Parks and Resorts Orlando entertainment complex has three parks that each provide distinct aquatic entertainment.
**SeaWorld® Orlando**, with its animal encounters and thrilling rides, is the most popular. Among the main attractions is **Antarctica: Empire of the Penguin**, where audience members follow the fictional adventures of a penguin named Puck, before exploring the icy world of a penguins' colony.
**Clyde & Seamore's Sea Lion High™** is an interactive, fun-filled show that follows the comic adventures of sea lions, walruses, and otters in an aquatic-themed high school. **Turtle Point** is home to rescued turtles, which are too injured to survive on their own in the wild. Other attractions include **Dolphin Cove**, **Pacific Point Preserve**, **Manatee Rescue** and **Shark Encounter**. **Kraken** and **Manta** are two much-favored roller-coaster rides.

Most of the presentations are walk-through exhibits or sit-down stadium shows. The stadiums seat so many that finding a good spot is seldom a problem and visitors will usually get a good seat by arriving 15 minutes before the show starts. Bear in mind that those who sit near the front may get wet.

The thrilling Manta® ride at SeaWorld® Orlando

SeaWorld®'s more gentle pace means that visiting after 3pm affords a cooler and less crowded experience. It is also worth noting that the shows are timed so that it's all but impossible to leave one show just in time for another.

For an overview of the park and a great view, take the six-minute ride up the 400 ft (122 m) Sky Tower. For help with problems or queries, go to Guest Relations near the exit gate.

Across the street, **Discovery Cove** has a capacity of up to 1,300 guests a day and, for a steep entry price, offers some unforgettable experiences, such as an opportunity to swim with Atlantic Bottlenose dolphins, or an underwater walking tour around the Grand Reef. Beyond the lush vegetation, beaches, and waterfalls, in the Explorer's Aviary, guests can feed the birds with food provided by the staff. Packages are available with and without the Dolphin Swim Experience.

**Aquatica, SeaWorld's Waterpark™**, captures the essence of an aquatic paradise, with more than 3 million gallons of water in lagoons and wave pools, relaxing rivers, racing rides and water slides. Vibrant flora represents exotic destinations from around the world.

SeaWorld® has a rehabilitation program of rescuing stranded marine animals and, whenever possible, releasing them back into the wild. However, less positive aspects of SeaWorld have come to light since the release of the 2013 documentary film *Blackfish*, which questioned the ethics and highlighted the dangers of keeping killer whales in captivity. SeaWorld has since come under strong criticism for its treatment of its killer whales, seeing a downturn in public opinion, and a drop in the number of visitors to its theme parks.

### Top Tips for SeaWorld®

- SeaWorld® allows guests to feed many of the animals, but restricts both the type and amount of food, which has to be purchased from them. If this is something you would like to do, check with guest services as soon as you enter the park for feeding times and food availablility.
- Bring a waterproof plastic bag for your camera because in some of the shows, people on the first 12 rows are sometimes splashed by corrosive salt water.

The gated entrance to Seaworld® Orlando

*For hotels and restaurants in this region see pp317–18 and pp336–9*

# ❸ The Orlando Eye and the Merlin Entertainment Complex

The Orlando Eye, along with Madame Tussauds Orlando and SEA LIFE Aquarium Orlando, forms a part of the Merlin Entertainment Complex, owned by a group that also includes LEGOLAND® Florida *(see pp196–7)*. Tickets can be bought individually, though packages often offer multiple entries and discounts. It is advisable to check the websites for details and book in advance.

### 🎡 The Orlando Eye
8401 International Dr **Road map** E3
**Tel** (866) 228-6438. 🚌 8, 38, 42 from Orlando. **Open** 10am–midnight daily.
W **officialorlandoeye.com**

This huge observation wheel can be seen for miles, especially at night, when it is ablaze with 64,000 lights. Similar to the London Eye, the wheel gives visitors a gentle, 18-minute bird's-eye view of Central Florida in one of 30 air-conditioned, transparent capsules. While visitors can see for miles from the top of the ride, using a pair of binoculars can be handy to pick out certain specific sights. Compass marks on the ceiling give directions, while an accompanying recorded commentary points out the landmarks. To the east, a carpet of green stretches 50 miles (80 km)to the Atlantic, where, on a very clear day, it is possible to see the Vertical Assembly building at the Kennedy Space Center. Even on a cloudy day, it can be seen how much of the area is still undeveloped forest. To the northeast lies downtown Orlando, and to the north, Universal's Hogwarts Castle and The Incredible Hulk Coaster. A western view, timed well, offers mesmerizing views of the sunset.

Disney lies to the southwest, and Epcot®'s iconic white golf ball and the peaks of Space Mountain® are clear, along with a glimpse of Cinderella Castle. The view at night is less spectacular, offering vast darkness, punctuated by lights from the theme parks and I-Drive.

### 🎡 Madame Tussauds Orlando
8387 International Dr. **Road map** E3
**Tel** (866) 630-8315. 🚌 8, 38, 42 from Orlando.**Open** 10am–midnight daily.
W **madametussauds.com/orlando**

Merlin Entertainment demonstrated amazing risk in bringing a waxworks to a state whose temperatures are scorching in the summer, but bring it they did. Faux celebrities from the worlds of music, movies, television, art, science, history, sports, as well as popular culture line the pathways of this medium-sized (and well air-conditioned) attraction. Snap a selfie on a bench with One Direction, stand next to Steve Jobs, or else share the table with Audrey Hepburn in her *Breakfast at Tiffany's* attire. Props are also provided with some of the more

popular figures to use in and enhance the visitor's photographs. The historical tableaux are often elaborate: President Donald Trump is seen standing in the Oval Office; physicist Albert Einstein is in his library; and astronaut Neil Armstrong is kitted out in his moon-walk suit. There is no time limit on the self-guided tour, and employees at Madame Tussauds, will happily snap photos of visitors with their favorite celebrity figurines.

Visitors getting a glimpse of a sea animal at SEA LIFE Aquarium Orlando

### 🐠 SEA LIFE Aquarium Orlando
8449 International Dr. **Road map** E3
**Tel** (866) 622-0607. 🚌 8, 38, 42 from Orlando.**Open** 10am–10pm daily.
W **visitsealife.com/orlando**

In the same building as Madame Tussauds Orlando, this educational aquarium offers visitors a glimpse into the underwater lives of more than 5,000 sea animals in 32 displays, arranged in tanks reflecting the different oceans of the world. In one room, sardines swim in a silvery vortex above visitors' heads; another area offers starfish and other rock-pool inhabitants. Sharks and rays swim above and below visitors walking through a 360-degree ocean tunnel. Staff members also offer insights on breeding, rescuing, and protecting the creatures of the sea.

The Orlando Eye offers a bird's-eye view of Central Florida

# ❹ Universal Orlando®

Once a single movie park, competing with the other area attractions, Universal Orlando® now boasts two major theme parks, a state-of-the-art water park, entertainment complex, and five resort hotels. Together, Universal Studios Florida®, Universal's Islands of Adventure®, and Universal CityWalk® present a formidable reason to spend at least some time away from Disney. Harry Potter and his world are the undeniable stars at Universal. A real British steam train carries passengers between Universal Studios® and Islands of Adventure®, since The Wizarding World spans both the parks.

Universal Globe marking the entrance to Universal Studios Park®

## Tackling the Parks

The busiest times of the year at Universal Studios Orlando® are the same as those at Walt Disney World® *(see p178)*.

When the parks are open until late, two full days are just about long enough to see everything. When the parks close early – the only disadvantage of visiting in off season – you really need three or four days. Those staying for longer can opt for one of Universal's multi-day packages, which offer cost-effective admission to the parks and CityWalk®, as well as several discounts.

Lines at Universal are longer and slower moving than those at Walt Disney World®, since The Wizarding World of Harry Potter™ arrived at Islands of Adventure® and then spilled over into Universal Studios®. For a complete Harry Potter experience, buy a Park-to-Park ticket, because The Wizarding World spans both parks. You may have to wait for up to two hours for the best rides. At peak times, combat lines by arriving early (the gates open an hour before the official opening time) and experience the popular rides *(see p186)* before it gets too busy. You will not be able

to ride them all early, so ride the others just before the park closes. You are unlikely to have to wait long for shows but you should arrive 15 minutes early in tourist season to secure a seat. Those shows with no displayed schedule run continuously and you will rarely have to wait longer than the show's duration. Note that lines for rides near the big shows grow considerably when the performances end. Another way of combating the lines is by purchasing the Universal Express Pass, which allows visitors to make a reserve an attraction and skip the line.

Most rides are likely to be too intense for very young children and some have minimum height restrictions; the exception is ET Adventure®. The attractions designed to appeal to children are Despicable Me Minion Mayhem, Flight of the Hippogriff, Woody Woodpecker's Nuthouse Coaster®, Pteranodon Flyers, Animal Actors on LocationSM, and Seuss and Jurassic Park Islands.

## Live Filming

While there is no guarantee that you will be able to see live filming on the day that you visit Universal Studios Florida®, there is a chance that cameras may be rolling on the backlot (within the theme park itself).

It is more probable, especially from September to December, that you could be in the audience for the taping of a TV show. It is possible to call ahead to check which shows are being filmed during your visit: call (407) 224-4233. Tickets for shows are issued on a first come first served basis (on the day of filming) at the Studio Audience Center located near Guest Services. It is wise to go there as soon as you enter the park to be sure of obtaining tickets.

Board showing the shooting schedule

On a very busy day, you might like to indulge in one of the VIP Tours, which can last up to eight hours. This provides priority admission to at least one of the parks, a walk around back-stage areas, and access to production facilities and sound stages.

If you stay at one of Universal's resorts, you can use your room key for more than just accessing your room. It is an

Hogwarts Castle at The Wizarding World of Harry Potter™, Universal Studios®

Despicable Me characters pose for photos outside the Minion Mayhem attraction

express pass, giving priority seating at many attractions and can be used like a credit card throughout the park.

## Exploring

The entrance to Universal Studios Florida® is known as **Front Lot** because it is made to look like the front lot of a working Hollywood movie studio from the 1940s. The shooting schedule notice board near the turnstiles, with details of shows being filmed, is real enough, however.

Immediately inside the park, the palm-lined Plaza of the Stars has several shops (*see p185*), but do not linger here on arrival: instead you should head off immediately to the main attractions before the lines reach their peak.

Poster showing Shrek 4-D mesmerizing its audience

## VISITORS' CHECKLIST

**Practical Information**
**Road map** E2. Orange Co. 1000 Universal Studios Plaza, exits 29 or 30B on I-4. **Tel** (407) 363-8000.
**Open** minimum opening hours 9am–6pm daily; extended evening opening in summer and on public hols. 🅿️ ♿ 🚻 📷
W **universalorlando.com**

**Transport**
🚌 21, 37, 40 from Orlando.

## Production Central

Probably the least aesthetic section of the park. Maps show the studios' main sound stages here, but these are actually off limits to those not on a VIP Tour.

**Despicable Me Minion Mayhem** takes visitors into the high-tech empire of Gru, one of the great super-villains of animation. After being transformed into mischievous Minions, guests set out on a 3-D digital adventure with characters from the movie – Gru along with his adopted daughters Agnes, Edith, and Margo – and descend into Gru's secret lab. There, guests join a Minion-inspired, interactive dance party.

**Shrek 4-D** is a fun-packed ride which includes a 13-minute 3D movie starring the voices of Cameron Diaz, Eddie Murphy, John Lithgow, and Mike Myers. "OgreVision" glasses enable you to see, hear, and almost feel the action from your seat.

Production Central also houses shops and restaurants, including the Universal Studios® Store.

## New York

This area has more than 60 façades, some of which replicate real buildings, others which reproduce those that have appeared only on screen. There are cut-outs of the Guggenheim Museum and New York Public Library, cleverly creating an illusion of depth and distance. Macy's, the famous department store, is there, as is Louie's Italian Restaurant, where a shootout took place in the original *Godfather* movie.

New York is also the location for the 3D motion simulator ride **Race Through New York Starring Jimmy Fallon**. Visitors join the host of *The Tonight Show Starring Jimmy Fallon* in a fun-filled race through, below, and above New York City.

Another reality ride at New York is the state-of-the-art **Revenge of The Mummy – The Ride℠**. The thrill ride is based on the popular *Mummy* movies and uses high-speed roller coaster engineering and space age robotics to propel riders through Egyptian sets, passageways and catacombs. The attraction includes an animated figure of the fearsome Mummy that thrills and frightens with its life-like movements.

The entrance to Race Through New York Starring Jimmy Fallon

Hollywood Boulevard, a fine example of the park's superbly created sets

## Hollywood

Hollywood Boulevard and Rodeo Drive are the most attractive streets in Universal Studios. While ignoring actual geography, these sets pay tribute to Hollywood's golden age from the 1920s to the 1950s.

The Brown Derby was a restaurant shaped like a hat where the movie glitterati once congregated – Universal's own version is a fun hat shop. Schwab's Pharmacy, where hopefuls hung out sipping sodas and waiting to be discovered, is brought back to life as an old-fashioned ice-cream parlor. Notice, too, the Hollywood Walk of Fame, with the names of stars embedded in the sidewalk, just as in the real Hollywood Boulevard.

**TRANSFORMERS: The Ride-3-D** is the ultimate next-generation ride for thrill-seekers. It uses 1460 ft (18 m) custom-built screens to take the 3-D-glasses-wearing audience into the Decepticon-versus-humanity war, as they hurtle along a 2,000 ft (610 m) long track.

The top attraction in Hollywood is **Terminator 2®: 3-D**. This exciting ride also uses the latest in 3-D movie technology and robotics, together with explosive live stunts, to catapult the audience into the action alongside the star of the *Terminator* films, Arnold Schwarzenegger.

Men in Black™ – Alien Attack™

**Hello Kitty** and her pals have ousted one of the few remaining original attractions in the park. Fans of film and television icon Lucille Ball may feel a twinge when they turn onto Rodeo Drive and find a more modern icon in her place. Hello Kitty now reigns over an interactive shop offering a wide range of items based on the popular Japanese cartoon character. Visitors can design their own, unique merchandise and even meet Hello Kitty.

**Universal Horror Make-Up Show** offers a fascinating, behind-the-scenes look at the skill of the make-up artist, and how the movie industry uses incredible make-up to create the most amazing scary monsters and creepy effects.

## Woody Woodpecker's Kid Zone

Everyone should ride the enchanting, if rather tame, **ET Adventure®** based on Steven Spielberg's 1982 movie. You are off to ET's home planet on a flying bicycle, soaring over a twinkling cityscape.

In **Animal Actors on Location<sup>SM</sup>,** animal look-alikes take the parts of canine superstars such as Lassie and Beethoven.

**A Day in the Park with Barney™** appeals only to young children. Set in a magical park, it features a goofy, purple Tyrannosaurus Rex called Barney from the pre-school age TV show.

**Fievel's Playland®** is inspired by the popular animated movies *An American Tail* and *An American Tail: Fievel Goes West*. Fievel is a mouse, and the playground's props, such as a cowboy hat, boots, glasses, and a tea cup, are oversized – just as they would seem to the star of the movie.

**Woody Woodpecker's Nuthouse Coaster®** is a gentle, child-friendly introduction to the world of amusement rides, and is fun for younger children.

**Curious George Goes to Town<sup>SM</sup>** has plenty of water to splash in and hundreds of foam balls.

Universal's Transformers™: The Ride-3-D, a state-of-the-art attraction

## World Expo

The inspiration behind World Expo's architecture is the Los Angeles 1984 Olympic Games and Expo '86 in Vancouver. The focus here is on the rides and shows.

**Men In Black™ – Alien Attack™** is an addictive ride in which you join Will Smith in a four-person simulator battling aliens using laser weapons and smoke bombs. Each person has their own cannon, and the scores reflect the team's ability to destroy aliens on a massive scale.

**The Simpsons Ride™** transports visitors into the middle of Springfield, the Simpsons' hometown. Guests can enjoy a drink at Moe's, grab a sandwich at Krusty Burger, or drop in for doughnuts at Lard Lad. The popular duo of aliens, Kang and Kodos, have their own, aptly named Kang and Kodos' Twirl 'n' Hurl ride, which sends visitors into an intergalactic spin.

## San Francisco

Most of this area is based on San Francisco, notably the city's Fisherman's Wharf district. Chez Alcatraz, for instance, is a snack bar closely modeled on the ticket booths for tours to Alcatraz island.

San Francisco's big attraction is **Fast & Furious Supercharged**. This full-throttle, high-octane experience will take visitors inside the heart-pounding activities of the action film

Transformers™ Optimus Prime at the Universal Orlando® Resort

franchise, which features fast cars and international crime cartels.

## The Wizarding World of Harry Potter™ – Diagon Alley™

Last, but definitely not least, you arrive in London, where King's Cross Station delivers Harry Potter fans to and from Diagon Alley™ and Hogsmeade™. If you arrive by train, be sure to pop through Platform 9 3/4™ before heading into the cool darkness of Diagon Alley™. The main attraction is Gringotts™ Bank and the **Escape from Gringotts™** ride. Blasts of fire from the dragon perched above the bank can be felt in the street below, where visitors can peruse shops such as Ollivanders, Weasley's Wizard Wheezes, and Quality

Quidditch Supplies. Visitors can buy a special wand at Ollivanders that interacts with parts of Diagon Alley™ and Hogsmeade™. Don't miss Knockturn Alley's Borgin and Burkes shop, a favorite haunt of practitioners of the Dark Arts.

## Eating, Drinking, and Shopping

The food at Universal Orlando's theme parks is generally good. The Hard Rock Café is the largest in the world but there are plenty of other options. Advance reservations are advisable for Lombard's Seafood Grille, which specializes in fish dishes and has a good-value buffet. Mel's Drive-In is definitely the place to go for fast food and shakes; the wonderful 1950s diner is straight out of the 1973 movie *American Graffiti*.

Most of the shops stay open after official closing times, and you can buy a full range of themed souvenirs from them. In the Front Lot you will find Universal Studios Store, which sells everything from fake Oscars to oven mitts bearing the Universal logo, and On Location, where a signed photo of your favourite movie star can set you back hundreds of dollars. Most of the attractions have their own store.

Dragon atop Gringotts™, a sequence from the Escape from Gringotts™ ride

# Exploring the Islands of Adventure®

One of the world's most technologically advanced theme parks, Islands of Adventure® requires a full day's visit. The themed islands include Jurassic Park®, with an educ-ational, interactive Discovery Center®, The Wizarding World of Harry Potter™ with the Dragon Challenge Coaster™, and the park's most popular ride: Harry Potter and the Forbidden Journey™. Marvel Super Hero Island® features Spiderman, the Incredible Hulk, Captain America, and Dr. Doom. Seuss Landing Island™ and Toon Lagoon Islands cater to younger visitors. King Kong is back in his home on Skull Island.

**TOP 5 RIDES**

① **Harry Potter and the Forbidden Journey™**

② **The Amazing Adventures of Spiderman®**

③ **The Incredible Hulk Coaster®**

④ **Skull Island: Reign of Kong**

⑤ **The Jurassic Park River Adventure®**

The river ride in Jurassic Park River Adventure®

## Tackling the Park

There is no transport system within the park other than small boats which crisscross the lake. A day will suffice to experience all the attractions, provided that you arrive at opening time. As with any theme park, a clearly organized schedule is essential if you are to make the most out of your visit.

## The Islands

The entrance to the park is marked by the Pharos Lighthouse which sounds a bell every few minutes. The first island you encounter moving clockwise is the **Marvel Super Hero Island®** where the theme draws from the Marvel Comics' Super Hero stable of characters. The Incredible Hulk Coaster®, probably the best coaster in Florida, is a green leviathan that accelerates you to more than 40mph in two seconds before inverting you at 110 ft (33.5 m) above the ground as a prelude to raging through a series of

seven inversions and two under-water dives.

Storm Force Accelatron® is just a faster and more intense version of Disney's Mad Hatter's Tea Party ride. It is incredibly fast-spinning and might induce motion sickness. Dr Doom's Fearfall®, although some-what daunting to watch, is actually a remarkably pleasant ride in which you are strapped into seats surrounding a pillar and then catapulted into the air before plunging down a 150 ft (46 m) fall. Next to Dr Doom is The Amazing Adventures of Spiderman®, a complex ride which achieves a stunning integration of 3D movie technology together with motion simulation, as well live special effects.

**Toon Lagoon**, where cartoons change form into reality, hosts two wet rides and scheduled performances of the riotous Toon Lagoon Beach Bash. Opposite is Popeye and Bluto's Bilge-Rat Barges®, a white-water raft ride that includes an encounter with a giant octopus. Me Ship, the OliveSM, a play area for young children overlooks the raft ride and provides water canons to soak riders on the rafts below. Dudley Do-Right's Ripsaw Falls®, the adjacent flume ride, is loosely based on the Rocky and Bull-winkle™ cartoons. It combines

a pleasant cruise with an excellent final drop in which you appear to submerge.

**Skull Island**: Reign of Kong, signals the return of the legend-ary ape to the park. Visitors board jungle transports for a thrill-ride through an ancient temple and a series of caves before confronting the colossal Kong himself. Director Peter Jackson helped to design the ride.

**Jurassic Park®**, based on the movies of the same name, boasts exotic vegetation and offers some shade. The Jurassic Park River Adventure® is an exquisitely crafted cruise through the Jurassic Park® compound where you encounter Hadrosaurs, Stegosaurs, and others before "accidentally" being diverted as a consequence of a "raptor" breakout. The ride ends with an 85 ft (26 m) drop into a lagoon. Camp Jurassic® is a playground area for pre-teenage children. Here, smaller children can enjoy amber mines, climb dinosaur nets, and explore the prehistoric playground to their heart's con-tent. Situated nearby are the Pteranodon Flyers, which lift pairs of riders on an 80 second flight over Jurassic Park Island. Raptor Encounter offers a photo-op with a truly magnif-icent velociraptor. The Discovery Center® is an interactive natural history exhibit where guests can view the results of mixing DNA from various species, including themselves.

**The Wizarding World of Harry Potter - Hogsmeade™** transports visitors to the iconic locations of Hogwarts™ and

Hogsmeade™, and is home to Harry Potter and the Forbidden Journey™, a magical tour beginning at Hogwarts™ and finishing with a thrilling aerial adventure, and Dragon Challenge™ – a pair of dueling high-speed roller coasters. The third ride, Flight of the Hippogriff™, is more family-friendly as it weaves its way through the pumpkin patch and Hagrid's hut. Hogsmeade™ Station is the gateway for Hogwarts™ Express, where guests board the train to King's Cross Station and Diagon Alley™.

Stage shows include The Eighth Voyage of Sindbad® Stunt Show, where stunts, flames, and explosions never fail to entertain. Poseidon's Fury® is an equally stunning show where the battle between Poseidon and Zeus is superbly executed through a myriad of extraordinary special effects.

**Seuss Landing™** is based on the fantastic Seuss children's books, and appeals mainly to the youngest and those familiar with the popular Seuss

Harry Potter™ Flight of the Hippogriff roller coaster ride

books. If I Ran The Zoo™ is another youngsters' playground. Discover some of the world's strangest creatures in this interactive play area for Dr Seuss fans of all ages. Caro-Suess-el™ is an extraordinary merry-go-round with several popular Dr Seuss characters as the horses. On the ride One Fish Two Fish Red Fish Blue Fish™, you have the added excitement of attempting to catch fish while avoiding water jets. For those people who have had no previous experience of Seuss, The Cat in the Hat™ is a somewhat bewildering journey through a manic display of cat-like characters on a whirling couch.

# Universal CityWalk®

A 30 acre (12 ha) entertainment complex of restaurants, nightclubs, shops, and cinemas, Universal CityWalk® offers visitors the opportunity to continue their Universal experience long after the parks have closed. The gateway to all of Universal's entertainment offerings, CityWalk®'s design was inspired by many of popular culture's innovators, such as Bob Marley, Thelonius Monk, and Motown.

### The Complex

CityWalk® appeals primarily to adults, and popular music and dance lovers are extremely well catered for. The complex is open from 11am–2am and while there is no entrance fee, each club makes a small cover charge. An All-Club pass can be purchased which may also include a movie.

CityWalk® offers a dazzling array of restaurants that range from Emeril's® Restaurant Orlando (a top TV chef), to the famous Hard Rock Café® Orlando. For sports fans, the NASCAR Sports GrilleSM and NBA City Restaurant provide athletic offerings, and the Bubba Gump Shrimp Co.™ offers the nostalgia. Bob Marley – A Tribute to Freedom is an exact replica of this famous musician's home. The complex is also home to several nightclubs, including the grooveSM dance club with live music from today's finest performers.

CityWalk® boasts specialty shops and state-of-the-art movie theaters and its outdoor stages and common areas are the setting for live concerts, art festivals, cooking demonstrations, celebrity personal appearances, and street performances. A sparkling lagoon running through the complex provides visitors with a picturesque location in which to relax while sipping a cool drink in the late-afternoon sun, or a perfect spot for a moonlight stroll.

The Hard Rock Café and music venue, Universal CityWalk®

The Orlando Eye, the largest observation wheel on the east coast ▶

Downtown Orlando, dominated by the SunTrust Center

# ❺ Orlando

**Road map** E2. Orange Co. 277,000.
8723 International Drive,
(407) 363-5872. **w** visitorlando.com

Until the 1950s, Orlando was not much more than a sleepy provincial town. Its proximity to Cape Canaveral and the theme parks, however, helped to change all that.

Downtown Orlando, where glass-sided high-rises mark a burgeoning business district, beckons mostly at night, when tourists and locals flock to the many bars and restaurants around Orange Avenue, Orlando's main street.

During the daytime, take a stroll in the park around **Lake Eola**, three blocks east of Orange Avenue. Here, you will get a taste of Orlando's (comparatively) early history. Overlooking the lake is a mix of high-rise condos and a few older homes. Alternatively, visit the **Orange County Regional History Center** on Central Blvd.

In the quieter residential areas just north of Downtown, there are parks and museums. If you are short of time, Winter Park should be your priority.

## 🏛 Orange County Regional History Center

65 E Central Blvd. **Tel** (407) 836-8500.
**Open** daily. **Closed** public hols.
**w** thehistorycenter.org

Housed in the 1927 courthouse in central Downtown, the Center crams 12,000 years of Central Florida's past into three floors. Do not miss the diorama of the sink-hole that swallowed buildings and cars in Winter Park in the 1980s.

## 🎭 Loch Haven Park

N Mills Ave at Rollins St. Orlando Museum of Art: **Tel** (407) 896-4231. **Open** 10am–4pm Tue–Fri, noon–4pm Sat & Sun. **Closed** public hols.
**w** omart.org Orlando Shakespeare Theater: **Tel** (407) 447-1700.

Loch Haven Park, 2 miles (3 km) north of Downtown, has a trio of small museums. The most highly regarded is the **Orlando Museum of Art**, which has three permanent collections: pre-Columbian artifacts, with figurines from Nazca in Peru; African art; and American paintings of the 19th and 20th centuries. The Park is home to the **Orlando Shakespeare Theater**, which includes the 350-seat Margeson Theater and the smaller Goldman

Fountain at the center of the rose garden, Harry P. Leu Gardens

Theater. The Center produces the classics throughout the year and is home to the Orlando Fringe Festival in spring (www.orlandoshakes.org).

## 🌳 Harry P. Leu Gardens

1920 N Forest Ave. **Tel** (407) 246-2620.
**Open** daily. **Closed** Dec 25.
**w** leugardens.org

The Harry P. Leu Gardens offer 50 acres of serenely beautiful gardens. Elements such as Florida's largest rose garden are formal, while elsewhere you find mature woods of spectacular live oaks and cypresses, festooned with Spanish moss. In winter, seek out the camellias.

## 🏛 Dr. Phillips Center for the Performing Arts

445 S Magnolia Ave. **Tel** (407) 839-0119 (showtime hotline). **Open** for performances. **w** drphillipscenter.org

The splendid new concert hall and entertainment venue is the crown jewel of downtown Orlando, hosting Broadway performances and internationally known musical artists.

## 🏛 Enzian Theater

1300 S Orlando Ave, Maitland.
**Tel** (407) 629-0054 (showtime hotline). **Open** daily.
**w** enzian.org

Home of the nationally recognized Florida Film Festival, this nonprofit, alternative cinema is set amid flourishing, green gardens and impressive ancient oaks. The sociable, open-air Eden Bar is a good place to mingle.

## 🏛 Maitland Art Center

231 W Packwood Ave, 6 miles (9 km) N of Downtown. **Tel** (407) 539-2181. **Open** daily. **Closed** public hols. Voluntary donations. (limited access). **w** maitlandartcenter.org

This art center located in the leafy suburb of Maitland occupies studios and living quarters which were designed in the 1930s by artist André Smith as a winter retreat for fellow artists. Set around courtyards and gardens, the buildings are delightful, with abundant use made of Mayan and Aztec motifs. The studios are still used, and there are exhibitions of contemporary American arts and crafts.

## 🏛 Orlando Science Center

777 East Princeton St. **Tel** (407) 514-2000 or (888) OSC 4FUN. **Open** 10am–5pm Sun–Fri, 10am–10pm Sat. 🖉 🔋 🖥 📷 **w** osc.org

The aim of this center is to provide a stimulating environment for experiential science learning, which it achieves by providing a huge range of exciting, state-of-the-art interactive exhibits. Covering 207,000 sq ft (19,200 sq m) of floor space, there are many fascinating attractions, including the Dr. Phillips CineDome, which surrounds people with amazing images and movies as well as functioning as a planetarium. The DinoDigs exhibit with its collection of dinosaur fossils is very popular with children, as is the orange packing plant, where youngsters eagerly pick and pack plastic oranges, while the Body Zone allows you to explore the intimate workings of the human body. The original museum was opened in 1960 at Loch Haven Park and was called the Central Florida Museum. It was not until 1984 that it was renamed the Orlando Science Center. The present building, six times larger than its previous home, was completed and opened in February 1997.

## ⑥ Winter Park

**Road map:** E2. Orange Co. 🚗 30,200. 🚉 🚌 ℹ 150 N New York Ave, (407) 644-8281. Scenic Boat Tour: **Tel** (407) 644-4056. 🖉 **w** winterpark.org

Bordering greater Orlando, this refined town took off in the 1880s, when wealthy northerners came south and began to build winter retreats here. The aroma of expensive perfume and coffee emanates from classy stores and cafés along its main street, Park Avenue, while at the country club up the road members all in white enjoy a game of croquet. At the northern end of Park Avenue, the **Charles Hosmer Morse Museum of American Art** holds probably the finest collection in the world of works by

Detail from Tiffany's *Four Seasons* window

Louis Comfort Tiffany (1848–1933). Magnificently displayed are superb examples of his Art Nouveau creations: jewelry, table lamps, and a large number of his windows, including the *Four Seasons* (1899). A reproduction of the superb terrace from Tiffany's home, with its columns topped by glass daffodils, should not be missed. The Tiffany Chapel is also stunning. Tiffany designed it for the 1893 World's Columbian Exposition in Chicago. For almost a century it was not seen by the general public.

Main door of Knowles Memorial Chapel, Rollins College

The galleries also exhibit pieces from the same period by luminaries such as Frank Lloyd Wright.

At the southern end of Park Avenue is **Rollins College**, with a delightful arboreal campus dotted with Spanish-style buildings erected in the 1930s. Noteworthy is the Knowles Memorial Chapel, whose main entrance features a relief of a meeting between the Florida natives and the Spanish conquistadors. The college's **Cornell Fine Arts Museum** has over 6,000 works of art, including an impressive collection of Italian Renaissance paintings, and is the oldest collection in Florida.

To see where the wealthy Winter Park residents live, take the narrated **Scenic Boat Tour**. Between 10am and 4pm, boats depart hourly from the east end of Morse Boulevard and chug around nearby lakes and along interconnecting canals overhung with hibiscus, bamboo, and papaya. The lakes are surrounded by magnificent live oaks, cypress trees, and huge mansions with green, sweeping lawns.

🏛 **Charles Hosmer Morse Museum of American Art**
445 Park Ave N. **Tel** (407) 645-5311. **Open** Tue–Sun. **Closed** public hols. 🖉 🔋 **w** morsemuseum.org

🏛 **Cornell Fine Arts Museum**
1000 Holt Ave. **Tel** (407) 646-2526. **Open** 10am–4pm Tue–Fri, noon–5pm Sat & Sun 🔋 **w** rollins.edu/cfam

Potthast's *The Conference*, Orlando Museum of Art, Loch Haven Park

Towering to 400 ft (122m), the magnificent Orlando Eye is located in the heart of Orlando

# ● International Drive

**Road map** E2. Orange Co. Orlando. Orlando. **Visitor Center**, 8723 International Drive. **Tel** (407) 363-5872. **orlandoinfo.com**

Just a stone's throw from Walt Disney World®, and anchored by Universal Studios® and SeaWorld® at either end, International Drive is here solely because of the theme parks. "I Drive," as everyone knows it, is a tawdry 3 mile (5 km) ribbon of restaurants, hotels, shops, and theaters. After dark, however, it becomes a lively neon strip with everything open until late.

I Drive's biggest attraction is the **Orlando Eye** (see p181), which towers over the area, giving visitors views as far as the coast. Adjacent to the Orlando Eye is the **I Drive 360** entertainment complex, that hosts several popular attractions. The fascinating **Skeletons: Museum of Osteology** features skeletons of more than 500 animals, along with facts about each one. There is the **7-D Dark Ride Adventure** which is a state-of-the-art shooting game with seven dimensions, including wind, sound, and movement. I Drive 360 also features **Madame Tussauds** waxworks as well as the **SEA LIFE Aquarium** (see p181). Filled with fantastic objects, illusions, and movie footage of strange feats, **Ripley's Believe It or Not!** is I-Drive's other quality attraction. It is one of a world-

wide chain of museums that was born out of the 1933 Chicago World Fair's so-called Odditorium – the creation of a famous American broadcaster and cartoonist, Robert Ripley, who traveled the globe in search of the weird and wonderful. You cannot miss Orlando's Ripley's Believe It or Not! – it is housed in a building that appears to be falling into one of Florida's infamous sinkholes (see p26). Other attractions include **Wonder-Works**, which offers interactive family fun with a simulated earthquake and laser tag games. **Pointe Orlando** is an ultra-modern, outdoor shopping mall with upscale eateries, nightclubs, and shops, along with attractions such as an IMAX® movie theater, B.B. King's Blues Club, and an Improv Comedy Club.

**Titanic – The Experience**, the world's first permanent Titanic attraction, with artifacts, movie memorabilia, and full-scale

re-creations of the ship's rooms and grand staircase. Orlando's excellent Official Visitor Information Center, which has coupons for many of Orlando and the surrounding area's most popular attractions, hotels, and restaurants, is well worth a visit, because you can save plenty of money (see p370).

**Pointe Orlando**
9101 I-Drive. **Tel** (407) 248-2838.
**Open** noon–10pm Mon–Sat, noon–8pm Sun. **pointeorlando.com**

**Ripley's Believe It or Not!**
8201 I-Drive. **Tel** (407) 363-4418.
**Open** daily. **ripleysorlando.com**

**Wonder Works**
9067 I-Drive. **Tel** (407) 351-8800.
**Open** daily. **wonderworksonline.com**

# ● Gatorland

**Road map** E3. Orange Co. 14501 S Orange Blossom Trail, Orlando. **Tel** (407) 855-5496. Orlando. Orlando. **Open** daily. **gatorland.com**

This giant working farm, open since the 1950s, has a license to raise alligators for their hides and meat.

On sale at Gatorland

Its breeding pens, nurseries, and rearing ponds hold thousands of alligators, from infants that would fit into the palm of your hand to 12 ft (4 m) monsters. The alligators can be observed from a boardwalk and tower as they bask in the shallows of a cypress swamp. The shows include alligator wrestling and the Gator Jumparoo, in which

The unmistakable sinking home of Ripley's Believe It or Not!

The gaping jaws of an alligator marking the entrance to Gatorland

the animals leap out of the water to grab chunks of chicken from the hands of trainers. There are also handling demonstrations of Florida's poisonous snakes.

The park's other highlights include an aviary, a zip line, and a petting zoo.

One of the typically offbeat shops in Kissimmee's Old Town

## ❾ Kissimmee

**Road map** E3. Osceola Co. 🚗 41,000.
🚌 🚆 *i* 1925 E Irlo Bronson Memorial Hwy. **Tel** (407) 847-5000. Old Town: 5770 W Irlo Bronson Mem. Hwy. **Tel** (407) 396-4888.
W **kissimmee.com**

In the early 1900s, cows freely roamed the streets of this cattle boom town. Now, the only livestock you are likely to see are those that appear in the twice-yearly rodeo at Kissimmee's **Silver Spurs Arena** *(see p39)*. Kissimmee (pronounced Ki-SIM-me) means "Heaven's Place" in the language

of the Calusa Native Americans *(see pp44–5)*, but the reason most people visit is to make use of the glut of cheap motels close to Walt Disney World®. They are strung out along the traffic-ridden US 192, amid chain restaurants and billboards advertising the latest attractions, shopping malls, and dinner shows. The latter are the chief appeal of Kissimmee after dark.

After a day in a theme park, however, you might prefer to visit Kissimmee's **Old Town**. This re-created pedestrian street of early 20th-century buildings has eccentric shops offering psychic readings, tattoos, Irish linen, candles, and so forth. There is also a moderately entertaining haunted house and a small fairground with antique equipment.

**Warbird Adventures**, by the Kissimmee municipal airport, offers visitors the unforgettable opportunity to fly in an original World War II Advanced T-6 Navy Trainer or, alternatively, a classic MASH helicopter.

Whether you want a thrilling acrobatic adventure or a smooth sightseeing flight, you will be allowed to take the controls and learn about flying one of these historical aircraft from an experienced instructor.

**Silver Spurs Arena**
Osceola Heritage Park. **Tel** (321) 697-3495. **Open** for shows. 🐾 ♿
W **silverspursrodeo.com**

**Ⅲ Warbird Adventures**
N. Hoagland Blvd. **Tel** (407) 870-7366.
**Open** Mon–Sat. **Closed** Dec 25. 🐾
♿ W **warbirdadventures.com**

## Dinner Shows

For great family fun, consider going to a dinner show *(see p359)*. The area boasts around a dozen – not including Disney's two shows *(see p177)* – strung along I Drive or off US 192 near Kissimmee. Tickets cost $40–75 for an adult and $20–25 for children, but discounts are available with coupons from the Orlando Visitor Center. The following are the best:

**Capone's Dinner and Show:** A 1931 Chicago speakeasy offers mobsters and Italian food. **Tel** (407) 397-2378.
W **alcapones.com**

**Blue Man Group:** A spectacular show of music and dance by the internationally acclaimed men in blue. **Tel** (407) 307-3407.
W **universalorlando.com**

**Pirate's Dinner Adventure:** A lavish show set around a pirates' ship, with boat races, acrobatics, and a tour of the studios beforehand. **Tel** (407) 248-0590.
W **piratesdinneradventure. com**

**Sleuth's Mystery Dinner Show:** Eight different shows, all with a suspicious death with plenty of twists. **Tel** (407) 363-1985.
W **sleuths.com**

**Medieval Times:** Jousting knights have top billing at this colorful and dramatic show. **Tel** (407) 396-1518.
W **medievaltimes.com**

**Outta Control Dinner Show:** A high-energy comedy magic show, aimed at adults, and accompanied by unlimited dishes. **Tel** (407) 351-8800.

A Knight preparing for battle in the dinner show Medieval Times

# ⑩ Lake Toho

**Road map** E3. Osceola Co. 3 miles (5 km) S of Kissimmee. 🚉 Kissimmee. 🚍 Kissimmee. 🚤 from Big Toho Marina on Lakeshore Blvd, downtown Kissimmee.

At the headwaters of the Florida Everglades, and approximately 20 miles (32 km) from downtown Orlando, Lake Tohopekaliga (or Toho, as the locals call it) is famous for its wide variety of exotic wildlife. Makinson Island, in the middle of the lake, is a 135 acre (55 ha) nature preserve and county park, where visitors can observe a wide variety of flora and fauna in their natural surroundings. Alligators, bald eagles, ospreys, herons, and egrets can be observed on a 2 mile (3 km) hiking trail around the preserve. Visitors must arrange their own transportation to reach the island. Approximately one third of the 19,000-acre lake is made up of maidencane grass and bullrush reeds. Anglers come from all over the world to compete in events at Lake Toho, which is one of the best places in Florida for catching trophy bass.

The reflection of the setting sun on Lake Tohopekaliga

Alternatively, visitors can go fishing with a local guide, or contact one of the many boat rental companies around the lake to explore the area and the Kissimmee River. Lake Toho is one of a series of lakes in the area, all of which offer recreational opportunities for adventurous travelers. Tours by airboats and swamp buggies take visitors deep into the swampy homes of alligators and snakes. Ziplines and hot-air balloon rides put a little

distance between the visitor and wildlife, allowing for a close observation from above.

# ⑪ Disney Wilderness Preserve

**Road map** E3. 2700 Scrub Jay Trail, 12 miles (18 km) SW of Kissimmee. **Tel** (407) 935-0002. 🚉 Kissimmee. 🚍 Kissimmee. **Open** 9am–5pm daily. **Closed** Sat & Sun Jun–Sep. 📷 📹 Sun 1:30pm. 🌐 **tnc.org**

Orlando's best maintained wilderness preserve is a wonderfully peaceful place, where visitors can escape from the crowds. A partnership between Disney and the Nature Conservancy opened to the public in 1992; the 12,000-acre preserve consists of tranquil lakes and swamps that are a haven for native plants and animals. The preserve is bordered by one of the last remaining undeveloped lakes in Florida.

More than 160 different species of wildlife live here, including Florida scrub-jays, Florida sandhill cranes, and Sherman's fox squirrels.

Unlike the other Disney attractions, there are no thrills or rides here, but there is still plenty to do. Visitors can follow one of the three hiking trails that lead to the shores of Lake Russell. The shortest walk is the interpretive trail, a pleasant 0.8 miles (1.2 km), where there is the opportunity to learn first-hand about nature along the way. The longer trails are partially

Amateur pilot in simulated combat at Fantasy of Flight

unshaded, so plenty of water and sunscreen should be brought along during the hotter months.

Visitors can also take an off-road buggy tour, which starts with a 20-minute introductory video about the preserve, before a embarking upon a trip through the swampland with a guide. Visitors do need to bear in mind that, despite its name, this is not a theme park. The alligators and snakes are very real. Visitors should always remain alert and exercise caution when they explore these regions.

# ⑫ Fantasy of Flight

**Road map** E3. Polk Co. 1400 Broad way Blvd SE, Polk City. **Tel** (863) 984-3500. 🚉 Winter Haven. 🚍 Winter Haven. **Open** daily. **Closed** Thanksgiving, Dec 25. 📷 ♿ 🌐 **fantasyofflight.com**

Fantasy of Flight may have the edge over Florida's many other

Lake Russell, one of the many lakes at The Disney Wilderness Preserve

aviation attractions because it provides the very sensations of flying. A series of vivid walk-through exhibits takes visitors into a World War II B-17 Flying Fortress during a bombing mission, and into World War I trenches in the middle of an air raid.

For an extra fee visitors can ride a World War II fighter aircraft simulator in a dogfight over the Pacific. In the cockpit, there will be a preflight briefing and advice from the control tower about takeoff, landing, as well as the presence of enemy aircraft.

A hangar full of the world's greatest collection of mint antique airplanes contains the first widely used airliner in the US, the 1929 Ford Tri-Motor, which appeared in the film *Indiana Jones and the Temple of Doom*, and the Roadair 1, a combined plane and car that flew just once, in 1959.

Several tours are available, including a look behind the scenes at the huge storage bays, or a visit to the Restoration Shop where visitors will meet expert craftsmen who rebuild the engines. There is also the opportunity to watch a pilot fly one of the aircraft in a private air show – or take to the skies.

# ⑬ LEGOLAND®

*See pp196–7.*

# ⑭ Bok Tower Gardens

**Road map** E3. Polk Co. 1151 Tower Blvd, Lake Wales. **Tel** (863) 676-1408. 🚉 Winter Haven. 🚌 Lake Wales. **Open** daily. 🅿️ ♿ 🌐 boktowergardens.org

Edward W. Bok arrived in the US from Holland in 1870 at the age of six, and subsequently became an influential publisher. Shortly before his death in 1930, he presented 128 acres of beautiful woodland gardens to the American public "for the success they had given him."

The striking, pink marble Singing Tower at Historic Bok Sanctuary

The sanctuary now encompasses 250 acres (100 ha) at the highest spot in peninsular Florida – a dizzying 298 ft (91 m) above sea level – in the center is the Singing Tower, which shelters Bok's grave at its base. The tower cannot be climbed, but try to attend its 45-minute live carillon concert, played daily at 3pm.

# ⑮ Yeehaw Junction

**Road map** E3. Osceola Co. Desert Inn, 5570 South Kenansville Road, Yeehaw Junction 34972. **Tel** (407) 436-1054. **Open** daily. ♿ 🌐 desertinnrestaurant.com

Yeehaw Junction was once known only as a watering hole for lumbermen and cowboys driving herds of cattle from the center of the state to the markets and railroads at the coast. Located at the crossroads of Florida's Turnpike and the scenic Highway 441, the **Desert Inn** is a good place to stop. The restaurant serves gator-and turtle-burgers, and there is a gift shop and a large outdoor area for festivals, as well as barbeques.

Dessert Inn on the scenic Highway 441, Yeehaw Junction

The 1880s building, which is listed on the National Registry of Historical Places, offers a fascinating look into the history of Cracker Country for busloads of tourists and bluegrass festival enthusiasts.

1930s police car, American Police Hall of Fame

# ⑯ American Police Hall of Fame

6350 Horizon Drive, Titusville. **Tel** (321) 264-0911. 🚉 Titusville. **Open** 10am–6pm daily. **Closed** Thanksgiving, Dec 25. 🅿️ ♿ 🌐 aphf.org

Few visitors are unmoved by the Hall of Fame's vast marble memorial, engraved with the names of more than 5,000 American police officers who have died in the line of duty. Yet some of the exhibits, while fascinating, are gory and sensationalist. The *RoboCop* mannequin, brass knuckles, and weapons disguised as lipstick and an umbrella, are innocuous enough. Some visitors, however, may find the prospect of strapping themselves into an electric chair, or inspecting the gas chamber, harder to stomach.

# ⓭ LEGOLAND® Florida

LEGOLAND® Florida, the largest of the LEGOLAND® parks, is another of Florida's impressive family-friendly theme parks. Conveniently located about halfway between Orlando and Tampa, the 150-acre (60-ha) park stretches across the beautiful shores of Lake Eloise, one of Central Florida's largest lakes. Little kids as well as older ones can enjoy an action-packed day of adventure and education amidst giant LEGO® figures, miniature LEGO® reproductions of cities, LEGO® rides, live shows, interactive games, and the LEGOLAND® Water Park. Built on the site of the former Cypress Gardens, the park also features native plants and exotic species.

Primary colors and not-so-mini figures greet visitors at the entrance to the park

**LEGOLAND® Water Park**
Hair-rising slides, splash pools, the LEGO wave pool, and the Build-A-Raft lazy river make this one of the most fun spots in the park.

Flying School

Driving School

Boati Scho

Cypress Gardens

①

## KEY

① The historic **Cypress Gardens** have been beautifully restored with great care.

② **MiniLand** has nine themed areas, including the Kennedy Space Center and the LEGO® STAR WARS™ set.

③ **LEGO® Kingdoms** transports kids to the medieval times with the LEGOLAND® Castle and its dragons.

④ **Fun Town** has the popular Grand Carousel and a 4-D movie theater.

⑤ **The Beginning**, features a 100 ft (30 m) high rotating platform offering a 360° view of the park.

**Pirate's Cove Ship**
Visitors are entertained by life-size versions of the popular Pirate series, complete with a pirate ship and an invading band of pirates on water-skis.

**Imagination Zone**
This area showcases several exciting hands-on models. At the Kid Power Towers, participants winch themselves up to the top of the colorful poles, then have a free fall to the bottom.

*For hotels and restaurants in this area see pp317–18 and pp336–9*

### Land of Adventure
Coastersaurus offers an old-fashioned, bone-rattling wooden coaster experience, in a prehistoric jungle of life-sized, animated LEGO brick dinosaurs.

## VISITORS' CHECKLIST

**Practical Information**
**Road map** E3. One LEGOLAND® Way, Winter Haven, about 45 minutes southwest of Orlando. **Tel** (877) 350-5346. **Open** 10am–7pm daily. **Closed** Tue & Wed during slow periods. Water Park **Open** 10:30am–6:30pm daily. 🏊 separate entry fee.
🆆 florida.legoland.com

**Transport**
LEGOLAND® shuttle buses run daily from I-Drive. The pick-up spot is outside Madame Tussauds Orlando, 8387 I-Drive.

### Duplo® Valley
Toddlers will recognize their familiar big LEGO blocks, as they ride the colorful train and tractors.

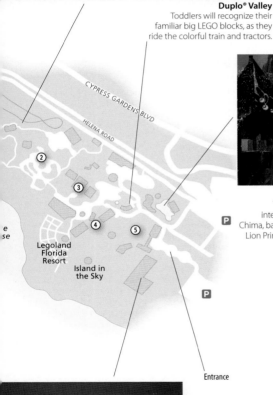

CYPRESS GARDENS BLVD

HELENA ROAD

② ③ ④ ⑤

Legoland Florida Resort

Island in the Sky

🅿

🅿

Entrance

### World of Chima™
The Quest for Chi™ takes visitors on an interactive boat ride through the world of Chima, battling water cannons to help Laval the Lion Prince defeat Cragger the Crocodile King.

### LEGOLAND® Hotel
A paradise for LEGO lovers, the hotel has 152 rooms in LEGO decor, interactive play areas, a pool, and a restaurant.

## Top Tips

- There are more than enough activities to fill two days, if you include the water park.
- Arrive early, and take older children straight to the coasters to beat lines
- Some coasters have a minimum height requirement, some require adult accompaniment.
- Save Aqua Zone Wave racers or NFPA Rescue Academy until the afternoon, when a drenching will be appreciated.
- Visit Kid Power Towers early, because it demands some work in the heat.
- Parents in particular will enjoy the gardens, and the magnificent banyan tree.

## ⑰ Canaveral National Seashore and Merritt Island

**Road map** F2. Brevard Co.
🚌 Titusville. **W** nps.gov/cana

These adjacent preserves on the Space Coast share an astounding variety of fauna and a wide range of habitats, including saltwater estuaries, marshes, pine flatwoods, and hardwood hammocks, all due to the meeting of temperate and subtropical climates here. You can often see alligators, as well as endangered species such as manatees, but it is the bird life that makes the greatest visual impact.

Many visitors simply head straight for the beach. The **Canaveral National Seashore** incorporates Florida's largest undeveloped barrier island beach – a magnificent 24-mile (39-km) strip of sand backed by dunes strewn with sea oats and sea grapes. Apollo Beach, at the northern end, is accessible along Route A1A, while Playalinda Beach is reached from the south, along Route 402; no road connects the two. The beaches are fine for sunbathing, but swimming conditions can be hazardous, and there are no lifeguards.

Behind Apollo Beach, Turtle Mound is a 40 ft (12 m) high rubbish dump of oyster shells created by Timucua Native Americans *(see pp44–5)* between AD 800 and

### Space Coast Bird Life

The magnificent and abundant bird life of the Space Coast is best viewed early in the morning or shortly before dusk. Between November and March, in particular, the marshes and lagoons teem with migratory ducks and waders, as up to 100,000 arrive from colder northern climes.

Sandhill crane

Brown pelican

Royal tern

Black skimmer

1400. Climb the boardwalk to the top for a view over Mosquito Lagoon, flecked with a myriad mangrove islets. Route 402 to Playalinda Beach also provides memorable views – of the Kennedy Space Center's shuttle launch pads, rising eerily out of the watery vastness. This route also crosses **Merritt Island National Wildlife Refuge**, which covers an area of 220 sq miles (570 sq km). Most of the refuge lies within the Kennedy Space Center and is out of bounds.

By far the best way to experience the local wildlife

**An alligator in the wild**

first hand is to follow the 6 mile (10 km) Black Point Wildlife Drive. An excellent leaflet, available at the start of the track near the junction of routes 402 and 406, explains such matters as how dikes control local mosquito populations (although visitors should still come armed with insect repellent in summer). Halfway along the drive you can stretch your legs by following the 5 mile (8 km) Cruickshank Trail, which starts nearby and has an observation tower.

East along Route 402 towards Playalinda, the Merritt Island Visitor Information Center has excellent displays on the habitats and unique flora and forna within the refuge. A mile (1.5 km) farther east, the Oak Hammock and Palm Hammock trails have short boardwalks across the marshland for bird-watching and photography.

🗺 **Canaveral National Seashore**
Route A1A, 20 miles (32 km) N of Titusville or Route 402, 10 miles (16 km) E of Titusville. **Tel** (321) 267-1110. **Open** daily.

🗺 **Merritt Island National Wildlife Refuge**
Route 406, 4 miles (6.5 km) E of Titusville. **Tel** (321) 861-0667. **Open** daily. **W** merrittisland. fws.gov

View from Black Point Drive, Merritt Island National Wildlife Refuge

## ⑱ Kennedy Space Center

*See pp200–205.*

## ⑲ Valiant Air Command Warbird Air Museum

**Road map** E2. Brevard Co. 6600 Tico Road, Titusville. **Tel** (321) 268-1941. 🚌 Titusville. **Open** 10am–6pm daily. **Closed** Thanksgiving, Dec 25. 🎫 ♿ 🆆 vacwarbirds.org

At this museum an enormous hangar houses military planes from World War II and later – all lovingly restored to flying condition. The pride of the collection is a working Douglas C-47 called Tico Belle: the aircraft saw service during World War II before becoming the official carrier for the Danish royal family.

Every March there is an air show, with mock dogfights. Several of the restored planes fly regularly, including a US Navy TBM Avenger, which has been recently undergone a 15-year rehabilitation. This plane honors the five bombers of the infamous Flight 19, which disappeared over the Bermuda Triangle in 1945. Visitors interested in aircraft restoration may explore the Larkin/Lindsay Restoration Hangar (accompanied by a staff member) and observe the detailed work on various ongoing warbird projects, carried out by its dedicated volunteers. Another section of the museum displays a large collection of military aviation memorabilia,

Porcher House, on the edge of Cocoa's leafy historic district

including uniforms, insignia, equipment, weapons, models, and artifacts.

## ⑳ Cocoa

**Road map** E3. Brevard Co. Cocoa Beach Chamber of Commerce. 🚹 20,000. 🚌 🛈 400 Fortenberry Rd, Merritt Island, (321) 459-2200. 🆆 cocoabeachchamber.com

Cocoa is the most appealing community among the sprawling conurbations along the Space Coast mainland. Its historic district, near where Route 520 crosses the Indian River to Cocoa Beach, is an attractive enclave known as Cocoa Village – with buildings dating from the 1880s (some of which house unpretentious boutiques), replica gas street-lamps, and brick sidewalks.

In Delannoy Avenue, on the eastern edge of the village, is the Classical Revival Porcher House, built of coquina stone *(see p219)* in 1916. Note the spade, heart, diamond, and

club carvings on its portico wall: Mrs. Porcher was an extremely avid bridge player.

## ㉑ Cocoa Beach

**Road map** F3. Brevard Co. 🚹 14,000. 🚌 Merritt Island. 🛈 400 Fortenberry Rd, (321) 459-2200.

The Space Coast's big, no-frills resort calls itself the east coast's surfing capital. Surfing festivals and bikini contests set the tone, along with win-your-weight-in-beer competitions on the pier. Motels, chain restaurants, and the odd strip joint characterize the main thoroughfare.

These are all eclipsed by the **Ron Jon Surf Shop**. This neon palace has surf boards galore (for sale and for rent) and a huge T-shirt collection. In front of its flashing towers, beach bum sports figures are frozen in modern sculpture.

🏠 **Ron Jon Surf Shop** 4151 N Atlantic Ave. **Tel** (321) 799-8888. **Open** daily: 24 hours. ♿

The Ron Jon Surf Shop in Cocoa Beach, with everything for the surfing or beach enthusiast

# ⑲ Kennedy Space Center

Situated on Merritt Island National Wildlife Refuge less than an hour's drive east of Orlando, the Kennedy Space Center has captured the world's attention. It was from here, with the launch of Apollo 11 in July 1969, that President Kennedy's dream of landing a man on the moon was realized. The center is one of the homes of NASA (National Aeronautics and Space Administration), and was the preparation and launch facility for the crewed Space Shuttle *(see p204)*. The Kennedy Space Center Visitor Complex offers events, attractions, and interactive programs to inform and entertain throughout the year.

★ **Apollo/Saturn V Center**
A Saturn V rocket, of the kind used by the Apollo missions, is the showpiece here. There is also a reconstructed control room where visitors experience a simulated launch *(see p202)*.

**Lunch with an Astronaut**
These sessions offer a one-of-a-kind opportunity to meet a veteran NASA astronaut.

★ **Rocket Garden**
Visitors can walk through a group of towering rockets, each of which represents a different period of space flight's history.

**KEY**

① Astronaut Encounter
② Children's Play Dome
③ Astronaut Memorial
④ Space shop
⑤ Shuttle Launch Experience®
⑥ Departure point for bus tours
⑦ Heroes & Legends
⑧ Information

**Visitor Complex**
*Each year, more than 1.5 million visitors from around the world experience their very own space adventure. Built in 1967, the Visitor Complex is one of Central Florida's most popular tourist destinations.*

★ **KSC Bus Tour**
Get exclusive access to the historic launch sites and working spaceflight facilities of NASA on a bus tour within the Kennedy Space Center.

**VISITORS' CHECKLIST**

**Practical Information**
**Road map** F2. Brevard Co. Off Route 405, 6 miles (9.5 km) E of Titusville. **Tel** (877) 313-2610. **Open** 9am daily. Closing times vary by season 🖼 all the exhibits are accessible; wheelchairs and strollers are available at Information. 🖉 🖾 W kennedyspacecenter.com

**Transport**
🚌 Titusville.

★ **Heroes & Legends**
Features the US Astronauts Hall of Fame. It displays personal items including journals, countdown recordings, and artifacts.

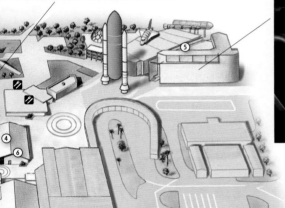

**Shuttle Launch Experience®**
Strap in and get vertical for a realistic simulation of a space shuttle launch.

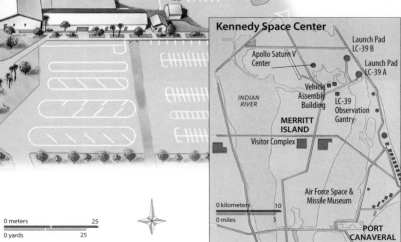

**Kennedy Space Center**

Apollo Saturn V Center
Launch Pad LC-39 B
Launch Pad LC-39 A
Vehicle Assembly Building
LC-39 Observation Gantry
INDIAN RIVER
MERRITT ISLAND
Visitor Complex
Air Force Space & Missile Museum
PORT CANAVERAL

0 kilometers        10
0 miles        5

0 meters        25
0 yards        25

# Exploring the Kennedy Space Visitor Complex

Built in 1967 for astronauts and their families to view space center operations, today the Visitor Complex is host to more than 1.5 million tourists each year. The 131 sq mile (340 sq km) facility offers guests a full-day, comprehensive space experience, including the Space Shuttle Atlantis, excellent IMAX® films, astronaut encounters, and the Apollo/Saturn V Center – the climax of the narrated, video-enhanced bus tour. The go-at-your-own-pace tour enables visitors to stop and explore the Apollo/Saturn V Center. One all-inclusive admission ticket admits visitors on the KSC Tour, both IMAX® space films, the US Astronaut Hall of Fame at Heroes & Legends, and all exhibits.

Discover NASA's plans to explore deep space at Journey to Mars: Explorers Wanted

## Visitor Complex

Organised into Mission Zones that are grouped by chronological events, the complex covers everything from the dawn of space exploration to current and future missions. The place everyone heads first is the **Shuttle: A Ship Like No Other** exhibit, where you can see the dramatic placement of the actual Atlantis orbiter, viewed as it would have been by space-walking astronauts. Visitors can then head to the Shuttle Launch Experience, described by astronauts as close to the

feeling of a real launch. You feel the G-forces as the simulation hurtles you toward space, then for an instant you hang weightless. Next on the list, or whenever you feel a need to escape the Florida heat, is the **IMAX® Theater** at Nasa Now and Next.

Top of the bill is *Hubble 3D*, an IMAX® film narrated by Leonardo DiCaprio, which offers an inspiring look into the legacy of the Hubble Space Telescope, launched into space in 1990 aboard the Space Shuttle Discovery. The film illustrates the impact the telescope has had on the way we

view the universe and features footage from the final Hubble repair mission. It also takes audiences through a space-shuttle launch sequence, and allows them to float next to astronauts. Another film on offer at the IMAX® is *Journey to Space*, narrated by Sir Patrick Stewart. The film uses actual space footage to explore NASA's plans to reach out into deep space. IMAX® films are included in the general admission ticket.

The 300-seat Astronaut Encounter Theater at the Visitor Complex offers visitors an opportunity to meet one of the people (there are more than 500) who have flown in space.

The **Astronaut Hall of Fame** commemorates the astronauts of Mercury, Gemini, Apollo, and the Space Shuttle Program, and has many of their personal items on display, plus artifacts, journals, and countdown recordings. Nearby, a "Space Mirror" tracks the movement of the sun, reflecting its light onto the names inscribed on the **Astronaut Memorial**. This honors the 16 astronauts, from the Apollo 1 to the Space Shuttle Challenger missions, who have given their lives in the service of space exploration.

Visitors clicking pictures with the Space Shuttle Atlantis at Kennedy Space Center

| | | | | | | |
|---|---|---|---|---|---|---|
| **1958** First American satellite, the *Explorer 1*, is launched (Jan 31) | **1962** John Glenn orbits the earth in *Mercury* spacecraft | **1966** *Gemini 8* makes first space docking (Mar 16) | **1968** *Apollo 8* orbits the moon (Dec 24) | **1977** The Space Shuttle *Enterprise* is tested aboard a Boeing 747 (Feb 18) | **1983** The first American woman goes into space, aboard Space Shuttle *Challenger* (Jun 18) | |
| **1955** | **1960** | **1965** | **1970** | **1975** | **1980** | |
| **1961** On May 5, Alan Shephard becomes the first American in space. Kennedy commits nation to moon landing | **1965** Edward White is the first American to walk in space (Jun 3) | **1969** Neil Armstrong and Buzz Aldrin (*Apollo 11*) walk on the moon (Jul 24) | **1975** American *Apollo* and Russian *Soyuz* vehicles dock in orbit (Jul 17) | **1981** *Columbia* is the first shuttle in space (Apr 12) **1982** The Space Shuttle Program begins | **1986** T Challeng explodes, killi all its cre (Jan 2 | |

## KSC Exhibits and Bus Tour

The entrance gate leads guests to a grand plaza and fountain where ticket stations and self-service kiosks can be found along with information stations, a retail store, and a restaurant. A fascinating walk-through exhibit shows visitors a comprehensive history of the major missions that provided the foundation for the space program. The all-glass rotunda leads to **Early Space Exploration**, which showcases key figures from the early days of rocketry. In the **Mercury Mission Control Room**, visitors view from an observation deck the actual components and consoles from which the first eight manned missions were monitored. Footage and interviews with some of the personnel are highlights of this area. Next are displays of the authentic Mercury and Gemini spacecraft so visitors can relive some of the excitement and intensity of early space exploration. KSC Tour buses leave

The Vehicle Assembly Building, which dominates the flat landscape

Rockets, missiles, and space launch vehicles on display at the Rocket Garden

every few minutes from the Visitor Complex and offer an exceptional tour of the space center's major facilities. The tour includes the **Apollo/Saturn V Center** and takes guests into secured areas, where guides explain the inner workings of each of the facilities. Visitors can take as long as they wish to explore the Apollo/Saturn V Center.

### Space Complex Tour

For each self-guided tour, allow between two and three hours to fully explore the facilities featured on the KSC Tour. The tours are fascinating and well worth the time it takes get around.

The Apollo/Saturn V Center features an actual 363 ft (110 m) Saturn V moon rocket. Visitors will see the historic launch of Apollo 8, the first manned mission to the moon in the Firing Room Theater, followed by a film at the Lunar Theater, which shows actual footage of the moon landing.

The **Apollo Treasures Gallery** is a celebration of 40 years of Apollo. Here visitors can see the actual Apollo 14 Command Module, as well as various pieces of rare equipment and spacesuits from the original moon missions. The only place in the world where guests can dine next to a genuine moon rock is also here, at the atmospheric Moon Rock Café.

There are additional special-interest tours, including: **Cape Canaveral: Then & Now Tour**, which is an historic tour of the Mercury, Gemini, and Apollo launch pads, as well as the Air Force Space and Missile Museum; and the **KSC Up-Close Tours**, which provide an insider's view of the entire space program. Tours may vary, and there are three available: The Vehicle Assembly Building, Launch Pad, and Launch Control Center. Tours sell out daily, so should be reserved in advance and taken on separate days, as they cover vast areas in great detail.

| | | | | |
|---|---|---|---|---|
| 3 *Discovery*, the shuttle since *Challenger* disaster, unched (Sep 29) | **1995** The *Atlantis* docks with Russian *Mir* space station (Jun 29) | **2001** Dennis Tito pays US$20 million to spend one week on board an International Space Center | **2008** NASA's *Phoenix* probe uncovers the existence of water ice on Mars (Jun) | **2012** SpaceX Dragon is the first private spacecraft to deliver cargo to the International Space Station |
| **1990** | **1995** | **2000** | **2005** | **2010** | **2015** |
| **1990** Hubble telescope is launched (Apr 24) | **1996** *Mars Pathfinder* gathers data from Mars | | **2006** The *New Horizons* spacecraft begins a nine-year journey toward Pluto (Jan 19) | **2011** Space Shuttle program ends (Aug 31) | **2015** NASA readies its ORION space capsule for deep-space exploration, and commercial aerospace companies developed more systems |
| | | **2003** Space Shuttle *Columbia* explodes on re-entry, killing all its crew (Feb 1) | | | |

# The Space Shuttle

By the late 1970s, the cost of sending astronauts into space had become too much for the American space budget. Hundreds of millions of dollars were spent lifting the Apollo missions into space, with little more than a scorched command module ever returning to Earth. The time had come to develop reusable spacecraft made for years of service. The answer was the Space Shuttle Columbia, which was launched into space on April 12, 1981 *(see pp56–7)*. The shuttle's large cargo capacity enabled it to take all kinds of satellites and probes into space, and it was used to lift materials for the construction of the International Space Station. The Space Shuttle program officially ended in 2011.

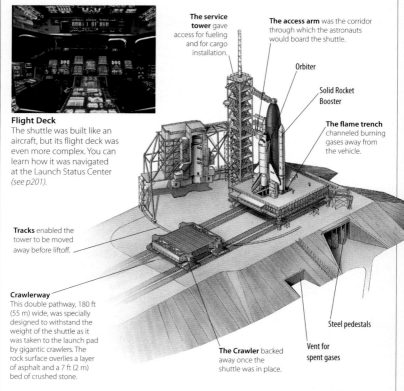

**The service tower** gave access for fueling and for cargo installation.

**The access arm** was the corridor through which the astronauts would board the shuttle.

Orbiter

Solid Rocket Booster

**The flame trench** channeled burning gases away from the vehicle.

**Flight Deck**
The shuttle was built like an aircraft, but its flight deck was even more complex. You can learn how it was navigated at the Launch Status Center *(see p201)*.

**Tracks** enabled the tower to be moved away before liftoff.

**Crawlerway**
This double pathway, 180 ft (55 m) wide, was specially designed to withstand the weight of the shuttle as it was taken to the launch pad by gigantic crawlers. The rock surface overlies a layer of asphalt and a 7 ft (2 m) bed of crushed stone.

**The Crawler** backed away once the shuttle was in place.

Vent for spent gases

Steel pedestals

## The Shuttle Launches

Since the shuttle made its maiden voyage in 1981, there were many missions shared between the *Columbia, Challenger, Discovery, Atlantis,* and *Endeavour* vehicles. The program was severely crippled when *Challenger* exploded shortly after liftoff in 1986, and again when *Columbia* disintegrated on re-entry in 2003. The safety of the other shuttles was later assured and regular launches were planned until 2011, when the program was retired. The launch of *Atlantis* on July 8, 2011 marked the final mission of this inspirational era of space exploration. Shuttle Atlantis can be seen at its permanent home at the Kennedy Space Center.

Shuttle clearing the launch tower

# Beyond the Shuttle Program

The future of space lies in the hands of private entrepreneurs – a band of billionaires made wealthy by various industries. Their companies, which include SpaceX, Virgin Galactic, and Blue Origin, have begun to take over the work traditionally undertaken by NASA, who shares its Kennedy Space Center launch pads and resources with them. Rockets designed by these companies launch from the Space Center regularly (launch schedules are available online), and visitors can see them during tours of the space center, or from across the lagoon.

SpaceX Falcon 9 rocket launcher with the Dragon spacecraft

## Space Privateers

Defense contractors and private companies have been developing launch systems and sending commercial communications satellites into space from KSC and Cape Canaveral for more than a decade. However, nothing set fire to the world's imagination as much as the efforts of high-tech entrepreneurs Elon Musk, Richard Branson, Jeff Bezos, Paul Allen, and others, who have turned their energies and wealth to space exploration.

## SpaceX

Founded in 2002 by PayPal co-founder Elon Musk, SpaceX made history in 2012 when its Dragon spacecraft became the first private spacecraft to launch from Cape Canaveral, to deliver cargo to the International Space Station, and to return safely to Earth. Since then Dragon has continued to carry cargo to and from the Space Station. It has many more launches scheduled to depart from Cape Canaveral – some from Launch Pad 39A. Entrepreneur Elon Musk's future plans include taking astronauts into space.

## Blue Origin

Amazon owner Jeff Bezos founded Blue Origin more than a decade ago, to develop safe, reliable, cost-effective human access to space. Working in partnership with NASA, the company has successfully tested an innovative launch-pad escape system, and launched sub-orbital rockets. In the future, Blue Origin plans to take tourists into space, and deliver astronauts into orbit.

## United Launch Alliance

Owned by Lockheed Martin and The Boeing Company, ULA is made up of two of the launch industry's most experienced teams – Atlas and Delta – which have been involved in America's presence in space since the 1960s. Formed in 2006, ULA regularly launches from Cape Canaveral Air Force Station, and continues its relationship with NASA, such as supplying rockets to launch spacecraft into orbit.

## Orion

Not all space exploration has moved to the private sector. Current NASA missions include the unmanned Exploration Flight Test-1 mission (EFT-1), which will test its Orion crew module systems for the beginning of human journeys toward deep space, asteroids, and Mars. Visitors to Kennedy Space Center can find out more about this flight test, launched atop a mammoth Delta 4 Heavy rocket, as well as updated details of the ambitious mission.

### Where to Watch the Launches

- Titusville, across the lagoon from KSC
- Marina Park: 501 Marina Road
- Sand Point Park: 101 N Washington Ave (US 1)
- Space View Park: 8 Broad Street
- Manzo Park: 3335 S Washington Ave (US 1)
- Rotary Riverfront Park: 4141 S. Washington Ave (US 1)
- Kennedy Point Park: 4915 S Washington Ave (US 1)
- Westbound SR 528 Causeway over the Banana River
- Cocoa Beach
- Jetty Park: East end of Port Canaveral off George King Blvd
- Cocoa Beach Pier: 401 Meade Ave
- Alan Shepard Park: East end of SR 520
- Fischer Park: East side of SR A1A, half a mile south of SR 520
- Lori Wilson Park: 1500 N Atlantic Ave

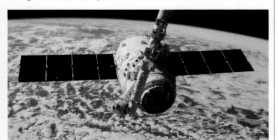

The Dragon spacecraft berths at the Space Station with help from Canadarm2

# THE NORTHEAST

The charms of the Northeast are more discreet than the glitz of Miami or the thrills of Orlando. Just a few miles from busy interstate highways, salty fishing villages, former plantations, and quaint country towns recall old-time Florida. Fabulous beaches lure sun-worshipers, while the historic town of St. Augustine can claim to be the longest inhabited European settlement in the US.

The state's recorded history begins in the Northeast, on the aptly named First Coast. Juan Ponce de León first stepped ashore here in 1513 (see p46), and Spanish colonists established St. Augustine, now a well-preserved town guarded by the mighty San Marcos fortress – one of the region's highlights.

The Northeast also saw the first influx of pioneers and tourists during the 19th-century steamboat era (see p52). At this time, Jacksonville was the gateway to Florida, with steamboats plying the broad St. Johns River and its tributaries. In the 1880s, Henry Flagler's railroad opened up the east coast, and wealthy visitors flocked to his grand hotels in St. Augustine and Ormond Beach. Those

in search of the winter sun headed farther south, too. Broad sandy beaches flank the popular resort of Daytona, which has been synonymous with car racing ever since the likes of Henry Ford and Louis Chevrolet raced automobiles on the beach during their winter vacations. Daytona is also a popular place for students to spend Spring Break: this is as lively as it gets in the Northeast.

Venturing inland, west of the St. Johns, is the wooded expanse of the Ocala National Forest; the woods then thin out to reveal the rolling pastures of Marion County's billion-dollar thoroughbred horse industry. Nearby, charming country towns and villages such as Micanopy have been virtually untouched by the 20th century.

St. Augustine's splendid Lightner Museum, occupying the former exclusive Alcazar Hotel

◀ Castillo de San Marcos at sunset, St. Augustine

# Exploring the Northeast

The first coast is a well-traveled route, unfurling along the Atlantic shore in a 120 mile (193 km) string of beaches and resorts, interrupted by dunes and marshland popular with bird-watchers. Resorts run the gamut from decorous Fernandina Beach to action-packed Daytona Beach. Between these two extremes lies the historic jewel of St. Augustine. Strike inland, and the Ocala National Forest offers dozens of hiking trails, boating, and fishing on spring-fed lakes. Snorkeling and diving are also popular pursuits in crystal-clear springs. Many of the region's Victorian homes are now bed-and-breakfasts, which make a pleasant change from hotels, and provide a more homely base for exploring.

## Sights at a Glance

Traditional American trailer, Ocala National Forest

**For additional map symbols** *see back flap*

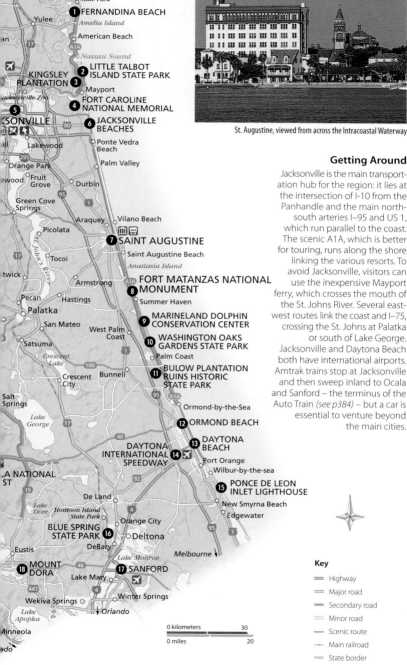

St. Augustine, viewed from across the Intracoastal Waterway

**Savannah**
Fort Clinch
State Park
Yulee
**1 FERNANDINA BEACH**
*Amelia Island*
American Beach
*Nassau Sound*
**2 LITTLE TALBOT
ISLAND STATE PARK**
KINGSLEY
PLANTATION **3** Mayport
*Jacksonville Zoo*
**4 FORT CAROLINE
NATIONAL MEMORIAL**
**5**
SONVILLE
**6 JACKSONVILLE
BEACHES**
Ponte Vedra
Beach
Lakewood
Orange Park
Palm Valley
wood Fruit
Grove
Durbin
Green Cove
Springs
Araquey Vilano Beach
Picolata
**7 SAINT AUGUSTINE**
Tocoi
Saint Augustine Beach
*Anastasia Island*
twick
Armstrong **FORT MATANZAS NATIONAL
8 MONUMENT**
Pecan Hastings
Summer Haven
Palatka
San Mateo **9 MARINELAND DOLPHIN
CONSERVATION CENTER**
West Palm
Coast
Satsuma
**10 WASHINGTON OAKS
GARDENS STATE PARK**
*Crescent
Lake*
Palm Coast
Crescent Bunnell **11 BULOW PLANTATION
RUINS HISTORIC
STATE PARK**
Salt
Springs
Ormond-by-the-Sea
*Lake
George*
**12 ORMOND BEACH**
**DAYTONA 13 DAYTONA
INTERNATIONAL BEACH
SPEEDWAY 14**
Port Orange
A NATIONAL
ST
Wilbur-by-the-sea
De Land **15 PONCE DE LEON
INLET LIGHTHOUSE**
*Lake
Dorr*
New Smyrna Beach
Hontoon Island
State Park Orange City
Edgewater
**BLUE SPRING
STATE PARK 16**
DeBary
Deltona
Eustis
*Lake Monroe*
Melbourne
**18 MOUNT
DORA 17 SANFORD**
Lake Mary
441
Winter Springs
Wekiva Springs
*Lake
Apopka*
Orlando
inneola
do

### Getting Around

Jacksonville is the main transportation hub for the region: it lies at the intersection of I-10 from the Panhandle and the main north–south arteries I–95 and US 1, which run parallel to the coast. The scenic A1A, which is better for touring, runs along the shore linking the various resorts. To avoid Jacksonville, visitors can use the inexpensive Mayport ferry, which crosses the mouth of the St. Johns River. Several east–west routes link the coast and I-75, crossing the St. Johns at Palatka or south of Lake George. Jacksonville and Daytona Beach both have international airports. Amtrak trains stop at Jacksonville and then sweep inland to Ocala and Sanford – the terminus of the Auto Train *(see p384)* – but a car is essential to venture beyond the main cities.

0 kilometers 30
0 miles 20

### Key

— Highway
— Major road
— Secondary road
— Minor road
— Scenic route
—·— Main railroad
— State border

Chinese Chippendale architecture in Fernandina

# ❶ Fernandina Beach

**Road map**: E1. Nassau Co. 🏛 12,000
🚉 Jacksonville. 🚌 Jacksonville.
ℹ 961687 Gateway Blvd, (904) 261-
3248. 🌐 ameliaisland.com

The town of Fernandina Beach
on Amelia Island, just across the
St. Marys River from Georgia, was
renowned as a pirates' den until
the early 1800s. Its deep-water
harbor attracted a motley crew
of foreign armies and adventurers, whose various allegiances
earned Amelia Island its
nickname, the Isle of Eight Flags.
Today, Fernandina is better known
as a charming Victorian resort
and Florida's primary source of
sweet Atlantic white shrimp –
more than two million pounds
(900,000 kilos) are caught by
the shrimping fleet each year.

The original Spanish settlement
was established at Old Fernandina,
a sleepy backwater just north
of the present town. In the
1850s the whole town moved
south to the eastern terminus
of Senator David Yulee's cross-
Florida railroad. The move,
coupled with the dawn of Florida
tourism in the 1870s (see pp52–3),
prompted the building boom
that created the much-admired
heart of today's Fernandina –
the 50-block **Historic District**.

The legacy of Fernandina's
golden age is best seen in
the Silk Stocking District, which
occupies more than half of the
Historic District, and is so-named
for the affluence of its original
residents. Sea captains and
timber barons built homes
here in a variety of styles: Queen
Anne houses decorated with
fancy gingerbread detailing and
turrets jostle graceful Italianate
residences and fine examples
of Chinese Chippendale.

Watching the shrimp
boats put into harbor
at sunset is a local
ritual. The fleet is
commemorated by
a monument at the
foot of downtown
Center Street, where
chandleries and naval
stores once held sway.
These weathered brick
buildings now house
antique shops and
upscale gift shops. The
1878 Palace Saloon still
serves a wicked Pirate's
Punch at the long
mahogany bar adorned
with hand-carved caryatids.

Down on 3rd Street, the 1857
Florida House Inn is the state's
oldest tourist hotel, and a couple
of blocks farther south, the
**Amelia Island Museum of
History** occupies the former

Peg Leg,
of Fernandina Beach

jail. Guided, 90-minute tours
cover the island's turbulent
past – from the time of the
first Native American inhabitants to the early 1900s.
Guided tours of the town are
also offered (reserve ahead).

🏛 **Amelia Island Museum
of History**
233 S 3rd St. **Tel** (904) 261-7378.
**Open** daily. **Closed** public hols.
📷 📹 compulsory; two tours
daily. ♿ limited. 🌐 amelia
museum.org

## Environs
Thirteen miles (21 km) long and
only 2 miles (3 km) wide at its
broadest point, **Amelia Island**
was first settled by the Timucua
tribe in the second century BC.
The rich fishing grounds and
abundant hunting suggest
that the island may have
supported around 30,000
people, although few signs
remain of their presence.
There's still excellent fishing,
and the island also offers five
golf courses and one of
Florida's rare opportunities to
ride horses along the beach.
The splendid sands are
backed by dunes that can
reach 40 ft (12 m) high
in places.

The northern tip of
the island is occupied
by the 1,121 acre
(453 ha) **Fort Clinch
State Park**, with trails, beaches,
and camp grounds, as well as a
19th-century fort built to guard
the Cumberland Sound at the
mouth of the St. Marys River.
Construction of the fort, an irregular brick pentagon with massive
earthworks, 4.5 ft (1.5 m) thick
walls, and a battery of Civil War
cannons, took from 1847 until
the 1860s.

Park rangers wear Civil War
uniforms. They are joined by
volunteers on the first full
weekend of each month in re-
enactments, when a variety of
duties are re-created. Candlelit
tours are given on the Saturday.

🏰 **Fort Clinch State Park**
2601 Atlantic Ave Tel: (904) 277-7274.
**Open** daily. 📷 ♿ limited. ⚠
🌐 floridastateparks.org

Amelia Island's Atlantic shore, in easy reach
of Fernandina Beach

# ❷ Little Talbot Island State Park

**Road map**: E1. Duval Co. 12157
Heckscher Drive, Jacksonville.
**Tel** (904) 251-2320. 🚆 Jacksonville.
🚌 Jacksonville. **Open** daily. 🅿️ ♿
limited. 🏕️ 🅦 **floridastateparks.org**

Much of Amelia Island and
the neighboring islands of Big
Talbot, Little Talbot, and Fort
George to the south remain
undeveloped and a natural
haven for wildlife.

Little Talbot Island State Park
has a good family campground,
trails through coastal hammocks
and marshlands, and great
fishing. There are otters, marsh
rabbits, fiddler crabs, herons,
and laughing gulls. Bobcats hide
out in the woods, manatees bob
about in the Intracoastal waters,
and in summer turtles lay their
eggs on the beach (see p121).
In Fall, whales travel here to
calve offshore.

View along a trail through marshland on
Little Talbot Island

# ❸ Kingsley Plantation

**Road map**: E1. Duval Co. 11676
Palmetto Ave, Fort George.
**Tel** (904) 251-3537. 🚆 Jacksonville.
🚌 Jacksonville. **Open** call first.
♿ 🅦 **nps.gov**

Located in the Timucuan
Ecological and Historic Preserve,
Kingsley Plantation is the oldest
plantation house in Florida. Built
in 1798 at the northern end of
Fort George Island, it takes its
name from Zephaniah Kingsley,
who moved here in 1814.
He amassed 32,000 acres

Ruins of the original slave cabins unique to the Kingsley Plantation

(12,950 ha) of land, stretching
from Lake George near the
Ocala National Forest north
to the St. Marys River. This area
used to encompass four major
plantations; the Kingsley plantation itself had as many as 100
slaves working in its fields of
cotton, sugarcane, and corn.

Kingsley was a rather liberal
thinker for his time, supporting
slavery while also advocating
a more lenient "task-system" for
his slaves. He married a slave,
Anna Jai, and later freed her.
They lived in the clapboard
plantation house (see p49)
until 1839.

Described at the time as "a
very nice commodious house,"
Kingsley's relatively simple home
is closed for restoration. The
building is topped by a small
rooftop parapet called a "widow's
walk," once used to survey the
surrounding fields. Nearby are
the barn and separate kitchen
house, but the plantation is best
known for the 23 slave cabins
located in woods near the
entrance gate. Built of durable
tabby (see p300), these basic
dwellings have survived the
years, and one is now restored.

Fort Caroline in 1564 by Theodore de Bry

# ❹ Fort Caroline National Memorial

**Road map**: E1. Duval Co. 12713
Fort Caroline Rd, Jacksonville.
**Tel** (904) 641-7155. 🚆 Jacksonville.
🚌 Jacksonville. **Open** daily.
**Closed** Thanksgiving, Dec 25, Jan 1.
♿ 🅦 **nps.gov/foca**

The actual site of Fort Caroline
was washed away when the St.
Johns River was dredged in the
1880s. At Fort Caroline National
Memorial, a reconstruction of
the original 16th-century
defenses clearly illustrates the
style of the first European forts
in the New World. Information
panels around the site explain
the fort's violent history, which
began shortly after French
settlers arrived in June 1564.

In the attempt to stake a
claim to North America, three
small French vessels carrying
300 men sailed up the St. Johns
and made camp 5 miles (8 km)
inland. René de Goulaine de
Laudonnière led the French,
who were helped by local
Timucua Native Americans, to
build a triangular wooden fort,
named La Caroline in honor of
Charles IX of France
(see p46). A year later,
with the settlers
close to starvation,
reinforcements
under Jean Ribault
arrived. The Spanish,
however, took
the fort.

In the park is a
replica of the stone
column erected
by Jean Ribault.

The glass and steel skyline that dominates Jacksonville's north bank

# ❺ Jacksonville

**Road map**: E1. Duval Co. 🗺 1,201,984. ✈ 🚇 🚌 ℹ 550 Water St, (904) 798-9111. 🌐 visitjacksonville.com

Jacksonville, the capital of the First Coast of Florida, was founded in 1822. Named after General Andrew Jackson (see p49), the town boomed as a port and rail terminus in the late 1800s. Today, financial businesses fuel the impressive downtown commercial district, which you can view from the Skyway (see p384).

Jacksonville, Florida's largest city in area, spans the St. Johns River, which provides a focus for visitors. Most people head for the pedestrian areas that flank the riverbanks and are connected by water taxi services (see p385).

The **Jacksonville Landing** shopping and dining complex and the Museum of Contemporary Art Jacksonville are located on the north side of the St. Johns. Riverside, a large residential area, is home to the Cummer Museum of Art. The pleasant 1.2 mile (2 km) long **Riverwalk** along the south

bank includes the impressive Museum of Science and History.

## 🏛 Museum of Science and History

1025 Museum Circle. **Tel** (904) 396-6674. **Open** daily. 🅿 ♿ 🌐 themosh.org

This ever-expanding museum houses an eclectic collection of exhibits, and provides a user-friendly guide to local history. The 12,000-year-old culture of the local Timucua Native Americans (see pp44–5) and their predecessors is illustrated with tools, arrowheads, pottery, and other archaeological finds.

There are sections dealing with the ecology and history of the St. Johns River and the Maple Leaf, a Civil War steamship that sank in 1864. The Bryan Gooding Planetarium runs 3-D laser shows on Fridays and Saturdays.

## 🏛 Museum of Contemporary Art Jacksonville

333 North Laura Street. **Tel** (904) 366-6911. **Open** varies. **Closed** Mon. 🅿 🌐 mocajacksonville.org

## Jacksonville City Center

① Jacksonville Landing
② Sweet Pete's Candy Factory
③ Riverwalk
④ Museum of Science and History
⑤ Cummer Museum of Art and Gardens
⑥ Museum of Contemporary Art Jacksonville

For keys to symbols see back flap

For hotels and restaurants in this area see p319 and pp339–41

Located in the heart of Jacksonville, this spacious museum of five galleries is home to the largest collection of modern and contemporary art in Southeast USA.

### 🏠 Sweet Pete's Candy Factory

400 N. Hogan St. **Tel** (855) 798-7393.
**Open** daily. **Closed** public hols.
🆆 sweetpetescandy.com

One of the largest independent candymakers in the United States, manufacturing handcrafted candies and quality chocolates, this shop is housed in a historic building in Jacksonville, once a political club visited by Presidents Teddy Roosevelt, John F. Kennedy and Dwight Eisenhower.

Rare white rhinos at the famous Jacksonville Zoo

### 🦓 Jacksonville Zoo & Gardens

870 Zoo Parkway. **Tel** (904) 757-4463.
**Open** daily. **Closed** Dec 25. 🅿️ 🅰️
🆆 jacksonvillezoo.org

Opened in 1914, Jacksonville Zoo lies north of the city, off I-95. Some 1,800 animals, from anteaters to zebras, are on view in their natural habitats. Lions, elephants, and kudu roam the African veldt, while diminutive dik-dik deer, African crocodiles, and porcupines can be found along the zoo's Okavango Trail. Other attractions include the largest collection of jaguars in the US, an aviary, and a Magellanic penguin area.

For a broader picture, take the 15-minute miniature rail journey that loops around half of the 89-acre site.

### 🏛 Cummer Museum of Art and Gardens

829 Riverside Ave. **Tel** (904) 356-6857.
**Open** Tue–Sun. **Closed** public hols.
🅿️ 🅰️ 🆆 cummer.org

This excellent museum stands in exquisite formal gardens that lead down to the St. Johns River. With a permanent collection of 4,000 objects, the 12 galleries exhibit a small but satisfying selection of both decorative and fine arts. These range from Classical and pre-Columbian sculpture and ceramics through Renaissance paintings to the Wark Collection of jewel-like early Meissen porcelain.

Other notable pieces include the tiny *Entombment of Christ* (c.1605) by Rubens, and a striking collection of Japanese netsuke. Also on show is work by American Impressionists and such 19th-and-20th-century artists as John James Audubon.

### ❻ Jacksonville Beaches

**Road map**: E1. Duval Co, St. Johns Co.
🚉 Jacksonville. 🚌 Jacksonville.
🚌 BH1, BH2, BH3. ℹ️ 325 Jacksonville Dr, (904) 249-3868. 🆆 **jacksonville beach.org**

Some 12 miles (19 km) east of downtown Jacksonville, half a dozen beaches stretch 28 miles (45 km) north and south along the Atlantic shore. In the south, Ponte Vedra Beach is known for its sports facilities, particularly golf. Jacksonville Beach is the busiest spot, and is home to

Swimmers enjoying the freshwater lakes of Kathryn Abbey Hanna Park

**Adventure Landing**, a year-round entertainment complex and summer season water park. Heading north, Neptune Beach and Atlantic Beach are both quieter and are popular with families.

By far the nicest spot is the **Kathryn Abbey Hanna Park**, with its fine white sand beach, woodland trails, freshwater lake fishing, swimming, and camping areas. The park lies just south of **Mayport**, one of the oldest fishing villages in the US, still with its own shrimping fleet and home to a US Navy aircraft carrier.

### 🎡 Adventure Landing

1944 Beach Blvd. **Tel** (904) 246-4386.
**Open** daily, weather permitting. 🅿️
🅰️ 🆆 adventurelanding.com

### 🏕 Kathryn Abbey Hanna Park

500 Wonderwood Drive. **Tel** (904) 249-4700. **Open** daily. 🅿️ 🅰️ ⚠️
🆆 coj.net

Shrimp boats moored at the picturesque docks of Mayport on the St. Johns

# ❶ Street-by-Street: St. Augustine

America's oldest continuously occupied European settlement was founded by Pedro Menéndez de Avilés *(see p46)* on the feast day of St. Augustine in 1565. The town burned down in 1702 but was soon rebuilt in the lee of the mighty Castillo de San Marcos. Many of the picturesque, narrow streets of the old town, lined by attractive buildings made of indigenous coquina rock, date from this early period.

When Henry Flagler *(see pp128–9)* honeymooned in St. Augustine in 1883, he was so taken by the place that he later returned to found the Ponce de León Hotel, now Flagler College, and soon the gentle trickle of visitors became a flood. St. Augustine has been a major stop on the tourist trail ever since. Today, it has many attractions for the modern tourist, not least its 43 miles (70 km) of beaches and its proximity to several golf courses and marinas.

**★ Flagler Colle**
Tiles and other Spanish touches were used in the architecture of th former Flagler ho

**★ Lightner Museum**
*Cleopatra* (c.1890) by Romanelli is one of the exhibits from Florida's Gilded Age on display here.

**Casa Monica**
became Flagler's third hotel in town in 1888.

**Government House**
This imposing building houses the University of Florida's Museum of History and Archaeology. The exhibit "First Colony: Our Spanish Origins" tells the story of the founding of St. Augustine.

**Prince Murat House**
Prince Achille Murat, nephew of Napoleon, resided in this house in 1824.

← To Oldest House

**★ Ximenez-Fatio House**
This was built as a private house in 1797. Later, a second floor with an airy verandah was added, and in the mid-19th century it became a boarding house.

**Plaza de la Constitución**
The heart of the Spanish settlement is this leafy square, which is host to a program of concerts, and flanked by Government House and the Cathedral Basilica.

## VISITORS' CHECKLIST

**Practical Information**
**Road map**: E1. St. Johns Co.
🏔 14,200. 🛈 10 Castillo Drive, (904) 825-1000. Arts & Crafts Spring Festival (Apr).
W FloridasHistoricCoast.com

**Transport**
🚌 52 San Marco Ave, (800) 231-2222.

**City Gate**
Dating from the 18th century, this city entrance leads to the Old Town via historic St. George Street.

**The Peña-Peck House**, dating from the 1740s, is the finest First Spanish Period home in the city.

➤ To City Gate

SPANISH STREET

ST GEORGE STREET

TREASURY STREET

CATHEDRAL PLACE

CHARLOTTE STREET

AVENIDA MENENDEZ

KING STREET

**Bridge of Lions**
Marble lions guard the bridge opened across Matanzas Bay in 1927.

| 0 meters | | 50 |
| 0 yards | | 50 |

**Key**

— Suggested route

**Spanish Military Hospital**
This reconstruction of a ward re-creates the spartan hospital conditions available to Spanish settlers in the late 18th century.

# Exploring St. Augustine

The historic heart of St. Augustine is compact and easy to explore on foot. Part of the fun is escaping off the busy main streets and wandering down shady side turnings, peering into courtyards, and discovering quiet corners where cats bask in the sunshine and ancient live oaks trail curtains of gray-green Spanish moss. Horsedrawn carriage tours are a popular way to get around – they depart from Avenida Menendez, north of the Bridge of Lions. Tourist trains and trolleys follow a more extensive route around the main sights while their drivers narrate an anecdotal history of St. Augustine.

St. George Street, the historic district's main thoroughfare, lit up at night

### A Tour of St. Augustine

Pedestrian St. George Street is the focus of the historic district, with shops and some of St. Augustine's main attractions, including the excellent Colonial Quarter Museum. The street leads from the old City Gate to the town square, the Plaza de la Constitucion. Attractive, brick-paved Aviles Street runs south from this square and has several interesting Colonial buildings.

King Street, west of the plaza, has a very different feel, with the Lightner Museum and Flagler College housed in hotels built by Henry Flagler (*see pp52–3*) in the late 19th century.

### 🏛 The Oldest Wooden Schoolhouse

14 St. George St. **Tel** (888) 653-7245.
**Open** 9am–5pm daily. **Closed** Dec 25.
🅿 ♿

Built some time before 1788, this is purportedly America's oldest wooden schoolhouse. Walls of cypress and red cedar are held together by wooden pins and cast-iron spikes, and a massive chain anchors it in high winds.

### 🏛 Colonial Quarter

33 St. George St. **Tel** (904) 342-2857.
**Open** 9am–8pm daily.
**Closed** Dec 25, for special events.
🌐 ColonialQuarter.com

Experience life in 16th–18th-century St. Augustine, and learn about the cultures that left their mark on it – from Minorcans and Native Americans to the Spanish, British, and African-Americans – on this two-acre plot in the downtown historic district. Guided tours operate several times a day, and interactive events, such as musket drills in the 17th-century fortified town, are fun for all ages.

The Colonial Quarter also showcases archaeological evidence of one of the town's first wooden forts, plus 16th-century boat-building and blacksmith skills. Climb the watchtower for views of the Castillo de San Marcos and the bay.

### 🏛 Peña-Peck House

143 St. George St. **Tel** (904) 829-5064.
**Open** Mon–Sat. 🅿 ♿ limited.

This restored house was built in the 1740s for the Spanish Royal Treasurer, Juan de Peña. In 1837 it became the home and office of

Dr. Seth Peck, and the Peck family lived here for almost 100 years. It is furnished in mid-19th century style, and many of the objects displayed are family heirlooms.

### 🏛 Museum of History and Archaeology at the Government House

48 King St. **Tel** (904) 825-5079.
**Open** daily. **Closed** Dec 25. 🅿 ♿
🌐 staugustine.ufl.edu

Government House, adorned with Spanish-style loggias copied from a 17th-century painting, over-looks the Plaza de la Constitucion, and houses the restored museum, managed by the University of Florida. The museum focuses on St. Augustine and North Florida history through changing exhibitions.

### 🏛 Spanish Military Hospital

3 Aviles St. **Tel** (904) 827-0807.
**Open** daily. **Closed** Dec 25.
🌐 ancientcitytours.net

Offering a rare glimpse into the care given to soldiers in the late 1700s, the hospital rooms include an apothecary and cot-lined ward. On display is a list of hospital rules and gory medical practices.

### 🏛 Prince Murat House

246 St. George St. **Tel** (904) 257-8994.
🅿 🌐 thecollectorinn.com

Once part of the Dow Museum of Historic Homes, this house, now a boutique hotel, was rented by Prince Murat, nephew of Napoleon Bonaparte. The atmospheric house has been renovated and turned into a hotel that offers the unbeatable experience of staying in one of the oldest buildings in the entire country.

The Oldest Wooden Schoolhouse, built in the 1700s

### 🏠 Ximenez-Fatio House

20 Aviles St. **Tel** (904) 829-3575. **Open** Tue–Sat. **Closed** public hols. 🐾 ♿ limited. 🅦 ximenezfatiohouse.org

This lovely house was built in 1797 as the home and store of a Spanish merchant. Today, run by the National Society of Colonial Dames, it is a museum that re-creates the genteel boarding house it became in the 1830s, decorated with period artworks and furnishings, when invalids, developers, and adventurers escaped to Florida from the harsh northern winters.

### 🏠 Oldest House

14 St. Francis St. **Tel** (904) 824-2872. **Open** daily. **Closed** Easter, Thanksgiving, Dec 25. 🐾 ♿ limited. 🅦 oldesthouse.org

Also known as the Gonzalez-Alvarez house, this building can be traced through almost 300 years. There is even evidence that the site was first occupied in the early 1600s, though the existing structure postdates the English raid of 1702 (see p47).

The coquina walls (see p219) were part of the original one-story home of a Spanish artilleryman, Tomas Gonzalez. A second story was added during the English occupation of 1763–83. Each room is furnished in a style relevant to the different periods of the house's history.

### 🏛 Lightner Museum

75 King St. **Tel** (904) 824-2874. **Open** 9am–5pm daily. **Closed** Dec 25. 🐾 ♿ 🅦 lightnermuseum.org

Formerly the Alcazar Hotel, set up by Henry Flagler, this three-story, Hispano-Moorish building is now, aptly, a museum devoted to the Gilded Age. It was selected by Chicago publisher Otto C. Lightner, who transferred his collections of Victorian arts to St. Augustine in 1948. There's a glittering display of superb glass (including work by Louis Tiffany), furnishings, sculpture, paintings, plus mechanical musical instruments and toys. The Grand Ballroom houses an exhibit of "American Castle" furniture.

The Gonzalez Room, named after the first residents of the Oldest House

### 🏛 Flagler College

King St at Cordova St. **Tel** (904) 829-6481. **Open** daily. 🐾 ♿ 🅦 flagler.edu

Starting out as the Ponce de León Hotel, another of Flagler's splendid endeavors, this building opened in 1888, heralded as "the world's finest hotel." A statue of Flagler greets visitors, but only the college dining room and marble-clad foyer in the rotunda are open to the public. Here, the cupola's symbolic motifs represent Spain and Florida: notably the golden mask of the Timucuan (see pp44–5) sun god. You can also visit the Flagler Room with its c. 1887 illusionary paintings.

Tiffany stained-glass window

### 🏛 Fort Mose Historic State Park

15 Fort Mose Trail. **Tel** (904) 823-2232. **Open** 9am–5pm daily. **Closed** Tue. 🐾 🅦 floridastateparks.org

In 1738, this site became America's first legal free African settlement, for those fleeing slavery from the colonies in the Carolinas. In 1994 the site became a National Historic Landmark, and in 2009, a precursor site on the National Underground Railroad Network to Freedom. Visitors can explore the land, visitor center, and museum.

### 🏛 St. Augustine Lighthouse

81 Lighthouse Ave. **Tel** (904) 829-0745. **Open** 9am–6pm daily. 🐾 🅦 staugustinelighthouse.com

This working historical lighthouse offers lofty views of St. Augustine, and visitors can learn about the changing coastline, the origins of the shrimping industry, and

traditional wooden boat-building (call for times). There are activities aplenty for children, from the walk-in kaleidoscope to knot tying and a play shipyard.

### 🐊 St. Augustine Alligator Farm Zoological Park

999 Anastasia Blvd. **Tel** (904) 824-3337. **Open** 9am–5pm daily. 🐾 🅦 alligatorfarm.com

Opened in the late 19th century, this farm of Florida reptiles was a quintessential Florida attraction. Today it is a zoo with educational shows and exhibits, plus research and worldwide conservation efforts. Daredevil visitors can zip-line across the alligator lagoon.

### 🏛 Villa Zorayda

83 King St. **Open** 10am–5pm Mon–Sat, 11am–4pm Sun. **Closed** Easter, Thanksgiving. 🅦 villazorayda.com

This is a one-tenth scale replica of part of the Alhambra Palace in Granada, Spain. Built in 1883 with 40 windows differing in size, shape, and color, it contains valuable art and artifacts from the Middle East.

Visitors can take self-guided audio tours in English or Spanish.

Moorish tracery and Arabic motifs decorating the Villa Zorayda

# Castillo de San Marcos

Despite its role as protector of the Spanish fleets en route back to Europe, St. Augustine was guarded for over a century only by a succession of wooden forts. After suffering a century of attacks, including one by Sir Frances Drake *(see p47),* and many more by pirates, the Spanish colonizers began to build a stone fortification in 1672.

The resulting Castillo de San Marcos, which took 23 years to finish, is the largest and most complete Spanish fort in the US. Constructed of coquina, it is a textbook example of 17th-century military architecture, with layers of outer defenses and walls up to 18 ft (6 m) thick.

After the US gained Florida in 1821, the castillo was renamed Fort Marion. It was used chiefly as a military prison and storage depot for the rest of the 19th century.

**Mortars**
Often highly decorated and bearing the royal coat of arms, these short-barreled weapons fired large, heavy projectiles on a curved trajectory. Bombs could thus clear obstacles or land on ships' decks.

**★ Guard Rooms**
No Spanish soldiers actually lived in the fort. During guard duty (usually 24-hour shifts), they would cook, eat, and shelter in these reinforced vaults.

**★ Glacis and Covered Way**
Across the moat, a walled area known as the "covered way" shielded soldiers who were firing on the enemy. Leading up to the wall, a slope (the "glacis") protected the fort from cannon fire.

## Coquina

This sedimentary limestone rock, formed by billions of compacted seashells and corals, had the consistency of hard cheese when waterlogged, and was easy to quarry. It hardened as it dried but could still absorb the impact of a cannonball without shattering. During the siege of 1740, the English attackers fired projectiles that buried themselves in the fort's coquina walls. Legend has it that they were then dug out and fired back.

The thick coquina walls of the powder magazine

### VISITORS' CHECKLIST

**Practical Information**
1 South Castillo Drive, St. Augustine. **Tel** (904) 829-6506. **Open** 8:45am–4:45pm daily. **Closed** Dec 25. 🖼 ♿ limited. 📷 call ahead for details.
ᴡ nps.gov/casa/

★ **Gun Deck**
From here, cannons could reach targets up to 3 miles (5 km) away. Strategic positioning made a deadly crossfire.

**La Necessaria**
Tucked under the ramp that leads up to the gun deck was the "necessary" room, a tidal-flush sewage system.

## KEY

① **The inner drawbridge and portcullis,** built of ironclad pine beams, were the fort's final defenses.

② **The ravelin** guarded the entrance from enemy attack.

③ **The moat,** which once encircled the entire fort, was usually kept dry. During sieges livestock was kept there.

④ **The Plaza de Armas** is ringed by rooms that were used to contain stockpiles of food and weapons.

⑤ **British room**

⑥ **Chapel**

⑦ **Watchtower** the fort's northeast bastion, this tower would have been manned day and night to look out for enemy ships.

⑧ **Powder magazine**

⑨ **Water battery**

⑩ **Sea wall**

⑪ **The shot furnace,** built in 1844 by the US Army, was designed to heat up cannon balls. The red-hot "shot" could set enemy ships on fire.

## ❽ Fort Matanzas National Monument

**Road map** E2. 8635 A1A South, St. Augustine. **Open** 9am–5:30pm daily. **Closed** Dec 25.

This Spanish outpost fort was built between 1740–1742 to guard the Matanzas Inlet, and to warn St. Augustine of enemies advancing from the south. Today, Fort Matanzas is a historical reminder of Spain's early empire in the New World.

The park is situated on barrier islands along the Atlantic shores and Matanzas estuary, providing salt marshes, scrub, and maritime hammock to attract and to protect endangered species.

## ❾ Marineland Dolphin Conservation Center

**Road map** E2. Flagler Co. 9600 Ocean Shore Blvd, Marineland. **Tel** (904) 471-1111. 🚌 St. Augustine. **Open** 8:30am–4:30pm daily. 🅿 ♿ 🆆 **marineland.net**

The center began in 1938 as Marine Studios, a set location for many movies, including *Tarzan*. It now puts dolphins at center stage, and visitors can swim with these gentle creatures, touch and feed them, or learn to be a trainer with one- or three-day trainer camp programs. The dolphins live in a habitat of 1.3 million gallons, ensuring their well-being. The center's aim is to foster the preservation of marine life.

## ❿ Washington Oaks Gardens State Park

**Road map** E2. Flagler Co. 6400 N Ocean Shore Blvd, 2 miles (3 km) S of Marineland. **Tel** (386) 446-6780. 🚌 St. Augustine. **Open** daily. 🅿 ♿ 🆆 **floridastateparks.org**

Beneath a canopy of oaks and palms, 400 acres (162 ha) of former plantation land have been transformed into beau gardens of hydrangeas, azaleas, and ferns, plus a rose garden and trails through a coastal hammock to

Ruins of the 19th-century sugar mill at Bulow Plantation

the Matanzas River. Across the A1A a boardwalk leads to the beach, strewn with coquina boulders, and tidal pools eroded from the soft stone.

## ⓫ Bulow Plantation Ruins Historic State Park

**Road map** E2. Flagler Co. Old Kings Rd, 3 miles (5 km) S of SR 100. **Tel**: (386) 517-2084. 🚌 Daytona Beach. **Open** daily. 🅿 ♿ 🆆 **floridastateparks.org**

Somewhat off the beaten track, the ruins of this 19th-century plantation stand in a dense hammock where sugar cane once grew. The site is part of the 4,675 acres (1,890 ha) of land adjacent to a creek that Major Charles Bulow bought in 1821. His slaves cleared half this area and planted rice, cotton, and sugar cane. The plantation, known as Bulowville, was abandoned after Native American attacks during the Seminole Wars (*see pp50–51*). Today, Bulow Creek is a state canoe trail, and you can rent canoes to explore this backwater.

On its banks are the foundations of the plantation house, a ten-minute stroll takes you to the ruins of the old sugar mill, which resemble the remains of some ancient South American temples.

**Environs**
About 10 miles (16 km) north of Bulow Plantation is historic **Flagler Beach**, a charming old-world town with a fishing pier, quaint museum, and ocean-front eateries.

🏠 **Flagler Beach**
S Ocean Shore Blvd. Tel: (386) 517-2000. 🆆 **cityofflaglerbeach.com**

## ⓬ Ormond Beach

**Road map** E2. Volusia Co. 🔼 42,000. 🚌 Daytona Beach. 🛈 126 E Orange Ave, Daytona Beach (386) 255-0415. 🆆 **ormondbeach.org**

Ormond Beach was one of the earliest winter resorts on Henry Flagler's railroad (*see pp52–3*). No longer standing, his fashionable Ormond Hotel boasted a star-studded guest list including Henry Ford and John D. Rockefeller.

The Rockefeller Room in The Casements, Ormond Beach

Rockefeller bought a house just across the street in 1918 after overhearing that another guest was paying less; despite his immense wealth, the millionaire chief of Standard Oil guarded his nickels and dimes closely. His winter home, **The Casements**, has been restored and is today a museum and cultural center, housing Rockefeller-era memorabilia, such as the great man's high-sided wicker beach chair. There's also a period-style room and a rather incongruous Hungarian arts and crafts display.

A short walk from The Casements, the **Ormond Memorial Art Museum** is set in a small but charming tropical garden. Shady paths wind around lily ponds inhabited by basking turtles. The museum hosts changing exhibitions of works by contemporary Florida artists.

Old Flagler engine, Ormond Beach

🎦 **The Casements**
25 Riverside Drive. **Tel** (386) 676-3216. **Open** Mon–Sat. **Closed** public hols. ♿ limited. 📷 Mon–Fri.

🏛 **Ormond Memorial Art Museum**
78 E Granada Blvd. **Tel** (386) 676-3347. **Open** daily. **Closed** public hols. 📷 ♿ 🌐 ormondartmuseum.org

❸ **Daytona Beach**

**Road map** E2. Volusia Co. 🏠 66,000. ✈ 🚌 🛈 126 E Orange Ave, (386) 255-0415. 🌐 daytonabeach.com

Extending south from Ormond Beach is brash and boisterous Daytona Beach. As many as 200,000 students descend on the resort for the Spring Break (see p38), even though Daytona has tried to discourage them. Its famous 23-mile (37-km) beach is one of the few in Florida where cars are allowed on the sands – a hangover from the days when motor enthusiasts raced on the beaches (see p223).

Daytona is still a mecca for motorsports fans. The nearby speedway (see p222) attracts huge crowds, especially during the Speedweek in February and the Motorcycle Weeks in March and October. Downtown Daytona, known simply as "Mainland," lies across the Halifax River from the beach. Most of the action, though, takes place on the beach, which is lined with hotels. The Boardwalk still retains some of its arcades and carnival-style atmosphere, but the area has been regenerated and offers updated rides, including a roller coaster. The Daytona Lagoon waterpark and the bandstand still draw crowds. Down on the beach, jet skis, windsurf boards, buggies, and bicycles can be rented.

Across the Halifax River, in the restored downtown area, the **Halifax Historical Society Museum** occupies a 1910 bank building. Local history displays include a model of the Boardwalk in about 1938, with chicken-feather palm trees and a Ferris wheel.

West of downtown is the excellent **Museum of Arts and Sciences**. The Florida prehistory exhibit is dominated by the 13-ft (4-m) skeleton of a giant sloth, while Arts in America features arts from 1640–1920. There are also notable Cuban and African collections, and a planetarium.

*Miss Perkins* (c.1840) by J Whiting Stock, Museum of Arts and Sciences

**Gamble Place** is run by the same museum. Built in 1907 for James Gamble, of Procter & Gamble, this hunting lodge, surrounded by open porches, sits on a bluff above Spruce Creek. The furnishings are all period pieces. Tours are available by reservation through the museum, and take in the Snow White House – an exact copy of the one in Disney's 1937 classic – built in 1938 for Gamble's great-grandchildren.

🏛 **Halifax Historical Museum**
252 S Beach St. **Tel** (386) 255-6976. **Open** Tue–Sat. **Closed** public hols. 📷 ♿ 🌐 halifaxhistorical.org

🏛 **Museum of Arts & Sciences**
1040 Museum Blvd. **Tel** (386) 255-0285. **Open** Tue–Sun. **Closed** Thanksgiving, Dec 24, Dec 25. 📷 ♿ **Gamble Place** 📷 🌐 moas.org

Sunbathers relaxing on the sands of Daytona Beach

## ⓮ Daytona International Speedway

**Road map** E2. Volusia Co. 1801 W International Speedway Blvd. **Tel** (866) 761-7223. 🚌 Daytona. 🚌 9 from bus terminal at 209 Bethune Blvd. **Open** daily. **Closed** Dec 25. 🅿️ ♿ 🅦 daytonainternational speedway.com

Daytona's very own "World Center of Racing," the Daytona International Speedway, attracts thousands of race fans and visitors every year. People come from around the world to attend the eight major racing weekends held annually at the track – which can hold about 160,000 spectators.

The Speedway is host to NASCAR (National Association for Stock Car Auto Racing) meets – the Daytona 500 being the most famous – and sports car, motorcycle, and karting races.

The Coca-Cola 3-D IMAX® Theater shows *NASCAR 3D: The IMAX® Experience*, which gives an inside look at the world of NASCAR's elite team and drivers.

A half-hour trolley tour around the speedway track is

The Daytona 500, held each February at Daytona International Speedway

1953 red Corvette, a classic sports car

available on days when no races take place. Other tours last between 30 minutes and three hours and take visitors to the Velocitorium, home to Sir Malcolm Campbell's Bluebird V, the car that set a land speed record on nearby Ormond Beach in 1935. A trip around the track, along the infield and down pit road gives visitors an idea of what the drivers go through. They can also get a closer look at the $400-million renovation project currently underway. Choose from one of the many driving experiences on offer, or opt to be the passenger as a professional instructor takes you at speeds of up to 165 mph.

## ⓯ Ponce de León Inlet Lighthouse

**Road map** E2. Volusia Co. 4931 S Peninsula Drive. **Tel** (386) 761-1821. **Open** daily. **Closed** Dec 25. 🅿️ ♿ limited. 🅦 ponceinlet.org

This imposing red brick lighthouse dates from 1887 and guards the entrance to a hazardous inlet at the tip of the Daytona peninsula. The lighthouse tapers skyward for 175 ft (53 m), its beacon is visible 19 miles (30 km) out to sea, and there are far-reaching views from the windswept observation deck, reached by a 203-step spiral staircase. One of the former keepers' cottages at its base has been restored to its 1890s appearance, another houses the small Museum of the Sea, and a third contains a magnificent 17-ft- (5-m-) high Fresnel lens.

### Daytona International Speedway

Lake Lloyd

Williamson Beltway

Daytona Beach

W International Speedway Blvd (92)

I-4
I-95

**Key**

☐ Visitor center
☐ Track
☐ Grandstand
☐ Sprint Tower

0 meters 500
0 yards 500

The striking Ponce de León Inlet lighthouse south of Daytona Beach

# The Birthplace of Speed

Daytona's love affair with the car started in 1903, when the first timed automobile runs took place on the sands at Ormond Beach, the official "Birthplace of Speed." That year, Alexander Winton achieved a land speed record of 68 mph (109 km/h). The speed trials were enormously popular and attracted large crowds. Wealthy motor enthusiasts gathered at Henry Flagler's Ormond Hotel *(see p220)*, and included the likes of Harvey Firestone and Henry Ford. Speed trials continued until 1935, when Malcolm Campbell set the last world record on the beach. Stock cars began racing at Ormond Beach in 1936, and the first Daytona 200 motorcycle race took place there the following year. Development forced the racetrack to be moved in 1948, and in 1959 Daytona International Speedway opened and racing on the beach was abandoned altogether.

### Racing on the Beach

*In 1902, a guest at the Ormond Hotel noticed just how easy it was to drive his car on the hard sandy beach. He organized the first speed trials, which continued for the next 32 years.*

**Ransom E. Olds' Pirate** was the first car to race on Ormond Beach in 1902. The first official race was held in 1903, when Olds challenged Alexander Winton and Oscar Hedstrom on a motorcycle. Winton won in his car, *Bullet No 1.*

**The *Bluebird Streamliner*** was driven to a new world record for the measured mile by Malcolm Campbell at Ormond Beach in 1935. Powered by a Rolls-Royce engine, the car reached speeds of greater than 276 mph (444 km/h).

### The "World Center of Racing"

*In 1953, Bill France, who had entered the inaugural stock car race, realized that the growth of Daytona Beach would soon put an end to the beach races. He proposed the construction of Daytona International Speedway, today one of the world's leading racetracks.*

**Go-karts** look like the fun machines that you can race on vacation, but the karts that compete at Daytona manage speeds of over 81 mph (130 km/h).

**Lee Petty** won the first Daytona 500 at Daytona International Speedway in 1959, beating Johnny Beauchamp, his fellow competitor, by a mere 2 ft (50 cm). The 500-mile (800-km) competition was watched by a crowd of 41,000 and involved 59 cars.

## ⓰ Blue Spring State Park

**Road map** E2. Volusia Co. 2100 W French Ave, Orange City. **Tel** (386) 775–3663. **Open** daily. 🚗 ♿
**W** floridastateparks.org

One of the country's largest first-magnitude artesian springs, Blue Spring pours out around 100 million gal (450 million liters) of water a day. The temperature of the water is at a constant 68° F (20° C), and consequently the park is a favorite winter refuge for manatees *(see p254)*. Between the months of November and March, when the manatees escape the cooler waters of the St. Johns River, you can see hundreds of them from the park's elevated boardwalks. Snorkeling or scuba diving are available in the turquoise waters of the spring head, as is canoeing on the St. Johns. **Thursby House**, atop one of the park's ancient shell mounds, was built in the late 19th century.

### Environs

About 2 miles (3 km) north as the crow flies is wooded **Hontoon Island State Park**. Reached by a free passenger ferry from Hontoon Landing, the island has an 80 ft (24 m) observation tower, camping and picnic areas, and a nature trail. Canoes and fishing skiffs can also be rented.

In 1955 a rare wooden owl totem made by the ancient local Timucua Indians *(see pp44–5)* was found here.

### 🏕 Hontoon Island State Park

2309 River Ridge Rd, De Land. **Tel** (386) 736–5309. **Open** daily. 🚗 **W** floridastateparks.org

Children playing in front of Thursby House, Blue Spring State Park

### Florida's Bubbling Springs

Most of Florida's 320 known springs are located in the upper half of the state. The majority are artesian springs, formed by waters forced up deep fissures from underground aquifers (rock deposits containing water). Those that gush more than 100 cu ft (3 cu m) per second are known as first-magnitude springs.

Filtered through the rock, the water is extremely pure and sometimes high in salts and minerals. These properties, plus the sheer beauty of the springs, have long attracted visitors for recreational and health purposes.

Juniper Springs in Ocala National Forest, adapted for swimmers in the 1930s

## ⓱ Sanford

**Road map** E2. Seminole Co. 🏙 58,600. 🚆 400 E 1st St, (407) 322–2212. 🚌 inc Auto Train. 🚌 Lynx buses from Orlando *(see p387)*. **W** sanfordfl.gov

Built during the Seminole Wars *(see pp48–51)*, Fort Mellon was the first permanent settlement on Lake Monroe. Sanford was founded nearby in the 1870s. It became a major inland port thanks to the commercial steamboat from Jacksonville on the St. Johns River, which eventually brought Florida's early tourists *(see p52)*.

Restored downtown Sanford dates from the 1880s, the height of this Steamboat era. Several of the old red brick buildings (a rarity in Florida) house antique shops, and the area can easily be explored on foot in a couple of hours. Today's visitors are more likely to arrive

Sanford town sign

on the Auto Train or by SunRail *(see p384)* than by river, but short pleasure cruises are still available.

## ⓲ Mount Dora

**Road map** E2. Lake Co. 🏙 13,800. 🚆 Sanford. 🛈 341 N Alexander St, (352) 383–2165. **W** mountdora.com

Set among the former citrus groves of Lake County, this town is one of the prettiest Victorian settlements left in the state. Its name comes from both the relatively high local elevation of 184 ft (56 m), and the small lake on which it sits. The town was originally known as Royellou, after Roy, Ella, and Louis, the children of the first postmaster.

Mount Dora's attractive tree-lined streets are laid out on a bluff above the lakeshore. The historic tour takes in quiet neighborhoods of late 19th-century clapboard homes and the restored downtown district, with its many antique shops. The tour starts from the Chamber of Commerce.

On Donnelly Street, the splendid Donnelly House, now a Masonic Hall, is a notable example of ornate Steamboat architecture. The Modernism Museum on 4th Avenue houses a collection which perfectly

Shingles and gingerbread decoration on Donnelly House, Mount Dora

showcases the movement. Nearby, the small Mount Dora History Museum depicts local history in the old fire station, which later became the jail. Down on Lake Dora, fishing and water sports are available.

**🏛 Mount Dora History Museum**
450 Royellou Lane. **Tel** (352) 383-0006. **Open** Tue–Sun. **Closed** Jan 1, Thanksgiving, Dec 25. ♿ limited.

# ⑲ Ocala National Forest

**Road map** E2. Lake Co/Marion Co. **Open** daily. 🏕 to camp site & swimming areas. ♿ ⚠ Visitor Center: 3199 NE Co. Rd. **Tel** (352) 236–0288. Juniper Springs canoe rental: (352) 625-2808. **W** fs.usda.gov

Between Ocala and the St. Johns River, the world's largest sand pine forest covers 366,000 acres (148,000 ha), crisscrossed by spring-fed rivers and numerous hiking trails. It is one of the last refuges of the endangered Florida black bear and also home to many more common animals such as deer and otter. Birds, including bald eagles, ospreys, barred owls, the non-native wild turkey, and many species of waders (which frequent the river swamp areas), can all be spotted here.

Dozens of hiking trails vary in length from boardwalks and short loop trails of under a mile (1.5 km), to a 66 mile (106 km) stretch of the cross-state National Scenic Trail (see p365). Bass-fishing is popular on the many lakes scattered through the forest, and there are swimming holes, picnic areas, and camp grounds at recreation areas such as Salt Springs, Alexander Springs, and Fore Lake.

Canoe rental is widely available; the 7 mile (11 km) canoe run down Juniper Creek from the Juniper Springs Recreation Area is one of the finest in the state, but reserve in advance. Bird-watching is particularly good along the Salt Springs Trail, and wood ducks congregate on Lake Dorr.

Information and guides can be picked up at the main visitor center on the western edge of the forest, or at the smaller centers at Salt Springs and Lake Dorr, both on Route 19.

# ⑳ Silver Springs

**Road map** E2. Marion Co. 5656 E Silver Springs Blvd. **Tel** (352) 236-7148. **Open** daily. 🏕 ♿ limited. **W** floridastateparks.org

Glass-bottom boat trips at Silver Springs have been revealing the natural wonders of the world's largest artesian spring since 1878.

Once Florida's oldest commercial tourist attraction, Silver Springs became a state park in 2013 after undergoing a $4-million makeover, which included removing exotic animals and amusement rides. The boat trips offer visitors a glimpse of the Florida outback, where the early Tarzan movies starring Johnny Weissmuller were filmed.

**Environs**
On a quieter note, at **Silver River State Park**, 2 miles (3 km) southeast, visitors can take a pleasant 15-minute walk along a trail through a hardwood hammock and a cypress swamp area, leading to a swimming hole in a bend of the crystal clear river.

**🏞 Silver River State Park**
1425 NE 58th Ave, Ocala. **Tel** (352) 236–7148. **Open** daily. 🏕 ♿ **W** floridastateparks.org

Boats cruise the Silver River from Silver Springs

The Young Shepherdess (1868) by
Bougereau, Appleton Museum

# ㉑ Ocala

**Road map** D2. Marion Co. 🚗 59,000.
🚌 🚆 ℹ️ Chamber of Commerce,
110 E Silver Springs Blvd, (352) 629-
8051. 🌐 **ocalacc.com**

Surrounded by undulating
pastures neatly edged by mile
upon mile of white wooden
fences, Ocala is the seat of
Marion County and center of
Florida's thoroughbred horse
industry. The grass in this region
is enriched by the subterranean
limestone aquifer *(see p224)*, and
the calcium-rich grazing helps
to contribute to the light, strong
bones of championship horses.
Florida's equine industry has
produced more than 37
champions, including five
Kentucky Derby winners.
   There are over 400 thoroughbred farms and specialized
breeding centers around Ocala.
Many are open for visits, which
are usually free of charge. Expect
to see Arabians, Paso Finos, and
miniature ponies on the farms;
contact the Ocala Chamber
of Commerce for up-to-date
information regarding farm visits.

Another reason to stop off in this
area is to visit the **Appleton
Museum of Art**, east of Ocala.
Built in 1984 of Italian marble by
the industrialist and horsebreeder
Arthur I. Appleton, the museum
houses stunning art from around
the world. His eclectic collection
includes pre-Columbian and
European antiquities, Oriental
and African pieces, and Meissen
porcelain, and is known for its
strong core of mainstream
19th-century European art.

🏛️ **Appleton Museum of Art**
4333 NE Silver Springs Blvd.
**Tel** (352) 291-4455. **Open** Tue–Sun.
**Closed** Dec 25, Jan 1. 🅿️ ♿

# ㉒ Marjorie Kinnan Rawlings Historic State Park

**Road map** D2. Alachua Co. S CR 325,
Cross Creek. **Tel** (352) 466-3672.
🚌 Ocala. **Open** grounds daily; house
Thu–Sun. **Closed** Aug–Sep. 🅿️ ♿
📷 🌐 **floridastateparks.org**

The author Marjorie Kinnan
Rawlings arrived in the tiny
settlement of Cross Creek,
which she was later to describe
fondly as "a bend in
a country road," in
1928. Her rambling
farmhouse remains
largely unchanged,
nestling in a well-
tended citrus grove
where ducks waddle
up from the banks
of Orange Lake.
   The writer remained
here during the 1930s
and then visited on and
off until her death in 1953. The
local scenery and characters fill
her autobiographical novel,

Herlong Inn,
stick collection

*Cross Creek* (1942), while the
big scrub country to the south
inspired her Pulitzer prize-
winning novel *The Yearling*
(1938), a coming-of-age story
about a boy and his fawn.
   Guided tours around the
site explore the Cracker-style
homestead, built in the 1880s,
which has been imaginatively
preserved and contains original
Rawlings' furnishings: bookcases
full of contemporary writings by
authors such as John Steinbeck
and Ernest Hemingway, a secret
liquor cabinet, a typewriter,
and a sunhat on the verandah.
Lived-in touches like fresh
flowers make it look as though
the owner has just popped out
for a stroll around the garden.

# ㉓ Micanopy

**Road map** D2. Alachua Co.
🚗 470. ℹ️ 30 East University Ave,
Gainesville, (352) 374-5260.
🌐 **micanopytown.com**

Established in 1821, Florida's
second oldest permanent white
settlement was a trading post
on Native American lands,
originally known as Wanton.
Renamed Micanopy in
1826, after a native
chief, this time-warp
village is now as
decorous as they come,
and a haven for film-
makers and antique
lovers. Planted with live
oaks trailing Spanish
moss, the main street,
Cholokka Boulevard, is
lined with Victorian
homes and a strip of
brick-fronted shops stuffed with
bric-a-brac and craft galleries.
Here, too, is the grandest
building in Micanopy, the
imposing red-brick antebellum
**Herlong Mansion**, supported
by four massive Corinthian
columns. Built by a 19th-century
lumber baron, today it serves
as a bed and breakfast.
   Micanopy's picturesque
cemetery, established in 1825, is
located on a canopied street off
Seminary Road, en route to I-75.
It is shaded by spreading live
oaks and majestic cedars, and
covered with velvety moss.

The airy porch where author Marjorie Kinnan Rawlings once wrote

*For hotels and restaurants in this area see p319 and pp339–41*

Lichen-stained gravestones in Micanopy's atmospheric cemetery

## Environs

During the 17th century one of the largest and most successful Spanish cattle ranches in Florida was located to the north of present-day Micanopy. Cattle, horses, and hogs once grazed on the lush grass of **Payne's Prairie State Preserve**, where a small herd of wild American bison can sometimes be seen, as well as more than 200 species of local and migratory birds.

Passing through the preserve is the pleasant 17 mile (27 km) **Gainesville-Hawthorne State Trail**, a rail trail used by hikers, riders, and cyclists.

🏞 **Paynes Prairie State Park**
100 Savannah Blvd, US 441,
1 mile (0.5 km) N of Micanopy.
**Tel** (352) 466-3397. **Open** daily.
♿ 🆆 floridastateparks.org

## ㉔ Gainesville

**Road map** D2. Alachua Co.
🚗 131,500. ➡ 🚌 ℹ 300 East University Avenue, (352) 334-7100.
🆆 gainesvillechamber.com

A university town, the cultural capital of north central Florida, and home of the Gators football team, Gainesville is a comfortable blend of town and gown. In the restored downtown historic district are brick buildings that date from the 1880s to the 1920s, several of which house cafés and restaurants. The campus is dotted with fraternity houses and two important museums.

Leave plenty of time for the first of these, the excellent **Florida Museum of Natural History**. The natural science collections contain more than 10 million fossil specimens, plus superb butterfly and shell collections. There are displays dedicated to the various Florida environments, and an anthropological journey through the state's history up to the 19th century. The striking **Samuel P. Harn Museum of Art** is one of the largest and best-equipped university art museums in the country. Its excellent, permanent collection of fine art and crafts includes a broad range of Asian ceramics, African

Shark tooth at the Florida Museum of Natural History

ceremonial objects, Japanese woodcuts, and European and American paintings.

🏛 **Florida Museum of Natural History**
Hull Rd at SW 34th St. **Tel** (352) 846-2000. **Open** daily.
**Closed** Thanksgiving, Dec 25.
♿ 🆆 flmnh.ufl.edu

🏛 **Samuel P. Harn Museum of Art**
Hull Road (off SW 34th St). **Tel** (352) 392-9826. **Open** Tue–Sun. **Closed** public hols. ♿ 🆆 harn.ufl.edu

## Environs

Just southwest of town, the lovely **Kanapaha Botanical Gardens** are at the height of their beauty from June to September, although visitors in springtime are rewarded by masses of azaleas in bloom. A trail circles the sloping 62-acre site, whose beauty was first noted by the naturalist William Bartram (see p49) in the late 1800s. The paths meander beneath vine-covered arches and through bamboo groves. Other distinct areas include a desert garden, a lakeside bog garden, and a colorful hummingbird garden.

🌺 **Kanapaha Botanical Gardens**
4700 SW 58th Drive (off Route 24).
**Tel** (352) 372-4981. **Open** Fri–Wed.
**Closed** Dec 25. ♿ 🆆 kanapaha.org

Giant Amazonian water lilies, the late-summer highlight of the bog garden in Kanapaha Botanical Gardens

# THE PANHANDLE

There is a saying in Florida that "the farther north you go, the farther south you get." Certainly, the Panhandle has a history and sensibility closer to that of the Deep South than to the lower part of the state. Geography, history, climate and even time (the western Panhandle is one hour behind the rest of the state), distinguish this intriguing region from other parts of Florida.

The Panhandle was the site of the first attempt by the Spanish at colonizing Florida and much subsequent fighting by Colonial powers. A community was set up near present-day Pensacola in 1559, predating St. Augustine, but was abandoned after a hurricane. It later re-emerged and was the main settlement in the region until the 1820s, when Tallahassee was chosen as the capital of the new Territory of Florida *(see p52)*. The site of the new city, equidistant from St. Augustine and Pensacola, was a compromise – the precise location reputedly being the meeting point of two scouts sent out on horseback from the two cities. Today, Tallahassee is a dignified state capital with elegant architecture but a small-town air. Thanks to the lumber and cotton trade, the 1800s experienced spells of prosperity, but the region was bypassed by the influx of wealth that came to other parts of Florida with the laying of the railroads. Tourism in the Panhandle is a more modern development, even though its fine white-sand beaches are unparalleled in the state. This stretch of coast has become increasingly popular with vacationers from the Deep South, but it is still often overlooked by overseas visitors. At the eastern end of the Panhandle, in the area known as the "Big Bend," the family resorts give way to quaint historic coastal towns like Cedar Key, a laid-back fishing village reminiscent of old-time Key West. Inland, large preserves and parks incorporating forests, springs, and navigable rivers provide the main attraction.

A beach on Okaloosa Island, one of the Panhandle's many dazzling quartz sand beaches

◀ The iconic Florida State Capitol building, Tallahassee

# Exploring the Panhandle

Most visitors to the Panhandle head straight for the famous beach resorts that stretch in an arc between Pensacola and Panama City Beach. Ideal for family vacations, resorts such as Fort Walton Beach and Destin offer all types of accommodations as well as activities ranging from water sports and deep-sea fishing to golf and tennis. While most attention is focused on the coast, the rest of the Panhandle should not be ignored – the resorts can be used as a good base for forays into the hilly, pine-forested interior, where it is possible to escape the crowds. Excellent canoeing can be enjoyed on the Blackwater and the Suwannee rivers, while near Tallahassee visitors will find some of Florida's prettiest countryside, crossed by unspoiled canopied roads.

Quietwater Beach, near Pensacola on Santa Rosa Island

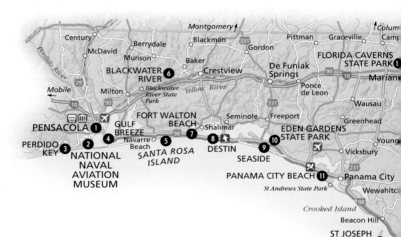

## Sights at a Glance

Elegant, plantation-style mansion at Eden Gardens State Park

## Getting Around

Although the Amtrak line ran through the region, following the line of I-10, passenger service was halted in 2005, when Hurricane Katrina damaged the lines, making car rental essential for exploring the Panhandle. There are two main driving routes: the fast but dull I-10, which streaks from Pensacola to Tallahassee and then on to the Atlantic Coast; and US 98, which parallels the coast all the way from Pensacola to the so-called "Big Bend," where it links up with the main north-south Gulf Coast highway, US 19. Country roads in the Panhandle are generally quiet, but be alert for logging trucks pulling out of concealed forest exits.

Waterfront buildings at the popular harbor of Destin

Pelicans enjoying the peace and quiet of Apalachicola

**For additional map symbols** *see back flap*

### Key

▬ Highway
▬ Major road
▬ Secondary road
═ Minor road
─ Scenic route
▬ Main railroad
▬ State border

# ❶ Street-by-Street: Pensacola

The city's first settlers were a party of Spanish colonists, led by Don Tristan de Luna, who sailed into Pensacola Bay in 1559. Their settlement survived for only two years before being wiped out by a hurricane. The Spanish returned, but Pensacola changed hands frequently: in the space of just over 400 years the Spanish, French, English, Confederate, and US flags all flew over the city. Pensacola took off in the 1880s, when much of the present downtown district was built. This area features a variety of architectural styles, ranging from quaint Colonial cottages to elegant Classical-Revival homes built during the late 19th-century timber boom. The route shown here focuses on the area known as Historic Pensacola Village *(see p234)*.

**Lavalle House**
The simple plan and bright color scheme of this early 19th-century two-room cottage was designed to appeal to its French Creole immigrant tenants.

**The Museum of Industry**
Recalls Pensacola's timber and maritime trades using a reconstructed sawmill, a ship's chandlery, and a replica logging train.

**Pensacola Historical Museum** Exhibits here focus on the history of the Pensacola area. There is a great wealth of material and artifacts which are available to the public.

**★ T.T. Wentworth, Jr. Museum**
A broad collection of Florida memorabilia, such as this 1870s bed, fill this unusual museum.

**Pensacola Museum of Art**
The old city jail, dating from 1908, was converted into a museum in the 1950s. This William Nell landscape is among the broad array of art exhibited.

**A British officers' compound** has been excavated in this parking lot. The exposed foundations form part of the city's Colonial Archaeological Trail *(see p234)*.

**Steamboat House**
Dating from the mid-19th-century steamboat era *(see p52)*, this delightful house echoes the shape of a riverboat. It comes complete with verandah "decks."

## VISITORS' CHECKLIST

**Practical Information**
**Road map** A1. Escambia Co.
🏙 294,400. 🛈 1401 E Gregory St, (850) 434-1234. 🎭 Fiesta of Five Flags (Jun).
🌐 **visitpensacola.com**

**Transport**
✈ 5 miles (8 km) N. 🚌 980 E Heinburg St, (850) 433-4966. 🚍 505 W Burgess Rd, (850) 476-4800.

★ **Seville Square**
Shaded by live oaks and magnolia trees, Seville Square lies at the heart of the Seville District, which was laid out by the British in the 1770s.

**Fountain Square**
centers around a fountain decorated with plaques showing local features.

**Dorr House**, a fine Greek-Revival mansion, is the last of its kind in western Florida.

★ **Museum of Commerce**
A fully equipped print workshop is one of the many interesting exhibits in the museum's cleverly constructed late-Victorian streetscape.

| 0 meters | | 200 |
| 0 yards | | 200 |

**Key**

— Suggested route

# Exploring Pensacola

Several historic districts provide the most interesting areas to explore in Pensacola. Foremost is the old downtown district, Historic Pensacola Village, which is centered on pretty Zarragossa Street. Farther north, in the North Hill Preservation District, you can stroll past the homes built by prominent local professionals and merchants during the 19th-century timber boom. Between the two, Palafox Place is a busy commercial district with a number of distinctive buildings and quaint shops.

Downtown Pensacola is linked by two bridges to its barrier island resort satellite, Pensacola Beach *(see p240)*. While sightseeing is focused on the mainland, visitors often stay in hotels by the beach.

Cell doors now standing open, Pensacola Museum of Art

Guides in 19th-century costume in Historic Pensacola Village

### 🚽 Historic Pensacola Village

Tivoli House, 205 E Zarragossa St. **Tel** (850) 595-5985. **Open** Tue–Sat. **Closed** public hols. 🎨 🚻 📷
**w** historicpensacola.org

This collection of museums and historic houses is located in Pensacola's oldest quarter, called the Historic Pensacola Village. You can enjoy an unhurried stroll through the village's streets, which offer a taste of the city as it was in the 19th century.

For a more in-depth look, take one of the guided tours that depart twice daily from Tivoli House on Zarragossa Street. In tourist season, tour guides liven up the proceedings by dressing in period costume. The tours visit the simply furnished French Creole Lavalle House (1805) and the gracious Dorr House (1871), the Old Christ Church (1832), and the Lear-Rocheblave House (1890), among others. A single ticket, available from Tivoli House, covers the tour and entrance to all village properties for one week. This ticket will be required to visit the Museum of

Industry and Museum of Commerce. Housed in a late 19th-century warehouse, the Museum of Industry on Church Street provides an informative introduction to Pensacola's early development. Exhibits cover brick-making, fishing, transportation, and the lumber trade.

Forming a backdrop to Zarragossa Street's Museum of Commerce is a Victorian street scene complete with reconstructed stores including a printer's shop with a working press, a pharmacy, a saddlery, and an old-time music store.

Overlooking leafy Seville Square is Old Christ Church, built in 1832, and one of the oldest churches in Florida still standing on its original site.

### 🏛 T.T. Wentworth, Jr. Florida State Museum

330 S Jefferson St. **Tel** (850) 595-5990. **Open** Tue–Sat. **Closed** public hols. 🚻
This museum is laid out in the former City Hall, an imposing Spanish Renaissance Revival building. The founder's eclectic collections include West Florida memorabilia, artifacts from Spanish shipwrecks, and weird

and wonderful oddities from all over the world. These run the gamut from arrowheads and a "shrunken head" from pre-Columbian Central America, to a 1930s telephone exchange and old Coca-Cola bottles.

The museum contains well thought-out historical displays and dioramas illustrating points along Pensacola's Colonial Archaeological Trail, which links remains of fortifications dating from 1752–1821. One of the exhibits chronicles over 450 years of Pensacola history.

### 🏛 Pensacola Museum of Art

407 S Jefferson St. **Tel** (850) 432-6247. **Open** Tue–Sat. **Closed** Jul 4, Thanksgiving, Dec 25, Jan 1. 📷 except Tue. 🚻
**w** pensacolamuseumofart.org

The cells of the old city jail, complete with steel-barred doors, have taken on a new life as whitewashed galleries for this Museum. Frequently changing exhibitions draw on the museum's broad-based collections, which include pre-Columbian pottery, 19th-century satinware glass, and Roy Lichtenstein's Pop Art.

The Spanish Renaissance-style home of the T.T. Wentworth, Jr. Museum

## 🏛 Pensacola Children's Museum

115 E Zarragossa St. **Tel** (850) 595-1559. **Open** 10am–4pm Tue–Sat. **Closed** Sun, public hols. 🎦 📷
**W** historicpensacola.org

Housed in an 1885 building first known as the Gulf Saloon, the museum, run by the West Florida Historic Preservation, Inc., offers an interactive learning experience of Pensacola history, showcasing military and multicultural histories plus the maritime and lumber industries. Child-friendly exhibits include the Panton Trading Post, Lavalle Cottage, the Fort, Native American Village, and Kiddie Corral. The second floor houses artifacts geared toward older children and adults, but also offers a rail set, building blocks, and dress-up clothes for younger kids.

## 🏛 North Hill Preservation District

This historic district (stretching for about ten blocks from Wright Street, north of Pensacola Historic Village) features

McCreary House in the North Hill Preservation District

The extensive, unspoiled sands at Johnson Beach on Perdido Key

elegant late 19th- and early 20th-century houses. They were built on the site of former British and Spanish forts, and even now cannonballs are occasionally dug up in their tree-shaded gardens. All the houses are privately owned. Among the most striking is the verandah-fronted McCreary House (see p34) on North Baylen Street, close to the intersection with De Soto Street.

## ❷ National Naval Aviation Museum

*See pp236–7.*

## ❸ Perdido Key

**Road map** A1. Escambia Co. Route 292, 12 miles (19 km) W of Pensacola. 🚖 Pensacola. 🚌 Pensacola. ℹ 15500 Perdido Key Dr, Pensacola, (850) 492-4600. **W** perdidochamber.com

A 30-minute drive southwest from Pensacola are the pristine shores of Perdido Key, which regularly features in the list of the top 20 US beaches. There are bars and restaurants and facilities for water sports, fishing, and diving, or you can simply swim or soak up the sun.

The whole eastern end of the island is accessible only by foot. The road runs as far as the **Johnson Beach Day Use Area**, just east of the bridge from the mainland. The sands extend for some 6 miles (10 km) on both gulf and bay sides, and there are facilities for visitors, and a ranger station.

On the mainland opposite Perdido Key, **Big Lagoon State Park** combines sandy beach with salt-marsh areas offering excellent bird-watching and hiking. Enjoy sweeping views from the observation tower.

### 🚖 Johnson Beach Day Use Area
13300 Johnson Beach Rd, off Route 292. **Tel** Federal Govt Office of National Seashore (850) 934-2600. **Open** daily. **Closed** Dec 25. 🎦 ♿

### 🏞 Big Lagoon State Park
12301 Gulf B each Highway. **Tel** (850) 492-1595. **Open** daily. 🎦 ♿

---

## Florida's Lumber Boom

In the 19th century, the demand for lumber and naval stores including tar and turpentine played an important part in northern Florida's development. Its vast stands of live oaks were particularly popular with shipbuilders for their disease- and decay-resistant wood. Flourishing lumber towns such as Cedar Key (see pp248–9) were established, and the fortunes made during the lumber boom of the 1870s–80s were transformed into Pensacola's elegant homes, including Eden Mansion (see p241).

By the 1930s, most of Florida's mature hardwood forest had been destroyed, and other building materials and forms of fuel had begun to replace wood. The lumber mills closed, leaving thousands unemployed.

Loggers in the 19th century, who worked long hours of hard manual labor

# ❷ National Naval Aviation Museum

Opened in 1963, this free museum has grown over the years to more than 350,000 sq ft (32,500 sq m) of exhibit space, making it the world's largest Naval Aviation museum. More than 150 aircraft and spacecraft, as well as models, artifacts, and technological displays, don the decks aboard Naval Air Station Pensacola, attracting nearly a million visitors, annually. Representing Navy, Marine Corps, and Coast Guard aviation, the museum offers tours by volunteers, many of whom are military veterans.

**Hangar Bay One**
The museum's Hangar Bay One exhibit displays aircraft of the post-World War II era, including a Marine One presidential helicopter and a replica of the Apollo 17 lunar module.

**Flying Tigers**
The painted jaws of these World War II fighters were the trademark of the Volunteer Flying Tiger pilots who fought in the skies over China and Burma.

**The USS *Cabot* Flight Deck** is a life-size reproduction of a World War II aircraft carrier deck, complete with fighter planes.

**Sunken Treasures** displays two aircraft recovered from Lake Michigan, where they sank during training in World War II.

**Spirit of Naval Aviation Monument**

**The IMAX® theater** shows four different features seven times daily.

## Gallery Guide

*The museum occupies two floors, or "decks," which are divided into two wings joined by an atrium. The west wing is devoted almost entirely to World War II carrier aircraft, while the south wing is more broadly historical. More aircraft can be found in Hangar Bay One, to the rear of the museum.*

**F-14 Tomcat**

**Entrance**

**Biplane**
Early aircraft include World War I training planes and biplanes once favored by circus barnstormers.

**K47 Airship**
America's "K"-type airships performed vital maritime patrol duties during World War II.

**The Space Capsule Display** features a Skylab Command Module, Mercury Capsule, Moon Rover Vehicle, astronaut suits, space films, and memorabilia.

**★ MaxFlight Simulators**
Visitors can experience mid-air combat and stunt flying in scenarios with dozens of different aircraft.

**Cockpit trainers** show actual layouts of various Naval Aviation aircraft.

**★ Blue Angels**
Four former Blue Angels A-4 Sky-hawks are suspended in a dramatic diamond formation from the ceiling of the seven-story glass atrium.

### Key

- ▢ WWII/Korean War aircraft
- ▢ Early aircraft
- ▢ Modern aircraft
- ▢ Theater
- ▢ Interactive exhibits
- ▢ Displays
- ▢ Art gallery
- ▢ Hangar Bay One
- ▢ Nonexhibition space

### Fort Barrancas

Enclosed by water on three sides, the strategic Naval Air Station site was fortified by Spanish colonists in 1698. The original ram-parts, built on a bluff (*barranca* in Spanish) overlooking Pensacola Bay, were replaced by a more substantial fort in 1781, and major additions were made by the US Army in the 1840s. The remains of the Spanish and US forts, concealed behind formidable defensive earthworks, are linked by a tunnel. The fort is a few minutes' walk from the museum, where you can arrange to go on a guided tour of the area.

View of the earthworks surrounding Fort Barrancas

## 4 Gulf Breeze

**Road map** A1. Santa Rosa Co.
🏠 6,600. 🚇 Pensacola. 🚌 Pensacola.
ℹ️ 409 Gulf Breeze Parkway, (850) 932-7888. 🖥️ gulfbreezechamber.com

The affluent community of Gulf Breeze lies at the western end of a promontory reaching out into Pensacola Bay. The area east of the town is heavily wooded and once formed part of the huge swathes of southern woodlands that were set aside in the 1820s to provide lumber for shipbuilding (see p235).

The **Naval Live Oaks Reservation**, off US 98, was originally a government-owned tree farm and now protects some of the remaining woodland. Visitors can follow trails through 1,300 acres (500 ha) of oak hammock woodlands, sand-hill areas, and wetlands, where wading birds feast off an abundance of marine life. A visitor center dispenses maps and information about local flora and fauna.

Ten miles (16 km) east of Gulf Breeze, **The Zoo** is a favorite family excursion, with more than 700 animals in residence. You can take a ride on the Safari Line train through 30 acres (12 ha) of land where animals roam freely, take in the views from the elevated boardwalk, or stroll through the botanical gardens.

The Safari Line train, on its tour around The Zoo, Gulf Breeze

You can even look a giraffe in the eye from the feeding platform.

🚻 **Naval Live Oaks Reservation**
1801 Gulf Breeze Parkway. **Tel** (850) 934-2600. **Open** daily. **Closed** Dec 25.
♿ limited. 🖥️ nps.gov/guis

🚻 **The Zoo**
5701 Gulf Breeze Parkway.
**Tel** (850) 932-2229. **Open** daily.
**Closed** Thanksgiving, Dec 25. 🚗 ♿
🖥️ gulfbreezezoo.org

## 5 Santa Rosa Island

**Road map** A1. Escambia Co, Okaloosa Co, Santa Rosa Co. 🚇 Pensacola. 🚌 Pensacola or Fort Walton Beach. ℹ️ 8543 Navarre Parkway, Navarre, (850) 939-2691. 🖥️ floridabeaches torivers.com

A long, thin streak of sand, Santa Rosa stretches all the way from Pensacola Bay to Fort Walton Beach, a distance of 45 miles (70 km). At its western tip **Fort Pickens**, completed in 1834, is the largest of four US forts constructed in the early 19th century to defend Pensacola Bay.

The Apache chieftain Geronimo was imprisoned here from 1886–8, during which time people came from far and wide to see him; the authorities supposedly encouraged his transformation into a tourist attraction. The fort remained in use by the US Army until 1947. Now, visitors are free to explore the brick fort's dark passageways and small museum.

The nature trail, Naval Live Oaks Reservation

Santa Rosa has several fine white beaches. Pensacola Beach and Navarre Beach are both popular, each with a fishing pier and plenty of water sports activities. Between them is a beautiful, undeveloped stretch of sand where visitors can relax away from the crowds. There is a campground at the western end of the island, near Fort Pickens.

🏰 **Fort Pickens**
1400 Fort Pickens Rd (Route 399).
**Tel** (850) 934-2621. **Open** daily. 🚗
♿ limited. ⚠️ 🖥️ nps.gov/guis

Boardwalk leading onto Pensacola Beach on Santa Rosa Island

## 6 Blackwater River

**Road map** A1. Santa Rosa Co.
🚇 Pensacola. 🚌 Pensacola. ℹ️ 5247 Stewart St, Milton, (850) 623-2339.
🖥️ santarosachamber.com

The Blackwater River starts in Alabama and flows for 60 miles (95 km) south to the Gulf of Mexico. One of the purest sand-bottom rivers in the world, its dark, tannin-stained waters meander prettily through the forest, creating oxbow lakes and sand beaches.

The river's big attraction is its canoeing: one of the state's finest canoe trails runs for 31 miles (50 km) along its course. Canoe and kayak trips can be arranged through several operators in Milton, the self-styled "Canoeing Capital of Florida." These trips range from half-day paddles to three-day marathons, with the option of

The Blackwater River, well-known for its canoeing trail

tackling the more challenging Sweetwater and Juniper creeks to the north.

The small **Blackwater River State Park**, located at the end of the canoe trail, offers swimming, picnicking areas, and the Chain of Lakes Trail. This 1 mile (1.5 km) nature trail runs through woodlands thick with oak, hickory, southern magnolia, and red maple trees.

**Blackwater River State Park**
Off US 90, 15 miles (24 km) NE of Milton. **Tel** (850) 983-5363.
**Open** daily. limited.
**floridastateparks.org**

## 7 Fort Walton Beach

**Road map** A1. Okaloosa Co. 20,500. Crestview. 34 Miracle Strip Parkway SE, (850) 244-8191, (800) 322-3319.
**fwbchamber.org**

Fort Walton Beach lies at the western tip of the so-called Emerald Coast, a 24 mile (40 km) strip of dazzling beach stretching east to Destin and beyond. Diving shops and marinas line US 98, which skirts the coast and links Fort Walton to Santa Rosa Island. Known locally as Okaloosa Island, this is where most local people and visitors go. There is superb swimming as well as pier and deep-sea fishing, and this is a prime location for water sports, too.

Also available is swimming, sailing, or windsurfing off the island's north shore, on sheltered Choctawhatchee Bay. Boat trips can be arranged at the numerous marinas. For those who prefer dry land, the Emerald Coast boasts a dozen golf courses.

**Gulfarium** marine park's most popular aquatic residents are its sea lions and dolphins. There are also seal and otter enclosures, as well as alligators and exotic birds. The glass walls of the Living Sea aquarium reveal sharks, rays, and huge sea turtles. There's not a great deal to lure you downtown except for the informative **Indian Temple Mound Museum**, which stands in the shadow of an ancient earthwork, a ceremonial and burial site of the Apalachee tribe *(see pp44–5)*. The museum exhibits artifacts recovered from the mound and other historic sites nearby, and houses one of the finest collections of pre-contact ceramics in the southeast, while well-illustrated displays trace more than 10,000 years of human habitation in the Choctawhatchee Bay area.

Indian pot, Temple Mound Museum

Three miles (5 km) north of town at Shalimar is the Eglin Air Force Base, the largest air force base in the world. Here, the **US Air Force Armament Museum** displays aircraft, missiles, and bombs dating from World War II to the present day. There is a SR-71 "Blackbird" spy plane as well as high-tech laser equipment. Tours of the 720 sq mile (1,865 sq km) base are available.

**Gulfarium**
1010 Miracle Strip Parkway.
**Tel** (850) 244-5169. **Open** daily.
**Closed** Thanksgiving, Dec 24, Dec 25.
limited. **gulfarium.com**

**Indian Temple Mound Museum**
139 SE Miracle Strip Parkway.
**Tel** (850) 833-9595. **Open** Mon–Sat.
**Closed** Jan 1, Thanksgiving, Dec 25. limited. **fwb.org**

**US Air Force Armament Museum**
100 Museum Drive (Route 85).
**Tel** (850) 651-1808. **Open** daily.
**Closed** public hols.

People strolling along the Gulf of Mexico's white powder sands at Fort Walton Beach

## 8 Destin

**Road map** A1. Okaloosa Co.
🏛 13,500. ✈ 🚌 Fort Walton Beach.
ℹ️ 4484 Legendary Dr, Suite A, (850)
837-6241. **W** destinchamber.com

Situated between the Gulf of
Mexico and Choctawhatchee
Bay, Destin is a narrow strip of
a town that runs parallel to the
coastal highway, US 98. It started
out in 1845 as a fishing camp but
the town has since grown into
what is claimed to be the "most
prolific fishing village" in the

Fisherman at work on his catches
at the harbor in Destin

United States. Deep-sea fishing
is the big attraction and charter
boats come and go full of
hopeful fishermen. The waters
near Destin are particularly rich
in fish because of a 100 ft (30 m)
drop in the continental shelf
only 10 miles (16 km) from the
shore. The prime catches
include amberjack, tarpon, and
blue marlin. There is a busy
calendar of fishing tournaments
in Destin, the most notable
being October's month-long
Fishing Rodeo. Another
important date is early October,
when people flock to Destin for
the annual Seafood Festival.
Cockles, mussels, shrimp, and
crab tempt the crowds.

With its stunning beaches and
the clear waters so typical of the
Emerald Coast, Destin has also
become a very popular seaside
resort. There are also plenty of
opportunities for diving
and snorkeling.

🏛 **Destin Seafood Festival**
Destin (Early Oct).
**W** destinseafoodfestival.org

A wooden tower characteristic of Seaside's
gulfshore homes

## 9 Seaside

**Road map** B1. Walton Co. 🏛 200.
ℹ️ (850) 231-4224. **W** seasidefl.com

When Robert Davis decided
to develop Seaside in the mid-
1980s, the vanished resorts of
his childhood provided his
inspiration. Davis's vision was of
a nostalgic vacation town of
traditional northwest Florida-
style wooden cottages, with
wraparound verandahs, steeply
pitched roofs, and white picket
fences. The original style was

# The Beaches of the Panhandle

Between Perdido Key and Panama City Beach lie some of
the most beautiful beaches in Florida. The finely ground sand –
90 per cent quartz, washed down from the Appalachian
mountains – sweeps into broad beaches and can be nearly
blinding in the sunlight. The hordes descend in June and July,
but the Gulf waters are still pleasantly warm as late as November.
Visitors can choose between quiet, undeveloped beaches and
the more dynamic resorts; there is also plenty of opportunity
for diving and other water sports.

③ **Pensacola Beach** has
miles of pristine sand overlooked by a string of shops,
hotels, and bars. A large
crowd gathers on
weekends *(see p238)*.

**Navarre**

① **Perdido Key** Some of
the state's most westerly
shores, on Perdido Key, are
inaccessible by car and are
therefore quieter than most
*(see p235)*.

② **Gulf Islands National Seashore**
offers camping, a superb beach for
popular coastal activities, and
historical fortifications to explore.

④ **Navarre Beach** is one of
the quieter of the island's
beaches. It has good facilities,
including a pier for fishing
*(see p238)*.

| 0 kilometers | 15 |
| 0 miles | 10 |

rapidly hijacked, however, by quaint gingerbread detailing, turrets, and towers *(see pp34–5)*.

The town's pastel-painted, Neo-Victorian charms have an unreal, Disneyesque quality, and when driving along US 98 it is hard to resist stopping for a quick peek. And then, of course, there is the additional appeal of the beach.

### Environs

1 mile (1.5 km) west of Seaside, the **Grayton Beach State Park** boasts another fine stretch of Panhandle shoreline, and one that regularly features high in the rankings of the nation's top beaches. In addition to its broad strand of pristine quartz-white sand, the park offers good surf fishing, boating facilities, a nature trail, and also a campground. During the summer, families can take part in ranger-led programs.

**Grayton Beach State Park**
County Rd 30A, off US 98, (1 mile) 1.5 km W of Seaside. **Tel** (850) 231-4210.
**Open** daily. 🏊 ♿
**w** floridastateparks.org

Statue amid the lush surroundings of the Eden Gardens State Park

### ❿ Eden Gardens State Park

**Road map** B1. Walton Co. Point Washington. **Tel** (850) 231-4214. Fort Walton Beach. Gardens: **Open** daily. House: **Open** Thu–Mon. 🅿 📷 10am–2pm.
**w** floridastateparks.org

Lumber baron William H. Wesley built this fine Greek Revival mansion overlooking the Choctawhatchee River in 1897. The gracious two-story wooden building, styled after an antebellum mansion, with high-ceilinged rooms and broad verandahs, is furnished with antiques. The gardens, planted with camellias and azaleas, are shaded by southern magnolia trees and live oaks. These lead to picnic tables by the river, near where the old lumber mill once stood. Whole trees were once floated from inland forests downriver to the mill, where they were sawed into logs, then sent by barge along the Intracoastal Waterway to Pensacola.

#### ⑦ Santa Rosa Beach
This undeveloped sandy beach is backed by dunes and marshlands teeming with birds and other wildlife.

#### ⑨ Panama City Beach
Condos, hotels, and amusement and water parks line buzzing Panama City Beach. Diving and water sports are popular pastimes *(see p242)*.

Valparaiso

*Choctawhatchee Bay*

⑳

③③①

⑨⑧

⑤ ⑥ ⑨⑧ ⑦ ⑧ • **Seaside** ⑨⑧

lton ach

Panama City

②③①

⑨

⑩

⑨⑧

#### ⑥ **Destin** attracts bathers to its gorgeous beach, as well as a macho deep-sea fishing crowd.

#### ⑧ **Grayton** provides boardwalks across the dunes to one of the finest beaches in the country.

#### ⑤ **Fort Walton Beach** is a relaxed, family-oriented resort and one of the best for water sports *(see p239)*.

#### ⑩ **St. Andrews** has a superb beach that, unlike Panama City Beach, is protected against developers *(see pp242–3)*.

Panama City Beach, the liveliest seaside resort in the Panhandle

# ⓫ Panama City Beach

**Road map** B1. Bay Co. 🚗 37,600.
🚌 🚐 ℹ️ 17001 Panama City Beach
Pkwy, (850) 233-5070. Captain
Anderson's: **Tel** (850) 234-3435.
Treasure Island Marina: **Tel** (850)
234-8944. 🅦 visitpanamacity
beach.com

A brash postcard type of place,
Panama City Beach is a 27 mile
(43 km) "Miracle Strip" of hotels,
amusement parks, and arcades,
bordered by a gleaming quartz
sand beach. The Panhandle's
biggest resort, it caters both to
the young crowds at Spring
Break (see p38), and to families,
who dominate in summer. The
sports facilities are excellent.

Panama City Beach, nick-
named the "wreck capital of the
south," is a famous diving destination. Besides a few natural reefs
formed from limestone ridges in
the sea bottom and the
presence of older shipwrecks, it
has more than 50 artificial diving
sites created by wrecked boats –
providing some of the best
diving in the Gulf. Dive operators
offer scuba and snorkeling trips
and lessons. For the less
energetic, Captain Anderson's
and Treasure Island Marina offer
dolphin feeding trips and
glass-bottomed boat tours.

### 🚢 Gulf World Marine Park
15412 Front Beach Rd.
ℹ️ (850) 234-5271. **Open** daily.
**Closed** Thanksgiving, Dec 25. 🎟️ 🅰️
🅦 gulfworldmarinepark.com
Dolphin and sea lion shows
are the highlights here. The
aquariums and a walkthrough
shark tank are set in lush tropical
gardens with a resident troupe
of performing parrots.

### 🏛️ Museum of Man in the Sea
17314 Panama City Beach Parkway.
Tel (850) 235-4101. **Open** daily.
**Closed** Jan 1, Thanksgiving, Dec 25.
🎟️ 🅰️ 🅦 maninthesea.org
The Museum of Man in the Sea
provides a homespun but
educational look at the history
of diving and marine salvage.
It has exhibits ranging from
ancient diving helmets to
salvaged treasures from the
17th-century Spanish galleon
*Atocha (see p32)*, and there is a
parking lot full of submarines.
A favorite exhibit is Moby
Dick, a whale rescue vessel
resembling a killer whale.

### 🐾 ZooWorld
9008 Front Beach Rd.
**Tel** (850) 230-1243. **Open** daily.
**Closed** Dec 25. 🎟️ 🅰️
🅦 zooworldpcb.net
ZooWorld is home to more than
350 animals, including bears, big
cats, alligators, camels, giraffes,
and orangutans, as well as more
than 15 endangered species.
The Gentle Jungle Petting
Zoo, which offers plenty of
opportunity to interact with the
wildlife, is particularly popular
with young children.

An orangutan, one of ZooWorld's more
entertaining residents

### 🌊 Shipwreck Island Water Park
12201 Hutchison Blvd. **Tel** (850) 234-
3333. **Open** Apr–May: Sat, Sun; Jun–
Aug: daily (subject to change). 🎟️
🅰️ limited. 🅦 shipwreckisland.com
This water park will have no
trouble keeping the family
entertained for the entire day.
The 1,600 ft (490 m) Lazy River
tube ride is great and there
are higher-energy options for
the more adventurous: try the
35 mph (55 km/h) Speed Slide,
the Raging Rapids, or the
370 ft (110 m) White Knuckle
Rapids. There are gentler rides
for youngsters, as well as a
children's pool. Other attractions
include a wave pool and
sunbathing areas.

Fun on the Lazy River ride at Shipwreck
Island Water Park

### 🌴 Coconut Creek Family Fun Park
9807 Front Beach Rd. **Tel** (850) 234-
2625, (888) 764-2199. **Open** 9am–
11:30pm daily. **Closed** Dec 24, 25.
🎟️ Children under 6 play free. 🅰️
🅦 coconutcreekfun.com
This park has two 18-hole
mini-golf courses, featuring an
African safari theme. There is
also a giant maze the size of a
football field, which has as its
theme voyaging from one
South Pacific island to another,
and is the largest of its kind in
the country.

### Environs
An easy 3 mile (5 km) hop
southeast of the main Strip,
**St. Andrews State Park** is a
good antidote to Panama City

A replica of a turpentine still in St. Andrews State Park

Beach, though it can become very busy in summer. The preserve has a pristine white sand beach and emerald green waters. The swimming is good, and there is excellent snorkeling around the rock jetties. Behind the dunes, lagoons and marshland are home to alligators and wading birds. Also within the park, not far from the fishing pier, is a modern re-creation of an early turpentine still, like those found throughout the state in the early 1900s *(see p235)*.

🏊 🛶 **St. Andrews State Park**
4607 State Park Ln. **Tel** (850) 233-5140.
**Open** daily. 🅿️ 🚻 limited. ⛺
🅦 **floridastateparks.org**

## ⑫ Florida Caverns State Park

**Road map** B1. Jackson Co. 3345 Caverns Rd, off Route 166, 3 miles (5 km) N of Marianna. 🚌 Marianna: **Tel** (850) 482-9598. **Open** daily. 🅿️ 🚻 📷 🅦 **floridastateparks.org**

The limestone that underpins Florida is laid bare in this series of underground caves hollowed out of the soft rock and drained by the Chipola River. The filtering of rainwater through the limestone rock over thousands of years has created a breathtaking subterranean cavescape of stalactites, stalagmites, columns, and glittering rivulets of crystals. Wrap up warm for the guided tours, since the caverns maintain a cool 61–66 °F (16–19 °C).

The park also offers hiking trails and horseback riding, and visitors can swim and fish in the Chipola River. A 52 mile (84 km) canoe trail slips through the high limestone cliffs along the river's route south to Dead Lake, just west of Apalachicola National Forest *(see p244)*.

## ⑬ Torreya State Park

**Road map** C1. Liberty Co. Route CR 1641, 13 miles (21 km) N of Bristol. 🚌 Blountstown. **Tel** (850) 643-2674. **Open** daily. 🚻 🅿️ limited.
🅦 **floridastateparks.org**

More off the beaten track than most other parks in Florida, Torreya State Park is well worth seeking out. Named after the torreya, a rare type of yew tree that once grew here in abundance, the park abuts a beautiful forested bend in the Apalachicola River. High limestone bluffs, into which Confederate soldiers dug gun pits to repel Union gunboats during the Civil War, flank the river, offering one of the few high natural vantage points in Florida.

**Gregory House**, a fine 19th-century Classical Revival mansion, stands on top of the 150 ft (45 m) bluff. In 1935 it was moved here by conservationists from its first site downriver and has since been restored.

It is a 25-minute walk from Gregory House down to the river and back, or you can take the 7 mile (11 km) Weeping Ridge Trail. Both paths run through woodland and offer a chance to spot all types of birds, deer, beaver, and the unusual Barbours map turtle (so-called for the maplike lines etched on its shell).

## ⑭ St. Joseph Peninsula State Park

**Road map** B1. Gulf Co. Route 30E. 🚌 Blountstown. **Tel** (850) 227-1327. **Open** daily. 🅿️ 🚻 limited. ⛺ open all year. 🅦 **floridastateparks.org**

At the tip of the slender sand spit that extends north from Cape San Blas to enclose St. Joseph's Bay, this beautifully unspoiled beach park is ideal for those in search of a little peace and quiet. The swimming is excellent, and snorkeling and surf fishing are also popular activities. Bird-watchers should pack their binoculars, since the birdlife is prolific along the shoreline: over 200 species of birds have been recorded here. Guests can stay in cabins overlooking the bay, and there are basic camping facilities, too.

Venture from the beach and explore the saw palmetto and pine woodlands, where you may see deer, raccoons, bobcats, and even coyotes.

The forested course of the Apalachicola River in Torreya State Park

Restored houses on the water's edge in Water Street, Apalachicola

## ⓯ Apalachicola

**Road map** B1. Franklin Co.
🏠 3000. 🚌 Tallahassee. 🛈 122
Commerce St, (850) 653-9419.
🌐 apalachicolabay.org

A riverside customs station established in 1823, Apalachicola saw its finest days during the first 100 years of its existence. It boomed first with the cotton trade, then sponge divers and lumber barons made their fortunes here. Today, a swath of pines and hardwoods still stands as the Apalachicola National Forest, extending from 12 miles (19 km) north of Apalachicola to the outskirts of Tallahassee.

At the end of the lumber boom in the 1920s, the town turned to oystering and fishing in the waters at the mouth of the Apalachicola River. Oyster and other fishing boats still pull up at the dockside, which is lined with refrigerated seafood houses and old brick-built cotton warehouses. Among the seafood houses on Water Street there are several places to sample fresh oysters.

The old town is laid out in a neat grid with many fine historic buildings dating from the cotton boom era. A walking map, available from the chamber of commerce, takes in such privately owned treasures as the 1838 Greek Revival Raney House.

Devoted to the town's most notable resident, the **John Gorrie Museum State Park** has a model of Gorrie's patent ice-making machine. Designed to cool the sickrooms of yellow fever sufferers, Dr. Gorrie's 1851 invention was the cutting edge of modern refrigeration and air conditioning.

🏛 **John Gorrie Museum State Park**
46 6th Street (Gorrie Square). **Tel** (850) 653-9347. **Open** Thu–Mon. **Closed** Jan 1, Thanksgiving, Dec 25. 🖼

## ⓰ St. Vincent, St. George, and Dog Islands

**Road map** B2, C2, C1. Franklin Co.
🚌 Tallahassee. 🛈 122 Commerce St, Apalachicola, (850) 653-9419. Jeannie's Journeys: **Tel** (850) 927-3259.
🌐 sgislandjourneys.com

This string of barrier islands separates Apalachicola Bay from the Gulf of Mexico. St. George is linked by a bridge to Apalachicola. However, a 9 mile (14 km) stretch of dunes at its eastern end is preserved as the **St. George Island State Park** – the main expanse of beach is on the gulf side. The beaches on St. George are consistently named among the best nationally.

To the west, the **St. Vincent National Wildlife Refuge** is uninhabited and accessible only by boat: Jeannie's Journeys, on East Gorey Drive, runs tours.

Surf fishing, a popular activity on the quiet sands of St. George Island

Kayak tours to the island's interior are available between May and October. Visitors can see nesting ospreys in spring, sea turtles laying their eggs in summer, and migrating waterfowl in winter.

To the east, little Dog Island can be reached only by boat from Carrabelle on the mainland. It has a small inn, big dunes, and excellent shell hunting.

🏖 **St. George Island State Park**
**Tel** (850) 927-2111. **Open** daily.

🏖 **St. Vincent National Wildlife Refuge**
**Tel** (850) 653-8808. **Open** Mon–Fri.

Fun in the pool at Wakulla Springs

## ⓱ Wakulla Springs State Park

**Road map** C1. Wakulla Co. 550. Wakulla Park Drive, Wakulla Springs. **Tel** (850) 926-0700. 🚌 Tallahassee. **Open** daily. 🖼 ♿
🌐 floridastateparks.org

One of the world's largest freshwater springs, the Wakulla pumps 700,000 gal (2.6 million liters) of water a minute into the large pool which is the big appeal of this park.

Visitors can swim or snorkel in the clear, limestone-filtered water, or take a ride in a glass-bottom boat. There are also trips on the Wakulla River – look out for alligators, ospreys, and wading birds – and woodland trails to follow.

Do not leave without visiting the Spanish-style Wakulla Springs Lodge hotel and restaurant, built as a hunting lodge in the 1930s.

# Fishing for Shellfish in Apalachicola Bay

Apalachicola Bay was one of the most productive estuarine systems in the world until water flow issues, water quality, and other concerns caused the oyster population to plummet. While oysters are still available locally, along with shrimp, blue crab, and fish, the numbers are not enough to support the local fishing industry. The government has closed some areas to harvesting, making life difficult for oystermen, who have made a living on the bay for generations. A federal grant is being used to help the fishery and local oystermen. Fed by the nutrient-rich Apalachicola River, the bay has always been a valuable nursery, breeding, and feeding ground for many marine species. The warm, shallow waters of the salt marshes between Apalachicola Bay and Cedar Key *(see pp248–9)* are important feeding grounds too, and the fishing tradition extends all along the coast.

**"Tongs,"** a pair of rakes joined like scissors, are used to lift the oysters from the sea.

**A "culler"** separates the oysters by size, throwing back any that are too small.

Fishing for oysters in Apalachicola Bay

## Oyster Fishing

Oystermen, known locally as "tongers" after the tools they use, fish from small wooden boats, primarily in public grounds called oyster bars. The oysters can be harvested all year, but there is usually a lull in the summer and fall, when fishermen focus on other species.

Fresh oysters, best served on ice

**Fresh seafood** is sold throughout the year around Apalachicola. On the first weekend of November, seafood lovers converge on the town for the annual Florida Seafood Festival.

**White, brown, and pink shrimps** are fished both from small boats in the bay, and off-shore in the Gulf of Mexico from larger vessels, which may be out for a week or more. The catch is brought back to seafood houses on land for sorting and distribution.

**Blue crabs**, both the hard-shell and soft-shell varieties (the latter known as "peelers"), are caught in baited wire traps, which are dropped and collected by small boats. The crabs appear in warm weather, sometimes as early as February.

# ⓲ Tallahassee

Just 14 miles (23 km) from the Georgia border, encircled by rolling hills and canopy roads, Tallahassee is the epitome of "The Other Florida" – gracious, hospitable, and uncompromisingly Southern. The former site of an Apalachee Indian settlement and a Franciscan mission, this remote spot was an unlikely place to found the new capital of Territorial Florida in 1824 *(see p229)*. However, from its simple beginnings, Tallahassee grew dramatically during the plantation era and after Florida's elevation to full statehood in 1845. The elegant town houses built by politicians, plantation owners, and businessmen during that period can still be enjoyed today.

## VISITORS' CHECKLIST

**Practical Information**
Road map C1. Leon Co.
🗺 190,900. ℹ 106 E. Jefferson Street, (850) 606-2305.
🎭 Springtime Tallahassee (Mar–Apr). 🌐 visittallahassee.com

**Transport**
✈ 8 miles (13 km) S. 🚆 918 Railroad Avenue, (800) 872-7245.
🚌 112 W Tennessee Street, (850) 222-4240.

### Exploring Tallahassee
The historic district, which contains the city's fine 19th-century homes, is focused around Park Avenue and Calhoun Street, both quiet, shady streets planted with century-old live oak trees and southern magnolias. The Brokaw-McDougall House on Meridian Street is a splendid Classical Revival building. Similar influences are evident in The Columns, an 1830 mansion (the city's oldest building) on Duval Street. The

**Woodcarving in the Old Capitol Senate**

Capitol Complex is at the very heart of downtown Tallahassee. Here, the venerable Old Capitol building has been beautifully restored to its 1902 state, with a pristine white dome and striped awnings. Inside, visitors can see the Supreme Court chamber, the old cabinet meeting room, and also the Senate. The 22-floor New Capitol building behind, where the March–May legislative sessions take place, casts a shadow over its predecessor. But although

it is a grim 1970s structure, it does at least offer a lovely view of Tallahassee from its top floor. The Visitor Center on Jefferson Street has walking-tour maps.

### 🏛 Knott House Museum
301 East Park Ave. **Tel** (850) 922-2459. **Open** Wed–Sat. 📷 ♿
🌐 museumoffloridahistory.com
This house is unusual in that it was built by a free black builder in 1843 – 20 years prior to the liberation of Florida's slaves. Now one of the most beautifully restored Victorian homes in Tallahassee, it is named after the Knotts, who moved here in 1928

## Tallahassee City Center

① Museum of Florida History
② Old Capitol
③ New Capitol
④ The Columns
⑤ Knott House Museum
⑥ Brokaw-McDougall House

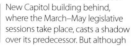

PENSACOLA
Greyhound Station
Goodwood Museum and Gardens
Florida State University
PANAMA CITY
VIRGINIA STREET
TENNESSEE HWY
CALL STREET
Brokaw-McDougall House ⑥
JACKSONVILLE
④ The Columns
WEST PARK AVENUE
COLLEGE AVENUE
JEFFERSON STREET
PENSACOLA STREET
MADISON STREET
MADISON AVENUE
Mary Brogan Museum of Art & Science
① Museum of Florida History
EAST PARK AVENUE
⑤ Knott House Museum
New Capitol ③ ② Old Capitol
Amtrak Station
GAINES STREET
ST FRANCIS STREET
ALL SAINTS STREET
Tallahassee Museum of History and Natural Science
BRONOUGH STREET
BLOXHAM STREET
DUVAL STREET
ADAMS STREET
Black Archives Research Center & Museum

0 meters 200
0 yards 200

Tallahassee Regional Airport
13 km (8 miles)
WAKULLA
Cascades Park

**Key to Symbols** *see back flap*

and completely refurbished the house. The attractive interior is evocative of the former owners. Poems that Luella Knott composed and tied to her antique furnishings are still in place today.

### 🏛 Museum of Florida History

500 S Bronough St. **Tel** (850) 488-1484. **Open** daily. **Closed** Thanksgiving, Dec 25. 👤
**W** museumoffloridahistory.com

The museum tackles 12,000 years of the region's history in entertaining style. Varied dioramas feature elements of paleo-Indian culture, massive armadillos, and a mastodon skeleton made of bones found in Wakulla Springs *(see p244)*. Numerous artifacts and succinct storyboards provide an excellent history from the Colonial era to the "tin can" tourists of the 1920s *(see p55)*.

### Environs

Three miles (5 km) southwest of the city, Lake Bradford Road leads to the **Tallahassee Museum**, which is very popular with children. The centerpiece is Big Bend Farm – a superb re-creation of late 19th-century rural life; employees dressed as farmhands tend goats and geese among authentic 1880s farm buildings. Bellevue, a small plantation home built in the 1830s, is among the other attractions. There is also an interactive discovery center and a zoo. On the shores of Lake Bradford, this woodland area provides natural habitat enclosures for black bears and bobcats, while alligators lurk amid

Boardwalk in the Tallahassee Museum

AB Maclay Gardens State Park near Tallahassee, at its best in the spring

the water lilies and cypress swamp areas. **Goodwood Museum and Gardens**, on the northeastern edge of Tallahassee, was a major producer of cotton and corn in the 19th century *(see pp50–51)*. The main house, built in the 1830s, retains many original features, including a mahogany staircase. After years of neglect, the plantation buildings are being restored.

### 🏛 Tallahassee Museum

3945 Museum Drive. **Tel** (850) 576-1636. **Open** daily. **Closed** Jan 1, Thanksgiving, Dec 24–25. 👤👤
**W** tallahasseemuseum.org

### 🏛 Goodwood Museum and Gardens

1600 Miccosukee Rd. **Tel** (850) 877-4202. **Open** Mon–Fri. 🕐 Mon–Sat
**W** goodwoodmuseum.org

## ⓳ AB Maclay Gardens State Park

**Road map** C1. 3540 Thomasville Rd, Leon Co. **Tel** (850) 487-4556. 🚉 Tallahassee. 🚌 Tallahassee. **Open** Mon–Sat. **Closed** Sun. 👤👤 (limited). **W** floridastateparks.org

These gorgeous gardens, 4 miles (6 km) north of Tallahassee, were originally laid out around Killearn, the 1930s winter home of New York financier Alfred B. Maclay. More than 200 varieties of plants are featured in the landscaped gardens that surround the shores of Lake Hall. They remain

eye-catching even in winter, when the camellias and azaleas are in full bloom (from January to April). Visitors can also swim, fish, go boating, or stroll along the Big Pine Nature Trail.

## ⓴ Monticello

**Road map** C1. Jefferson Co.
🏔 13,000. 🚉 Tallahassee.
🚌 Tallahassee. 🛈 420 W Washington St, (850) 997-5552.
**W** monticellojeffersonfl.com

Founded in 1827, Monticello (pronounced "Montisello") was named after the Virginia home of former President Thomas Jefferson. Lying at the heart of northern Florida's cotton-growing country, the town prospered and funded the building of elegant homes. Some of these are now guesthouses, making the town an ideal base from which to explore the Tallahassee area.

Monticello radiates from the imposing courthouse on US 90. The historic district lies to the north, where there are tree-canopied streets and a wealth of lovely old buildings, ranging from 1850s antebellum mansions to Queen Anne homes with decorative woodwork and Gothic features. Every year at the end of June, the town hosts its Watermelon Festival to celebrate a mainstay of the local agricultural economy. Pageants, dancing, rodeos, and the traditional watermelon seed spitting contest are among the festival's many attractions.

Unadorned Presbyterian church, Monticello

## ㉒ Suwannee River State Park

**Road map** D2. Suwannee Co. 13 miles (21 km) W of Live Oak. 🚌 Live Oak. **Tel** (386) 362–2746. **Open** daily. 🅿️ ♿ limited. ⚠️ 🆆 floridastateparks.org

Made internationally famous by the song *Old Folks at Home*, written by Stephen Foster in 1851, the Suwannee's sources are in Georgia and it runs 265 miles (425 km) to the Gulf of Mexico.

The Park offers some of the best back-country canoeing in Florida. The river is easy flowing here with low banks, and canoeists have a good chance of seeing a range of wildlife, including herons, American coots, and turtles. Canoe rental is available, and there is a boat ramp and a shady campground.

The nearby **Stephen Foster Folk Culture Center State Park** is the oldest park on the river, and offers similar sporting activities.

Enjoying the sun at a wharf in Suwannee River State Park

### 🎭 Stephen Foster Folk Culture Center State Park

11016 Lillian Saunders Drive. **Tel** (386) 397-4331. **Open** daily. 🅿️ 🆆 floridastateparks.org

## ㉓ Steinhatchee

**Road map** D2. Taylor Co. 🔼 1,000. 🚌 Chiefland. ℹ️ 428 N Jefferson, Perry, (850) 584-5366. 🆆 taylorcountychamber.com

Set back from the mouth of the Steinhatchee River, this is a sleepy old fishing town along the riverbank. To get a flavor of the place, ignore the trailer parks and stroll among the fish camps, bait shops, and boats tied up to the cypress wood docks. Trout fishing is big here, and people go crabbing along the coast.

About 26 miles (42 km) northwest is **Keaton Beach**, a tiny but popular coastal resort.

## ㉔ Cedar Key

**Road map** D2. Levy Co. 🔼 950. 🚌 Chiefland. ℹ️ 525 2nd Street, (352) 543-5600. 🆆 cedarkey.org

At the foot of a chain of small bridge-linked keys jutting out into the Gulf of Mexico, Cedar Key is a picturesque, weathered Victorian fishing village. In the 19th century it flourished as the gulf terminal of Florida's first cross-state railroad, and from the burgeoning lumber trade. However, within a few decades its stands of cedar forest had

## ㉑ Cotton Trail Tour

In the 1820s and 1830s, the area around Tallahassee was the most important cotton-growing region in Florida. From the outlying plantations, horse-drawn wagons creaked along red clay roads to market in the capital. Today, these old roads pass through one of the last corners of unspoiled rural Florida.

This tour follows the old Cotton Trail, along canopied roads, and past cattle pastures and paddocks carved out of deep green woodlands. It takes about 3.5 hours, or it could be completed en route between Tallahassee and Monticello *(see p247)*.

④ **Bradley's Country Store**
Famous for its home made sausages, this traditional country store is still run by the Bradleys, who established the business in 1927.

③ **Old Pisgah United Methodist Church**
This unadorned Greek Revival church, built in 1858, is the oldest Methodist building in Leon County.

② **Miccosukee Road**
Originally an Indian trail, this canopy road was used by 30 local plantations in the 1850s.

① **Goodwood Plantation**
This former cotton plantation *(see p247)* retains its attractive 1840s mansion shaded by live oak trees.

**Key**

▬▬ Tour route
══ Other road

been transformed into pencils, and the logging boom ended. A few of the old lumber warehouses have been turned into shops and restaurants, but the Cedar Key of today is blissfully quiet.

Visitors can take a boat from the docks to an offshore island beach in the Cedar Keys National Wildlife Refuge, or take a bird-watching trip along the salt-marsh coast. Various boats run trips from the docks.

Alternatively, visit the entertaining **Cedar Key Historical Society Museum**, in which eclectic exhibits include some fossilized tapir teeth, Indian pottery shards, and crab traps. There is also a map of the town's historic buildings available.

**🏛 Cedar Key Historical Society Museum**
Corner of D and 2nd Streets.
**Tel** (352) 543-5549. **Open** 1–4pm Sun–Fri, 11am–5pm Sat. **Closed** Jan 1, Thanksgiving, Dec 25. 🅿 ♿

### Environs
Thirty miles (50 km) to the north of Cedar Key is **Manatee Springs State Park**, where a spring gushes from a cave mouth 30 ft (9 m) below the surface of an azure pool. The spring water feeds the Suwannee River, which is as clear as glass and popular with divers and snorkelers. Sightings of manatees, which occasionally winter here, are unreliable, but it is easy to spot dozens of turtles, fish, and egrets feeding in the shallows, and the turkey vultures hovering overhead. Visitors can also swim, rent a canoe, take a boat tour, or follow one of the hiking trails; along which they may spot an armadillo in the undergrowth.

**🦌 Manatee Springs State Park**
Route 320, 6 miles (10 km) W of Chiefland. **Tel** (352) 493-6072.
**Open** daily. 🅿 ⛺
**Ⓦ floridastateparks.org**

Weather-beaten hut on stilts off the coast of Cedar Key

---

#### ⑤ Miccosukee
This community was a Native American village until it was destroyed by Andrew Jackson's army in 1818, during the First Seminole War (see pp48–9).

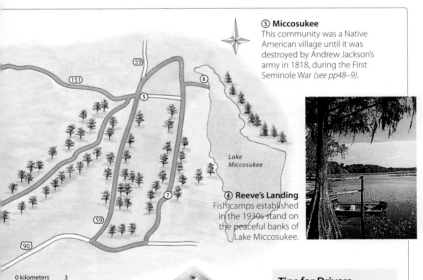

*Lake Miccosukee*

#### ⑥ Reeve's Landing
Fishcamps established in the 1930s stand on the peaceful banks of Lake Miccosukee.

#### ⑦ Magnolia Road
One of Florida's last unpaved canopy roads, this track led to the now-vanished port of Magnolia, from which cotton was shipped to New York.

### Tips for Drivers
**Length:** 50 miles (80 km).
**Stopping-off points:** There are no restaurants along the route, so take your own provisions or buy a snack at Bradley's Country Store, and enjoy a picnic on the banks of Lake Miccosukee.

0 kilometers    3
0 miles    3

# THE GULF COAST

For many visitors the Gulf Coast begins and ends with its fabulous beaches and their accompanying resorts, bathed by the warm, calm waters of the Gulf of Mexico. However, with only a little effort visitors can kick the sand from their shoes and visit some of Florida's most interesting cities, or explore wilderness areas that have been left virtually untouched by the vagaries of time.

Ever since the Spanish colonization, the focus of activity along the Gulf Coast has been around Tampa Bay, the large inlet in Florida's west coast. Pánfilo de Narváez anchored in the bay in 1528, and Hernando de Soto *(see p47)* landed nearby in 1539. The bay was a perfect natural port and became a magnet to pioneers in the 19th century. The favorable climate even attracted the odd sugargrower: Gamble Plantation near Bradenton is the southernmost plantation house in the US *(see p270)*.

After the Civil War, the Gulf Coast became a significant center for trade between the US and the Caribbean. This was due in part to Henry Plant, whose rail line from Virginia, laid in the 1880s, helped to fuel both Tampa's and the region's greatest period of prosperity. Pioneers flooded in, from ethnic groups such as the Greek sponge fishermen who settled in Tarpon Springs, to wealthier American immigrants – chief among whom was circus king John Ringling, whose splendid Italianate home, and impressive European art collection, is the city of Sarasota's top attraction. Henry Plant, like Flagler in eastern Florida *(see pp52–3)*, used the promise of winter sunshine to lure wealthy travelers from the north. The west coast's much-advertised average of 361 days of sunshine a year still helps to attract great hordes of tourists to the generous miles of white sand beaches. Lively beach scenes are the norm around St. Petersburg and Clearwater, but visitors can easily escape the cosmopolitan vacation atmosphere: only a short distance inland are quirky cattle towns, rivers perfect for canoeing, and swamps and forests where wild animals reside undisturbed.

A beautiful sunny morning at Clearwater Beach

◀ The city skyline is reflected in Tampa Bay at dusk

# Exploring the Gulf Coast

The beaches that run in an almost continuous line along the Gulf Coast, interrupted only by a series of bays and inlets, are hard to resist. However, the joy of this region is that it is easy to spice up a Gulf Coast vacation with some sightseeing. The abundant accommodation by the water, from quaint cottages to no-expense-spared resorts, makes this a natural base with all the main cities and inland sights within easy reach. Visitors will find some of Florida's best museums in St. Petersburg, Tampa, and Sarasota, as well as high-profile attractions such as Busch Gardens and The Florida Aquarium in Tampa. There are also other interesting sights: from the world's largest concentration of Frank Lloyd Wright buildings at Florida Southern College, to the weird and wonderful mermaids of Weeki Wachee Springs.

The glistening towers and dome of the old
Tampa Bay Hotel, a part of the University of Tampa *(see p248)*

Exploring the pristine landscapes of Myakka River State Park

*For hotels and restaurants in this area see pp320–23 and pp343–5*

## Getting Around

The region is easy to get around by car. US 19 runs along the coast north of Tampa Bay, crossing the mouth of the bay over the magnificent Sunshine Skyway Bridge, while US 41 links the coastal communities south of Tampa. If speed is of the essence you will want to use I-75, which runs farther inland.

As in every other region of Florida, life is hard without a car. Greyhound buses link the main towns, but rail services are more limited. Amtrak trains run only as far as Tampa, but its connecting "Thruway" buses (see p384) provide a link to St. Petersburg, and south along the coast as far as Fort Myers.

Deserted Clearwater Beach at sunset

### Key

Mascotte
Orlando

━━ Highway
══ Major road
▬▬ Secondary road
⋯⋯ Minor road
── Scenic route
▬▬ Main railroad

0 kilometers    30
0 miles    25

akeland
**2 FLORIDA SOUTHERN COLLEGE**
Bartow
Fort Meade
Bowling Green
chula
Zolfo Springs
Gardner

**19 ARCADIA**

eace River Shores
Babcock
otte Park  **20 BABCOCK WILDERNESS ADVENTURES**
Fort Myers Shores
West Palm Beach
Lehigh Acres
Cape Coral

**22 KORESHAN STATE HISTORIC SITE**
Naples

The old-fashioned pier on Anna Maria Island, a well-known local landmark west of Bradenton

## Sights at a Glance

**For additional map symbols** see back flap

# ❶ Crystal River

**Road map** D2. Citrus Co. 3,000.
🚌 ℹ️ 28 NW US 19, (352) 795-3149.
🌐 **crystalriverfl.org**

Crystal River has two main attractions. In winter, people come to watch the manatees, which gather in herds of up to 300 to bask in the warm local springs, between January and March. You need to make a reservation with one of the boat operators in the area for an early morning trip around the **Crystal River National Wildlife Refuge**, which was set up specifically to protect the manatees. Manatees are active only in the very early morning hours, and the clear water makes spotting them easy.

A year-round attraction is the **Crystal River Archaeological State Park**, a complex of six mounds 2 miles (3 km) west of the town. The site, now a National Historic Landmark, is thought to have been occupied for 1,600 years, from 200 BC to AD 1400, one of the longest continually occupied sites in Florida. An estimated 7,500 Native Americans visited the complex every year for ceremonial purposes. Excavation of 400 of the possible 1,000 graves at the site has also revealed that local tribes had trade links far to the north of Florida.

Climb up to the observation deck for a bird's-eye view of the site. Just below is the main temple mound, built in around AD 600. Beyond, two stelae, or carved ceremonial stones, erected in around AD 440 can be seen flanking two of the site's three burial mounds. This stone is typical of the pre-Columbian cultures of Mesoamerica, but no evidence exists to link them with Crystal River. On the western edge of the site is an area marked by two midden mounds *(see p44)* on a midden ridge. A model of the site in the visitor center has examples of the pottery found.

*Pottery at Crystal River*

**Ⓧ Crystal River National Wildlife Refuge**
1502 SE Kings Bay Drive. **Tel** (352) 563-2088. **Open** daily (Apr–mid-Nov: Mon–Fri). 🌐 **fws.gov/crystalriver**

**Ⓜ Crystal River Archaeological State Park**
3400 N Museum Point. **Tel** (352) 795-3817. **Open** daily. 🅿️ ♿ limited.
🌐 **floridastateparks.org**

## The Manatee in Florida

You cannot go far in Florida without hearing about the sea cow, or manatee, an animal that was at serious risk of extinction. A 'Save the Manatee' program over the past two decades has allowed for recovery of numbers, from 2,500 a decade ago to around 6,600 in 2017. Once plentiful, the animals were extensively hunted for meat and sport until the beginning of the 20th century. Since then, habitat destruction and boat collisions have done most of the damage.

The manatee, which grows to an average length of 10 ft (3 m), is a huge but gentle creature. It lives in shallow coastal waters, rivers, and springs, spending about five hours a day feeding – sea-grass is its favorite food.

*The manatee, an inhabitant of both salt and fresh water*

# ❷ Homosassa Springs Wildlife State Park

**Road map** D2. Citrus Co. 4150 South Suncoast Blvd, Homosassa. 🚌 Crystal River. **Tel** (352) 628-5343. **Open** daily. 🅿️ ♿ 🌐 **floridastateparks.org**

One of the best places to see manatees is at Homosassa Springs Wildlife State Park, where a floating observatory enables visitors to get close up to the animals.

Injured manatees, usually the victims of boat propellers, are treated and rehabilitated here before being released into the wild. There are often half a dozen in the recovery pool, and more outside the park fence in winter: in cold weather manatees are attracted by the warm spring water.

# ❸ Weeki Wachee Springs

**Road map** D2. 6131 Commercial Way, Spring Hill, Hernando Co. Junction of US 19 & SR 50. **Tel** (352) 592-5656. 🚌 Brooksville. **Open** daily. 🅿️ ♿ 🌐 **weekiwachee.com**

This long-standing theme park is built on one of Florida's largest freshwater springs. In the 1940s, ex-Navy frogman Newton Perry thought of using women swimmers to take the part in "live mermaids" performing a kind of

*A performing "mermaid" at Weeki Wachee Springs*

underwater ballet. A theater was built 15 ft (5 m) underwater with strategically placed air pipes for the swimmers to take in air.

Other attractions include a water park, a Misunderstood Creatures show, and a popular wilderness river cruise.

# ❹ Tarpon Springs

**Road map** D3 Pinellas Co. 🔼 24,000. 🚌 Clearwater. 🛈 11 E Orange St, (727) 937-6109. 🔟 **tarponsprings chamber.com**

This lively town on the Anclote River is most famous as a center of Greek culture – the legacy of the immigrant fishermen lured here at the start of the 20th century by the prolific local sponge beds. Visitors will find restaurants specializing in Greek food, an Athens Street, and a Poseidon gift shop, as well as a Parthenon bakery.

Alongside Dodecanese Boulevard are the Sponge Docks, which are busy once more – thanks to the recovery of the nearby sponge beds, decimated by bacterial blight in the 1940s. Boat trips organized by local sponge fishermen include a demonstration of sponge diving by a diver fitted out in a traditional suit.

The **Spongeorama** museum and shopping village is housed in former dockside sheds, and the Sponge Exchange, now refurbished, is an upscale complex with galleries, boutiques, and quaint restaurants. Two miles (3 km) south rises

Trimming natural sponges before sale in Tarpon Springs

The nature trail through unspoiled woodland on Caladesi Island

**St. Nicholas Greek Orthodox Cathedral**, a symbol of Tarpon Springs' Greek heritage. The Byzantine Revival church, a replica of St. Sophia in Istanbul, was erected in 1943 using marble transported from Greece. It is the starting point for the Epiphany Festival *(see p41)*.

**📷 Spongeorama**
510 Dodecanese Blvd.
**Tel** (727) 943-2164. **Open** daily.
🔟 spongeorama.com

**🛕 St. Nicholas Greek Orthodox Cathedral**
36 N Pinellas Ave at Orange St.
**Tel** (727) 937-3540. **Open** daily. ♿

# ❺ Dunedin

**Road map** D3. Pinellas Co. 🔼 38,000. 🚌 Clearwater. 🛈 301 Main St, (727) 733-3197. 🔟 **visitdunedinfl.com**

Dunedin was founded by a Scotsman, John L Branch, who in 1870 opened a store to supply ships on their way down the Gulf Coast to Key West. Passing sea and rail routes brought trade and prosperity, and this soon attracted a number of his compatriots. Dunedin's Scottish heritage is still expressed in its annual Highland Games festival held in late March or early April.

The renovated properties on and around Main Street impart the authentic flavor of early 20th-century, small-town Florida. The **Historical Museum**, which occupies Dunedin's former railroad station, has a fine collection of photographs

and artifacts from the town's early days. Nearby Railroad Avenue is now part of the **Pinellas Trail**, a paved walking and cycling path running for 47 miles (76 km) from Tarpon Springs to St. Petersburg, along the route of a former railroad.

**🏛 Historical Museum**
349 Main St. **Tel** (727) 736-1176.
**Open** Tue–Sat. **Closed** public hols. ♿

**Environs**
Three miles (5 km) north of Dunedin, a causeway crosses to **Honeymoon Island State Park**. You can swim and fish there, but this barrier island is largely undeveloped, in order to preserve its status as an important osprey nesting site. It is also the departure point for the passenger ferry to the even more alluring **Caladesi Island State Park**, which can also be reached from Clearwater Beach *(see p256)*.

Caladesi's 3 mile (5 km) beach, fronting the Gulf of Mexico, was rated in 2008 as the beast beach in the nation. The beach gives way to dunes fringed by sea oats, and there is a 3 mile (5 km) nature trail through cypress and mangrove woods.

**🏞 Honeymoon Island State Park**
Route 586, 3 miles (5 km) NW of Dunedin. **Tel** (727) 469-5942.
**Open** daily. 🚗 ♿ limited.

**🏞 Caladesi Island State Park**
1 Causeway Blvd. **Tel** (727) 469-5918. **Open** daily. 🚗 ♿
🔟 floridastateparks.org

Interior of the McMullen Log House, Pinellas County Heritage Village

## ➏ Clearwater Beach

**Road map** D3. Pinellas Co. 🚍 23,000.
✈️ 🚌 Clearwater. 🚎 tourist trolley
from Cleveland St. ℹ️ 1130 Cleveland
St, (727) 461-0011.
🌐 **clearwaterflorida.org**

The satellite of Clearwater city,
this lively resort sits amid the
long strip of barrier islands that
line the Gulf shore. Hotels
and bars, often filled with
European tourists,
dominate the
waterfront, but
Clearwater Beach
manages to retain
some character. A
nightly sunset festival
at Pier 60 on the beach
has been celebrating
the setting sun for
20 years.

Screech owls in
the Suncoast
Sanctuary

The broad sandy beach
is consistently voted among
the nation's top beach
destinations, and the water
sports facilities are excellent.
Boat trips of all kinds (from
diving and fishing expeditions,
to cruises to watch Atlantic
bottlenose dolphins), depart
from the marina.

### Environs

Across Clearwater Pass is Sand
Key, which runs south for 12
miles (19 km). **Sand Key Park**,
near the top, has a popular palm-
fringed beach.

About 7 miles (11 km) to the
south – beyond the chic
residential district of Belleair,
complete with a hotel built by
Henry Plant *(see pp52–3)* – is the
**Suncoast Seabird Sanctuary**.
Up to 500 injured birds live
at this sanctuary.

Pelicans, owls, herons, egrets,
and other species are all on
view, while Ralph Heath, who
runs the sanctuary, and his
helpers offer guided tours.

It is well worth making the
diversion inland to Largo, 8 miles
(13 km) southeast of Clearwater
Beach, to visit the **Pinellas
County Heritage Village**. This
consists of 16 historic buildings,
brought here from various
sites, such as the
McMullen Log House
*(see p34)*, and the
Seven Gables Home
(1907), which offers a
taste of the lifestyle of
a wealthy Victorian
family. Spinning,
weaving, and other
skills are demonstrated
in the museum.

🦅 **Suncoast Seabird Sanctuary**
18328 Gulf Blvd, Indian Shores,
33785. **Tel** (727) 391-6211.
**Open** 9am–sunset daily. ♿

🏛️ **Pinellas County
Heritage Village**
11909 125th Street N. **Tel** (727)
582-2123. **Open** Tue–Sun.
**Closed** public hols. ♿ limited.
🌐 **pinellascounty.org/heritage**

## ➐ St. Petersburg Beaches

**Road map** D3. Pinellas Co.
✈️ 🚍 Tampa. 🚌 St. Petersburg.
🚢 many services from St. Petersburg.
ℹ️ Tampa Bay Beaches Chamber of
Commerce, 6990 Gulf Blvd, (727)
360-6957. 🌐 **visitstpete
clearwater.com**

South of Clearwater and Sand
Key Park are a series of small
beach communities, which offer
quiet beauty, and lots of beach
access. **Madeira Beach** is a
good place to stay if you prefer
a laid-back atmosphere to the
buzzing scenes of the bigger
resorts. John's Pass Village, a
re-created fishing village nearby,
also offers a quirkier-than-
average choice of restaurants
and shops. There is also a fishing
pier and a marina.

Farther south, monotonous
ranks of hotels characterize
Treasure Island. Next in line, **St.
Pete Beach** (St. Petersburg was
officially shortened to St. Pete
because it was considered more
evocative of a fun-filled resort),
has a 7 mile (11 km) strip of
white sand and a buzzing scene
along the waterfront. At its
southern end towers the Don
CeSar Resort. Built in the 1920s,
the hotel's scale and list of
celebrity guests are typical of
the grand hotels of that era.

At the southern tip of the
barrier island group, **Pass-a-
Grille** is a breath of fresh air after
crowded St. Pete Beach. Skirted
by the main coastal road, this
sleepy community has some
lovely homes from the early
1900s, and beaches still in their
natural state. A word of warning:
take plenty of change for the
parking meters.

The extravagant Don CeSar Resort overlooking St. Pete Beach

# Gulf Coast Beaches

With an average of 361 days of sunshine a year and just two hours' drive from Orlando, the coast between St. Petersburg and Clearwater is the busiest resort area along the Gulf Coast, attracting hordes of overseas visitors. The strip encompasses 28 miles (45 km) of superb barrier island beaches. Due to the high quality of the sand and water, plus the booming local food and craft beer scene, the St. Pete-Clearwater area regularly appears in lists of the nation's top beaches and is frequently selected as one of the best places to visit and live. Farther south, Sarasota's barrier island beaches are of an equally high standard: they attract more Floridians than package tourists. Wherever you are, you can expect a more laid-back mood than on the east coast.

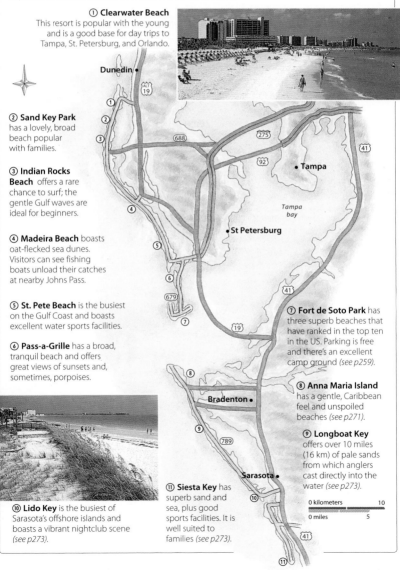

① **Clearwater Beach**
This resort is popular with the young and is a good base for day trips to Tampa, St. Petersburg, and Orlando.

② **Sand Key Park** has a lovely, broad beach popular with families.

③ **Indian Rocks Beach** offers a rare chance to surf; the gentle Gulf waves are ideal for beginners.

④ **Madeira Beach** boasts oat-flecked sea dunes. Visitors can see fishing boats unload their catches at nearby Johns Pass.

⑤ **St. Pete Beach** is the busiest on the Gulf Coast and boasts excellent water sports facilities.

⑥ **Pass-a-Grille** has a broad, tranquil beach and offers great views of sunsets and, sometimes, porpoises.

⑦ **Fort de Soto Park** has three superb beaches that have ranked in the top ten in the US. Parking is free and there's an excellent camp ground (see p259).

⑧ **Anna Maria Island** has a gentle, Caribbean feel and unspoiled beaches (see p271).

⑨ **Longboat Key** offers over 10 miles (16 km) of pale sands from which anglers cast directly into the water (see p273).

⑩ **Lido Key** is the busiest of Sarasota's offshore islands and boasts a vibrant nightclub scene (see p273).

⑪ **Siesta Key** has superb sand and sea, plus good sports facilities. It is well suited to families (see p273).

Dunedin

Tampa

*Tampa bay*

St Petersburg

Bradenton

Sarasota

0 kilometers 10
0 miles 5

# ❽ St. Petersburg

This city of broad avenues grew up in the great era of 19th-century land speculation. In 1875, Michigan farmer John Williams bought a plot of land beside Tampa Bay, with a dream of building a great city. An exiled Russian nobleman called Peter Demens soon provided St. Petersburg with both a railroad and its name – the latter in honor of his birthplace.

"St. Pete," as it is often called, used to be best known for its ageing population. However, times have changed, and the city now has a much more vibrant image. Extensive renovation has brought new life to the waterfront area downtown, and St. Petersburg's claim to be a lively cultural center is greatly boosted by the presence of the prestigious Salvador Dalí Museum *(see pp260–61)*.

The pink landmark in downtown, The Vinoy Renaissance Resort

### Exploring St. Petersburg

Most people visit the area for its stunning miles of beach, although the city itself is well worth a visit for its idylic Tampa Bay waterfront lined with marinas and distinctive buildings. Art museums, with the Dalí Museum at the forefront exhibiting surrealist art works, and other galleries also offer visitors a world-class experience.

The **Vinoy Renaissance Resort** *(see p322)*, an attractive building built in the 1920s as the Vinoy Hotel and much modernized, dominates the downtown skyline. Away from the waterfront is the massive **Tropicana Field**, St. Petersburg's other main landmark. This is a popular place for large-scale activities ranging from rock concerts to sports events.

### 🏛 St. Petersburg Museum of History

335 2nd Ave NE. **Tel** (727) 894-1052. **Open** Wed–Sun. **Closed** Thanksgiving, Dec 25, Jan 1. 🅿 ♿ 🅦 spmoh.org

This museum tells the story of St. Petersburg from prehistoric times to the present. Exhibits range from mastodon bones, fossils, and native pottery to an entertaining mirror gallery, which gives visitors a comic idea of how they would have looked in Victorian fashions.

A special pavilion houses a replica of a sea plane called the *Benoist*, which marks St. Petersburg as the birthplace of commercial aviation. This aircraft made the first flight with a paying passenger across Tampa Bay in 1914.

## St. Petersburg City Center

① Tropicana Field
② St. Petersburg Museum of History
③ Florida Holocaust Museum
④ The Chihuly Collection
⑤ Museum of Fine Arts
⑥ Mahaffey Theater
⑦ Sunken Gardens
⑧ Great Explorations
⑨ Fort De Soto Park
⑩ Salvador Dalí Museum

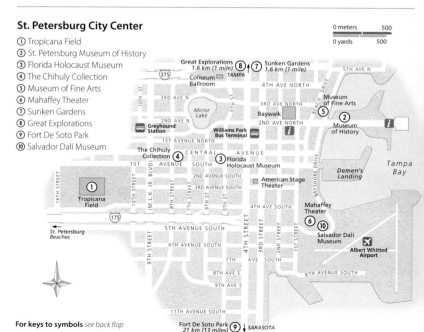

*Poppy*, one of Georgia O'Keeffe's acclaimed flower paintings, in the Museum of Fine Arts

### 🏛 Florida Holocaust Museum

55 Fifth St S, St. Petersburg **Tel** (727) 820-0100 or (800) 960-7448.
**Open** daily. **Closed** Thanksgiving, Dec 25, Jan 1, Jewish hols. 🅿 ♿
**w** flholocaustmuseum.org

This museum, located in downtown St. Petersburg, honors the millions of people who suffered or died during the Holocaust.

### 🏛 The Chihuly collection

720 Central Ave. **Tel** (727) 822-7872
**Open** daily. **w** moreanartscenter.org/chihuly

The work of world-renowned glass artist Dale Chihuly is displayed in a building designed specifically to show the large works of glass art. Across the street is the Morean Arts Center Glass Studio and Hot Shop where glassblowers create unique works.

### 🏛 Museum of Fine Arts

255 Beach Dr NE. **Tel** (727) 896-2667.
**Open** daily. **Closed** Jan 1, Martin Luther King Day, Thanksgiving, Dec 25.
🅿 ♿ 🎫 **w** fine-arts.org

Housed in a striking Palladian-style building overlooking the bay, the Museum of Fine Arts is renowned for its wide-ranging collection of European, American, pre-Columbian, and Asian works. Supreme among the French Impressionist paintings are *A Corner of the Woods* (1877) by Cézanne, and Monet's classic *Parliament, Effect of Fog, London* (1904). Other prominent works are the vivid *Poppy* (1927) by Georgia O'Keeffe, *La Lecture* (1888) by Berthe Morisot, and Auguste Rodin's *Invocation* (1886), which

stands in the sculpture garden.

A large collection of photographs, dating from the early 1900s to the present, rounds off the collection.

### 🏛 Mahaffey Theater

400 1st St S. **Tel** (727) 982-5767. **Open** daily.
🅿 ♿ **w** mahaffey theater.com

This modern, glass-enclosed building on the waterfront provides stunning views across Tampa Bay. It contains a 2,031-seat, state-of-the-art theater that features box-style seating, along with a ballroom area. Named for the St. Petersburg family who contributed significantly to the capital campaign, the theater hosts Broadway roadshows, music and dance events, celebrity entertainers, special exhibitions, and children's theater. It is also home to Florida Orchestra's classical music concerts.

### 🌿 Sunken Gardens

1825 4th Street N. **Tel** (727) 551-3102.
**Open** daily. 🎫 🅿 ♿ **w** stpete.org/sunken

Thousands of tropical plants and flowers flourish in this large walled garden, which descends to 10 ft (3 m) below the street outside. The site was once a water-filled sinkhole *(see p26)*; its soil is kept dry by a network of hidden pipes.

Lush tropical plants flanking a stream at the Sunken Gardens

## VISITORS' CHECKLIST

**Practical Information**
**Road map** D3. Pinellas Co.
🗺 260,000. 🛈 100 2nd Ave N, (727) 821-4715. **w** visitstpete clearwater.com

**Transport**
✈ St. Petersburg/Clearwater International Airport, 10 miles (16 km) N of Downtown. 🚌 180 9th St North, (727) 898-1496; also Amtrak bus to Pinellas Square Mall, Pinellas Park, (800) 872-7245.

Wander among the bougain-villea and hibiscus, and visit the extensive orchid garden. Other features include a walk-through butterfly encounter and a horticulture program.

### 🏛 Great Explorations

1925 4th Street N. **Tel** (727) 821-8992.
**Open** daily. 🅿 ♿ **w** greatex.org

"Hands on" is the ethos of this museum, which is aimed at children but is equally fascinating to adults.

Youngsters are encouraged to crawl, climb, and touch everything. For example, the popular Orange Grove has children picking, packing, and shipping oranges from a mock grove, making pizza, or creating animated videos. The emphasis here is on teamwork.

### 🏖 Fort De Soto Park

3500 Pinellas Bayway South, Tierra Verde. **Tel** (727) 582-2267.
**Open** daily. ♿ **w** fortdesoto.com

Five islands in Boca Ciega Bay south of St. Petersburg make up **Fort De Soto Park**. The park offers great views of the Sunshine Skyway Bridge, and superb beaches, especially along the southern and western coasts. The islands are thick with vegetation and bird colonies.

History fans should head for the chief island, Mullet Key, where massive gun emplacements concealed by high concrete walls mark the remains of Fort De Soto. The fort was begun during the Spanish-American War *(see p53)*, but was never finished.

# The Salvador Dalí Museum

Although far from the native country of Spanish artist Salvador Dalí (1904–89), this museum boasts the most comprehensive collection of his work outside of Spain, spanning his entire career. The first museum opened in 1982, 40 years after Ohio businessman Reynolds Morse saw the first exhibition of Dalí's work, and began collecting his works. The museum moved to a spectacular waterfront location in 2011. In addition to 96 original oil paintings, the museum has more than 100 watercolors and drawings, along with 1,300 graphics, sculptures, and other objects. The works range from Dalí's early figurative paintings to his first experiments in Surrealism, and the biggest collection of mature, large-scale compositions described as his "masterworks."

**The Building**
Crawling along the building's concrete walls is the impressive *Enigma*, a large geodesic bubble containing more than 1,000 triangular pieces of glass.

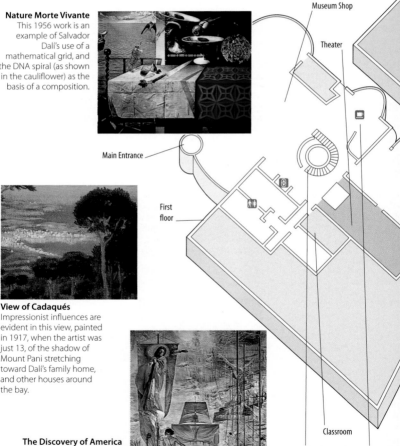

**Nature Morte Vivante**
This 1956 work is an example of Salvador Dalí's use of a mathematical grid, and the DNA spiral (as shown in the cauliflower) as the basis of a composition.

Museum Shop

Theater

Main Entrance

First floor

**View of Cadaqués**
Impressionist influences are evident in this view, painted in 1917, when the artist was just 13, of the shadow of Mount Pani stretching toward Dalí's family home, and other houses around the bay.

**The Discovery of America**
Inspired by a "cosmic dream," this work (1958–9) pays homage to the Spanish painter Velázquez while predicting man's first step on the moon.

Classroom

**The helical spiral staircase** represents Dalí's interest in science.

Café Gala

**Don Quixote and Sancho Panza**
This 1968 etching is just one of over 1,000 drawings and other illustrations produced during Dalí's Classic Period. Examples appear in the museum's special exhibitions.

## VISITORS' CHECKLIST

**Practical Information**
1 Dalí Boulevard, St. Petersburg.
**Tel** (727) 823–3767.
**Open** 10am–5:30pm daily
(8pm Thu). **Closed** Thanksgiving,
Dec 25. 🅿️ 🚻 ♿ 🎥 📷
Ⓦ thedali.org

**Transport**
🚌 4, 32, trolley.

**The Sick Child**
This early painting was composed in 1914, when Dalí was just ten years old and already showing huge talent.

**Daddy Longlegs of the Evening–Hope!**
This image was the foundation stone of the collection. Painted in 1940, it shows a daddy-longlegs crawling over the face of a hideously distorted violinist.

Third floor

## Gallery Guide

*The collection of Dalí's paintings is displayed on the third floor. The theater, on the first floor, shows a short film about the museum, and the second floor houses the library, which is used by researchers and scholars.*

### Key to Floor Plan

- Introduction
- Early Works
- Anti-Art
- Surrealism
- Nuclear Mysticism
- Collection Galleries
- Special exhibitions
- Nonexhibition space

## How Dalí's Art Came to St. Petersburg

Reynolds Morse and his wife Eleanor were fascinated by Salvador Dalí after seeing an exhibition of his art in 1942. They bought their first Dalí work, *Daddy Longlegs of the Evening–Hope!*, one year later and met the artist soon after. Thus began the Morses' life-long friendship with Dalí and his wife, Gala. During the next 40 years the Morses amassed the largest private collection of Dalí's art in the world. After a nationwide search, Morse chose St. Petersburg for the collection because of its resemblance to the artist's childhood summer home of Cadaqués. The museum was rehoused in a stunning, hurricane-proof building, which opened in 2011.

# ❾ Tampa

Tampa is one of the fastest-growing cities in Florida. Modern skyscrapers have replaced many original buildings, but vestiges of a colorful history remain – mainly in the historic Latin quarter, Ybor City *(see pp264–5)*, where Tampa's famous cigar industry took root in the 1880s, and in some quirky architecture downtown. The Spanish arrived here in 1539, but Tampa was just a small town until the late 1800s, when Henry Plant *(see pp52–3)* extended his railroad here. Today, Tampa's big attraction is Busch Gardens *(see pp268–9)*, one of the top theme parks in the US, but the sleek Florida Aquarium in the Channel District is attracting an increasing number of people into the heart of Tampa.

Sunrise over downtown Tampa's office buildings and bridge

## Exploring Downtown

You can easily explore Tampa's compact downtown area on foot. Here, you will find the historic Tampa Theatre and several examples of the public art on which the city justifiably prides itself.

Situated at the mouth of the Hillsborough River, Tampa can also be enjoyed from the water. *Yacht Star Ship (see p361)* runs lunch and dinner cruises around Tampa Bay. For an intimate experience of the city's waterways, paddleboards, electric boats, and water bikes can be rented out. Water taxis also provide good views of the city's chief sights, including the old Tampa Bay Hotel, (now the University of Tampa), and the Museum of Art.

For another view of the city, ride the uptown–downtown connector free of charge. This is a rubber-wheeled trolley that travels from Harbour Island north to Tampa Street, stopping on every block to pick up passengers.

Another way of traveling through downtown is to ride one of the streetcars of the TECO Line Streetcar System, which runs from downtown through the Channel District and into Ybor City. The streetcars are replicas of the Birney Safety Cars that ran on Tampa's streets until 1946. Running seven days a week, they are air-conditioned and take around 22 minutes to complete the route. The uptown–downtown connector trolley meets with the TECO Line Streetcar.

## 🏛 Henry B. Plant Museum

401 W Kennedy Blvd. **Tel** (813) 254-1891. **Open** Tue–Sun. **Closed** Jan 1, Thanksgiving, Dec 25. Donation requested. ♿
**W** plantmuseum.com

The former Tampa Bay Hotel, now home to the University of Tampa, houses the Henry B. Plant Museum. The famous landmark has Moorish minarets that are visible from all over downtown.

Henry Plant commissioned the building in 1891 as a hotel for the well-to-do passengers of his newly built railroad. The construction alone cost $3 million, with an additional $500,000 spent on furnishings. The hotel was not a success, however, and it fell into disrepair soon after Plant's death in 1899. The hotel was bought by the city in 1905 and became part of the University of Tampa in 1933. The south wing of the ground floor was set aside and preserved as a museum.

Complete with a solarium, the museum is splendidly furnished and equipped, with 90 percent of the exhibits on display original to the hotel. Wedgwood china, Venetian mirrors, and 18th-century French furniture effortlessly evoke the sense of a lost age. Visitors are welcome to walk around what is now the university campus to appreciate the sheer size of the building.

## 🏛 Tampa Museum of Art

120 W Gasparilla Plaza.**Tel** (813) 274-8130. **Open** daily. **Closed** Easter, Thanksgiving, Dec 25, Jan 1. ♿♿
**W** tampamuseum.org

The Tampa Museum of Art houses a growing collection of

The elegant solarium at the Henry B. Plant Museum

The sweeping views of the Tampa Riverwalk

world-class art ranging from Classical Greek, Roman, and Etruscan antiquities, to contemporary American, Cuban, and European works and world-class traveling exhibitions. The museum houses both permanent and temporary collections of photography, sculpture, paintings, and sketches. The museum itself is considered a work of art, made with aluminum, glass, and fiber-optic lights. Part of Tampa's scenic Riverwalk, it also hosts outdoor events.

### 🎭 Tampa Theatre

711 N Franklin St. **Tel** (813) 274-8981. **Open** daily. **Closed** Dec 25. 🎦 ♿ 🎦 🌐 tampatheatre.org

In its day, the Tampa Theatre was one of the most elaborate movie theaters in America. The building was designed in 1926 by the architect John Eberson in an architectural style known as Florida-Mediterranean. The lavish result was described by the historian Ben Hall as an "Andalusian bonbon."

In an attempt to create the illusion of an outdoor location, Eberson fitted the ceiling with

lights designed to twinkle like stars. Other effects included artificial clouds, produced by a smoke machine, and lighting to simulate the rising sun.

The easiest way to visit the beautifully restored theater, is to see a movie here (see p359). Movie festivals, plays, and special events are all held here. Guided tours, which take place twice a month, include a 20-minute movie about the theater, and a mini-concert on a traditional 1,000-pipe theater organ.

## Tampa City Center

① Henry B. Plant Museum
② Tampa Museum of Art
③ Tampa Theatre
④ Ybor City
⑤ Florida Aquarium
⑥ Hyde Park
⑦ Museum of Science and Industry
⑧ Lowry Park Zoo
⑨ Tampa Heights

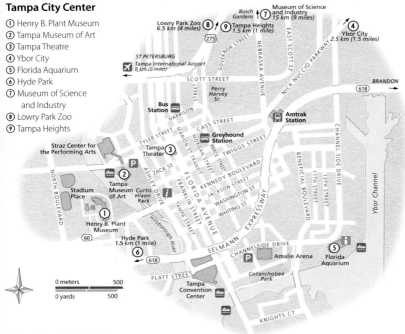

For keys to symbols see back flap

# Street-by-Street: Ybor City

A Spaniard named Don Vicente Martinez Ybor moved his cigar business from Key West to Tampa in 1886. About 20,000 migrant workers, mostly from Cuba and Spain, eventually joined him. The legacy of the cigar boom of the late 1800s and early 1900s is still visible in Ybor City. Its main street, 7th Avenue, with its Spanish-style tiles and wrought-iron balconies, looks much as it did then. Today the district is enjoying a new lease of life. What were once cigar factories and workers' cottages now house shops, restaurants, and clubs. Quiet during the day, Ybor City comes to life in the evening.

**Cigar Museum and Visitor Center**
Housed in the world's largest cigar box, the Visitor Center provides information about accommodation and events in the city.

**Historic Clubs**
Built between 1917–18, the landmark Tampa Cuban Club (El Circulo Cubano de Tampa) is one of several cultural societies in Ybor City.

**Cigar City Cider and Mead**
The only business of its kind in Tampa, is part of the city's booming craft beer industry.

9TH AVENUE

13TH STREET

AVENIDA REPUBLICA DE CUBA

8TH AVENUE

15TH STREET

7TH AVENUE

**The Ritz**, a stunning 1917 movie theater, now houses one of Ybor's top nightclubs.

**José Martí Park**
A statue commemorates José Martí, the Cuban freedom fighter who made several visits to Ybor City to rally support for Cuba's independence campaign.

**Key**

— Suggested route

0 meters 100
0 yards 100

*For hotels and restaurants in this area see pp320–23 and pp343–5*

### ★ Cigar Worker's House
This tiny house (attached to Ybor City State Museum) is furnished to look like a cigar worker's home. "La Casita" is a fine example of the shotgun houses (see p304) built for the flood of immigrants who came to work in Ybor city in the late 1800s.

**Centennial Park**, has an open-air market selling fresh produce.

**Ybor City State Museum**, housed in a former bakery, explores the history of Ybor City and also organizes walking tours of the district. There is a small ornamental garden attached.

9TH AVENUE

19TH STREET

18TH STREET

17TH STREET

LA SEPTIMA

Columbia Restaurant

**Columbia Restaurant**
Florida's oldest restaurant takes up a whole block on 7th Avenue. The Spanish-Cuban food and lively flamenco make it popular with tourists (see p341).

**La Tropicana** serves traditional Cuban fare to its crowd of regulars.

## The Cigar Industry in Tampa

With ships able to bring a regular supply of tobacco from Cuba to its port, Tampa was ideally located for cigar-making. Several huge cigar factories sprang up soon after V.M. Ybor moved here, and by 1900 Ybor City was producing over 111 million cigars annually. Each cigar was skillfully rolled by hand by workers who were often entertained by a lector reading aloud to them. Automation and the growing popularity of cigarettes changed all this. Cigars are still made in Tampa (mostly with leaves grown in Honduras), but now usually made by machine. The Gonzalez y Martínez Cigar Company is one of the few companies to hand roll cigars.

Workers in an Ybor City cigar factory, 1929

**El Sol Cigars**
Although Ybor's oldest cigar store (opened in 1929) no longer rolls its cigars by hand, it is a good place to buy them.

A diver amid reefs and exotic fish at the Florida Aquarium

### 🐟 Florida Aquarium

701 Channelside Drive. **Tel** (813) 273-4000. **Open** daily. **Closed** Thanksgiving, Dec 25. 🅿️ ♿
**W** flaquarium.org

This enormous aquarium is located on the waterfront, and unmistakable with its blue, shell-shaped dome, it is a state-of-the-art interpretation of a modern aquarium. Inside, visitors will not only find tanks of fish but will also come face to face with baby alligators, birds, otters, and all kinds of other creatures living in their authentic habitats. The aquarium also offers a 90 minute cruise around the bay.

The purpose of the Florida Aquarium is to enable visitors to follow the passage of a drop of water from its first appearance in an underground spring to its arrival in the sea, passing through various habitats along the way.

The conditions of each habitat are re-created in separate galleries. The Florida Coral Reefs Gallery, for instance, takes visitors under-water for a panoramic view of a coral colony and its tropical fish. Recorded commentaries by experts at different stages of the tour can be rented, and there are regular hands-on labs, with special projects and activities, and biologists and botanists standing by to explain them.

### 🏛 Hyde Park

Across the river, southwest of Downtown off Bayshore Boulevard, Hyde Park is a charming historic area in Tampa. Dating from the late 19th century, its houses display a striking mix of architectural styles from Colonial to Gothic Revival. The quiet residential streets of Hyde Park are best explored by foot. Visitors can park at Hyde Park Village, off Snow Avenue, where you'll find several upscale shops and restaurants. On some days, musicians come out to entertain the shoppers.

An open-air concert for visitors to Hyde Park Village

### 🏛 Museum of Science and Industry

4801 E Fowler Ave. **Tel** (813) 987-6100. **Open** daily. 🅿️ ♿ **W** mosi.org

With plans for the museum to move downtown in a few years, it has been reduced in size and the IMAX® dome is closed temporarily.

In the meantime, many exhibits have closed or been re-imagined. The Museum of Science and Industry operates in the Kids In Charge area and the adjoining Welcome Center building. The playground and Sky Trail Ropes Course and Zip Line remain open, as does the planetarium.

MOSI is also home to the Saunders Planetarium, which hosts regular astronomical shows. On every Friday and Saturday evening, there are special star-viewing sessions at which, weather permitting, telescopes are set up in the parking lot so that visitors can observe the night sky.

### 🦁 Lowry Park Zoo

1101 West Sligh Ave. **Tel** (813) 935-8552. **Open** daily. **Closed** Thanksgiving, Dec 25. 🅿️ ♿ **W** lowryparkzoo.com

This zoo, 6 miles (10 km) north of downtown Tampa, is one of the best in North America. One of the main attractions is the manatee center, which has a rehabilitation pool, and up to 20 animals in residence at any one time. Visitors can learn more about this endangered species by taking part in the "Manatee Sleepover," a special program that offers the chance to explore the zoo after closing time, learn about the rehabilitation program, and spend the night at the manatee center.

The zoo's Florida Wildlife Center, a special sanctuary for native animals such as alligators and the Florida panther, is another highlight. Other areas worth visiting are Primate World, the Asian Domain, (home to

The eye-catching dome of the Museum of Science and Industry

*For hotels and restaurants in this area see pp320–23 and pp343–5*

## The Legend of Gaspar

José Gaspar was a legendary pirate who preyed on ships and communities between Tampa and Fort Myers in the 19th century. His stronghold was among the isles of the Lee Island Coast *(see pp282–3)*, many of whose modern names recall the association – including Gasparilla and Captiva, where Gaspar is said to have kept his female captives. Legend has it that the pirate was eventually cornered by a US warship, and that he drowned himself in anchor chains rather than be taken prisoner.

Tampa suffered from several of Gaspar's raids, and now holds a Gasparilla Festival each January *(see p41)*. The highlight of this celebration is a mock invasion of the city by hundreds of rowdy villains aboard the world's only fully-rigged "pirate ship."

"Pirates" celebrating Tampa's Gasparilla Festival in the 1950s

Sumatran tigers and an extremely rare Indian rhino), and a free-flight aviary. There is also a delightful children's museum, an amusement center, and a pleasant picnic area.

### ▦ Tampa Heights

This historic neighborhood, located north of downtown, has undergone a major transformation. It is also accessible from the Tampa Riverwalk. Two food halls opened in late 2017, which house a coffeehouse, meadery, microbrewery and numerous other activities which attract a diverse mix of entrepreneurial companies.

### ❿ Busch Gardens

*See pp268–9.*

### ⓫ Hillsborough River

**Road map** D3. Hillsborough Co. 🚉 Tampa. 🚌 Tampa.

Extending through the countryside northeast of Tampa, the Hillsborough River provides a pleasant respite from the hustle and bustle of the city. It is flanked on both sides by dense backwoods of live oak, cypress, magnolia, and mangrove trees, which once covered great swathes of Florida's terrain.

One of the best ways to experience the Hillsborough River is by canoe: **Canoe Escape**

organizes trips along a stretch of the river about 15 minutes' drive from downtown Tampa. Located just beyond the city line, the area is surprisingly wild, and there is a good chance of spotting a great variety of wildlife, including herons, egrets, alligators, turtles, and otters. Canoeing conditions are ideal for beginners. Visitors can choose from three main itineraries, each of which covers about 5 miles (8 km). All journeys involve roughly two hours' paddling which allows plenty of time to absorb the surroundings. Longer day trips are also available.

A section of the river is protected as **Hillsborough River State Park**. Canoeing is a popular way to explore this section; there are also walking trails, and the chance to swim and fish. The park has a large and popular campground, which is open all year round, and there are picnic sites.

Developed in 1936, the Hillsborough River State Park became one of Florida's earliest state parks partly due to the historic significance of Fort Foster, built during the Second Seminole War *(see p50)* to guard a bridge at the confluence of the Hillsborough River and Blackwater Creek. The fort and bridge have been reconstructed, and a battle is re-enacted here annually in December. Tours visit the fort every weekend and on holidays; a shuttle bus runs to it from the park's entrance.

### 🛶 Canoe Escape

12702 US 301, Thonotosassa, 12 miles (19 km) NE of Tampa. **Tel** (813) 986-2067. **Open** daily. **Closed** Thanksgiving, Dec 24 & 25. 🅿

### 🛶 Hillsborough River State Park

15402 US 301 N, 12 miles (19 km) NE of Tampa. **Tel** (813) 987-6771. **Open** daily. 🅿 ♿ limited. 🅰 🆆 floridastateparks.org

Re-created buildings at Fort Foster in Hillsborough River State Park

# ⑩ Busch Gardens

Busch Gardens is one-of-a-kind – a theme park that incorporates one of America's top zoos. To fulfill its unusual aim of re-creating life in Colonial-era Africa, the park supports more than 12,000 animals, with giraffes and zebras roaming freely over the "Serengeti Plain". Lions, gorillas, and other African animals can also be seen from a safari ride. Bird Gardens features macaws, cockatoos, and birds of prey. Animals are the main attraction, but the park's numerous thrill rides attract visitors of all ages. SheiKra, North America's first dive coaster is one of Florida's tallest roller coasters. Adventure Island, adjacent to Busch Gardens, is a 30 acre (12 ha) Key West-themed water park.

**Congo River Rapids**
Rapids, geysers, waterfalls, and a dark cave await rafters set adrift on a swift river current.

**Kumba**
Participants on this roller coaster plunge 135 ft (41 m) at more than 60 mph (100 km/h) while spiraling 360°, and tearing through one of the world's largest vertical loops.

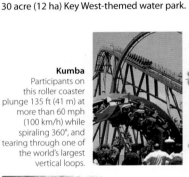

★ **Jungala**
Explore a three-story play land of climbing nets and mazes, and then connect up close with exotic jungle animals.

★ **SheiKra**
This dive coaster sends riders on a breathtaking 3-minute journey through a loop and into a water feature finale.

## KEY

① **Bird Gardens**

② **Stanleyville**

③ **Falcon's Fury**

④ **Pantopia**

⑤ **Pantopia Theater**

⑥ **Serengeti Plain**

⑦ **A train** can be taken around all the major areas within the park.

⑧ **Guest Relations**

| 0 meters | | 100 |
| 0 yards | | 100 |

### Edge of Africa
This safari experience, on the southern edge of the Serengeti Plain, offers visitors a chance to have a close-up view of giraffes, lions, hippos, hyenas, and other African animals.

## VISITORS' CHECKLIST

**Practical Information**
**Road map** D3. 10165 N McKinley Dr. Tampa. **Tel** (813) 987 5082.
W buschgardens.com
**Open** 10am–6pm daily, extended hours for summer and holidays.

**Transport**
Tampa. Tampa. 5 from Marion St, downtown Tampa, 39 from Netpark Transfer Center.

### Egypt
The hair-raising ride, Montu, is found here, as well as the exciting family spin coaster, Cobra's Curse.

### Myombe Reserve
This simulated rainforest is the habitat of western lowland gorillas and chimpanzees, both of which are endangered species.

### ★ Cheetah Hunt
A high-speed roller coaster that climbs high above the African landscape before racing across the plains above the heads of visitors. It can reach speeds of up to 60 mph (97 kph).

Entrance

## ⓬ Florida Southern College

Road map E3. Polk Co. 111 Lake Hollingsworth Drive, Lakeland. **Tel** (863) 680-4111. 🚆 Lakeland. 🚌 Lakeland. **Open** daily. **Closed** Jul 4, Thanksgiving, Dec 25, Jan 1. Visitor Center: **Open** until 2pm Mon–Sat. **Closed** Sun. ♿ 🌐 **flsouthern.edu**

This small college has the world's largest collection of buildings designed by Frank Lloyd Wright. Amazingly, the college president persuaded Wright (one of the most eminent architects of his day), to design the campus at Lakeland with the promise of little more than the opportunity to express his ideas – and payment when the money could be raised. Work began in 1938

The light and spacious interior of the Annie Pfeiffer Chapel

on what Wright, already famous as the founder of organic architecture, termed his "child of the sun." His aim of blending buildings with their natural surroundings made special use of glass to bring the outdoor light to the interiors. The original plan was for 18 buildings, but only seven had been completed by the time Wright died in 1959 – five were finished or added later.

The Annie Pfeiffer Chapel is a particularly fine expression of his ideas. Windows of stained glass break the monotony of the building blocks, and the entire edifice is topped by a spectacular tower in place of the traditional steeple; Wright called it a "jewel box."

As a whole, the campus has the light and airy feel that Wright sought to achieve. The buildings are linked to each other by the Esplanades – a covered walkway, stretching for 1.5 miles (2 km), in which light, shade, and variations in height draw attention from one building to the next.

Visitors can wander around the campus at any time, but the interiors can be explored only during the week. The Thad Buckner Building, complete with clerestory windows, now houses a visitor center, where there are drawings and furniture by Wright, and photographs of the building work.

The antebellum Gamble Mansion

## ⓭ Gamble Plantation Historic State Park

Road map D3. Manatee Co. 3708 Patten Ave, Ellenton (Highway 301, 1.5 miles west of I-75). **Tel** (941) 723–4536. 🚆 Tampa. 🚌 Bradenton. **Open** daily. **Closed** Thanksgiving, Dec 25, Jan 1. ♿ ♿ limited. 🌐 **floridastate parks.org/gambleplantation**

The only Antebellum home left in southern Florida, this whitewashed mansion is on the main road into Bradenton.

It was built in 1845–50 by Major Robert Gamble, who settled along the fertile Manatee River after the Second Seminole War *(see p50)*. Today only a fraction of the plantation's 3,500 acres (1,416 ha) remains. The site

### Florida Southern College

① Emile Watson Building
② Benjamin Fine Building
③ J. Edgar Wall Waterdome
④ Raulerson Building
⑤ Thad Buckner Building
⑥ Annie Pfeiffer Chapel
⑦ William Danforth Chapel
⑧ Polk County Science Buildings
⑨ Lucius Pond Ordway Building

### Key

═══ Esplanade

0 meters          100
0 yards           100

of the old slave quarters, for instance, is now a school. The house is furnished just as it was in its heyday, and the garden, flourishing with live oak trees draped with Spanish moss, is pure Deep South.

However, romantic notions about Gamble's life are swept away in the small museum in the visitor center. Gamble fell into financial difficulties and was forced to sell the house to pay his debts. Among the artifacts on display in the museum is a document showing that the plantation, along with the grounds and 191 slaves, was sold in 1856 for the sum of $190,000.

## ⑭ Bradenton

**Road map** D3. Manatee Co.
🚗 54,400. ✈ 🚌 including Amtrak Thruway bus. 🛈 222 10th St W, (941) 748–3411.

The seat of Manatee County, Bradenton is best known as the home of the Nick Bollettieri Tennis Academy *(see p362)*, the school that has nurtured the early promise of such world tennis stars as Andre Agassi and Pete Sampras.

The local beaches are a big attraction, but a couple of sights deserve a visit before heading off to the beach. **Manatee Village Historical Park** recounts the story of the Florida frontier a century ago through a fascinating collection of restored buildings. These include a boathouse, a general store, and an early settler's house, and all have been furnished as they would have originally looked.

The **South Florida Museum** is both educational and fun. "Florida from Stone Age to Space Age" is the theme, with exhibits ranging from dinosaur dioramas to life-size replicas of 16th-century Spanish-style buildings and early cars. Laser shows add excitement to the Bishop Planetarium program, while the

The kitchen of an early settler's house at Manatee Village Historical Park

Parker Aquarium provides a lively overview of local marine life.

### 🏛 Manatee Village Historical Park
1404 Manatee Ave E. **Tel** (941) 749–7165. **Open** Mon–Fri (Winter: Sun pm). **Closed** public hols. ♿

### 🏛 South Florida Museum
201 10th St W. **Tel** (941) 746–4131. **Open** daily. **Closed** Apr–May & Aug–Dec: Mon; 1st Sat Nov; Thanksgiving, Dec 25, Jan1. ♿ 🅿 ⊒ **south floridamuseum.org**

### Environs
Five miles (8 km) west of central Bradenton, the **De Soto National Memorial** commemorates the landing near here in 1539 of Hernando de Soto *(see p47)*. He and his 600 men set out on an epic four-year 4,000-mile (6,500-km) trek into the southeastern US in search of gold. They discovered the Mississippi, but the trek was disastrous and de Soto and half his army died. A monument recalls the luckless explorers and

Stone monument to explorer De Soto

marks the start of the De Soto Trail, which follows part of the route they took. The park also has a replica of de Soto's base camp. This is staffed by costumed volunteers, who give a memorable insight into the daily routines of the Spanish conquistadors. A visitor center has a museum, a bookstore, and exhibits of 16th-century weapons and armor. There is also a half-mile (1 km) nature trail through mangroves.

Two bridges link Bradenton to **Anna Maria Island**, whose sandy shoreline, backed by dunes, is largely undeveloped but is washed by breakers big enough to attract a handful of surfers. There is a scattering of small resorts based around the three main communities of Anna Maria, Holmes Beach, and Bradenton Beach. In the north stands the picturesque Anna Maria Pier, which was built in 1910.

### 🏛 De Soto National Memorial
8300 DeSoto Memorial Hwy. **Tel** (941) 792–0458. **Open** daily. **Closed** Thanksgiving, Dec 25, Jan 1. ♿ ⊒ **nps.gov/deso**

Anna Maria Island's beautiful, unspoiled beach

# ⑮ Sarasota

This city is known as Florida's cultural center, a fact often credited to John Ringling *(see p274)*, who was one of many influential people attracted to the up-and-coming town in the early 1900s. Ringling poured money into the area, and his legacy is seen everywhere, though nowhere more so than in his house and fine art collection, the city's biggest attraction *(see pp274–7)*. Sarasota's other great asset is that it seems to have escaped the worst excesses of the state's other cities. Promoted as "Florida's Mild Side," Sarasota is an attractive and clean community, with the bonus of a waterfront setting. Visitors can join its affluent inhabitants browsing around its stylish shops or lying on the beach. Fabulous barrier island beaches are just a short drive from downtown Sarasota and are the best places to stay.

Flamingos gather at a small lake at Sarasota Jungle Gardens

## Exploring Sarasota

The most pleasant area of downtown Sarasota focuses on Palm Avenue and Main Street, where restored storefronts dating from the early 20th century house antique shops, bars, and restaurants. Shopping and eating are also the main activities at nearby Sarasota Quay, and you can sign up for dinner cruises and other boat trips at the adjacent marina.

Dominating the waterfront to the north is the striking Van Wezel Performing Arts Hall *(see p361)*. Opened in 1970, this distinctive pink and lavender building is worth a visit, both to admire its sweeping, seashell-inspired lines, and to attend one of the many events, including concerts and Broadway shows, which are staged here *(see p358)*.

## 🏛 Sarasota Classic Car Museum

5500 N Tamiami Trail. **Tel** (941) 355-6228. **Open** daily. **Closed** Dec 25. 🅿 ♿ 📷 **W** sarasotacarmuseum.org

One of the oldest of its kind in the world, Sarasota Classic Car Museum opened its doors to the public in 1953. It is now home to 120 classic cars acquired either through exchanges with other car museums, or as donations from collectors.

An 1890s carousel organ at the museum

Highlights of the collection are a rare 1954 Packard Model 120 convertible, a 1955 Rolls-Royce Silver Wraith, a 1981 De Lorean in mint condition, and a Cadillac station wagon – one of only five ever made. John Lennon's Mercedes Roadster is also on show here, as is Paul McCartney's beloved Mini Cooper.

## 🌿 Sarasota Jungle Gardens

3701 Bay Shore Rd. **Tel** (941) 355-1112. **Open** daily. **Closed** Dec 25. 📷 ♿ **W** sarasotajunglegardens.com

Originally developed as a botanical garden, this 10-acre (4-ha) former banana grove offers an oasis of tropical plants, trees, and flowers from around the world, with palm forests and gardens of hibiscus, ferns, roses, gardenias, and bougainvillea. The flamingo lagoon is a big attraction.

Other attractions, including a children's petting zoo and butterfly garden, place an emphasis on education and conservation. Simple entertainment is offered by the exotic bird shows and a reptile show. There is also a café and a gift shop.

## 🌿 Marie Selby Botanical Gardens

811 S Palm Ave. **Tel** (941) 366-5731. **Open** daily. **Closed** Dec 25. 📷 📷 ♿ **W** selby.org

You needn't be a gardener to appreciate the former home of wealthy Sarasota residents, William and Marie Selby. Set among laurel and banyan trees overlooking Sarasota Bay, the estate was designed by Marie during the early 1920s as an escape from the modern world: the bamboo curtain she had planted to obscure the growing Sarasota skyline can still be seen.

The gardens have more than 20,000 tropical plants and are particularly famous for their collection of orchids and

Christy Payne House in the Marie Selby Botanical Gardens

*For hotels and restaurants in this area see pp320–23 and pp343–5*

epiphytes. There are also areas devoted to all sorts of exotic plants, from tropical foods and herbs to colorful hibiscus plants. The Tropical Display House has an impressive array of jungle vegetation.

The Spanish-style house, now a gift shop, is of less interest than the 1930s Christy Payne House. This delightful plantation-style mansion holds a Museum of Botany and Arts.

### 🏛 St. Armands Circle

This upscale shopping and dining complex on St. Armands Key was one of John Ringling's creations. He purchased the island in 1917 and produced an adventurous plan for a housing development, which centered on a circular shopping mall featuring gardens and classical statues. The area flourished briefly before being caught up in the Depression but was revived in the 1950s. It now looks much as Ringling planned, with shady avenues radiating from a central point.

St. Armands Circle, well placed between Downtown and the beaches, is popular both during the day and at night. The shops are mostly expensive, but anyone can enjoy the street entertainers who often congregate here.

### 🐟 Mote Aquarium and Mote Marine Laboratory

1600 Ken Thompson Parkway. **Tel** (941) 388-4441. **Open** daily. 🅿 ♿ 🎫 📶 **mote.org**

This aquarium is located on City Island, between Lido and Longboat Keys. It has a bay walk with an excellent view of the

Tropical fish at the Mote Aquarium and Mote Marine Laboratory

Sarasota skyline, but the real attractions can be found inside. Among the most popular exhibits is a huge shark tank, complete with underwater observation windows, and a "touch tank," where you can come to grips with all kinds of marine creatures, from horseshoe crabs and whelks to stingrays. More than 30 other aquariums are stocked with local fish and plants, and there is a display on the rivers, bays, and estuaries of the surrounding area.

Explanatory leaflets provide a useful insight into every exhibit, while guides explain how the aquarium ties in with the work of the attached laboratory, prominent in the study of sharks and pollution.

### 🎭 Asolo Repertory Theatre

5555 North Tamiami Tr. **Tel** (941) 351-8000. **Open** Sep–Jul. 📶 **asolorep.org**

For more than 50 years, the Asolo has been Florida's premier professional theater, and one of the most important cultural forces in the Sarasota's rich arts scene in the southeastern US. It stages up to 15 productions

every season, a diverse repertoire of newly commissioned plays, reinterpretations, and musical theater. Asolo Rep is the creative home of more than 100 artists and technical craftsmen, and its resident acting company is complemented by award-winning directors, designers, and guest artists.

Asolo Repertory Theatre – an important cultural center of Sarasota

### 🏖 Sarasota Beaches

The nearby barrier islands, Longboat Key, Lido Key, and Siesta Key, boast superb sandy beaches facing the Gulf of Mexico, and they are understandably popular (*see p257*). Development has been intense, with camps along the shore in places, but there are several quieter areas, too. The beach in South Lido Park, on Lido Key, is peaceful during the week and has a pleasant woodland trail.

On Siesta Key the main residential area is in the north, focused around a network of canals. The broad Siesta Key Beach nearby is lively at any time. A quieter scene can be found at Turtle Beach, which also has the only campground on these Keys. Longboat Key is well-known for its golf courses. Wherever you are, the water sports are excellent.

South Lido Park beach, with a view south of nearby Siesta Key

# The Ringling: Museum of Art

John Ringling was an Iowa-born circus owner whose phenomenally successful show *(see p276)* made him a multimillionaire. In 1925, he decided to build an art collection and a museum to house it, both as a memorial for himself and his wife, Mable, and as a gift to the people of Florida. He spent the next six years amassing a remarkable collection of European paintings, from Italian and Flemish Baroque works to a collection of Asian art. Following John Ringling's death in 1936, his estate was bequeathed to the state.

**Statuary**
The courtyard is dotted with bronze casts of Classical sculpture, such as this chariot.

The James Turrell "Skyspace" is in the William G. and Marie Selby Courtyard

A replica of Michelangelo's David

**Center for Asian Art**
The newest of the museum's galleries, The Dr. Helga Wall-Apelt Gallery of Asian Art, fosters exploration of historical and contemporary Asian cultures.

12
13
14
15
16
17
18

**Spanish Gallery**
This gallery contains Spanish works of the 17th century, including paintings by El Greco and Velázquez, such as this magnificent portrait of Philip IV of Spain, possibly Velázquez's earliest military portrait of Philip.

**★ Astor Rooms**
These lavish 19th-century interiors came from a New York mansion.

## Gallery Guide

*The galleries are arranged around a sculpture garden. Starting with the galleries to the right of the entrance hall, the rooms roughly follow a chronological order counterclockwise, ranging from late medieval painting to 20th-century European art; 16th- and 17th-century Italian painting is well represented. Modern art and special exhibitions are displayed in the Searing Wing. The Visitors Pavilion is home to the Historic Asolo Theater.*

**Bayfront Gardens**
The Ringling sits on 66 acres (26 ha) on the shores of Sarasota Bay. The grounds contain impressive banyan trees and Mable Ringling's Rose Garden, planted in 1913.

The Ulla R. and Arthur F. Searing **wing** houses contemporary art special exhibitions.

★ **Courtyard**
A gallery of antique columns of various styles surrounds the courtyard.

**VISITORS' CHECKLIST**

**Practical Information**
5401 Bay Shore Road, Sarasota.
**Tel** (941) 359-5700. Museums, Theater, and Gardens: **Open** 10am–5pm daily (to 8pm Thu). **Closed** Thanksgiving, Dec 25, Jan1. 1st floor only of the Ca'd'Zan.
**w** ringling.org

**Transport**
2, from the corner of 1st St and Lemon St, Downtown.

Fountain of Oceanus

**The Building of a Palace**
This Italian Renaissance painting by Piero di Cosimo is one of the gallery's proudest possessions. Painted tempera on a wood panel, it dates from around 1515.

★ **Rubens Gallery**
This gallery has great treasures, including *The Gathering of the Manna*, painted around 1625.

11
10
9
8
7
6
5
4
3
2
1
21

Entrance

Statue of Apollo

Fountain of the Tortoises

**Key to Floor Plan**

- Dutch and Flemish 1600–1700
- Rubens Gallery
- Medieval and Renaissance
- Italian 1500–1700
- Spanish 1600–1700
- European 1700–1800
- Astor Rooms
- French 1600–1700
- Flemish 1600–1700
- Ringling Master Plan
- Center for Asian Art

# Ringling Museum: Cà' d'Zan

The Ringlings' winter residence, Cà' d'Zan, was the first part of the Ringling estate to be completed, providing a spectacular foretaste of what was to come. The Ringlings' love of Italy, nurtured during frequent visits to Europe, was displayed for all to see in the building's design as well as in its Venetian name, meaning "House of John." The property, which overlooks Sarasota Bay, was modeled on a Venetian palace, but there are also features drawn from French and Italian Renaissance architecture.

Set off by a 200 ft (60 m) marble terrace and crowned by a distinctive tower, Cà' d'Zan took two years to build and was finished in 1926. The ballroom, court, formal dining room, and bedrooms all provide glimpses into the life of the American super-rich of the period, with modern conveniences, including one of the first private elevators in Florida.

★ **Terracotta Decoration**
The exterior of Cà' d'Zan boasts some of the finest examples of terracotta work in the country.

★ **Ballroom**
The ballroom was designed with an elaborate coffered ceiling gilded in gold, reflecting the extravagance of the 1920s. The ceiling painting, titled *Dancers of the Nations,* is composed of 22 vignettes that depict dancing couples from around the world in their native costumes.

## KEY

① **The court**, with its marble floors and onyx columns, was the Ringlings' living room and is the focal point of the house.

② **Solarium**

③ **The tower**, was lit up when the Ringlings were at home.

④ **Mable Ringling's bedroom**, features an elegant 1920s Louis XV-style suite and pillowcases she made herself.

⑤ **Servants' rooms**

⑥ **Kitchen**

⑦ **John Ringling's Office**

⑧ **Exercise room**

## The Ringling Circus

What started as a traveling wagon show, founded in 1884 by five of the seven Ringling brothers, developed into one the most successful circuses of the era. The Ringlings' varied bill of entertainment proved more enduring than their rivals' offerings, and the brothers gradually bought up their competitors. In 1907, they formed a partnership with Phineas T. Barnum. The Ringling's first director and curator, A. Everett Austin Jr., established the Circus Museum in 1948. It was the first museum in the country to document the rich history of the circus.

In 2006, the Tibbals Learning Center opened and houses the Howard Bros. Circus Model, the largest miniature circus in the world.

*Five Graces* circus wagon, 1878

### Taproom
With its vaulted ceiling and stained-glass windows, the Taproom illustrates Ringling's love of collecting objects from far afield; he bought the bar from Cicardi's Restaurant in St. Louis, Missouri.

### John Ringling's Bedroom
The handsome, 19th-century Neo-Classical furniture lends an elegance to this room. Jacob de Wit's *Dawn Driving Away the Darkness* (1735) adorns the ceiling.

### Breakfast Room
This simply decorated room was used mainly for informal family occasions. The Venetian blinds are original.

### Historic Asolo Theater
Built in Italy in 1798 for the exiled queen of Cyprus, the theater was acquired by The Ringlings in 1949 and is considered the birthplace of Sarasota's performing arts culture. America's only 18th-century European theater serves as the city's primary playhouse and can be found in the Visitors Pavilion across from the FSU Center for the Performing Arts.

Lush vegetation overhanging the river in Myakka River State Park

although the main shelling beaches are farther south *(see pp282–3)*. The area is famous for the fossilized sharks' teeth brought in by the tide. Brohard Paw Park on Harbor Drive South is a haven for dog lovers.

## ⑯ Myakka River State Park

**Road map** D3 Sarasota Co. 13207 SR 72, 9 miles (14 km) E of Sarasota.
🚌 Sarasota. **Tel** (941) 361-6511.
**Open** daily. 🅿️ ♿ limited. 📷 ⛺
🌐 myakkariver.org

In spite of its proximity to the city of Sarasota, in the Myakka River State Park you can imagine how the region must have looked to its first settlers. Dense oak, palm thickets, pine flatwoods, and an expanse of dry prairie are interspersed with marshland, swamps, and lakes.

The parkland's 28,000 acres (11,300 ha), which stretch along the Myakka River and around Upper Myakka Lake, form an outstanding wildlife sanctuary. More than 200 species of birds have been recorded here, including egrets, blue herons, vultures, and ibis, all of which are plentiful, as well as much rarer ospreys, bald eagles, and wild turkeys. Alligators and deer can usually be seen, though other non-native animals such as foxes are glimpsed only rarely. Observation platforms, from which you can view the wildlife, are dotted throughout the park.

Ambitious explorers can take to the park's 39 miles (63 km) of marked hiking trails or 15 miles (24 km) of bridle trails. Alternatively, there are guided tours by trolley between December and May, the best time to visit, and narrated river tours by airboat all year round.

## ⑰ Venice

**Road map** D4. Sarasota Co.
🚹 22,500. 🚌 ℹ️ 597 Tamiami Trail S, (941) 488-2236.
🌐 venicechamber.com

Venice is a sleepy seaside town, situated slightly off the beaten track and awash with flowers and palm trees, which line the center of the main shopping street, Venice Avenue. The town has a fine collection of carefully restored historic buildings, including the Venice Little Theater on Tampa Avenue, which dates from 1927.

**Caspersen Beach**, fringed by sea oats and palmettos, lies at the southern end of Harbor Drive. It is a popular place to swim, to fish, and to collect shells,

Fossil hunting, Caspersen Beach

## ⑱ Gasparilla Island

**Road map** D4. Lee Co, Charlotte Co.
🚌 Venice. ℹ️ 5800 Gasparilla Rd, Boca Grande, (941) 964-0568.
🌐 bocagrandechamber.org

Discovered originally by fishermen, and later by the wealthy who were fleeing northern winters, Gasparilla is a perfect island hideaway midway between Sarasota and Fort Myers.

Activity is centered around the community of Boca Grande, which is joined by a causeway to the mainland. The restored former railroad station, the San Marco Theater, and the grand Gasparilla Inn are eloquent reminders of times past. Many old wooden buildings have been saved and given a fresh coat of paint, giving the place a pleasant, tropical feel. Fishing has been big business here for a long time – Boca Grande is known as the "tarpon capital of the world" – and there are a number of marinas where you can arrange boat trips, some of which go to nearby barrier islands

The Range Light, which warns ships away from Gasparilla Island's coast

*(see pp282–3)*. Another way to explore is to follow the bike trail that runs down the island.

At the island's southern tip, the **Gasparilla Island State Park** has quiet beaches where visitors can fish and swim as well as hunt for shells. A squat late 19th-century lighthouse overlooks Boca Grande Pass, but its function is fulfilled by the more modern Range Light.

**⌘ Gasparilla Island State Park**
880 Belcher Rd, Boca Grande. **Tel** (941) 964-0375. **Open** daily.

The colorful 1920s Schlossberg-Camp Building in Arcadia

## ⑲ Arcadia

**Road map** E3. De Soto Co. 🚗 7,600. 🚌 🛈 16 S Volusia Ave, (863) 494-4033. **W** **desotochamber.net**

It is a pleasure to stroll around the old cattle ranching town of Arcadia. Local cowboys are more likely to ride around in a pickup truck than on horseback, but the horse is still very much part of the local culture. Cowboy fever reaches a peak twice a year, in March and July, when competitors and devotees from all over the US converge for the All-Florida Championship Rodeo, the oldest rodeo in the state.

Arcadia's flamboyant and sometimes colorful architecture recalls the prosperity and confidence of the 1920s. The best examples are the Florida Mediterranean-style Koch Arcade Building, on West Oak Street, and the Schlossberg-Camp Building, on West Magnolia Street.

Many earlier buildings were destroyed by a fire in 1905; the striking J.J. Heard Opera House on Oak Street was constructed the following year. Only a few buildings from the late 1800s survive, and these can be seen by arrangement with the Chamber of Commerce.

## ⑳ Babcock Ranch Eco Tours

**Road map** E4. Charlotte Co. 8000 SR 31. **Tel** (800) 500-5583. 🚌 Punta Gorda. **Open** daily. **Closed** Dec 25. 🎥 🛈 compulsory. **W** **babcock wilderness.com**

The huge Crescent B Ranch was originally owned by lumber baron, E.V. Babcock, who bled the cypress swamp for timber in the 1930s. It is still run by the phenomenally rich Babcock family, and part of the 90,000-acre (36,420-ha) working ranch is open as the Babcock Ranch Eco Tours. During 90-minute trips led

Swamp buggy exploring Babcock Ranch Eco Tours

by trained naturalists, swamp buggies take visitors through deep woods and a dense patch of cypress swamp, offering the opportunity to see a wide variety of wildlife. Panthers, which are bred successfully here, are in a specially designed paddock; alligators cruise just a short distance away. The ranch's herds of horses and Cracker cattle are also on view. Babcock's tours are very popular and must be reserved well in advance.

### Rodeos in Florida

Much of Florida's interior scrubland is ranching country, focused around cattle towns such as Arcadia, Kissimmee *(see p193)*, and Davie *(see p141)*, where rodeos are a feature of everyday life. Speed is the key during competitions. In events such as calf roping and steer wrestling (in which the cowboy must force the animal to the ground), the winner is the one with the fastest time – usually well under ten seconds. In bareback or saddle bronco riding the cowboys must stay on the bucking horse for at least eight seconds, but they are also judged on their overall skill and technique. During the competition a commentator keeps the audience informed of the cowboys' current form, giving details of any titles held.

Whip popping at Arcadia's All-Florida Championship Rodeo

# ㉑ Fort Myers

The approach to Fort Myers across the Caloosahatchee River is stunning, a fine introduction to a city that still has an air of old-time Florida. Following the sweep of the river is McGregor Boulevard, lined with ranks of royal palms; the first of these were planted by the inventor Thomas Edison, who put Fort Myers on the map in the 1880s, when it was just a small fishing village.

In addition to Edison's home and a few other sights, the old downtown area around First Street, with its many shops and restaurants, is worth exploring; a trolley service runs regularly through the downtown area linking the main sights. When visitors have had their fill of the city, there are beaches just a short distance away.

## VISITORS' CHECKLIST

**Practical Information**
**Road map** E4. Lee Co.
🚗 68,000. 🅹 2310 Edwards Drive, (239) 332–3624, (800) 366-3622. 🎪 Edison Festival of Lights (Feb). 🆆 fortmyers.org

**Transport**
✈ 7 miles (11 km) SE. 🚌 2275 Cleveland Avenue, (800) 231-2222; also Amtrak Thruway bus, (800) 872-7245.

The original equipment on show in Thomas Edison's laboratory

### 🏛 Edison and Ford Winter Estates
2350 McGregor Blvd. **Tel** (239) 334-7419. **Open** daily. **Closed** Thanksgiving, Dec 25. 🐾 🎫 ♿
🆆 edisonfordwinterestates.org

The waterfront retreat of one of America's most famous inventors, the Edison Winter Home is Fort Myers' most enduring attraction. Thomas Edison (1847–1931) built the estate in 1886, and the house, laboratory, and botanical gardens are much as he left them.

The two-story house and adjoining guesthouse were among the first prefabricated buildings in the US, built in sections to Edison's specifications in Maine, and shipped to Fort Myers by schooner. This precluded extravagance, but the house is large and comfortable, and spacious overhanging porches around the ground floor kept the buildings cool. Many of the original furnishings are inside.

Edison was the holder of more than 1,000 patents, and his interests ranged from the light bulb to the phonograph, which recorded on wax cylinders. His laboratory, on the opposite side of McGregor Boulevard from the house, contains the original equipment he used in his later experiments in synthetic rubber production. The museum displays samples of Edison's work as an inventor, including the telegraph, telephone, and X-ray machine, personal items, dozens of phonographs, and a 1916 Model T car that was given to him by Henry Ford.

Thomas Edison was also an enthusiastic horticulturalist, and the gardens around the house and laboratory contain a great variety of exotic plants. The giant banyan tree, which was given to Edison by the tire magnate Harvey Firestone in 1925, boasts a circumference in excess of 400 ft (120 m).

Edison was a popular man locally, and tours of the home are notable for the breadth of knowledge and enthusiasm shown by the guides.

### 🏛 Ford Winter Home
2350 McGregor Blvd. **Tel** (239) 334-3614. **Open** daily. **Closed** Thanksgiving, Dec 25. 🐾 🎫 ♿

Next to the Edison home (and viewable on the same ticket) is Mangoes, the small estate bought in 1916 by the car manufacturer Henry Ford. The Fords were great friends of the Edisons, and following Thomas Edison's death in 1931 never returned here.

The rooms have been faithfully re-created with period furnishings and still have the homely air favored by Clara Ford. Some early Ford cars are displayed in the garage.

### 🏛 Imaginarium Hands-On Museum and Aquarium
2000 Cranford Ave. **Tel** (239) 321-7420. **Open** 10am–5pm Tue–Sat, noon–5pm Sun. **Closed** Thanksgiving, Dec 25. 🐾 ♿ 📷
🆆 imaginariumfortmyers.com

The Imaginarium Hands-On Museum and Aquarium has something to offer the entire family. It has over 60 exciting interactive exhibits which are designed for all ages, where visitors can touch a cloud, feel

One of the several beautiful beaches to be found at Fort Myers

Young visitors on the boardwalk at the Calusa Nature Center

the huge force of a hurricane, or run through a thunderstorm. There is a movie theater, dinosaur dig, and children can also become a TV weatherperson in a ministudio as part of a daily program of shows and interactive presentations. The aquarium houses a variety of different fish, including sharks and moray eels, as well as other animals, such as turtles, swans, and iguanas.

### 🏛 Southwest Florida Museum of History

2031 Jackson St. **Tel** (239) 321-7430. **Open** 10am–5pm Tue–Sat. 🅿 🅐 🆆 swflmuseumof history.com

Housed in the former railroad station, this museum recalls Fort Myers' heyday as a cattle town and delves into the area's early history as represented by the Calusa Native Americans and Spanish explorers. Highlights include a scale model of Fort Myers in 1900 and a refurbished 1930 private railroad car – the type used to bring northerners to the area for the winter sunshine. There is also an exhibit of prehistoric art and artifacts.

### 🦋 Calusa Nature Center and Planetarium

3450 Ortiz Ave. **Tel** (239) 275-3435. **Open** daily. **Closed** Jan 1, Thanksgiving, Dec 25. 🅿 🅐 🆉 by request. 🆆 calusanature.org

This 105 acre (42 ha) patch of wilderness is an excellent introduction to the flora and fauna of southwest Florida. There is a large aviary, and

wooden walkways past ferns and mangrove, where it is often possible to spot herons, egrets, and the occasional ibis. The museum provides illustrated talks on snakes and alligators, and there are also regular guided nature walks and tours of the aviary.

The center also boasts a butterfly aviary and butterfly plant nursery where visitors can buy plants to grow a butterfly garden.

The planetarium features star and laser shows, for which there is a separate charge.

### Environs

A souvenir shop on a massive scale, **The Shell Factory** lies 4 miles (6 km) north of Fort Myers. On sale are shell ornaments and jewelry, but most impressive is the collection of shells and coral, claimed to be the largest in the world. The shop also stocks sponges, sculpted driftwood, posters, books, and other gift items. A zoo and fun park keep all members of the family amused.

### 🏠 The Shell Factory

2787 N Tamiami Trail. **Tel** (239) 995-2141. **Open** 10am–9pm Mon–Sat, 10am–8pm Sun. 🅐 🆆 shellfactory.com

## ㉑ Koreshan State Historic Site

**Road map** E4. Lee Co. Estero, 14 miles (23 km) S of Fort Myers. **Tel** (239) 992-0311. 🚌 Fort Myers. **Open** daily. 🅿 🅐 🆉 🛆 🆆 floridastateparks.org

Those interested in obscure religions mix with nature lovers at the Koreshan State Historic Site, the former home of the Koreshan Unity sect.

In 1894 the sect's founder, Dr. Cyrus Teed, had a vision telling him to change his name to Koresh (Hebrew for Cyrus) and to move to southwest Florida, where he was to establish a great utopian city with streets 400 ft (122 m) wide. He chose this beautiful location on the Estero River, where members pursued a communal lifestyle, with equal rights for women and shared ownership of property.

Far from the city of ten million people that Teed had envisaged, the Koreshan Unity sect had a mere 250 followers at its peak, and membership dwindled after his death in 1908. The last four members donated the site to Florida in 1961. Twelve of the sect's 60 buildings and their gardens survive; they include Cyrus Teed's home, which has been completely restored.

The park has canoe and nature trails, camping facilities, opportunities for fresh and saltwater fishing, and also arranges guided tours.

Cyrus Teed's restored home at the Koreshan State Historic Site

# ㉓ Lee Island Coast

The Lee Island Coast offers an irresistible combination of sandy beaches (famous for their shells), exotic wildlife, lush vegetation, and stupendous sunsets. Most people head for Sanibel and Captiva islands, with their chic resorts, marinas, and golf courses. However, other less developed islands – where there are few distractions from the beaches and natural beauty – are just a short boat trip away. Boat tours and charters can be picked up at many places, and there are also some regular boat services, whose routes are marked on the map below.

Tranquil beachfront cottages on Sanibel Island

## Sanibel and Captiva Islands

Despite being more accessible than the other islands, Sanibel and Captiva have a laid-back, Caribbean air. They are famous both as havens for lovers of the good life and for their shells. Most visitors soon get drawn into the shell-collecting culture, which has given rise to the expressions "Sanibel Stoop" and "Captiva Crouch" for the posture adopted by avid shell hunters. Sanibel may not be most people's idea of an island retreat – with its manicured gardens and rows of shops and restaurants along Periwinkle Way, the hub of Sanibel town – but there are no condos, and two areas are protected as preserves. Most of the beaches with public access are along Gulf Drive, the best being Turner and Bowman's beaches.

Captiva is less developed than Sanibel, but you'll still find the odd resort, including the South Seas Plantation Resort (*see p320*), with its busy marina – a starting point for boat trips to Cayo Costa.

### 🖂 Sanibel Captiva Conservation Foundation

Mile Marker 1, Sanibel-Captiva Rd. **Tel** (239) 472-2329. **Open** May–Nov: Mon–Fri; Dec–Apr: Mon–Sat. 🅆 sccf.org

This private foundation oversees the protection of a chunk of Sanibel's interior wetland. Its 4 miles (6 km) of boardwalk trails are much quieter than those in the better known "Ding" Darling refuge nearby. An observation tower provides a perfect vantage point.

### 🏛 Bailey-Matthews National Shell Museum

3075 Sanibel-Captiva Rd. **Tel** (239) 395-2233. **Open** daily. 🅆 shellmuseum.org

Even if you aren't interested in shelling, this museum is well worth a visit. The centerpiece Great Hall of Shells includes displays grouped

**Boca Grande**
**Gasparilla Island**
**Cayo Costa**
**Cayo Costa Island State Park**
**North Captiva Club Resort**
**Bokeelia**
**Cabbage Key**
**Useppa Key**
**Matlacha**
**Pine Island**
**Pine Island Sound**
**North Captiva Island**
**South Seas Plantation Resort**
**Captiva Island**
**J.N. "Ding" Darling**
**St James City**
**Turner Beach**
**Bowman's Beach**
**Sanibel Island**
**Sanibel**
**Fort Myers**
**Sanibel Captiva Conservation Foundation**
**Bailey-Matthews National Shell Museum**

0 meters 4
0 yards 4

**Key**
--- Boat service
▬▬ Road

For map symbols *see back flap*

according to habitat, from barrier islands to the Everglades. It claims to have one-third of the world's 10,000 shell varieties.

### 🖼 J.N. "Ding" Darling National Wildlife Refuge

1 Wildlife Dr, Sanibel.
**Tel** (239) 472-1100. **Open** daily.
**Closed** public hols. 🖼 🔲
**W** fws.gov/dingdarling

This refuge occupies two-thirds of Sanibel. Resident wildlife, including raccoons, alligators, and birds such as roseate spoonbills, bald eagles, and ospreys, are surprisingly easy to spot. The popular 5 mile (8 km) scenic "Wildlife Drive" can be covered by bike as well as by car, and there are trolley tours, too. Paths and canoe trails are lined with sea grape, red mangrove, and cabbage palm. Canoes, fishing boats, and bikes can be rented.

Roseate spoonbills in the J.N. "Ding" Darling National Wildlife Refuge

### 🖼 Cayo Costa State Park

Cayo Costa Island. **Tel** (941) 964-0375.
**Open** daily. 🖼 🔲 🔺
**W** floridastateparks.org

Cayo Costa Island is one of the state's most unspoiled barrier islands. Much of it is planted with non-native Australian pine and Brazilian pepper trees. These were originally imported during the 1950s for their shade and wood, but are now gradually being cleared to let domestic species take over.

There are 9 miles (14 km) of dune-backed beach and, on the eastern side, several mangrove swamps. Inland, there is a mix of pine flatwoods, grassy areas, and hammocks. The whole island offers plenty of bird-watching opportunities and excellent shelling, especially in winter. Boat trips take visitors to Cayo

Yachts at anchor in the peaceful marina of Cabbage Key

Costa all year round; Tropic Star, from Bokeelia on Pine Island, offers the most frequent service. A trolley links the bayside dock to the gulf side. Cayo Costa has a basic camp ground with 12 cabins.

### Cabbage Key

This island was chosen by the novelist Mary Roberts Rinehart for her home in 1938. Her house, built in the shade of two 18th-century Cuban laurel trees, is now the Cabbage Key Inn. This is best known for its restaurant, which is decorated with around 30,000 autographed one-dollar bills. The first bill was left by a fisherman anxious to make sure he had funds to buy drinks on his next visit. When he returned, he had money to spare and left the bill where it was. Other visitors then took up the idea.

A 40 ft (12 m) water tower nearby provides a lovely view of the small island, and there is also a short nature trail. Tropic Star from Pine Island, and Captiva Cruises from Captiva Island run the most regular trips to the Cabbage Key.

### Pine Island

This island, fringed with mangrove rather than beaches, is useful mainly as an access point to nearby islands. You can arrange all kinds of boat trips at the marina in Bokeelia; but allow time to enjoy its fine collection of fishing piers.

### Shells and Shelling

Junonia

The beaches of Sanibel and Captiva are among the best in the US for shelling. The Gulf of Mexico has no offshore reef to smash the shells, and the waters are relatively shallow and warm, with a flat bed – all factors that encourage growth. The wide plateau off the southern tip of Sanibel also acts as a ramp, helping to roll the shells ashore. Live shelling is a federal offense on Sanibel and subject to restrictions elsewhere, so collect only empty shells.

The best advice is to go early, and look just beneath the surface of the sand where the surf breaks. Seabirds feeding along the shore are a good indication of a good crop of shells. Shelling is best in winter or directly following a storm. The Junonia and the Lion's paw scallop are particularly sought after.

Florida fighting conch

Common fig shell     Lion's paw scallop     Janthina

# THE EVERGLADES AND THE KEYS

Southwest Florida is mostly occupied by the world-famous Everglades – low-lying wetlands of huge ecological importance. Resorts and towns pepper the Keys, where both Floridians and visitors come to enjoy the region's other natural wonder – the coral reef.

Before the arrival of the Europeans, south Florida was home to tribes such as the Calusa and the Matecumbe *(see pp44–5)*. From the 1500s, the Keys were visited by a succession of settlers, pirates, and wreckers *(see p307)*, but the mosquito-infested mainland was not settled until the mid-19th century, with the establish-ment of what is now the thriving coastal resort of Naples.

The first road to open up the area by linking the Atlantic and Gulf coasts was the Tamiami Trail, built in 1928. Pioneer camps located off it, such as Everglades City and Chokoloskee, have barely changed since the late 1800s, and today seem caught in a time warp. They mark the western entrance of the Everglades National Park. This broad river of

sawgrass, dotted with tree islands, possesses a peculiar beauty and is a paradise for its thrilling and prolific wildlife. Running southwest off the tip of the peninsula are the Keys, a chain of jewel-like islands protected by North America's only coral reef. Henry Flagler's Overseas Railroad once crossed the Keys; it has since disappeared and has been replaced by the Overseas Highway – the route of one of the country's classic road trips. The farther south you travel, the easier it is to agree with the saying that the Keys are more about a state of mind than a geographical location. At the end of the road is legendary Key West, where there is plenty to see and do, but where the relaxed Keys approach to life reigns supreme.

A vibrant mural in Key West's Bahama Village, reflecting the Caribbean origins of its inhabitants

◀ A warm summer's day in a Florida swamp

# Exploring the Everglades and the Keys

Naples and Marco Island in the northwest are the best bases for enjoying the Gulfshore beaches, and they boast some superb golf courses, too. They also offer easy access to the wild and expansive scenery of Big Cypress Swamp and Everglades National Park, which together take up a great proportion of the region. The Florida Keys are justifiably famous for their activities focused on the nearby coral reef, such as fishing, diving, and snorkeling. Islamorada and Key Largo in the Upper Keys both have plenty of accommodation to choose from, while bustling Marathon and colorful Key West, with its picturesque guesthouses, are excellent bases from which to explore the more laid-back Lower Keys.

The Overseas Highway, the main artery through the Florida Keys

## Sights at a Glance

1. Naples
2. Big Cypress Swamp
3. Ah-Tah-Thi-Ki Museum
4. Miccosukee Indian Village
5. *Everglades National Park pp290–95*
6. Biscayne National Park
7. Key Largo
8. John Pennekamp Coral Reef State Park
9. Tavernier
10. Theater of the Sea
11. Islamorada
12. Indian and Lignumvitae Keys
13. Dolphin Research Center
14. Marathon
15. Pigeon Key
16. Lower Keys
17. *Key West pp302–7*
18. Dry Tortugas National Park

DRY TORTUGAS
NATIONAL PARK

0 kilometers        25
0 miles            25

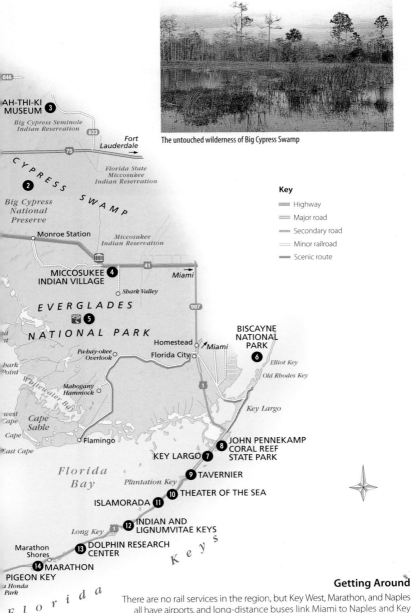

The untouched wilderness of Big Cypress Swamp

**Key**

〓〓 Highway

〓〓 Major road

── Secondary road

┅┅ Minor railroad

── Scenic route

## Getting Around

There are no rail services in the region, but Key West, Marathon, and Naples all have airports, and long-distance buses link Miami to Naples and Key West. The Tamiami Trail (US 41) and I-75 connect Miami and Fort Lauderdale with Naples. The Overseas Highway (US 1) begins at Florida City, but the Card Sound Road (Route 997), which has less traffic and better views, offers an alternative approach to the Keys. The Overseas Highway is most scenic after the 7-Mile Bridge, where the islands are less built up and the views are more panoramic. Directions and addresses in the Keys are often given in Mile Markers, which refer to the small green and white signs at the roadside indicating the distance from Key West.

**For map symbols** *see back flap*

# ❶ Naples

**Road map** E4. Collier Co. 🗺 21,845.
🚆 🚌 🛈 2390 Tamiami Trail N, (239)
262-6141. **W** paradisecoast.com

A conservative and affluent
beach city, Naples prides itself on
its manicured appearance and
on its 55 golf courses; it has the
greatest per capita concentration of courses in the state.

Downtown, most of what is
called "historic" Naples dates
from the early 20th century, and
with its pastel-colored buildings
is a pleasant area to explore.
Many of the 19th-century
houses were destroyed by
hurricane Donna in 1960, which
also claimed the original 1887
pier. Rebuilt in 1961, this is now
a popular spot for both anglers
and pelicans; the latter are a
common sight perched upon
the railings.

A beautiful white sandy beach
stretching for 10 miles (16 km) is
flanked mostly by condos, but it
offers easy public access and safe
swimming in warm Gulf waters.

The informative **Collier
County Museum** focuses on
local history and includes a
re-created Seminole village.
Exhibits at the five museums
range from ancient indigenous
tribal artifacts to those
connected with the region's
pioneering past and the building
of the Tamiami Trail (US 41), on
which the museum stands.

Beautiful sunset at the Naples pier

🏛 **Collier County Museums**
3331 Tamiami Trail E. **Tel** (239) 252-
8476. **Open** 9am–5pm Mon–Fri.
**Closed** public hols. ♿
**W** colliermuseums.com

## Environs

Developed as a resort since the
1960s, **Marco Island** is the most
northerly of the Ten Thousand
Islands chain, and is a good base
for exploring the western fringe
of the Everglades *(see p290)*. Outstanding archaeological items,
some 3,500 years old, were found
here. These are now kept in
museums elsewhere, but you can
still see the remains of midden
mounds – giving clues to the
lifestyle of the ancient Calusa
Native Americans *(see pp44–5)*.

# ❷ Big Cypress Swamp

**Road map** E4. Collier Co, Monroe Co.
**Tel** (239) 695-1201.

Home to several hundred
species such as the endangered
Florida panther, this vast,
shallow wetland basin is not, in
fact, a true swamp. It features a
range of habitats, determined
by only slight differences in
elevation, which include sandy
islands of slash pine, wet and
dry prairies, and hardwood
hammocks *(see p291)*. One-third
of the swamp is covered by
cypress trees, growing in belts
and long narrow forests
("strands"). It is the scale of these
strands as opposed to the size
of the trees that gives the area
its name.

The swamp functions as a wet
season water storage area for
the greater Everglades system
and as a buffer zone for the
Everglades National Park *(see
pp290–91)*. Finished in 1928,
the Tamiami Trail, also known
as US 41, cuts through the
swamp and has opened
up the area. The road skirts the
Everglades and stretches from
Tampa to Miami, hence its
name. Today, such engineering
feats are environmentally
questionable, because they
block the natural movement of
water and wildlife essential to
the fragile balance of southern
Florida's unique ecosystem.

**Big Cypress National
Preserve** is the largest of the

Boardwalk winding through Fakahatchee Strand, Big Cypress Swamp

### The Seminoles of Florida

"Seminole" (meaning "wanderer" or "runaway") was first used in the 1700s for several Creek Native American tribes, forced to flee south to Florida by land-hungry Europeans and later retreated into the Everglades *(see p51)*.

Today, the Seminole tribe is officially distinct from the other main grouping, the Miccosukee tribe, but members of both are known as Seminoles.

Historic land disputes led the US Government to allocate reservation lands to the Florida tribes in 1911. Here, Seminoles maintain their traditions but also incorporate elements of modern American life. Since then, bingo halls and gambling casinos have significantly increased tribal wealth *(see p141)*. Billie Swamp Safaris offers tours of Seminole tribe backcountry.

Seminole dress in the late 1800s, showing European influence

Wood storks nesting in the trees of Corkscrew Swamp Sanctuary

protected areas. Most visitors here enjoy the views from US 41, and stop at the Oasis Visitor Center for information.

On the western edge of the swamp is the **Fakahatchee Strand Preserve State Park**, one of Florida's wildest areas. A huge natural drainage ditch, or slough (pronounced "slew"), it is 20 miles (32 km) long and 3–5 miles (5–8 km) wide.

Logging ceased here in the 1950s, having destroyed 99 per cent of old growth cypresses. The Preserve's only remaining examples, some dating from the 15th century, are found at Big Cypress Bend. Here, a short trail passes through a mosaic of plant communities, including magnificent orchids and nestlike epiphytes *(see p294)*. Here too is the US's largest stand of native royal palms. Route 846, running northeast from Naples, takes you to the popular

**Audubon of Florida's Corkscrew Swamp Sanctuary**. A 2 mile (3 km) boardwalk traverses various habitats, including Florida's largest stand of old growth cypress trees. The sanctuary is famous for its many birds, and is an important nesting area for endangered wood storks, which visit during the winter.

**✹ Big Cypress National Preserve**
Oasis Visitor Center, US 41. **Tel** (239) 695-2000. **Open** daily. **Closed** Dec 25.
🚻 🆆 nps.gov/bicy

**✹ Fakahatchee Strand Preserve State Park**
137 Coast Line Dr, Copeland. **Tel** (239) 695-4593. **Open** daily. 🚻

**✹ Audubon of Florida's Corkscrew Swamp Sanctuary**
375 Sanctuary Rd W, off Route 846. **Tel** (239) 348-9151. **Open** daily.
🚻 🆆 corkscrew.audubon.org

### ❸ Ah-Tah-Thi-Ki Museum

**Road map** F4. Hendry Co. 30290 Josie Billie Hwy, PMB 1003, Clewiston. **Tel** (863) 902-1113. **Open** 9am–5pm daily. **Closed** public hols. 🚻 🗹 2:30pm daily. 🚻 🆆 ahtahthiki.com

This museum is located on 64 acres (26 ha) of the Big Cypress Seminole Reservation. On site is a traditional village where Seminole tribal members tell stories and demonstrate crafts.

The museum is dedicated to the understanding of Seminole culture and history; Ah-Tah-Thi-Ki means "a place to learn." There is an impressive 180-degree, five-screen film.

### ❹ Miccosukee Indian Village

**Road map** F5. Dade Co. US 41, 25 miles (40 km) W of Florida Turnpike. **Tel** (877) 242-6464. **Open** daily. 🚻 🚻 🆆 miccosukee.com

Most of the Miccosukee tribe live in small settlements along US 41. The best way to find out more about them is to visit the Miccosukee Indian Village near Shark Valley *(see p291)*.

Here, visitors can see traditional *chickees (see p34)* and crafts like basket-weaving, doll-making, and beadwork. Native artifacts, clothing, paintings, and cooking utensils are displayed at the Miccosukee Museum. There is also a luxurious resort and gaming facility, which offers spa facilities, a golf course, and a country club.

Palmetto dolls and beadwork for sale in the Miccosukee Indian Village

# ⑤ Everglades National Park

Covering 1.5 million acres (566,580 ha), this huge park, also a World Heritage Site, makes up only one-fifth of the entire Everglades area. The main entrance on its eastern boundary is 10 miles (16 km) west of Florida City. The park's walking trails are mostly elevated boardwalks, about half a mile (1 km) long and clearly marked – some are suitable for bicycles. Boats and canoes can be rented, and there is a variety of boat trips to choose from. Lodgings consist of campgrounds, including more primitive sites where visitors stay in *chickees* (*see p34*), most of which are accessible only by canoe. There is a small charge for backcountry camping permits which must be obtained in person at ranger stations in Everglades City or Flamingo; reservations can be made only in the 24 hours prior to departure.

**Everglades City**
The Ten Thousand Islands archipelago and the national park's west coast are accessible from Everglades City.

**Whitewater Bay**
Open water, in the form of rivers, tidal creeks, and shallow lakes, (such as Whitewater Bay), appear only where the Sheet of the Everglades meets the Gulf of Mexico and Florida Bay.

Naples

**Everglades City**

Tamiami Trail

Chokoloskee

Ten Thousand Islands

**BIG CYPRESS NATIONAL PRESERVE**

**GULF OF MEXICO**

## Safety Tips

Protection against biting insects is vital, especially during the summer months. Follow the advice given by rangers and on information boards, and respect all wildlife: alligators can jump and move quickly on land; some trees and shrubs like the Brazilian pepper tree are poisonous, as are some caterpillars and snakes. If planning to go off the beaten path, let some-one know your itinerary. Always drive slowly: much wildlife can be seen from the road – and may also venture onto it.

**Coral snake**

0 kilometers     15
0 miles     10

**Canoeing in the Everglades**
Along the western coast and around Florida Bay are countless opportunities to explore the park's watery trails. These range from short routes, to the week-long adventure of the challenging and remote Wilderness Waterway.

**Shark Valley**
Take a narrated trolley ride or cycle along this 15 mile (25 km) loop road. At its end is a 60 ft (18 m) tower that offers great views.

**Anhinga Trail**
Starting at the Royal Palm Visitor Center, this is one of the most popular trails in the park. Its namesake, the anhinga bird, is often seen drying its distinctive plumage in the sun after diving for fish.

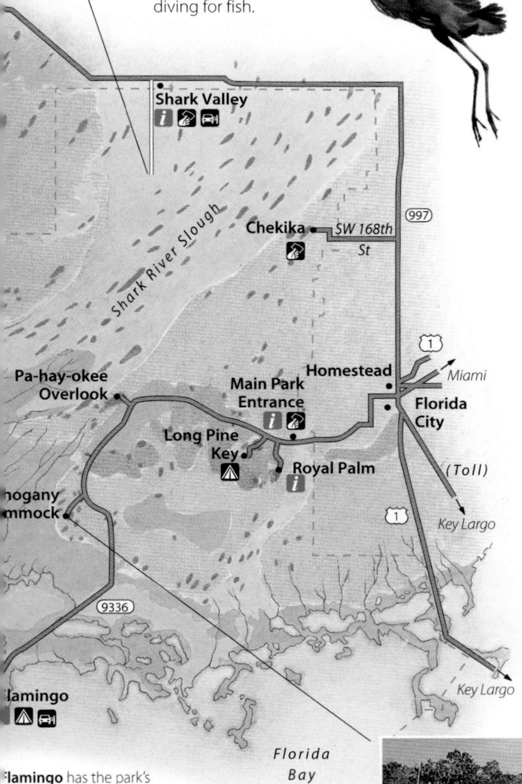

**VISITORS' CHECKLIST**

**Practical Information**
Road map E4, E5, F5. Monroe Co, Dade Co, Collier Co. **Open** daily.
ℹ️ all visitor centers open Dec– Apr daily; during rest of year, call in advance to check. Main Visitor Center: **Tel** (305) 242-7700. **Open** 8am–5pm. Gulf Coast Visitor Center: (in Everglades City) **Tel** (239) 695-3311; for boat tours and canoe rental call (239) 695-2591. **Open** 9am–4:30pm. Shark Valley Information Center: **Tel** (305) 221-8776; for trolley tour reservations and bicycle rental (305) 221-8455.
**Open** 8:30am–5:15pm. Royal Palm Visitor Center: **Tel** (305) 242-7700. **Open** 8am–4:15pm. Flamingo Visitor Center: **Tel** (239) 695-2945; for canoe, boat, or bicycle rental, boat tours, marina, call (239) 695-3101.
**Open** 8:30am–5:30pm. ♿ most park boardwalks are accessible. Call (305) 242-7700. ⛺ call (800) 365-2267 to reserve.
Excellent interactive map:
🌐 nps.gov/ever

**Shark Valley** ℹ️🚲🚌

Chekika 🏊 — SW 168th St

(997)

**Shark River Slough**

**Pa-hay-okee Overlook** •

**Main Park Entrance** ℹ️🚲

**Homestead**
1 → *Miami*

• **Florida City**

**Long Pine Key** ⛺

**Royal Palm** ℹ️

*(Toll)*

*Key Largo*

...hogany ...mmock •

(9336)

1

*Key Largo*

...lamingo ⛺🚌

**Florida Bay**

**Key**

| ▨ | Mangrove |
|---|---|
| ▨ | Saltwater prairie |
| ▨ | Cypress trees |
| ▨ | Freshwater prairie |
| ▨ | Freshwater slough |
| ▨ | Pinelands |
| ▨ | Hammock |
| – – | Wilderness Waterway |
| – – | Park boundary |
| ▬ | Paved road |
| ═ | Road closed to private vehicles |

**Flamingo** has the park's largest campground. Several hiking and canoe trails are to be found in its vicinity.

**Mahogany Hammock Boardwalk**
This trail meanders through a large, dense tropical hardwood hammock. It is noted for its colorful tree snails *(see p293)* and epiphytes *(see p294)*, and for being the home of the largest mahogany tree in the country.

**For additional map symbols** *see back flap*

# The Wildlife of the Everglades

The Everglades is a vast sheet river system – the overspill from Lake Okeechobee *(see p132)* that moves slowly across a flat bed of peat-covered limestone. Some 200 miles (322 km) long and up to 50 miles (80 km) wide, its depth rarely exceeds 3 ft (1 m).

Tropical air and sea currents act on this temperate zone to create combinations of flora that are unique in North America. Clumps of vegetation, such as cypress domes *(see p29)*, tropical hardwood hammocks, and bayheads, break the expanse of sawgrass prairie. There are also hundreds of animal species – some 350 species of birds, for which the Everglades is particularly renowned. This unique ecosystem, with its rich vegetation and associated wildlife, can be sustained only by the cycle of dry (winter) and wet (summer) seasons – the Everglades' life force.

**Osprey**
This fish-eating bird is seen around the park's coast, bays, and ponds. Its large nests are easily recognizable.

**The strangler fig**
starts life as a seed that is carried in bird droppings to a crevice of another tree. In time, it completely engulfs the host tree.

**Snowy Egret**
Beautiful breeding plumage, yellow feet, and a black bill identify this bird.

**Bromeliad**
*(see p294)*

**Green Tree Frog**
This endearing amphibian has a resonant call that can be heard throughout the Everglades.

**Bayheads**
are hammocks dominated by bay trees, that thrive on rich organic soil.

Sweet bay

Wax myrtle

Sawgrass

Cattail

## Tree Islands

*Hammocks or tree islands are areas of elevated land found in freshwater prairies. They support a fantastic variety of flora and fauna.*

Alligator flag

Bladderwort

Water Lily

**'Gator holes** are made by alligators hollowing out ponds and depressions during the dry season to reach the water below. The water-filled holes sustain many species during the winter.

**American Alligator**
With its rough hide and toothy grin, the alligator is one of the park's best known (and most feared) residents.

Royal palm

**Great Blue Heron**
Found all over Florida, this wading bird has a 6 ft (2 m) wingspan. In south Florida its plumage is sometimes completely white.

**Roseate Spoonbill**
These striking birds winter in the park and use their spatulate bills to fish for food in shallow water.

**The mahogany** is just one of the West Indian species that predominates in tropical hardwood hammocks.

**The gumbo-limbo's** bark is red and peeling, hence its nickname the "tourist tree."

Saw palmetto

Peat

**Red mangrove trees** are easily recognized by their distinctive roots. Salt-tolerant, they play a crucial role in protecting the shoreline and act as a nursery for marine animals.

**Tree Snail**
There are 58 varieties of the colorful tree snail, which live in hammocks and move around only during the wet season.

**Otter**
Related to the weasel, this delightful animal is often seen frolicking in freshwater ponds.

# Exploring Everglades National Park

Most visitors come to Everglades National Park for the day, which can easily be spent exploring just one or two of the trails. However, a popular excursion involves stopping at the different boardwalk trails along the Main Park Road (Route 9336); it is an easy drive down and back to Flamingo on Florida Bay. Try to include at least one of the less-visited trails and ponds located off the southern part of the road between Mahogany Hammock and Flamingo. Information boards abound to help you identify the flora and fauna. Remember to bring insect repellent and protection against the sun.

Long Pine Key, which boasts a lovely camp ground and shady trails

Rangers and visitors examining wildlife on a "slough-slog"

### Around the Royal Palm Visitor Center

The highly informative Royal Palm Visitor Center, and two nearby boardwalk trails, are located on the site of Florida's first state park, created in 1916. The popular **Anhinga Trail**, passing over Taylor Slough, contains slightly deeper water than the surrounding terrain; in the dry winter months it attracts wildlife to drink. Its open site provides better photo opportunities and fewer insects, but the intense sun can be hazardous. Alligators congregate at the 'gator hole *(see p292)* at the beginning of the trail, and a wide range of fauna, including deer, raccoons, and the splendid anhinga bird, can also be spotted.

The shady **Gumbo Limbo Trail**, on the other hand, is mosquito paradise in summer. However, it is an easy walk, and, if your visit is confined to the park's eastern half, it offers the best chance to explore a tropical hardwood hammock. Watch out for *bromeliads*, members of the pine-apple family and a type of *epiphyte*. This nonparasitic plant grows on other plants but obtains its nourishment from the air and rainwater. There are also many types of orchids and the trail's namesake, the gumbo limbo tree *(see p293)*.

Bromeliads on a mahogany tree

### Long Pine Key

This area takes its name from a large stand of slash pines that are unique to southern Florida. Insect- and rot-proof, they have long been a popular building material. Pinelands need fire for survival – without it, they progress to hardwoods. Since roads and canals act as fire breaks, park rangers set controlled fires to encourage regeneration of the pinelands and that of associated species such as the saw palmetto.

The camp ground here occupies a stunning position and is one of the main reasons that people stop at Long Pine Key. Several shady trails lead off from it, and there's a half mile (1 km) loop of the Pineland Trail, located 2 miles (3 km) to the west. Don't stray from the path: the limestone bedrock contains "solution holes" created by rain eroding away the rock. These can be deep and difficult to spot.

## Trails Around Flamingo

As a general rule, canoe trails through open water offer an ideal way to escape the summer's insects, while the hiking trails are undoubtedly most agreeable during the winter months.

**Key**

–– Hiking trail

-- Canoe trail

▬▬ Paved road

══ Unpaved road

### From Pa-hay-okee to Flamingo

The open expanse of sawgrass prairie that can be viewed from the elevated **Pa-hay-okee Overlook** is the epitome of the Everglades. The observation tower here is a perfect spot from which to watch the fluid light changes dancing across this sea of grass, especially in the late afternoon. Tree islands or hammocks break the horizon, and you will see a multitude of wading birds, hawks, and snail kites, whose only food, the apple snail, lives on the sawgrass. This prairie is also home to cattails and other wetland plants.

The **Mahogany Hammock Trail** (see p291), by contrast, leads through one of the park's largest hammocks. This area is home to a wide variety of fauna and flora; the bromeliads here are very impressive, and the junglelike vegetation is especially dense during the wet summer months.

The various trails and ponds between Mahogany Hammock and Flamingo tend to attract fewer people but are no less rewarding, especially for the bird life. Try exploring West Lake Trail or Snake Bight Trail, which ends on Florida Bay.

The settlement of **Flamingo** lies 38 miles (60 km) from the main park entrance. In the late 1800s, it was a remote outpost and hideaway for hunters and fishermen. These days, a few park rangers are the only long-

Stunning views of the prairie from the Pa-hay-okee Overlook

term residents. Flamingo's position on Florida Bay offers visitors a wide choice of activities such as hiking, fishing, boating, and watching wildlife. An overnight stay at the camp ground is recommended especially for bird-watching, which is most rewarding in the early morning and late afternoon.

Apart from countless species of birds and animals, the bay and creeks around Flamingo contain manatees (see p254) and the endangered American crocodile. This is easily distinguished from the alligator by its gray-green color and the fact that the teeth of both jaws show when its mouth is shut. You may spot one in this area.

Flamingo's visitor center has wildlife guides and information about local ranger-led activities. These include evening slideshows and talks, and daytime "slough-slogs" – intrepid walks through the swamp.

### ❻ Biscayne National Park

**Road map** F5. Dade Co. 9700 SW 328th St, Convoy Point. 🚉 Miami. 🚌 Homestead. **Tel** (305) 230-7275. **Open** daily. **Closed** Dec 25. Visitor Center: **Open** 9am–5pm. Boat tours: **Tel** (305) 230-1100. ♿ limited. ⚠ 🅦 nps.gov/bisc

Dense mangrove swamp protects the shoreline of Biscayne National Park, which incorporates the northernmost islands of the Florida Keys. Its shallow waters hold the park's greatest draw – a living coral reef with myriad forms, and around 200 types of tropical fish. The barrier islands are untouched, so the coral here is healthier, and the water even clearer than in the more popular underwater parks farther south around Key Largo.

You can take glass-bottom boat tours, and there are also diving and snorkeling trips; which all leave from the visitor center. It is advisable to reserve tours and trips in advance.

### The Everglades Under Threat

Everglades National Park enjoys good protection within its boundaries, but threats from outside are more difficult to control. Since it was created in 1947, the park's greatest problems have been water related. The Everglades ecosystem and Florida's human population are in direct competition for this priceless commodity: irrigation canals and roads disrupt the natural through-flow of water from Lake Okeechobee (see p132), and the drainage of land for development has also had detrimental effects on wildlife. Agriculture in central Florida uses vast amounts of water, and high levels of chemical fertilizers promote the unnatural growth of swamp vegetation. The state and federal governments are studying how best to protect the area and return water flow to its natural state.

Agriculture near the Everglades requires great quantities of water

Elkhorn coral and tropical fish in Biscayne National Park

## ❼ Key Largo

**Road map** F5. Monroe Co. 🏕 11,000.
🚌 ℹ MM 106, (305) 451-1414, (800)
822-1088. **African Queen: Tel** (305)
451-4655. 🌐 fla-keys.com/key-largo

The first of the inhabited Keys,
this is the largest island in the
chain and was named "long
island" by Spanish explorers.
Its proximity to Miami
makes it also the
liveliest, especially
on weekends when
it is crowded.

The island's great-
est attractions are
the diving and
snorkeling
opportunities along the
coral reef found just
offshore, in the John
Pennekamp Coral
Reef State Park and
the National Marine Sanctuary.

Another Key Largo attraction
is the *African Queen*, the boat
used in the 1951 movie of the
same name. This makes short
pleasure trips between

Gold ornament from
a treasure ship

extensive periods of restoration.
It is moored at MM 100, which
is also the base for a casino
ship offering a different type of
trip – one that provides a rare
chance to gamble *(see p360)*.

Local legend tells of a
mysterious and secretive former
government official who lives
in the hammocks and returns
to civilization only when
an ecological need
arises. His various
exploits over the
years have resulted
in land, (once
slated for
development),
being returned to
pristine wilderness.
Much of Florida's
wetlands, hammocks,
and beaches have
been bulldozed and
replaced with apartments,
resorts, and shopping malls.
However, with the help of
concerned citizens, there is
hope that Florida's delicate
ecosystem can be kept intact.

## ❽ John Pennekamp Coral Reef State Park

**Road map** F5. Monroe Co. MM 102.5.
🚌 Key Largo. **Tel** (305) 451-1202.
**Open** daily. 🐾 ♿ limited.
🌐 floridastateparks.org

Just less than five per cent of
this park is on dry land, and its
facilities include a visitor's center,
a small museum on the ecology
of the reef, swimming areas, and
woodland trails. The park is best
known for its fabulous underwater reaches, which extend
3 miles (5 km) east from Key
Largo, and provide an unforgettable glimpse of the vivid colors
and extraordinary forms of coral
reef life.

There are canoes, dinghies,
or motorboats for rent, as well
as snorkeling and scuba gear.
Snorkeling and diving trips can
easily be arranged, and there is
a diving school that offers certified courses. Those who are less
inclined to get wet can take a

# Florida's Coral Reef

North America's only live coral reef system extends
200 miles (320 km) along the length of the Keys, from
Miami to the Dry Tortugas. A complex and extremely
delicate ecosystem, it protects these low-lying islands
from storms and heavy wave action emanating from the
Atlantic Ocean. Coral reefs are created over thousands
of years by billions of tiny marine organisms known as
polyps. Lying 10–60 ft (3–18 m) below the surface, the
reef is an intricate web of countless cracks and cavities,
and is home to a multitude of plants and diverse sea
creatures, including more than
500 species of fish.

The scaleless green moray, fearsome in looks but
generally harmless to humans

Longspine squirrelfish, characterized
by the pronounced dorsal fin

Sea fans, "soft" corals
that have no skeleton

### Key to Corals

① Smooth starlet coral
② Sea fan
③ Flower coral
④ Elliptical star coral
⑤ Sea rod
⑥ Pillar coral

⑦ Orange tube coral
⑧ Elkhorn coral
⑨ Brain coral
⑩ Staghorn coral
⑪ Large flower coral
⑫ Sea plume

A scuba diver exploring corals at the John Pennekamp Coral Reef State Park

glass-bottom boat trip. Most tours visit destinations that are actually located in the neighboring section of the Florida Keys National Marine Sanctuary, known as the Key Largo National Marine Sanctuary, which extends 3 miles (5 km) farther out to sea.

Some parts of the reef here are favored by snorkelers, such as the shallow waters of White Bank Dry Rocks, with its impressive array of corals and colorful tropical fish. Nearby Molasses Reef offers areas for both snorkelers and divers, who may encounter a wide variety of fish such as snapper and angelfish. Farther north, French Reef has swim-through caves where divers can find darting shoals of glassy sweepers. At Key Largo Dry Rocks, the *Christ of the Deep* statue lies submerged at 20 ft (6 m) and is a popular underwater photo stop.

## 9 Tavernier

**Road map** F5. Monroe Co. 🚾 2,500.
ℹ️ MM 106 (305) 451-1414.

Henry Flagler's railroad (*see pp52–3*) reached this part of the Keys around 1910. Today, a number of buildings, constructed in the 1920s and 1930s as the settlement grew, are located around MM 92; of these only the Tavernier Hotel is open to the public.

Tavernier's most notable attraction is the **Florida Keys Wild Bird Rehabilitation Center**. Here, sanctuary is offered to injured birds, most of whom have been harmed by humans, involving cars or fishing tackle. They recuperate in spacious cages set in tranquil surroundings, contrasting with the bustle of the rest of the island.

**🦅 Florida Keys Wild Bird Rehabilitation Center**
92080, Overseas Highway.
**Tel** (305) 852-4486. **Open** daily.
♿ 🌐 keepthemflying.org

---

**A hard coral polyp** secretes a limescale skeleton to protect its fleshy body. Coral heads and branches are eventually formed by the growth cycles of countless polyps. Microscopic plants, which live in the polyps' tissues, determine the color of the coral.

Mouth — Fleshy tentacles

Stony base

Stomach

An attractive stoplight parrotfish, grazing on coral polyps with its beaklike teeth

Giant tube sponge

Plume worm

Sea anemone

Queen angelfish, one of the reef's most intensely colored (and inquisitive) fish

Barrel sponge

Vase sponge

## ⑩ Theater of the Sea

**Road map** F5. Monroe Co. MM 84.5.
**Tel** (305) 664-2431. **Open** daily. 🚫
♿ 🅦 theaterofthesea.com

Windley Key is home to the
Theater of the Sea, which opened
in 1946 and is Florida's second
oldest marine park. Situated in a
former quarry created during the
construction of Flagler's railroad
*(see pp52–3)*, the attraction is
famous for its traditional sea lion
and dolphin shows. It is also possible to take boat trips to explore
wildlife in the local lagoons. This
series of lagoons provide a
home to Atlantic bottlenose
dolphins, California sea lions, sea
turtles, tropical and game fish,
sharks, stingrays, alligators, and
marine invertebrates. Many of
the animals have been rescued,
and need care and treatment.

The observation tower and original ruined water cisterns on Indian Key

Turquoise waters of Islamorada, ideal for game fishing

## ⑪ Islamorada

**Road map** F5. Monroe Co. 🅰 8,500.
🚌 ℹ MM 82.5, (305) 644-4503.
🅦 islamoradachamber.com

Proudly declaring itself "The Sport
fishing Capital of the World,"
Islamorada, pronounced "Eye-luh-
mo-rada," encompasses seven
islands and is best known for its
outstanding big game fishing.

Whale Harbor Marina in the
town of Islamorada, on Upper
Matecumbe Key, bristles with
impressive deep-sea charter craft
used to catch blue-water fish.
Fishing party boats based here
take people of all levels of experience, so even those who are not
dedicated anglers can enjoy half
a day out at sea on one of these

trips. Back in town at MM 82, the
Art Deco Hurricane Monument
marks the grave of 500 people
killed by a tidal surge in the
hurricane of 1935 *(see p30)*.

## ⑫ Indian and Lignumvitae Keys

**Road map** F5. Monroe Co.
🚌 Islamorada. 🚤 Lower Matecumbe
Key. ℹ Islamorada, (305) 664-4503.

These uninhabited islands, on
opposite sides of the Ocean
Highway, are accessible only
by boat.

Tiny Indian Key has a surprising
amount of history for its size. Once
occupied by native people, it
was settled in 1831 by Captain
J. Houseman, an opportunistic
wrecker *(see p307)*. A small community flourished under his rule,
but in 1840 Seminoles attacked,
killing these settlers. The Key was
abandoned, and today only the
outlines of the village and its
cisterns remain, amid vegetation

The Ocean Highway passing through the Indian and Lignumvitae Keys

impressive for both its variety and
rampant growth. An observation
tower provides splendid views
of the island.

Larger Lignumvitae Key, which
can be explored only on a guided
tour, is of even greater botanical
interest. It boasts 133 native tree
species, including its namesake, a
blue-flowering tree that can live
for 1,000 years. Scientists believe
that other vegetation here is as
old as 10,000 years. Notable wildlife includes some colorful tree
snails *(see p293)* and impressively
large spiders. Be prepared for
mosquitoes.

## ⑬ Dolphin Research Center

**Road map** E5. Monroe Co. MM 59.
**Tel** (305) 289-1121. **Open** daily.
**Closed** public hols. 🚫 ♿
🅦 dolphins.org

A nonprofit-making concern,
the Dolphin Research Center on
Grassy Key is a serious establishment whose main function is to
research dolphin behavior. The
Center also acts as a rest home
for sick and injured dolphins, or
for those just worn out from the
stresses of a busy life as a theme
park attraction.

There are exhibits, regularly
scheduled lagoon-side walking
tours, and special programs
such as the college-credit
Dolphin Lab. The center is
part of the Marine Mammal
Stranding Network, dedicated
to rescuing and rehabilitating
whales and dolphins. It is the
only facility in the Keys allowed
to assist manatees in distress..

# Fishing in the Florida Keys

There are three main fishing zones in South Florida, each offering its own type of experience and rewards. Near the warm Gulf Stream, offshore gamefish such as marlin abound in conditions excellent for deep-sea (or blue-water) angling. The Atlantic coastal waters up to and including the coral reef itself contain tropical species such as snapper and grouper. To the north of the Keys, the shallow backcountry flats of the Gulf are home to game fish such as tarpon. Islamorada, Marathon, and Key West are the area's major fishing centers, and small marinas throughout the region have boats for rent. There are enough options to suit most tastes, budgets, and abilities, but visitors might have a greater chance of success if they reserve a place on a fishing party boat, or rent an experienced guide. Weather conditions and seasonal variations determine the available species, but visitors can fish the waters of the Florida Keys all year round.

### Deep-Sea versus Backcountry

Deep-sea fishing, one of the most exhilarating options available, appeals to the Hemingway spirit of the trophy angler. Renting a sports boat, however, is expensive. Skiffs fish the tranquil and scenic backcountry reaches, where cunning and stealth help to secure a catch.

**Flat-bottom skiffs** are poled through inshore waters; motors can become snarled up in the seagrass.

**Fishermen** in sports boats fitted with fighting chairs wear harnesses to battle deep-sea fish.

**Bait and tackle shops** are found along the Overseas Highway and in marinas. They not only rent and sell equipment and licenses (*see p363*), but are often the best places to find out about guides and fishing trips offered locally.

**Big game fish** are the ultimate trophy. Local restaurants can clean and cook their guests' catch, but for a long-lasting memento, let a taxidermist prepare and mount them (*see p363*).

**Fishing party boats** are a popular and economical way to fish around the reef. The per-person price usually includes a fishing license, tackle, and bait, as well as the crew's expertise.

Marathon's Boot Key Harbor, with the 7-Mile Bridge in the distance

## ⑭ Marathon

**Road map** E5. Monroe Co. ![icon] 9,000.
![icons] **ⅈ** MM 53.5, (305) 743-6555.
**w** floridakeysmarathon.com

Marathon was originally named Vaca ("cow") Key by the Spanish settlers, probably for the herds of manatees or sea cows (see p254) once found offshore. It was renamed in the early 1900s by the men who had the grueling task of laying the Overseas Railroad (see p285).

The main center of the Middle Keys, this island is rather heavily developed and at first glance appears to be an uninviting strip of shopping plazas and gas stations. Marathon's principal appeal lies in the surrounding fishing grounds, and those located under the bridges where the Atlantic Ocean and the Gulf of Mexico meet are considered to be particularly fertile.

Devotees can choose from a broad range of angling techniques (see p299). These include spear-fishing (illegal in the Upper Keys but allowed here), and line-fishing off what may be the longest pier in the world – a 2 mile (3 km) stretch of the old 7-Mile Bridge. There are several pleasing waterfront resorts with small beaches, created artificially from imported sand. Turn south off the Overseas Highway in order to find these.

Door detail, Crane Point Hammock

Definitely worth a visit is **Crane Point Hammock**, consisting of 64 acres (26 ha) of tropical hardwood forest and wild mangrove wetlands. There are nature trails and a traditional conch-style house (see p305) built out of tabby – a type of local home-made concrete, made of burned seashells and coral rock. The entrance to the hammock is via the **Crane Point Museum**, opened on Earth Day in 1991. The interesting collection explains the history and geology as well as the ecology of the islands, and is designed to appeal in particular to younger visitors.

**Ⅲ Crane Point Museum**
MM 50.5. **Tel** (305) 743-9100.
**Open** daily. **Closed** Dec 25. ![icons]
**w** cranepoint.net

## ⑮ Pigeon Key

**Road map** E5. Monroe Co. MM 47.5, via the old 7-Mile Bridge. **Tel** (305) 289-0025. **Open** daily. ![icons]
**w** pigeonkey.net

This tiny Key was once the construction base for Henry Flagler's 7-Mile Bridge, described by some as the eighth wonder of the world when it was eventually completed in 1912. Seven wooden structures, originally used by building and maintenance crews, are today part of a marine research and educational foundation, and form one of the last intact railroad villages from the Flagler era.

There is a historical museum in the Bridge Tender's House, but many people visit simply to enjoy the island's tranquil surroundings. The old bridge, running parallel to the "new" 7-Mile Bridge built in 1982, marches across the Key on concrete piles and provides a stunning backdrop to the island. It is also the only way to reach the Key. No cars are allowed on the Key, so go by foot or by bicycle, or take the shuttle bus from the foundation's headquarters at MM 48.

## ⑯ Lower Keys

**Road map** E5. Monroe Co. ![icon] Key West. **ⅈ** MM 31, (305) 872-2411.
**w** lowerkeyschamber.com

Once beyond the 7-Mile Bridge, the Keys appear to change. The land is rugged and less developed than in the Upper

The Negro Quarters, an example of Pigeon Key's original dwellings

Bahia Honda's beautiful beach in the Florida Keys

Keys, and the vegetation is more wooded, supporting different flora and fauna. The pace of life slows right down, upholding the local claim that the Lower Keys are more about a state of mind than a geo-graphical location.

Just 37 miles (60 km) from Key West is **Bahia Honda State Park**, a protected area of 524 acres (212 hectares) that boasts the finest beach in all the Keys. Brilliantly white sand is backed by a dense, tropical forest crossed by a number of trails. If you follow these you will find various unusual species of tree, such as silver palm and yellow satinwood, and plenty of birds. The usual water sports equipment is available to rent, but visitors should remember that the current here can be very strong.

Trips out to the **Looe Key National Marine Sanctuary** are also available from the park. This 5 mile (8 km) section of the reef is a spectacular dive location, with unique coral formations and abundant marine life.

From Bahia Honda, the highway swings north and reaches the next major point of interest, and the second largest island in the chain, **Big Pine Key**. This

island is the Lower Keys' main residential community and the best place to see the diminutive Key Deer, most often spotted at dusk or in the early morning. Take the turning for Key Deer Boulevard near MM 30 to reach the **Blue Hole**, a flooded quarry set in woodlands. The viewing platform here is ideal from which to watch the deer and other wildlife that come to drink. Nearby, the 1 mile (2 km) looped path of the Jack Watson Nature Trail has markers to help in the identification of the trees and plants.

Perky's Bat Tower

Continuing on down the Overseas Highway, while crossing Cudjoe Key, keep a lookout for **"Fat Albert"**, a large white surveillance blimp.

Tethered at a height of 1,400 ft (427 m), Fat Albert's job is to monitor anything from drug smugglers to political activities in Cuba.

Neighboring Sugarloaf Key, once the location of a sponge-farming enterprise, is now famous for its **Bat Tower**, reached by turning north off the Overseas Highway just after MM 17. It was built in 1929 by Richter C. Perky, a property speculator, for the purpose of attracting the bats that he believed would rid the island of its ferocious mosquitoes, allowing him to develop it as a resort. However, not a single bat came and the tower remains as a testament to the failure of his plans.

🏊 **Bahia Honda State Park**
MM 37. **Tel** (305) 872-2353.
**Open** daily. 🅿️ ♿ limited.
🌐 **floridastateparks.org**

### Key Deer

Related to the white-tailed deer, Florida's endangered Key Deer are found only on Big Pine Key and the surrounding islands. They swim between these keys, but are more often sighted as they roam around the slash pine woodlands. Despite the enforcement of strict speed restrictions, and the establishment of a refuge on Big Pine Key, around 50 deer are killed in road accidents each year. The number of deer has stabilized at around 300. It is strictly forbidden to feed them.

A fully grown Key Deer, no bigger than a large dog

# ⑰ Key West: Street-by-Street

The southernmost settlement in the continental US, Key West is a city like no other, and a magnet for people who want to leave the rest of Florida, and even America, behind. This is a place to join in with locals busy dropping out, and to indulge in the laid-back, tropical lifestyle.

First recorded in 1513, the island soon became a haven first for pirates and then for "wreckers" *(see p307)*, both of whom preyed on passing merchant ships and their precious cargos. Key West grew to be the most prosperous city in Florida, and the opportunistic lifestyle on offer lured a steady stream of settlers from the Americas, the Caribbean, and Europe. Visitors will find their legacy in the island's unique architecture, cuisine, and spirit. A large gay community, writers, and New-Agers are among the more recent arrivals who have added to Key West's cultural cocktail.

**The Curry Mansion**
This opulent 19th-century home's interior reflects the wealth of Key West's wreck captains *(see p306)*.

**Sloppy Joe's** was Ernest Hemingway's favorite haunt. The bar moved here from its former site on Greene Street in 1935.

**Pier House Resort**
Just off Mallory Square, this resort has a popular terrace where people gather to watch the famous Key West sunsets.

★ **Mel Fisher Maritime Museum**
All sorts of shipwreck treasures, and the gear used to find them, are displayed in this excellent museum *(see p306)*.

**Audubon House,**
built in the 1840s, contains period pieces and ornithological prints by John James Audubon *(see p50)*.

**The Oldest House Museum** *(see p306)*

**Duval Street**
Key West's main thoroughfare, Duval Street is lined with souvenir shops and is often busy with tourists. Several of the Old Town's sights are located here.

**Key**

— Suggested route

| 0 meters | 100 |
| 0 yards | 100 |

### Fleming Street
Typical of the quiet, shady residential roads of the Old Town, Fleming Street boasts many beautiful wooden houses. These are fine examples of traditional Key West architecture *(see p305).*

## VISITORS' CHECKLIST

**Practical Information**
Road map E5. Monroe Co. 🏠 27,000. ℹ️ 402 Wall Street, (305) 294-2587. 🌐 **keywestchamber. org** Audubon House: **Tel** (305) 294-2116. **Open** daily. 🎉 Conch Republic Independence Celebration (Apr), Hemingway Days Festival (Jul), Fantasy Fest (mid-Oct).

**Transportation**
✈️ 2 miles (3 km) E of Duval St. 🚌 Simonton and Virginia sts, (305) 296-9072. ⛴️ Mallory Sq, (305) 292-8158.

### St. Paul's Episcopal Church
This 1912 church is dedicated to the patron saint of shipwrecked sailors. Some of its 49 stained-glass windows feature nautical imagery.

### Margaritaville
Jimmy Buffet, the Floridian singer, owns this café and adjoining shop, where T-shirts and memorabilia are for sale *(see p349).*

### The San Carlos Institute
was founded by Cubans in 1871. Today it occupies a beautiful Baroque-style building, which dates from 1924 and functions as a Cuban heritage center.

Bahama Village

### ★ Bahama Village
As yet relatively undeveloped, this old Key West neighborhood is filled with brightly painted clapboard buildings.

# Exploring Key West

Most of the sights are either on or within two or three blocks of Duval Street, which links the Gulf of Mexico with the Atlantic, and is the main axis of Old Key West. Focused between Whitehead and White streets, this district boasts the largest concentration of 19th-century wooden buildings in Florida. Simple shotgun houses, which were erected to house Cuban cigar-workers, contrast with the whimsically Romantic style of the homes of wealthier citizens. Take the Conch Train or Old Town Trolley tour, rent a bicycle, or just wander around the back streets. In the south of the island, there are plenty of beautiful, sandy beaches.

Shady palms lining a subtropical beach in southern Key West

**A Tour of Key West**

On the northern edge of the old town, **Mallory Square** is the famous place to watch the sunset, while performance artists vie with each other to amuse the crowds. During the day, to get the feel of the city, head down Duval Street and take side streets at random. These pretty streets are lined with Key West's distinctive gingerbread houses, set among shady tropical trees and drooping bougainvillea.

Even more rewarding, and named after Key West's earliest settlers, is **Bahama Village**. This historic neighborhood on the western fringe of the old town is bordered by Fort, Virginia, Petronia, and Whitehead streets. Life here is lived outside, with animated domino games on street corners and chickens wandering freely – a taste of the Caribbean in North America. The typical shotgun houses have largely escaped the enthusiastic renovations found elsewhere.

## 🏛 Fort East Martello Museum and Gallery

3501 S Roosevelt Blvd. **Tel** (305) 296-3913. **Open** daily. **Closed** Dec 25. 🅿 ♿ limited. 🆆 kwahs.com

Located in the east of the island, the East Martello tower was begun in 1861 to protect Fort Zachary's defensive position (see p306). It was never completed, because its design quickly became outmoded.

Today, the squat tower is an informative museum that provides the visitor with an excellent introduction to Key West and its checkered past. Everything is included here, from stories about Key West's many literary connections, to the island's changing commercial history. Visitors can also see one of the unbelievably flimsy rafts used by Cubans to flee Castro's regime (see pp56–7).

The tower itself offers fine views and houses works of art by a number of local artists.

## 🏛 Hemingway Home

907 Whitehead St. **Tel** (305) 294-1136. **Open** daily. 🅿 ♿ limited. 🆆 hemingwayhome.com

Probably the town's major (and most hyped) attraction, this Spanish colonial-style house built of coral rock is where Ernest Hemingway lived from 1931 to 1940. Above the carriage house is the room where the novelist penned several works; *To Have and Have Not* was the only book set in Key West. His library and mementos from his travels are displayed, as are memorabilia such as the cigar-maker's chair upon which he sat and wrote. Guides describe the hard-living writer's nonliterary passions of fishing and hell-raising in Sloppy Joe's (see p302). Descendants of his six-toed cats still prowl around the house and its luxuriant garden.

## 🏛 Lighthouse Museum

938 Whitehead St. **Tel** (305) 294-0012. **Open** daily. **Closed** Dec 25. 🅿 🆆 kwahs.com

Across the road from Heming-way House stands the town's lighthouse, built in 1848. The clapboard keeper's cottage at its foot houses a modest museum containing lighthouse and other historical artifacts.

Original Lighthouse flag

The greatest attraction is the tower itself. Make the 88-step climb for panoramic views and the chance to step inside and look through the old lens, once capable of beaming light some 25 miles (40 km) out to sea.

*Boza's Comparsa* (1975), Duval Street by M Sanchez, East Martello Museum

*For hotels and restaurants in this area see pp323–5 and pp345–7*

# Key West Architecture

The architecture of Key West is striking above all for its simplicity, a response to the hot climate, and the limited materials available – principally wood – which was either salvaged or imported. Early "conch" houses, built at the beginning of the 19th century, were often built by ships' carpenters who introduced elements they had seen on their travels. From the Bahamas came various devices to increase shade and ventilation against the Florida sun. Later, Classical Revivalism filtered in from the north, while the Victorian style of the late 1800s introduced a highly decorative influence. Key West's prosperous inhabitants favored often extravagant gingerbread details, but carvings also adorn humbler dwellings. Since the 1970s, when the town's architectural legacy was first properly acknowledged, many houses have been renovated, especially inside. However, their essential flavor remains.

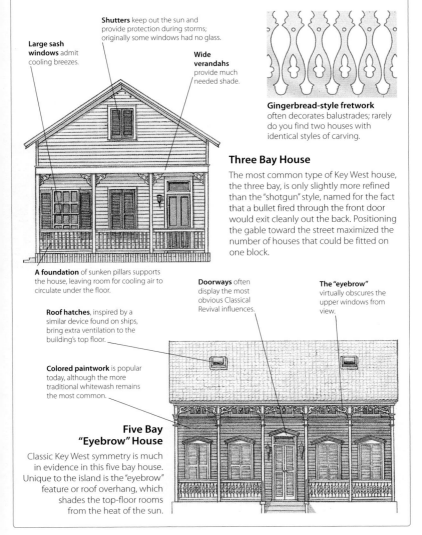

**Shutters** keep out the sun and provide protection during storms; originally some windows had no glass.

**Large sash windows** admit cooling breezes.

**Wide verandahs** provide much needed shade.

**Gingerbread-style fretwork** often decorates balustrades; rarely do you find two houses with identical styles of carving.

## Three Bay House

The most common type of Key West house, the three bay, is only slightly more refined than the "shotgun" style, named for the fact that a bullet fired through the front door would exit cleanly out the back. Positioning the gable toward the street maximized the number of houses that could be fitted on one block.

**A foundation** of sunken pillars supports the house, leaving room for cooling air to circulate under the floor.

**Roof hatches**, inspired by a similar device found on ships, bring extra ventilation to the building's top floor.

**Colored paintwork** is popular today, although the more traditional whitewash remains the most common.

**Doorways** often display the most obvious Classical Revival influences.

**The "eyebrow"** virtually obscures the upper windows from view.

## Five Bay "Eyebrow" House

Classic Key West symmetry is much in evidence in this five bay house. Unique to the island is the "eyebrow" feature or roof overhang, which shades the top-floor rooms from the heat of the sun.

The impressive brick vaulting of Fort Zachary Taylor

### 🏛 Fort Zachary Taylor Historic State Site

End of Southard St. **Tel** (305) 292-6713.
**Open** daily. 🚗 🅿 ♿ limited.
**W** floridastateparks.org

As part of the national coastal defense system begun in the mid-19th century, this brick fort was completed in 1866. During the Civil War, Union troops were stationed here to keep the island loyal to the north. Originally, the fort was three stories high and had toilets that were flushed by the tides. It was remodeled in the 1890s.

Today, it houses a museum which contains a fine collection of Civil War artifacts. Visitors can also explore the grounds and enjoy the view from an observation deck. Nearby is Key West's best public beach, which has shady picnic areas.

### 🏛 The Mel Fisher Maritime Museum

200 Greene St. **Tel** (305) 294-2633.
**Open** 9:30am–5pm daily. 🅿 ♿
**W** melfisher.com

A plain stone exterior belies the opulence of some of the treasures this museum holds. The late Mr. Fisher grabbed the headlines in 1985 when he discovered the wrecks of the Spanish galleons *Nuestra Señora de Atocha (see p32)* and *Santa Margarita*, about 40 miles (64 km) west of Key West. Inside were 47 tons of gold and silver bars and 70 lbs (32 kg) of raw emeralds that sank with them in 1622.

Items on display include jewelry, coins, and crucifixes. The story of the salvage operation is also told, but do check out the fantastic website.

### 🏛 The Oldest House Museum

322 Duval St. **Tel** (305) 294-9502.
**Open** daily. ♿ limited.
**W** oirf.org

Originally the home of wreck captain, Francis B. Watlington, this is thought to be the oldest house in Key West. Built in 1829, its design reveals some rather idiosyncratic maritime influences, such as the hatch used for ventilation in the roof. The house is stuffed full of nautical bric-a-brac, ships' models and paintings, and an array of documents concerning wrecking – the industry that first made Key West (and Captain Watlington) rich. Visitors are greeted by volunteer staff, whose anecdotes make the history of the house come alive.

Don't miss the separate kitchen house in the backyard, the oldest of the few examples that still remain in the Keys. Located away from the main building, it minimized the risk of fire and in addition helped to keep the temperature down in the rest of the house.

The ship-style hatch in the attic of the Oldest House Museum

### 🏠 The Curry Mansion

511 Caroline St. **Tel** (305) 294-5349.
**Open** daily. 🚗 ♿
**W** currymansion.com

This grand and embellished mansion was begun in 1855 by William Curry, a Bahamian wreck captain who became Key West's first millionaire. His son Milton completed the work 44 years later.

In addition to its sweeping verandas, the house boasts many original features, including wood-paneled rooms and electrical fittings. The rooms are furnished with Victorian and later objects, from Tiffany-stained glass to a rifle once owned by Ernest Hemingway – all collected by the present owner. It is said that key lime pie *(see p328)* was first made here by Aunt Sally, the cook, using canned condensed milk (first available in 1895). The Curry Mansion is also a guest house *(see p324)*.

The charming Robert Frost Cottage in the garden of Heritage House

### 🏛 Heritage House Museum and Robert Frost Cottage

410 Caroline St. **Tel** (305) 296-3573.
**Open** Mon–Sat. **Closed** Thanksgiving, Dec 25, Jan 1. 🅿 ♿

Built in 1834 and originally the home of a British captain, this house is one of Key West's oldest buildings. It is in near-original condition and contains period furnishings and travel curios that belonged to the Porters, a wealthy Key West family. The garden contains an outdoor kitchen house and, beneath a fine banyan tree, the Robert Frost cottage; this is named after the American poet who stayed here during his many visits to Key West between 1945 and 1960.

### 🏛 Key West Cemetery

701 Passover Lane. **Tel** (305) 292-8177.
**Open** daily. 🔓 Tue & Thu only. ♿

Due to the proximity of the limestone bedrock and water table, most of the tombs here are above ground. Laid out on a grid system, the cemetery holds the remains of many of Key West's earliest residents. Within the compound there are separate areas for Jews and Roman Catholics, while many of the Cuban crypts are crowned with a statue of a chicken, probably associated with the Santería religion *(see p81)*. There is even a special burial area devoted to pets. A statue of a lone sailor commemorates the loss of 252 crewmen on the battleship USS *Maine*, which was sunk in Havana's harbor at the onset of the Spanish-American War in 1898 *(see p53)*. Stroll around to read the often amusing inscriptions and epitaphs, "I told you I was sick" among others. Many of the town's early settlers were known simply by their first names or nicknames, and this Key West informality followed them to their graves. There are references to Bunny, Shorty, Bean, and so forth. Dismissive of this tradition, Ernest Hemingway is reported to have said "I'd rather eat monkey manure than die in Key West."

**Statue of the Lone Sailor**

### The Business of Wrecking

In the late 1700s, the waters off the Keys were fished mainly by Bahamians of British descent, who patrolled the reef in order to salvage shipwrecks. Lookouts, or "Wreckers," at their vantage points would shout "Wreck ashore!" to send salvage vessels racing toward the reef to be the first to claim a grounded ship. In this way, goods from around the world ended up in the Keys; these ranged from basics such as timber to luxury goods like lace, wine, and silver. This opportunistic scavenging came to be known as "wrecking." It grew so popular that in 1825 an act of the US Congress legislated for much tighter control and decreed that only US residents could have such salvage rights. Key West boomed, and in the years that followed, it became the richest city in Florida.

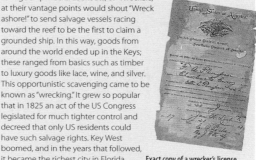

Exact copy of a wrecker's license

### 🔵 Dry Tortugas National Park

**Road map** D5. Monroe Co. 🚌 Key West. ℹ️ 1601 N Roosevelt Blvd, (305) 292-5000. 🌐 **keywestinfo.com**

The Dry Tortugas consists of seven reef islands lying 68 miles (109 km) west of Key West. Of these, Garden Key is the most visited, being the site of **Fort Jefferson**, the largest brick fortification in the US. The hexagonal design included a moat 70 ft (21 m) wide, and walls up to 8 ft (2.5 m) thick and 50 ft (15 m) high.

It was originally envisaged that the fort would control the Florida Straits with a garrison of 1,500 men and 450 cannons.

Beginning in 1845, construction continued for the next 30 years, but the fort was never completed or involved in any battle. During the Civil War, after being occupied by Union forces, it was downgraded to a prison for captured deserters.

The only access is by boat or seaplane. Most people come on organized trips from Key West, which often include an opportunity to snorkel in the crystal-clear water. The bird-watching is especially good between March and October, when the islands are home to migrant and nesting birds, such as boobies, sooty terns, and magnificent frigatebirds with their 7 ft (2 m) wingspan.

Remote Garden Key in Dry Tortugas National Park, occupied by the imposing 19th-century Fort Jefferson

# TRAVELERS' NEEDS

# WHERE TO STAY

Florida has a huge variety of accommodation suitable for all budgets and tastes – from rustic cabins with minimal facilities to luxurious resorts that can cater to every need and whim. In between, guests can choose from hotels, charming guesthouses, intimate inns, motels, fully equipped apartments, cabins, and camp sites, where campers can pitch a tent or hook up an RV or mobile home. Prices tend to fluctuate greatly according to the season, location, and even the day of the week. Local tourist offices can help to provide more detailed information about options in their particular areas.

Lobby of the Eden Roc Resort and Spa in Miami *(see p314)*

## Hotels and Resorts

Hotels range from historic Spanish and stylish Art Deco to the ultra modern. Chain hotels are popular, and have the advantage of being familiar, though prices vary depending upon the location. They range from the upscale Ritz-Carlton and W Hotels through the mid-range Marriott and Hilton.

Several hotels are large complexes often set in immaculately kept grounds – the best ones come with their own private beach. Prices at these are high, but larger properties provide all types of amenities, from swimming pools – sometimes Olympic-sized – to shops and usually a choice of restaurants. Many resorts have excellent sports facilities, including golf courses and tennis courts, and may also provide instructors for individual lessons. Spas and health clubs are increasingly popular, some with services designed to pamper and some offering daily fitness classes. With their well-equipped games rooms, special children's programs, and other facilities, these resorts can be good options for families.

## Bed and Breakfasts

Anyone in search of a more traditional sense of hospitality might choose to stay in a bed and breakfast (B&B). These are often private homes where the owner is the host. Breakfast is usually excellent, with home-made breads and coffee, and guests often eat together in an informal atmosphere.

Any place called an inn tends to be slightly larger and pricier than a B&B and may even have a restaurant. However, it is likely to be friendlier and more intimate than a standard hotel.

The drawbacks with B&Bs are that they may have restrictions with regards to children, or may not provide extra room or beds for them. They may also require a minimum stay during the tourist season. Moreover, since most have just a few rooms, an advance reservation is essential.

Several agencies specialize in arranging B&B accommodation. These include **Florida B&B Inns**, which lists historic establishments across the state, and the **Key West Innkeepers Association**. Regional publications and local tourism guides offered by the **AAA** are useful sources as well.

## How to Reserve

While it is relatively easy to reserve a room at short notice in a hotel of your choice off season, securing a room in season, particularly in Orlando or Miami, may require making a reservation several months in advance. However, given the many options at one's disposal, it is possible to find a room any time of the year, as long as your choice is not only limited to the high-end resorts and luxury hotels.

Reservations can be made online or by phone with a credit card; note that a deposit is often required. To avoid losing a reservation, give advance notice if arriving after 5pm.

Shady gardens and pool typify many plush Florida resorts

◀ The buzzing Lincoln Road Mall in Miami Beach

## Facilities

Competition in Florida's hotel trade is fierce so facilities are generally good. Rooms without a TV, private bath, and air conditioning are extremely rare, even in B&Bs. Most have a refrigerator and desk; some hotels also provide microwaves or kitchenettes. Bedrooms usually have two queen-size beds and can accommodate up to four people.

People with disabilities will be best provided for in a modern, conventional hotel or resort. In addition to elevators, ramps, and pool lifts, a few hotels have rooms designed for people in wheelchairs. Visitors with special needs should inform the hotel when reserving a room.

## Prices

Room rates vary enormously depending on the time of year, with prices in tourist season often 30–50 per cent more than in off season. In south Florida, the high season runs from mid-November to Easter, while in the Panhandle and the Northeast, where it is cooler in winter, hotels charge their highest rates in spring and summer. Wherever you are, however, expect to pay peak rates at Christmas, Easter, school holiday periods, and Thanksgiving. At any time of the year, a room facing the water may cost 25 per cent more, so it is worth asking for the full range of prices.

Winter rates are considerably lower in January after the holidays. Another way to save would be to stay mid-week rather than weekends; even Sunday nights are often less expensive, since many weekenders tend to check out on Sunday.

It is difficult to find even a motel room these days for less than $150 in popular beach locations during high season. Rates are usually calculated per room rather than per person. This means that only a small reduction is made on the cost of a double room when calculating the price of a single guest.

Many hotels offer special deals on their own websites, such as discounts for stays over three or four nights, and package deals including breakfast. A number of hotels also offer discounts for senior citizens and families.

## Hidden Extras

Room rates are generally quoted exclusive of both sales tax *(see p350)* and the so-called resort tax, which is 2–5 per cent of the price of the room (depending on the area). So taxes can add as much as 15 per cent to the rate quoted.

The cost of making phone calls from a hotel room can be exorbitant. A few places offer free local calls from rooms, but as a general rule using your own cell phone is far cheaper. Do consider using free Wi-Fi instead. There are also often charges for receiving faxes.

Many hotels charge for valet parking: a fee of anything from $10 to $30 a day, not including the optional tip for the attendant.

The fashionable Delano Hotel in South Beach, Miami *(see p315)*

Some hotels can also have a hidden resort fee, a charge that covers amenities such as beach chairs and towels, as well as Wi-Fi access. This is an automatic charge, not an option, and can add $30 a day to the bill in some resorts. Be sure to ask before reserving.

Given the hugely inflated price of most hotel breakfasts, guests would do well to go out to a nearby café or diner instead. Be warned too that there are charges for watching certain in-room movies: read the screen before pressing the remote control button.

## Motels

Motels lack charm but are a good budget or last-minute option, particularly during the tourist season. City or town outskirts are classic motel territory. Parking is free and located conveniently near the rooms.

Offerings range from the more upscale Hampton Inns to the budget Days Inn chain. Larger chains may offer free breakfast and amenities including pools, and rooms with a microwave and refrigerator. Feel free to inspect rooms before checking in.

Local tourist offices have lists of available motels, and the AAA regional guides give ratings in their motel listings.

A sumptuous bedroom at the Casa Monica Hotel, St Augustine *(see p319)*

Cabins for rent by the ocean at Bahia Honda in the Keys *(see p301)*

## Accommodation in Orlando

For anyone planning to visit the theme parks, proximity is a major consideration: arriving early is the best way to avoid the worst lines. Waiting in traffic for an hour or more just to get to the park only reduces quality time. Furthermore, staying nearby means that the option to return to the hotel for a break during the day, or when the lines are too long, is available.

Universal Orlando® has on-site hotels, and Walt Disney World® Resorts offers a host of on-site and adjacent options. Rooms at these mega-resorts are costlier, but convenient, and may offer great package deals. However, both Universal and Disney have "good neighbor hotels," which are conveniently located, less expensive, and also offer admission packages to guests.

Lodgings are in big demand at these hotels near the parks and must be reserved six months to a year in advance, especially if visiting at Easter or Christmas. There are so many hotels in Greater Orlando, though, that you need never worry about finding a room. When choosing where to stay, ask how long it takes to get to the parks, whether shuttle buses are available, and when they run.

## Apartment Rentals

Being a much sought-after family destination, apartment accommodation is popular among those visiting Florida. Condominiums (condos), consisting of complete apartments, are available for rent and are found mainly on beach resorts. They may seem expensive ($1,200 per week is on the low side), but can be good value especially for large families. **TripAdvisor**, **HomeAway** and **Airbnb** are among the many agencies that arrange condo rentals and often organize rentals of a private apartment or a house.

Rooms with cooking facilities are known as efficiencies, and are available in some hotels and motels. These may cost more than standard rooms but enable families to avoid expensive restaurant meals. In rural areas efficiency cabins can be found attached to campgrounds.

Visitors can also choose to stay in a private home for free by doing a house swap. To arrange this, enroll as a member of a home-exchange organization; **Guest to Guest** and others have members worldwide and use social media to connect.

## Camping

Florida has a huge number of camp sites. These range from the basic, where there may be no running water, to the luxurious, with swimming pools, shops, restaurants, and boat rentals. RV parks have space for tent campers as well, and some rent out trailers and cabins too.

Florida has dozens of state parks with camping grounds. In addition, some 20 parks also offer comfortable cabin accommodation that is among the state's most reasonable lodgings, often costing less than $100 for cabins that can accommodate a family of four. These range from rustic with shared bath lodges, to fully equipped modern facilities. The **Florida State Parks** has a complete roster with pictures on its website.

State parks charge $10–25 per site, while charges at a private campground increase to about $40 per night. Most sites take advance reservations, but state parks hold back some spaces for people who arrive on the day.

The **Florida Association of RV Parks and Campgrounds (FARVC)** produces the free *Florida Camping Directory*, listing its licensed members – copies can be ordered online directly from the FARVC website. Additionally, **Kampgrounds of**

One of the luxurious rooms at the Sandestin Resort, Destin *(see p320)*

**America (KOA)** runs a number of good quality sites in Florida and issues its own directory.

## Youth Hostels

Florida has several youth hostels, some in South Beach and some in Orlando. The Florida chapter of **Hostelling International** can also provide useful information.

Facilities can be excellent, sometimes with swimming pools and game rooms, and rates are very low: around $15–$25 per night. Reserve ahead in tourist season to avoid disappointment.

## Traveling with Children

Most hotels provide basic facilities such as cribs (cots) for families – a babysitting service may be available, too. Some places, however, particularly in Orlando and popular beach locations, place children higher

The Honeymoon Cottage at The Moorings Village, Islamorada *(see p323)*

A trailer in a tranquil spot in a Panhandle park

on their list of priorities and provide children's swimming pools and play areas. Some also have children's programs, with organized activities, though these may cost extra.

Most hotels do not charge for children younger than 12 sharing the room with their parents; in some cases this could be extended to those under 18. Some rooms have a sofa that folds out into a bed; otherwise an extra bed may be set up for a small additional fee.

### Recommended Hotels

The hotels listed in the following pages are a sample of the many available, chosen for their special value, facilities, and location. From five-star luxury resorts to boutique hotels, humble B&Bs and inns, to the standard modern hotels,

they are all characterful and usually in great locations. Entries are listed by region, beginning with Miami.

Since there are too many motels to be included; see local tourism guides for a comprehensive list. While many beachfront hotels call themselves resorts, those listed here as resorts have extensive tennis facilities and/or golf in addition to a beach and pool. Spas and exercise facilities are available in even moderately priced hotels these days. Rates are for a standard room for two during high season, and will be less the rest of the year. Taxes will add 13 per cent to all rates.

The entries marked as DK Choice are those that are judged exceptional within their categories. The majority of these are quite popular, so be sure to reserve well ahead.

## DIRECTORY

### Bed and Breakfasts

**AAA Auto Club South**
W aaasouth.com

**Florida B&B Inns**
Tel (561) 223-9550.
W florida-inns.com

**Key West Innkeepers Association**
316A Simonton St,
Key West, FL 33040.
Tel (305) 295-9500.
W keywestinns.com

### Apartment Rentals

**Airbnb**
W airbnb.com

**Guest to Guest**
Tel (203) 808-3809.
W guesttoguest.com/en

**HomeAway**
W homeaway.com

**TripAdvisor**
W tripadvisor.com

### Camping

**FARVC**
1340 Vickers Dr,
Tallahassee,
FL 32303.
Tel (800) 395-2267.
W farvc.org

**Florida State Parks**
3900 Commonwealth
Blvd, Tallahassee,
FL 32399.
Tel (850) 245-2118.
W myflorida.com

### KOA
PO Box 30558, Billings,
MT 59114.
Tel (406) 248-7444.
W koa.com/where/fl

### Youth Hostels

**Hostelling International**
8401 Colesville Rd, Suite 600, Silverspring, MD 20910.
Tel (240) 650-2100.
W hiusa.org

# Where to Stay

## Miami

### Miami Beach

**Aqua** $$
Modern Map 2 F2
*1530 Collins Ave, 33139*
**Tel** *(305) 538-4361*
**w** aquamiami.com
Well-equipped modern rooms in
an Art Deco building. Fabulous
terrace and tropical garden.

**Clay Hotel** $$
Historic Map 2 E3
*1438 Washington Ave, 33139*
**Tel** *(305) 250-0759*
**w** clayhotel.com
Built in the 1930s, this atmospheric hotel has bright rooms with
modern decor, some with balconies.

**Freehand Miami** $$
Hostel **Road map** F1
*2727 Indian Creek Dr, 33140*
**Tel** *(305) 531-2727*
**w** thefreehand.com
A block away from the beach, this
stylish hostel offers double and
dorm rooms. Pool and bar on site.

**The Kent** $$
Historic Map 2 F3
*1131 Collins Ave, 33139*
**Tel** *(305) 604-5068*
**w** thekenthotel.com
With a fabulous Art Deco exterior,
this hotel offers comfortable
rooms with contemporary decor.

**Lord Balfour** $$
Boutique Map 2 E4
*350 Ocean Dr, 33139*
**Tel** *(305) 673-0401*
**w** lordbalfourmiami.com
Lord Balfour offers accommodation
with British-inspired, modern
decor and contemporary art.

Relaxing terrace with pool at Clinton Hotel,
Miami Beach

**The Marlin Hotel** $$
Boutique Map 2 E4
*1200 Collins Ave, 33139*
**Tel** *(305) 695-3000*
**w** themarlinhotel.com
Steps from the beach, this Art
Deco landmark has been fully
redesigned. It offers luxury, and
sophisticated dining.

**Nassau Suite Hotel** $$
Historic Map 2 F3
*1414 Collins Ave, 33139*
**Tel** *(305) 532-0043*
**w** nassausuite.com
Built in 1937, this landmark hotel
provides a full-service experience.
Suites are equipped with kitchens.

**The Albion** $$$
Historic Map 2 F2
*1650 James Ave, 33139*
**Tel** *(305) 913-1000*
**w** rubellhotels.com
This beautiful 1939 building has
been decorated in minimalist
tones and trendy furnishings.

### DK Choice

**The Angler's** $$$
Luxury Map 2 E4
*660 Washington Ave, 33139*
**Tel** *(305) 534-9600*
**w** theanglersresort.com
Stay in a spacious suite, studio,
or villa in one of the four majes-
tic buildings that make up this
Mediterranean Revival complex.
Relax in the private gardens,
Jacuzzis, or rooftop terraces. Spa
treatments are also available.

**The Beach Plaza Hotel** $$$
Boutique Map 2 F3
*1401 Collins Ave, 33139*
**Tel** *(305) 531-6421*
**w** beachplazahotel.com
Art Deco hotel with large, tropically
themed rooms, a courtyard bar,
and evening wine reception.

**Cadet Hotel** $$$
Historic Map 2 F2
*1701 James Ave, 33139*
**Tel** *(305) 672-6688*
**w** cadethotel.com
Once home to Captain Clark Gable's
cadets, this hotel has comfortable
rooms, luxurious suites, and a spa.

**Celino** $$$
Luxury Map 2 E4
*640 Ocean Dr, 33139*
**Tel** *(786) 574-4090*
**w** thecelinohotel.com
A modern, loft-style luxury hotel,
with a rooftop glass-bottomed
swimming pool.

### Price Guide

Prices are based on one night's stay in
high season for a standard double room,
inclusive of service charges and taxes.

| | |
|---|---|
| $ | up to $100 |
| $$ | $100 to $200 |
| $$$ | over $200 |

**Clinton Hotel** $$$
Boutique Map 2 E4
*825 Washington Ave, 33139*
**Tel** *(305) 405-5070*
**w** clintonsouthbeach.com
Modernist building with con-
temporary interior design. Some
suites have balconies with a spa.

**The Delano** $$$
Luxury Map 2 F2
*1685 Collins Ave, 33139*
**Tel** *(305) 672-2000*
**w** delano-hotel.com
This Philippe Starck-inspired
hotel, famous for its decor and
celebrity clientele. Crisp all-white
rooms, and a great pool and bar.

**Eden Roc Miami Beach** $$$
Boutique **Road map** F5
*4525 Collins Ave, 33140*
**Tel** *(305) 531-0000*
**w** edenrocmiami.com
Elegant Art Deco landmark with
spacious rooms, a lavish pool, and
beach. Wonderful ocean views.

**Fontainebleau Hotel** $$$
Resort **Road map** F5
*4441 Collins Ave, 33140*
**Tel** *(305) 538-2000*
**w** fontainebleau.com
Fabulously retro, this hotel
features Las Vegas-style glitzy
decor. Spectacular pool and spa.

**Hotel Astor** $$$
Luxury Map 2 E3
*956 Washington Ave, 33139*
**Tel** *(305) 531-8081*
**w** hotelastor.com
The sleek Astor has large suites,
warm decor, and high quality linen.
It has a popular restaurant, too.

**Hotel St. Augustine** $$$
Boutique Map 2 E4
*347 Washington Ave, 33139*
**Tel** *(305) 532-0570*
**w** hotelstaugustine.com
A chic hotel and spa with loft-
style rooms and steam baths.

**The Hotel of South Beach** $$$
Luxury Map 2 E4
*801 Collins Ave, 33139*
**Tel** *(305) 531-2222*
**w** thehotelofsouthbeach.com
Decorated by fashion designer
Todd Oldham. All accommodation
has fantastic balcony views.

**Impala Hotel** **$$$**
Boutique **Map** 2 F3
*1228 Collins Ave, 33139*
**Tel** *(305) 673-2021*
w impala-miami.com
Mediterranean-style intimate
boutique hotel with Murano glass
fixtures and custom furnishings.

**The Mondrian** **$$$**
Boutique **Map** 2 D3
*1100 West Ave, 33139*
**Tel** *(305) 514-1500*
w morganshotelgroups.com
This glamorously designed hotel,
on the waterfront, is the ultimate
in comfort and stunning views.

**National Hotel** **$$$**
Historic **Map** 2 F2
*1677 Collins Ave, 33139*
**Tel** *(305) 532-2311*
w nationalhotel.com
Quiet Art Deco classic with
an authentic 1940s vibe, and
a luxurious swimming pool.

**The Palms Hotel & Spa** **$$$**
Luxury **Road map** F5
*3025 Collins Ave, 33140*
**Tel** *(305) 534-0505*
w thepalmshotel.com
With private gardens leading
to the beach, The Palms offers
guests a quiet, relaxed ambience.

**Pelican Hotel** **$$$**
Boutique **Map** 2 F4
*826 Ocean Dr, 33139*
**Tel** *(305) 673-3373*
w pelicanhotel.com
Quirky hotel with themed rooms
including a Viva Las Vegas and a
Tarzan Jungle Room.

**Ritz-Carlton South Beach** **$$$**
Luxury **Map** 2 F2
*1 Lincoln Rd, 33139*
**Tel** *(786) 276-4000*
w ritzcarlton.com
Experience utter indulgence at
the Ritz-Carlton. Some rooms
have sea views, and there are two
opulently large swimming pools.

**The Sagamore** **$$$**
Luxury **Map** 2 F2
*1671 Collins Ave, 33139*
**Tel** *(305) 535-8088*
w sagamorehotel.com
Indulgent hotel famed for its
stunning art collection. All rooms
have a kitchenette and spa bath.

**The Setai** **$$$**
Luxury **Map** 2 F1
*2001 Collins Ave, 33139*
**Tel** *(305) 520-6000*
w thesetaihotel.com
This oceanfront hotel has
gorgeous accommodation
as well as world-class dining
and spa facilities.

The Spanish-style exterior of Biltmore Hotel in Coral Gables

**Townhouse Hotel** **$$$**
Modern **Map** 2 F1
*150 20th St, 33139*
**Tel** *(305) 534-3800*
w townhousehotel.com
Chic hotel offering simple rooms
with modern decor, a rooftop
bar, and sushi restaurant.

**Villa Paradiso** **$$$**
Modern **Map** 2 F3
*1415 Collins Ave, 33139*
**Tel** *(305) 532-0616*
w villaparadisohotel
Former apartment building with
bright, airy suites and studios,
as well as a tranquil garden.

## DK Choice

**W South Beach** **$$$**
Luxury **Map** 2 F1
*2201 Collins Ave, 33139*
**Tel** *(305) 938-3000*
w wsouthbeach.com
This stunning flagship of W
Hotels has spacious rooms with
balconies, kitchenettes, and
ocean vistas. Guests are spoiled
for choice between the private
beach, swimming pool, rooftop
tennis, basketball courts, and
many dining options.

**Whitelaw Hotel** **$$$**
Boutique **Map** 2 E4
*808 Collins Ave, 33139*
**Tel** *(305) 398-7000*
w whitelawhotel.com
Whitelaw's snug, quirky rooms
have a lively vibe to match its
motto of "clean sheets, hot
water, stiff drinks".

## Downtown and Little Havana

**Conrad Hotel** **$$$**
Modern **Map** 4 E3
*1395 Brickell Ave, 33131*
**Tel** *(305) 503-6500*
w conradmiami.com
This 36-story tower building offers
fantastic views from most of its
comfortably furnished rooms.

**The Four Seasons** **$$$**
Luxury **Map** 4 E3
*1435 Brickell Ave, 33131*
**Tel** *(305) 358-3535*
w fourseasons.com/miami
Business-oriented skyscraper
favored by jet-setters. Fantastic
accommodation and skyline views.

**Mandarin Oriental** **$$$**
Luxury **Map** 4 F2
*500 Brickell Key Dr, 33131*
**Tel** *(305) 913-8288*
w mandarinoriental.com
Frequented by celebrities, this
extravagant hotel boasts lavish
rooms, a spa, and five-star dining.

## Coral Gables and Coconut Grove

**Courtyard by Marriott** **$$**
Modern **Map** 5 C1
*2051 LeJeune Rd, 33134*
**Tel** *(305) 443-2301*
w marriott.com
This contemporary building has
comfortable rooms with traditional
decor and a rooftop pool.

**Hotel St. Michel** **$$**
Boutique **Map** 5 C1
*162 Alcazar Ave, 33134*
**Tel** *(305) 444-1666*
w hotelstmichel.com
No two rooms are alike at this
hotel with an old-world ambience
and traditional furnishings.

## DK Choice

**Biltmore Hotel** **$$$**
Resort **Map** 5 A2
*1200 Anastasia Ave, 33134*
**Tel** *(305) 445-1926*
w biltmorehotel.com
Large rooms and fabulous suites
match the flair of this luxurious
Spanish-style 1920s landmark,
complete with a Giralda-inspired
bell tower. Facilities include a
golf course, tennis courts, a gigantic pool, and four restaurants.

**For more information on types of hotels** *see pages 310–13*

**Mayfair Hotel and Spa** $$$
Boutique     **Map** 6 F4
3000 Florida Ave, 33133
**Tel** (305) 441-0000
W mayfairhotelandspa.com
With gorgeous Art Nouveau detailing, the Mayfair has bright, tastefully furnished rooms with private balconies. Pets welcome.

**Ritz-Carlton Coconut Grove** $$$
Luxury     **Map** 6 F4
3300 SW 27th Ave, 33133
**Tel** (305) 644-4680
W ritzcarlton.com
Expect stunning accommodation and exceptional service at this intimate tropical retreat that overlooks the bay.

## Farther Afield

**Ritz-Carlton Key Biscayne** $$$
Resort     **Road map** F5
455 Grand Bay Dr, Key Biscayne, 33149
**Tel** (305) 365-4500
W ritzcarlton.com
This luxurious hotel has a private beach and excellent spa facilities.

**Turnberry Isle Resort** $$$
Resort     **Road map** F5
19999 W Country Club Dr, Aventura, 33180
**Tel** (305) 932-6200
W turnberryislemiami.com
This expansive holiday escape has a spa, a private beach, and tennis and golf courses.

**The Vagabond Hotel** $$$
Boutique     **Road map** 4 F1
7301 Biscayne Blvd., Miami, 33138
**Tel** (305) 400-8420
W thevagabondhotel.com
Located near Wynwood, this beautifully restored mid-century modern hotel, has a retro-luxe vibe that recalls the Rat-Pack glitz.

## The Gold and Treasure Coasts

**BOCA RATON: Ocean Lodge** $$
B&B     **Road map** F4
531 N Ocean Blvd, 33432
**Tel** (561) 395-7772
W oceanlodgeflorida.com
Two-story upscale motel located across from a beach, featuring large rooms with kitchenettes.

**BOCA RATON:**
**Boca Raton Resort** $$$
Resort     **Road map** F4
501 E Camino Real, 33432
**Tel** (561) 447-3000
W bocaresort.com
Exquisite historic building designed by architect Addison

Mizner, this retreat has kids' camp facilities, golf, boating, and a private beach. Charming rooms.

**CLEWISTON: Clewiston Inn** $$
Historic     **Road map** F4
108 Royal Palm Ave, 33440
**Tel** (863) 983-8151
W clewistoninn.com
This inn, with reasonably priced rooms and a simple decor, is said to be the oldest in the Lake Okeechobee area.

**DELRAY BEACH:**
**Sundy House** $$$
Boutique     **Road map** F4
106 S Swinton Ave, 33444
**Tel** (561) 272-5678
W sundyhouse.com
Beautiful historic cottages in a garden setting, with homely decor, uniquely themed rooms, and a freshwater swimming pond.

**FORT LAUDERDALE:**
**The Hotel Deauville** $
Hostel     **Road map** F4
2916 N Ocean Blvd, 33308
**Tel** (954) 568-5000
W thedeauvillehotel.com
Clean dorms and private rooms with communal kitchen and pool. Located close to the beach.

**FORT LAUDERDALE:**
**The Atlantic Hotel & Spa** $$$
Luxury     **Road map** F4
601 Fort Lauderdale Beach Blvd, 33304
**Tel** (954) 567-8020
W atlantichotelfl.com
Beachfront hotel that boasts large rooms with kitchenettes and balconies. There is also a pool and spa.

**FORT LAUDERDALE: Harbor Beach Marriott Resort & Spa** $$$
Luxury     **Road map** F4
3030 Holiday Dr, 33316
**Tel** (954) 525-4000
W marriottharborbeach.com
Located on a secluded beach, this Marriott hotel has attractive rooms, a large pool, and a spa.

**FORT LAUDERDALE:**
**The Pillars Hotel** $$$
Luxury     **Road map** F4
111 N Birch Rd, 33304
**Tel** (954) 467-9639
W pillarshotel.com
Richly furnished hideaway on the Intracoastal Waterway. Gorgeous pool and an extensive library.

**FORT LAUDERDALE:**
**Riverside Hotel** $$$
Historic     **Road map** F4
620 E Las Olas Blvd, 33301
**Tel** (954) 467-0671
W riversidehotel.com
Downtown 1930s landmark with great rooms, a palm-fringed pool, a fitness room, and a terrace.

**FORT LAUDERDALE:**
**W Fort Lauderdale** $$$
Luxury     **Road map** F4
401 N Fort Lauderdale Beach Blvd, 33304
**Tel** (954) 414-8200
W wfortlauderdalehotel.com
Trendy beachfront hotel with stylish rooms and a popular bar.

**HOBE SOUND: Jonathan Dickinson State Park** $
Lodge     **Road map** F4
16450 SE Federal Hwy, 33455
**Tel** (772) 546-2771
W floridastateparks.com
Located near Loxahatchee River. Cabins with kitchens and other modern amenities, accommodating up to six people.

**HOLLYWOOD: Diplomat Resort** $$$
Resort     **Road map** F4
3555 S Ocean Dr, 33019
**Tel** (954) 602-6000
W diplomatresort.com
Glitzy hotel with a lagoon pool with two waterfalls, an oceanfront spa, and a private beach.

The exterior of Seminole Hard Rock Hotel and Casino and its lagoon-style pool

The playful interior of a suite in PGA National Resort, Palm Beach Gardens

### HOLLYWOOD: Seminole Hard Rock Hotel and Casino $$$
Luxury     **Road map** F4
1 Seminole Way, 33314
**Tel** (954) 327-7625
W seminolehardrockhollywood.com
Spacious rooms and a lavish pool, though the casino is the main attraction for choosing this hotel.

### JUPITER: La Quinta Inn $$
Motel     **Road map** F4
34 Fisherman's Way, 33477
**Tel** (561) 575-7201
W laquintainn.com
Traditionally furnished rooms and modern facilities, including a gym and pool.

### LAUDERDALE BY THE SEA: Beachside Village Resort $$
Motel     **Road map** F4
4564 N Ocean Dr, 33308
**Tel** (954) 652-1216
W thebeachsidevillageresort.com
Relaxed resort with two pools, rooftop deck, kayaks, tennis court, and a pet-friendly reputation.

### NORTH HUTCHINSON ISLAND: The Mellon Patch Inn $$
B&B     **Road map** F3
3601 N Hwy A1A, Fort Pierce, 34949
**Tel** (772) 462-6699
W themellonpatchinn.com
Small, welcoming cottage-style B&B operating since 1949. Simple furnishings and good breakfasts.

### PALM BEACH: Palm Beach Historic Inn $$
Inn     **Road map** F4
365 S County Rd, 33480
**Tel** (561) 832-4009
W palmbeachhistoricinn.com
This antique-filled historic inn offers comfortable rooms within walking distance of the beach.

### PALM BEACH: Chesterfield Hotel $$$
Historic     **Road map** F4
363 Cocoanut Row, 33480
**Tel** (561) 659-5800
W chesterfieldpb.com
A landmark hotel with gorgeous rooms and a shaded courtyard,

epitomising the relaxed Palm Beach lifestyle. Do not miss the elaborate high tea.

### PALM BEACH: The Colony $$$
Luxury     **Road map** F4
156 Hammon Ave, 33480
**Tel** (561) 655-5430
W thecolonypalmbeach.com
Elegant, vibrant rooms and suites with British-colonial decor.

### PALM BEACH: Four Seasons Palm Beach $$$
Resort     **Road map** F4
2800 S Ocean Blvd, 33480
**Tel** (561) 582-2800
W fourseasons.com
Elegant beach haven with sleek furnishings, fine dining, a bar and lounge, as well as sports facilities.

### PALM BEACH GARDENS: PGA National Resort $$$
Resort     **Road map** F4
400 Ave of the Champions, 33418
**Tel** (561) 627-1800
W pgaresort.com
Famed championship golf courses, 19 tennis courts, and a lavish spa are the highlights of this resort. It also has nine restaurants, each with different culinary concepts.

### PORT ST. LUCIE: Club Med Sandpiper Bay $$$
Resort     **Road map** F3
4500 SE Pine Valley St, 34952
**Tel** (772) 398-5100
W clubmed.com
Family-oriented, all-inclusive resort with golf and tennis academies, and beach volleyball.

### SEBASTIAN: Floridana Beach Motel $
Motel     **Road map** F3
6580 S Hwy A1A, Melbourne Beach, 32951
**Tel** (321) 726-6560
W motelfloridana.com
Budget lodging, some with kitchenettes. The owner can show those keen on fishing the best local spots. Plenty of facilities for surfing and sunbathing.

### SINGER ISLAND: Hilton Singer Island Resort $$$
Resort     **Road map** F3
3700 N Ocean Dr, 33404
**Tel** (561) 848-3888
W hilton.com
This elegant establishment offers comfortable rooms with sea views, and a private beach.

### SOUTH HUTCHINSON ISLAND: Dockside Inn $$
Inn     **Road map** F3
1160 Seaway Dr, 34949
**Tel** (772) 468-3555
W docksideinn.com
Lovely inn with nautically-themed rooms, waterfront balconies, five fishing piers, and a small marina.

### VERO BEACH: The Driftwood Resort $$
Historic     **Road map** F3
3150 Ocean Dr, 32963
**Tel** (772) 231-0550
W verobeachdriftwood.com
Rustic-chic accommodation in nine cabins with balconies and all the modern amenities.

### VERO BEACH: Islander Inn $$
Motel     **Road map** F3
3101 Ocean Dr, 32963
**Tel** (772) 231-4431
W islanderinnverobeach.com
This inn – with its ceiling fans, wicker furniture, courtyard, and pool – exudes an old-Florida feel.

### VERO BEACH: Disney's Vero Beach Resort $$$
Resort     **Road map** F3
9250 Island Grove Terrace, 32963
**Tel** (772) 234-2000
W disneybeachresorts.com
Family resort with studios and villas, a Mickey-shaped pool, mini-golf, and plenty of kids' activities.

### WEST PALM BEACH: Hotel Biba $$
Boutique     **Road Map** F4
320 Belvedere Rd, 33407
**Tel** (561) 832-0094
W hotelbiba.com
A 1940s motor lodge re-imagined with flair. The rooms are comfortable and with colorful decor.

## Orlando and the Space Coast

### CELEBRATION: Bohemian Hotel $$
Inn     **Road map** E3
700 Bloom St, 34747
**Tel** (407) 566-6000
W celebrationhotel.com
Elegantly furnished inn located in a lakeside setting. Great option away from the Disney crowds.

**For more information on types of hotels** see pages 310–13

**COCOA BEACH:**
**Doubletree Hotel** $$
Modern **Road map** F3
*2080 Atlantic Ave, 32931*
**Tel** *(321) 783-9222*
W cocoabeachdoubletree.com
Comfortable oceanfront spot
with snug rooms and freshly
baked cookies on arrival.

**COCOA BEACH:**
**The Inn at Cocoa Beach** $$
Inn **Road map** F3
*4300 Ocean Blvd, 32931*
**Tel** *(321) 799-3460*
W theinnatcocoabeach.com
Located by the beach, with each
room individually styled. Fantastic
wine and cheese evenings.

**KISSIMMEE: Quality Inn & Suites** $
Motel **Road map** E3
*2945 Entry Point Blvd, 34747*
**Tel** *(407) 390-0204*
W choicehotels.com
Budget choice near the Disney
parks. Clean rooms, with free
breakfast and guest laundry.

**KISSIMMEE: Gaylord Palms**
**Resort** $$$
Resort **Road map** E3
*6000 W Osceola Pkwy, 34747*
**Tel** *(407) 586-0000*
W marriott.com
Lavish resort with its own water
park. The atrium contains re-cre-
ations of major Florida landmarks,
splendid gardens, and pools.

**NEW SMYRNA BEACH:**
**Riverview Hotel** $$$
Historic **Road map** E2
*103 Flager Ave, 32169*
**Tel** *(386) 428-5858*
W riverviewhotel.com
Overlooking the Halifax River, this
charming Victorian hotel has com-
fortable rooms, a pool, and a spa.

**ORLANDO: Grand**
**Bohemian** $$$
Luxury **Road map** E3
*325 S Orange Ave, 32801*
**Tel** *(407) 313-9000*
W grandbohemianhotel.com
One of the finer hotels in
downtown Orlando, featuring
great rooms, fine art, a pool, and
a jazz-themed bar.

## DK Choice

**ORLANDO: Villas of**
**Grand Cypress** $$$
Resort **Road map** E3
*1 N Jacaranda, 32836*
**Tel** *(407) 239-4700*
W grandcypress.com
This lush, beautifully landscaped
complex has extravagant villas
with kitchens, patios, and
bathrooms with Roman tubs.
Choose from four golf courses, a
racquet club, climbing wall, and
pools with waterfalls and slides.
Free shuttle to the theme parks.

**UNIVERSAL ORLANDO®:**
**Hyatt Place Universal** $$
Modern **Road map** E3
*5895 Caravan Court, 32819*
**Tel** *(407) 351-0627*
W orlandouniversal.place.hyatt.com
Located near three major theme
parks. The large suites are tastefully
decorated and have kitchenettes.

**UNIVERSAL ORLANDO®:**
**Hard Rock Hotel** $$$
Luxury **Road map** E3
*5800 Universal Blvd, 32819*
**Tel** *(407) 503-2000*
W hardrockhotelorlando.com
This Hard Rock flagship has,
as expected, a fun rock and roll
theme. Spacious rooms and
spa facilities.

## DK Choice

**UNIVERSAL ORLANDO®:**
**Loews Portofino**
**Bay Hotel** $$$
Luxury **Road map** E3
*5601 Universal Blvd, 32819*
**Tel** *(407) 503-1000*
W loewshotels.com
A beautifully re-created Italian
village, complete with a boat-
filled waterfront and festive
piazza, this extravagant complex
has spacious rooms, three pools,
and spa facilities. Enjoy the hotel's
exclusive theme park benefits,
such as early admission and
skipping the regular lines.

**WALT DISNEY WORLD®:**
**Disney's All Star Resorts** $$
Hotel **Road map** E3
*World Dr & Osceola Pkwy, Lake
Buena Vista, 32830*
**Tel** *(407) 934-7639*
W disneyworld.com
Disney's least expensive lodgings.
Small rooms with three themed
towers and lots of fun activities.

**WALT DISNEY WORLD®: Disney's**
**Caribbean Beach Resort** $$
Resort **Road map** E3
*900 Cayman Way, Lake Buena Vista,
32830*
**Tel** *(407) 934-3400*
W disneyworld.com
Five island "villages" set around a
huge lake, with pirate boats and
mini-golf. Fantastic experience.

**WALT DISNEY WORLD®: Disney's**
**Coronado Springs Resort** $$
Resort **Road map** E3
*1000 W Buena Vista Dr, 32830*
**Tel** *(407) 939-1000*
W disneyworld.com
A luxury haven, with a Mayan
pyramid pool and evening camp-
fires. Mini-golf and fitness center.

**WALT DISNEY WORLD®: Disney's**
**Port Orleans Resort** $$
Resort **Road map** E3
*2201 Orleans Dr, Lake Buena Vista,
32830*
**Tel** *(407) 934-5000*
W disneyworld.com
Wrought-iron balconies, horse-
drawn carriages, a lagoon lake, and
a fantastic New Orleans ambience.

**WALT DISNEY WORLD®:**
**Animal Kingdom Lodge** $$$
Luxury **Road map** E3
*2901 Osceola Pkwy, Lake Buena
Vista, 32830*
**Tel** *(407) 938-3000*
W disneyworld.com
Luxury safari lodge with African-
style decor and art, offering
views of zebras and giraffes.

The large swimming pool and opulent terrace at Grand Bohemian in Orlando

## The Northeast

### DK Choice

**AMELIA ISLAND: Omni Amelia Island Plantation $$$**
Resort      Road map E1
*6800 First Coast Hwy, 32035*
**Tel** *(904) 261-6161*
**W** omnihotels.com
This sprawling retreat has everything needed for an active vacation: a beach, indoor and out-door pools, golf courses, tennis center, and nature trails. Comfort-able rooms offer splendid views.

**DAYTONA BEACH: The Villa Inn    $$**
B&B      Road map E2
*801 N Peninsula Dr, 32118*
**Tel** *(386) 248-2020*
**W** thevillabb.com
Spanish-style mansion with elegant European furnishings, antiques, and a walled garden. Guests must be aged 16 or older.

**DAYTONA BEACH: Hilton Daytona Beach    $$$**
Luxury      Road map E2
*100 N Atlantic Ave, 32118*
**Tel** *(386) 254-8200*
**W** daytonahilton.com
Oceanfront high-rise with attractive rooms and great views. There is also a kids' pool, a special area for activities, and numerous fine dining options.

**DAYTONA BEACH: The Plaza Resort & Spa    $$$**
Historic      Road map E2
*600 N Atlantic Ave, 32118*
**Tel** *(386) 255-4471*
**W** plazaresortandspa.com
Well-refurbished beachfront hotel featuring traditionally furnished rooms with kitchenettes. There is a spa and a relaxing steam room.

**DAYTONA BEACH: The Shores Resort & Spa    $$$**
Resort      Road map E2
*2637 S Atlantic Ave, 32118*
**Tel** *(386) 767-7350*
**W** shoresresort.com
Fantastic resort with Atlantic or Intracoastal views from rooms. Free shuttle to attractions.

**FERNANDINA BEACH: Hampton Inn & Suites    $$**
Historic      Road map E1
*19 S 2nd St, 32034*
**Tel** *(904) 491-4911*
**W** hamptoninn3.hilton.com
Located on the harbor and in the heart of old town. Elegant rooms, breakfast included. Pet-friendly.

Stylish Spanish decor at Casa Monica Hotel, St Augustine

### DK Choice

**FERNANDINA BEACH: Elizabeth Pointe Lodge    $$$**
B&B      Road map E1
*98 S Fletcher Ave, 32034*
**Tel** *(904) 277-4851*
**W** elizabethpointelodge.com
Elizabeth Pointe is an award-winning, Nantucket-style shingled beach house with gorgeous ocean views from the wide porch and windows. Offers elegantly decorated rooms, scrumptious breakfasts, evening wine and *hors d'oeuvres*.

**JACKSONVILLE: Hyatt Regency Riverfront    $$**
Modern      Road map E1
*225 E Coastline Dr, 32202*
**Tel** *(904) 588-1234*
**W** jacksonville.hyatt.com
Modern high-rise by the Riverwalk with comfortable rooms, a roof-top pool, and a spa.

**JACKSONVILLE: The Omni    $$$**
Modern      Road map E1
*245 Water St, 32202*
**Tel** *(904) 355-6664*
**W** omnihotels.com
High-rise with spectacular views of the river and bridges, the hotel has a sophisticated bar and restaurant.

**NEPTUNE BEACH: Seahorse Oceanfront Inn    $$**
Motel      Road map E1
*120 Atlantic Blvd, 32266*
**Tel** *(904) 246-2175*
**W** jacksonvilleoceanfronthotel.com
Old-fashioned motel with spacious rooms and ocean-front balconies and patios. Complimentary breakfast.

**PONTE VEDRA BEACH: Ponte Vedra Inn    $$$**
Historic      Road map E1
*200 Ponte Vedra Blvd, 32082*
**Tel** *(904) 285-1111*
**W** pontevedra.com
A landmark since 1928, this five-star resort has Spanish-style decor, beautiful rooms, and a golf course.

**ST. AUGUSTINE: The Pirate Haus Inn    $**
Hostel      Road map E1
*32 Treasury St, 32084*
**Tel** *(904) 808-1999*
**W** piratehaus.com
Popular budget inn with doubles, family rooms, bunk dorms, and an unlimited pancake breakfast.

**ST. AUGUSTINE: Best Western Bayfront Inn    $$**
Historic      Road map E1
*16 Avenida Menedez, 32084*
**Tel** *(904) 824-4482*
**W** bestwesternbayfront staugustine.com
This hotel has comfortable rooms with modern amenities and a pool overlooking Matanzas Bay.

**ST. AUGUSTINE: Casa de Solana    $$**
Historic      Road map E1
*21 Aviles St, 32094*
**Tel** *(904) 824-3555*
**W** casadesolana.com
This inn has homely rooms with British-Colonial decor and fireplaces. Lavish breakfasts.

**ST. AUGUSTINE: Victorian House    $$**
Historic      Road map E1
*11 Cadiz St, 32084*
**Tel** *(904) 824-5214*
**W** victorianhousebnb.com
This 1897 charming Victorian hotel has eclectic decor and generous breakfasts.

### DK Choice

**ST. AUGUSTINE: Casa Monica Hotel    $$$**
Historic      Road map E1
*95 Cordova St, 32084*
**Tel** *(904) 827-1888*
**W** casamonica.com
Old Spanish charm pervades in this restored 1888 beauty, from the frescoed lobby to the atmospheric guest rooms and the acoustic guitar music in the Cobalt lounge. The rooms have modern amenities, and the pool deck is a welcome private haven.

**For more information on types of hotels** *see pages 310–13*

Spectacular pool and magnificent beach house at Watercolor Inn, Santa Rosa Beach

# The Panhandle

### APALACHICOLA: Coombs House Inn $$$
Inn                    Road map B1
80 6th St, 32320
**Tel** (850) 653-9199
Ⓦ coombshouseinn.com
Charming Victorian houses with antique furniture and four-poster beds in the rooms.

### APALACHICOLA: Gibson Inn $$$
Inn                    Road map B1
51 Ave C, 32320
**Tel** (850) 653-2191
Ⓦ gibsoninn.com
Built in 1907, this stunning inn, featuring wraparound porches and great period furnishings, is a local landmark. Free breakfasts.

### DESTIN: Summer Place Inn $$
Inn                    Road map A1
14047 Emerald Coast Pkwy, 32541
**Tel** (850) 650-8003
Ⓦ summerplaceinn.com
Well-appointed rooms with modern amenities. Enjoy a selection of pools and free breakfasts.

### DESTIN: Sandestin Resort $$$
Resort                 Road Map A1
9300 Emerald Coast Pkwy, 32541
**Tel** (850) 267-8000
Ⓦ sandestin.com
Range of lodgings from cottages to high-rise accommodation. Golf, tennis, pools, beach, and a zip line.

### FORT WALTON BEACH: Aunt Martha's B&B $$
B&B                    Road map A1
315 Shell Ave, 32548
**Tel** (850) 243-6702
Ⓦ auntmarthasbedandbreakfast.com
Resembling an old Florida beach house. Charming rooms with views and big Southern breakfasts.

### FORT WALTON BEACH: Ramada Plaza Beach Resort $$
Modern                 Road map A1
1500 E Miracle Strip Pkwy, 32548
**Tel** (850) 243-9161
Ⓦ ramadafwb.com
A beach, waterfall, grotto pool, and playground. Comfortable rooms.

### FORT WALTON BEACH: Holiday Inn $$$
Luxury                 Road map A1
1299 Miracle Strip Pkwy, 32548
**Tel** (877) 859-5095
Ⓦ hifwb.com
This beachfront high-rise offers family suites with kitchen facilities. Waterfall pool and kids' activities.

### FORT WALTON BEACH: Islander Beach Resort $$$
Luxury                 Road map A1
790 Santa Rosa Blvd, 32548
**Tel** (850) 986-7600
Ⓦ wyndhamvacationrentals.com
Comfortable condos, studios, and three-bedroom apartments with kitchenettes, balconies, and a pool.

### GRAYTON BEACH: Grayton Beach State Park $$
Lodge                  Road map B1
357 Main Park Rd, 32459
**Tel** (800) 326-3521
Ⓦ floridastateparks.com
Get back to nature at this cabin site near the beach. No phone and TV policy. Two-day minimum stay.

### PANAMA CITY BEACH: Beachcomber by the Sea $$
Modern                 Road Map B1
17101 Front Beach Rd, 32413
**Tel** (850) 233-3600
Ⓦ beachcomberbythesea.com
Seven-story hotel by the beach where rooms have kitchenettes. Continental breakfasts.

### PANAMA CITY BEACH: Flamingo Motel $$
Motel                  Road map B1
15525 Front Beach Rd, 34213
**Tel** (850) 324-2232
Ⓦ flamingomotel.com
Family-owned beachfront motel. Basic but comfortable rooms with kitchens. Good value.

### PANAMA CITY BEACH: Sunset Inn $$
Inn                    Road map B1
8109 Surf Dr, 32408
**Tel** (850) 234-7370
Ⓦ sunsetinnfl.com
Sunset Inn has comfortable self-contained units and suites as well as a fabulous sundeck.

### PENSACOLA: Lee House $$$
Boutique               Road map A1
400 Bayfront Pkwy, 32502
**Tel** (850) 912-8770
Ⓦ leehousepensacola.com
Elegant hotel amid an historic district. Wide porches overlook Pensacola Bay, and nearby cottages are part of the property.

### PENSACOLA BEACH: Portofino Island Resort $$$
Resort                 Road map A1
10 Portofino Dr, 32561
**Tel** (877) 605-0746
Ⓦ portofinoisland.com
Apartments in five Mediterranean-style condos with kitchens, spa, pools, golf, plus kids' activities.

---

## DK Choice

### SANTA ROSA BEACH: Watercolor Inn $$$
Inn                    Road map B1
34 Goldenrod Circle, 32459
**Tel** (850) 534-5000
Ⓦ watercolorresort.com
Watercolor is a luxurious but relaxed beach retreat with spacious, comfortable rooms, king-size beds, walk-in showers, and balconies. Complimentary bikes, canoes, and kayaks are also available.

---

### TALLAHASSEE: Governors Inn $$$
Historic               Road map C1
209 S Adams St, 32301
**Tel** (850) 681-6855
Ⓦ thegovinn.com
Convenient downtown choice with old-fashioned warmth, and rooms named after past governors. Free Continental breakfasts.

# The Gulf Coast

### CAPTIVA ISLAND: Captiva Island Inn $$
Inn                    Road map E4
11508 Andy Rosse Ln, 33924
**Tel** (239) 395-0882
Ⓦ captivaislandinn.com
Delightful complex near the beach with cottages including kitchenettes. Complimentary breakfast at nearby restaurants.

### CAPTIVA ISLAND: South Seas Island Resort $$$
Resort                 Road map E4
5400 Plantation Rd, 33924
**Tel** (239) 472-5111
Ⓦ southseas.com
Expansive retreat with golf and tennis facilities and a 2.5 mile (4 km) private beach. Luxurious rooms with plenty of amenities.

**CAPTIVA ISLAND:**
**Tween Waters Inn**          $$$
Resort          Road map E4
*15951 Captiva Dr, 33924*
**Tel** *(239) 472-5161*
W tween-waters.com
Rooms and cottages spread over
a huge private area between Gulf
and Bay Beach. Spa, tennis, and
golf facilities. Continental breakfast.

**CLEARWATER:**
**Amber Tides Motel**          $
Motel          Road map D3
*420 Hamden Dr, 33767*
**Tel** *(727) 445-1145*
W ambertides-motel.com
Old-fashioned motel close to the
beach. Clean, basic rooms with
microwaves and refrigerators.

**CLEARWATER BEACH:**
**Clearwater Beach Marriott**  $$$
Luxury          Road map D3
*1201 Gulf Blvd, 33767*
**Tel** *(727) 596-1100*
W marriott.com
Pleasant hotel located on the
beautiful Sand Key. All suites have
cooking facilities and balconies.

**CLEARWATER BEACH: Hyatt**
**Regency Clearwater**          $$$
Luxury          Road map D3
*301 S Gulfview Blvd, 33767*
**Tel** *(727) 373-1234*
W clearwaterbeach.hyatt.com
This beachfront hotel has extrav-
agant suites with balconies and
kitchens. Kids camp available.

**FORT MYERS BEACH:**
**Diamond Head Resort**          $$
Luxury          Road map E4
*2000 Estero Blvd, 33931*
**Tel** *(239) 765-7654*
W diamondheadfl.com
All-suite hotel by the beach
with screened balconies, a pool,
outdoor whirlpools, and a spa.

A spacious villa with beach views at Pink
Shell Beach Resort, Fort Myers Beach

**FORT MYERS BEACH:**
**Palm Terrace Resort**          $$
Modern          Road map E4
*3333 Estero Blvd, 33931*
**Tel** *(239) 765-5783*
W palm-terrace.com
Modestly furnished self-contained
apartments set around an enticing
pool. Most suites have balconies.

**DK Choice**

**FORT MYERS BEACH:**
**Edison Beach House**          $$$
Inn          Road map E4
*830 Estero Blvd, 33931*
**Tel** *(239) 463-1530*
W edisonbeachhouse.com
This beachside hotel cannot be
beaten for space and amenities.
Airy suites with beach-style
wicker, balconies, kitchens, and
laundry facilities. There is also a
pool and a children's playhouse.

**FORT MYERS BEACH:**
**Outrigger Beach Resort**          $$$
Luxury          Road map E4
*6200 Estero Blvd, 33931*
**Tel** *(239) 463-3131*
W outriggerfmb.com
Choose between self-contained
suites or motel-style rooms, some
with beach views. Large pool.

**FORT MYERS BEACH:**
**Pink Shell Beach Resort**          $$$
Luxury          Road map E4
*275 Estero Blvd, 33931*
**Tel** *(239) 463-6181*
W pinkshell.com
Expansive luxury hotel by a
white-sand beach. Studios and
villas with cooking facilities.

**LONGBOAT KEY: The Resort**
**at Longboat Key Club**          $$$
Resort          Road map D3
*220 Sands Point Rd, 34228*
**Tel** *(941) 383-8821*
W longboatkeyclub.com
Spacious, upscale resort on the
Sugar Sand Beach, with tennis
courts, pools, and golf.

**PALM HARBOR:**
**Innisbrook Golf Resort**          $$
Resort          Road map D3
*36057 US Hwy 19N, 34683*
**Tel** *(727) 942-2000*
W innisbrookgolfresort.com
Deluxe rooms, kids' club, and four
championship golf courses.

**SAFETY HARBOR:**
**Safety Harbor Resort & Spa**  $$
Resort          Road map D3
*105 N Bayshore Dr, 34695*
**Tel** *(727) 726-1161*
W safetyharborspa.com
Choose from the many fitness
and spa packages at this

bayside resort with natural
mineral springs. Beautifully
presented rooms.

**SANIBEL ISLAND: Seaside Inn**  $$
Inn          Road map E4
*541 E Gulf Dr, 33957*
**Tel** *(866) 565-5092*
W theinnsofsanibel.com
Pleasant 1960s beachside inn.
Golf and tennis club privileges
and complimentary breakfast.

**SANIBEL ISLAND:**
**Tarpon Tale Inn**          $$
Inn          Road map E4
*367 Periwinkle Way, 33957*
**Tel** *(239) 472-0939*
W tarpontale.com
This friendly Inn features bright,
airy studios and cottages. Each has
a kitchenette, is individually styled,
and surrounded by lush gardens.

**SANIBEL ISLAND: Casa Ybel**  $$$
Resort          Road map E4
*2255 W Gulf Dr, 33957*
**Tel** *(239) 472-3145*
W casaybelresort.com
Upscale condo beachfront retreat.
Suites have great balcony views
and fully-equipped kitchens.
Plenty of children's activities.

**SANIBEL ISLAND: Island Inn**  $$$
Inn          Road map E4
*3111 W Gulf Dr, 33957*
**Tel** *(239) 472-1561*
W islandinnsanibel.com
Vintage cottages and modern
lodges set in expansive grounds
near a beach. Tennis, lawn games,
and Continental breakfasts.

**SANIBEL ISLAND: Sanibel**
**Inn**          $$$
Inn          Road map E4
*937 E Gulf Dr, 33957*
**Tel** *(239) 472-3181*
W sanibelinn.com
Spacious and well-equipped
rooms and condos. Great beach,
plus tennis and biking facilities.

**SANIBEL ISLAND:**
**Sundial Beach Resort**          $$$
Resort          Road map E4
*1451 Middle Gulf Dr, 33957*
**Tel** *(239) 395-6031*
W sundialresort.com
Studio to three-bedroom condos
by the beach with tennis and golf
club privileges, pools, and a spa.

**SARASOTA: Holiday Inn**
**Sarasota Airport**          $$
Motel          Road map D3
*8009 15th St E, 34243*
**Tel** *(941) 355-9000*
W holidayinn.com
Ultra-modern six-story motel
with excellent rooms and an
indoor pool. A short drive to town.

**For more information on types of hotels** *see pages 310–13*

**SARASOTA:
La Quinta Inn & Suites** $$
Modern     **Road map** D3
*1803 N Tamiami Trail, 34234*
**Tel** *(941) 366-5128*
W laquintasarasota.com
Tastefully decorated and furnished
budget hotel. Free breakfasts.

**SARASOTA:
Captiva Beach Resort** $$$
Resort     **Road map** D3
*6772 Sara Sea Circle, Siesta Key,
34242*
**Tel** *(941) 349-4131*
W captivabeachresort.com
Near Sonesta Key's white-sand
beach, this resort is a complex of
clean, modern units with kitchens.

**SARASOTA: The Cypress** $$$
B&B     **Road map** D3
*621 Gulfstream Ave, 34236*
**Tel** *(941) 955-4683*
W cypressbb.com
A great find nestled amid mango
and palm trees overlooking the
bay. Lovely antiques and Oriental
rugs in rooms. Excellent breakfast.

**SARASOTA: The Ritz-
Carlton** $$$
Resort     **Road map** D3
*1111 Ritz-Carlton Dr, 34236*
**Tel** *(941) 309-2000*
W ritzcarlton.com
Relax in typical Ritz-style
luxury. Spa and tennis facilities,
private golf club, and Lido Key
beach club.

**SARASOTA:
Sandcastle Hotel** $$$
Luxury     **Road map** D3
*1540 Benjamin Franklin Dr, 34236*
**Tel** *(941) 388-2181*
W sandcastlelidobeach.com
Located by Lido Beach, this
hotel offers beach game
facilities, pools, and outdoor
dining. Some rooms have
beach views and balconies.

---

### DK Choice

**SARASOTA:
Turtle Beach Resort** $$$
Resort     **Road map** D3
*9049 Midnight Pass Rd, Siesta Key,
34242*
**Tel** *(941) 349-4554*
W turtlebeachresort.com
This private bayside cottage
complex, tucked away on the
quiet southern end of Siesta
Key, has an Old Florida charm.
It offers individually-styled
studios and suites with private
patios and hot tubs. Amenities
include a pool, shaded
hammocks and complimentary
kayaks and bikes.

---

**ST PETE BEACH: Beach Haven** $$
Motel     **Road map** D3
*4980 Gulf Blvd, 33706*
**Tel** *(727) 367-8642*
W beachhavenvillas.com
Located on the beachfront,
these simple motel-style units
offer excellent value. The one-
bedroom units have kitchens.

**ST PETE BEACH:
Don CeSar Hotel** $$$
Historic     **Road map** D3
*3400 Gulf Blvd, 33706*
**Tel** *(727) 360-1881*
W doncesar.com
This vast pink palace by the
sea offers vintage charm with
modern amenities, including a
pool and a spa.

**ST PETE BEACH:
Tradewinds Island Grand** $$$
Resort     **Road map** D3
*5500 Gulf Blvd, 33706*
**Tel** *(727) 367-6461*
W tradewindsresort.com
This luxurious beachfront
resort has five huge pools and
waterways with paddleboats.
Some rooms have kitchenettes.

**ST PETERSBURG:
Dickens House** $$
B&B     **Road map** D3
*335 8th Ave NE, 33701*
**Tel** *(727) 822-8622*
W dickenshouse.com
A stunning 1912 Arts and Crafts
house with five beautiful rooms,
some with whirlpools. Enjoy the
fantastic gourmet breakfasts.

**ST PETERSBURG: Hotel Indigo** $$
Modern     **Road map** D3
*234 3rd Ave NE, 33706*
**Tel** *(727) 822-4814*
W hotelindigo.com
Comfortable hotel with modern
rooms. Facilities include 24-hour
fitness center, pool, and whirlpool.

Tranquil lounge beside the pool at Turtle
Beach Resort, Sarasota

---

**ST PETERSBURG: Treasure Island
Beach Resort** $$
Resort     **Road map** D3
*10800 Gulf Blvd, 33706*
**Tel** *(727) 322-7022*
W treasureislandbeachresort.com
Surrounded by the white
beach, this resort offers suites,
equipped with kitchens, that
provide great views of sunsets,
as well as the Gulf, from the
balconies.

---

### DK Choice

**ST PETERSBURG: The Vinoy
Renaissance** $$$
Historic     **Road map** D3
*501 5th Ave NE, 33701*
**Tel** *(727) 894-1000*
W marriott.com
This beautifully restored
building has retained the
grandeur of the past while
adding top resort amenities
including a lavish pool, tennis,
golf, spa facilities, and a highly
regarded restaurant. Worth the
expense to experience Florida
as it was in its 1920s heyday.

---

**ST PETERSBURG: Watergarden
Inn at the Bay** $$$
Inn     **Road map** D3
*126 4th Ave NE, 33701*
**Tel** *(727) 822-1700*
W innatthebay.com
Tastefully restored period homes
with luxuriously comfortable
beds. Delicious buffet breakfasts.

**TAMPA: Embassy Suites
Westshore** $$
Modern     **Road map** D3
*555 N Westshore Blvd, 33609*
**Tel** *(813) 875-1555*
W embassysuites.com
Good option for families, with
two-room suites and cooking
facilities. Free breakfasts.

**TAMPA: Hilton Garden Inn** $$
Inn     **Road map** D3
*1700 E 9th Ave, 33602*
**Tel** *(813) 769-9267*
W hiltongardeninn.com
Tastefully decorated rooms
and suites. Facilities include a
pool, spa, fitness center, and
kid's activities.

**TAMPA: Sheraton Riverwalk
Hotel** $$
Luxury     **Road map** D3
*200 N Ashley Dr, 33602*
**Tel** *(813) 223-2222*
W sheratontampariverwalk.com
Comfortable downtown
hotel with an outdoor pool
and access to pleasant river-
side walks. Good restaurant
with patio seating.

A cottage porch overlooking lush gardens and the ocean at The Moorings Village, Islamorada

**TAMPA:**
**Marriott Waterside** **$$$**
Luxury **Road map** D3
*700 S Florida Ave, 33602*
**Tel** *(813) 221-4900*
W marriott.com
Centrally located, 22-story opulent hotel with comfortable rooms, a rooftop pool, and good views.

**TAMPA:**
**Westin Harbour Island** **$$$**
Luxury **Road map** D3
*725 S Harbour Island Blvd, 33602*
**Tel** *(813) 229-5000*
W westintampaharbourisland.com
This contemporary hotel with modern rooms is located on a private island. Great water views.

**VENICE:**
**Inn at the Beach** **$$$**
Luxury **Road map** D4
*725 W Venice Ave, 34285*
**Tel** *(941) 484-8471*
W innatthebeach.com
Comfortable motel-style lodgings by the beach with a bohemian vibe. Cooking facilities and complimentary Continental breakfasts.

## The Everglades and the Keys

**EVERGLADES CITY:**
**Ivey House** **$$**
B&B **Road map** E5
*107 Camelia St, 34139*
**Tel** *(239) 695-3299*
W iveyhouse.com
Choose to stay in either a comfortable, modern guesthouse or an inexpensive 1920s-era lodge with shared bathrooms. The hosts also run Everglades Adventures outings.

**FLORIDA CITY: Best Western**
**Gateway** **$$**
Motel **Road map** F5
*411 S Krome Ave, 33034*
**Tel** *(305) 246-5100*
W bestwestern.com
Conveniently located for the Keys or Everglades, this motel has a pool and offers free breakfasts.

**FLORIDA CITY: Everglades**
**International Hostel** **$$**
Hostel **Road map** F5
*20 SW 2nd Ave, 33034*
**Tel** *(305) 248-1122*
W evergladeshostel.com
Great for backpackers and budget travelers. Dorms as well as family rooms, a communal kitchen, and pancake breakfasts.

**ISLAMORADA: Ragged**
**Edge Resort** **$$**
Resort **Road map** F5
*243 Treasure Harbor Rd, 33036*
**Tel** *(305) 852-5389*
W ragged-edge.com
Comfortable rooms and cottages in this quiet, spacious oceanfront resort. Large pool and free bike hire.

**ISLAMORADA: Casa Morada** **$$$**
Boutique **Road map** F5
*136 Madeira Rd, 33036*
**Tel** *(305) 664-0044*
W casamorada.com
This upscale Caribbean-style hideaway features suites, some with Jacuzzis, and great views. Continental breakfast included.

**ISLAMORADA: Cheeca**
**Lodge & Spa** **$$$**
Resort **Road map** F5
*81801 Overseas Hwy, US 1 at MM 82, 33036*
**Tel** *(305) 664-4651*
W cheeca.com
Relaxed luxurious retreat. Spacious rooms with West Indian decor and marble baths. Snorkeling, nature trails, and a fun kids' camp.

**ISLAMORADA: Postcard Inn**
**Beach Resort & Marina** **$$$**
Inn **Road map** F5
*84001 Overseas Hwy, US1 at MM 84, 33036*
**Tel** *(305) 664-2321*
W holidayisle.com
With its lively ambience and legendary Tiki bar, Postcard Inn is a reliable favorite. There are panoramic views from some rooms and beach, pool, and watersports on site.

### DK Choice

**ISLAMORADA:**
**The Moorings Village** **$$$**
Luxury **Road map** F5
*123 Beach Rd, 33036*
**Tel** *(305) 664-4708*
W themooringsvillage.com
Eighteen beautifully furnished cottages with porches and balconies spread over an expansive area, including one of the best beaches in the Keys. Excellent spa offers yoga classes and outdoor massages. There is also a lap pool, tennis court, and hammocks under the palms.

**KEY LARGO:**
**Jules' Undersea Lodge** **$$$**
Luxury **Road map** F5
*51 Shoreland Dr, 33037*
**Tel** *(305) 451-2353*
W jul.com
Amazing underwater lodge for diving enthusiasts that has fish swimming past windows. Rates include breakfast and dinner.

### DK Choice

**KEY LARGO: Kona Kai**
**Resort & Gallery** **$$$**
Resort **Road map** F5
*97802 Overseas Hwy, 33037*
**Tel** *(305) 852-7200*
W konakairesort.com
Individual cottages, glowing with tropical colors, set in a lush botanical garden with hundreds of orchids and other rare plants. This 'adults only' paradise features garden tours, beach games, kayaks, paddleboats, a pool, a splendid art gallery, and hammocks for those who simply want to unwind.

**KEY LARGO:**
**Ocean Pointe Suites** **$$$**
Luxury **Road map** F5
*500 Burton Dr, Tavernier, 33070*
**Tel** *(305) 853-3000*
W providentresorts.com
Comfortable suites spread out over an extensive area with a private marina and beach.

**For more information on types of hotels** *see pages 310–13*

Tastefully decorated suite at Marquesa Hotel, Key West

**KEY WEST: Key West Hostel & Seashell Motel** $
Motel      **Road map** E5
*718 South St, 33040*
**Tel** *(305) 296-5719*
ⓦ keywesthostel.com
Basic rooms with en suites as well as bunk-bed dorms. Laundry and common kitchen facilities.

**KEY WEST:**
**Angelina Guest House** $$
Inn      **Road map** E5
*302 Angela St, 33040*
**Tel** *(305) 294-4480*
ⓦ angelinaguesthouse.com
Once a brothel, Angelina is now a popular guesthouse. Continental breakfasts. No children allowed.

**KEY WEST: Southernmost Point Guest House** $$
Inn      **Road map** E5
*1327 Duval St, 33040*
**Tel** *(305) 294-0715*
ⓦ southernmostpoint.com
Airy Victorian guesthouse on the quiet end of Duval, with porches, a pool, and shaded hammocks.

**KEY WEST:**
**Ambrosia Key West** $$$
B&B      **Road map** E5
*622 Fleming St, 33040*
**Tel** *(305) 296-9838*
ⓦ ambrosiakeywest.com
Charming B&B in a spacious garden, with themed rooms and suites, three pools and hot breakfasts.

**KEY WEST:**
**Amsterdam's Curry Mansion Inn** $$$
Historic      **Road map** E5
*511 Caroline St, 33040*
**Tel** *(305) 294-5349*
ⓦ currymansion.com
Lovely Victorian inn with wide porches, wicker furnishings, and antique fixtures. Fantastic breakfasts and evening cocktail hour.

**KEY WEST: Doubletree by Hilton Hotel Grand Key Resort** $$$
Luxury      **Road map** E5
*3990 Roosevelt Blvd, 33040*
**Tel** *(305) 293-1818*
ⓦ doubletreekeywest.com
Comfortable rooms in this island-styled hotel with a waterfall pool. Pet-friendly, free shuttle.

**KEY WEST: The Duval House** $$$
B&B      **Road map** E5
*815 Duval St, 33040*
**Tel** *(305) 924-1666*
ⓦ theduvalhouse.com
Attractive cottage complex around a courtyard with a pool and gardens. Continental breakfast.

---

### DK Choice

**KEY WEST:**
**The Gardens Hotel** $$$
Luxury      **Road map** E5
*526 Angela St, 33040*
**Tel** *(305) 294-2661*
ⓦ gardenshotel.com
Located in a secluded botanical garden estate, The Gardens has attractive rooms with Island-style furnishings, marble baths, and Jacuzzis. Enjoy the Continental breakfast on a porch overlooking the lush gardens. For age 16 and older.

---

**KEY WEST: The Grand** $$$
B&B      **Road map** E5
*1116 Grinnell St, 33040*
**Tel** *(305) 294-0590*
ⓦ thegrandguesthouse.com
Friendly guesthouse offers snug rooms and self-catering suites. The Continental breakfast is free.

**KEY WEST:**
**Island City House Hotel** $$$
Historic      **Road map** E5
*411 William St, 33040*
**Tel** *(305) 294-5702*
ⓦ islandcityhouse.com
Housed in three historic buildings sharing a patio and pool, the suites here have kitchens and old-fashioned decor.

---

### DK Choice

**KEY WEST:**
**Marquesa Hotel** $$$
Historic      **Road map** E5
*600 Fleming St, 33040*
**Tel** *(305) 292-1919*
ⓦ marquesa.com
Three beautifully restored 1880s homes and a contemporary unit form an oasis within walking distance from the town center. Airy rooms with ceiling fans. On-site Café Marquesa is one of the town's best. Reserved for adults.

---

**KEY WEST: Ocean Key Resort** $$$
Luxury      **Road map** E5
*Zero Duval St, 33040*
**Tel** *(305) 296-7701*
ⓦ oceankey.com
Located near the busy Mallory Square. Airy rooms with balconies, and a gorgeous seafront pool.

**KEY WEST: La Pensione** $$$
Historic      **Road map** E5
*809 Truman Ave, 33040*
**Tel** *(305) 292-9923*
ⓦ lapensione.com
Victorian hotel dating back to 1891. Rooms have king-size beds and balconies. Continental breakfast.

**KEY WEST: The Reach Waldorf Astoria** $$$
Resort      **Road map** E5
*1435 Simonton St, 33040*
**Tel** *(305) 296-5000*
ⓦ reachresort.com
Attractive rooms, overlooking, and with access to, the town's only natural beach. Lavish spa and exceptional service.

**KEY WEST:**
**Sunset Key Cottages** $$$
Luxury      **Road map** E5
*245 Front St, 33040*
**Tel** *(305) 292-5300*
ⓦ sunsetkeycottages.com
Set on a private island just offshore, this lavish cottage colony offers kitchen facilities and a free 24-hour ferry to town.

**KEY WEST:**
**The Weatherstation Inn** $$$
Inn      **Road map** E5
*57 Front St, 33040*
**Tel** *(305) 294-7277*
ⓦ weatherstationinn.com
Located in a gated community, this restored weather station offers airy rooms with breakfast baskets at the door. Age 15 and older only.

**KEY WEST: Westwinds Inn** $$$
Historic      **Road map** E5
*914 Eaton St, 33040*
**Tel** *(305) 296-4440*
ⓦ westwindskeywest.com
Stay in a unique 1900s clapboard home. Rooms with modern amenities, plus a pool and library. Continental breakfasts.

**LITTLE TORCH KEY:**
**Parmer's Resort** $$
Hotel      **Road map** E5
*565 Barry Ave, 33043*
**Tel** *(305) 872-2157*
ⓦ parmersresort.com
Waterfront resort with elegant rooms, some with kitchens, and a Lagoon Cottage that offers total privacy. Mini-golf, a bocce court, and Continental breakfast.

### LITTLE TORCH KEY:
**Little Palm Island** $$$
Luxury **Road map** E5
*28500 Overseas Hwy, US 1 at MM 28.5, 33042*
**Tel** *(305) 872-2524*
**W** littlepalmisland.com
Experience paradise on this private island with thatched villas and a wide range of amenities. Age 16 and older.

### LONG KEY:
**Lime Tree Bay Resort** $$
Resort **Road map** F5
*68500 Overseas Hwy, US 1 at MM 68.5, 33001*
**Tel** *(305) 664-4740*
**W** limetreebayresort.com
This quiet Gulfside getaway has pleasant rooms, beach access, a pool and free kayak rental.

### MARATHON: Banana Bay Resort and Marina $$
Resort **Road map** E5
*4590 Overseas Hwy, US 1 at MM 49.5, 33050*
**Tel** *(305) 743-3500*
**W** bananabay.com
Well-located by the bay, this romantic getaway has attractive rooms, a pool, bocce court, and tennis and snorkeling facilities.

### MARATHON: Holiday Inn Express & Suites $$
Modern **Road map** E5
*13201 Overseas Hwy, 33050*
**Tel** *(305) 289-0222*
**W** holidayinnkeys.com
Comfortable modern hotel in the Keys. Offers top-class fitness and business facilities, and a pleasant pool. Free hot breakfasts.

### MARATHON:
**Conch Key Cottages** $$$
Luxury **Road map** E5
*US 1 at MM 62/3, 33050*
**Tel** *(305) 289-1377*
**W** conchkeycottages.com
A great option on a tiny private island with a small

The bright interior of a suite at Hawk's Cay Resort, Marathon

beach. Guests are accommodated in tin-roof cottages built from old Florida pine.

### MARATHON:
**Hawk's Cay Resort** $$$
Luxury **Road map** E5
*61 Hawk's Cay Blvd, 33050*
**Tel** *(305) 743-7000*
**W** hawkscay.com
Observe dolphins at the on-site research center of this stylish resort. Rooms feature West Indies-style decor. There is also a fishing dock and kids' programs.

### MARCO ISLAND:
**The Boat House Motel** $$
Motel **Road map** E5
*1180 Edington Pl, 34145*
**Tel** *(239) 642-2400*
**W** theboathousemotel.com
Family-owned motel on Marco River. Clean rooms, kitchenettes, a pool, and a fishing dock.

### MARCO ISLAND:
**Olde Marco Inn & Suites** $$
Historic **Road map** E5
*100 Palm St, 34145*
**Tel** *(239) 394-3131*
**W** oldemarcoinn.com
Dating to 1883, this historic building houses modern rooms and condo suites with kitchenettes. It also has a beautiful garden and a fantastic French restaurant.

### MARCO ISLAND:
**Hilton Marco Beach Resort** $$$
Luxury **Road map** E5
*560 s Collier Blvd, 34145*
**Tel** *(239) 394-5000*
**W** hiltonmarcoisland.com
Spacious, well-furnished rooms with balconies in this beachfront hotel. Spa and tennis courts.

### MARCO ISLAND:
**JW Marriott Marco Island Beach Resort** $$$
Resort **Road map** E5
*400 S Collier Blvd, 34145*
**Tel** *(239) 394-2511*
**W** jwmarco.com
A huge resort with a wide range of facilities including a 3 mile (5 km) beach, two golf courses, tennis courts, and several pools.

### MARCO ISLAND:
**Marco Beach Ocean Resort** $$$
Luxury **Road map** E5
*480 S Collier Blvd, 34145*
**Tel** *(239) 393-1400*
**W** marcoresort.com
Stay in this luxury high-rise located by a 4 mile (6.5 km) beach. Suites with balconies, a rooftop pool, and a stunning sundeck.

### NAPLES: Sea Shell Motel $
Motel **Road map** E4
*82 9th St S, 34102*
**Tel** *(239) 262-5129*
This no-frills budget motel has simply furnished rooms and some self-catering units.

### NAPLES: Lighthouse Inn Motel $$
Motel **Road map** E4
*9140 Gulf Shore Dr, 34108*
**Tel** *(239) 597-3345*
Old-fashioned motel. Spotless and simple rooms and suites with small kitchens. Great value.

### NAPLES: Staybridge Suites $$
Modern **Road map** E4
*4805 N Tamiami Trail, 34103*
**Tel** *(239) 643-8002*
**W** igh.com
Full-service suites with on-site laundry and fully-equipped kitchens. Free buffet breakfasts.

### NAPLES: Hotel Escalante $$$
Boutique **Road map** E4
*290 5th Ave S, 34102*
**Tel** *(239) 659-3466*
**W** hotelescalante.com
Small hotel in a secluded area close to the beach. Attractive rooms and garden, plus many spa services.

### NAPLES: Inn on Fifth $$$
Inn **Road map** E4
*699 Fifth Ave S, 34102*
**Tel** *(239) 403-8777*
**W** innonfifth.com
Elegant rooms and special golf and tennis club privileges makes Inn on Fifth a good choice.

### NAPLES:
**Naples Beach Hotel** $$$
Resort **Road map** E4
*851 Gulf Shore Blvd, 34102*
**Tel** *(239) 261-2222*
**W** naplesbeachhotel.com
Golf course, tennis courts, on-site beach, and an excellent kids' program make this family-owned resort a perennial favorite.

### NAPLES:
**Naples Grande Beach Resort** $$$
Resort **Road map** E4
*475 Seagate Dr, 34103*
**Tel** *(239) 597-3232*
**W** naplesgrande.com
Luxurious resort with lavish rooms, a pool with slides, and sports facilities.

### NAPLES: La Playa Resort $$$
Resort **Road map** E4
*9891 Gulf Shore Dr, 34108*
**Tel** *(239) 597-3123*
**W** laplayaresort.com
Popular resort with a prime beachfront location, huge rooms, and an exclusive golf club.

**For more information on types of hotels** *see pages 310–13*

# WHERE TO EAT AND DRINK

While fast food is a staple in Florida as it is anywhere in the US, the real joy of dining here comes from abundant fresh produce – from tropical fruits to seafood – all used to great effect by restaurants across the state. Waterfront views add to the pleasure of dining in the many eateries located along the bountiful coastline. Restaurants in Florida, from the trendiest establishments that set or follow the latest culinary fashions, to more homely and traditional places, cater to every palate and budget. Wherever you travel, it is possible to find unique locally-owned restaurants as well as the familiar chains.

The dining area at the very glitzy Barton G. The Restaurant

## Types of Restaurants

Florida's elite restaurants tend to have European-style (often French) menus, while still making the most of local fare. "New American" is another name for more creative takes on familiar dishes, using imaginative combinations and sauces. A breed of innovative chefs has combined Florida's fine produce with zesty Caribbean flavors to create a unique cuisine that people call New Florida or "Floribbean". Menus often change daily or weekly to ensure that the freshest of ingredients are used.

Fine dining can be found throughout the state, but Miami, the cities of the Gold and Gulf coasts, and the Orlando area have a special reputation for their restaurants. Some of the most famous chefs from across America have established outposts here, as well as in eateries at Walt Disney World® and Universal® in Orlando.

Florida boasts a large concentration of Caribbean and South American-inspired restaurants and cafés. There is also a special emphasis on Cuban food, especially in Miami and Tampa where the Cuban population is large. Southern dishes such as shrimp and grits and New Orleans-style blackened fish are popular as well.

Restaurants of every size and shape serve seafood, with coastal areas offering delectable freshly caught fish. One popular institution, The Raw Bar, offers fresh raw oysters or clams as well as steamed shrimp.

Vegetarians need not worry because almost every restaurant will have a choice of vegetarian dishes on the menu. Cafés and bars, for drinking and for more informal eating, are listed on pages 348–9.

## Eating Hours

Breakfast can usually be eaten anytime from 7am to 11am. Sunday brunch is an especially popular tradition served from around 10am to 2pm. Some establishments offer lavish brunch buffets.

Lunch is generally available from 11:30am to 2:30pm, and the most popular hours for dining are between 6pm and 9pm. Many places stay open later on Friday and Saturday evenings. The early-bird special, generally offered before 6pm at special rates, is intended for those who like to eat early. Eating hours can always change, so it would be wise to check.

## Reservations

To avoid disappointment it is always wise to reserve a table, especially on weekends or at the more upscale or popular eateries. At some places, such as Joe's Stone Crab in Miami Beach (see p330), diners cannot reserve ahead and instead must wait in line for a table. In such cases, it might be prudent to dine early or late to minimize the waiting time. It is always wise to reserve during peak season.

## Tips on Eating Out

Dining out in Florida is mostly an informal affair. There are very few restaurants that require a jacket or tie, and those that do will provide these for diners to wear. "Casual but neat" is the general rule.

Old-world Spanish decor at the Columbia Restaurant, Tampa (see p345)

All eateries in Florida are non-smoking establishments so smokers should be prepared to step outside if they want to light up.

Tips range from 15 to 20 per cent. At sophisticated places, guests frequently tip a generous amount if the service has been good. The state sales tax of 6 per cent is added automatically to all checks, but the tip should be calculated on the food amount alone.

Most credit cards are readily accepted at almost all eateries.

## Dining on a Budget

There are several ways to cut the food budget. Helpings in restaurants tend to be large, so an appetizer is often enough for a light meal. Patrons may also share dishes, but there may be a small charge for this. Some restaurants offer small plates or a choice of small servings of entrées, and most restaurants now have menus on their websites, making it easier to choose wisely.

All-you-can-eat buffets are a bargain, and some restaurants offer cheaper meals on a prix fixe menu. It may be wise to call the restaurant ahead for such details because the times and conditions may vary.

Smaller restaurants sometimes advertise BYOB which means that you are welcome to bring your own bottle of wine, and openers and glasses will be provided. This option, when available, can be a welcome saving.

If keen to eat in a chic place, remember that lunches are usually cheaper than dinners. Breakfast in hotels, however, can be shockingly over-priced. Instead, join the locals at a nearby deli or diner. Choosing a hotel with Continental breakfast included is a real money-saver.

Some bars also serve reasonably priced food. Many offer free or half-priced hors d'oeuvres, late afternoon or early evening, during happy hours. Sports bars have TVs for watching games, and also have inexpensive snacks on their menus.

Outside dining at Aunt Catfish's On the River in Daytona Beach *(see p339)*

Delis and supermarkets are good for picnic provisions; the former also often provide cooked dishes and sandwiches to be eaten on or off the premises. Many state parks have barbecue grills where you can grill your catch or whatever food you care to bring along. Many restaurants in the Keys will also grill your catch for a reduced price.

## Menus

Menus throughout the state rely heavily on fresh fish and other seafood items such as clams, lobsters, shrimp, crab, and conch. You can also find crawfish, blackened fish (coated with Cajun spices and cooked quickly in a smoking hot pan), and gumbos. Beef, chicken, and pork are also readily available. Surf 'n' Turf is a popular combination of seafood and beef, usually steak and lobster. If "dolphin" appears on a Florida menu, it refers to mahi mahi. If guests are unsure about menu items or require a special menu, feel free to ask. Restaurant staff are normally very pleased to help.

## Children

Most restaurants are happy to accommodate the needs of younger diners. Many offer kids' menus with smaller portions of child-friendly dishes such as pasta, pizza, burgers, hot dogs, and fries. Most also provide highchairs or booster chairs. Call ahead to check what is

available. Children are not allowed in bars, but if food is served on the premises they can accompany adults and have a meal in an area away from the bar. Apart from this, almost all places will welcome well-behaved youngsters.

## Recommended Restaurants

A tourist mecca, Florida has thousands of restaurants to choose from. Serving diner food to fancy cuisine, the establishments listed on pages 329–47 are some of the best, and have been selected for their quality of food and service. The listings also reflect factors such as authentic cuisine, outdoor dining, or live music. DK Choices represent the best of the best – be it value for money, a celebrity chef, unusual features, great ambience, or exceptional food. Within each price category, the entries are listed alpha-betically by location.

Customers at the popular waterside café, Big Pink, in Miami

# The Flavors of Florida

With an ideal climate, Florida is blessed with a profusion of tropical fruits, year-round bountiful vegetables, and fresh seafood from both ocean and gulf, and these are the major elements found in the state's cuisine. In the cities of central and south Florida, the large Cuban and Caribbean populations have had a strong culinary impact, and Latin America contributes dishes such as *ceviche*. In the north, food reveals the influence of neighboring southern states. However, in order to please the thousands of tourists who visit the "sunshine state," almost every type of international cuisine is available.

Giant shrimp

Fish straight from the ocean, ready for sale to local restaurateurs

## Florida Seafood

Among the best of the local catch to watch for on Florida menus are amberjack, mahi-mahi, pompano, snapper, tuna, and wahoo. Grouper, part of the sea bass family, is especially popular. The fillets appear both as main dishes and in delicious sandwiches. Florida shrimp, another favorite, is large, sweet, and tender. It may be boiled, peeled, and served cold with cocktail sauce, cooked in a spicy sauce and served in the shell, or used in numerous other main courses.

## Latin Cuisine

In cities with large Cuban or Mexican populations, such as Miami and Tampa, many dining places serve dishes that show a strong Spanish influence. Roast pork, *arroz con pollo* (chicken with spiced rice), and paella are mainstays. Cuban sandwiches, and flan for dessert, are also typical.

## Tropical Treats

Florida's tropical climate produces much of the exotic fruit found in America, from kumquats and papaya to lychees and star fruit. The variety grown means that a bountiful supply of top-quality produce is always in season. Weekly local farmers' markets, found in almost every community, are fun to visit.

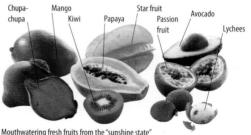

Chupa-chupa    Mango    Star fruit    Avocado
                 Kiwi    Papaya    Passion    Lychees
                                    fruit

Mouthwatering fresh fruits from the "sunshine state"

## Regional Dishes and Specialties

Stone crabs, rich, sweet, and firm in texture, are the most prized of Florida seafoods, perhaps partly because they are available only from mid-October to mid-May. The meat is always cooked, but is usually served chilled, with melted butter and mustard sauce. Conch (a giant sea snail), another important shellfish, may be served as an appetizer, in salads, or as the base for chowder. Shrimp comes in two varieties – large and pink-hued from the Gulf, or white and delicate from the Atlantic. The state's signature dessert is Key Lime Pie, truly authentic only when its tangy filling is made with the small, round, yellow-green aromatic limes grown in the Florida Keys. Fish dishes may be grilled, sautéed, or pan-seared; but are often marinated with lime juice and served with sauces or side dishes made with local fruits.

Limes

**Stone crab claws** The claws are the only part of this local delicacy to be eaten – delicious dipped in butter and sauce.

# Where to Eat and Drink

## Miami

### Miami Beach

**11th Street Diner** $
American     Map 2 F3
*1065 Washington Ave, 33139*
**Tel** *(305) 534-6373*
Classic old-time diner with a
fun ambience. Serves favorites
such as meatloaf, fried chicken,
sandwiches, and burgers.

**Big Pink** $
American     Map 2 E5
*157 Collins Ave, 33139*
**Tel** *(305) 532-4700*
Popular waterside diner featuring
all-day breakfasts and an ironic
"TV Dinner" selection. Good
sandwiches and salads.

**Café Charlotte** $
Argentinian/Italian     Map 2 F3
*1497 Washington Ave, 33139*
**Tel** *(305) 535-1522*
No-frills setting and delicious
Argentinian specialties including
skirt steak, *empanadas* (pastry
filled with meat, vegetables and
cheese), and lime chicken.

**Lime Fresh** $
Mexican     Map 2 D3
*1439 Alton Rd, 33139*
**Tel** *(305) 532-5463*
Part of a reliable chain, with
reasonably priced Mexican
favorites including tacos, burritos,
quesadillas, and fajitas.

**Puerto Sagua** $
Cuban     Map 2 E4
*700 Collins Ave, 33139*
**Tel** *(305) 673-1115*
A favorite since 1962 with a
good Cuban menu, as well as
American turkey and grilled
cheese sandwiches.

**Roasters 'n Toasters** $
Deli     Map F4
*525 Arthur Godfrey Rd, 33140*
**Tel** *(305) 531-7691*
New York-style deli with everything
from corned beef and pastrami, to
wraps, sandwiches, and soups.

**Rosinella** $
Italian     Map 2 E2
*525 Lincoln Rd, 33139*
**Tel** *(305) 672-8777*
Comfortable family-style dining
with home-made pastas and
budget-priced pizzas. Selection
of Italian and American wines.

**Shake Shack** $
American     Map 2 D2
*1111 Lincoln Rd, 33139*
**Tel** *(305) 434-7787*
Quality burgers at bargain prices,
plus great fries and shakes worth
standing in line for.

### DK Choice

**Tap Tap Haitian** $
Haitian     Map 2 E4
*819 5th St, 33139*
**Tel** *(305) 672-2898*
Since 1994, this restaurant, art
gallery, and cultural center all
rolled into one has attracted a
vibrant, multi-cultural crowd.
Known for its authentic Haitian
dishes such as steamed whole
fish in lime sauce, shrimp in
Creole sauce, goat stew, sweet
potato pie, and banana fritters.

**405 Deli** $$
Deli     Map 4 F1
*405 NW 26th St, 33127*
**Tel** *(786) 347-7100*     **Closed** *Sat*
Enjoy traditional Jewish delights
from the kitchen of the James
Beard Award-nominated Zak The

**Price Guide**
Prices are based on a three-course meal
for one with glass of house wine, and all
unavoidable extra charges including tax.

| $ | up to $35 |
|---|---|
| $$ | $35 to 50 |
| $$$ | over $50 |

Baker. The corned beef and
smoked salmon are served on
some of Florida's best bread.

**Balans** $$
International     Map 2 D2
*1022 Lincoln Rd, 33139*
**Tel** *(305) 534-9191*
With jambalaya, crab linguine, Thai
curry, and burgers, Balans has
something for everyone. Good
brunches and a busy bar.

**Fratelli la Bufala** $$
Italian     Road Map F4
*437 Washington Ave, 33139*
**Tel** *(305) 532-0700*
Legendary in Italy, this chain
from Naples imports fresh
buffalo mozzarella and wines
from Campania, and serves
Neapolitan pizza direct from
a blazing wood-fired oven.

**Front Porch Café** $$
American     Map 2 F3
*1458 Ocean Dr, 33139*
**Tel** *(305) 531-8300*
An excellent choice for breakfast
and brunch, this café has its own
versions of traditional American
dinner entrées, and exclusive
poolside dining for hotel guests.

**News Café** $$
American     Map 2 F4
*800 Ocean Dr, 33139*
**Tel** *(305) 538-6397*
Large crowds flock to this round-
the-clock café serving crab cakes,
grilled salmon, pizza, and pasta.

The colorful exterior of Big Pink

**For more information on types of restaurants** *see page 326–7*

**Nexxt Café** $$
International Map 2 E2
*700 Lincoln Rd, 33139*
**Tel** *(305) 532-6643*
Nexxt offers a range of choices, from small plates and tapas to mains, including Cajun chicken and Miso salmon. Good cocktails.

**Barton G. The Restaurant** $$$
American Map 2 D3
*1427 West Ave, 33139*
**Tel** *(305) 672-8881*
Glitzy spot, with whimsical decor and a focus on extravagant presentation and enticing aromas. Try the king salmon and samurai tuna.

**Casa Tua** $$$
Italian Map 2 E4
*1700 James Ave, 33139*
**Tel** *(305) 673-1010*
Cozy boutique eatery combining immaculate Italian and European cuisines. Dine in the magical lantern-lit garden space, romantic library, or 20-seater chef's table.

**A Fish Called Avalon** $$$
Seafood Map 2 E4
*700 Ocean Dr, 33139*
**Tel** *(305) 532-1727*
Fresh seafood on offer, with some surprises such as orzo paella and crab-crusted grouper. Enjoy live music on the verandah.

**Forte dei Marmi** $$$
Italian Map 2 E4
*150 Ocean Dr, Miami Beach, 33139*
**Tel** *(786) 276-3095*
Local, organic fare from two-time Michelin-starred chef Antonio Mellino. The suckling pig, slow-cooked for 36 hours, is a must try.

**Grillfish** $$$
Seafood Map 2 F2
*1444 Collins Ave, 33139*
**Tel** *(305) 538-9908*
A local favorite for its extremely fresh seafood served with tasty sauces. There are also plenty of seafood pasta combinations.

**Joe's Stone Crab** $$$
Seafood Map 2 E5
*11 Washington Ave, 33139*
**Tel** *(305) 673-0365* **Closed** *Aug–Oct*
Despite the long lines, Joe's is a must-visit for fresh seafood and absolutely wonderful stone crabs. Or pop in at Joe's Takeaway next door and avoid the wait.

**Las Vacas Gordas** $$$
Argentinian Road Map F4
*933 Normandy Dr, 33141*
**Tel** *(305) 867-1717*
Enjoy large portions of juicy steak and well-priced Argentinian fare in an eclectic, lively, and contemporary setting.

**Leynia** $$$
Argentinean Map 2 F1
*1685 Collins Ave, Miami Beach, 33139*
**Tel** *(305) 674-5752*
Argentine beef meets Japanese flavors at Leynia – Patagonian lamb is served alongside sushi.

**Nobu Miami Beach** $$$
Japanese Map 2 F1
*4525 Collins Ave, 33139*
**Tel** *(305) 695-3232*
A classy international brand, with fantastic sushi and Japanese specialties. Reserve in advance.

**Osteria del Teatro** $$$
Italian Map 2 F3
*1200 Collins Ave, 33139*
**Tel** *(786) 475-1364*
An intimate oasis renowned for its traditional North Italian veal, pasta dishes, and wine list.

**Prime One Twelve** $$$
Steakhouse Map 2 E5
*112 Ocean Dr, 33139*
**Tel** *(305) 532-8112*
Join Prime One Twelve's celebrity clientele and enjoy luscious steaks, dry-aged beef, and truffled lobster mac 'n' cheese.

**Sardinia Enoteca Ristorante** $$$
Italian Map 2 D2
*1801 Purdy Ave, 33139*
**Tel** *(305) 531-2228*
Choose from dozens of Italian wines, paired with delicious pastas and entrées. Truly Italian–style service and atmosphere.

**Spiga** $$$
Italian Map 2 E3
*1228 Collins Ave, 33139*
**Tel** *(305) 534-0079*
Handmade pastas are the specialty at this quiet, romantic restaurant.

The sophisticated bar at Azul, with ice-cold champagne nestled in the bar top

Try the green veal ravioli with mushrooms, or fettucine with shrimp and asparagus.

**Yuca** $$$
Cuban Map 2 E2
*501 Lincoln Rd, 33139*
**Tel** *(305) 532-9822*
Serves contemporary Cuban cuisine including guava baby-back ribs and plantain-coated mahi mahi.

## Downtown and Little Havana

**La Casita** $
Cuban/Mexican Road Map F4
*3805 SW 8th St, 33134*
**Tel** *(305) 448-8224*
Cuban café that also offers Mexican standards such as tacos, burritos, and enchiladas at great prices.

Striking decor at Joe's Stone Crab

**Islas Canarias** $
Cuban **Road Map** F4
*13695 SW 26th St, 33135*
**Tel** *(305) 559 6666*
Decent Cuban favorites
including sandwiches, pork,
and chicken dishes. Great value.

**S&S Restaurant** $
Diner
*2699 Biscayne Blvd, 33139*
**Tel** *(305) 456-8876*
Recently re-homed after 79 years,
this classic eatery still has the
same owners and menu of
tasty diner fare. Friendly staff.

**Velvet Creme Doughnuts** $
Café **Map** 4 F2
*1555 SW 8th St, 33135*
**Tel** *(305) 301-5257*
The 70-year-old Velvet has
been rebuilt in Calle Ocho and
offers artisan donuts and coffee.

**Versailles** $
Cuban **Map** 4 E2
*3335 8th St, 33135*
**Tel** *(305) 444-8358*
Choose from two sampler plates
for a delicious introduction to
Cuban cuisine at Little Havana's
best-known restaurant.

**Ella's Oyster Bar** $$
Seafood **Road Map** F4
*1615 SW 8th St, 33135*
**Tel** *(786) 332-4436*
Come here for seafood cooked
with an eclectic mix of Florida,
Cuba and New England style.
Favorites include fish tostadas
and Maine lobster rolls.

**Miami Smokers** $$
BBQ **Road Map** F4
*306 NW 27th Ave, 33125*
**Tel** *(786) 520-5420*
House-cured meats from heritage-
bred pigs feature on the menu
here. The stacked sandwiches
come with fillings such as sausage,
slab bacon, sweet ham, and more.

**Arson** $$$
Continental **Road Map** F4
*104 NE 2nd Ave, 33132*
**Tel** *(786) 717-6711*
Every dish on the menu at
Arson is cooked on a Spanish
open-fire wood grill. Try the pork
shoulder, dorado cooked in salt,
and the Angus rib eye steak.

**DB Bistro Moderne** $$$
French **Map** 4 F1
*255 Biscayne Blvd, 33131*
**Tel** *(305) 421-8800* **Closed** *Sun*
Run by celebrity chef Daniel
Boulud, this chic bistro is known
for its *escargot* (snails), duck
confit, and the extravagant
but delectable sirloin burger.

**Il Gabbiano** $$$
Italian **Map** 4 F1
*One Miami Tower, 335 S Biscaye*
*Blvd, 33131*
**Tel** *(305) 373-0063* **Closed** *Sun*
Enjoy inspired Italian cuisine in a
sublime bayside setting. Delicious
pastas and fantastic veal dishes.

**Michael's Genuine Food**
**& Drink** $$$
American **Road Map** F4
*130 NE 40th St, 33137*
**Tel** *(305) 573-5550*
Trendy spot where all the
ingredients are sourced fresh from
the sea or from nearby farms.
Serves a range of dishes, from
small to extra-large helpings.

**Naoe** $$$
Japanese **Map** 4 F2
*661 Brickell Key Dr, 33131*
**Tel** *(305) 947-6263* **Closed** *Mon*
Divine Japanese cuisine is served
in a multi-course format, priced
by the number of courses.

**The River Seafood and**
**Oyster Bar** $$$
Seafood **Map** 4 E2
*650 S Miami Ave*
**Tel** *(305) 530-1915*
Enjoy seafood prepared in every
way imaginable. Grand, sophisticated setting. The crab fried
brown rice should not be missed.

**DK Choice**

**Tuyo** $$$
American **Map** 4 E1
*415 NE 2nd Ave, 33132*
**Tel** *(305) 337-3200* **Closed** *Sun*
*& Mon*
The creative chef here prepares
delicious "Floribbean" cuisine by
blending fresh local ingredients
with Latin spices. Some stand-
outs from the menu include
marinated duck breast, Keys
yellowtail with citrus butter, *foie*
*gras*, and cornbread-stuffed quail.
Romantic setting and great views
atop the Miami Culinary Institute.

## Coral Gables and Coconut Grove

**Jaguar** $$
Latin American **Road Map** F5
*3067 Grand Ave, 33133*
**Tel** *(305) 444-0216*
Artfully seasoned Latin and
many grilled items feature
in Jaguar's colorful tropical
menu. Seafood taster platters
are available.

**DK Choice**

**Seasons 52** $$
American **Road Map** F4
*321 Miracle Mile, 33134*
**Tel** *(305) 442-8552*
Choose from a range of fresh,
healthy food, with no entrée
over 475 calories. Dishes
include cedar plank roasted
salmon and grilled T-bone
lamb chops. Also sample from
an extensive wine and drinks
list that features pomegranate
margarita martini and mandarin
orange cosmopolitan. Live
piano music in the bar adds
to the charm.

**Ariete** $$$
American **Road Map** F5
*3540 Main Hwy, Coconut Grove,*
*33133*
**Tel** *(305) 640-5862*
This chef-driven eatery is great
for adventurous diners, with
shareable entrées and family-
style plating of smoked pork
chops, venison tartare, and
pasta made from green nettles
on the menu.

**Le Bouchon du Grove** $$$
French **Map** 6 F4
*3430 Main Hwy, 33133*
**Tel** *(305) 448-6060*
With delightful French posters
on the walls, this chef-owned
casual bistro serves award-
winning French cuisine. The
service is excellent.

The elegant lounge and bar at DB Bistro Moderne

**For more information on types of restaurants** *see page 326–7*

**Caffe Abbracci** $$$
Italian **Map** 5 C1
*318 Aragon Ave, 33134*
**Tel** *(305) 441-0700*
This is where Miami's elite
head for authentic Italian.
The owner is very welcoming.
Wide choice of American
and European wines.

**George's in the Grove** $$$
French **Road Map** F5
*3145 Commodor Plaza, 33133*
**Tel** *(305) 444-7878*
French bistro with lively
ambience serving everything
from mussels and steak frites to
burgers and pizza. The free glass
of champagne offered on arrival
is a nice touch.

**Ortanique on the Mile** $$$
Caribbean **Map** 5 C1
*278 Miracle Mile, 33134*
**Tel** *(305) 446-7710*
Trendy Caribbean restaurant with
plenty of seafood and fresh fruit
on the menu. Try one of their
delicious Bacardi mojitos.

**Palme d'Or** $$$
French **Map** 5 A2
*1200 Anastasia Ave, 33134*
**Tel** *(305) 913-3201* **Closed** *Sun
& Mon*
A great choice for formal dining
and special occasions. Exquisite
surroundings and traditional
French food including venison,
rack of lamb, and lemon sole.

**Pascal on Ponce** $$$
French **Map** 5 C2
*2611 Ponce de Leon Blvd, 33134*
**Tel** *(305) 444-2024* **Closed** *Sun*
This small, classy café covered
with beautiful art pieces has a
reputation for fine food and a
bargain prix fixe bistro menu.

**Red Fish Grill** $$$
Seafood **Road Map** F5
*9610 Old Cutler Rd, 33156*
**Tel** *(305) 668-8788* **Closed** *Mon*
Enjoy fine seafood and excellent
wines in a romantic seaside
setting in Matheson Hammock
Park. Ask for a table on the palm-
lined outdoor terrace to admire
spectacular views over the bay.

**Zucca** $$$
Italian **Map** 6 D1
*162 Alcazar Ave, Coral Gables,
33134*
**Tel** *(786) 580-3731*
Located in the historic Hotel St.
Michel, this restaurant offers a
creative fine dining experience in
a casual space. Homemade pasta
and steaks are combined with
hand-crafted cocktails and an
extensive wine list.

## Farther Afield

**Mario the Baker** $
Italian **Road Map** F4
*14691 Biscayne Blvd, North Miami
Beach, 33181*
**Tel** *(305) 891-7641*
For a quick pizza and pasta fix,
Mario does not disappoint. Try
the white sauce Alfredo pizza or
over-stuffed nine-inch subs,
available to dine-in, takeout or
for delivery.

**Shorty's BBQ** $
Southern **Road Map** F5
*9200 Dixie Hwy, South Miami, 33156*
**Tel** *(305) 670-7732*
A southern Florida institution,
well-known for its delectable ribs,
barbecued brisket, pulled pork
sandwiches, and chicken. Don't
miss their legendary BBQ sauce.
Good bargain lunch platters and
excellent service.

**Mignonette Uptown** $$
Seafood/American **Road Map** F4
*13951 Biscayne Blvd, North Miami
Beach, 33181*
**Tel** *(305) 705-2159*
This new inhabitant of the
old Gourmet Diner location
has kept the silver Airstream
design. The menu features
fish dip, po' boy sandwiches,
oysters, and a superb brunch
and dinner service.

**Sushi House** $$
Asian **Road Map** F4
*15911 Biscayne Blvd, North Miami
Beach, 33160*
**Tel** *(305) 947-6002* **Closed** *Mon*
Along with its specialty sushi, this
chic Asian eatery offers a wide-
ranging menu including Szechwan
cuisine and dishes cooked on a
*hibachi* (Japanese grill).

**Cantina Beach** $$$
Mexican **Road Map** F4
*Ritz Carlton, 455 Grand Bay Dr, 33149*
**Tel** *(305) 365-4500*
Great oceanside restaurant under
a thatched roof. Enjoy Mexican
favorites prepared with the usual
Ritz pizzazz, and choose from
over 85 kinds of tequila.

**Kitchen 305** $$$
American **Road Map** F4
*16701 Collins Ave, Sunny Isles, 33160*
**Tel** *(305) 749-2110*
Located in the lobby of the
Newport Beachside Resort, this
trendy restaurant has an eclectic
menu including paella, crab cakes,
and veal shank stew. All-you-can-
eat lobster on Wednesdays.

### DK Choice

**Rusty Pelican** $$$
American **Road Map** F4
*3201 Rickenbacker Causeway, 33149*
**Tel** *(305) 361-3818*
With a creative chef at the helm
and spectacular bay and city
views from the dining room,
Rusty Pelican is a great choice.
It offers sushi, land or sea
entrées, a bargain prix fixe
menu, and small plates for
sharing. Try signature dishes
including lobster bouilabaisse
and seafood en papillote.

**Timo** $$$
Mediterranean **Road Map** F4
*17624 Collins Ave, Sunny Isles,
33160*
**Tel** *(305) 936-1008*
An upscale eatery highly
rated for its seasonal Italian-
Mediterranean dishes. Try the
*zuppa di pesce* (lobster, shellfish,
and Sardinian couscous).

The Rusty Pelican restaurant, next to the Rickenbacker Marina in Miami

The facade of Mexican restaurant Casa Maya Grill in Deerfield Beach

# The Gold and Treasure Coasts

**BOCA RATON: Ben's Kosher Deli**
Deli        **Road Map** F4   $
*9942 Clint Moore Rd, 33496*
**Tel** *(561) 470-9963*
Ben's is a busy New York-style deli with an extensive menu featuring corned beef, pastrami, potato pancakes, and stuffed cabbage. There is an inventive kids' menu.

**BOCA RATON: Tin Muffin Café** $
American       **Road Map** F4
*364 E Palmetto Park Rd, 33432*
**Tel** *(561) 392-9446*   **Closed** *Sun*
Appealing bakery and café with delicious sandwiches, salads, and home-made soups. Popular lunch spot. Credit cards not accepted.

**BOCA RATON: Abe & Louie's** $$$
Steakhouse    **Road Map** F4
*2200 Glades Rd, 33431*
**Tel** *(561) 447-0024*
Top-quality meats, and an impressive wine list. Fun club ambience with leather seats and spacious booths. The bone-in filet mignon is a must try.

**BOCA RATON: Kathy's Gazebo** $$$
Continental    **Road Map** F4
*4199 N Federal Hwy, 33431*
**Tel** *(561) 395-6033*   **Closed** *Sun*
An old-fashioned café known for specialties such as rack of lamb, veal medallions, scampi, and Dover sole. Excellent wine and champagnes available.

**BOCA RATON: Max's Grille** $$$
American      **Road Map** F4
*404 Plaza Real, 33432*
**Tel** *(561) 368-0080*
Diners are spoilt for choice at this popular, lively bistro offering everything from chicken wings and salads to grilled meat and fish. Good brunches.

---

## DK Choice

**BOCA RATON: Sapori**   $$$
Italian      **Road Map** F4
*301 via de Palmas, 33432*
**Tel** *(561) 367-9779*
The Italian word for 'flavors', Sapori is a small, unpretentious restaurant rightly known for its flavorful fish dishes and some of the city's best pasta. Expect surprises such as short rib ravioli or sweet-and-sour salmon filet. Visit on one of their pasta Thursdays when chef Marco Pindo explains ingredients and shows how each dish is made.

---

**DANIA BEACH: Jaxson's** $
Ice Cream Parlor   **Road Map** F4
*128 S Federal Hwy, 33004*
**Tel** *(954) 923-4445*
Jaxson's serves fine sandwiches and salads, but its delicious ice creams, in flavours such as rocky road, butter pecan, and cookie dough, are the big draw. Fun, old-fashioned ambience with colorful memorabilia on the walls.

**DANIA BEACH: Le Petit Café De Dania** $$
French      **Road Map** F4
*3308 Griffin Rd, 33312*
**Tel** *(954) 967-9912*   **Closed** *Mon*
Authentic French favorites prepared by chefs from Brittany in a welcoming, intimate bistro setting. Try the specialty crepes and the 'Sunset Dinner'.

**DAVIE: Buca di Beppo** $
Italian      **Road Map** F4
*3355 S University Dr, 33328*
**Tel** *(954) 577-3287*
Chain restaurant offering large portions of tomato sauce-based Italian perennials, family-style meals and delicious desserts at affordable prices. Lively vibe.

---

**DEERFIELD BEACH: Casa Maya Grill** $
Mexican     **Road Map** F4
*301 SE 15th Terrace, Cove Shopping Ctr, 33441*
**Tel** *(954) 570-6101*
Authentic Mexican enchiladas, tacos, and burritos served in a pleasant setting. Try the refreshing margaritas and sangrias.

**DEERFIELD BEACH: Little Havana** $
Cuban      **Road Map** F4
*721 S Federal Hwy, 33441*
**Tel** *(954) 427-6000*
Family-owned eatery serving authentic Cuban fare and home-made bread. Good daily dinner specials. Music on weekends.

**DELRAY BEACH: Caffe Luna Rosa** $$
Italian      **Road Map** F4
*34 S Ocean Blvd, 33483*
**Tel** *(561) 274-9404*
Serving a varied menu during the day and exclusively Italian cuisine in the evening, Caffe Luna Rosa guarantees a great meal in a beautiful beach-side setting.

**DELRAY BEACH: Sundy House Restaurant** $$$
American     **Road Map** F4
*106 S Swinton Ave, 33444*
**Tel** *(561) 272-5678*   **Closed** *Mon*
Savor well-prepared American fare in a romantic garden setting with an outdoor bar. Great weekend brunch with plenty of seafood and Mediterranean dishes.

**FORT LAUDERDALE: The Floridian** $
Diner      **Road Map** F4
*1410 E Las Olas Blvd, 33301*
**Tel** *(954) 463-4041*
An old-time diner open round-the-clock. Serves large portions of hearty fare, including ham-burgers and meatloaf. The all-day breakfasts are popular.

**For more information on types of restaurants** *see page 326–7*

**FORT LAUDERDALE:**
**Tarpon Bend**                $$
American                **Road Map** F4
*200 SW 2nd Ave, 33301*
**Tel** *(954) 523-3233*
A lively sports bar known for its happy hour and young clientele. Decent grilled fish, burgers, and beer on tap.

**FORT LAUDERDALE: 15th Street**
**Fisheries & Dockside Café**  $$$
Seafood                **Road Map** F4
*1900 SE 15th St, 33316*
**Tel** *(954) 763-2777*
Watch the boats and feed the tarpons at this café by the marina. Delicious seafood on offer, along with a more casual menu for light snacking. Good bar.

**FORT LAUDERDALE:**
**Blue Moon Fish Co.**          $$$
Seafood                **Road Map** F4
*44405 Tradewinds Ave, 33308*
**Tel** *(954) 267-9888*
Dine on fresh seafood while watching yachts sail along the Intracoastal. Good two-for-one lunches. Reserve ahead and ask for alfresco seating.

**FORT LAUDERDALE:**
**Café Seville**                $$$
Spanish                **Road Map** F4
*2768 Oakland Park Blvd, 33306*
**Tel** *(954) 565-1148*        **Closed** *Sun*
Plentiful tapas, gazpacho and paella among the many Spanish favorites at Café Seville. Extensive list of Spanish wines.

**FORT LAUDERDALE: Canyon** $$$
American                **Road Map** F4
*1818 E Sunrise Blvd, 33304*
**Tel** *(954) 475-1950*
Popular spot known for big portions made from locally-sourced produce, and its prickly pear margaritas. No reservations taken so expect long lines.

**FORT LAUDERDALE:**
**Casablanca Café**             $$$
American                **Road Map** F4
*3049 Alhambra St, 33304*
**Tel** *(954) 764-3500*
Casablanca has a beautiful, romantic setting with ocean views and a piano bar. The extensive menu features chili-dusted sea scallops, walnut chicken, and Atlantic swordfish.

**FORT LAUDERDALE:**
**Eduardo de San Angel**        $$$
Mexican                **Road Map** F4
*2822 E Commercial Blvd, 33308*
**Tel** *(954) 772-4731*        **Closed** *Sun*
Great Mexican fine-dining experience. The chef-owner serves truly gourmet food in a warm hacienda-style setting.

The dining room of The Floridian in Fort Lauderdale

**FORT LAUDERDALE:**
**Greek Islands Taverna**       $$$
Greek                **Road Map** F4
*3300 N Ocean Blvd, 33308*
**Tel** *(954) 565-5505*
Owned by the Kantzavelos brothers for more than 16 years where hoards of loyal patrons line up to sample the *meze*, fresh fish, and lamb. Specializes in little-known wines from Greece.

**FORT LAUDERDALE:**
**Lobster Bar Sea Grille**      $$$
Seafood/Steakhouse  **Road Map** F4
*450 E Las Olas, 33301*
**Tel** *(954) 772-2675*
Delectable fresh seafood, live lobsters, and prime steaks served in an upscale yet casual atmosphere. Try their home-made ice creams and sorbets.

**DK Choice**

**FORT LAUDERDALE:**
**Market 17**                   $$$
American                **Road Map** F4
*1850 SE 17th St, 33316*
**Tel** *(954) 835-5507*  **Closed** *May–Oct: Mon*
The elegant food at Market 17 is prepared using fresh farm-to-table organic produce. Choose from delectable dishes made with local seafood and game, or the homemade charcuterie. A special dining-in-the-dark option is offered.

**FORT LAUDERDALE: Nisi**       $$$
Greek                **Road Map** F4
*3330 E Oakland Park Blvd, 33308*
**Tel** *(954) 200-6006*
Upscale, modern cuisine takes on traditional Greek staples including steak, seafood and lamb sausage. Great appetizers.

**FORT LAUDERDALE:**
**Sette Bello**                 $$$
Italian                **Road Map** F4
*6241 N Federal Hwy, 33308*
**Tel** *(954) 351-0505*        **Closed** *Sun*
Decorated with traditional Italian flare, this restaurant is run by an attentive chef known for his well-prepared classics and ricotta cheesecake. Good daily specials.

**FORT LAUDERDALE: Valentino's**
**Cucina Italiana**             $$$
Italian                **Road Map** F4
*620 S Federal Hwy, 33301*
**Tel** *(954) 523-5767*        **Closed** *Sun*
Innovative Italian cuisine and superb service are hallmarks of this chef-owned sophisticated restaurant. Fine dining at its best.

**HOLLYWOOD:**
**Las Vegas Cuban Cuisine**       $
Cuban                **Road Map** F4
*1212 N State Rd 7, 33021*
**Tel** *(954) 792-4713*
Part of a small chain that promises large portions of tasty Cuban fare at low prices. Good lunch specials and a kids' menu.

**HOLLYWOOD: Le Tub**
**Saloon**                        $
American                **Road Map** F4
*1100 N Ocean Dr, 33019*
**Tel** *(954) 921-9425*
A busy outdoor seating saloon in a trendy gas station setting. Serves legendary burgers and brews, and delicious key lime pie.

**HOLLYWOOD: Taverna Opa**      $$
Greek                **Road Map** F4
*410 N Ocean Dr, 33019*
**Tel** *(954) 929-4010*
A fun place with belly dancers and Intracoastal

views. Choose from delicious *meze*, grilled fish, lamb, and souvlaki platters, accompanied by Greek wines.

**JENSEN BEACH:**
**11 Maple Street** $$$
American **Road Map** F4
*3224 NE Maple Ave, 34957*
**Tel** *(772) 334-7714* **Closed** *Sun*
Quaint homely eatery with a sophisticated menu. Artful small plates for sharing, with octopus, quail, ribs, and steak on offer.

**PALM BEACH: Pizza**
**Al Fresco** $$
Italian **Road Map** F4
*14 Via Mizner, 33480*
**Tel** *(561) 832-0032* **Closed** *Sun*
Savor delicious thin-crust pizza straight from a wood-burning oven along with a range of entrées in a lovely garden setting. Great choice for breakfast.

**PALM BEACH:**
**Bice Ristorante** $$$
Italian **Road Map** F4
*313 1/2 Worth Ave, 33480*
**Tel** *(561) 835-1600*
Upscale, high-quality Italian cuisine served in a swanky setting. Fantastic landscaped patio and attentive service.

**PALM BEACH: Bonefish**
**Grill** $$$
Seafood **Road Map** F4
*4635 PGA Blvd, Palm Beach Gardens, 33418*
**Tel** *(561) 799-2965*
This chain outlet near Palm Beach serves reliably fresh fish, oysters, lobsters, and more. Good martinis. Lively spot, though rather noisy.

**DK Choice**
**PALM BEACH: Buccan** $$$
American **Road Map** F4
*350 S County Rd, 33480*
**Tel** *(561) 833-3450*
With a highly renowned chef, an energetic vibe, and a creative menu featuring many small plates to share, Buccan stands out from the rest. The menu extends beyond steak and swordfish to offer a range of meals from short rib *empanadas* (stuffed pastry), hot dog paninis to wood-fired pizza with quail or lamb chop toppings.

**PALM BEACH: Café**
**Boulud** $$$
French **Road Map** F4
*301 Australian Ave, 33480*
**Tel** *(561) 655-6060*
New York's star chef Daniel Boulud brings elegant French cuisine to the south. The prix fixe lunch here is a great bargain.

**PALM BEACH:**
**Chez Jean-Pierre** $$$
French **Road Map** F4
*132 N County Rd, 33480*
**Tel** *(561) 833-1171* **Closed** *Sun*
With arty surroundings and elegant cuisine, Chez Jean-Pierre is worth the splurge. Specialties include dover sole and profiteroles.

**PALM BEACH: Echo** $$$
Asian **Road Map** F4
*230A Sunrise Ave, 33480*
**Tel** *(855) 435-0061* **Closed** *Mon*
Sample excellent sushi and delicious entrées such as Thai roast duck and lemon chicken. Sleek interior with a lively bar.

**PALM BEACH:**
**Palm Beach Grill** $$$
American **Road Map** F4
*340 Royal Poinciana Way, 33480*
**Tel** *(561) 835-1077*
Lively restaurant serving reliably delicious ribs and snappers among other American favorites. Key lime pie and burgers for the thrifty.

**POMPANO BEACH: Calypso** $$
Caribbean **Road Map** F4
*460 S Cypress Rd, 33060*
**Tel** *(954) 942-1633* **Closed** *Sat & Sun*
Relish island favorites such as Jamaican jerk chicken, West Indian curries, and conch chowder in Calypso's no-frills setting.

**DK Choice**
**POMPANO BEACH:**
**Café Maxx** $$$
American **Road Map** F4
*2601 E Atlantic Blvd, 33062*
**Tel** *(954) 782-0606*
Lovers of fine cuisine have been making pilgrimage to Café Maxx since 1984. An impressive wine list and innovative offerings that include jerk-spiced scallops, pine nut-crusted rack of lamb, and pumpkin bisque.

**VERO BEACH: Ocean Grill** $$$
American **Road Map** F3
*1050 Beachland Blvd, 32963*
**Tel** *(954) 941-7830*
Enjoy fine dining on a sand dune with beautiful ocean views. There is a varied menu with many sea-food options. Kids' menu available.

**WEST PALM BEACH: Agora** $
Turkish **Road Map** F4
*2505 North Dixie Hwy, 33407*
**Tel** *(561) 651-7474* **Closed** *Sun*
Traditional Turkish classics and modern interpretations of Mediterranean dishes paired with unusual Turkish wines.

**WEST PALM BEACH:**
**Hot Pie Pizza** $
Pizza **Road Map** F4
*123 S Olive Ave, 33401*
**Tel** *(561) 655-2511*
Thin-crust pizzas, burgers, and pastas are on offer at this eatery. The authentic New York-style coal oven, exposed brick, and wooden booths add to the ambience.

**WEST PALM BEACH: Pistache** $$$
French **Road Map** F4
*101 N Clematis St, 33401*
**Tel** *(561) 833-5090*
The menu at this French bistro features mussels, *coq au vin*, and crepes. Terrace seating overlooking the Intracoastal Waterway.

The interior of Italian restaurant Sette Bello in Fort Lauderdale

The entrance and terrace of French bistro Pistache in West Palm Beach

**WEST PALM BEACH:**
**Rhythm Café**                    **$$$**
American          **Road Map** F4
*3800A S Dixie Hwy, 33405*
**Tel** *(561) 833-3406*    **Closed** *Mon*
Located in a converted gas
station, this quirky café in
the antique district offers
tapas and the catch of the
day cooked in a variety of
different ways.

## Orlando and the Space Coast

**COCOA: Café**
**Margaux**                        **$$$**
French             **Road Map** F3
*220 Brevard Ave, 32922*
**Tel** *(321) 639-8343*    **Closed** *Sun*
French fine dining with
creative choices such as
filo-encased Norwegian
salmon, and pear, brie, and
walnut-stuffed pork loin.
Exceptional wines.

**COCOA BEACH: Keith's**
**Oyster Bar**                        **$**
Seafood            **Road Map** F3
*401 Meade Ave, 32931*
**Tel** *(321) 783-7549*
Casual open-air dining located
on a pier. Menu includes oysters,
coconut beer shrimp, and crab
legs. Home-made Key lime pie.

**COCOA BEACH:**
**Pompano Grill**                  **$$**
Seafood            **Road Map** F3
*110 N Brevard Ave,*
*32931*
**Tel** *(321) 784-9005*    **Closed** *Sun*
*& Mon*
Extremely popular family-run
café offering fresh local catch
and excellent seafood crepes.
Decent variety of chicken and
steak dishes. A small place,
so reserve ahead.

**COCOA BEACH: The Fat Snook  $$**
Seafood            **Road Map** F3
*2464 Atlantic Ave, 32931*
**Tel** *(321) 784-1190*
Family-owned restaurant offering
creative seafood specialties, as
well as beef, chicken, and
Caribbean-inspired dishes. Indulge
in boutique-style wines and craft
beers from around the world.

**INTERNATIONAL DRIVE:**
**Bahama Breeze**                  **$$**
Caribbean          **Road Map** E2
*8849 International Dr, 32819*
**Tel** *(407) 248-2499*
Part of the top-quality chain
popular for its great Caribbean
menu and tropical drinks. Try the
coconut shrimp and pulled pork
sliders. Great island ambience.

**INTERNATIONAL DRIVE:**
**The Capital Grille**            **$$$**
Steakhouse         **Road Map** E2
*9101 International Dr, 32819*
**Tel** *(407) 370-4392*
This upscale restaurant chain
serves only the choicest of steaks
and delicious side dishes. Try the
chef's daily seafood platter.
Expensive but worth it.

**INTERNATIONAL DRIVE:**
**Cuba Libre**                     **$$$**
Cuban              **Road Map** E2
*9101 International Dr, 32819*
**Tel** *(407) 226-1600*
Decent Cuban fare offered in
a festive ambience reminiscent
of Havana, complete with
refreshing mojitos, sangrias, and
salsa dancing on Saturdays.

**INTERNATIONAL DRIVE:**
**Everglades**                     **$$$**
Steakhouse         **Road Map** E2
*Rosen Center Hotel, 9840*
*International Dr, 32819*
**Tel** *(407) 996-2385*
This restaurant celebrates
"everything Florida" including

fresh Florida grouper, rock
shrimp, venison steak, and
their specialty dish – gator
chowder soup. Also try the
Key lime pie.

**INTERNATIONAL DRIVE:**
**The Oceanaire**                  **$$$**
Seafood            **Road Map** E2
*9101 International Dr, 32819*
**Tel** *(407) 363-4801*
Perfectly prepared seafood
and attentive service. Sleek
setting with ocean liner
decor. Opt for the quieter
patio seating.

**INTERNATIONAL DRIVE:**
**Urban Tide**                     **$$$**
Seafood            **Road Map** E2
*9801 International Dr, 32819*
**Tel** *(407) 345-4570*
Chef Jared Gross highlights
fresh Florida seafood in
flawlessly executed dishes.

**KISSIMMEE: Pacino's Italian**
**Ristorante**                     **$$$**
Italian            **Road Map** E3
*5795 W Hwy 192, 34746*
**Tel** *(407) 239-4141*
Elegant, traditional Italian
restaurant serving wood-fired
brick-oven pizzas, grilled steaks
and chops, pastas, and seafood.
Friendly ambience.

**LAKE BUENA VISTA:**
**Hemingway's**                    **$$$**
Seafood            **Road Map** E2
*Hyatt Regency Resort, 1 Grand*
*Cypress Blvd, 32836*
**Tel** *(407) 239-1234*
Inspired by Ernest Hemingway's
fishing exploits, this restaurant
offers fantastic seafood
including local swordfish,
Florida rock shrimp, mahi
mahi, and Cayo Huesto crab
cakes. Ask for its signature
drink Papa's Doble, designed
by Hemingway himself.

**ORLANDO: Lee & Rick's** $
Seafood                 Road Map E2
*5621 Old Winter Garden Road, 32811*
**Tel** *(407) 293-3587*
An area landmark for more
than 65 years, Lee & Rick's is a
throwback to a simpler time.
Long-time oyster shuckers work
their craft here for a uniquely
Floridian experience.

**ORLANDO: Little Saigon** $
Vietnamese              Road Map F2
*1106 Colonial Dr, 32803*
**Tel** *(407) 423-8539*
A neighborhood favorite, Little
Saigon offers well-priced, authentic
Vietnamese fare. Delicious appe-
tizers and noodle and rice dishes.

**ORLANDO: Artisan's Table** $$
American                Road Map E2
*22 E Pine St, 32801*
**Tel** *(407) 730-7499*
Intimate restaurant in the heart
of Downtown's old district.
Distinctive use of seasonal and
local ingredients offers a perfect
balance of freshness and flavor.

**ORLANDO: Rusty Spoon** $$
American                Road Map F2
*55 West Church Street, 32801*
**Tel** *(407) 401-8811*
James Beard-nominated chef
Kathleen Blake will not serve
produce out of season or fish out
of state. Try the combo of local
shrimp, fish, and clams over
hearty Florida grits. Superb
selection of craft beers.

**ORLANDO: Seasons 52** $$
American                Road Map E2
*7700 Sand Lake Rd, 32819*
**Tel** *(407) 354-5212*
Seasons 52 is proof that healthy,
low-calorie meals can still be
utterly delicious. Good happy-
hour "Flights and Flatbreads",
with exceptional hand-selected
wines and tasty flatbreads.

**ORLANDO: Smokey Bones** $$
American                Road Map F2
*3400 E Colonial Dr, 32803*
**Tel** *(407) 894-1511*
Part of a chain, this popular
sports bar offers a hearty
menu of generous wings, baby-
back ribs, pulled pork, brisket, and
burgers. Create your own combos
and special party packs.

**ORLANDO: The Boheme** $$$
American                Road Map F2
*325 S Orange Ave, 32801*
**Tel** *(407) 313-9000*
Fine dining in a gorgeous setting
replete with elegant art, stately
columns, and music and cocktails
in the piano lounge. Renowned
Jazz brunch on Sundays.

## DK Choice

**ORLANDO: Christini's
Ristorante** $$$
Italian                 Road Map E2
*7600 Dr. Phillips Blvd, 32819*
**Tel** *(407) 545-6867*
Having received several awards
for both its food and wine, this
bastion of fine dining has been
a favorite for over 25 years.
Beautiful wood paneling, celebrity photographs, and paintings
add to the warm ambience.
Those who find the meat dishes
expensive can choose from the
equally delicious, and more
affordable, chicken or pasta
dishes on the menu.

**ORLANDO: Le Coq au Vin** $$$
French                  Road Map F2
*4800 S Orange Ave, 32806*
**Tel** *(407) 851-6980*     **Closed** *Mon*
Quality French café renowned
for bronzed fish with roasted
pecans and citrus *beurre blanc*
(butter sauce), cooked in
cast-iron skillet.

**ORLANDO: FishBones** $$$
Steakhouse/
Seafood                 Road Map E2
*6707 Sand Lake Rd, 32819*
**Tel** *(407) 352-0135*
Savor steak, prime ribs, chops and
chicken prepared in an open pit
grill. Extensive menu of fresh
seafood as well. Attentive staff will
assist in pairing food and wine.

**UNIVERSAL ORLANDO®:
Bubba Gump Shrimp** $$
Seafood                 Road Map E3
*6000 Universal Blvd, 32819*
**Tel** *(407) 903-0044*
Shrimp mac 'n' cheese and
popcorn shrimp are favorites
at this familiar chain outlet
with plenty of options on the
extensive menu. Fun atmosphere
and a kids' menu available.

**UNIVERSAL ORLANDO®:
Emeril's Orlando** $$$
Creole                  Road Map E3
*6000 Universal Blvd, 32819*
**Tel** *(407) 224-2424*
New Orlean's Creole favorites re-
created in an open kitchen. There
is a 10,000 bottle wine gallery
and a special chef's tasting
room. Kids' menu also available.

**UNIVERSAL ORLANDO®:
Emeril's Tchoup Chop** $$$
Asian                   Road Map E3
*6300 Hollywood Way, 32819*
**Tel** *(407) 503-2467*
Choose from an interesting
Asian menu featuring banana
leaf-wrapped pork, Chinese
spiced lamb shank, grilled garlic
tiger shrimp, and more. Superb
tiki classics and signature cocktails.

**WALT DISNEY WORLD®:
Chef Mickey's** $
American                Road Map E3
*Contemporary Resort, 4600 N
World Dr, 32830*
**Tel** *(407) 824-1000*
Gorge on the bountiful American
buffet and meet Mickey, Minnie,
Donald, and other Disney friends.
The sundae bar is very popular.

## DK Choice

**WALT DISNEY WORLD®:
Boma-Flavors of Africa** $$
African                 Road Map E3
*Animal Kingdom Lodge, 2901
Osceola Pkwy, 32830*
**Tel** *(407) 938-4744*
Boma features all the color and
flavor of an African market– with
a thatched roof, tree trunk table-
tops, and an array of serving
stations offering delicately
spiced meats and fish, along
with curries, and mac 'n' cheese.
For dessert, try the Zebra Dome:
a chocolate mousse striped
with dark and white chocolate.

The warmly decorated dining room with exceptional views at Seasons 52 in Orlando

For more information on types of restaurants *see page 326–7*

The well-stocked bar at Flying Fish Café in Walt Disney World®

### WALT DISNEY WORLD®:
**Bongos Cuban Café®** $$
Cuban **Road Map** E3
*Disney Springs, 1498 E Buena Vista Dr, 32830*
**Tel** *(407) 828-0999*
Bongos serves cuban specials such as shrimp criolla, shredded beef, and fried rice. There is a good kids' menu and fun late-night dancing for adults. Gorgeous setting in a re-created 1950s Havana nightclub.

### WALT DISNEY WORLD®:
**Cape May Café** $$
Seafood **Road Map** E3
*Beach Club Resort, 1800 Epcot Resorts Blvd, 32836*
**Tel** *(407) 939-3463*
Admiral Goofy and other favourite Disney characters preside over breakfast, while evenings bring traditional New England seafood in Cape May Café's relaxed beach-like setting.

### WALT DISNEY WORLD®:
**Ohana** $$
Polynesian **Road Map** E3
*Polynesian Resort, 1600 Seven Seas Dr, 32836*
**Tel** *(407) 824-1334*
Amidst storytellers, coconut races, and other festive fun, Ohana serves up excellent Polynesian food cooked in an open pit and served on skewers. Join Lilo and Stitch for breakfast.

### WALT DISNEY WORLD®: Raglan
**Road™ Irish Pub** $$
Irish **Road Map** E3
*Disney Springs, 1640 Buena Vista Dr, 32830*
**Tel** *(407) 938-0300*
Modern and classic Irish pub fare courtesy of celebrity chef Kevin Dundon. Some of the best fish and chips in Orlando are served here. There is nightly fiddle playing entertainment.

### WALT DISNEY WORLD®:
**Whispering Canyon Café** $$
American **Road Map** E3
*Wilderness Lodge Resort, 901 Timberline Dr, 32830*
**Tel** *(407) 939-3463*
A log cabin feast complete with sing-alongs and hobby horse races. Try the bottomless shakes, and s'mores cheesecakes.

### WALT DISNEY WORLD®:
**California Grill** $$$
International **Road Map** E3
*Contemporary Resort, 4600 N World Dr, 32830*
**Tel** *(407) 939-3463*
Sushi is served here along with creative takes on Florida snapper, oak-fired beef, and organic chicken. Excellent wine list.

---

### DK Choice

### WALT DISNEY WORLD®:
**Les Chefs de France** $$$
French **Road Map** E3
*Epcot World Showcase, 32830*
**Tel** *(407) 827-8709*
Located in Epcot's France Pavilion, Les Chefs de France offers a great dining experience. The brasserie menu created by famous French chefs, with dishes such as Coquille St. Jacques and duckling with cherries, appeals to the adults while kids have their own menu and visits from Ratatouille's Chef, Remy. The prix fixe menu is unbeatable value.

---

### WALT DISNEY WORLD®:
**Cinderella's Royal Table** $$$
American **Road Map** E3
*Fantasyland, Magic Kingdom Dr, 32830*
**Tel** *(407) 934-2927*
Experience fairytale dining in a grand hall with windows that afford views of Fantasyland. Disney princesses, including

Cinderella and her prince, visit guests at their tables. A souvenir photo is included in the tab.

### WALT DISNEY WORLD®:
**Flying Fish** $$$
Seafood **Road Map** E3
*Boardwalk Inn, 2101 Epcot Resorts Blvd, 32830*
**Tel** *(407) 939-2359*
Updated in 2017, this restaurant sports a modern, sophisticated style and is one of the best on the Disney property. The menu focuses on local, freshly-caught seafood.

### WALT DISNEY WORLD®:
**Terralina Crafted Italian** $$$
Italian **Road Map** E3
*Disney Springs, 1650 E Buena Vista Dr, 32830*
**Tel** *(407) 934-8888*
Revamped by James Beard Award-winning chef Tony Matuano, Terralina boasts a menu that aims to replicate the food of Italy's Lake District. Diners enjoy lovely views of the Disney Springs lagoon.

### WALT DISNEY WORLD®:
**Todd English's Bluezoo** $$$
Seafood **Road Map** E3
*Swan and Dolphin, 1500 Epcot Resorts Blvd, 32830*
**Tel** *(407) 934-1111*
Bluezoo features a stunning "undersea" setting for celebrity chef Todd English's out-standing seafood creations. Kids' menu is available.

### WALT DISNEY WORLD®:
**T-REX Café™** $$$
American **Road Map** E3
*1676 E Buena Vista Dr, 32830*
**Tel** *(407) 828-8739*
Dinosaurs abound at T-REX. The quirky menu offers paleo shrimp, bronto burgers, fossil fish and chips, chocolate extinction, and much more.

**WALT DISNEY WORLD®:**

**Victoria & Albert's** $$$
American        Road Map E3
*Grand Floridian Resort, 4401
Floridian Way, 32830*
**Tel** *(407) 939-3862*
Where Victorian elegance meets
haute American cuisine. One of
the top fine-dining choices in the
area with an elegant multi-
course prix fixe menu. There
is also an excellent wine list.

**WINTER PARK:**

**Café de France** $$$
French        Road Map E2
*526 Park Ave S, 32789*
**Tel** *(407) 647-1869*        **Closed** *Sun
& Mon*
Reliable favorites at this chic
French café, entrenched in
Central Park since 1982, include
duckling, *coq au vin*, and grilled
salmon. A wide range of French
and other European wines is
also on offer.

**WINTER PARK: Luma on
Park** $$$
American        Road Map E2
*290 S Park Ave, Winter Park, 32789*
**Tel** *(407) 599-4111*
Sophisticated seafood, delectable
steaks, and one of the best wine
lists in town are on offer at this
modern restaurant. Luma prides
itself on using locally-sourced
ingredients and has an open
kitchen.

**WINTER PARK:**

**Ravenous Pig** $$$
Gastropub        Road Map E2
*565 W Fairbanks Ave, 32789*
**Tel** *(407) 628-2333*        **Closed** *Sun
& Mon*
The owner-chef has put an
emphasis on seasonal ingredients
with a sophisticated gastronomic
twist, such as tea-smoked salmon
and pork porterhouse.

# The Northeast

**DAYTONA BEACH:**

**Hog Heaven** $
American        Road Map E2
*37 N Atlantic Ave, 32118*
**Tel** *(386) 257-1212*
Standard barbecue joint with
all the trimmings: ribs, pulled
pork, chicken, and four types of
sauce. Good kids' baskets.

## DK Choice

**DAYTONA BEACH: Aunt
Catfish's On the River** $$$
American        Road Map E2
*4009 Halifax Dr, Port Orange, 32127*
**Tel** *(386) 767-4768*
A laid-back Old South outpost
by the river, well-known for its
buffet bar. Feast on grilled or
fried catfish, fried alligator, ribs,
coconut shrimp, and great salads
served with hush puppies
(deep-fried cornmeal) and the
restaurant's famous cinnamon
rolls. Big, delicious brunch on
Sundays, and music every night.

**DAYTONA BEACH: Azure** $$$
American        Road Map E2
*2637 S Atlantic Ave, 32118*
**Tel** *(386) 767-7356*
One of Daytona Beach's best
restaurants, Azure has an
elegant dining room with an
oceanfront terrace. Specialties
include *étouffée* (seafood and
rice covered in thick sauce),
and house-cured steak.

**DAYTONA BEACH:**

**Down the Hatch** $$$
Seafood        Road Map E2
*4894 Front St, 32127*
**Tel** *(386) 761-4831*
This informal eatery overlooking
Ponce Inlet offers large portions
of fresh seafood, as well
as steaks and pasta.
Interesting daily specials.

**FERNANDINA BEACH:**

**29 South** $$$
American        Road Map E1
*29 S 3rd St, 32034*
**Tel** *(904) 799-7919*
An eclectic menu with small
plates and creative entrées
such as shrimp and grits
(cornmeal), wild salmon, and
short ribs. Large salads and
pizzas also available.

**FERNANDINA BEACH:**

**Joe's 2nd Street Bistro** $$$
American        Road Map E1
*14 S 2nd St, 32034*
**Tel** *(904) 321-2558*
Set in a restored early 20th-
century home with a pleasant
courtyard, this elegant eatery
offers a varied menu featuring
almond-crusted tilapia, leg of
lamb, pork schnitzel, and pastas.

**FERNANDINA BEACH: Salt** $$$
American        Road Map E1
*4750 Amelia Island Pkwy, 32034*
**Tel** *(904) 277-1100*        **Closed** *Mon*
Sophisticated, award-winning
dining with wood-burning grilled
dishes and a unique menu of
salted meats. Great for special
occasions. Decadent soufflés
provide the perfect finish.

**GAINESVILLE: Harry's
Seafood Bar & Grill** $$
Seafood/Creole        Road Map D2
*110 SE 1st St, 32601*
**Tel** *(352) 372-1555*
Sample a range of New Orleans
favorites such as jambalaya,
crawfish, and shrimp creole, along
with crab cakes, fried platters, and
large salads.

**GAINESVILLE:**

**Paramount Grill** $$
American        Road Map D2
*12 SW 1st Ave, 32601*
**Tel** *(352) 378-3398*
An appealing downtown
restaurant, whose innovative
chef-owner uses the freshest
ingredients to create brilliant
combinations. Pair the dishes with
their excellent American and
international wines.

**JACKSONVILLE:**

**Clark's Fish Camp** $$
American        Road Map E1
*12903 Hood Landing Rd, 32258*
**Tel** *(904) 268-3474*
Featuring standard seafood
along with alligator, kangaroo,
and ostrich dishes, Clark's is a
rustic and quirky eatery also
known for its taxidermy collection.

Beautifully presented dish from the menu at Café de France in Winter Park

**For more information on types of restaurants** *see page 326–7*

Local art adorns the walls at Florida Cracker Café in St. Augustine

### JACKSONVILLE: bb's $$$
American      **Road Map** E1
*1019 Hendricks Ave, 32207*
**Tel** *(904) 306-0100*     **Closed** *Sun*
This popular restaurant and
bar offers light fare as well as
fine cuisine featuring specialty
seafood. Bargain prix fixe
on weeknights.

### JACKSONVILLE: Biscottis $$$
American      **Road Map** E1
*3556 St. Johns Ave, 32205*
**Tel** *(904) 387-2060*
An elegant place which displays
local art on exposed brick walls.
Big salads, nightly entrée
specials, great desserts, and a
kids' menu are on offer.

### JACKSONVILLE: Bistro Aix $$$
American      **Road Map** E1
*1440 San Marco Blvd, 32207*
**Tel** *(904) 398-1949*
This hip bistro in Jacksonville's
historic area offers small plates as
well as pizzas and French treats,
such as mussels and steak frites.

### JACKSONVILLE:
**Matthew's Restaurant** $$$
American      **Road Map** E1
*2107 Hendricks Ave, 32207*
**Tel** *(904) 396-9922*    **Closed** *Sun*
This is a great fine-dining
choice with sleek and elegant
surroundings and a 2,000-bottle
wine cellar. Matthew Meure's
beautifully presented fare is
well-priced, given the high
quality. Excellent entrées
including pistachio-crusted
Arctic char, steak with
portobello mushrooms, and
Gorgonzola cheese. Choose
from great desserts like flourless
chocolate cake and ricotta
cheesecake. Music on weekends.

### JACKSONVILLE: Orsay $$$
French      **Road Map** E1
*3630 Park St, 32205*
**Tel** *(904) 381-0909*
Charming restaurant with a
classic brasserie menu featuring
dover sole, *duck a l'orange*, and
*coq au vin*. Good weekday prix
fixe bargains.

### JACKSONVILLE BEACH: Mojo $
American      **Road Map** E1
*1500 Beach Blvd, 32250*
**Tel** *(904) 247-6636*
A smokehouse, barbecue pit, and
blues bar rolled into one. Promises
good old Southern barbecue
with great sides. Check the
schedule for blues music nights.

### JACKSONVILLE BEACH:
**Marker 32** $$$
Seafood/American    **Road Map** E1
*14549 Beach Blvd, 32250*
**Tel** *(904) 223-1534*    **Closed** *Sun*
Enjoy choice specialties such as
Florida pompano and thick pork

chops while watching the sun
set over the Intracoastal
Waterway.

### OCALA: Sonny's Real American $
Barbecue      **Road Map** E2
*4102 E Silver Springs Blvd, 34470*
**Tel** *(352) 236-1012*
Sonny's may be an ubiquitous
chain, but has consistently good
barbecue at fantastic prices.

### OCALA: Arthur's Bistro $$$
Southern      **Road Map** E2
*3600 SW 36 Ave, 34474*
**Tel** *(352) 390-1515*
Sample Southern treats such as
rib eye, bayou shrimp, and char-
grilled grouper. Sandwiches and
snacks are also available.

### ORMOND BEACH:
**Frappe's North** $$$
American      **Road Map** E2
*123 W Granada Blvd, 32174*
**Tel** *(386) 386-4888*
Come to Frappe's for tasty, eclectic,
and often organic choices such as
pork *saltimbocca* (marinated
meat topped with prosciutto and
sage), Cajun chicken, shrimp, and
yellowfin tuna.

### ORMOND BEACH:
**Stonewood Grill & Tavern** $$$
Steakhouse      **Road Map** E2
*100 S Atlantic Ave, 32176*
**Tel** *(386) 671-1200*
Comfortable tavern with specialty
grilled steaks and chops. The
varied menu also offers amazing
seafood, burgers, and sandwiches.

### PONTE VEDRA BEACH:
**Palm Valley Fish Camp** $$
Seafood      **Road Map** E1
*299 N Roscoe Blvd, 32082*
**Tel** *(904) 285-3200*
Offering a wide choice of
delectable fresh fish, oysters, and
other seafood, this small eatery
has a loyal clientele so it is best to
reserve ahead. Take-out available.

### ST. AUGUSTINE:
**Florida Cracker Café** $$
American      **Road Map** E1
*81 St George St, 32084*
**Tel** *(904) 829-0397*
This pleasant café features local
art and has an eclectic menu
that includes shrimp and
grits (cornmeal), meat loaf,
and sandwiches, along with
the famous Key lime pie.
Good selection of beers.

### ST. AUGUSTINE: The Floridian $$
American      **Road Map** E1
*72 Spanish St, 32084*
**Tel** *(904) 829-0655*   **Closed** *Tue: lunch*
Head to the Floridian for Southern
comfort – house-smoked brisket,

The stylish interior of Orsay in Jacksonville

Atmospheric dining at 95 Cordova in St. Augustine

"Church Picnic" chicken – along with sandwiches, salad bowls, and vegetarian choices.

**ST. AUGUSTINE:**
**Gypsy Cab Company** $$
Seafood **Road Map** E1
838 Anastasia Blvd, 32808
**Tel** (904) 824-8244
A renowned restaurant with creative combinations such as salmon and scallop Provençale, and steak and shrimp carbonara.

**ST. AUGUSTINE: Columbia** $$$
Spanish **Road Map** E1
98 St. George St, 32084
**Tel** (904) 824-3341
A branch of the famed Tampa that dates back to 1905, this festive restaurant features hacienda-style decor and a well-prepared Spanish-Cuban menu.

### DK Choice

**ST. AUGUSTINE: Costa Brava**
**at 95 Cordova** $$$
International **Road Map** E1
95 Cordova St, 32084
**Tel** (904) 810-6810
Settle into high-back tapestry chairs amid columns, arches, and chandeliers in this restaurant inside the magnificent Casa Monica Hotel, and sample skillfully-blended Spanish and Mediterranean flavors. Small plates include the famed Kessler calamari, seared scallops and lamb lollipop chops.

**ST. AUGUSTINE: Raintree** $$$
American **Road Map** E1
102 San Marco Ave, 32084
**Tel** (904) 824-7211
This popular restaurant, set in a romantic Victorian home with a courtyard, serves up delectable traditional steak,

beef Wellington, and the top-quality seafood. Service is friendly and attentive.

## The Panhandle

**APALACHICOLA: Up the**
**Creek Raw Bar** $
Seafood **Road Map** B2
313 Water St, 32320
**Tel** (850) 653-2525
This casual spot with a waterfront deck is the place to discover why Apalachicola oysters are as famous as they are. Try the chef's house specialties washed down with local beers. Great value and excellent service.

**APALACHICOLA: Owl**
**Café** $$
Seafood/American **Road Map** B2
15 Ave D, 32320
**Tel** (850) 653-9888
A very pleasant café and tap room offering local oysters, grouper, pastas, and crab cakes. There is also a decent wine list. A good spot for Sunday brunch.

**APALACHICOLA: Tamara's**
**Café Floridita** $$
Spanish **Road Map** B2
71 Market St, 32320
**Tel** (850) 653-4111 **Closed** Mon
This pleasant upstairs café, with brick walls and bright decor, offers decent Spanish fare including tapas, paella, pecan-crusted grouper, and margarita chicken. Attentive service.

**DESTIN: Donut Hole** $
American **Road Map** A1
635 Harbor Blvd, 32541
**Tel** (850) 837-8824
Great choice for all-day breakfast food with corned beef hash, omelets, eggs Benedict,

sandwiches, burgers, and salads. Wide range of fresh doughnuts.

**DESTIN: The Back Porch** $$
Seafood **Road Map** A1
1740 Old Hwy 98, 32541
**Tel** (850) 837-2022
Informal seafood shack with a porch facing the beach and the Gulf. Specials on the menu include oysters and grilled amberjack. Good lunch deals.

**DESTIN: Marina Café** $$$
American/Seafood **Road Map** A1
404 Hwy 98 E, 32541
**Tel** (850) 653-7960
Elegant nautical dining room with outdoor deck seating and great harbor views. Formal cuisine such as steaks and seafood paired with delicious wines. Also offers wood-fired pizza, pasta, and sushi.

**FORT WALTON BEACH:**
**The Gulf** $$
Seafood **Road Map** A1
1284 Marler Ave, Okaloosa Island, 32548
**Tel** (850) 387-1300
This unique beachside eatery built from shipping containers, offers casual seasonal menus including specialities such as grouper sandwiches, and a signature crawfish roll. Offers great cocktails and occasional full moon parties on the beach.

**GRAYTON BEACH: Piccolo's**
**Restaurant and the Red Bar** $$
Seafood **Road Map** B1
70 Hotz Ave, 32459
**Tel** (850) 231-1008
This restaurant, with its laid-back vibe and live music, offers a small but excellent seafood menu. No credit cards.

**For more information on types of restaurants** see page 326–7

**PANAMA CITY BEACH:**
**Hunt's Oyster Bar**          $$
Seafood              **Road Map** B1
*1150 Beck Ave, 32401*
**Tel** *(850) 763-9645*      **Closed** *Sun*
This family-owned, no-frills
restaurant offers some of
the freshest Apalachicola oysters
– both raw and cooked. Well-
priced weekday lunch specials.

**PANAMA CITY BEACH:**
**Schooners**              $$
Seafood              **Road Map** B1
*5121 Gulf Dr, 32408*
**Tel** *(850) 235-3555*
With a fantastic location near
the beach, this restaurant serves
decent seafood and often has live
music. Good early bird specials.

**PANAMA CITY BEACH:**
**Capt. Anderson's**          $$$
Seafood              **Road Map** B1
*5551 N Lagoon Dr, 32408*
**Tel** *(850) 234-2225*      **Closed** *Sun*
Watch the boats unload the
day's catch at this seafood
standout – a marina fixture
since 1953. Try the specialty
grilled shrimp and South
African lobster tails. Expect
long lines in high season.

## DK Choice

**PANAMA CITY BEACH:**
**Firefly**              $$$
American              **Road Map** B1
*535 Richard Jackson Blvd, 32407*
**Tel** *(850) 249-3359*
Firefly provides a fantastic
dining experience beneath a giant oak
tree with twinkling lights, and is
a great choice for a romantic
meal. The sophisticated menu
on offer features she-crab
soups, rack of lamb, double-cut
pork chops, andouille-crusted
red snapper, and lobster tail.
Great martini menu in the
Library Lounge, a sushi happy
hour, and a children's menu.

**PENSACOLA: Cactus Flower**
**Café**              $$
Mexican              **Road Map** A1
*3425 N 12th Ave, 32503*
**Tel** *(850) 432-8100*      **Closed** *Sun*
Popular for its mahi mahi
fish tacos, tortilla soup, freshly-
made salsa, and traditional
favorites such as quesadillas
and burritos.

**PENSACOLA:**
**Five Sisters Blues Café**      $$
American              **Road Map** A1
*421 W Belmont St, 32501*
**Tel** *(850) 912-4856*
Enjoy live music and relish
Southern specials including

gumbo, fried chicken, crab
cakes, pulled pork, and pot
roast. Excellent Sunday brunch.

## DK Choice

**PENSACOLA: Dharma Blue** $$$
American       **Road Map** A1
*300 S Alcaniz St, 32502*
**Tel** *(850) 433-1275*      **Closed** *Sun*
Dharma Blue is located in a
lovely Victorian home over-
looking the historic Seville
Square. Sample exquisite
cuisine such as blackened fish
with sautéed shrimp, grilled
duck breast, beef filet, and thick
pork chops. Great lunch specials
including portobello focaccia,
fish tacos, or quiche of the day.

**PENSACOLA: McGuire's Irish**
**Pub**              $$$
Steakhouse           **Road Map** A1
*600 E Gregory St, 32502*
**Tel** *(850) 433-6789*
Steakhouse, pub, brewery, and
wine cellar all rolled into one.
Offers excellent Irish stew, meats,
corned beef and cabbage, and
seafood. The huge burgers come
highly recommended.

**SANTA ROSA: Fish Out of**
**Water**              $$$
Seafood              **Road Map** B1
*Watercolor Inn, 34 Goldenrod*
*Circle, 32459*
**Tel** *(850) 534-5050*
Located between Grayton Beach
and Seaside, this award-winning
restaurant has a relaxed setting.
The Southern-inspired kitchen
uses some of the freshest
ingredients to deliver outstanding
results. Delicious sunset cocktails.

**SEAGROVE BEACH: Café 30A** $$$
American              **Road Map** B1
*3899 E County Hwy 30A, 32459*
**Tel** *(850) 231-2166*
Café 30A has a striking multi-
level dining room and offers

a choice of wood-oven
roasted seafood, grilled
meats, and pizzas.

**SEASIDE: Bud & Alley's**      $$$
American              **Road Map** B1
*2236 E County Rd 30A, 32459*
**Tel** *(850) 231-5900*
With a menu emphasizing fresh
seafood, this lively waterfront
restaurant also serves tacos and
pizza, and has a children's menu.

**SEASIDE: Great**
**Southern Café**          $$$
American              **Road Map** B1
*83 Central Square, 32459*
**Tel** *(850) 231-7327*
True to its name, this restaurant
serves great Southern favorites
all through the day. Do not
miss the Grits a Ya Ya.

**TALLAHASSEE: Dog et Al**      $
American              **Road Map** C1
*1456 Monroe St, 32301*
**Tel** *(850) 222-4099*      **Closed** *Sun*
A classic joint serving a wide
range of hot dogs: big ones,
little ones, footlongs, corn dogs,
and turkey dogs, with the option
to add chili, cheese, and kraut.

**TALLAHASSEE: Mom & Dad's** $$
Italian              **Road Map** C1
*4175 Apalachee Pkwy, 32311*
**Tel** *(850) 877-4518*      **Closed** *Sun*
& Mon
Family-owned eatery that has
been serving exquisite old-
fashioned Italian fare for more
than 50 years. Good wine list.

**TALLAHASSEE: Azu Lucy**
**Ho's**              $$$
Asian              **Road Map** C1
*3220 Apalachee Pkwy, 32311*
**Tel** *(850) 893-4112*
Savor some of the city's best
Chinese fare along with delicious
Japanese teriyaki, sushi, tempura,
and fusion dishes. The mango
beef and honey pineapple
shrimp are favorites.

Enjoy the fantastic vista at Schooners in Panama City Beach

**TALLAHASSEE:**
**Cypress Restaurant** **$$$**
American **Road Map** C1
*320 E Tennessee St, 32301*
**Tel** *(850) 513-1100* **Closed** *Sun & Mon*
This chef-owned restaurant boasts a sophisticated menu featuring kumquat glazed duck breast, pecan-crusted grouper, and some of the best shrimp and grits (cornmeal) in town.

**TALLAHASSEE:**
**Kool Beanz Café** **$$$**
Caribbean **Road Map** C1
*921 Thomasville Rd, 32303*
**Tel** *(850) 224-2466*
This trendy and noisy café serves terrific fare: try the jerk spiced scallops and lime basil shrimp. Excellent brunches.

# The Gulf Coast

## DK Choice

**ANNA MARIA ISLAND:**
**Beach Bistro** **$$$**
American **Road Map** D3
*6600 Gulf Dr, Holmes Beach, 34217*
**Tel** *(941) 778-6444*
One of Florida's top-rated restaurants, Beach Bistro is a great spot for a romantic meal, with beautiful sunset views over the sea. Some of the delicacies on offer include Floridian grouper with cashew-toasted coconut crust, *boullabaise* filled with lobster tail, sinful sliders of sirloin, *foie gras*, and *bearnaise* sauce on a sweet roll.

**ANNA MARIA ISLAND:**
**Sign of the Mermaid** **$$$**
American/European **Road Map** D3
*9707 Gulf Dr, 34216*
**Tel** *(941) 778-9399*
Wonderfully decorated restaurant in a restored 1912 cottage. Sample from an unusual and extensive variety of formal Floridian and European cuisine. Delicious desserts, and a good range of wines, both American and international.

**CAPTIVA ISLAND:**
**Bubble Room** **$$$**
American **Road Map** E4
*15001 Captiva Rd, 33924*
**Tel** *(239) 472-5558*
Enjoy steaks and seafood in kitschy surroundings with toys, trains, juke boxes, old records, and Christmas lights at this very colorful restaurant.

The romantic setting of Beach Bistro, Anna Maria Island

**CAPTIVA ISLAND:**
**Mucky Duck** **$$$**
American/Seafood **Road Map** E4
*11546 Andy Rosse Ln, 33924*
**Tel** *(239) 472-3434*
Informal beachfront café serving grouper, coconut shrimp, roast duckling, and chicken marsala. Lovely sunset views.

**CAPTIVA ISLAND:**
**Old Captiva House** **$$$**
American/Seafood **Road Map** E4
*15951 Captiva Dr, 33924*
**Tel** *(239) 472-5161*
Fine dining in a charming 1931 home. Choose from a varied menu, while enjoying piano music and sunset views.

**CLEARWATER BEACH: Clear Sky**
**Beachside Café** **$$**
American **Road Map** D3
*490 Mandalay Ave, 33767*
**Tel** *(727) 442-3684*
Located in a stripmall, this eatery offers a superb and almost neverending breakfast (including bloody marys and mimosas), as well as full seafood and steak dinner menus.

**CLEARWATER BEACH:**
**Marina Cantina** **$$$**
Mexican **Road Map** D3
*25 Causeway Blvd, 33767*
**Tel** *(727) 443-1750*
Opened in 2016, this glitzy upscale marina restaurant serves tweaked Mexican fare such as seared mojo tuna and whole fish straight from the Gulf.

**DUNEDIN: Bon Appetit** **$$$**
American **Road Map** D3
*148 Marina Plaza, 34698*
**Tel** *(727) 733-2151*
Upscale dining on the waterfront with indoor and alfresco seating. There is a formal menu as well as a choice of comfort foods. Good prix fixe dinner bargains.

**FORT MYERS: The Veranda** **$$$**
American **Road Map** E4
*2122 2nd St, 33901*
**Tel** *(239) 332-2065* **Closed** *Sun*
Located in a charming historic home, the Veranda offers Southern-style fine dining. Try the grouper on grits (cornmeal), chicken with bay shrimp, and crawfish-topped snapper.

## DK Choice

**LONGBOAT KEY:**
**Euphemia Haye** **$$$**
European **Road Map** D3
*5540 Gulf of Mexico Dr, 34228*
**Tel** *(941) 383-3633*
Located in a cottage amid tropical greenery, this restaurant addresses two distinct needs. Find romantic fine dining downstairs, with dishes such as pistachio-crusted snapper, lamb shank, and the signature duckling. The Haye Loft upstairs has live music, drinks, pizza, and a dazzling dessert bar with apple walnut crumble pie and banana foster treats.

**LONGBOAT KEY: Maison**
**Blanche** **$$$**
French **Road Map** D3
*2605 Gulf of Mexico Dr, 34228*
**Tel** *(941) 383-8088*
A minimalist yet exotic restaurant in the casual beachside area. Crowd favorites include blue crab in cauliflower mousse, slow-cooked short ribs and an excellent three-course prix fixe menu.

**SANIBEL ISLAND: Island Cow** **$$**
American **Road Map** E4
*2163 Periwinkle Way, 33957*
**Tel** *(239) 472-0606*
Very well-priced breakfast, burgers, sandwiches, and fish cooked nine ways. Kids love the nightly mooing contest.

### SANIBEL ISLAND:
**Mad Hatter** $$$
American          Road Map E4
*6467 Sanibel-Captiva Rd, 33957*
**Tel** *(239) 472-0033*     **Closed** *Mon*
This romantic waterfront café
has creative seasonal menus
featuring shrimp wrapped in
filo, black truffle scallops, and
duckling with berry sauce.

### SANIBEL ISLAND: Timbers
**Restaurant and Fish Market** $$$
Seafood          Road Map E4
*703 Tarpon Bay Rd, 33957*
**Tel** *(239) 395-2722*
Big, busy eatery with fresh
seafood, a raw bar, chowder,
and platters. Try the specialty
crunchy grouper and
delicious steaks.

### SARASOTA: Nancy's Bar-B-Q $
America          Road Map D3
*301 S Pineapple Ave, 34236*
**Tel** *(941) 366-2271*     **Closed** *Sun*
Worth waiting in line at the
counter for some great barbecue,
including pulled pork, brisket,
chicken, ribs, and salmon, along
with scrumptious sides.

### SARASOTA: Yoders $
American          Road Map D3
*3434 Bahia Vista St, 34239*
**Tel** *(941) 955-7771*     **Closed** *Sun*
Serving Amish treats since
1975. Big breakfasts, delicious
fried chicken, and famous pies
such as the peanut butter
cream pie. No alcohol.

### SARASOTA: Café L'Europe $$$
French          Road Map D3
*431 St. Armands Circle, 34236*
**Tel** *(941) 388-4415*
Long-established bastion of
fine dining with great ambience.
This café counts Dover sole and
*chateaubriand* (particular cut of
steak) among its specialties. Prix
fixe early bird dinner.

### SARASOTA: Michaels on
**East** $$$
American          Road Map D3
*1212 E Ave S, 34239*
**Tel** *(941) 366-0007*     **Closed** *Sun*
This sophisticated restaurant offers
terrific "Epicurean Adventures"
menus focusing on particular
world cuisines, as well as prix fixe
dinners. Over 350 exceptional
wines to choose from.

### ST. PETE BEACH: Madfish $$$
American          Road Map D3
*5200 Gulf Blvd, 33706*
**Tel** *(727) 360-9200*
Casual yet upscale retrofit diner
with great breakfasts as well as
late night menus. Delicious prime
rib. Early bird specials.

### ST. PETE BEACH:
**Maritana Grille** $$$
European          Road Map D3
*Don Cesar Hotel, 3400 Gulf Blvd,
33706*
**Tel** *(727) 360-1882*
Upscale restaurant with an airy
dining room. Try its specialty
griddled seafood or choose from
top-notch steak, venison, and
wood grilled rack of lamb.

### ST. PETERSBURG:
**The Moon Under Water** $$
Gastropub          Road Map D3
*332 Beach Dr NE, 33701*
**Tel** *(727) 896-6160*
Trendy pub with British and
Indian influences. Seventeen
traditional and craft beers on
tap. Serves fish and chips,
along with curries, burgers,
and pot pies.

### ST. PETERSBURG:
**Red Mesa Cantina** $$
Mexican          Road Map D3
*128 3rd St S, 33701*
**Tel** *(727) 896-8226*
Excellent Mexican fare including
tortillas, tacos, burritos, and
*ceviche* (seafood cooked using
citrus juice) in the colorful
interiors or beautiful courtyard.
Live music and hand-crafted
cocktails in the tequila bar.

### ST. PETERSBURG: Cassis
**American Brasserie** $$$
French/American     Road Map D3
*170 Beach Dr NE, 33701*
**Tel** *(727) 827-2927*
This elegantly decorated, trendy
brasserie serves great seafood,
and offers pleasant sidewalk
seating. There is a separate
menu for pet dogs.

### TAMPA: Cigar City Cider
**& Mead** $
Taproom          Road Map D3
*1812 N 15th St, Ybor City, 33605*
**Tel** *(813) 242-6600*
Modern tap room in the heart of
Ybor City's Spanish district offers
dozens of ciders and an array of
meads, making it the perfect
cooling rest stop.

### TAMPA: Mel's Hot Dogs $
American          Road Map D3
*4136 Busch Blvd, 33617*
**Tel** *(813) 986-8000*     **Closed** *Sun*
This local legend near Busch
Gardens has been a favorite since
the early 1970s. Serves hot dogs
plus great burgers.

### TAMPA: Bella's Italian Café $$
Italian          Road Map D3
*1413 S Howard Ave, 33606*
**Tel** *(813) 254-3355*
A local favorite for over 25 years,
this warm and informal café has
a wood-burning pizza oven and
serves traditional Italian fare.
Excellent late-night happy hour.

### TAMPA: Bern's Steakhouse $$$
Steakhouse          Road Map D3
*1208 S Howard Ave, 33606*
**Tel** *(813) 251-2421*
Known for its opulent decor,
prime steaks, and delicious
desserts, this Steakhouse also
offers amazing wine cellar tours.
Has a decadent dessert room.

### TAMPA: Ceviche Tapas Bar
**and Restaurant** $$$
Spanish          Road Map D3
*2500 W Azeele St, 33609*
**Tel** *(813) 250-0203*
Trendy restaurant with live music
and flamenco dance shows. Offers

The Columbia Restaurant in Tampa exudes old-world Spanish charm

over a hundred kinds of tapas for sharing, plus paella and *ceviche* (seafood cooked using citrus juice).

### DK Choice

**TAMPA:**
**Columbia Restaurant** $$$
Spanish **Road Map** D3
*2117 E 7th Ave, Ybor City, 33605*
**Tel** *(813) 248-4961*
Filled with old-world Spanish atmosphere, Florida's oldest restaurant has now grown to fill a city block. But despite its size and the crowds who flock here, this family-owned institution has maintained the quality of its Spanish-Cuban menu and signature dishes such as paella and snapper Alicante. Flamenco dancers nightly, except Sunday, add to the atmosphere.

**TAMPA: Mise en Place** $$$
American **Road Map** D3
*442 W Kennedy Blvd, 33606*
**Tel** *(813) 254-5373* **Closed** *Sun & Mon*
Elegant restaurant perfect for a special occasion. The Kobe beef and rack of lamb are highly recommended. Prix fixe options, too.

**TAMPA: The Refinery** $$$
American **Road Map** D3
*5137 N Florida Ave, 33603*
**Tel** *(813) 237-2000*
Multi-James Beard Award nominee chef Greg Baker changes the menu weekly, and uses local ingredients in-house to prepare everything from sausage to salad dressing.

### DK Choice

**TAMPA: Restaurant BT** $$$
French **Road Map** D3
*2507 S MacDill Ave, 33629*
**Tel** *(813) 258-1916* **Closed** *Sun*
Food lovers come from afar to savor the subtle blend of French and Vietnamese techniques and seasonings by the talented chef at this stylish café. Some of the chef's most memorable creations include snapper Saigon with lemongrass and curry, Viet bouillabaisse, Cote Basque prawns, and duckling with mango sauce.

**VENICE: Sharky's on the Pier** $$
Seafood **Road Map** D4
*1600 S Harbor Dr, 34285*
**Tel** *(941) 488-1456*
Located right on the beach, this restaurant and tiki bar serves

The creative drinks menu at The Refinery, Tampa

delightful snacks, sandwiches, and full meals. Live music Wednesdays through Saturdays.

## The Everglades and the Keys

**EVERGLADES: City Seafood and Market** $
Seafood **Road Map** E5
*702 Begonia St, 34139*
**Tel** *(239) 695-4700*
This riverside café offers sandwiches and freshly-caught seafood such as stone crabs and shrimp, as well as alligator tail and frog legs. For dessert, try the Key lime pie and ice creams.

**EVERGLADES: Coopertown Restaurant** $
Seafood **Road Map** E5
*22700 SW 8 St, 33194*
**Tel** *(305) 226-6048*
Grab a paper plate and devour swamp specialties such as alligator tail, frog legs, and catfish. Delicious sandwiches and great breakfasts, too.

**ISLAMORADA: Marker 88** $$$
Seafood **Road Map** F5
*88000 Overseas Hwy, 33070*
**Tel** *(305) 852-9315*
Enjoy upscale dining in a casual beachside setting. A range of fresh seafood on the menu as well as excellent meat choices. Extensive wine list available.

**ISLAMORADA: Pierre's** $$$
French **Road Map** F5
*81600 Overseas Hwy, MM 81.6, 33036*
**Tel** *(305) 664-3225*
Elegant, romantic, and perfect for special occasions, Pierre's promises exquisite fine dining with gorgeous views from the verandahs. Savor elegant gourmet seafood and steaks as well as innovative cocktails.

**ISLAMORADA:**
**Wahoo's Bar and Grill** $$$
Seafood **Road Map** F5
*83413 Overseas Hwy, MM 83.5, 33036*
**Tel** *(305) 664-9888* **Closed** *Sun*
Watch the fishing fleet come in while feasting on freshly caught snapper, grouper, tuna, and more. For the thrifty, a range of sandwiches is available.

**KEY LARGO:**
**Mrs. Mac's Kitchen** $$
Seafood **Road Map** F5
*99336 Overseas Hwy, MM 99.4, 33037*
**Tel** *(305) 451-3722* **Closed** *Sun*
Head to Mrs. Mac's for some good old down-South cooking. Chili, conch chowder, crab cakes, fresh fish of the day, and homemade pies are on the menu.

**KEY LARGO: Fish House Restaurant and Market** $$$
Seafood **Road Map** F5
*102401 Overseas Hwy, MM 102.4, 33037*
**Tel** *(305) 451-4665*
Have the catch of the day cooked to your liking: broiled, fried, grilled, or blackened. Shrimp, crab and other seafood. as well as meats and pasta, are also on offer.

**KEY WEST: Banana Café** $$
French **Road Map** E5
*1215 Duval St, 33040*
**Tel** *(305) 294-7227*
Small bistro with specialty seafood crepes as well as fantastic ribeye and sauteed local snapper. Good breakfast selections.

**KEY WEST: Camille's** $$
American **Road Map** E5
*1202 Simonton St, 33040*
**Tel** *(305) 296-4811*
This family-friendly restaurant has quirky decor and serves great breakfast (crab Benedict) and reasonable dinner options (stone crab meat cake).

**For more information on types of restaurants** *see page 326–7*

### KEY WEST: Mangia Mangia Pasta Café $$
Italian/Seafood    Road Map E5
*900 Southard St, 33040*
**Tel** *(305) 294-2469*
Home-made pastas reign supreme at Mangia Mangia, both as mains or as a side dish with scampi, mahi mahi, or chicken. The lobster linguini is a must-try. Island-inspired decor.

### KEY WEST: Mangoes $$
American    Road Map E5
*700 Duval St, 33040*
**Tel** *(305) 294-8002*
Offers a varied menu with many seafood choices and, true to its name, signature drinks including mangorita and mango colada. Great patio seating, ideal for people-watching.

### KEY WEST: Sarabeth's Kitchen $$
American    Road Map E5
*530 Simonton St, 33040*
**Tel** *(305) 293-8181*    **Closed** *Mon & Tue*
Florida import of the New York favorite, known for its brunch and lunch menus. Excellent soups, salads, pancakes, and dinner choices ranging from meat loaf to snapper.

## DK Choice

### KEY WEST: Seven Fish $$
American    Road Map E5
*921 Truman Ave, 33040*
**Tel** *(305) 296-2777*    **Closed** *Tue*
Step away from the tourist crowds to discover this locals' favorite: a corner bistro where mahi mahi and meatloaf share the menu with surprises such as banana chicken and crab and shitake mushroom pasta. Everything is prepared expertly and is well priced. Space is tight, so reserve well ahead.

### KEY WEST: El Siboney $$
Cuban    Road Map E5
*900 Catherine St, 33040*
**Tel** *(305) 296-4184*
Savor home-cooked Cuban fare at excellent prices at this family-friendly restaurant. To order the paella, call in an hour ahead. Good daily specials.

### KEY WEST: Sloppy Joe's Bar $$
American    Road Map E5
*201 Duval St, 33040*
**Tel** *(305) 294-5717*
Ernest Hemingway's famous haunt, this friendly pub features live music and standard but delicious pub grub. Beer on tap and an extensive drinks menu.

The exterior of Mangia Mangia Pasta Café in Key West

### KEY WEST: La Trattoria Restaurant $$
Italian    Road Map E5
*3593 S Roosevelt Blvd, 33040*
**Tel** *(305) 295-6789*
Enjoy traditional Italian favorites in a relaxed setting with fantastic ocean views. Excellent martinis and live music.

### KEY WEST: A&B Lobster House $$$
Seafood    Road Map E5
*700 Front St, 33040*
**Tel** *(305) 294-5880*
Occupying a prime spot on the harbor, this restaurant offers freshly caught seafood, excellent lobster tail with coconut pecan rice, and great steaks.

### KEY WEST: Antonia's Restaurant $$$
Italian    Road Map E5
*615 Duval St, 33040*
**Tel** *(305) 294-6565*
Upscale and romantic, this highly rated Italian restaurant has an extensive menu and wine list. Reservations are essential.

### KEY WEST: Blue Heaven $$$
American    Road Map E5
*729 Thomas St, 33040*
**Tel** *(305) 296-8666*
Trendy spot with live music and mismatched decor. Terrific seafood including lobster, stone crab, and seared sea scallops. Excellent brunch options.

### KEY WEST: Café Marquesa $$$
American    Road Map E5
*600 Fleming St, 33040*
**Tel** *(305) 292-1244*
Sophisticated and intimate restaurant with a highly rated menu featuring dishes such as duck breast with chicken and apple sausage.

## DK Choice

### KEY WEST: Café Sole $$$
French/American    Road Map E5
*1029 Southard St, 33040*
**Tel** *(305) 294-0230*
This small café with a romantic garden has at its helm a talented chef whose fantastic menus combine the best of Provence and Florida. Think lobster bisque and French onion soup, conch *carpaccio* and *duckling a l'orange*. Try the specialty hog snapper, a delicate white meat fish served with roasted red pepper sauce.

### KEY WEST: Hot Tin Roof $$$
Seafood    Road Map E4
*0 Duval Street, 33040*
**Tel** *(305) 296-7701*
Located at the Ocean Key Resort, this restaurant has a menu filled with Key West shrimp, snapper, and Angus beef. Hand-painted murals compliment the views of Sunset Pier and Mallory Square.

### KEY WEST: La Te Da $$$
American    Road Map E5
*1125 Duval St, 33040*
**Tel** *(305) 296-6706*
Upscale but laid-back restaurant. Offers a varied menu with meat loaf, scampi, snapper, and Tahitian roasted chicken.

### KEY WEST: Louie's Backyard $$$
American    Road Map E5
*700 Waddell Ave, 33040*
**Tel** *(305) 294-1061*
With the ocean as its backyard, Louie's promises dazzling views and fantastic fare with just a touch of Caribbean spices. Popular, so reserve well ahead.

**KEY WEST: Michael's Key West** $$$
American                Road Map E5
*532 Margaret St, 33040*
**Tel** *(305) 295-1300*
A local favorite, Michael's has three gorgeous settings in which to enjoy the gourmet cuisine: a formal dining room, a romantic patio, and a garden bar serving fantastic fondue.

**KEY WEST: One Duval** $$$
Seafood                Road Map E5
*Pier House Resort, 1 Duval St, 33040*
**Tel** *(305) 296-4600*
Lovely waterfront restaurant serving fresh local seafood and old favorites all day, with more formal dinner options. Dine on the deck with gorgeous views, and enjoy live music at the piano bar.

**KEY WEST: Pisces** $$$
Seafood                Road Map E5
*1007 Simonton St, 33040*
**Tel** *(305) 294-7100*
With interesting contemporary decor, including artwork by Andy Warhol, Pisces dishes up superb seafood such as lobster tango mango and yellowtail atocha.

**MARATHON: Butterfly Café** $$
American/
Caribbean                Road Map E5
*2600 Overseas Hwy, 33050*
**Tel** *(305) 289-7177*
Attractive dining room at the Tranquility Bay resort, serving up delicious conch chowder, coconut shrimp, burgers, and meals for kids, all with a Caribbean touch.

**MARATHON: Herbie's Restaurant** $$
Seafood                Road Map E5
*6350 Overseas Hwy, 33050*
**Tel** *(305) 743-6373*      **Closed** *Sun & Mon*
Justifiably popular for its conch fritters and fresh seafood, offered at fair prices and served in a low-key Old Florida setting.

**MARATHON: Lazy Days South** $$$
American                Road Map E5
*725 11th St Ocean, 33050*
**Tel** *(305) 289-0839*
Very popular oceanfront restaurant. Varied menu with seafood, steaks, pasta, and sandwiches. Great sunset views.

**MARCO ISLAND: Arturo's** $$$
American                Road Map E5
*844 Bald Eagle Dr, 34145*
**Tel** *(239) 642-0550*
Elegant restaurant that offers a wide choice, from frog legs and chicken Parmesan to its specialty, stuffed pork chops. Popular bar.

**MARCO ISLAND: Old Marco Lodge Crab House** $$$
Seafood                Road Map E5
*401 Papaya St, Goodland, 34145*
**Tel** *(239) 642-7227*
Picturesque lodge restaurant with a large outdoor deck and water views. Serves fresh seafood, as well as soups, salads, and sandwiches. Kids' menu, too.

**MARCO ISLAND: Sale e Pepe** $$$
Italian                Road Map E5
*480 S Collier Blvd, 34145*
**Tel** *(239) 393-1600*
Elegant resort dining with Gulf views and sophisticated preparation of home-made pastas, fresh seafood, and prime meats.

**MARCO ISLAND: Snook Inn** $$$
Seafood/American    Road Map E5
*1215 Bald Eagle Dr, 34145*
**Tel** *(239) 394-3313*
Casual waterfront dining at the Snook Inn, where the menu ranges from sandwiches to formal entrées. Specialties include stuffed shrimp and Carribean-style barbecue ribs.

**NAPLES: First Watch** $$
Café                Road Map E4
*225 Banyan Blvd, 34102*
**Tel** *(239) 434-0005*
Head to First Watch for hearty and healthy breakfasts with multi-grain pancakes and skillet hashes. The lunch sandwiches are served with a soup or salad.

**NAPLES: Noodles Italian Café and Sushi Bar** $$
Italian/Japanese    Road Map E4
*1585 Pine Ridge Rd, 34109*
**Tel** *(239) 592-0050*
Traditional Italian and sushi bar coexist happily here. Choose from the low-carb menu that features gourmet pizzas and

Stylish decor with Italian flare at Sea Salt in Naples

specialties such as beef Oscar and salmon florentine.

**NAPLES: Barbatella Spirited Italian Trattoria** $$$
Italian                Road Map E4
*1290 3rd St, 34102*
**Tel** *(239) 263-1955*
With a trendy dining room and courtyard seating, this gourmet Italian restaurant offers excellent rotisserie and grill specialties, along with wood-fired pizzas, home-made pastas, and gelati.

**NAPLES: Bistro 821** $$$
International        Road Map E4
*821 5th Ave, 34102*
**Tel** *(239) 261-5821*
With a distinctly South Beach vibe, this upscale bistro has a varied menu featuring pot pie, paella, risotto, trademark miso-sake, and roasted sea bass. Excellent wine list.

**NAPLES: Café Lurcat** $$$
American                Road Map E4
*494 5th Ave, 34102*
**Tel** *(239) 213-3357*
A trendy and popular hangout serving delicious tapas and small plates at the bar. Upstairs and outside, savor American fine dining, with creative cuisine and several low-calorie choices.

**NAPLES: Cote d'Azur** $$$
French                Road Map E4
*11224 Tamiami Trail N (US41), 34110*
**Tel** *(239) 597-8867*      **Closed** *Mon*
This top-rated intimate bistro features fantastic provincial French cuisine. Try its specialty roasted seafood, boned and filleted at the table.

**NAPLES: Sea Salt** $$$
Italian                Road Map E4
*1186 3rd St S, 34102*
**Tel** *(239) 434-7258*
A stylish, modern setting and a talented Venetian-born chef make Sea Salt one of Naples's top restaurants. Start with raw oysters, hand-cut carpaccio, or a cured meats selection and move on to swordfish on Parmesan polenta, halibut with beluga lentil ragu, or venison tenderloin. Excellent wines.

**NAPLES: USS Nemo** $$$
Seafood                Road Map E4
*3745 Tamiami Trail (US 41), 34103*
**Tel** *(239) 261-6366*
Sample superb seafood with Asian influences amidst whimsical undersea decor at this award-winning restaurant. Try the signature dish, miso-broiled bass with citrus-ginger butter.

# Bars and Cafés

Florida's easy-going lifestyle helps to ensure an abundance of bars and cafés. The term café often denotes an informal, bistro-style restaurant but can also refer to a coffee house or, indeed, a bar. Sports bars are very popular and usually have several television sets, each tuned to a different station – but often the sound is turned off while loud music plays in the background. Many bars and cafés have a happy hour, generally from 4 to 7pm, when drinks are less expensive and snacks are served free of charge; the bars and cafés included here are good for just a drink as well as a meal, or a coffee and a snack.

## Miami

**Miami Beach:** News Café
*800 Ocean Drive.* **Map** 2 F4.
**Tel** *(305) 538-6397.*

With ample sidewalk tables, this laid-back café is the top meeting place in South Beach and is open 24 hours a day. People gather to drink, eat, and to take in the Ocean Drive scene. The eclectic menu features good breakfasts and huge bowls of pasta as well as light, healthy meals. There are a dozen types of coffee, and the pastry list is equally long. ☐ ☐ *AE DC MC V*

**Miami Beach:** Front Porch Café
*1458 Ocean Dr.* **Map** 2 F4.
**Tel** *(305) 531-8300.*
This popular neighborhood hot spot is best known for its delicious breakfasts. Enjoy drinks in the lobby of the Z Hotel or decadent homemade pastries and desserts. ☐ ☐ *AE MC V*

**Downtown:** Hard Rock Café
*401 Biscayne Blvd.* **Map** 4 F1.
**Tel** *(305) 377-3110.*

Tourists and locals alike fill the Hard Rock Café, which is festooned with rock memorabilia, and throbs with loud music. There is a bar for those intent on drinking and soaking up the atmosphere, but reserve ahead if you want to eat. The food is American, from juicy burgers to hot, tasty apple pie, and the portions are generous. ☐ *AE DC MC V*

**Coral Gables:** Café at Books & Books
*265 Aragon Ave.* **Map** 5 C1.
**Tel** *(305) 448-9599.*

Located in the courtyard of Books & Books, this European-style deli serves soup, sandwiches, and fantastic desserts, all made by Lyon & Lyon

Caterers. There is a coffee bar open 9am–7pm daily. ☐ ☐ *AE MC V*

**Coconut Grove:** Monty's in the Grove
*2550 S. Bayshore Dr.* **Map** 6 E4.
**Tel** *(305) 856-3992.*

With stunning water views, island music, and a wide variety of seasonal seafood, Monty's is a popular weekend spot. It is child-friendly on weekends. ☐ *AE DC MC V*

**Coconut Grove:** Fat Tuesday
*Coco Walk, 3015 Grand Ave.* **Map** 6 E4.
**Tel** *(305) 441-2992.*

This former sports bar has three satellite dishes, 51 TVs, and five pool tables. It is now one of the Fat Tuesday's chain bars/cafés, which serves as a meeting place for the young at heart. US and imported beer are available, and the menu offers light meals and snacks, such as buffalo wings, veggie pizza, giant burgers, and Mississippi mud pie. ☐ *AE DC MC V*

## The Gold and Treasure Coasts

**Boca Raton:** Tin Muffin Café
*364 East Palmetto Park Rd.*
**Road map** F4. **Tel** *(561) 392-9446.*

This tiny café offers delightful sandwiches and quiches, plus the

home made desserts are a treat. Try the shrimp salad or the banana cake while you sit and watch the world go by. Tin Muffin Café is not a destination restaurant, but worth a visit if you are in the neighborhood. ☐ ☐

**Fort Lauderdale:** Shooters Waterfront
*3033 NE 32nd Ave.* **Road map** F4.
**Tel** *(954) 566-2855.*

This waterfront bar and restaurant is a people-watcher's paradise, always packed with a casual crowd eating, drinking, and watching the boats sail by. The menu is quite extensive and reasonably priced. You can nibble on shrimp and crab cakes, or tuck into more substantial food like a Florida grouper sandwich. ☐ ☐ *AE DC MC V*

**Palm Beach:** The Leopard Lounge
*363 Cocoanut Row.* **Road map** F4.
**Tel** *(561) 659-5800.*

Located in the Chesterfield Hotel, the Leopard Lounge is strikingly decorated with scarlet and black drapes, and the leopard theme is picked out in the plush carpeting and tablecloths. On weekends the place is jammed with locals who dance to the sounds of the "big band" era, performed live. A full menu is served. ☐ *AE DC MC V*

## Orlando and The Space Coast

**Orlando:** Bongos Cuban Café
*1498 E Buena Vista Drive.*
**Road map** E3. **Tel** *(407) 828-0999.*

This hip café in the middle of Downtown Disney® is owned by Gloria Estefan and husband Emilio, and features outstanding Cuban cuisine and hot dance music. Try the *arroz con pollo* and black bean soup.

The News Café on Ocean Drive, Miami Beach

There are two floors of indoor and outdoor tables – the upstairs balcony is a great place to people watch. 🏃 🪑 *AE DC MC V*

## The Northeast

**Jacksonville:** River City Brewing Company
*835 Museum Circle.* **Road map** E1.
**Tel** *(904) 398-2299.*

Home-brewed beer and a varied selection of food at reasonable prices make this a popular spot with the locals. On Friday there is a live band, and Saturday nights offers a local DJ. There is no cover charge. 🏃 🪑 *AE DC MC V*

**St. Augustine:** A1A Ale Works
*1 King St.* **Road map** E1.
**Tel** *(904) 829-2977.*

Situated at the foot of the Bridge of Lions, this friendly pub and restaurant has a microbrewery on site. Ale aficionados come for the seven varieties of home-brewed ale that are available. Live bands play on weekends. 🏃 🪑 *AE DC MC V*

**St. Augustine:** OC White's Seafood and Spirits
*118 Avenida Menendez.*
**Road map** E1. **Tel** *(904) 824-0808.*

In an 18th-century building found across the street from St. Augustine's marina, OC White's offers a great view and live entertainment nightly. The interior is decorated with wax figures of pirates, and a full menu of seafood, steaks, and burgers is served. 🏃 🪑 *AE D MC V*

**Daytona Beach:** Oyster Pub
*555 Seabreeze Blvd.* **Road map** E2.
**Tel** *(386) 255-6348.*

Just one block from the beach, this pub has a raw bar serving fresh oysters, shrimp, and other seafood. During happy hour, prices are cut for drinks and seafood. There is sports coverage on 27 TVs, a pool room, and a disc jockey on weekends. 🏃 *AE MC V*

**Gainesville:** 2 Bits Lounge
*1714 SW 34th Street.* **Road map** D2.
**Tel** *(352) 371-3600.*

Located in the Hilton Hotel near the University of Florida campus, this popular bar is dedicated to sports, and shows all the favorite games. Snacks are also available. *AE DC MC V*

## The Panhandle

**Panama City Beach:** Shuckum's Oyster Pub
*15614 Front Beach Rd.* **Road map** B1.
**Tel** *(850) 235-3214.*

The bar at this unpretentious and popular watering hole is covered with signed dollar bills left by satisfied customers. Shuckum's is best known for its local oysters, which are served raw, baked, steamed, or fried in a sandwich. Other seafood dishes are also available. 🏃 🪑 *MC V*

**Pensacola Beach:** Sidelines Sports Bar and Restaurant
*2 Via de Luna Drive.* **Road map** A1.
**Tel** *(850) 934-3660.*

This informal meeting place in Pensacola Beach has a different special for each night of the week; on "Cajun Night," for example, it serves Cajun Bloody Marys. There is seating in booths, and the ubiquitous sports memorabilia and giant-screen televisions adorn the walls. 🏃 *AE MC V*

## The Gulf Coast

**Lee Island Coast:** The Mucky Duck
*11546 Andy Rosse Lane, Captiva Island.*
**Road map** E4. **Tel** *(239) 472-3434.*

This British-style pub occupies a charming 1930s building in Captiva town. Its creator, a former British policeman, named it after his favorite pub back home. Visitors can play darts, enjoy a beer, and watch the sunset. The eclectic menu has English meals such as fish and chips, and vegetarian platters. 🏃 🪑 *AE DC MC V*

**Tampa:** Elmer's Sports Café
*2003 E 7th Ave, Ybor City.* **Road map** D3. **Tel** *(813) 248-5855.*

Ybor City's original sports bar is renowned for its thick and chewy pizzas, great wings, and good beers. Elmer's has giant-screen TVs scattered all around the café, and there is also a pool table. Tasty home made food served in a pleasant atmosphere. 🏃 *AE MC V*

**St. Petersburg:** Ferg's Sports Bar & Grill
*1320 Central Ave.* **Road map** D3.
**Tel** *(727) 822-4562.*

This former gas station, located across the street from Tropicana Stadium, has been converted into a two-story bar with a large covered patio and sidewalk café seating. The menu features chicken wings, burgers, sandwiches, and steaks. There are more than 40 televisions, and big games attract throngs of locals and visitors. 🏃 🪑 *AE DC MC V*

## The Everglades and The Keys

**Naples:** HB's On The Gulf
*851 Gulf Shore Blvd N.* **Road map** E4.
**Tel** *(239) 435-4347.*

Sophisticated HB's On The Gulf, opened in 1946, is located in the Naples Beach Hotel on Naples Pier. It is a fine place for watching the sun go down, although you need to arrive early to get a seat. After sunset, the huge outside bar is packed with people, and a live band provides musical entertainment. HB's serves a full menu, but the food is not the highlight here. 🏃 🪑 *AE DC MC V*

**Key West:** Hog's Breath Saloon
*400 Front St.* **Road map** E5.
**Tel** *(305) 296-4222.*

The original Hog's Breath Saloon moved down to Key West in 1988. It is now a local favorite, offering a raw bar, local seafood dishes, and tasty desserts (including a fine version of the famous Key Lime Pie). There is live music every day from 1pm until 2am. 🏃 🪑 *AE MC V*

**Key West:** Jimmy Buffet's Margaritaville Café
*500 Duval St.* **Road map** E5.
**Tel** *(305) 292-1435.*

There are plenty of Jimmy Buffet trinkets here, both on display and for sale (see p303), though the local singer-songwriter is rarely seen. Frosty Margaritas are the house specialty, and light meals, sandwiches, burgers, and local seafood are also available. 🏃 *AE MC V*

**Key West:** Sloppy Joe's
*201 Duval St.* **Road map** E5.
**Tel** *(305) 294-5717.*

Formerly Ernest Hemingway's favorite drinking place (see p302), Sloppy Joe's is more commercial than in the novelist's day, attracting mainly tourists. However, it retains its Key West character. The menu includes typical bar fare, with jalapeño or conch fritters, chicken fingers and fries, and the renowned "original Sloppy Joe" burger. 🏃 *MC V*

# SHOPPING IN FLORIDA

Shopping is a popular pastime in Florida, and many use it as an enjoyable way of escaping the heat for a few hours. Orlando and Miami in particular, attract many overseas shoppers. The state is known for its discount stores, but at the other end of the scale, it also boasts some extraordinarily upscale shops, usually clustered in fashionable shopping districts or malls. For first-time visitors to Florida, the shopping culture might require some getting used to. Rather than shopping in town or city centers, Floridians generally gravitate toward huge shopping malls, where department stores and other shops sell everything from clothes to computers. For souvenirs and gifts *(see pp352–3)*, however, the small specialty shops are the best bet. If you are looking for something specific, local tourist offices can provide listings of stores in their area. Shops in Miami are described on pages 98–9.

Mizner Park in Boca Raton, with shops as elegant as its architecture

## When to Shop

Most stores open from 10am to 6pm Monday to Saturday, often staying open late once a week. Shopping mall shops, and many department stores, stay open until 9pm. Some stores, including those in the shopping malls, open Sundays, typically from 10am to 6pm, while others (mostly in the larger cities) never close.

During the festive month of December, many stores extend their opening and closing times by one or two hours, to allow ample time for people to do their holiday shopping.

## Sales Tax

Florida levies a six per cent sales tax (may vary in different counties) on all goods except drugs, groceries, and children's clothes. Tax is not included in displayed prices, but is automatically added to the check. It is worth noting that some years, usually in the last week of July or the first week of August, the state allows for a "tax-free shopping week" for the benefit of families who need to shop for the upcoming school year. Take advantage of the tax-free status on most clothing and reserve purchases up to $50. This way, you will be able to save a rather considerable six per cent off your total check.

## Department Stores

Most shopping malls include at least one department store. These are often huge affairs, offering an amazing range of products and services, from complimentary gift-wrapping to assistants who will help you with your shopping.

Most of the department stores can be found all over the US, and all of them have a particular reputation for the quality of their merchandise. For example, Bloomingdale's has a good name for its stock of new fashions, as well as its gourmet food. Some stores specialize only in designer fashion such as the elegant Saks Fifth Avenue, Neiman Marcus, and the conservatively classy Lord & Taylor. The well-known national department store Macy's also has several branches throughout the state. Shopping stalwarts Sears and JCPenney offer everything from clothing and cosmetics to appliances and power tools.

For essentials, from pencils to toothpaste, as well as grocery and electronics, you need look no farther than the no-frills superstores such as Target, Kmart, and Walmart, all of which can be found in many locations throughout the state. You can also find basic necessities and sundries, along with snacks and one-hour photo developing at stores such as Walgreens and CVS Pharmacy. Many of these stores remain open around the clock, especially in larger cities.

A stylish fashion boutique in Bal Harbour Shops in Miami

## Shopping for Bargains

For some people, the chief appeal of Florida's shops are their cut-price goods. Discount stores carry all kinds of general merchandise, but electronic equipment, household goods, and clothes are the biggest draw. Some stores specialize in inexpensive fashion, chief among them being Ross, T.J. Maxx, and Marshalls, all of which have branches in all the major cities. Best Buy is a great store for discounts on computers and electronics.

Factory outlet malls are particularly popular among bargain hunters. In these stores, you can buy slightly imperfect or discontinued merchandise at 50 to 75 per cent below the retail price. Most factory outlet malls also contain brand-name stores selling household items and all types of clothing, such as Benetton sweaters and Levi's jeans at throwaway prices.

Orlando's International Drive (see p192) is lined with a multitude of discount and factory outlet stores. You can even find cheaper Disney souvenirs here, but be warned that the quality is usually not as good as the quality of those available in the theme parks themselves. You are better off visiting Disney's Character Warehouse stores in several of the city's factory outlet malls, because these sell the previous season's official theme park merchandise at a discount of up to 75 per cent.

Flea markets, usually large, lively affairs that function on weekends, are popular territory for bargains. Used goods may

The famous Orange World fruit stand in Kissimmee, selling top-quality Florida fruit

not interest you, but at most markets you'll find crafts, antiques, and other merchandise you may consider taking home. The food stands are an added bonus. Some markets are equally good for their entertainment value, such as the Fort Lauderdale Swap Shop (see p138).

## Gifts and Souvenirs

Fresh oranges are a popular buy for Florida's visitors. The best-quality fruit is grown by the Indian River (see p119), where oranges are sold by the sackful, from November to March. Another popular citrus is the key lime, which can be found statewide in a variety of food products, from sauces to pies. Shops usually deliver the fruit home for you if you live within the US. Fresh fruit can't be shipped or carried into

Sponges for sale in Key West

certain states, such as California or Arizona, and international shipping is usually forbidden by customs.

Artisanal hot pepper sauces have become wildly popular in Florida, where peppers grow like weeds. Shops specializing in the spicy condiments can be found from Key West to Jacksonville.

Seashells also have wide appeal, but check their origins. The Lee Island Coast (see pp282–3) is most famous for its shells. You can buy harvested specimens in the Shell Factory near Fort Myers (see p281). The shells and corals touted by roadside stalls along US 1 in the Keys are often imported. Such stalls also sell natural sponges, but Tarpon Springs (see p255) is the classic place for them.

Native Americans sell crafts made on their reservations in Miccosukee Indian Village (see p289) and Hollywood (see p140), but Florida is not the best place for crafts. However, many towns are known for antiques, such as Dania (see p140), Micanopy (see p226), and Mount Dora (see p224).

Disney has honed merchandising into an art. Shopping is a major activity at Walt Disney World® and other theme parks. Museum stores also sell souvenirs, from reproduction artifacts to educational games.

One of Florida's many factory outlets, advertising its bargain prices

# What to Buy in Florida

People will probably tell you that you can buy just about anything you could ever want in Florida, from a designer bikini to state-of-the-art electronics – or even a new home. Indeed some overseas visitors go to Florida specifically to shop. Even if you are searching for more humble souvenirs or gifts, you will have your choice in the state's theme parks and seaside tourist centers. You may have to search around if you want to avoid kitsch memorabilia – though, in fact, this is what Florida probably does best, and is what evokes (more than anything else) the flavor of the Sunshine State.

Miami Dolphins cap

### Unmistakably Florida
All across Florida you can buy fun souvenirs from towels to ashtrays, often at reasonable prices. They are frequently emblazoned with "Florida," a palm tree, alligator, or some other characteristic image.

Keyring

Dried meal from the Kennedy Space Center

Fake Oscar from Universal Studios®

### Theme Park Fare
All the theme parks, from Universal Studios® to Busch Gardens, produce their own merchandise, designed to appeal to all ages.

Tile with flamingos – a favorite motif

Alligator money bank

### Seminole Crafts
Crafts made by Seminoles are available in a few places in the city (see p351). You can pick up dolls and jewelry for just a few dollars. Apart from these, brightly colored clothes, bags, and blankets can be a good buy, too.

### Hand-Rolled Cigars
The Cuban tradition of hand-rolling cigars survives in Ybor City in Tampa (see pp264–5), and in Miami's Little Havana (see p99), though many are now made by machine. They make a fine gift for cigar-smoking friends.

### Books
Books about Miami's Art Deco district often feature superb photos and make a lasting souvenir of the city. Alternatively, take home the flavors of Florida in the form of a cookbook.

### Latin Music
If you get a taste for the Latin rhythms of Miami's Hispanic community, there is plenty of locally produced music to buy.

## Inexpensive Goods

Many overseas visitors to the US will find that because of lower taxes, a whole range of goods are cheaper than they are at home, including jeans, sunglasses, running shoes, CDs, cameras, books, and so on. Florida also has many discount stores (see p351) that offer even lower prices; small electrical appliances are often a good buy. Downtown Miami is famous for its bargain shops (see pp98–9), which sell primarily low-cost gold, jewelry, and electronic equipment. Feel free to bargain if you have the nerve. Note that if you buy electronic equipment you may need to get a transformer for it to work outside the US. Most shops are used to foreign visitors and can send bulky purchases back home for you.

### T-Shirts
Sold everywhere from gift shops to ordinary discount stores, T-shirts can be very cheap – but you should check the quality before buying.

### Western Gear
The leather goods sold in stores such as JW Cooper are not necessarily made in Florida, but are as authentic as you'll find out West. The state has real cowboy culture and the gear is often a good value by international standards.

Authentic cowboy boots

Leather belt

## The Flavors of Florida

*Florida is famous worldwide for its citrus fruits, which you can buy either fresh (mostly in the winter months) or preserved – as colorful candies, jams, or jellies, or as tasty marinades and oils for cooking. For those with a sweet tooth there are all sorts of sugary goodies, from sticky coconut patties to chewy sweets such as salt water taffy. Locally made chocolate is not of great quality, but often comes in fun shapes.*

Coconut patties

A basket of jellied citrus fruit, a favorite edible souvenir

Florida-grown oranges, sold by the sack

Colorful salt water taffy, popular among visitors

Mango marinade

Key lime oil for cooking

Lime marmalade     Tangerine jelly or "butter"     Hot jalapeño pepper jelly

# Florida Shopping Malls and Districts

Shopping malls in Florida offer the very best in retail therapy, with a wide variety of stores, restaurants, and entertainment, all located in one complex. Many malls are anchored by two or more department stores *(see p350)*, and include an array of shops covering everything from clothing, health, and beauty to books, music, and DVDs. While most malls are fully enclosed, there are some open-air structures as well. There are also several factory outlet malls *(see p351)*, which sell branded goods at dramatically reduced prices. Parking is easily available and most shopping centers are accessible by the city's public transportation system.

Shoppers who want to enjoy Florida's sunny weather as they stroll from store to store may prefer the state's numerous outdoor shopping districts. These fashionable areas are mainly home to chic and exclusive boutiques, as well as to some down-to-earth stores.

## Shopping Districts

For those who dislike the idea of shopping malls, Florida's open-air shopping districts are a fine alternative, offering a selection of shops over a five or six block radius, rather than a cluster of shops operating in one complex.

These shopping areas have breathed new life into historic districts, and the stores here are predominantly upscale.

## Miami Area

Miami's largest mall, **Aventura Mall**, has more than 250 stores, followed closely by **Dadeland Mall** and **Dolphin Mall**. The smaller **Bal Harbour Shops** in Miami Beach caters to upscale shoppers, with its chic designer boutique. Downtown, the **Bayside Marketplace** offers waterfront shops, restaurants, and entertainment.

The best shopping districts in the Miami area *(see pp98–9)* include Coral Gables' **Village of Merrick Park** and **Downtown Coral Gables and Miracle Mile**. Downtown Coconut Grove is also superb, with malls such as **CocoWalk** and the shopping area, **Mayfair in the Grove**. Other leading districts include South Beach's chic, eight-block-long **Lincoln Road Mall**, and **Cauley Square Historic Village**, which is closer to the Everglades than to downtown Miami.

## Gold & Treasure Coasts

Travelers looking to cut costs will adore **Sawgrass Mills** in Fort Lauderdale. With over 300 budget department stores and outlet shops, this place could occupy you for an entire day. For more upscale shopping, visit **The Galleria**.

Palm Beach's **Worth Avenue**, fashionable since the 1920s, is now one of the world's most exclusive shopping streets. Just down the coast in Boca Raton, **Mizner Park**, named after the famous architect who designed it, also indulges the rich and famous. Not far away in Boca Raton, the large, upscale **Town Center Mall** in Glades Road is a convenient place to shop.

## Orlando & the Space Coast

Orlando has the highest number of outlet malls in Florida. International Drive is home to **Premier Outlets**, as well as the **East End Market**. Orlando **Premium Outlets** and Lake Buena Vista Factory Stores are near Walt Disney World®.

A shopping tradition for Orlando visitors, **The Florida Mall** has many tourist-oriented shops, while **Pointe Orlando** and **Mall at Millenia** are more upscale. **Park Avenue** in Winter Park *(see p191)* is full of boutiques and gourmet restaurants.

## The Northeast

Shoppers in Jacksonville can see the beautiful St. Johns River from The **Jacksonville Landing** complex, while **The Avenues** offers a slightly more traditional mall experience.

Farther down the coast, bargain shoppers should visit **St. Augustine Premium Outlets**. No visit to Daytona Beach is complete without a stop at **Ocean Walk Shoppes**, which as its name suggests, faces the sea.

## The Panhandle

Visitors to Destin can choose between the open-air **Destin Commons** mall or **Silver Sands Premium Outlets**, which specializes in budget designer clothes.

In Tallahassee, the state capital of Florida, **Governor's Square Mall** offers the widest selection of stores.

## The Gulf Coast

Bargain shoppers will find three outlet malls along the Gulf Coast's I-75 corridor. From north to south, discount shopping is offered at **Ellenton Premium Outlets** near Sarasota, and **Miromar Outlets** in Estero.

For more upscale shopping, go to **International Plaza and Bay Street** near Tampa airport, or **Centro Ybor**, situated in Ybor City, Tampa's Latin Quarter district. Shopping districts of note include Sarasota's **St. Armands Circle**, a haven for gourmets, **Hyde Park Village** in Tampa, and **Johns Pass Village** near Madeira Beach, which is modeled on a late 19th-century fishing village.

## The Everglades & The Keys

Cost cutters will enjoy the **Outlets** in both Naples and Florida City.

The upscale district of **Fifth Avenue South** in Naples has a variety of boutiques. Any trip to Key West has to include the artsy **Mallory Square**, with its gift shops, boutiques, and street vendors.

# DIRECTORY

## Miami Area

**Aventura Mall**
19501 Biscayne Blvd,
Aventura.
**Tel** (305) 935-1110.
🅦 aventuramall.com

**Bal Harbour Shops**
9700 Collins Ave,
Bal Harbour.
**Tel** (305) 866-0311.
🅦 balharbourshops.
com

**Bayside Marketplace**
401 Biscayne Blvd, Miami.
**Map** 4 F1.
**Tel** (305) 577-3344.
🅦 baysidemarketplace.
com

**Cauley Square
Historic Village**
22400 Old Dixie Hwy
(US 1), Miami.
**Road Map** F5.
**Tel** (305) 258-3543.
🅦 cauleysquare.com

**CocoWalk**
3015 Grand Ave,
Coconut Grove.
**Map** 6 E4.
**Tel** (305) 444-0777.
🅦 cocowalk.net

**Dadeland Mall**
7535 N Kendall Drive,
Kendall.
**Tel** (305) 665-6226.

**Dolphin Mall**
11401 NW 12th St, Miami.
**Tel** (305) 365-7466.
🅦 shopdolphinmall.
com

**Downtown Coral
Gables and Miracle
Mile**
224 Miracle Mile,
Coral Gables.
**Map** 5 C1.
**Tel** (305) 569-0311.
🅦 shopcoralgables.com

**Lincoln Road Mall**
Lincoln Rd at Meridian
Ave, Miami Beach.
**Map** 2 E2.
**Tel** (305) 531-3442.

**Mayfair in the Grove**
3390 Mary St.,
Coconut Grove.
**Map** 6 E4.
**Tel** (305) 448-1700.
🅦 mayfairinthegrove.
com

**Village of Merrick Park**
358 San Lorenzo Ave,
Coral Gables.
**Map** 5 C4.
**Tel** (305) 529-0200.
🅦 villageofmerrick
park.com

## Gold & Treasure Coast

**The Galleria**
2414 E Sunrise Blvd, Fort
Lauderdale.
**Tel** (954) 564-1015.
🅦 galleriamall-fl.com

**Mizner Park**
327 Plaza Real, Boca Raton.
**Tel** (561) 362-0606.
🅦 miznerpark.com

**Sawgrass Mills**
12801 W Sunrise Blvd,
Fort Lauderdale.
**Tel** (954) 846-2350.
🅦 sawgrassmills.com

**Town Center Mall**
6000 Glades Road,
Boca Raton.
**Tel** (561) 368-6000.
🅦 simon.com

**Worth Ave**
Palm Beach.
**Tel** (561) 659-6909.
🅦 worth-avenue.com

## Orlando and the Space Coast

**East End Market**
3201 Corrine Dr, Orlando.
**Tel** (321) 236-3316.

**The Florida Mall**
8001 S Orange Blossom
Trail, Orlando.
**Tel** (407) 851-6255.

**Lake Buena Vista
Factory Stores**
15591 Apopka Vineland
Rd, Orlando.
**Tel** (407) 238-9301.
🅦 lbvfs.com

**Mall at Millenia**
4200 Conroy Rd, Orlando.
**Tel** (407) 363-3555.
🅦 mallatmillenia.com

**Orlando Premium
Outlets**
8200 Vineland Av, Orlando.
**Tel** (407) 238-7787.
4951 International Drive,
Orlando.
**Tel** (407) 352-9600.

**Park Avenue**
Winter Park, Orange Co.
**Tel** (877) 972-4262.
🅦 wpfl.org

**Pointe Orlando**
9101 International
Drive, Orlando.
**Tel** (407) 248-2838.
🅦 pointeorlando.com

## The Northeast

**The Avenues**
10300 Southside Blvd,
Jacksonville.
**Tel** (904) 363-3060.

**Jacksonville Landing**
2 Independent Drive,
Jacksonville.
**Tel** (904) 353-1188.
🅦 jacksonvillelanding.
com

**Ocean Walk Shoppes**
250 N Atlantic Ave,
Daytona Beach.
**Tel** (386) 258-9544.
🅦 oceanwalk shoppes.
com

**St. Augustine
Premium Outlets**
2700 State Rd 16, St.
Augustine.
**Tel** (904) 825-1555.

## The Panhandle

**Destin Commons**
4300 Legendary Drive,
Destin.
**Tel** (850) 337-8700.
🅦 destincommons.com

**Governor's Square Mall**
1500 Apalachee Pkwy,
Tallahassee.
**Tel** (850) 877-8106.
🅦 governorssquare.
com

**Silver Sands
Premium Outlets**
10562 Emerald Coast
Pkwy, W Destin.
**Tel** (850) 654-9771.
🅦 premiumoutlets.
com

## The Gulf Coast

**Centro Ybor**
1600 E 8th Ave,
Tampa.
**Tel** (813) 242-4660.
🅦 centroybor.com

**Ellenton Premium
Outlets**
5461 Factory Shops Blvd,
Ellenton.
**Tel** (941) 723-1150.
🅦 primeoutlets.com

**Hyde Park Village**
1509 W Snow Ave, Tampa.
**Tel** (813) 251-3500.
🅦 hydeparkvillage.net

**International Plaza
and Bay Street**
2223 N Westshore Blvd,
Tampa.
**Tel** (813) 342-3790.
🅦 shopinternational
plaza.com

**Johns Pass Village**
12901 Gulf Blvd, Madeira
Beach.
**Tel** (727) 394-0756.
🅦 johnspass.com

**Miromar Outlets**
10801 Corkscrew Rd,
Estero.
**Tel** (239) 948-3766.
🅦 miromaroutlets.com

**St. Armands Circle**
300 Madison Drive,
Sarasota.
**Tel** (941) 388-1554.
🅦 starmandscircle
assoc.com

## The Everglades & The Keys

**Fifth Avenue South**
649 5th Ave S, Naples.
**Tel** (239) 692-8436.
🅦 fifthavenue south.
com

**Florida Keys
Outlet Center**
250 E Palm Drive,
Florida City.
**Tel** (305) 248-4727.

**Mallory Square**
400 Wall St, Key West.
**Tel** (305) 809-3700.
🅦 mallorysquare.com

**Naples Outlet Center**
6060 Collier Blvd, Naples.
**Tel** (239) 775-8083 .
🅦 premiumoutlets.
com/naples

# Specialty Shops in Florida

Shopping is as natural as breathing in Florida, and there is a plethora of stores specializing in all kinds of merchandise statewide. From antiques to outdoor gear and music, there is a store to fulfill every shopping need.

Most specialty stores are not found in major shopping areas, so public or private transportation is needed to access them. However, the vast selection of goods available, and the opportunity to interact with knowledgeable sales staff, make these shops well worth a visit.

## Antiques

Just northwest of Orlando, Mount Dora (see p224) is the self-proclaimed antiques capital of Florida. **Renninger's** is one of the largest antiques markets in this haven for collectors. Micanopy (see p226), another hub for vintage goods, has more than 18 antiques stores.

Other notable destinations for antiques shopping include **Waldo's Antique Village**, a flea market in the tiny town of Waldo near Starke, and the **Hillsboro Antique Mall** in Pompano Beach. For sheer volume, visit the **Historic Antique District** in Dania (see p140), which offers over 100 shops within a one-block radius.

## Arts and Craft Galleries

The Florida Keys are a great place to shop for locally-made arts and crafts. In Key Largo (see p296), drop into **Happy Feathers** for unique Florida crafts that also make fantastic gifts. Farther down the road in Key West, Duvall Street has a multitude of local craft and art galleries, including **Alan S. Maltz Gallery**, which features the photographer's award-winning works.

In downtown St. Petersburg (see p258), **Florida CraftArt** is a joy for art lovers. This 2,500 sq ft (232 sq m) retail space and gallery displays the works of crafters from around the state.

## Farmers' Markets

Farmers' Markets are excellent places in which to buy fresh Florida citrus fruits and other produce straight from local farms and orchards. Many markets also offer a variety of crafts and other attractive and interesting merchandise.

**Downtown Farmer's Market** in Orlando opens for business every Sunday morning, and offers baked goods, farm produce, and flowers. **Lincoln Road Mall**, which opens on Sunday, is very popular with South Beach locals, while in the Panhandle, **Tallahassee Downtown Marketplace** opens on Tuesday, Thursday, and Saturday.

In the Gulf Coast, explore **Clearwater Downtown Farmer's Market**, which opens Wednesday and Saturday, from mid-October to mid-April. **Ybor City Fresh Market** is held year-round, every Saturday.

## Gifts and Souvenirs

Not surprisingly, Miami, with its Little Havana neighborhood, has many treats in store for cigar aficionados. **El Titan de Bronze,** has an excellent collection of hand-rolled cigars. **Sosa Family Cigars** at Walt Disney World® also stocks quality cigars and cigar accessories. For a less smoky experience, try **Little Havana To Go**, which advertises itself as the official souvenir store for Cuban art, music, books, and more.

Items from **Key West Aloe**, with its vast range of Aloe-based beauty products, have a distinct Floridian touch. The frangipani soaps are a fragrant reminder of the Keys.

Get your motor running with a visit to **Orlando Harley-Davidson**, Florida's largest motorcycle dealership. Its logo merchandise is guaranteed to delight the motorcycle enthusiast back home.

## Gourmet Food and Drink

Key West has a wide variety of tasty gourmet offerings. Try the fiery flavorings of **Peppers of Key West**, the fresh-baked artisan breads of **Cole's Peace**, and the incredibly fresh fish sold by the **Conch Republic Seafood Company**.

**St. Augustine Distillery** handcrafts small batches of whiskey, rum, vodka, and gin, using Florida crops. **Lakeridge Winery** offers a range of reds, whites, and rosés made from Florida's Muscadine grape.

For desserts, try **Peterbrooke** for delicious custom-made chocolate treats, and take its fascinating factory tour.

**International Food Club** sells a vast range of foods from all over the world, from bangers and mash to Indian teas and Chinese spices.

## Music and DVDs

Carrying a wide range of music and movies, the **F.Y.E. chain** has several locations throughout Florida, including Miami and Orlando.

For more genre-specific options, try an independent store. **Park Ave CDs** specializes in indie rock. **Sweat Records** in Miami offers a similar selection.

## Outdoor and Watersports

With its perennial sunshine, Florida is a great place for outdoor and watersports. Happily, it also has the stores to supply outfits for any activity.

Soccer enthusiasts will find everything they desire at **Soccer Locker** in Miami. Farther up the coast, Cocoa Beach is home to **Ron Jon Surf Shop**. This legendary watersports store is open 24 hours for all your sun, sea, and sand needs. For camping and fishing fans, **Bass Pro Shops** has several locations in Florida, with its newest, and possibly largest branch, located in Orlando.

# DIRECTORY

## Antiques

**Hillsboro Antique Mall and Café**
2900 W. Sample Rd,
Pompano Beach.
**Tel** (954) 571-9988.
w hillsboroantiquemall.
com

**Historic Antique District**
Federal Hwy, Dania Beach
Blvd, Dania.
**Tel** (954) 925-6935.

**Renninger's**
20651 US Hwy 441,
Mount Dora.
**Tel** (352) 383-8393.
w renningers.com/dora

**Waldo's Antique Village**
17805 NE US Hwy 301,
Waldo.
**Tel** (407) 877-5921.
w waldosfleamarket.
com

## Arts and Crafts Galleries

**Alan S. Maltz Gallery**
1210 Duval St, Key West.
**Tel** (305) 295-0005.
w alanmaltz.com

**Florida CraftArt**
501 Central Ave,
St. Petersburg.
**Tel** (727) 821-7391.

**Happy Feathers**
99150 Overseas Hwy,
Key Largo.
**Tel** (305) 453-1800.

## Farmers' Markets

**Clearwater Downtown Farmer's Market**
112, S Osceola,
Clearwater.
**Tel** (727) 461-7674.
w clearwaterfarmers
market.com
(Open 8am–1pm)

**Downtown Farmer's Market**
Lake Eola Park, Orlando.
**Tel** (321) 202-5855.
w orlandofarmers
market.com
(Open 10am–4pm)

**Lincoln Road Mall**
Lincoln Rd at 16th St,
Miami Beach.
**Map** 2 E2.
**Tel** (305) 531-3442.
w lincolnroad.org

**Tallahassee Downtown Marketplace**
115 E Park, Tallahassee.
**Tel** (850) 224-3252.
w downtownmarket.
com
(Open 8am–2pm)

**Ybor City Fresh Market**
8th Ave and 19th St,
Ybor City.
**Tel** (813) 241-2442.
w ybormarket.com

## Gifts and Souvenirs

**El Titan de Bronze**
1071 SW 8th St, Miami.
**Map** 3 B2.
**Tel** (305) 860-1412.

**Key West Aloe**
1075 Duval St..
**Tel** (305) 517-6365.
w keywestaloe.com

**Little Havana To Go**
1442 SW 8th St, Miami.
**Map** 3 B2.
**Tel** (305) 857-9720.

**Orlando Harley-Davidson**
3770 37th St, Orlando.
**Tel** (407) 423-0346.
w orlandoharley.com

**Sosa Family Cigars**
1502 E Buena Vista Drive,
Lake Buena Vista.
**Tel** (407) 827-0114.
w sosacigars.com

## Gourmet Food and Drink

**Cole's Peace**
1111 Eaton St, Key West.
**Tel** (305) 292-0703.
w colespeace.com

**Conch Republic Seafood Company**
631 Greene St, Key West.
**Tel** (305) 294-4403.
w conchrepublic
seafood.com

**International Food Club**
4300 LB McLeod Rd,
Orlando.
**Tel** (321) 281-4300.

**Lakeridge Winery**
19239 US 27 N, Clermont.
**Tel** (800) 768-9463.
w lakeridgewinery.
com

**Peppers of Key West**
602 Greene St, Key West.
**Tel** (800) 597-2823.
w peppersofkeywest.
com

**Peterbrooke**
1470 San Marco Blvd,
Jacksonville.
**Tel** (800) 771-0019.
w peterbrooke.com

**St. Augustine Distillery**
112 Riberia St,
St. Augustine.
**Tel** (904) 825-4962.
w staugustinedistillery.
com

## Music and DVDs

**F.Y.E.**
Coral Square,
9009 W Atlantic Blvd,
Coral Springs.
**Tel** (954) 755-8052.
Altamonte Mall,
451 E Altamonte Dr.,
Altamonte Springs.
**Tel** (407) 332-8851.

**Park Ave CDs**
2916 Corrine Dr., Orlando.
**Tel** (407) 447-7275.
w parkavecds.com

**Sweat Records**
5505 NE 2nd Ave, Miami.
**Tel** (786) 693-9309.

## Outdoor and Watersports

**Bass Pro Shops**
Artegon Marketplace,
5156 International Drive,
Orlando.
**Tel** (407) 563-5200.
w basspro.com

**Ron Jon Surf Shop**
4151 N Atlantic Ave,
Cocoa Beach.
**Tel** (888) 757-8737.
w ronjons.com

**Soccer Locker**
9601 S Dixie Hwy,
Miami.
**Road map** F5.
**Tel** (305) 670-9100.
w soccerlocker.com

# ENTERTAINMENT IN FLORIDA

Whether your preference is for a Broadway drama, a lavish Las Vegas-style floorshow, a night in a disco, or a bit of gambling, Florida has something for everyone. You'll find the greatest range of entertainment in South Florida, particularly along the Gold Coast and in Miami *(see pp100–101)*, but Sarasota and Tampa are also major cultural centers. Walt Disney World® and Orlando offer the best choice of family entertainment, with theme parks galore to thrill the children during the daytime, and dinner shows at

night. In the Northeast and the Panhandle the entertainment is more limited, the best offered in resorts such as Panama City Beach, and university cities such as Gainesville and Tallahassee.

Within cities with distinct mainland and beach areas, such as Fort Lauderdale, the liveliest nightlife is on the waterfront. As far as the performing arts are concerned, most high-quality shows take place between October and April, although there is a good choice of events throughout the year.

The Raymond F. Kravis Center for the Performing Arts, West Palm Beach

## Sources of Information

Most regional newspapers in Florida have a special weekend section that lists all local attractions and events, as well as details of venues. Local Convention and Visitors' Bureaus and chambers of commerce are also filled with useful brochures.

## Making Reservations

The easiest way to purchase tickets for a concert, play, football game, or other event is to call the relevant box office and pay by credit card. Some places, however, will require a reservation to be made through **Ticketmaster**. This company runs an extensive pay-by-phone operation and also has outlets in music and discount stores. It charges a commission of $2–8 per ticket above the ticket's face value, depending on the event.

## Major Venues

Florida's largest venues, some of which are known as performing arts centers, are used for a whole range of performances, from operas to rock concerts, as well as for special events including, in some cases, sports events. This is where major national touring companies or artists usually perform, though visitors can sometimes see local productions here, too.

Some of the most important venues in Florida include the **Raymond F. Kravis Center for the Performing Arts** in West Palm Beach; Fort Lauderdale's **Broward Center for the Performing Arts**; the **Adrienne Arsht Center for the Performing Arts** in Miami *(see p100)*; the huge **Straz Center**; the **MIDFLORIDA Credit Union Amphitheatre** in

Tampa; and the **Van Wezel Performing Arts Hall** in Sarasota. Other major theaters include the **Camping World Stadium** in Orlando, a 70,000-seat arena where stars from Paul McCartney to Metallica perform. The **EverBank Field** in Jacksonville also hosts major rock concerts.

## Theater

Road shows, often lavish productions with extravagant sets and big casts, originate on Broadway and are the highest-quality productions you are likely to see in Florida. The state has several good theater companies of its own, whose shows are performed in smaller, more atmospheric places such as the **Mann Performing Arts Hall** in Fort Myers or Key West's **Red Barn Theatre**. The **Florida State University Center for the Performing Arts** is home to Sarasota's own Asolo Theater Company. The building, originally built for the Queen of Cyprus was brought to Sarasota in the 1940s. The **Players of Sarasota** is the city's longest established theater company, where such famous actors

Theater emblem, Pensacola

as Montgomery Clift launched their careers. Its performances of musicals and plays usually earn widespread praise.

## Classical Music, Opera, and Dance

Most major cities have their own symphony orchestra. The **Symphony of the Americas** performs mainly in Fort Lauderdale and in the cities along the Gold Coast, as well as touring internationally. Miami's New World Symphony *(see p100)* also tours inter-nationally. Look out for performances by the Jacksonville Symphony Orchestra, which is based at the city's **Times-Union Center for the Performing Arts**.

The **Florida Grand Opera**, the state's largest opera company, currently performs at the Adrienne Arsht Center for the Performing Arts. The Broward Center for the Performing Arts is the home of the Gold Coast Opera, a private theatrical company that presents classical operas such as *Carmen* and *The Barber of Seville*. For a more intimate experience, visit the small **Monticello Opera House**, which hosts opera between September and May.

The best ballet company is the Miami City Ballet *(see p100)*, whose choreographer is Edward Villella, a protégé of the late George Balanchine.

## Movies

New York or Los Angeles offer the best arts movies, but Florida has plenty of multi-screen movie theaters showing blockbuster movies. The state's most famous movie is the historic **Tampa Theatre** *(see p263)*, which hosts a variety of live acts but shows mainly a mixture of classic and foreign movies.

Also look out for annual movie festivals: Sarasota has one in November, and the Miami International Film Festival is in February, when films are shown at the Olympia Theater *(see p100)*. Orlando hosts the Florida Film Festival at the Enzian Theater in the spring *(see p190)*.

## Dinner Shows

Dinner shows are a popular form of family entertainment in Florida, especially in Orlando *(see p193)*. Here, diners sit at communal tables and are served huge meals that are generally themed to the show that you are watching. Audience participation is normally *de rigueur*.

Outside Orlando, the dinner shows tend to be less raucous but still provide varied entertainment, from conventional plays to comedies, musicals, and even murder-mystery dinners. The **Mai Kai** in Fort Lauderdale, a long-running and superbly tacky Polynesian revue, entertains with dancers dressed in grass skirts, fire eaters, and so forth. Jacksonville's **Alhambra Dinner Theater** puts on ambitious musicals of the *Oklahoma* and *South Pacific* school.

A singer entertains at Miami's Latin Carnival *(see p38)*

## Live Music and Nightclubs

Some of the most entertaining places to dance are clubs where you can dance to live instead of canned music. The best are often clubs where the music is provided by a big band or orchestra –"supper clubs" offer food as well as a band. The music can be varied: the **Coliseum Ballroom**, a Moorish-style gem in St. Petersburg, attracts a crowd for both ballroom and country dancing. South Beach has the greatest choice of conventional discos *(see p101)*, but good clubs can be found in popular vacation spots. **Razzles** in Daytona Beach offers high-energy music, and **Cheers** in Fort Lauderdale showcases current rock bands and has a busy dance floor. **Cowboys Orlando** is a popular country music dance club. Nightclubs require you to show ID to prove that you are over 18 or, in some cases, 21.

Festivals are fertile territory for live music, and there are also countless spots where dancing to the music isn't compulsory. Key West has several well-established places, like the Hog's Breath Saloon *(see p349)*. Tampa's **Skipper's Smokehouse** offers reggae and blues. Country and western music is popular, for which Pace's **Farmers' Opry House** is a major venue. Some of the bars listed on pages 348–9 also offer live entertainment.

Sign for Hog's Breath Saloon in Key West

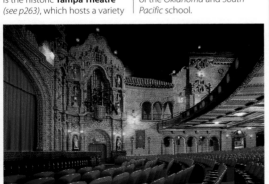

The lavish interior of the Tampa Theatre, an historic cinema

Street performers in Mallory Square in Key West, providing nightly entertainment at sunset

## Cruise and Boat Trips

Florida is the world's leading departure point for cruises to the Caribbean, and ships set off regularly from Miami, Port Everglades, and other ports. Companies offering cruises for several days or more include **Disney, Royal Caribbean,** and the **Carnival Cruise Line**.

You can also go on mini-cruises, for a day or just an evening – the cost of which starts at around $40. Evening cruises usually entail dinner and dancing, and sometimes on-board gambling. The proximity of Freeport, Grand Bahama, allows one-day mini-cruises on lines such as **Balearia Bahamas Express** in Fort Lauderdale.

Day cruises are a great way to explore Florida and offer unparalleled views. Pleasure boat trips are available all over the state. The Jungle Queen in Fort Lauderdale (see p139), the **Manatee Queen** in Jupiter (see p121), and St. Petersburg's **Starlite Cruises**, are popular boats.

## Gambling

Gambling on cruise ships is popular because conventional casinos are illegal on most of the mainland: once a ship is in international waters, about 3 miles (5 km) from shore, the law no longer applies. But you can visit one of the state's six **Seminole Indian Casinos**: two are in Hollywood (see p141), one in Coconut Creek, another in Immokalee near Naples, one near Tampa, and one in Okeechobee. The Miccosukee tribe owns a casino near Miami. Gulfstream Park Racetrack and Mardi Gras at Hollywood Racetrack, both in Hallandale, and Pompano Park Harness Track in Pompano Beach also have casinos.

## Children's Entertainment

Children are catered to all over Florida, not just at the theme parks. Museums often have excellent hands-on exhibits, and in many zoos and some parks there are "petting zoos," where children can enjoy direct contact with the animals. Children can also have great fun at the water parks (see p363), found all over the state. With **Walt Disney World® Resort, Universal Orlando®, SeaWorld®**, and other big attractions, Orlando has no shortage of family entertainment; look out for what is on at the **Amway Center**, which hosts everything from ice-skating shows to circuses and NBA games.

There is also plenty of free entertainment. Children often enjoy street entertainers, and there are festivals to choose from all year round (see pp38–41).

## Gay and Lesbian Venues

South Beach in Miami is well-known for its vibrant LGBT scene, with popular bars such as **Twist**, SoBe's largest gay venue, and **The Cabaret South Beach** attracting an increasing number of visitors from home and abroad each year. Key West's **801 Bourbon Bar** and nearby **Aqua Night Club** feature raucous nightly drag shows, and in Fort Lauderdale, **Scandal's Saloon** offers music and drinks along with cowboy cool and tongue-in-cheek humor.

For information on popular nightlife venues, restaurants, accommodation, and local activities visit the **Gay and Lesbian Community Center**, Key West.

The Rivership Romance on the St. Johns River

Festivities during the Gay Pride celebration in Fort Lauderdale

# DIRECTORY

## Making Reservations

**Ticketmaster**
Tel (800) 745-3000.
w ticketmaster.com

## Major Venues

**Adrienne Arsht Center for the Performing Arts**
1300 Biscayne Blvd, Miami.
Tel (786) 468-2000.

**Broward Center for the Performing Arts**
201 SW Fifth Ave, Fort Lauderdale.
Tel (954) 522-5334.

**Camping World Stadium**
1 Citrus Bowl Place, Orlando.
Tel (407) 440-5700.

**EverBank Field**
1 Stadium Blvd, Jackson-ville.
Tel (904) 633-6100.

**MIDFLORIDA Credit Union Amphitheatre**
4802 US 301 North, Tampa.
Tel (866) 614-4183.

**Raymond F. Kravis Center for the Performing Arts**
701 Okeechobee Blvd, West Palm Beach.
Tel (561) 832-7469.

**Straz Center**
1010 N MacInnes Place, Tampa.
Tel (813) 229-7827.

**Van Wezel Performing Arts Hall**
777 N Tamiami Trail, Sarasota.
Tel (941) 955-7676.
w vanwezel.org

## Theater

**Florida State University Center for the Performing Arts**
5555 N Tamiami Trail, Sarasota.
Tel (941) 351-8000.

**Mahaffey Theater**
400 First St South, St Petersburg.
Tel (727) 892-5798.

**Mann Performing Arts Hall**
8099 College Parkway, Fort Myers.
Tel (239) 481-4849.

**Players of Sarasota**
838 N Tamiami Trail, Sarasota.
Tel (941) 365-2494.

**Red Barn Theatre**
319 Duval St, Key West.
Tel (305) 296-9911.

## Classical Music, Opera, and Dance

**Florida Grand Opera**
8390 NW 25th St, Miami.
Tel (305) 854-7890.

**Monticello Opera House**
West Washington St, Monticello.
Tel (850) 997-4242.

**Symphony of the Americas**
2425 E Commercial Blvd, Fort Lauderdale.
Tel (954) 335-7002.

**Times-Union Center for the Performing Arts**
300 W Water St, Jacksonville.
Tel (904) 633-6110.

## Movies

**Tampa Theatre**
711 N Franklin St, Tampa.
Tel (813) 274-8981.
w tampatheatre.org

## Dinner Shows

**Alhambra Dinner Theater**
12000 Beach Blvd, Jacksonville.
Tel (904) 641-1212.

**Mai Kai**
3599 N Federal Highway, Fort Lauderdale.
Tel (954) 563-3272 or (800) 262-4524.

## Live Music and Nightclubs

**Cheers**
941 E Cypress Creek Rd, Fort Lauderdale.
Tel (954) 771-6337.

**Coliseum Ballroom**
535 4th Ave North, St. Petersburg.
Tel (727) 892-5202.

**Cowboys Orlando**
1108 S Orange Blossom Trail, Orlando.
Tel (407) 422-7115.

**Farmers' Opry House**
8897 Byron Campbell Rd, Pace, Florida.
Tel (850) 994-6000.

**Razzles**
611 Seabreeze Blvd, Daytona Beach.
Tel (386) 257-6236.

**Skipper's Smokehouse**
910 Skipper Rd, Tampa.
Tel (813) 971-0666.

## Cruise and Boat Trips

**Balearia Bahamas Express**
Terminal 1, Port Everglades, Fort Lauderdale.
Tel (866) 699 6988.

**Carnival Cruise Line**
3655 NW 87th Ave, Miami.
Tel (800) 764-7419.

**Manatee Queen**
1065 N Ocean Blvd, Jupiter.
Tel (561) 744-2191.

**Royal Caribbean Cruise Line**
Miami, Fort Lauderdale, Port Canaveral.
Tel (800) 561-7225.

**Starlite Cruises**
3400 Pasadena Ave South, St. Petersburg.
Tel (727) 462-2628.

**Yacht Star Ship**
601 Channelside Drive, Tampa.
Tel (813) 223-7999.

## Gambling

**Seminole Hard Rock Hotel and Casino**
5223 N Orient Rd, I-4 Exit 5, Tampa.
Tel (866) 502-7529.
506 South 1st St, Immokalee.
Tel (800) 218-0007.
5550 NW 40th St, Coconut Creek.
Tel (866) 222-7466.

## Children's Entertainment

**Amway Center**
400 W Church St, Orlando.
Tel (407) 440-7000.

**SeaWorld®/Busch Gardens**
Tel (407) 363-2613.
w buschgardens.com

**Universal Orlando®**
Tel (407) 363-8000.
w universalorlando.com

**Walt Disney World®**
Tel (407) 934-7639.
w disneyworld.com

## Gay and Lesbian Venues

**801 Bourbon Bar**
801 Duval St, Key West.
Tel (305) 294-473.
w 801bourbon.com

**Aqua Night Club**
711 Duval St, Key West.
Tel (305) 294-0555.

**The Cabaret South Beach**
Shelborne South Beach, 1801 Collins Ave, South Beach.
Tel (305) 504-7500.
w thecabaretsouthbeach.com

**Gay and Lesbian Community Center, Key West**
513 Truman Ave, Key West.
Tel (305)292-3223.
w glcckeywest.org

**Scandal's Saloon**
1373 NE 6th Ave, Wilton Manors.
Tel (954) 567-2432.
w scandalsfla.com

**Twist**
1057 Washington Ave, South Beach.
Tel (305) 538-9478.
w twistsobe.com

# SPORTS AND OUTDOOR ACTIVITIES

Thanks to Florida's climate, you can take part in many sports and outdoor activities all year round, making the state a top destination for all sports enthusiasts, from golfers and tennis players to canoeists and deep-sea divers – some people even base their entire vacation around the sports opportunities available. Water sports of all kinds are well represented, with wonderful beaches on both the Atlantic and Gulf coasts. Florida also boasts approximately 10 million acres (4 million ha) of protected land, which can be explored on foot, horseback, bicycle, or boat. For those who prefer to watch rather than to take part, Florida has a wide range of spectator sports on offer, which are described on pages 36–7.

A seaside golf course at Boca Raton on the Gold Coast

## Source of Information

The two best sources of general information are the **Florida Sports Foundation** and the **Department of Environmental Protection (DEP)**, which can provide information on most outdoor activities. The *Florida Vacation Guide*, available from Florida tourist board offices abroad, provides useful addresses, or local tourist offices can be contacted for information about specific areas. Further sources are given in individual sections.

## Golf

Florida is a golfer's paradise, and with over 1,100 courses, it is the country's top golfing destination. Palm Beach offers so many courses (160 total) it claims to be the "golfing capital of the world," even though Naples boasts the greatest concentration.

Courses in Florida are flat by most standards, but landscaping provides some relief. Many of the most challenging courses are attached to resort hotels along the coast (some offer vacation packages). Courses can also be found inland, including at Walt Disney World®. Approximately two-thirds of courses are open to the public.

Golf is a year-round sport, but winter is the busiest season. If you play in summer, start early in the day to avoid late afternoon thunderstorms and lightning. Greens fees vary from less than $20 to more than $75 per person and are highest in the peak winter season.

The *PLAY FLA GOLF* guide, from the Florida Sports Foundation, lists all public and private courses.

## Tennis

Tennis, like golf, is very popular in Florida. Many hotels have courts, and some resorts offer vacation packages that include lessons. Contact the **United States Tennis Association (Florida Section)** for information on coaching, clubs, and competitions. The state's most famous tennis school is the **Nick Bollettieri Tennis Academy** *(see p271)*, which offers weekly training programs for $800 or more, as well as one-day sessions.

## Diving and Snorkeling

Florida is superb diving and snorkeling territory. The country's only living coral reef skirts the state's southeast coast, stretching the length of the Keys, where there is a magnificent variety of coral and fish *(see pp296–7)*. The reef lies 3–5 miles (5–8 km) offshore and is easily accessible to amateur snorkelers. Guided snorkeling trips are available throughout the Keys and are generally excellent.

The state's estimated 4,000 diving sites have increased, thanks to the artificial reefs program. All over Florida, everything from bridge spans to freighters have been used to create a habitat for coral and colorful fish; there is even a Rolls Royce off Palm Beach. Sunken Spanish galleons also provide fascinating dive sites, mainly in south Florida.

Without a Certified Divers Card visitors will need to take a course. Recognized NAUI or PADI courses are widely

Freshwater swimming at Wakulla Springs, near Tallahassee

Colorful jet ski and boat rental outlet in the Panhandle

available, and novices can learn in just four days for $300–400.

For more information, the Florida Sports Foundation's *Florida Boating and Diving Guide* is helpful, or visitors can call the **Keys Association of Dive Operators (KADO)**.

## Swimming and Water Sports

Swimming is as natural as breathing to most Floridians. Many hotels have pools, but the joy of Florida is the chance to swim in the ocean or in the many lakes, springs, and rivers.

The Atlantic provides the best waves and Florida's only surfing beaches, including Cocoa Beach *(see p199)*. The warm, gentle swells of the Gulf of Mexico are better for children. These western beaches are beautiful, with white sands and dunes in the Panhandle. Coastal erosion means that the southeastern beaches are often quite narrow, while there are only a couple of sandy beaches in the Keys.

Beach access is sometimes controlled: many lie within parks, which charge admission. Some hotels like to give the impression that their beach is for guests only, but they can't stop public access. Lifeguards monitor the most popular beaches in high season.

Many inland parks have freshwater swimming areas, including some beautifully clear spring water holes, such as those in Blue Spring State Park *(see p224)*. Another alternative are the water parks, with all types of rides and pools, found throughout the state.

The full range of water sports, from windsurfing to jet skiing, is offered at Florida's resorts; water-skiing can also be enjoyed on freshwater lakes and inland waterways. Avoid swimming in the interior lakes during summer, as algae growth can pose danger.

## Fishing

Florida's numerous lakes and rivers are overflowing with fish, and fishing is not so much a sport as a way of life for a great many Floridians. The opportunities are endless, both inland and all along the coast.

The Atlantic and Gulf shores are dotted with dedicated fishermen. Fishing right off the pier is popular at many coastal spots, but for those who enjoy angling on a different scale there is plenty of sport fishing for which the state is probably better known.

Deep-sea fishing boats can be chartered at many seaside resorts. The biggest fleets are found in the Panhandle, especially around Fort Walton Beach and Destin, and in

the Keys. With the Gulf Stream nearby, the waters off the Keys offer the most varied fishing in the state *(see p299)*. Organized group excursions are an excellent option for novices. If you want to take a big fish home, a taxidermist will preserve it; the more eco-conscious alternative these days is to have a model made of it. Bait and tackle shops or the charter boat operator can give you the names of local taxidermists.

Florida has thousands of lakes, as well as rivers and canals, for freshwater fishing. Boat rentals and fishing guides are available along the larger rivers, such as the Anclote and the St. Johns, and in other popular fishing areas such as Lake Okeechobee *(see p132)*. Fishing is also permitted in many state and other parks. In rural parts, fish camps offer simple accommodation and basic supplies, though some are open only during the summer.

Licenses, costing from $12 to $30, are required for freshwater and saltwater fishing. The *Fishing Handbook*, available from the **Florida Fish and Wildlife Conservation Commission**, provides information on locations and licensing. It also gives details of the entry dates, fees, regulations, and prizes of Florida's fishing tournaments; one of the best known is Destin's Fishing Rodeo *(see p40)*.

For more information on fishing or hunting, contact the Department of Environmental Protection, or the Florida Fish and Wildlife Conservation Commission *(see p365)*.

Pelicans observing anglers on a pier on Cedar Key

The Intracoastal Waterway at Boca Raton, on the Gold Coast

## Boating

Florida's waterways attract boats of every description, from state-of-the-art yachts to wooden skiffs. With over 8,000 miles (12,870 km) of tidal coastline and 4,500 sq miles (11,655 sq km) of inland waters, the state is a paradise for boaters. Having a boat is as normal as having a car for some Floridians; the state has over 700,000 registered boats, and this does not include the 300,000 brought in annually from outside Florida.

The Intracoastal Waterway, extending 500 miles (800 km) down the east coast to the tip of the Keys *(see pp26–7)*, is very popular. Often sheltered from the Atlantic Ocean by barrier islands, the route runs through rivers, creeks, and dredged canals. Although most of the west coast is open, the most interesting territory for boaters is where the Intracoastal Waterway resumes among the islands of the Lee Island Coast *(see pp282–3)*.

The 135-mile (217-km) Okeechobee Waterway, which cuts through the state, is another popular route, becoming extremely busy during the summer. It runs along the St. Lucie Canal from Stuart, across Lake Okeechobee and then on to Sanibel Island via the Caloosahatchee River.

These inland waterways, like many of the state's 166 rivers, are suitable for small boats or houseboats. Many of the latter are more like floating apartments, often being equipped with air-conditioning, microwave ovens, and even televisions.

Houseboats can be rented from several marinas, in Sanford on the St. Johns River, for example *(see p224)*, while small to medium-size boats are available at many fish camps or marinas.

Florida has an astonishing 1,250 marinas. Those along the coast usually have excellent facilities, with accommodation and rental outlets for boats and fishing tackle; inland marinas tend to be more basic. *Florida Boating and Diving*, a brochure available from the **Florida Sports Foundation**, lists most marinas in the state, with details of their facilities.

**Florida State Park emblem**

## Backcountry Pursuits

Florida's protected areas vary from popular beaches to much wilder areas like the Everglades. The provision of facilities varies too, but most parks have some sort of visitors' center, dispensing maps and other information.

Some also organize guided tours. Winter is the best time to explore, when the summer rains and mosquitoes are no longer around.

Over 110 areas are protected by the state, classified variously as State Parks and State Preserves. They all charge admission and usually open from 8am to sunset daily. The Department of Environmental Protection (DEP) has a free guide, *Florida State Parks*, which lists all these areas plus their facilities, or visit www.floridastateparks.org

Information on the fewer federally-run national parks is available from the **National Park Service** in Georgia. Many other parks are private, including sanctuaries run by the **Florida Audubon Society**; these are particularly good for bird life. The *Florida Trails* guide, issued by the national tourist board *(see p371)*, has a complete list of private, state, and national parks. As a result of the Florida Rails-to-Trails Program, old train tracks have been turned into trails, suitable for hiking, biking, in-line skating, and riding. Best are the 16 mile (26 km) Tallahassee–St. Marks Historic Railroad State Trail, south of Tallahassee, and the Gainesville–Hawthorne State Trail *(see p227)* in the Northeast. The DEP's Office of Greenways and Trails has information on these and many other trails.

Outdoor adventure tours are organized by a few companies. One is **Build a Field Trip**, which arranges trips all over the state.

Visitors on a boardwalk in the Everglades National Park

# Biking

There is plenty of opportunity for both on-road and off-road biking in Florida, where the flatness of the landscape makes for easy cycling territory – though avid bikers may find it rather dull. The rolling countryside of the Panhandle is by far the most rewarding area to explore, while the Northeast also has some good trails, for example in Paynes Prairie *(see p227)*.

If visitors need one, a bicycle can usually be rented on site or from a local source. For general biking information, visit the **Florida Trails and Greenways** website.

Canoeing in the Blackwater River State Park

# Walking

Florida might not seem ideal walking country, but the variety of habitats makes up for the flat landscape. Most state parks have hiking trails, and there is a project currently underway to create the National Scenic Trail – starting at the Big Cypress National Preserve *(see p288)* in south Florida, and ending near Pensacola. So far, 1,000 miles (1609 km) of the planned 1,292 mile (2,079 km) route have been completed.

The **Florida Trail Association** is the best place to obtain information about hiking trails.

## Canoeing

There is ample opportunity for canoeing in Florida; the Florida Canoe Trail System is comprised of 36 routes along creeks and rivers totaling 950 miles (1,520 km). A number of parks are known for their canoe runs, the most famous being the exhilarating, 99 mile (160 km) Wilderness Waterway in the Everglades National Park *(see pp290–95)*. Some of the best rivers, such as the Blackwater River *(see p238)*, can be found in the North, while the Hillsborough River on the Gulf Coast is also popular *(see p267)*.

Enjoying the countryside near Ocala on horseback

Always check the water level before setting off, because both high and low levels can be dangerous.

## Horseback Riding

The Ocala National Forest in the Northeast *(see p225)* has over 100 miles (160 km) of trails suited to horseback riding. There are 15 state parks with riding trails, including Myakka River *(see p278)*, Jonathan Dickinson *(see p121)*, and the Florida Caverns *(see p243)*, and about half the parks have facilities for overnight stays.

Information is available from the *Florida Horse Trail Directory*, issued by the **Department of Agriculture and Consumer Services**, or from the DEP.

---

# DIRECTORY

## Sources of Information

**Department of Environmental Protection (DEP)**
3900 Commonwealth Blvd, Tallahassee, FL 32399. **Tel** (850) 245-2052.

**Florida Sports Foundation**
Tallahassee, FL 32308.
**Tel** (850) 488-8347.
W flasports.com

## Tennis

**Nick Bollettieri Tennis Academy**
5500 34th St West, Bradenton, FL 34210.
**Tel** (800) 872-6425.
W imgacademies.com

**United States Tennis Association (Florida Section)**
Deuce Court, Daytona Beach, FL 32124.
**Tel** (386) 671-8949.
W florida.usta.com

## Diving and Snorkeling

**Keys Association of Dive Operators (KADO)**
3128 N Roosevelt Blvd, Key West, FL 33040.
W divekeys.com

## Fishing

**Florida Fish and Wildlife Conservation Commission**
**Tel** (850) 488-4676.

**Tel** (888) 347-4356.
(fishing licenses).
**Tel** (888) 486-8356
(hunting licenses).
W myfwc.com

## Backcountry Pursuits

**Build a Field Trip**
3440 NE 12th Ave, Oakland Park, 33334.
**Tel** (954) 772-7800.

**Florida Audubon Society**
**Tel** (407) 539-5700.
**Tel** (305) 371-6399.
W fl.audubon.org

**National Park Service (Southeast)**
100 Alabama St SW, Atlanta, GA 30303.
**Tel** (404) 507-5600.

## Biking

**Florida Trails and Greenways**
W visitflorida.com/trails

## Walking

**Florida Trail Association**
PO Box 13708, Gainesville, FL 32604.
**Tel** (352) 378-8823 or (800) 343-1882.

## Horseback Riding

**Department of Agriculture and Consumer Services**
**Tel** (407) 888-8700.
W doacs.state.fl.us

# WEDDINGS IN FLORIDA

Apart from its fame as an immensely popular vacation spot, Florida is widely recognized as one of the most sought-after wedding and honeymoon destinations. The state's picture-perfect weather is ideal for wedding ceremonies that range from inexpensive backyard affairs to theme park extravaganzas that cost thousands of dollars. Themed weddings are extremely popular and organizers can create anything the bride and groom desires, even tying the knot near Cinderella's Castle. Florida is also famous for its unusual weddings. Couples can exchange vows while golfing, fishing, on the beach, or in a hot-air balloon. Many local planners offer ceremonies to fulfill every fantasy, and honeymoon packages to suit all budgets.

Romantic ceremony at the beach

## Wedding Packages

Most resorts and hotels in Florida offer a wide range of wedding and vacation combination packages to those getting married in the state.

The **Grand Bohemian Hotel** in Orlando offers a Bohemian-themed wedding, with the ceremony conducted at its rooftop garden. Prices, including a one-night stay in the Art Deco-inspired hotel, range from $1,600 to more than $3,000. **The Inn on Fifth** in Naples is housed in a renovated 1930s bank, and retains most of the original architecture and decor, including crystal chandeliers, stairs lined with burgundy carpeting, and wrought-iron railings. The hotel's rooftop pool area, complete with waterfalls, also makes a scenic setting for a wedding. The legendary **Biltmore Hotel** in Coral Gables offers a variety of stunning locations in which to exchange vows, from a lovely rose-strewn pool gazebo to the spacious ballroom, with packages starting at $3000.

Key West sunsets are absolutely gorgeous, and getting married in front of one can make the ceremony even more romantic. The **Westin Key West Resort & Marina** and its sister resort, **Westin Sunset Key Guest Cottages**, allow couples to do just that. Tie the knot on the Hilton Pier with the setting sun in the background, or on the beach at Sunset Key, which is a separate island, a three-minute boat ride away from the Hilton. For the ultimate tropical wedding, **Little Palm Island Resort & Spa**, just off Little Torch Key, offers an unmatched island ambience. Packages start at $1500, barring accommodation, but come with a guarantee that there will be no other weddings held on the island that day.

## Theme Parks

Call it romantic, child-like, or corny, a **Walt Disney World® Resort** wedding is always special. More than 2,000 couples take the plunge every year, and the wedding packages start at around $3,000, while custom arrangements begin at about $7,500 and can skyrocket for large gatherings. Couples could opt for a fairytale wedding at Magic Kingdom® where the bride arrives in Cinderella's glass coach, a safari-themed affair in Animal Kingdom®, star in their own movie at Disney's Hollywood Studios®, or marvel at dazzling shows in a choice of country pavilions at Epcot®. There are plenty of other options too – check their official website for details.

If couples are keen on giraffes and gazelles, **Busch Gardens** will host a ceremony in one of its exotic habitats while providing unique tailor-made live entertainment.

Bride and groom at their beach wedding

## Outdoor Extravaganzas

Located close to downtown Orlando, **Harry P. Leu Gardens** (*see p190*) is a lush 50 acres (20 ha) of horticultural splendor. It offers several garden settings for weddings amid masses of roses and camellias. The Rose Garden, the Floral Clock, and the Butterfly Garden here are very popular wedding venues.

**Historic Bok Sanctuary** (*see p195*) in Lake Wales is one of the highest points in Florida, and is a National Historic Landmark. Exchange marriage vows in a romantic setting of palm trees, flowering plants, and a 57-bell carillon.

## The Unusual

Couples who wish to have a truly unique wedding have a range of options. **Orlando Balloon Rides** offers hot-air balloon weddings, including transport to the flight site, a ground-based ceremony, an hour long balloon flight for two, and a champagne toast. The **Medieval Times Dinner & Tournament** allows couples to wed against a backdrop of 11th-century England, while

Orange Blossom Balloons, which offers hot-air balloon weddings

biker couples can tie the knot at **Orlando Harley-Davidson®**. The bride and groom ride on Harleys, followed by a cavalcade of bikes. At **Daytona International Speedway** the ceremony is performed in the winner's circle and includes a victory lap. High-fliers will love the **Fantasy of Flight**, where the wedding ceremony is held in an aircraft-laden hangar. **Brevard Zoo** offers its Serengeti Pavilion, Flamingo Pond, and Australian Aviary for weddings and receptions.

## Wedding Details

There are entire books filled with lists of wedding planners, caterers, and photographers. The free publications, **Perfect Wedding Guide** and **The Knot**, are great starting points. Order invitations from print stores and office supply shops. Flowers can be bought from budget dealers or boutique florists. Haute couture shops and stores in upscale shopping malls supply wedding gowns. Wedding planners can take care of all these details.

## Legalities

Marriage licenses are available at any courthouse in the state. The **State of Florida Official Marriage Guide** lists all their addresses. The bride and groom need to present proper identification such as a driver's license or a passport. The license will be issued at the time of application and is effective immediately; it must be used within 60 days. No blood test or waiting period is needed for out-of-state residents. If previously married, the date of divorce or date of the spouse's death is required.

# SURVIVAL
# GUIDE

# PRACTICAL INFORMATION

With more than 112 million visitors a year, Florida is very well geared to catering to tourists' needs. It is the ultimate family vacation destination. A strong emphasis is placed on entertaining children, and the informal lifestyle and excellent facilities make traveling with youngsters a real pleasure. The only complaint a child is likely to have is if the lines at Walt Disney World®, or the other theme parks, are too long (which is likely in peak season), or if the sun too hot. Given its warm climate, for most visitors Florida is a winter destination. The peak season runs from December to April, when rates for flights and hotels are at their height, and the beaches and attractions are at their busiest.

Tourist information center, Florida

Children, card-carrying students, and senior citizens can often claim a discount, and anyone can use the coupons found in brochures available at tourist offices. These can significantly cut the price of admission fees and also buy budget meals in local restaurants. Coupons from the information center on International Drive in Orlando (see p192) can save you hundreds of dollars.

## Visas and Passports

British citizens, members of EU countries, citizens of Australia and New Zealand do not need a visa provided they have a return ticket and their stay in the US does not exceed 90 days. However, they must register online with the Electronic System for Travel Authorization (ESTA) at least 72 hours before (and preferably well in advance of) departure (www.cbp.gov). Note that a fee is charged.

Canadians need only a valid passport, while other citizens must apply for a nonimmigrant visa from a US consulate.

Before travel, it is advisable to check the latest information at www.uscis.gov.

## Travel Safety Advice

Visitors can get up-to-date travel safety information from the **UK Foreign and Commonwealth Office** (www.gov.uk/foreign-travel-advice), the **US Department of State** (www.travel.state.gov) and the **Australian Department of Foreign Affairs and Trade** (www.dfat.gov.au or www.smartraveller.gov.au).

## Customs Allowances

Customs allowances for visitors over 21 years of age are: 0.95 liter (1 quart) of alcohol, gifts worth up to $100, and 200 cigarettes, 50 cigars (not Cuban ones), or 4.4 pounds (2 kg) of tobacco. Prohibited goods include cheese, fresh fruit, meat products, and illegal drugs.

## Tourist Information

Most large cities in Florida have a Convention and Visitors' Bureau (CVB), where you will find a huge array of brochures. The majority of hotels have free "WHERE" magazines that list entertainment, museums, shopping, and restaurants. Also, there is usually a brochure rack in the hotel lobby.

For information before leaving home, contact **Visit Florida** for a vacation pack.

## Admission Charges

Museums, parks, and other attractions generally charge an admission fee. This can vary enormously, from $2 at a small museum to more than $100 for a day pass into Walt Disney World®'s Magic Kingdom®.

## Opening Times

State parks are usually open every day from sunrise to sunset, though attached visitor centers may close earlier. The theme parks extend their opening hours during summer months and holiday periods. Most sights close on major national holidays: typically New Year, Thanksgiving, and Christmas (see p41).

## Etiquette

Dress in Florida is casual, except in a few top restaurants (see p326). On the beach itself it is illegal for women to go topless, except in a few places, such as Haulover Beach near Miami, and Playalinda Beach near Cape Canaveral. Drinking alcohol on beaches and in other public places is also illegal.

It is against the law to smoke in buses, trains, taxis, restaurants, and in most public buildings.

In restaurants unless a tip is already added to the bill (usually for parties of six or more people), you should tip 15–20 per cent of the check. Taxi drivers expect a similar tip. For hotel porters, $1 per bag is usual.

◄ An aerial view of boats and yachts docked at a marina in Port Orange, Daytona Beach

## Travelers with Specific Needs

US federal law demands that all public buildings be accessible to people in wheelchairs, although some old buildings are exempt. This guide specifies whether or not a sight is accessible, but you are advised to call ahead for details.

A few rental companies have cars adapted for people with disabilities, and some buses have "kneeling" wheelchair access – watch for a sticker on the windshield or by the door. Amtrak and Greyhound offer reduced fares.

**Mobility International** offers general advice for travelers with disabilities. Visit Florida, the state-run tourism board, issues a useful services directory, and Walt Disney World® has its own special guide, both online and in print form.

## Traveling with Children

As a top family destination, Florida places the needs of children high on its list of priorities (see p360). Strollers or small wagons can be rented at the major theme parks; car rental firms must supply children's seats; and many restaurants offer special menus (see p327). On planes, buses, and trains, children younger than 12 usually pay only half the standard fare, less if they are very young. For information on hotel facilities, see page 313. The main concern is the sun. Just a few minutes' exposure to the midday sun can burn young skin. Use sunblock and hats, and carry or buy water.

Boy enjoying a ride in a dolphin stroller, SeaWorld®

## Senior Travelers

Florida is a Mecca for senior citizens, both to visit and to settle. Anyone over 65 (less in some instances) is eligible for all kinds of discounts – at attractions, hotels, restaurants, and on public transit. The **National Parks Service** offers lifetime entrance to its sites for a one-time, $10 fee.

The **American Association of Retired Persons** can help members plan their vacation, and offers discounts on air fares, car rental, and rooms.

## Traveling on a Budget

Traveling off peak is a good way to reduce costs. Check online reservations and hotel websites for special deals. Hotels near theme parks are usually cheaper than those in the parks. Many restaurants offer cheap deals and happy hour specials before 6pm.

## Electricity

A voltage converter and an adapter is needed to use the American 110–120 volts AC system; adapters for the two-prong plugs used in the US can be bought abroad or locally. Many hotels, however, have plugs that power both 110- and 220-volt electric shavers, and often supply wall-mounted hair dryers.

## Responsible Tourism

As one of the country's great natural wonderlands, Florida offers prime ecotourism opportunities. The multitude of natural parks, from the Panhandle to the sprawling Everglades to the Florida Keys, is second to none. Guide-led river cruises through ancient Florida woodlands are available at Wakulla Springs State Park in the northwest, and you can rent a houseboat to tour along the unspoiled Suwannee River that flows across the state to the Gulf of Mexico. Local tour companies offer guided excursions through pristine nature preserves, some with overnight stays available,

Florida Green Lodging Program

and several former cattle ranches have been converted into resorts for horse trails and nature preserve touring. As an alternative to camping, the **Florida Green Lodging Program** provides a list of nearly 700 designated properties that conserve energy, reduce water usage, and protect air quality.

# Personal Security and Health

As in any city, there are parts of Miami, Orlando, Jacksonville, and other Florida towns that are not tourist-friendly. Visitors should be alert in urban areas, but anyone who takes precautions should enjoy a trouble-free trip. Police officers are friendly and helpful to tourists, and staff at hotel front desks can offer recommendations.

## Law Enforcement

Enforcement of the law is shared by three agencies: the city police forces, county sheriffs, and the Florida Highway Patrol, which deals with traffic accidents and offenses outside the cities. Major tourist centers are well policed, and Miami and Orlando also have Tourist Oriented Police (TOP) units.

Given Florida's eagerness to attract and to protect tourists, police officers are friendly and helpful to visitors.

## What to be Aware Of

Most cities in Florida, like elsewhere in the world, have "no-go" areas that should be avoided. The staff at the local tourist office or in your hotel should be able to advise. Some downtown areas are first and primarily business districts, which are quiet at night and can be unsafe. However, the past few years have seen an upsurge in locals living and dining downtown, and Fort Lauderdale, Jacksonville, and Orlando downtowns have blossomed. If in doubt, take a taxi or ride share rather than walking.

Burglaries within hotels are not unheard of. Leave your best jewelry at home and lock valuables in the safe in your room, or hand them in at the reception desk – few hotels will guarantee the security of items kept in your room.

If someone knocks on your door claiming to be hotel staff, you may want to check with reception before letting the person in.

Carry as little money as possible, keep your passport separate from your cash or credit cards, and leave your duplicate room key with the desk clerk. If you are unlucky enough to be attacked, hand over your wallet immediately. Do not try to resist.

## Staying Safe in Miami

Although visitors are rarely victims, Miami has one of the highest crime rates in the US. Certain districts are to be avoided at all costs. These include Liberty City and Opa-Locka, both located between the airport and Downtown. Farther north, Little Haiti is an interesting area, but should be treated with caution (*see p95*). Avoid all deserted areas at night, including the transit terminals and Downtown. Lively night spots such as Coconut Grove and South Beach are the safest areas after dark, but avoid quiet back streets (such as south of 5th Street in South Beach).

Miami's Tourist Oriented Police provide extra cover at the airport, especially around car rental outlets.

In an emergency dial 911, or contact **Miami-Dade Police Information** if you do not need immediate help.

Police officers on patrol, Florida-style, in St. Augustine

## In an Emergency

In an emergency, the police, ambulance, and fire services can be reached by dialing 911. Motorist Aid Call Boxes roughly every half a mile (1 km). If you are robbed in the street, go directly to the closest police station – dial 911 should you need help to locate it.

If you need emergency cash, check if your credit card offers emergency cash access; ask someone to transfer funds from your bank at home to your hotel or a specified bank in Florida. You can also use **PayPal** or **Moneygram** services, which allow cash transfers.

## Lost Property

Even though you have only a slim chance of retrieving stolen property, you should report all lost or stolen items to the police. Keep a copy of the police report if you are planning to make an insurance claim.

Most credit card companies have toll-free numbers for reporting a loss, as do **Thomas Cook** and **American Express** for lost cash cards. If you lose your passport, contact your embassy or consulate immediately (*see p371*).

## Hospitals and Pharmacies

Larger cities in the state, and some smaller towns, have 24-hour walk-in medical and dental clinics, where minor

Florida Sheriffs Officers at a training course on Harley Davidson Motorcycles

Emergency ambulance

Fire engine

Orange County sheriff patrol car

casualties and ailments can be treated. For less serious complaints, many drugstores such as Walgreens and CVS (some of which stay open late or for 24 hours), have registered clinics.

If you have a serious accident or illness, you can rely on high-quality treatment at a hospital. Stories of medics making accident victims wait while they haggle over money are largely questionable; even so, take great care of your insurance documents. Nothing comes for free: a straightforward visit to the doctor can cost more than $50. Hospitals accept the majority of credit cards, as do most doctors and dentists. Those without insurance may need to pay in advance.

Anyone on prescribed medication should take a supply with them and ask their doctor to provide a copy of the prescription in case of loss, or the need for more.

## Natural Hazards

Hurricanes are infrequent but devastating *(see pp30–31)*. If the worst should happen, follow the announcements on local television and radio. You can call the **National Hurricane Center** in Miami, which provides information on impending hurricanes.

The climatic hazard to affect most visitors is the sun. Use sun screen or sun block, and try to wear a hat; make sure that your children are well protected, too. Drink plenty of fluids to prevent dehydration.

As for the animal world, alligators are a thrilling sight, but they can and do kill – so treat them with respect, and bear in mind that any large body of water probably contains one or two. There are also several venomous snakes native to Florida, including the water moccasin, whose bite can be fatal. Do not touch unfamiliar vegetation, and steer clear of Spanish moss; it houses the red mite, which causes skin irritation. Wear insect repellent to fend off biting and stinging insects, particularly in areas close to fresh water, and from June to November.

Beaches are usually well supervised by lifeguards, but watch young children closely. Riptides are a danger in some places.

## Travel Insurance

Travel insurance coverage of a minimum of $1 million is highly recommended, mainly because of the high cost of medical care.

Lifeguard at Pier Park on Panama City Beach

Prices depend on the length of your trip, but make sure the policy covers accidental death, emergency medical care, trip cancelation, and baggage or document loss. Your insurance company or travel agent should be able to recommend a suitable policy, but it is worth shopping around for the best deal.

## DIRECTORY

### In an Emergency

**All Emergencies**
**Tel** 911 to alert police, fire, or medical services.

**Miami-Dade Police Information**
**Tel** (305) 595-6263.

**Moneygram**
**Tel** (800) 926-9400.

**PayPal**
W paypal.com

### Lost Property

**American Express**
**Tel** (800) 528-4800 (cards).

**Diners Club**
**Tel** (800) 234-6377.

**MasterCard**
**Tel** (800) 826-2181.

**Thomas Cook**
**Tel** (888) 713-3424 (cash passports).

**VISA**
**Tel** (800) 336-8472.

### Hospitals and Pharmacies

**Baptist Hospital of Miami**
8900 North Kendall Drive Miami, FL 33176.
**Tel** (786) 596-1960.
W baptisthealth.net

**Dental Care**
W dentists.com/florida_dentists.php

**Florida Hospital**
601 E Rollins St, Orlando, FL 32803.
**Tel** (407) 303-2800.
W floridahospital.com

### Natural Hazards

**National Hurricane Center**
**Tel** (305) 229-4470 recorded message with hurricane details.

# Banking and Currency

Foreign currency exchange is available at the main branches of any large city bank. In addition, most of the major airports have exchange desks. For the convenience of residents and visitors alike, automated cash machines (ATMs) throughout the state allow transactions 24 hours a day. Keep credit cards ready because they can be used to pay for most things.

## Banking

Banks are generally open from 9am to 3 or 4pm on weekdays, but some keep slightly longer hours. Banks include Regions Bank, **Bank of America**, Chase, **Fifth Third Bank**, SunTrust, and Wells Fargo, all of which have a number of branches throughout the state. The majority of banks have drive-through banking with live tellers and ATM machines.

Automatic teller machine (ATM)

## ATMs

Most banks and supermarkets in Florida have ATMs (Automatic Teller Machines) in their lobbies or in an external wall. These machines enable you to withdraw US bills, usually in $20s, from your bank or credit card account at home, and tend to offer a better exchange rate than a bank or currency exchange.

Before leaving home, ask your credit card company or bank which American ATM systems or banks will accept your bank card, and check the cost of each transaction; often there is a conversion charge. Inform your bank that you will be traveling to avoid the inconvenience of delays

or declined charges. Make sure that you know your PIN number.

## Credit and Debit Cards

Credit cards are a part of everyday life in Florida. The most widely accepted credit cards are **VISA**, **American Express**, **MasterCard**, and Discover. Debit cards, which draw funds directly from your bank account, are the easiest way to get cash, with better exchange rates than banks or currency exchanges. Thomas Cook offers a prepaid currency card, thus protecting your bank information. It can be purchased online or in person before you leave.

Credit cards can be used to pay for everything from admission fees to hotel bills to emergency medical care. To make a payment, your card will be swiped and then a signature will be required.

It is standard practice for car rental companies (which generally do not accept debit cards), to take an imprint of your card as security; often the only alternative is to pay a hefty deposit in cash. Some hotels adopt the same practice: a "phantom" sum of $200–300 may be debited for one night in a hotel. This should be automatically restored to your credit when you check out, but it

is a good idea to remind the clerk when you leave. Travelers' checks, while accepted at larger locations, have become an unrecognized curiosity at most stores or restaurants.

## Currency Exchange

Currency exchanges can be found in a surprising number of places in Florida. In Orlando, **Currency Exchange International** has locations at the Mall at Millenia and Florida Mall. Branches can also be found at the Dolphin, Dadeland, and Aventura Malls in Miami, and two at the Sawgrass Mills Mall in Fort Lauderdale. **Interchange** has four locations at Orlando International Airport.

Disney offers currency exchange at Epcot® and Magic Kingdom® Guest Services, and major hotels on Disney property will exchange currency in limited amounts. This is also true for the main hotels at other theme parks.

Most banks, though not all, exchange money, but you usually have to make arrangements in advance. Changing money at a bank is usually a cheap option, but you might feel it is worth paying more for the convenience of changing money at your hotel or at a currency exchange.

## Currency

American dollar bills are all the same size and color, so check the number before paying. The $1 coin is still legal but is rarely seen in circulation.

Always carry cash for giving tips, and to pay public transportation and taxi fares.

Branch of the Fifth Third Bank

## Coins

*American coins (actual size shown) come in 1-dollar, 50-, 25-, 10-, 5-, and 1-cent pieces. Also in circulation are State quarters, which feature a historical scene on one side. Each coin has a popular name: 1-cent pieces are called pennies, 5-cent pieces are nickels, 10-cent pieces are dimes, and 25-cent pieces are quarters.*

25-cent coin
(a quarter)

10-cent coin
(a dime)

5-cent coin
(a nickel)

1-cent coin
(a penny)

## Bank Notes (Bills)

*Units of currency in the United States are dollars and cents. There are 100 cents to a dollar. Notes come in $1, $5, $10, $20, $50, and $100 denominations, and have slight variations in color. The $10, $20, and $50 bills with extra security features are now in circulation. Paper bills were first issued in 1862, when coins were in short supply and the Civil War needed financing.*

1-dollar bill ($1)

5-dollar bill ($5)

10-dollar bill ($10)

20-dollar bill ($20)

50-dollar bill ($50)

100-dollar bill ($100)

### DIRECTORY

#### Banking

**Bank of America**
Tel (800) 732-9194.
w bankofamerica.com

**Fifth Third Bank**
Tel (800) 972-3030. w 53.com

#### Credit and Debit cards

**American Express**
Tel (800) 528-4800.
w americanexpress.com

**Mastercard/Cirrus**
Tel (800) 627-8372.
w mastercard.us

**Thomas Cook Cash Passport**
w cashpassport.com

**VISA**
Tel (800) 847-2911 (information).

#### Currency Exchange

**Currency Exchange International**
Tel (305) 937-4999. w ceifx.com

**Interchange**
Orlando International Airport.
Tel (407) 825-4563.

# Communications and Media

Communicating with people both within and outside Florida, whether by mail or by telephone, rarely causes problems – though no one claims that the United States' postal system is the world's fastest (at least as far as domestic mail is concerned). Cell phones and Wi-Fi-connected computers have almost completely replaced public payphones, which can be found at airports, but at few other places. A prudent way to save money is to avoid making telephone calls from your hotel room, for which often exorbitant surcharges are usually imposed.

## International and Local Telephone Calls

Toll free numbers (which are prefixed by 800, 866, 888, or 877) are common in the US. Note, however, that they are not toll free if calling from outside the US, and be aware that some hotels may impose an access charge for these calls.

Travelers should check with their phone service pro-vider before leaving home to determine their rates for calls made in the US. Phone services at hotels invariably include an additional and exorbitant service charge.

Most telephone calls are possible without the aid of an operator (whose inter-vention raises the price of a normal call). Collect calls can be made only by the operator and are therefore very expensive.

Cell phones have largely replaced public payphones

## Cell Phones

Inexpensive no-contract cell phones, using prepaid minutes, can be found at supermarkets, convenience stores (such as **7-Eleven**), and big-box electronic and discount department stores, including Target, **Walmart**, and Best Buy. The differences in American and European phone systems mean that removable SIM cards are not generally used in the US, and European phones may not work during your visit to Florida. It is worth checking this with your provider before you set off.

## Public Telephones

Public telephones are extremely rare and have almost completely disappeared from the streets. However, they can sometimes be found at airports.

Most public telephones take coins – you will need at least $8 worth of quarters to make an international call. There are also phonecard-operated telephones that take special prepaid debit cards, which involve dialing a toll-free number to gain access to your required number. Alternatively, you can use your credit card from both the coin- and phonecard-operated phones. To do this you must simply dial (800) CALLATT, key in your credit card number, and wait to be connected – you will be charged at normal rates.

Telephone directories are supplied at most public phones and provide details of rates.

## Internet and Wi-Fi

Many hotels in Florida offer guests wireless Internet access (Wi-Fi) in their rooms. Some hotels, usually the more expensive ones, charge by the day for in-room Internet access, but have free access in public areas. Value-priced hotels, paradoxically, often include full wired or wireless access in the room rate. Coffee shops, restaurants, libraries, and some city parks offer free Wi-Fi hotspots (search the Internet for locations or look for a sign in the window). Combining free Internet access with a voice-over-IP service such as Skype is a great way to save money and to stay in touch with people back home.

---

### Useful Dialing Codes

- Direct-dial calls to another area code: dial **1** followed by the area code and the 7-digit number. Calls within Florida require dialling the full ten-digit number, even if you're calling across the street.
- International direct-dial calls: dial **011**, then the code of the country (Australia 61, New Zealand 64, UK 44), followed by the local area/city code (minus the first 0) and the number.
- International operator assistance: dial **01**.
- International directory inquiries: dial **00**.
- Local operator assistance: dial **0**.
- Local directory inquiries: dial **411**.
- Long-distance information: dial **1**, then the appropriate area code, followed by **555-1212**.
- An **800, 866, 888,** or **877** ("toll-free") prefix means the call will be free; **900** numbers are not.
- For the police, fire, or ambulance service, dial **911**.

## Postal Services

Post office opening hours vary but are usually 9am to 5pm on weekdays, with some offices opening on Saturday mornings, too. There are 24-hour Automated Postal Centers inside post office lobbies, which dispense stamps and postage for larger packages. Drugstores, supermarkets, and hotels often sell stamps, but stamps not bought from a post office may cost more.

Surface mail sent overseas from the US takes weeks, so it is better to send letters by air mail, which is much quicker.

All domestic mail goes first class and takes one to five days – longer if you forget to include the zip code. You can pay extra for Priority Mail, for a delivery in two to three days, or Express Mail, which offers next-day delivery in the US, and within two to three days to many countries. Be sure to use the right mailbox. Mailboxes are painted blue, and Express and Priority mailboxes are silver and blue, and are clearly marked.

Many Americans use private courier services, such as **UPS** and **Federal Express**, for both domestic and international mail, or **DHL** for overseas packages; they can offer next-day delivery to most places.

Many shops can mail purchases home for you; mailing a parcel yourself involves the use of approved materials available from post offices.

A rank of newspaper-dispensing machines in Palm Beach

Standard mailbox

## Newspapers and Magazines

Most large cities have their own daily newspaper. Among the most widely read are the *Miami Herald, Tampa Bay Times,* and the *Orlando Sentinel.* The *Miami Herald* also has a widely read Spanish-language edition, *El Nuevo Herald.* Free weekly newspapers are the best source for local events and entertainment listings; glossy city monthlies (*Orlando Magazine, Miami Monthly, Jacksonville Magazine*) offer a look into the upscale local lifestyle and are great for restaurant recommendations.

You can usually pick up a national paper such as *USA Today* from street dispensers, but most of these are given over to local papers. For other national US dailies, such as the *New York Times,* and foreign newspapers, you will usually have to rely on bookstores, convenience stores, and good newsstands.

## Television and Radio

Television in Florida, much like anywhere else in the US, tends to be dominated by daytime talk shows and primetime cop shows. The cable channels offer more variety: ESPN is devoted to sports, and CNN to news, for example. Hotel rooms usually have cable TV, but you may have to pay to see a movie *(see p311).*

Most radio stations pump out pop and easy listening music, but if you hunt around (especially on the FM band), you can often pick up entertaining local stations, including Spanish-language ones in south Florida.

More serious broadcasting is left to the likes of PBS-TV (Public Broadcasting System) and NPR (National Public Radio), which offer jazz and classical music, along with documentaries, talk shows, and dramas – including re-broadcasts of BBC series.

## DIRECTORY

### Cell Phones

**7-Eleven**
812 8th St, Miami.
**Tel** (305) 854-7011.
124 W Pine St Suite 116, Orlando.
**Tel** (407) 648-8208.
**W** 7-eleven.com

**Target**
8350 S Dixie Hwy, Miami.
**Tel** (305) 668-0262.
**W** target.com

**Walmart**
8400 Coral Way, Miami.
**Tel** (305) 351-0725.
3101 W Princeton St, Orlando.
**Tel** (321) 354-2096.
**W** walmart.com

### Postal Services

**DHL**
**W** dhl.com

**Federal Express**
**W** fedex.com

**United States Postal Service**
**W** usps.com

**UPS**
**W** ups.com

# TRAVEL INFORMATION

Florida is the top holiday destination in the US, and is well served by flights from all over the world. The state's chief gateways are Miami, Orlando, and Tampa, and the growing number of charter flights is raising the profile of other airports. Flying is also worth considering if you plan to travel any distance within Florida. The hop between Miami and Key West, for example, takes 40 minutes, compared with four hours by car. However, when it comes to traveling around the state, the car reigns supreme, with fast interstates, major highways, and quieter county roads to choose from. Trains and buses are an alternative if you plan your routes carefully.

Miami International Airport, bustling with travelers

## Arriving by Air

All the major US carriers, including **Southwest**, **JetBlue**, **American Airlines**, **United Airlines**, and **Delta Air Lines** have hundreds of scheduled domestic services to Orlando and Miami. Many also offer direct flights from abroad, but this usually entails a stop at a US airport en route.

From the UK, **British Airways** and **Virgin Atlantic** have scheduled direct flights to Miami and Orlando; British Airways also has a service between London and Tampa. American Airlines runs daily flights to Miami from London's Gatwick and Heathrow airports. Delta Air Lines flies to Florida from Ireland via Atlanta, Georgia, or New York.

European carriers such as Air France, KLM, and Iberia also offer a range of flights, and Icelandair flies into Orlando from Manchester and Glasgow in the summer months. Qantas and several US airlines offer one- or two-stop flights from Australia and New Zealand.

Charter flights are less popular these days, but still offer direct and relatively inexpensive access to Florida. Most charter flights emanate from Canada, the Caribbean, and Latin America, but there are some from Europe, serving Fort Lauderdale and Orlando via Sanford, from Gatwick, Manchester, and Prestwick in the UK.

Any arrival into a US airport can be long and confusing due to increased security measures. Plan time into your vacation for this.

## Air Fares

The cheapest round-trip fares to Florida are generally economy on a scheduled flight (which must be reserved in advance). The competition between travel agencies and between the numerous airlines serving Florida means that it is worth shopping around. Check on-line reservation services for promotional fares. Some specialty operators offer good deals on charter flights.

Fares can be surprisingly cheap in the off season, and you'll often get a better deal if you are able to fly midweek.

| Airport | Information | Distance from City | Taxi Fare to City (Approx) | Shuttle Bus Fare to City (Approx) |
|---|---|---|---|---|
| Miami | (305) 876-7000 miami-airport.com | Miami Beach 10 miles (16 km) | $32 to Miami Beach | $14–20 to Miami Beach |
| Orlando | (407) 825-2001 orlandoairports.net | Walt Disney World® 18 miles (28 km) | $55–60 to Walt Disney World® | $20 per person to Walt Disney World®, or $ 4 by Lynx bus |
| Sanford | (407) 585-4000 orlandosanfordairport.com | Walt Disney World® 40 miles (64 km) | $90–110 to Walt Disney World® | $20–50 to Walt Disney World® |
| Tampa | (813) 870-8700 tampaairport.com | Downtown 9 miles (14 km) | $15–25 to Downtown | $12–32 to Downtown |
| Fort Lauderdale | (954) 359-1200 broward.org/airport | Fort Lauderdale 8 miles (13 km), Miami 30 miles (48 km) | $20 to Fort Lauderdale, $100 to Miami | $10 to Fort Lauderdale, $15 to Miami |

During vacation periods, seats are in big demand and air fares can rocket to more than double their usual rates, being highest during December.

Note that US airlines sometimes offer discounted seats on domestic flights if you buy an inbound ticket from them.

## Domestic Flights

Small and medium-size airlines fly within the state and are a quick way to get additional time in the Florida sun. Several airlines fly between Orlando and the Panhandle; Spirit flies from Fort Lauderdale to Tampa; Atlantic Airlines links Central Florida with both coasts, Key West to the south, and Pensacola to the north. Larger airlines fly from Orlando or Miami to every major city in the US, but it may take one or two connections to complete the journey.

## Florida Airports

Florida's top international airports are well equipped with information desks, banks, car rental desks, and other facilities. If you're collecting a rental car, you may be taken by bus to a pick-up point nearby. If you are heading into town, check out the shuttle buses (or "limos"), which offer a door-to-door service to and from the airport – they operate like shared taxis but are cheaper than regular cabs. Major hotels usually offer a courtesy bus service to their guests. Ask about this when you make your reservation.

## Miami Airport

Miami International Airport is one of the busiest in the world, which can mean long lines at immigration. The walk between concourses and gates is often long, too.

Tourist information desks are found outside all customs exits, and car rental counters, taxis, private limos, and shuttle buses are on the lower level

The People Mover monorail at Orlando International Airport

concourse. Companies such as **SuperShuttle** run 24-hour shuttle bus services to all the main districts of Miami. City buses in theory serve the airport, but these services should not be relied upon.

## Orlando and Sanford Airports

Orlando International Airport, the country's 13th busiest airport, welcomes 40 million passengers a year and is cont-inually expanding. It offers excellent overall customer convenience. Moving walkways and the automated monorail system help passengers to move around the two terminals easily. Multi-lingual tourist information centers by the security check-points are open from 7am to 11pm.

Many hotels have their own courtesy buses, but there are also shuttle buses; the **Mears Transportation Group** serves most destinations in the area. A less expensive way to travel to International Drive or to downtown Orlando is by Lynx bus (see p387). Services leave from outside the "A Side" terminal every half hour. Both trips take about 50 minutes.

Serving just over one million passengers a year, the Orlando Sanford International Airport, 30 miles (48 km) north of downtown Orlando, is much quieter than the main Orlando airport and is a hub for charter flights. Taxi ranks and several car rental outlets are conveniently located right outside the terminal building.

## Package Deals

The cheapest vacation deal to Florida is a package that throws in car rental and/or accommodation with the cost of the flight. Fly-drive deals offer a rental car "free" or at a vast discount, but be warned: there are heavy surcharges to pay (see pp382–3).

Double deals are popular – combining, for example, a week in Orlando with a week at a Gulf Coast resort. Package deals to all the major theme parks are worth considering if you are spending the whole time there. Information is available from travel agencies and theme park websites.

(see pp382–3).

## DIRECTORY

### Airline Numbers

**American Airlines**
Tel (800) 433-7300.

**British Airways**
Tel (800) 247-9297.

**Delta Air Lines**
Tel (800) 221-1212.

**JetBlue**
Tel (800) 538-2583.

**Southwest**
Tel (800) 435-9792.

**United Airlines**
Tel (800) 864-8331.

**Virgin Atlantic**
Tel (800) 862-8621.

### Shuttle Buses

**Mears Transportation Group**
Tel (407) 423-5566.

**SuperShuttle**
Tel (305) 871-2000.

# Driving in Florida

Driving in Florida is a delight. Most highways are well-paved, and Floridians are generally courteous and considerate drivers. Gasoline is relatively inexpensive and car rental rates are the lowest in the United States *(see pp382–3)*.

Visitors can survive without a car in Orlando *(see p387)*, but wherever they are, life is much easier with one. Many rest areas on interstate highways are covered by 24-hour armed security patrols, and direction signs have been improved in Miami *(see p386)*.

The toll plaza on Florida's Turnpike at Boca Raton

## What you Need

You must have a valid driver's license in order to drive a car in Florida. When renting a car, stated rates do not include accidental or liability insurance. Remember that when you rent a car, you are the liable party if there is an accident. Check with your credit card or auto insurance company regarding their insurance coverage when you use rental vehicles. The state of Florida requires that you carry a copy of the rental agreement in the car – store it safely out of sight.

While there are many state and federal regulations on the equipment requirements of cars, there are very few that pertain to occupants. Unlike some European countries, there is no requirement to carry warning triangles or safety flares in a car. Drivers and passengers can be fined for not wearing seatbelts, and at certain times of the year state-wide campaigns make it particularly expensive; fines of as much as $116 can be levied at checkpoints on major roads by the Florida Highway Patrol.

If you want to explore off-road trails on a motorbike, be aware that riders younger than 16 years are required to wear eye protection, over-the-ankle boots, and a safety helmet.

## Roads and Tolls

Florida has an excellent road network. The fastest and smoothest routes are the interstate highways, referred to as I-10, I-75, and so on. These usually have at least six lanes with rest areas generally located about 45 minutes' traveling time apart. Major highways may be fast at the best of times, but slow to an interminable crawl near downtown areas such as Miami, Orlando, and Jacksonville, especially during rush hours before and after work.

Interstates form part of the expressway system of roads (sometimes called "freeways"), to which access is permitted only at specified junctions or exits. Among other expressways are turnpikes and toll roads. Chief among the latter are the BeachLine Expressway (between Orlando and the Space Coast) and the Florida Turnpike, which runs from I-75, northwest of Orlando, to Florida City south of Miami. The toll you have to pay is dependent, logically, on the distance covered; if you travel the entire 329 miles (530 km) of the Turnpike, for example, the trip will cost around $20. Tolls can be paid to a collector in a booth or, if you have the correct change and do not need a receipt, dropped into a collecting bin, where the money is counted automatically. Certain sections of the Turnpike near Miami have been converted to an electronic collection system and cash is

**Highway Patrol insignia**

## Tips for Drivers

- Traffic travels on the right-hand side of the road.
- Seat belts are compulsory for both drivers and passengers, and children under three must sit in a child seat.
- You can turn right on a red light unless there are signs to the contrary, but you must come to a stop first.
- A flashing amber light at intersections means slow down, look for oncoming traffic, and then proceed with caution.
- Passing is allowed on both sides on any multilane road, including interstate highways.
- It is illegal to change lanes across a double yellow or double white solid line.
- If a school bus stops on a two-way road to drop off or pick up children, traffic traveling in both directions must stop. On a divided highway, only traffic traveling in the same direction need stop.
- Do not drink even one beer. Driving under the influence (DUI) is very serious; you can be fined hundreds of dollars, have your driver's license suspended, or even be imprisoned.

no longer accepted. Tolls are collected via Sunpass transponders or from having your license plate photographed at each toll booth; your rental car agency can provide information regarding this.

Be warned that local drivers change lanes frequently on expressways. Stick to the right to stay out of trouble and take care when approaching exits, which can be on both sides of the highway; most accidents occur during left turns.

Other routes include the US highways, which are usually, but not always, multilaned. These are also slower than expressways and often less scenic, because they are lined with motels and gas stations. State Roads and County Roads are smaller and better for touring. Unpaved routes exist in some of Florida's more rural areas; note that some car rental companies may not permit you to drive on these.

## Navigating

A recent, good road map is vital for touring Florida by car. The *Florida Transportation Map*, available free from most Convention and Visitor's Bureaus, and Florida tourist offices abroad, is adequate for general purposes; it gives the location of rest areas on interstate highways and includes maps of the main cities. If you plan to spend any length of time in a city, however, you should try to pick up a local detailed map. The city maps in tourist offices are often inadequate for driving – in

## Road Signs

Most road signs are clear and self-explanatory. If you are caught disregarding instructions you might be fined.

Generally, road numbers or names rather than destinations are marked, and different types of roads are indicated by signs of different shapes and colors. Directional signs are usually green. Traffic signals often have cameras.

| City parking restrictions | Mile marker in the Keys | Interstate Highway 4 | US Highway 1, heading south |

Overhead signs at the junction of two routes — Speed limit (in mph) — Rest area, indicated off an interstate

which case a good bookstore would be the best source. Check with your car rental company about the availability of GPS rental.

Navigating your way around Florida is comparatively easy. Major east–west routes have even numbers, and north–south routes have odd numbers. Signs on the roadside, including mile markers in the Keys *(see p287)*, tell you which road you are on; while the name hanging over intersections is not the road you are on but the one you are crossing. Junctions have two

numbers – when through routes follow the same course for a time.

## Speed Limits

Speed limits in the US are set by individual states. The limits in Florida are as follows:
• 55–70 mph (90–105 km/h) on highways.
• 20–30 mph (32–48 km/h) in residential areas.
• 15–20 mph (24–32 km/h) near schools.

Speed limits can vary every few miles, so look out for the signs. On an interstate you can be fined for driving slower than 40 mph (64 km/h). Speed limits are rigorously enforced by the Florida Highway Patrol, whose representatives issue tickets on the spot. A fine can set you back as much as $300.

Florida's "Move Over Act" requires highway and interstate road drivers to move over to the next lane or to slow down to at least 20 miles below the posted speed limit when approaching stopped emergency vehicles.

A typical Florida road intersection, Tallahassee

Mobile gas station, International Drive, Orlando

## Gasoline

Unleaded gasoline is used by most modern cars and vans and comes in three grades – regular, super, and premium. Diesel is usually also available.

Gasoline is less expensive in the US than in many other countries, but the price varies according to the location and service. Almost all gas stations are self-service; it is rare to find one that has an attendant to fill the tank. Gas prices are marked inclusive of tax per gallon – the US gallon, that is, which is 3.8 liters, about a liter less than an Imperial gallon. At most gas stations you can pay with cash (in advance) or credit card, and can pay by card at the pump without going inside the station.

## Safety for Drivers

Take care wherever you are. Various measures have been introduced to safeguard foreign drivers. For example, the license plate code identifying rental cars was dropped and an orange sunburst sign guides drivers along the main routes to and from the airport. Here are a few tips to help you to stay safe:

- If arriving in Florida by air at night, you could arrange to pick up your rental car the next morning in order to avoid driving in unfamiliar territory after dark.
- Avoid having purses or other valuable items visible inside the car; pack them out of sight in the trunk.
- Keep car doors locked, especially in urban areas.
- Ignore any attempt by a pedestrian or motorist to stop you, e.g., by pointing out some alleged fault on your car or, less subtly, by ramming you from behind. Another ruse is to stand by a "broken-down" vehicle, signaling for help.
- If you need to refer to a map in a city, do not stop until you are in a well-lit and preferably busy area.
- Avoid sleeping in the car off the highway, although some rest areas on expressways have security patrols.
- Avoid taking short cuts in urban areas. Stick to the main highways if possible.
- Bear in mind that while Florida highways are in reasonable repair, they have been rated by the National Highway Traffic Safety Admin-istration as the most dangerous thoroughfares in the country, particularly Interstate 95 (#1) and Interstate 4 (#3).

Highway sign in Miami

## Breakdowns

If your car breaks down, pull off the road, turn on the emergency flashers, and wait for the police. On expressways you can make use of one of the Motorist Aid Call Boxes (see p372). It is worth considering renting a cell phone – offered at a small cost by most car rental firms – or buying one at a convenience or electronics store (see also p376).

If you have rented a car, you will find an emergency number on the rental agreement, so try that first. In the event of a serious breakdown, the rental agency will provide a new vehicle. The **American Auto-mobile Association** (AAA) will assist its members. Alternatively, call the Florida Highway Patrol (511 on a cell phone) or the free Road Ranger service (*347).

## Parking

Finding a parking space is rarely a problem at theme parks and other major tourist attractions, shopping malls, or in most downtown districts. Parking near city beaches is more difficult (see p386).

You will find small and multi-level parking lots in cities, but usually you will have to use parking meters. Feed the meter generously: the fee varies from 25c to $1 per hour. Overstay and you risk a fine or the possibility of your car being clamped or towed away. Be sure to read parking signs carefully. Restrictions may be posted on telephone poles, street lights, or roadside walls or curbs. Cars parked within 10 ft (3 m) of a fire hydrant will be towed away.

## Car Rental

Car rental costs in Florida are already cheap by most standards, and you can save more by reserving and paying before leaving home. Fly-drive deals can knock more than 50 per cent off the cost, but do not be fooled by offers of "free" car rental. State tax and insurance will not be included in these offers.

If you wait until you arrive to organize your car rental, it is usually cheaper to rent a vehicle at the airport rather than from a downtown outlet.

All you need to rent a car is your driver's license, passport, and a credit card. If you present a debit card, you may be required to allow a large deposit to be charged. The minimum age for car rental is 21, but drivers under 25 may need to pay a surcharge.

Make sure your car rental agreement includes Collision Damage Waiver (CDW) – also known as Loss Damage Waiver (LDW) – or you'll be liable for any damage to the car, even if it was not your fault. Rental agreements include third-party insurance, but this is rarely adequate. It is advisable to buy additional or supplementary Liability Insurance, which should provide coverage of up to $1 million. These extras, plus taxes, can add $35–40 to each day's rental.

Most companies add a premium if you want to drop the car off in another city, and all impose high charges for gas: if you return the car with less fuel than it had initially, the difference can cost you as much as $9 per gallon. Gas stations near airports are notoriously expensive.

## Motorcycle Rental

If cruising the streets and high-ways on a Harley-Davidson is your dream, you may want to visit **Harley-Davidson** or **EagleRider** (both in several cities). Charges exceed $100 for

24 hours plus a substantial deposit, and the minimum age is 21. You may be eligible for a discount for advance booking.

## RV Rental

Recreational vehicles (RVs) or mobile homes are great for groups or families. It costs $500 and more to rent one for a week. RV rental outlets are surprisingly scarce. The largest in the United States is **Cruise America**, which also has agents in other countries.

Rental conditions are usually similar to those for car rental. Size and facilities vary greatly, but most RVs have every imaginable convenience.

## Great Drives

Great natural beauty, stretches of pristine and ancient woodlands and coastline, and an almost completely flat terrain – the highest part of Florida is only 345 ft (105 m) above sea level – means that there are some incredibly beautiful places in which to drive.

One of the most scenic and exciting drives is from Miami to the Florida Keys, spanning 160 miles (257 km), changing from big city to rustic scrub woods, and crossing Seven Mile Bridge to the majestic turquoise waters surrounding the Keys. If you have an adventurous nature, heading west from Fort Lauderdale across the Everglades offers a thrilling look at ancient Florida, and the drive around Apalachicola Bay on US 98 takes in unspoiled wildlife

and the sight of shrimp boats and oystermen plying their trade. The A1A coastal drive from Daytona to Jacksonville offers views of historical Spanish castles, unspoiled state parks, and a mostly unobstructed landscape of white sand beaches and the Atlantic Ocean.

## DIRECTORY

### Breakdowns

**AAA General Breakdown Assistance**
Tel (800) 222-4357.
NOTE: Rental companies provide 24-hour roadside assistance.

**American Automobile Association (AAA)**
1000 AAA Drive, Heathrow, FL 32746. **Tel** (800) 222-1134.
W aaasouth.com

### Car Rental

**Alamo**
Tel (800) 651-1223.
W goalamo.com

**Avis**
Tel (800) 352-7900.
W avis.com

**Budget**
Tel (800) 218-7992.
W budget.com

**Dollar**
Tel (800) 800-4000.
W dollarcar.com

**Enterprise**
Tel (855) 266-9565.

**Hertz**
Tel (800) 704-4473.
W hertz.com

**National**
Tel (877) 222-9058.
W nationalcar.com

**Thrifty**
Tel (800) 847-4389.
W thrifty.com

### Motorcycle Rental

**Eagle Rider**
Tel (888) 900-9901.

**Harley-Davidson**
Tel (407) 944-3700 (Orlando); (239) 275-4647 (Fort Myers).

### RV Rental

**Cruise America**
Tel (800) 671-8042.
W cruiseamerica.com

Channel Five Bridge, Florida Keys

# Traveling Around Florida

Visitors to Florida who rely on public transportation will find their horizons rather restricted. The rail network is limited, leaving buses – which link most sizable towns – as the main form of long-distance land transportation. Places outside the main urban areas will often elude those without cars. Some local bus services are good, but you'll need time and flexibility to make use of these. Public transportation within cities is more useful. Here, the emphasis is on serving commuters rather than visitors, but the main tourist centers have some services that cater to sightseers.

## Green Travel

As small towns are swallowed up by the ever-expanding mass of cities, it becomes increasingly harder to travel from one end of Orlando or Miami to the other without a car. However, there are several green travel options available.

While public transportation is not a high priority in Florida in general, some cities are aware of its ecological impact. In Fort Lauderdale's downtown area, **Sun Trolley** runs environmentally-friendly bio-diesel vehicles that offer air-conditioned comfort, while Orlando's **Lynx** operates a number of bio-diesel buses on its routes. For theme park visitors, the Lynx system also offers other car-alternative incentives as it is the best and cheapest way to get to Disney and Universal, and also eliminates parking fees. Buses leave from either downtown Orlando or from the International Drive hotel district. The Jacksonville's Skyway system runs elevated tracks across the St. John's River and connects downtown hotels, restaurants, and the Convention Center with the free trolley service that runs along the riverside.

For those concerned about their carbon footprint from air travel or driving, carbon offsets can be bought through companies such as TerraPass: www.terrapass.com.

## Arriving by Train

**Amtrak**, the national passenger rail company, serves Florida from the east coast. There are three daily services from New York City. This Silver Service takes about 25 hours (with sleepers and meals available), and runs via Washington D.C., down through Jacksonville and Orlando, terminating in Miami or Tampa. The Palmetto serves the same route but offers a business-class service.

If you want to travel by train but take your own car, there is Amtrak's Auto Train, which runs daily from Lorton in Virginia to Sanford, 30 miles north of Orlando, taking about 18 hours.

## Exploring by Train

Amtrak trains serve only a limited number of towns and cities in Florida (see the map on pages 16–17). Other than Tampa, the Gulf Coast is linked only by Amtrak buses, known as "Thruway" buses. These run from Winter Haven, near Orlando, to Fort Myers via St. Petersburg and Sarasota, with guaranteed connections with Amtrak rail services.

Rail fares do not compete well with those of buses, but trips are obviously more relaxing. When traveling overnight, you can choose between the ordinary (but reclining) seats of "coach class" or a cabin. Both options have decent meal services available on longer stretches.

Anyone planning to make more than a couple of trips by train might consider buying a rail pass, which gives unlimited travel on Amtrak's network during a set period of time. The pass must be bought before you arrive – either online with Amtrak or through a travel agent that deals with Amtrak.

Another train service is the south Florida regional **Tri-Rail**, which links 15 stations between Miami airport and West Palm Beach, including Fort Lauderdale and Boca Raton. Primarily for commuters, these trains can also be useful for tourists. One-way fares range from about $2.50 to $7, depending on the number of zones you pass through, with discounts for weekends and holidays. Transfers to Miami's Metrorail and Metromover services (see p386) are free. Transfers are also available on **SunRail** for Orlando's Lynx Bus service and Volusia County's Votran Bus service.

Spanish Revival-style Tri-Rail station in West Palm Beach

## Long-distance Buses

Whether you are traveling from other parts of the country or within Florida, **Greyhound** buses offer the cheapest way to get around. Some services are "express," with few stops en route, while others serve a greater number of destinations.

A few routes have "flag stops," where a bus may stop to deposit or collect passengers in places without a bus station. Pay the driver direct, or, if you want to reserve in advance, visit the website or go to the nearest Greyhound agent – usually in a local store or post office.

Passes provide unlimited travel for set periods of time (from between four and sixty days), but are useful only if you have a very full itinerary. Overseas visitors should also note that passes are cheaper if bought from a Greyhound agent outside the United States. Timetables, information about the different types of ticket, and details of baggage limits are available on the Greyhound website.

**Red Coach** runs smaller, premium buses, with movies, Wi-Fi Internet, and reclining seats, from Miami to Orlando, Jacksonville, Tampa, Tallahassee, and Gainesville.

## Taxis

Taxis are easily found at airports, transit terminals, and major hotels. Taxi stands are rare elsewhere, and since taxis are not generally licensed to pick people up from the curb, it is best to order one by phone: numbers are listed in the *Yellow Pages*. Alternatively, ask someone at your hotel to call a taxi for you – the concierge or bellman will be happy to do this and will not expect a tip.

If you are traveling off the beaten track in a city, it will help to have your destination marked on a map. Do not assume that the driver will know the way. All taxi fares should be metered according to the distance traveled, unless stated as a fixed fare. Many

Horse and carriage, a pleasant way to go sightseeing in St. Augustine

cabs accept credit cards, but you should check in advance.

Ride share services Uber and Lyft are commonplace in Florida cities, and operate even in some small towns. You have to download the app to your phone.

## Water Taxis

In several cities water taxis add a new dimension to urban travel. You'll find them in Jacksonville, Tampa, Fort Lauderdale, and the islands around Fort Myers. Routes are generally geared to tourists, and as a result they are fairly limited in scope – linking hotels, restaurants, and shops, for example. However, they are great for sightseeing and often offer special fares.

A yellow water taxi in Fort Lauderdale

## Transportation for Tourists

Most popular tourist centers provide special transportation for visitors. This often comes in the form of old-fashioned trolley buses: Tallahassee has a replica streetcar with wooden seats and brass handrails. In Daytona Beach (from mid-

January to September) and Fort Lauderdale, trolleys are a useful link between downtown and the beach, and Orlando has a trolley that runs along the International Drive hotel district.

A familiar sight in Key West is the Conch Train, which consists of open-sided cars towed by a butane-powered jeep disguised as an old locomotive. St. Augustine has a similar train, as well as horse-drawn carriages through its narrow streets.

## DIRECTORY

### Rail Information

**Amtrak**
Tel (800) 872-7245. W amtrak.com

**SunRail**
Tel (407) 487-4035. W sunrail.com

**Tri-Rail**
Tel (800) 874-7245. W tri-rail.com

### Bus Information

**Greyhound**
Tel (800) 229-9424.
W greyhound.com

**Jacksonville Transportation Authority**
Tel (904) 630-3181.
W jtafla.com

**Lynx**
Tel (407) 841-2279.
W golynx.com

**Metrobus Miami**
Tel (305) 891-3131.
W miamidade.gov/transit

**Red Coach**
Tel (877) 733-0724.
W redcoachusa.com

**Sun Trolley**
Tel (954) 761-3543.
W suntrolley.com

# Traveling Around Miami

Public transportation in Miami is run by **Miami-Dade County Transit**, which operates the buses, the Metrorail commuter train network, and Downtown's elevated Metromover. It is hard to make the most of Miami without a car unless you're happy to stay in South Beach. Taxis are reliable and widely available.

## Arriving in Miami

For information on getting away from Miami airport, *see page 379*. If you arrive at the **Amtrak** station, or at one of the **Greyhound** terminals, there are no car rental outlets but plenty of taxis and stops for buses going to Downtown and Miami Beach.

Arriving in Miami by car is direct but not hassle-free. Interstate 95 (I-95), the main road from the north is one of the busiest – and most dangerous – highways in the country. It heads straight through Downtown before joining US 1. The Airport Expressway, or State Road 112, is a toll road that connects Miami International with I-95, and costs around $1.25. Avoid the very hectic Palmetto and Dolphin Expressways. Route A1A is a slower way in from the north that takes you directly into South Beach, and is a far more scenic route. From the west, US 41 runs through Little Havana to the coast, where it links up with the main north–south routes.

## Metrorail, Metromover, and Metrobus

Metrorail, a 25-mile (40-km) rail line between the northern and southern suburbs of Miami, provides a useful link between Coral Gables or Coconut Grove, and the downtown area. Services run daily every 10 minutes or so from 6am until midnight, and cost $2 per ride. Purchase an Easy card or Easy ticket at any of the 22 Metrorail stations. This can be used throughout the Metro system, which does not accept cash. All Metrorail stations have elevators, escalators, and/or stairs. You can transfer free from Metrorail to the Tri-Rail line *(see p384)* in Hialeah, and also to the

The Metromover, looping around downtown Miami

Metromover system at Government Center and Brickell stations.

The free Metromover monorail has three loops, connecting the heart of Downtown with the Omni entertainment and Brickell financial districts on separate elevated lines, with 20 stations in total. The Inner Loop provides a quick way to see the downtown area *(see pp76–7)*. Cars operate from 5am to midnight daily, arriving every 90 seconds during rush hours and every 3 minutes during off-peak hours.

Metrobus runs throughout Miami-Dade County, from Miami Beach and Key Biscayne to West Miami-Dade, north to Broward County and south to Homestead, Florida City, and the Middle Keys. A single ride costs $2 and transfers are free. A 24-hour unlimited pass costs $5, while a seven-day pass is $26. There is a fee to transfer between bus and rail services.

## Taxis

Taxis charge approximately $3 per mile; the trip from South Beach to Coconut Grove, for example, will cost around $35.

Don't try to hail a passing cab from the curb; it is best to order one by phone *(see p385)*. **Central Cab** and Yellow Taxi are both reliable.

## Traveling By Car

Driving in Miami is not as intimidating as you might think. Biscayne Bay is a useful reference point, and you can't go far wrong if you stick to the main through streets. Navigation inside the Miami grid is relatively straightforward; streets run from east to west, while everything else runs north to south.

Parking can be a nightmare in South Beach. On weekends avoid it; at other times bring change for the meters, which operate from 9am to 9pm, and pay heed to the signs threatening to tow away your vehicle. Contact the **Miami Parking Authority** for directions to specific parking lots.

## Bicycling

Miami is becoming increasingly bicycle friendly. The network of cycle lanes is expanding, making it safer for bikers to get around the city. With its seafront trail, South Beach is one of the best places to explore by bike. **Bike and Roll** rents bikes, provides maps, and offers daily tours across the city.

## DIRECTORY

**Amtrak**
8303 NW 37th Ave, Miami
**Tel** (305) 835-1222.

**Bike and Roll**
210 l0th Street (10th & Collins), South Beach.
**Tel** (305) 604-0001.
Ⓦ bikeandroll.com/miami

**Central Cab**
**Tel** (305) 532-5555.

**Greyhound**
**Tel** (305) 871-1810 (Miami terminal). Ⓦ greyhound.com

**Miami-Dade County Transit**
Ⓦ miamidade.gov/transit

**Miami Parking Authority**
**Tel** (305) 373-6789.

# Traveling Around Orlando

If you are in Orlando for the theme parks, driving is pretty straightforward, and public transportation offered by the Lynx bus system will take you where you want to go. Getting around outside the prime tourist areas is a bit trickier, as Orlando is very spread out, so usually a car or taxi is needed if you want to explore. For the devoted walker or bicyclist, a connected system of hiking and biking trails is a pleasure.

A Lymmo bus, serving downtown Orlando

## Arriving in Orlando

Taxis and ride share services from Orlando International Airport are the easiest ways to get into the city. A taxi to Disney will cost around $50. The express **Lynx** bus leaves Orlando Airport from level one of the A Terminal, and is a bargain at $2–4, but can take an hour to arrive downtown. Most hotels offer free shuttle buses from the airport. Driving into Orlando takes you along Interstate 4, running east–west across the state from Daytona to Tampa, which is quick and convenient if you remember to avoid early morning and afternoon commuters, and late-night theme park devotees. The Florida 528 toll road (called the Beachline) runs directly from the airport to the Disney World gates, and costs around $1.75 – have coins ready.

## Rail

Built in 1926, Orlando's charming main **Amtrak** station is minutes from downtown and has taxi stands outside. Its waiting room is open 7:30am–8:15pm. A cab ride to International Drive costs around $35. The SunRail runs from Sand Lake Road in south Orlando to Deltona in Volusia County. A one-way fare is $3–4.

## Buses

You can survive in Orlando without a car thanks to the Lynx buses. While some residential areas have few or no bus routes, the main tourist areas of the airport, downtown Orlando, International Drive (including Universal Studios® and Sea-World®), and Walt Disney World® are quite well served. A one-way fare costs $2, while a single-day unlimited pass is $4.50, and a seven-day pass is $16. If you will need to use a different route to complete your journey, ask for a free transfer when you board the first bus. Have the exact fare, as drivers don't give change.

Orlando's Lynx buses logo

The free Lymmo service (run by Lynx) travels within downtown Orlando and offers rides to and from the Amway Center sports arena, as well as through the dining and nightlife area.

## Taxis

Taxis from **Mears Transportation Group** (Yellow Cab – not always yellow – City Cab, and Checker Cab), along with Uber and Lyft, blanket the city and offer efficient service. A phone call is necessary to get a cab unless you're at a taxi stand at a hotel or the airport.

## Traveling by Car

There are close to two dozen rental car agencies at Orlando Airport, so cars are popular here. On-street parking is free outside of downtown Orlando, where meters and ticketed garages are generally the only places to park. Many downtown restaurants will validate parking. Avoiding the often-jammed Interstate 4 highway is recommended when traveling locally. While street level roads in Orlando are generally in good repair, the multitude of lakes means very few of them run in a straight line; ask your rental car agent for a map.

## Bicycling and Walking

Orlando's old and unused railway tracks have undergone conversion to bicycling and walking trails, with plans for a 200-mile loop of trails around Central Florida. The connected South Lake and West Orange Trails run for 29 miles (47 km) from Clermont, just north of Disney, to Apopka, near Wekiva State Park (with 13 miles/21 km of trails), featuring paved walking and cycling paths. **West Orange Trail Bikes and Blades** rents bicycles for use on the trail hourly or by the day and will deliver bikes to your hotel. The delightful Cady Way Trail runs 4 miles (6 km) right through downtown Orlando, taking bikers, joggers, and skaters through some lovely areas. For more information visit the **Rails-to-Trails** website.

### DIRECTORY

**Amtrak**
1400 Sligh Blvd, Orlando.
Tel (407) 843-7611.

**Lynx**
Tel (407) 841-5969.
W golynx.com

**Mears Transportation Group**
Tel (407) 422-2222.

**Rails-to-Trails**
W railstotrails.org

**SunRail**
Tel (407) 487-4035.
W sunrail.com

**West Orange Trail Bikes and Blades**
W orlandobikerental.com

# General Index

# Acknowledgments

Dorling Kindersley would like to thank the following people whose contributions and assistance have made the preparation of this book possible.

## Main Contributors

Richard Cawthorne is a freelance travel writer specializing in the United States.

David Dick is a postgraduate at University College London, specializing in US history.

Guy Mansell writes travel articles for British magazines and newspapers, including The Sunday Telegraph, as well as guidebooks.

Fred Mawer is a travel journalist who contributes regularly to the Daily Telegraph and the Mail on Sunday. He is also the author of half a dozen guidebooks and has contributed to various Eyewitness guides.

Emma Stanford has traveled extensively in Florida and has written several books and articles about the state. She has written guidebooks for Berlitz, the AAA, and Fodor's.

Phyllis Steinberg lives in Florida. She writes about food, travel, and lifestyle for various US magazines and newspapers.

Jennifer Greenhill-Taylor is from Edinburgh but lives in Orlando. She writes about travel for print and online outlets and has contributed to several Eyewitness guides.

## Other Contributors and Consultants

Frances and Fred Brown, Monique Damiano, Todd Jay Jonas, Marlena Spieler, David Stone.

## Additional Photography

Lucy Clark, Steven Greaves, Dave King, Ian O'Leary, Magnus Rew, Rough Guides/ Demetrio Carrasco, Rough Guides/Angus Oborn, Tony Souter, Arvin Steinberg, James Stevenson, Clive Streeter , Stephen Whitehorn, Peter Wilson.

## Additional Illustrations

Julian Baker, Joanna Cameron, Stephen Conlin, Gary Cross, Chris Forsey, Paul Guest, Stephen Gyapay, Ruth Lindsay, Maltings Partnership, Paul Weston.

## Design and Editorial

Researcher Fred Brown
Managing Editor Vivien Crump
Managing Art Editor Jane Ewart
Deputy Editorial Director Douglas Amrine
Deputy Art Director Gillian Allan
Production David Proffit
Picture Research Monica Allende
Revisions Team Lesley Abravanel, Umesh Aggarwal, Shahnaaz Bakshi, Claire Baranowski, Hansa Babra, Vandana Bhagra, Hilary Bird, Rohan Bolton, Louise Boulton, Neha Chander, Sherry Collins, Dipika Dasgupta, Cathy Day, Surya Deogun, Caroline Elliker, Alice Fewery, Emer FitzGerald, Niki Foreman , Fay Franklin, Jo Gardner, Aishwarya Gosain, Emily Green, Jennifer Greenhill-Taylor, Donald Greig , Vinod Harish, Joseph Hayes, Leanne Hogbin, Laura Jones, Bharti Karakoti, Kim Kemp, Sumita Khatwani, Desiree Kirke, Maite Lantaron, Jude Ledger, Carly Madden, Tanya Mahendru, Hayley Maher, Nicola Malone, Alison McGill, Sam Merrell, Ella Milroy, Sonal Modha, Claire Naylor, George Nimmo, Mary Ormandy, Helen Partington, Sangita Patel, Susie Peachey, Rada Radojicic, Mani Ramaswamy, Lee Redmond, Lucy Richards, Rockit Design, Harvey de Roemer, Ellen Root, Anuroop Sanwalia, Michael Sasser, Shailesh Sharma, Payal Sharotri, Farah Sheikh, Anupama Shukla, Jonathan Shultz, Azeem Siddiqui, Lucy Sienkowska, Asavari Singh, Rituraj Singh, Akanksha Siwach, Susana Smith, Michelle Snow, Arvin Steinberg, Phyllis Steinberg, Paul Steiner, Lia Sussman, Alka Thakur, Rachel Thompson, Conrad Van Dyk, Vinita Venugopal, Deepika Verma, Ingrid Vienings, Ros Walford, Laura Walker, Penny Walker, Marian Virginia Warder, Michael Wise, Ed Wright, Sophie Wright.

## Cartography

Malcolm Porter, David Swain, Holly Syer and Neil Wilson at EMS Ltd. (Digital Cartography Dept), East Grinstead, UK;
Alok Pathak, Kunal Singh.
Map Co-ordinators Emily Green, David Pugh.

## Proofreader Stewart Wild

## Indexer Hilary Bird

## Special Assistance

Dorling Kindersley would like to thank all the regional and local tourist offices in Florida for their valuable help. Particular thanks also to: Rachel Bell, Busch Gardens; Alison Sanders, Cedar Key Area Chamber of Commerce; Marie Mayer, Collier County Historical Museum, Naples; Mr. and Mrs. Charlie Shubert, Coombs House Inn, Apalachicola; Nick Robbins, Crystal River State Archaeological Site; Emily Hickey, Dali Museum, St. Petersburg; Gary B. van Voorhuis, Daytona International Speedway; James Laray, Everglades National Park; Sandra Barghini, Flagler Museum, Palm Beach; Ed Lane, Florida Geological Survey, Florida Department of Environmental Protection, Tallahassee; Dr. James Miller, Archaeological Research, Florida Department of State, Tallahassee; Florida Keys National Marine Sanctuary; Jody Norman, Florida State Archives; Damian O'Grady and Tanya Nigro, Florida Tourism Corporation, London; Larry Paarlberg, Goodwood Plantation, Tallahassee; Dawn Hugh, Historical Museum of Southern Florida; Ellen Donovan, Historical Society of Palm Beach County; Melissa Tomasso, Kennedy Space Center; Valerie Rivers, Marjorie Kinnan Rawlings State Historic Site, Cross Creek; Carmen Smythe, Micanopy County Historian; Bob McNeil and Philip Pollack, Museum of Florida History, Tallahassee; Frank Lepore and Ed Rappaport, National Hurricane Center, Miami; Colonel Denis J. Kiely, National Museum of Naval Aviation, Pensacola; Richard Brosnaham and Tom Muir, Historic Pensacola Preservation Board; Ringling Museum of Art, Sarasota; Ardythe Bromley-Rousseau, Salvors Inc., Sebastian; Arvin Steinberg; Wit Tuttell, Universal Studios; Holly Blount, Vizcaya, Miami; Melinda Crowther, Margaret Melia and Joyce Taylor, Walt Disney Attractions, London.

## Photography Permissions

Dorling Kindersley would like to thank the following for their assistance and kind permission to photograph at their establishments: The Barnacle Historic Site; © 1996 FL Cypress Gardens, Inc.; all rights reserved, reproduced by permission; © Disney Enterprises, Inc.; Dreher Park Zoo: The Zoo of the Palm Beaches; Fish and Wildlife Service, Department of the Interior; Florida Park Service; Harry P. Leu Gardens, Orlando, FL; Key West Art and Historical Society: Lighthouse Museum and East Martello Museum; Metro-Dade Culture Center, Historical Museum of Southern Florida; Monkey Jungle Inc., Miami, FL; National Park Service, Department of Interior; Pinellas County Park Department; National Society of the Colonial Dames of America in the State of Florida; Suncoast Seabird Sanctuary Inc., Indian Shores, FL; and all other museums, churches, hotels, restaurants, stores, galleries, and sights too numerous to thank individually.

## Picture Credits

a-above; b-below/bottom; c-center; f-far; l-left; r-right; t-top.

Works of art have been reproduced with the permission of the following copyright holders: Courtesy of General Services Administration, Public Building Services, Fine Arts Collection: Denman Fink, *Law Guides Florida's Progress* (1940) at US Federal Courthouse, Miami 76cl.

Dorling Kindersley would like to thank the following individuals, companies, and picture libraries for their kind permission to reproduce their photographs:
**123RF.com:** fotoluminate 308–309, Tom Gilligan 147br, 177t; **Pisit Khambubpha** 192tl; **philipus** 288tr; **Alamy Stock Photo:** All Canada Photos 28bc; America 351tr; Pat & Chuck Blackley 15br; Pat Canova 340tl; Ian Dagnall 195bc, 280br, 382tl; Danita Delimont 295tr; Findlay 29br ; Dylan Garcia Photography 273cr; Jeff Greenburg 123bl, 123br; Jeff Greenberg 6 of 6 298bc; Chris Gug 297tl; imageBROKER 332bl; JeffG 95bl; Andre Jenny 138bl; Lordprice Collection 52cl; Dennis MacDonald 38cr; NASA Photo 56–7; NATUREWOELRD 115b; Nikreates 71cra; PF-(space1) 205tr; Peter Titmuss 370cla; RosalreneBetancourt 1 77bl, 102tr 40bl; RosalreneBetancourt 14 114; RosalreneBetancourt 7 72br; Stephen Saks Photography 232tr; James Schwabel 290br; State Archives of Florida / Florida Memory 55tl; ZUMA Press, Inc 36br; **Allsport/Getty Images:** Brian Bahr 37cr; Steve Swope 37bc; **Appleton Museum of Art, Ocala:** *Jeune Bergere (Young Shepherdess),* William Adolphe Bouguereau (1825–1905), French. Oil on canvas 226tl; **Archive Photos, New York:** 53ca, 56clb; Bert & Richard Morgan 122br; **Archivo de Indias, Seville:** 46cb; **Tony Arruza:** 27cb, 30clb, 42, 132tl, 294c, 301br, 359tr; **Aunt Catfish Restaurant, Daytona Beach:** Gerald Sprankel 327tr; **Avalon Hotel, Miami:** 65tl; **Azul:** 331tr. www.barefoot weddings.net: 366cla; **Barton G. The Restaurant:** 326cla; **Beach Bistro:** 343tr; **Larry Benvenuti:** 297cr; **Biblioteca Nacional, Madrid:** *Codice Osuna* 47cb; **Big Pink:** 329b; **The Biltmore Hotel:** 315tr; **The Bridgeman Art Library, London:** *The Agony in the Garden (Christ in the Garden of Olives),* 1889 by Gauguin, Paul (1848–1903), Norton Gallery, Palm Beach 131tc; **British Museum:** 45tl, 49cr; **Busch Gardens Tampa Bay.** All Rights Reserved.: 112bl, 268b, 268clb, 269tl, 269br, 296bc. All Rights Reserved, **Discovery Cove:** 187c, 187b. **Café de France:** 339bl; **Camera Press:** Steve Benbow 170bl; **John Carter:** 25bl; **Casa Maya Grill:** 333t; **Courtesy of Carnival Center for the**

**Performing Arts:** 100bl; Robin Hill 101tl; **Courtesy of The Charleston Museum, Charleston, South Carolina:** Osceola portrait 50cla; **Robert Clayton:** 58–9, 382clb; **Clinton Hotel:** 314bl; **Pat Clyne:** 118tr; **Bruce Coleman, London:** Raimund Cramm GDT 198cla; Library of Congress, LC-USF33-30491-M3 55cr; **Columbia Restaurant:** 326br, 344br; **Corbis:** 47tl, 48–9c; Morton Beebe 328cla; Jonathan Blair 150t; Richard Cummins 263tl; Demotix/Kelly Smy 372bl; Photononstop/Russel Kord 123cl; Reuters/Pierre Ducharme 204cla; **Cuban Club:** © Burget Brothers, photo courtesy of the Tampa Hillsborough County Public Library 264tr; **Salvador Dali Museum, St. Petersburg:** 260tr; All works of art by Salvador Dali © Kingdom of Spain, Gala – Salvador Dali Foundation, DACS, London 2011, *Nature Morte Vivante* 260ca, *The Sick Child* 261cra, *Cadaques* 260clb, *Don Quixote y Sancho Panza* 261t, *Discovery* 260bc, *Daddy Longlegs of the Evening–Hope!* (1940) 261ctr; Salvador Dali by Marc Lacroix 261br; **© International Speedway Corporation, Daytona:** 222tr, 223cl, 223bl; Nascar 223crb; **DB Bistro Moderne:** 331br; **The Charles Deering Estate:** 96tr; **© Disney Inc.:** 146br, 147tl, 156cl, 156cl, 157b, 158b, 166tr, 168cl, 172–3 all, 174–75 all, 176br; ©LEGO 173br; **Dreamstime.com:** Aiisha 188–9; Americanspirit 55cra, 65tr; John Anderson 292bl; Walter Arce 10cl; John Bilous 206; Mike Brown 204br; Steve Byland 293cra; Feng Cheng 29clb; 291ca; Keith Childers 28crb; Ivan Cholakov 2–3; Jerry Coli 164–5; Songquan Deng 74; Anne M. Fearon-wood 198ca; Caleb Foster 292cl; Fotoluminate 92, 293tc; Fotomak 21tl; 34tr; Giovanni Gagliardi 87t; 298cl; Jorg Hackemann 284; Hakoar 29tr; Matthew Hill 146clb; 170ca; Tom Hirtreiter 221br; Eduard Ionescu 227c; Jerryway 293bc; Ritu Jethani 125br; 130t; Wangkun Jia 177c; Judy Kennamer 262cl; Kmiragaya 62; Daniel Korzeniewski 13tl; Peter Leahy 296cr; 296bl; Miroslav Liska 144bl; Lunamarina 58–9, 368–9; Luvemak 251b; Maijaliisa 95tr; Gilles Malo 29cl, 29bl; Martha Marks 28cra; Meinzahn 101b; 303br; Meunierd 20tr; Mike711 293bl; Mirador-pictures 195tr; Felix Mizioznikov 57tc, 68clb, 348br; Glenn Nagel 110–11; Natalie11345 254tr; Offaxisproductions 11br; Jason Ondreicka 290bl; Sean Pavone 4tr, 5cl, 15tr, 117br; Ruth Peterkin 290tr; Ondřej Prosický 198cra; Rcavalleri 139b; Jason P Ross 25c; William Rothstein 258cl; Julie Rubacha 29cla; Craig Sims 14tr; TasFoto 61crb; Tommy Schutz 373bc; Tinamou 69cra; Peter Titmuss 57crb, 229b; Typhoonski 82, 140tl; Sergey Uryadnikov 4cb; Edwin Verin 203tr; Birute Vijeikiene 76tr; Wisconsinart 148–9; Michael Wood 22; Mary Katherine Wynn 366br; **David Dye, University of Memphis:** South Florida Museum 44crb, 47cla. **Eden Roc Renaissance Resort And Spa:** Jon Moe 310cla; **ET Archive:** Natural History Museum 49ca. **Fairchild Tropical Garden:** 96b; **Fifth Third Bank:** 374br; **© Henry Morrison Flagler Museum, Palm Beach:** 53tl, 126tr, 128cl, 128bc, 129tc, 129cra, 129crb; Archives 128tr, 129bl; **Florida Department of Environmental Protection:** 371tr; **The Floridian:** 334tr; **The Phillip and Patricia Frost Museum of Science:** Robin Hill 79tl; **Fontainebleau Hilton, Miami:** 73bl. **Pet Gallagher:** 24bl; **Genesis Space Photo Library:** NASA 204tl; **Getty Images:** Steve Bly 383bl; John Coletti 14br; Sir John Lavery/The Bridgeman Art Library 8–9; Leemage 211bc; J. Baylor Roberts 54–5c; David Rojas /FilmMagic 376c; Peter Unger 271br; **Giraudon, Paris:** Bridgeman 47cr; Laurus 43b; **Grand Bohemian:** 318bl; **The Granger Collection, New York:** 50clb, 50crb, 53cr; 54cl; **Gulfstream Park Racetrack:** 100cc; G.WIZ. **Hawk's Cay Resort:** 325bl; **© The Miami Herald:** © Al Diaz 37cl, 130bc; © Guzy 57cla;

© Charlie Trainor 81cr; **Division Historical Resources, State Department, Tallahassee**: 45crb, 118cla; **Courtesy of Hibel Museum of Art, Palm Beach, FL**: *Brittany and Child*, oil, gesso, and gold leaf on silk, Edna Hibel 24½" x 20½" (1994) 125cl; **Historical Museum of Southern Florida, Miami**: 54clb, 55clb, 56c, 67tr, 289tc; **Images Colour Library**: 61cra; **Index Stock Photography, Inc., New York**: 27b, 40ca, 41cra, 52t, 267tr, 358c; © Bill Bachmann 28cl; © James Blank 21br, 286cla; J. Christopher 31cr; © Henry Fichner 29cr; © Warren Flagler 57cra; Scott Kerrigan 299cr; Larry Lipsky 181bc, 295br; Wendell Metzen 36cla, 198cra, 292tr; Jim Schwabel 275tl, 287tr; Randy Taylor 38bl; **Indian Temple Mound**: 44cla; **Island Cow**: 344br; **iStockphoto.com**: gregobagel 89tr; **Joe's Stone Crab**: 330tr; **The John and Mable Ringling Museum of Art**: 274cb, 274br, 277br; **Kennedy Space Center**: 12bl, 200tr, 200c, 200clb, 201tc, 201cla, 202tr, 202clb, 203clb; **Kennedy Space Center – Visitors Center, Cape Canaveral**: 201cr; **The Kessler Collection**: 311bl, 319tr, 341t; **Kobal Collection**: Michael Fineman 141b; **Ken Laffal**: 27tc, 60bl, 113tr, 121bc; **Frank Lane Picture Library**: © Dembinsky 28clb, 297bl; © David Hosking 28br, 29br, 198tr, 292cr; Maslowski 120cra; © Leonard Lee Rue 29crb; **LEGOLAND Florida © Merlin Entertainments Group**: Chip Litherland 25tr, 196tr, 196cl, 196clb, 196br, 197tl, 197tc, 197cr, 197bl, 197cla; **Lightner Museum, St. Augustine, FL**: 53cb; **Lowe Art Museum**: 87c; **The Lynn Conservatory**: 134tr; **LYNX**: 387cla; **Barry Mansell**: 289cl; **Macmillan Publishers**: Pan Books *Native Tongue* and *Tourist Season* Carl Hiassen 88bl; **Mangia Mangia Pasta Café**: 346tr; **Provided Courtesy of Marineland Dolphin Conservation Center**: 220bl; **Marquesa Hotel**: 324tl; **Marvel Entertainment Group, NY**: Spider-Man TM and © 1996, Marvel Characters, Inc. All rights reserved 134t; **Fred Mawer, London**: 140br, 145tr; **Miami World Jai-Alai**: 37tr; **Miami-Dade Aviation Museum Foundation**: 237crb, 237cra; **Miami Dade Aviation**: 378cla; **Miami-Dade Transit**: 77br, 386ca; **Jason Mitchell**: 69crb; **The Moorings Village**: 313tr, 323tl; **Museum of Art, Fort Lauderdale**: *Big Bird with Child*, Karel Appel (1972) © DACS, London 2006 136tr; **Museum of Fine Arts, St. Petersburg**: *Poppy*, Georgia O'Keeffe (1927) © ARS, NY and © DACS, London 2006 259tl; © **NASA**: 204tr; **Naval Aviation Museum Foundation**: 236tr; **Museo Naval, Spain**: 32cl; **Peter Newark's Pictures**: American Pictures 49clb; Historical Pictures 33crb; Military Pictures 51crb; **The New York Public Library**: Print Collection, Miriam and Ira D. Wallach Division of Art, Prints and Photographs, Astor, Lenox and Tilden Foundations 46–7c; **Jesse Newman Associates**: 123br; **Glenn Van Nimwegen, Wyoming**: 294cla, 295bl; **NOAA National Hurricane Center, Miami**: 30–31, 31tc; **Orange Blossom Balloons**: 367tc; **The Orlando Eye**,

**Madame Tussauds Orlando & SEA LIFE Orlando**: 181cr; 181bl; **Orlando Harley-Davidson**: 176cl; **Orlando Museum of Art**: On long-term loan from the Gross Family Collection *The Conference* (d.) Edward Potthast (American, 1857–1927) 193bl; **Oronoz, Madrid**: 46cl; **Orsay**: 340br. **The Palm Beach Post, FL**: © Thomas Hart Shelby 122cl; © Greg Lovett 39cla; © Loren Hosack 123bl, 126bl; © E.A. Kennedy III 26b; © Mark Mirko 41clb; © Sherman Zent 39br; **Pérez Art Museum**: 78br; **PGA National Resort**: 317tl; **Pictures Colour Library**: 307b; **Pink Shell Beach Resort**: 321bl; **Pistache**: 336t; **The Refinery**: 345tr; **The John and Mable Ringling Museum of Art, Sarasota**: 276br; Bequest of John Ringling, *The Building of a Palace*, Piero di Cosimo (1515–1520) 275cra, *Abraham and Melchizedek*, Peter Paul Rubens (c.1625) 275crb, *Philip IV, King of Spain*, Diego Rodriguez de Silva y Velazquez, c.1625–1635 274cla; Giovanni Lunardi, 2002 276cl, 277tr, 277cr, 277bl. **Sandestin Golf and Beach Resort**: 312br; **Schooners**: 342br; **Seasons 52**: 337br; **Sea Salt**: 347bc; **SeaWorld Orlando**: 180tr, 180br; **Seminole Hard Rock Hotel & Casino**: 141tl, 316br; **Sette Bello**: 335bl; **Smithsonian Institution**: Department of Anthropology catalogue no. 240915 44clb; **SpaceX**: 205bl; **St. Augustine, Ponte Vedra & the Beaches VCB**: 214clb, 215tl, 215cra, 216cla; **STA Travel Group**: 370crb; **Florida State Archive, Tallahassee**: 49tl, 51tl, 51ca, 52clb, 55ca, 124br, 127cra, 223cra, 235b, 265br: Museum of Florida History 55crb, 119bl; **Tony Stone Images**: Randy Wells 290c; **Superstock**: 250, Oronoz / Album orz235138 48cl; **Tampa Theatre**: 359bl; **Turtle Beach Resort**: 322bl; **Florida Department of Commerce, Division of Tourism**: R Overton 45cra; © **2010 Universal Orlando Resort**. All Rights Reserved: 182br, 183br, 185bl, 185tl, 185br, 186c, 186br, 187tr, 187b, 188–9 all. **WaterSoundVacationRentals.com**: 320tl; **Prof L. Glenn Westfall, FL**: 52–3; **West Florida Historic Preservation. Inc**: 232ca; **Wet n'Wild**: 190–91 all; **Wish Restaurant**: 336br; **Wolfsonian Foundation, Miami**: Mitchell Wolfson, J.R. Collection 71br; **Wynwood Yard**: Masson Liang 101crb; **Ybor City Chamber of Commerce**: 264tr.

**Front Endpaper**: **Alamy Stock Photo**: RosalreneBetancourt 14 Rclb; **Corbis**: John Bilous 206-Rtr; **Dreamstime.com**: Benkrut Rtr; Songquan Deng Lcl; Fotoluminate Lbl; Jorg Hackemann Rbl; Kmiragaya Lbr; Typhoonski Lbc; **Superstock**: Stock Connection Lcra.

**Cover images**: Front: **4 Corners**: Susan Kremer; Spine: **4Corners**: Susan Kremer; Back: **123RF.com**: Songquan Deng

All other images © Dorling Kindersley. See **www.DKimages. com** for further information.

## Special Editions of DK Travel Guides

DK Travel Guides can be purchased in bulk quantities at discounted prices for use in promotions or as premiums. We are also able to offer special editions and personalized jackets, corporate imprints, and excerpts from all of our books, tailored specifically to meet your own needs.

To find out more, please contact:
(in the United States) **specialsales@dk.com**
(in the UK) **travelguides@uk.dk.com**
(in Canada) DK Special Sales at **specialmarkets@dk.com**
(in Australia) **penguincorporatesales@ penguinrandomhouse.com.au**